EYEWITNESS

PARIS

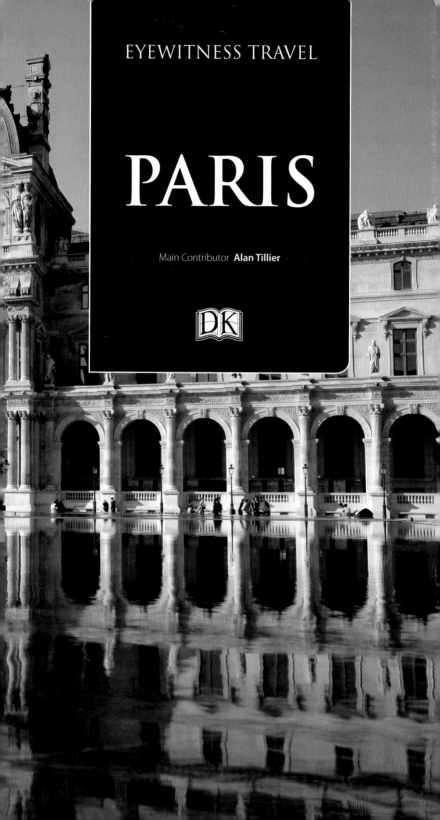

EYEWITNESS TRAVEL

PARIS

Main Contributor **Alan Tillier**

LONDON, NEW YORK,
MELBOURNE, MUNICH AND DELHI
www.dk.com

Project Editor Heather Jones
Art Editor Janis Utton
Editor Alex Gray
Designer Vanessa Hamilton
Design Assistant Clare Sullivan

Contributors
Chris Boicos, Michael Gibson, Douglas Johnson

Photographers
Max Alexander, Neil Lukas, Robert O'Dea

Illustrators
Stephen Conlin, Stephen Gyapay,
Maltings Partnership

This book was produced with the assistance of
Websters International Publishers.

Printed and bound in China

First published in Great Britain in 1993
by Dorling Kindersley Limited
80 Strand, London WC2R 0RL, UK

15 16 17 18 10 9 8 7 6 5 4 3 2 1

**Reprinted with revisions 1994, 1995, 1997 (twice), 1999, 2000,
2001, 2002, 2003, 2004, 2005, 2006, 2007, 2008, 2009, 2010,
2011, 2012, 2013, 2014, 2015**

Copyright © 1993, 2015 Dorling Kindersley Limited, London
A Penguin Random House Company

A CIP catalogue record is available from the British Library.

ISBN 978 0 2410 0729 7

Floors are referred to throughout in accordance with French
usage; ie the "first floor" is the floor above ground level.

Front cover main image: View of the forecourt to the Musée du Louvre

◄ Architect I M Pei's iconic glass pyramid that serves as the main entrance to the Musée du Louvre

Contents

How to Use this Guide **6**

Henri II (1547–59)

Introducing Paris

Pont Alexandre III

The Kiss by Rodin (1886)

Sacré-Coeur in Montmartre

An island in the Bois de Boulogne

Charles de Gaulle airport RER station

The Panthéon

HOW TO USE THIS GUIDE

This Eyewitness Travel Guide helps you get the most from your stay in Paris with the minimum of practical difficulty. The opening section, *Introducing Paris*, locates the city geographically, sets modern Paris in its historical context and explains how Parisian life changes through the year. *Paris at a Glance* is an overview of the city's specialities. The main sightseeing section of the book is *Paris Area by Area*. It describes all the main sights

with maps, photographs and detailed illustrations. In addition, eight planned walks take you to parts of Paris you might otherwise miss.

Carefully researched tips for hotels, shops and markets, restaurants and bars, sports and entertainment are found in *Travellers' Needs*, and the *Survival Guide* has advice on everything from posting a letter to catching the metro.

Paris Area by Area

The city has been divided into 14 sightseeing areas. Each section opens with a portrait of the area, summing up its character and history, with a list of all the sights to be covered.

These are clearly located by numbers on an *Area Map*. This is followed by a largescale *Street-by-Street Map* focusing on the most interesting part of the area. Finding your way about

the section is made simple by the numbering system used throughout for the sights. This refers to the order in which they are described on the pages that complete the section.

Colour-coding on each page makes the area easy to find in the book.

Recommended restaurants in the area are listed and plotted on the map.

A locator map shows you where you are in relation to surrounding areas. The area of the *Street-by-Street Map* is highlighted.

Numbered circles pinpoint all the listed sights on the area map. The Conciergerie, for example, is ❽

1 Area Map
For easy reference, the sights in each area are numbered and located on an area map. To help the visitor, the map also shows metro and mainline RER stations and car parks.

Stars indicate the sights that no visitor should miss.

St-Séverin ❸ is shown on this map as well.

A suggested route for a walk takes in the most attractive and interesting streets in the area.

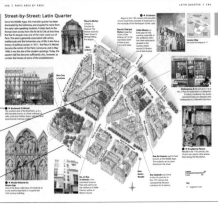

2 Street-by-Street Map
This gives a bird's-eye view of the heart of each sightseeing area. The most important buildings are picked out in stronger colour, to help you spot them as you walk around.

Paris at a Glance

Each map in this section concentrates on a specific theme: *Museums and Galleries, Churches, Squares, Parks and Gardens, Remarkable Parisians.* The top sights are shown on the map; other sights are described on the following two pages.

Each sightseeing area is colour-coded.

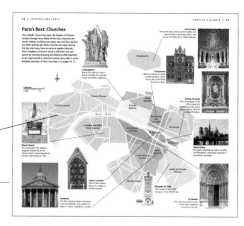

Practical Information lists all the information you need to visit every sight, including a map reference to the Street Finder at the back of the book.

Numbers refer to each sight's position on the area map and its place in the chapter.

3 Detailed information on each sight
All important sights in each area are described in depth in this section. They are listed in order, following the numbering on the *Area Map*. Practical information on opening hours, telephone numbers, websites, admission charges and facilities available is given for each sight. The key to the symbols used can be found on the back flap.

The Visitors' Checklist provides the practical information you will need to plan your visit.

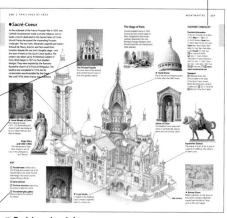

The façade of each major sight is shown to help you spot it quickly.

Stars indicate the most interesting architectural details of the building, and the most important works of art or exhibits on view inside.

Numbered circles point out key features of the sight listed in a key.

4 Paris's major sights
These are given two or more full pages in the sightseeing area in which they are found. Historic buildings are dissected to reveal their interiors; and museums and galleries have colour-coded floor plans to help you find important exhibits.

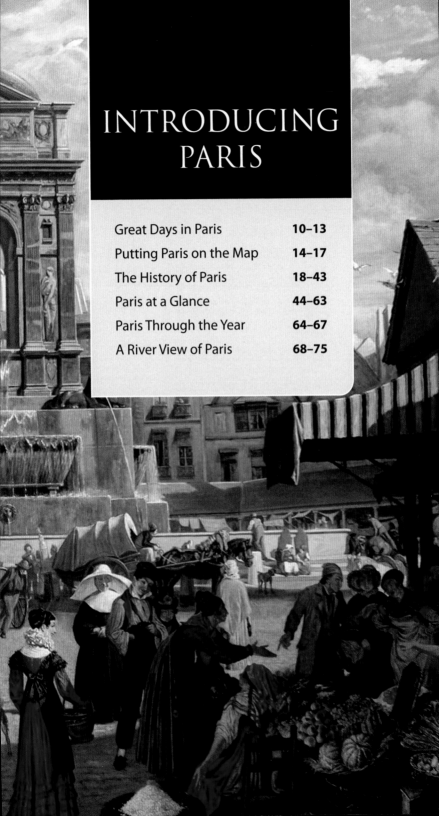

INTRODUCING PARIS

GREAT DAYS IN PARIS

Paris is a city packed with treasures and wonderful things to see and do. Here are itineraries for some of the best of the attractions, arranged first under themes and then by length of stay. Sightseers should manage everything on these itineraries, but the selections can also be dipped into for ideas. All sights are reachable by public transport. Price guides on pages 10–11 are for two adults or for a family of two adults and two children, excluding meals and transport costs.

Pyramide du Louvre, from across the fountain pools

Artistic Treasures

Two adults
allow at least €70

- Fabulous art at the Louvre
- Lunch at chic Café Marly
- A visit to the Rodin sculpture garden or take in the Pompidou Centre
- Dine at Tokyo Eat

Morning
Begin with the **Musée du Louvre** *(see pp122–9)*, one of the world's most impressive museums. Beat the crowds by using the little-known entrance at the Carrousel du Louvre (99 Rue de Rivoli). Save time by getting a floorplan and working out where you want to go and sticking to it.

Lunch
There are many cheap eateries nearby, but for a great lunch experience, head to smart **Café Marly** *(see p310)*. On warm days, sit in the outside gallery or revel in the cozy red velvet and gilt splendour of the interior.

Afternoon
Choose from three destinations for the afternoon. The fatigued should head to the sublime **Musée Rodin** *(see p191)* for a soothing stroll in the sculpture garden and a pensive moment next to *The Thinker*. Those seeking modern masterpieces should visit the **Pompidou Centre** *(see pp110–13)*, an intriguing inside-out building housing works from 1905 to the modern day. To go even more modern, explore the Marais *(Map 14 D3)* for world-renowned contemporary art galleries such as **Yvon Lambert** *(see p329)*, which includes works of artists such as David Shrigley and Carlos Amorales.

Evening
The **Palais de Tokyo** *(see p205)* is one of Paris' most fashionable exhibition spaces, with its multi-media displays open till midnight. After a quick tour around, stop at restaurant Tokyo Eat.

Retail Therapy

Two adults
allow at least €40

- Buy foody treats at Le Bon Marché
- Lunch at a top department store restaurant
- Drinks and dinner at Kong

Morning
One-stop shops for gourmets and gluttons include **Fauchon, Hédiard** and **La Grande Epicerie** at **Le Bon Marché** *(see pp325–6)*. In fact, anything that is edible – as long as it's delicious – can be found here. Specialist shops include **Poilâne** for bread, **Richart** for chocolate, **Legrand** for wine and **Pierre Hermé** for cakes. Or head down the Rue Mouffetard, one of the city's best market streets.

Lunch
Shopaholics can eat in one of the main department stores. The World Bar at **Printemps**, designed by Paul Smith, is a super-cool eatery *(see pp312–13)*, for example. The surrounding area is a busy shopping and

Ultra-hip interior of Kong, which also has stunning rooftop views

◄ View of the market at Fontaine des Innocents by John James Chalon eating hub, so you can combine the two with no difficulty.

Afternoon
Either shop on till you drop, or go esoteric and visit the **Musée des Arts Décoratifs** near the Louvre *(see p132)*; a true temple to the decorative arts with a fabulous shop to pick up gifts. Boutique lovers should go to **Claudie Pierlot, Agnès B, Isabel Marant, Vanessa Bruno** *(see pp316–19)*.

Evening
Head for restorative drinks and dinner at **Kong** on top of Kenzo's flagship store and fashion shrine *(see pp309–10)*.

Reflections in La Géode, giant sphere at the Parc de la Villette

Child's Play

Family of four
allow at least €190

- **Explore Parc de la Villette**
- **See animals at the zoo at Jardin des Plantes**
- **Stop for a café lunch**
- **Go up the Eiffel Tower**

Morning
Take receptive young minds to **Parc de la Villette**, which has an impressive children's programme. **La Cité des Sciences et de l'Industrie** (Science City) is packed with interesting interactive exhibits for budding Einsteins *(see pp240–41)*. Family fun can be found at the **Ménagerie** *(see p166)* in the Jardin des Plantes

area where the zoo is very popular. Even more exciting than the live animals for some are the skeletons and stuffed beasts in the **Muséum National d'Histoire Naturelle** *(see p169)*.

Lunch
There are lots of cafés in the Jardin des Plantes area or a more formal lunch can be had at **Mavrommatis** *(see p304)*.

Afternoon
No child can resist a trip up the **Eiffel Tower**, so take them up in the afternoon for a proper view of the city, or wait until nightfall and time your trip to coincide with the changing of the hour when thousands of lights twinkle for ten minutes *(see pp196–7)*. If there's time, take a tour of the waxworks at the **Grévin** museum *(see p220)*. Most of the models are of French celebrities, but big international names in art and sport can also be spotted.

The Great Outdoors

Two adults
allow at least €65

- **Boat trip on the Seine**
- **Lunch on the Rue de Rivoli**
- **A walk to Luxembourg Garden**
- **Take a balloon ride**

Morning
For today's trip, the Metro is banned, so instead take the hop-on-hop-off batobus up the Seine. The first "stop" is near the **Eiffel Tower** so a quick look

Modern water sculpture and glasshouse, Parc André Citroën

around the **Champ-de-Mars** underneath Gustave Eiffel's monument is recommended *(see p193)*. Continue on the batobus to the Louvre stop, jump off and wander around the **Jardin des Tuileries** *(see p132)*.

Lunch
The tea salon **Angélina** *(see p310)* is a cut above other cafés on Rue de Rivoli. Leave space for the famous Mont Blanc cake of chestnut purée and cream.

Afternoon
Reboard the boat and head up to **Notre-Dame** *(see pp82–5)*, then it's a good walk down the Boulevard St Michel to the **Jardin du Luxembourg** *(see p174)*. There's lots to see – chess tables, beehives and donkey rides – and the **Musée du Luxembourg**, which hosts blockbuster exhibitions. For a final blast of fresh air, cross the city to the **Parc André Citroën** and take a tethered balloon ride *(see p249)*.

A floral display in the Jardin des Plantes

The medieval Gothic cathedral of Notre-Dame on Ile St-Louis

2 days in Paris

- Explore Ile St-Louis and visit majestic Notre-Dame
- Admire Old Masters and antiquities in the Louvre
- Ascend the Eiffel Tower at sunset for fabulous views across the city

Day 1

Morning Explore tranquil **Ile St-Louis** (p79) before crossing Pont St-Louis to take in glorious **Notre-Dame** (pp82–5), with its buttresses and gargoyles. Head west across **Ile de la Cité** (pp80–81) to the Gothic jewel of **Sainte-Chapelle** (pp88–9). Walk over to the Right Bank and make for the world-famous **Musée du Louvre** (pp122–9), home to da Vinci's *Mona Lisa* and countless other treasures.

Afternoon Stroll through the charming **Jardin des Tuileries** (p132) to the architectural set piece of **Place de la Concorde** (p133). Follow **Avenue des Champs-Elysées** (p211), taking a detour down **Avenue Montaigne** (p211) to marvel at its many grand fashion houses, including Dior and Chanel. Continue on to the **Arc de Triomphe** (pp212–13), which promises fabulous views from the top, before heading east again, to the pretty **Jardin du Palais-Royal** (p131). Drop in at the foodie paradise of **Place de la Madeleine** (p218) on your way, if time allows. Dine in **Montmartre** (pp224–5), where the **Sacré-Coeur** (p226–7) is splendidly illuminated at night.

Day 2

Morning Walk up bohemian **Rue Mouffetard** (p168), which has a lively market at weekends, to the ancient scholarly haunt of the **Latin Quarter** (pp152–3). Be sure to glimpse the bombastic **Panthéon** (pp160–61) and the city's celebrated university, the **Sorbonne** (p159), here. Then cross the river to the chic streets of the **Marais** (pp94–5), and eat lunch under the shaded arcades of **Place des Vosges** (p98).

Afternoon Stay in this colourful district, enjoying the hip shops on **Rue des Francs Bourgeois** (p98) and the historic Jewish Quarter around **Rue des Rosiers** (p99). Be wowed by the cutting-edge exhibits in the dazzling **Pompidou Centre** (pp110–13), before heading across town, past Louis XIV's imposing **Hôtel des Invalides** (p186–7), to the legendary **Eiffel Tower** (pp196–7). At sunset, the views from the top can be marvellous.

3 days in Paris

- See the Champs-Elysées and the Arc de Triomphe
- Enjoy the Impressionists in the Musée d'Orsay
- Climb up to Montmartre and Sacré-Coeur

Day 1

Morning Start your day in the charming **Café de Flore** (p141) in **St Germain-des-Prés** (p138–40), which was at the heart of the city's intellectual life in the 1950s. Take in medieval **St-Séverin** (p158) before crossing to **Ile de**

la Cité (pp80–81), site of the Gothic wonder **Notre-Dame** (pp82–5) and beautiful **Sainte-Chapelle** (pp88–9). Nearby, **Ile St-Louis** (p79) is an oasis of calm.

Afternoon Visit the huge **Musée du Louvre** (pp122–9), making a beeline for the work of the Old Masters in the Denon wing. Walk through the pretty **Jardin des Tuileries** (p132) to historic **Place de la Concorde** (p133), and catch a bus along the **Avenue des Champs-Elysées** (p211) to the **Arc de Triomphe** (pp212–13).

Day 2

Morning Devote your morning to the **Latin Quarter** (pp152–3), home to the stately **Panthéon** (pp160–61), the great **Sorbonne** university (p159) and the superb **Musée National du Moyen Age** (pp154–7), which has Roman baths beneath it. Peer down ancient **Rue Mouffetard** (p168) before a rest in the **Jardin du Luxembourg** (p174).

Main gallery of the Musée d'Orsay, converted from a railway station into a museum

Afternoon Immerse yourself in the grandeur of **Invalides** (pp186–7), the final resting place of Napoleon Bonaparte. Here, you'll find the compact **Musée Rodin** (p191), with its impressive collection of works by the great sculptor, and the monumental **Eiffel Tower** (pp196–7). Next stop is the **Musée d'Orsay** (pp146–9) and its collection of Impressionist masterpieces. Wind down after a busy day with an evening stroll in lively **Montparnasse** (pp178–9).

Day 3

Morning For a dose of modern art, head to the mesmerizing **Pompidou Centre** (pp110–13). Cross the vibrant **Marais** (pp94–5) for a coffee in peaceful **Place des Vosges** (p98), then make for **Place de la Bastille** (p102), the site of Charles V's giant fortress of the same name. Nearby **Musée Carnavalet** (pp96–7) offers captivating insights into the history of Paris.

Afternoon Contemplate **Palais-Royal** (p130), the childhood home of Louis XIV, from the delightful **Jardin du Palais-Royal** (p131). Duck in and out of the 19th-century passages off Rue Vivienne on your way to **Galeries Lafayette** (pp38–9), the classic Parisian department store. Take in the evening light from **Sacré-Coeur** (pp226–7) on top of **Montmartre** (pp224–5).

5 days in Paris

- View the sculptures in the superb Musée Rodin
- Marvel at Monet's art in the Musée Marmottan
- Take a train to Versailles – Louis XIV's splendid palace

Day 1

Morning View Paris from atop the **Arc de Triomphe** (pp212–13) before walking east along the **Avenue des Champs-Elysées** (p211). Cross the grand expanse of **Place de la Concorde** (p133) and the formal **Jardin des Tuileries** (p132) to the historic **Palais-Royal** (p130), set in immaculate grounds.

Afternoon Get to know the islands of the Seine, **Ile St-Louis** (p79) and **Ile de la Cité** (pp80–81), where you'll find the Gothic masterpieces **Notre-Dame** (pp82–5) and **Sainte-Chapelle** (pp88–9). While away the rest of the day in the spectacular **Musée du Louvre** (pp122–9).

Day 2

Morning Move east across the vibrant **Marais** (pp94–5) district from the **Pompidou Centre**

(pp110–13), with its stunning contemporary art. Pop into the **Musée Carnavalet** (pp96–7) for a dose of Parisian history, and have a much-needed coffee at the calm **Place des Vosges** (p98). Finish your morning in the historic, and now hugely trendy, **Place de la Bastille** (p102).

Sunny café terrace in the elegant Marais

Afternoon Visit the city's most famous cemetery, the **Cimetière du Père Lachaise** (pp242–3), to see the tombs of notable figures, including the writer and great wit Oscar Wilde. Follow the **Canal St-Martin** (p236) to the futuristic **Parc de la Villette** (pp238–9). See the exhibits in the **Cité de la Musique** (p238), where you may also catch a concert.

Day 3

Morning See the Impressionists at **Musée d'Orsay** (pp146–9) and, if your artistic appetite allows, walk on to **Musée Rodin** (p191) in the impressive **Invalides** (pp186–7). For a change of scene, seek out **Rue Cler** (p192), with its street market and bistros.

Afternoon Scale the **Eiffel Tower** (pp196–7), then come down to earth at the Modernist **Palais de Chaillot** (p202) across

the river. Walk through elegant Passy to the **Musée Marmottan Claude Monet** (p256), which contains Monet's *Water Lily* paintings. Beyond it is the **Bois de Boulogne** (pp256–7), replete with lakes and gardens.

Day 4

Morning Spend the day out of the city, at magnificent **Versailles** (pp250–55) – Louis XIV's palace. Tour the sumptuous apartments on the first floor.

Afternoon Explore the palace's fabulous gardens, landscaped by André Le Nôtre, and the smaller **Grand Trianon** and **Petit Trianon** palaces (p251).

Day 5

Morning Sample intellectual Paris in **Café de Flore** (p141) in **St Germain-des-Prés** (pp138–40), a long-time haunt of writers and philosophers. Visit the **Latin Quarter** (pp152–3), home of the sublime church of **St-Séverin** (p158), fine medieval art in the **Musée National du Moyen Age** (pp154–7), the **Panthéon** (pp160–61) and the **Sorbonne** (p159) university. Step back in time on old **Rue Mouffetard** (p168) before having lunch in **Montparnasse** (pp178–9).

Afternoon Relax in **Jardin du Luxembourg** (p174), then head north to the Right Bank and the opulent **Opéra Garnier** (pp218–19). Treat yourself at **Galeries Lafayette** (pp38–9), and then climb **Montmartre** (pp224–5) to the ethereal **Sacré-Coeur** (pp226–7) to watch the sun set.

The beautiful formal gardens at Louis XIV's palace, Versailles

Putting Paris on the Map

Paris, the capital of France, is a city of over two million people covering 105 sq km (40.5 sq miles) of northern France. It is on the River Seine at the centre of the Ile-de-France, the region which is home to 11.5 million people, around one-fifth of the French population. An important European business and cultural centre, it is the focus of activity in the north of France.

Western Europe

North Sea

NORWAY

SWEDEN

DENMARK

UNITED KINGDOM

REP. OF IRELAND

NETHERLANDS

BELGIUM

GERMANY

POLAND

CZECH REPUBLIC

SLOVAKIA

Atlantic Ocean

FRANCE

SWITZ.

AUSTRIA

HUNGARY

SLOV.

CROATIA

BOSNIA HERZ.

SERBIA

MONTEN.

KOS.

MAC.

ITALY

ALBANIA

GREECE

PORTUGAL

SPAIN

● Paris

Harwich

North Sea

Sheerness

Ramsgate

Zeebrugg

Ostend (Oostende)

Dover

Channel Tunnel

Dunkirk (Dunkerque)

Folkestone

Calais   A16

A16

Boulogne   A26

Rouba

Lille

Le Touquet   A16

A1

Lens   D939   Douai

Arras   A1

A2

Abbeville   A28

N29

A28   Amiens   A29

A29

Le Havre

Rouen ✈

Beauvais   A16

A1

Compièg

N2

Chantilly

A13

See inset map above

Caen   A13

A28

Seine

PARIS ✈

A88   Argentan   N12

Dreux

A6   A5

Sées

Fontainebleau

Chartres   N20

A10

A19

Nogent-le-Rotrou   A11

Orléans   A77

Key

☐ Greater Paris

— Motorway

— Major road

--- Railway

— Country border

0 kilometres   50

0 miles   50

For additional map symbols *see back flap*

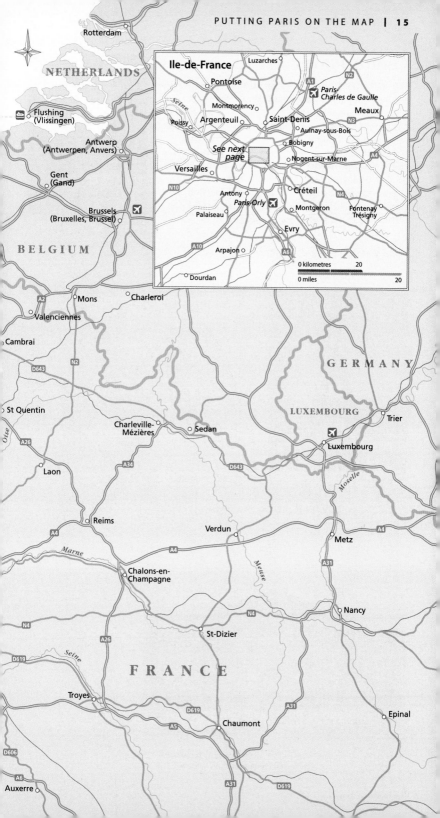

Rotterdam

NETHERLANDS

Flushing
(Vlissingen)

Antwerp
(Antwerpen, Anvers)

Gent
(Gand)

Brussels
(Bruxelles, Brussel)

BELGIUM

A2   Mons   Charleroi

Valenciennes

Cambrai

D643   N2

St Quentin

Charleville-
Mézières   Sedan

Oise   A26

Laon

Reims

A4

Marne

Chalons-en-
Champagne

GERMANY

LUXEMBOURG   Trier

D643   Luxembourg

Moselle

Verdun   Metz   A4

A4

Meuse   A31

N4   Nancy

N4   A26   St-Dizier

Seine   FRANCE

D619

Troyes   D619   A31

A5   Chaumont   A31   Epinal

D606

A6   A31   D619

Auxerre

Ile-de-France

Luzarches

Pontoise

A1   N2

Paris-
Charles de Gaulle

Seine   Montmorency   Meaux

Poissy   Argenteuil   Saint-Denis   N3

Aulnay-sous-Bois

See next   Bobigny
page

Versailles   Nogent-sur-Marne   A4

N10   Créteil

Antony   N4

Paris-Orly   Montgeron   Fontenay
Trésigny

Palaiseau

Evry

A10   A6

Arpajon

0 kilometres   20

Dourdan   0 miles   20

Central Paris

This book divides Paris into 14 areas, comprising central Paris and the nearby area of Montmartre. Most of the sights covered in the book lie within these areas, each one of which has its own chapter. Each area contains a range of sights that convey some of its history and distinctive character. The sights of Montmartre, for example, reveal its village charm and its colourful history as a thriving artistic enclave. In contrast, Champs-Elysées is renowned for its wide avenues, expensive fashion houses and opulent mansions. Most of the city's famous sights are within reach of the heart of the city and are easy to reach on foot or by public transport.

Dôme Church
The gilded Dôme Church *(see pp188–9)* lies at the heart of the Invalides.

Eiffel Tower
Named after the engineer who designed and built it in 1889, the Eiffel Tower is the city's best-known landmark *(see pp196–7)*. It towers more than 320 m (1,050 ft) above Champ-de-Mars park.

Musée du Louvre
Right in the heart of Paris, adjacent to the River Seine and the Tuileries garden, lies the city's most impressive museum, with an unrivalled collection of artifacts from around the world *(see pp122–9)*.

0 meters	800
0 yard	800

For keys to symbols *see back flap*

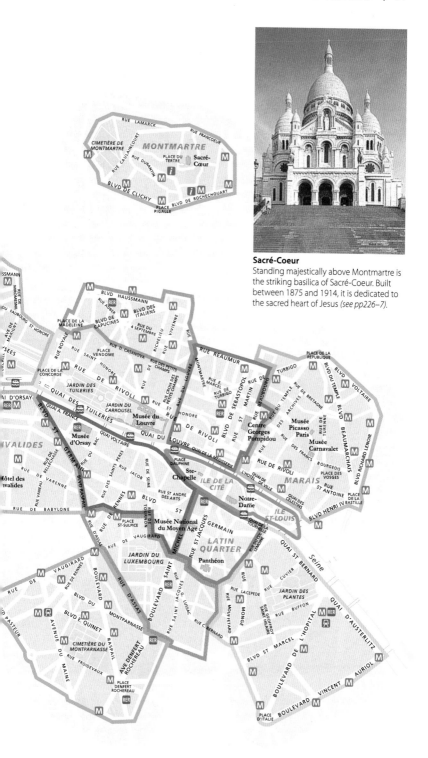

Sacré-Coeur

Standing majestically above Montmartre is the striking basilica of Sacré-Coeur. Built between 1875 and 1914, it is dedicated to the sacred heart of Jesus *(see pp226–7)*.

REPUBLIQUE FRANCAISE
LIBERTE EGALITE · FRATERNITE

THE HISTORY OF PARIS

The Paris conquered by the Romans in 55 BC was a small flood-prone fishing village on the Ile de la Cité, inhabited by the Parisii tribe. A Roman settlement soon flourished and spread on to the Left Bank of the Seine. The Franks succeeded the Romans, named the city Paris and made it the centre of their kingdom.

During the Middle Ages the city flourished as a religious centre and architectural masterpieces such as Sainte-Chapelle were erected. It also thrived as a centre of learning, enticing European scholars to its great university, the Sorbonne.

Paris emerged during the Renaissance and the Enlightenment as a great centre of culture and ideas, and under the rule of Louis XIV it also became a city of immense wealth and power. But rule by the monarch gave way to rule by the people in the bloody Revolution of 1789. By the early years of the new century, revolutionary fervour had faded and the brilliant militarist Napoleon Bonaparte proclaimed himself Emperor of France and pursued his ambition to make Paris the centre of the world.

Soon after the Revolution of 1848 a radical transformation of the city began. Baron Haussmann's grand urban scheme replaced Paris's medieval slums with elegant avenues and boulevards. By the end of the century, the city was the driving force of Western culture. This continued well into the 20th century, interrupted only by World War I and II and German military occupation. Since then, the city has revived and expanded dramatically, as it strives to be at the heart of a unified Europe.

The following pages illustrate Paris's history by providing snapshots of the significant periods in the city's evolution.

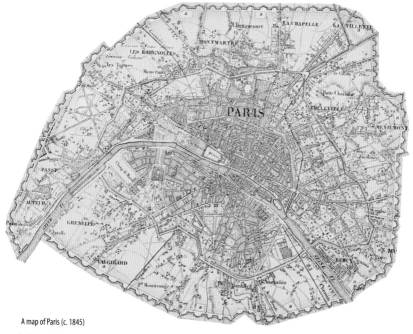

A map of Paris (c. 1845)

◀ *Allegory of the Republic* (1848) by Dominique Louis Papety

Kings and Emperors in Paris

Paris became the power base for the kings of France at the beginning of the Capetian dynasty, when Hugh Capet ascended the throne. Successive kings and emperors have left their mark and many of the places mentioned in this book have royal associations: Philippe-Auguste's fortress, the Louvre Palace, is now one of the world's great museums; Henri IV's Pont Neuf bridge links the Ile de la Cité with the two banks of the Seine; and Napoleon conceived the Arc de Triomphe to celebrate his military victories. The end of the long line of kings came with the overthrow of the monarchy in 1848, during the reign of Louis-Philippe.

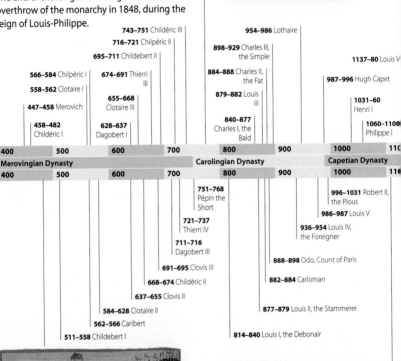

768–814 Charlemagne

743–751 Childéric III

716–721 Chilpéric II

695–711 Childebert II

566–584 Chilpéric I

558–562 Clotaire I

447–458 Merovich

458–482 Childéric I

674–691 Thierri III

655–668 Clotaire III

628–637 Dagobert I

954–986 Lothaire

898–929 Charles III, the Simple

884–888 Charles II, the Fat

879–882 Louis III

840–877 Charles I, the Bald

1137–80 Louis V

987–996 Hugh Capet

1031–60 Henri I

1060–1108 Philippe I

400	500	600	700	800	900	1000	110
Merovingian Dynasty				**Carolingian Dynasty**		**Capetian Dynasty**	
400	500	600	700	800	900	1000	110

751–768 Pépin the Short

721–737 Thierri IV

711–716 Dagobert III

691–695 Clovis III

668–674 Childéric II

637–655 Clovis II

584–628 Clotaire II

562–566 Caribert

511–558 Childebert I

996–1031 Robert II, the Pious

986–987 Louis V

936–954 Louis IV, the Foreigner

888–898 Odo, Count of Paris

882–884 Carloman

877–879 Louis II, the Stammerer

814–840 Louis I, the Debonair

482–511 Clovis I

1108–37 Louis VI, the Fat

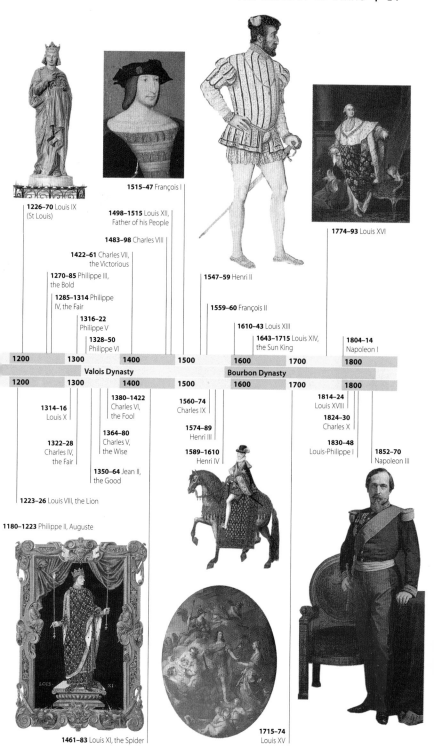

1226–70 Louis IX
(St Louis)

1515–47 François I

1498–1515 Louis XII,
Father of his People

1483–98 Charles VIII

1422–61 Charles VII,
the Victorious

1270–85 Philippe III,
the Bold

1285–1314 Philippe
IV, the Fair

1316–22
Philippe V

1328–50
Philippe VI

1547–59 Henri II

1559–60 François II

1610–43 Louis XIII

1643–1715 Louis XIV,
the Sun King

1774–93 Louis XVI

1804–14
Napoleon I

| 1200 | 1300 | 1400 | 1500 | 1600 | 1700 | 1800 |

Valois Dynasty   **Bourbon Dynasty**

| 1200 | 1300 | 1400 | 1500 | 1600 | 1700 | 1800 |

1314–16
Louis X

1380–1422
Charles VI,
the Fool

1560–74
Charles IX

1574–89
Henri III

1589–1610
Henri IV

1814–24
Louis XVIII

1824–30
Charles X

1322–28
Charles IV,
the Fair

1364–80
Charles V,
the Wise

1350–64 Jean II,
the Good

1830–48
Louis-Philippe I

1852–70
Napoleon III

1223–26 Louis VIII, the Lion

1180–1223 Philippe II, Auguste

1461–83 Louis XI, the Spider

1715–74
Louis XV

Gallo-Roman Paris

Paris would not have existed without the Seine. The river provided early peoples with the means to exploit the land, forests, marshes and islands. Excavations have unearthed canoes dating back to 4,500 BC, well before a Celtic tribe, known as the Parisii, settled there in the 3rd century BC, in an area known as Lutetia. From 59 BC, the Romans undertook the conquest of Gaul (France). Seven years later Lutetia was sacked by the Romans. They fortified and rebuilt it, especially the main island (the Ile de la Cité) and the Left Bank of the Seine.

Extent of the City
200 BC · Today

Bronze-Age Harness
Everyday objects like harnesses continued to be made of bronze well into the Iron Age, which began in Gaul around 900 BC.

Baths

Theatre

Fired-Clay Vase
Pale ceramics with coloured decoration were common in Gaul.

Forum

Iron Daggers
From the 2nd century BC, short swords of iron replaced long swords and were sometimes decorated with human and animal shapes.

Present-day
Rue Soufflot

Glass Beads
Iron-Age glass beads and bracelets have been found on the Ile de la Cité.

Present-day Rue
St-Jacques

Helmet worn by Gaulish warriors

52 B
Labienus, Caesa
lieutenant, defeats the Gau
under Camulogenes. Th
Parisii destroy their own c

4500 BC
Early boatmen operate from the banks of the Seine

4500	400 BC	300 BC	200 BC	100 BC

300 BC
Parisii tribe settle on the Ile de la Cité

Parisii gold coin minted on the Ile de la Cité

100 BC
Romans rebuild the Ile de la Cité, and create a new town on the Left Bank

Roman Oil Lamp
The inhabitants of the densely populated Ile de la Cité derived comfort during the dark winter months from the warmth of central heating and the light from oil lamps.

Gallo-Roman Goddess
Found in the arena, this head dates from the 2nd century AD.

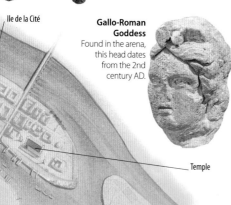

Ile de la Cité

Temple

Where to see Gallo-Roman Paris

Since the mid-19th century, excavations have yielded evidence of the boundaries of the Roman city which had as its central axes the present-day Rue St-Jacques and Rue Soufflot (in the fifth arrondissement). Under the Parvis de Notre-Dame (Place Jean-Paul II) in the Crypte Archéologique *(see p87)* the remains of Gallo-Roman houses and Roman ramparts can be seen. Other Roman sites in Paris are the Arènes de Lutèce *(p167)* and the baths at the Musée de Cluny – Musée National du Moyen Age *(pp154–7)*.

The baths *(thermae)* at Cluny had three huge rooms of water with different temperatures.

Stage backdrop

Spectator seats

Arènes de Lutèce
This huge arena, built in the 1st century AD, was used for circuses, theatrical performances and gladiatorial combat.

Ring Flask
From about 300 AD, this flask was found on the Ile de la Cité.

Lutetia in AD 200

Paris, or Lutetia, was laid out in a grid pattern with bridges linking the Ile de la Cité and the Left Bank.

Roman floor mosaic from the Cluny baths

285 Barbarians advance, Lutetia swept by fire

200 Romans add arena, baths and villas

360 Julien, prefect of Gaul, is proclaimed Emperor. Lutetia changes its name to Paris after the Parisii

0 BC	100	200	300	400

250 Early Christian martyr, St Denis, beheaded in Montmartre

451 Sainte Geneviève galvanizes the Parisians to repulse Attila the Hun

485–508 Clovis, leader of the Franks, defeats the Romans. Paris becomes Christian

Medieval Paris

Throughout the Middle Ages, strategically placed towns like Paris, positioned at a river crossing, became important centres of political power and learning. The Church played a crucial part in intellectual and spiritual life. It provided the impetus for education and for technological advances such as the drainage of land and the digging of canals. The population was still confined mainly to the Ile de la Cité and the Left Bank. When the marshes *(marais)* were drained in the 12th century, the city was able to expand.

Extent of the City
 1300   Today

Sainte-Chapelle
The upper chapel of this medieval masterpiece *(see pp88–9)* was reserved for the royal family.

The Ile de la Cité,
including the towers of the Conciergerie and Sainte-Chapelle, features in the pages for June.

Octagonal Table
Medieval manor houses had wooden furniture like this trestle table.

Drainage
allowed more land to be cultivated.

Weavers' Window
Medieval craftsmen formed guilds and many church windows were dedicated to their crafts.

A rural life
was led by most Parisians, who worked on the land. The actual city only occupied a tiny area.

512
Death of Sainte Geneviève. She is buried next to Clovis

725–732
Muslims attack Gaul

845–862
Normans attack Paris

| 500 | 600 | 700 | 800 | 900 |

543–556
Foundation of St-Germain-des-Prés

800
Charlemagne crowned Emperor by the Pope

Golden hand reliquary of Charlemagne

Notre-Dame
The great Gothic cathedrals took many years to build. Work continued on Notre-Dame from 1163 to 1334.

The Monasteries
Monks of many different orders lived in monasteries in Paris, especially on the Left Bank of the Seine.

University Seal
The University of Paris was founded in 1215.

The Louvre of Charles V
with its defensive wall is seen here from the Ile de la Cité.

The Nobility
From the mid-14th century, dress was considered to be a mark of class; noble ladies wore high, pointed hats.

The Months: June and October
This illuminated prayer book and calendar, the Très Riches Heures *(left and above), was made for the Duc de Berri in 1416. It shows many Paris buildings.*

A Medieval Romance

It was in the cloisters of Notre-Dame that the romance between the monk Pierre Abélard and the young Héloïse began. Abélard was the most original theologian of the 12th century and

was hired as a tutor to the 17-year-old niece of a canon. A love affair soon developed between the teacher and his pupil. In his wrath, Héloïse's uncle had the scholar castrated; Héloïse took refuge in a convent for the rest of her life.

1010–22
Christians burn Jews and heretics

1167
Les Halles food market created on the Right Bank of the Seine

1245
Work starts on Sainte-Chapelle

1253
The Sorbonne opens

1380
The Bastille fortress completed

1000	1100	1200	1300	1400

1079
Birth of Pierre Abélard

1163 Work starts on Notre-Dame cathedral

1215
Paris University founded

1226–70
Reign of Louis IX, St Louis

Joan of Arc

1430
Henry VI of England crowned King of France after Joan of Arc fails to defend Paris

Renaissance Paris

At the end of the Hundred Years' War with England, Paris was in a terrible state. By the time the occupying English army had left in 1453, the city lay in ruins, with many houses burned. Louis XI brought back prosperity and a new interest in art, architecture and clothes. During the course of the 16th and 17th centuries, French kings came under the spell of the Italian Renaissance. Their architects made the first attempts at town planning, creating elegant, uniform buildings and open urban spaces like the magnificent Place Royale (the present Place des Vosges).

Extent Of The City
🔲 1590   🔲 Today

Printing Press (1470)
Religious tracts, mainly in Latin, were printed on the first press at the Sorbonne.

A Knight Preparing to Joust
The Place Royale was the setting for jousting displays well into the 17th century.

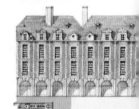

Jewel-Encrusted Pendant
A sign of the new prosperity, jewels became an important part of dress.

Place Royale

Built by Henri IV in 1609, with grand symmetrical houses round an open, central space, this was Paris's first square. Home to the aristocracy, it was renamed Place des Vosges in 1800 (see pp98–9).

Pont Notre-Dame
This bridge with its row of houses was built at the start of the 15th century. The Pont Neuf (1589) was the first bridge without houses.

1453 End of the Hundred Years' War with England

1516 François I invites Leonardo da Vinci to France. He brings the *Mona Lisa* with him

François I

| 1450 | 1460 | 1470 | 1480 | 1490 | 1500 | 1510 | 1520 |

1469 First French printing works starts operating at the Sorbonne

1528 François I takes up residence in the Louvre

16th-Century Knife and Fork Set
Ornate knife and fork sets were used in the dining rooms of the wealthy to carve joints of meat. Diners used hands or spoons for eating.

Where to see Renaissance Paris Today

Besides the Place des Vosges, there are many examples of the Renaissance in Paris. Churches include St-Etienne-du-Mont (p159), St-Eustache (p116), as well as the nave of St-Gervais–St-Protais (p103). Mansions such as the Hôtel de Bethune-Sully (p99) and the Hôtel Carnavalet (pp96–7) have been restored, and the staircases, courtyard and turrets of the Hôtel de Cluny (pp154–5) date from 1485–96.

The rood screen of St-Etienne-du-Mont (about 1520) is of outstanding delicacy.

Queen's Pavilion

Uniform houses with arcades flank the pavilion.

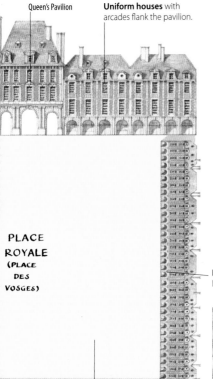

PLACE ROYALE (PLACE DES VOSGES)

Walnut Dresser (about 1545)
Elegant carved wooden furniture decorated the homes of the wealthy.

Nine symmetrical houses line each side of the square.

Hyante and Climente
Toussaint Dubreuil and other artists took up Renaissance mythological themes.

King's Pavilion

Duels were fought in the centre of the square in the 17th century.

1534 Ignatius of Loyola founds the Society of Jesus	**1546** Work starts on new Louvre palace; first stone quay built along Seine	**1559** Primitive street lanterns introduced; Louvre completed		**1572** St Bartholomew's Day massacre of Protestants			**1609** Henri IV begins building Place des Vosges	
						1589 Henri III assassinated at St-Cloud, near Paris		

530   **1540**   **1550**   **1560**   **1570**   **1580**   **1590**   **1600**   **1610**

1534 Founding of the Collège de France

1533 Hôtel de Ville rebuilt

1547 François I dies

1559 Henri II killed in a Paris tournament

1589 Henri IV completes Pont-Neuf and improves capital's water supply

1593 Protestant Henri of Navarre converts to Catholicism, and is crowned as Henri IV in 1594

1610 Henri IV is assassinated by Ravaillac, a religious fanatic

The Sun King's Paris

The 17th century in France, which became known as *Le Grand Siècle* (the great century), is epitomized by the glittering extravagance of Louis XIV (the Sun King) and his court at Versailles. In Paris, imposing buildings, squares, theatres and aristocratic *hôtels* (mansions) were built. Beneath this brilliant surface lay the absolute power of the monarch. By the end of Louis' reign the cost of his extravagance and of waging almost continuous war with France's neighbours led to a decline in the monarchy.

Extent Of The City

▨ 1657   ▨ Today

The mansard roof, with its slopes at both sides and both ends, came to typify French roofs of this period.

An open staircase rose from the internal courtyard.

Cross section of the living quarters

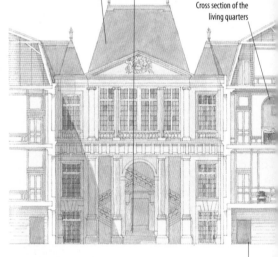

The Gardens of Versailles
Louis XIV devoted a lot of time to the gardens, which were designed by André Le Nôtre.

The ground floor contained the servants' quarters.

Louis XIV as Jupiter
On ascending the throne in 1661, Louis, depicted here as Jupiter triumphant, ended the civil wars that had been raging since his childhood.

Chest of Drawers
This gilded piece was made by André-Charles Boulle for the Grand Trianon at Versailles.

1610 Louis XIII's accession marks the start of *Le Grand Siècle*

Louis XIII

1622 Paris becomes an episcopal see

1624 Completion of Tuileries Palace

Cardinal Mazarin

1631 Launch of *La Gazette*, Paris's first newspaper

1643 Death of Louis XIII. Regency under control of Marie de Médicis and Cardinal Mazarin

1661 Louis XIV becomes absolute monarch. Enlargement of Château de Versailles begun

| 1610 | 1620 | 1630 | 1640 | 1650 | 1660 |

1614 Final meeting of the Estates Council (the main legislative assembly) before the Revolution

1629 Richelieu, Louis XIII's first minister, builds Palais Royal

1627 Development of the Ile St-Louis

1638 Birth of Louis XIV

1662 Colbert, Louis XIV's finance minister, founds Gobelins tapestry works

Weaving frame

Ceiling by Charles Le Brun
Court painter to Louis XIV, Le Brun decorated many ceilings like this one at the Hôtel Carnavalet (see p96).

Madame de Maintenon
When the queen died in 1683, Louis married Madame de Maintenon, shown here in a framed painting by Caspar Netscher.

Decorated Fan
For special court fêtes, Louis XIV often stipulated that women carry fans.

The Galerie d'Hercule with Le Brun ceiling

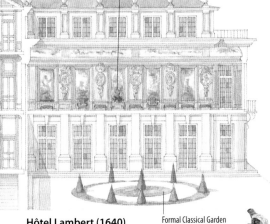

Where to See the Sun King's Paris

Many 17th-century mansions such as the Hôtel Lambert still exist in Paris, but not all are open to the public. However, Hôtel des Invalides (p191), the Dôme Church (pp188–9), the Palais du Luxembourg (p174) and Versailles (pp250–55) give a magnificent impression of the period.

Dôme Church (1706)

Formal Classical Garden

Hôtel Lambert (1640)
In the 17th century, the aristocracy built luxurious town houses with grand staircases, courtyards, formal gardens, coach houses and stables.

Neptune Cup
Made from lapis lazuli with a silver Neptune on top, this cup was part of Louis' vast collection of art objects.

Statue of Louis XIV at Musée Carnavalet

1667 Louvre rebuilt and observatory established

1682 Court moves to Versailles where it stays until the Revolution

1686 Le Procope, Paris's first café

1715 Louis XIV dies

1670	**1680**	**1690**	**1700**	**1710**

1670 Hôtel des Invalides built

1689 Pont Royal built

1692 Great famines due to bad harvests and wars

1702 Paris first divided into 20 arrondissements (districts)

Paris in the Age of Enlightenment

The Enlightenment, with its emphasis on scientific reason and a critical approach to existing ideas and society, was centred on the city of Paris. In contrast, nepotism and corruption were rife at Louis XV's court at Versailles. Meanwhile, the economy thrived, the arts flourished as never before and intellectuals, such as Voltaire and Rousseau, were renowned throughout Europe. In Paris, the population rose to about 650,000; town planning was developed, and the first accurate street map of the city appeared in 1787.

Extent Of The City
⬜ 1720   ⬜ Today

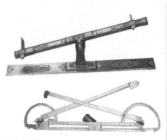

Nautical Instruments
As the science of navigation advanced, scientists developed telescopes and trigonometric instruments (used for measuring longitude and latitude).

The auditorium
with 1,913 seats, was the largest in Paris.

18th-Century Wigs
These were not only a mark of fashion but also a way of indicating the wearer's class and importance.

Comédie Française

The Age of Enlightenment saw a burst of dramatic activity, and new theatres opened. Among them was the Comédie Française (see p130), still one of the most prestigious theatres in the world.

1734 Fontaine des Quatre Saisons built

1748 Montesquieu's *L'Esprit des Lois* (an influential work about different forms of government) published

| 1720 | 1730 | 1740 | 1750 |

1722 City's first fire brigade founded
Fireman

1733 Voltaire's *Lettres Philosophiques* published

1751 First volume of Diderot's *Encyclopedia* published

Madame de Pompadour
Although generally remembered as the mistress of Louis XV, she was renowned as a patron of the arts and had great political influence.

Chocolate Pot
By the 18th century, bourgeois families could afford tobacco, tea, chocolate and coffee from Asia and the New World.

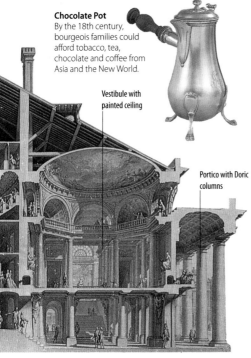

Vestibule with painted ceiling

Portico with Doric columns

The Catacombs
These were set up in 1785 as a more hygienic alternative to Paris's cemeteries (*see p181*).

Where to See Enlightenment Paris

The district around the Rue de Lille, the Rue de Varenne and the Rue de Grenelle (*p191*) has many luxurious town houses, or hôtels, which were built by the aristocracy during the first half of the 18th century. Memorabilia from the lives of the great intellectuals Voltaire and Jean-Jacques Rousseau are in the Musée Carnavalet (*pp96–7*), along with 18th-century interior designs and paintings. The imposing Hôtel des Monnaies (royal mint), which houses the Musée de la Monnaie (*p143*), is a fine example of the rational Neo-Classicism of architecture during the Enlightenment.

Churches were built throughout the Enlightenment. St-Sulpice (*p174*) was completed in 1776.

Le Procope (*p142*) is the oldest café in Paris. It was frequented by Voltaire and Rousseau.

1757 First oil street lamps

1764 Madame de Pompadour dies

1774 Louis XV, great grandson of Louis XIV, dies

1778 France supports American independence

1785 David paints the *Oath of the Horatii*

1760

1770

1780

c.1760 Place de la Concorde, Panthéon and Ecole Militaire built

1762 Rousseau's *Emile* and the *Social Contract* published

Rousseau, philosopher and writer, believed that humans were naturally good and had been corrupted by society.

1782 First pavements built, in the Place du Théâtre Français

1783 Montgolfier brothers make the first hot-air balloon ascent

Paris During the Revolution

In 1789 most Parisians were still living in squalor and poverty, as they had since the Middle Ages. Rising inflation and opposition to Louis XVI culminated in the storming of the Bastille, the king's prison; the Republic was founded three years later. However, the Terror soon followed, when those suspected of betraying the Revolution were executed without trial: more than 60,000 people lost their lives. The bloody excesses of Robespierre, the zealous revolutionary, led to his overthrow and a new government, the Directory, was set up in 1795.

Extent Of The City

▨ 1796 ▨ Today

The prison turrets were set alight.

Declaration of the Rights of Man and the Citizen
The Enlightenment ideals of equality and human dignity were enshrined in the Declaration. This illustration is the preface to the 1791 Constitution.

The French guards, who were on the side of the revolutionaries, arrived late in the afternoon with two cannons.

Paper Money
Bonds, called *assignats*, were used to fund the Revolution from 1790–93.

Drawbridge

Republican Calendar

The revolutionaries believed that the world was starting again, so they abolished the existing church calendar and took 22 September 1792, the day the Republic was declared, as the first day of the new era. The Republican calendar had 12 equal months, each sub- divided into three ten-day periods, with the remaining five days of each year set aside for public holidays. All the months of the year were given poetic names which linked them to nature and the seasons, such as fog, snow, seed-time, flowers and harvest.

A coloured engraving by Tresca showing *Ventôse*, the windy month (19 Feb–20 Mar) from the new Republican calendar

4 Aug Abolition of feudalism

26 Aug Declaration of the Rights of Man and the Citizen

14 Jul Fall of the Bastille

17 Sep Law of Suspects passed: the Terror begins

10 Aug The storming of the Tuileries

| 1789 | 1790 | 1791 | 1792 |

Cartoon on the three Estates: the clergy, the nobility and the awakening populace

Lafayette, Commander of the National Guard, takes his oath to the Constitution

17 Jul Champ de Mars massacre

25 Apr *La Marseillaise* composed

5 May The Estates council meets

14 Jul Fête de la Fédération

"Patriotic" Chair
The back of this wooden chair is topped by red bonnets, symbol of revolutionary politics.

The Sans Culottes
By 1792, the wearing of trousers instead of breeches *(culottes)* was a political symbol of Paris's artisans and shopkeepers.

La Marseillaise
The revolutionaries' marching song is now the national anthem.

The dead and wounded totalled 171 by the end of the day.

Wallpaper
Commemorative wallpaper was produced to celebrate the Revolution.

Coin tower

Great court

Well court

Guillotine
This was used for the first time in France in April 1792.

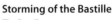

Storming of the Bastille

The Bastille was overrun on 14 July 1789 and the seven prisoners held there released. The defenders (32 Swiss guards, 82 wounded soldiers and the governor) were massacred.

20 Jun Invasion of the Tuileries

10 Aug Overthrow of Louis XVI

21 Jan Execution of Louis XVI

Autumn Robespierre in control of Committee of Public Safety

16 Oct Execution of Marie-Antoinette

24 Nov Churches closed

5 Apr Execution of Danton and supporters

19 Nov Jacobin Club (a revolutionary pressure group) closed

22 Aug New constitution: the Directory

1793

1794

1795

20 Sep Battle of Valmy

2–6 Sep September massacres

13 Jul Assassination of Marat, founder of *L'Ami du Peuple*, the revolutionary newspaper

27 Jul Execution of Robespierre

Robespierre, revolutionary and architect of the Terror

Napoleonic Paris

Napoleon Bonaparte was the most brilliant general in the French army. The instability of the new government after the Revolution gave him the chance to seize power, and in November 1799 he installed himself in the Tuileries Palace as First Consul. He crowned himself Emperor in May 1804. Napoleon established a centralized administration and a code of laws, reformed France's educational system and set out to make Paris the most beautiful city in the world. The city was endowed with grand monuments and embellished with the spoils of conquest. His power was always fragile and dependent on incessant wars. In March 1814 Prussian, Austrian and Russian armies invaded Paris and Napoleon fled to Elba. He returned to Paris in 1815 but was defeated at Waterloo and died in exile in 1821.

Extent Of The City
◻ 1810   ◻ Today

Ladies-in-Waiting
hold Josephine's train.

Château de Malmaison
This was the favourite home of Josephine, Napoleon's first wife.

Opaline-Glass Clock
The decoration on this clock echoed the fashion for draperies.

Elephant Project
This monument was planned for the centre of the Place de la Bastille.

Eagle's Flight
Napoleon's flight to Elba in 1814 was satirized in this cartoon.

1799 Napoleon seizes power

1797 Battle of Rivoli

1800 Banque de France founded

1802 Legion of Honour established

1809 Napoleon divorces Josephine and marries Marie-Louise

1815 Waterloo; second abdication of Napoleon. Restoration of the monarchy

1800	1805	1810	1815	1820

1804 Napoleon crowned

1800 Napoleon returns from Egypt on his ship *L'Orient*

1806 Arc de Triomphe commissioned

1812 Russian campaign ends in defeat

1814 Napoleon abdicates

Napoleon's death mask

1821 Napoleon dies

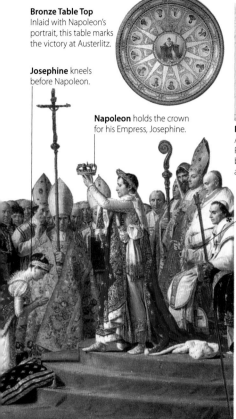

Bronze Table Top
Inlaid with Napoleon's portrait, this table marks the victory at Austerlitz.

Josephine kneels before Napoleon.

Napoleon holds the crown for his Empress, Josephine.

The Pope makes the sign of the cross.

Russian Cossacks in the Palais-Royal
After Napoleon's defeat and flight in 1814, Paris suffered the humiliation of being occupied by foreign troops, including Austrians, Prussians and Russians.

Where to see Napoleonic Paris

Many of the grand monuments Napoleon planned for Paris were never built, but two triumphal arches, the Arc de Triomphe (pp212–13) and Arc de Triomphe du Carrousel (p122), were a major part of his legacy. La Madeleine church (p218) was also inaugurated in his reign and much of the Louvre was rebuilt (pp122–3). Examples of the Empire style can be seen at Malmaison (p257) and at the Carnavalet (pp96–7).

Napoleon's Coronation

Napoleon's rather dramatic crowning took place in 1804. In this recreation by J L David, the Pope, summoned to Notre-Dame, looks on as Napoleon crowns his Empress just before crowning himself.

The Empress
Josephine was divorced by Napoleon in 1809.

The Arc de Triomphe du Carrousel was erected in 1806 and crowned with the horses looted from St Mark's, Venice.

1842 First railway line between Paris and St-Germain-en-Laye opens

1825	1830	1835	1840	1845

1830 Revolution in Paris and advent of constitutional monarchy

1831 Victor Hugo's *Notre-Dame de Paris* published. Cholera epidemic hits Paris

1840 Reburial of Napoleon at Les Invalides

Napoleon's tomb

The Grand Transformation

In 1848 Paris saw a second revolution which brought down the recently restored monarchy. In the uncertainties that followed, Napoleon's nephew assumed power in the same way as his uncle before him – by a *coup d'état*. He proclaimed himself Napoleon III in 1851. Under his rule Paris was transformed into the most magnificent city in Europe. He entrusted the task of modernization to Baron Haussmann. Haussmann demolished the crowded, unsanitary streets of the medieval city and created a well-ordered capital within a geometrical grid of avenues and boulevards. Neighbouring districts such as Auteuil were annexed, creating the suburbs.

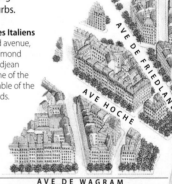

Extent Of The City
▨ 1859   ▢ Today

Boulevard des Italiens
This tree-lined avenue, painted by Edmond Georges Grandjean (1889), was one of the most fashionable of the new boulevards.

Twelve avenues
formed a star (*étoile*).

AVE DE FRIEDLAND

AVE HOCHE

AVE DE WAGRAM

AVE MAC-MAHON

AVE CARNOT

PLAC

Laying the Sewers
This engraving from 1861 shows the early work for laying the sewer system *(see p192)* from La Villette to Les Halles. Most was the work of the engineer Belgrand .

Circular Hoarding
Distinctive hoardings advertised opera and theatre performances.

Grand mansions
were built around the Arc de Triomphe between 1860 and 1868.

1851 Napoleon III declares the Second Empire

1852 Haussmann begins massive town-planning schemes

Viewing the exhibits at the World Exhibition

1855 World Exhibition

1850	1852	1854	1856	1858

1853 Baltard starts work on new Les Halles buildings

20 centimes stamp showing Napoleon III

1857 The poet, Baudelaire, prosecuted for obscenity for *The Flowers of Evil*

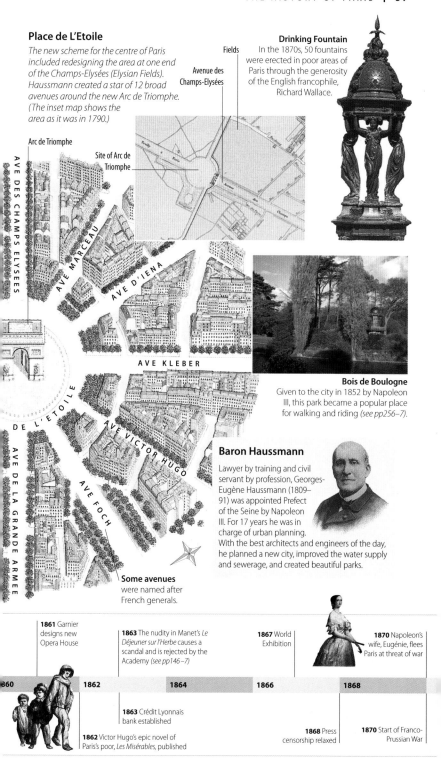

Place de L'Etoile

The new scheme for the centre of Paris included redesigning the area at one end of the Champs-Elysées (Elysian Fields). Haussmann created a star of 12 broad avenues around the new Arc de Triomphe. (The inset map shows the area as it was in 1790.)

Fields

Avenue des Champs-Elysées

Arc de Triomphe

Site of Arc de Triomphe

Drinking Fountain
In the 1870s, 50 fountains were erected in poor areas of Paris through the generosity of the English francophile, Richard Wallace.

AVE DES CHAMPS ELYSEES

AVE MARCEAU

AVE D'IENA

AVE KLEBER

DE L'ETOILE

AVE VICTOR HUGO

AVE FOCH

AVE DE LA GRANDE ARMEE

Bois de Boulogne
Given to the city in 1852 by Napoleon III, this park became a popular place for walking and riding *(see pp256–7)*.

Baron Haussmann

Lawyer by training and civil servant by profession, Georges-Eugène Haussmann (1809–91) was appointed Prefect of the Seine by Napoleon III. For 17 years he was in charge of urban planning. With the best architects and engineers of the day, he planned a new city, improved the water supply and sewerage, and created beautiful parks.

Some avenues were named after French generals.

1861 Garnier designs new Opera House

1863 The nudity in Manet's *Le Déjeuner sur l'Herbe* causes a scandal and is rejected by the Academy *(see pp146–7)*

1867 World Exhibition

1870 Napoleon's wife, Eugénie, flees Paris at threat of war

860   **1862**   **1864**   **1866**   **1868**

1863 Crédit Lyonnais bank established

1862 Victor Hugo's epic novel of Paris's poor, *Les Misérables*, published

1868 Press censorship relaxed

1870 Start of Franco-Prussian War

The Belle Epoque

The Franco-Prussian War culminated in the terrible Siege of Paris. When peace came in 1871, it fell to the new government, the Third Republic, to bring about economic recovery. From about 1890 life was transformed: the motor-car, aeroplane, cinema, telephone and gramophone all contributed to the enjoyment of life and the *Belle Époque* (beautiful age) was born. Paris became a glittering city where the new style, *Art Nouveau*, decorated buildings and objects. The paintings of the Impressionists, such as Renoir, reflected the *joie de vivre* of the times, while later those of Matisse, Braque and Picasso heralded the modern movement in art.

Extent of the City
▨ 1895   ▢ Today

The interior was arranged as tiers of galleries around a central grand staircase.

Cabaret Poster
Toulouse-Lautrec's posters immortalized the singers and dancers of the cafés and cabaret clubs of Montmartre, where artists and writers congregated in the 1890s.

Electricity illuminated the window displays.

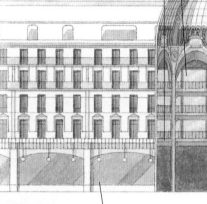

Central Hall of the Grand Palais
The Grand Palais *(p210)* was built to house two huge exhibitions of French painting and sculpture at the World Exhibition of 1889.

Windows facing on to the Boulevard Haussmann displayed the goods on offer.

The Naughty Nineties
The Lumière brothers captured the daring negligée fashions of the 1890s in the first moving images of the cinematograph.

1871 Third Republic established

1874 Monet paints first Impressionist picture: *Impression: Soleil levant*

1885 Louis Pasteur discovers rabies vaccine

1891 First metro station opens

1889 Eiffel Tower built

| 1870 | 1875 | 1880 | 1885 | 1890 |

Zoo animals were shot to feed the hungry (see p226)

1870 Siege of Paris

Entrance ticket to the exhibition

Louis Pasteur

1889 Great Exhibition

Citroën 5CV
France led the world in the early development of the motor-car. By 1900, the Citroën began to be seen on the streets of Paris, and long-distance motor racing was popular.

The glass dome could be seen from all parts of the store.

Moulin Rouge (1890)
The old, redundant windmills of Montmartre became nightclubs, like the world-famous Moulin Rouge (red windmill) (see p230).

Galeries Lafayette (1906)
This beautiful department store, with its dome a riot of coloured glass and wrought ironwork, was a sign of the new prosperity.

Art Nouveau Cash Till
Even ordinary objects like this cash till were beautified by the new style.

Where to see the Belle Epoque

Art Nouveau can be seen in monumental buildings like the Grand Palais and Petit Palais (p210), while the Galeries Lafayette (p313) has beautiful belle époque interiors. The Musée d'Orsay (pp146–9) has many objects from this period.

The entrance to the metro at Porte Dauphine was the work of leading Art Nouveau designer Hector Guimard (p148).

The doorway of No. 29 Avenue Rapp (p193), in the Eiffel Tower quarter, is a fine example of Art Nouveau.

Captain Dreyfus was publicly humiliated for selling secrets to the Prussians. He was later found innocent.

1894–1906 Dreyfus affair

1907 Picasso paints *Les Demoiselles d'Avignon*

1913 Proust publishes first volume of *Remembrance of Things Past*

| 1895 | 1900 | 1905 | 1910 |

1898 Pierre and Marie Curie discover radium

1895 Lumière brothers introduce cinematography

1909 Blériot flies across the English Channel

1911 Diaghilev brings the Russian ballet to Paris

Avant-Garde Paris

From the 1920s to the 1940s, Paris became a mecca for artists, musicians, writers and film-makers. The city was alive with new movements such as Cubism and Surrealism represented by Cézanne, Picasso, Braque, Man Ray and Duchamp. Many new trends came from the USA, as writers and musicians including Ernest Hemingway, Gertrude Stein and Sidney Bechet took up residence in Paris. In architecture, the geometric shapes created by Le Corbusier changed the face of the modern building.

Extent Of The City
1940   Today

Occupied Paris
Paris was under occupation for most of World War II. The Eiffel Tower was a favourite spot for German soldiers.

Napoleon by Abel Gance
Paris has always been a city for film-makers. In 1927 Abel Gance made an innovative movie about Napoleon, using triple screens and wide-angle lenses.

Josephine Baker
Arriving in Paris in 1925, the outlandish dancer catapulted to fame in "La Revue Nègre" wearing nothing but feathers.

Living space was made into a picture gallery.

Sidney Bechet
In the 1930s and 1940s the jazz clubs of Paris resounded to the swing music of black musicians such as the saxophonist Sidney Bechet.

Stilts supported the concrete shell.

La Roche Villa By Le Corbusier
Made from concrete and steel, with straight lines, horizontal windows and a flat roof, this house (1923) epitomized the new style.

1919 Treaty of Versailles signed in the Hall of Mirrors

1924 Olympic Games held in Paris

1924 André Breton publishes Surrealist Manifesto

1925 Art Deco style first seen at the Exposition des Arts Décoratifs

1914	1916	1918	1920	1922	1924	1926	1928

1914–18 World War I. Paris is under threat of German attack, saved by the Battle of the Marne. A shell hits St-Gervais- St-Protais.

World War I soldier in uniform

1920 Interment of the Unknown Soldier

An eternal flame for the Unknown Soldier burns under the Arc de Triomphe

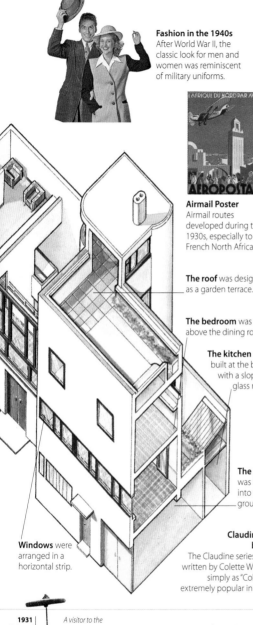

Fashion in the 1940s
After World War II, the classic look for men and women was reminiscent of military uniforms.

Airmail Poster
Airmail routes developed during the 1930s, especially to French North Africa.

The old Trocadéro was changed to the Palais de Chaillot *(see p202)* for the World Exhibition.

Where to See Avant-Garde Paris

La Roche Villa is now part of the Fondation Le Corbusier *(p256)* and can be visited in the Paris suburb of Auteuil. Hemingway's haunt, the bar-brasserie La Closerie des Lilas in Montparnasse *(p181)*, has retained much of its period decor. For fashion don't miss the Musée Galliera *(p205)*.

The roof was designed as a garden terrace.

The bedroom was above the dining room.

The kitchen was built at the back with a sloping glass roof.

The garage was built into the ground floor.

Windows were arranged in a horizontal strip.

Claudine in Paris by Colette
The Claudine series of novels, written by Colette Willy, known simply as "Colette", were extremely popular in the 1930s.

1931 Colonial Exhibition

A visitor to the exhibition in colonial dress

1937 Picasso paints Guernica in protest at the Spanish Civil War

1940 World War II: Paris bombed and occupied by Nazis

| 1930 | 1932 | 1934 | 1936 | 1938 | 1940 | 1942 |

Symbol of Free French super-imposed on the victory sign

Aug 1944 Liberation of Paris

1934 Riots and strikes in response to the Depression

1935 The talented Edith Piaf discovered dancing in the Paris streets

1937 Palais de Chaillot built

The Modern City

In 1962 a programme of renovation began, with run-down districts like the Marais being restored. This work was continued by François Mitterrand's *Grands Travaux* (great works) scheme. Access was improved to historical monuments and art collections, such as the Musée du Louvre *(see pp122–9)* and the Musée d'Orsay *(pp146–9)*. The scheme produced several monuments to the modern age, including the Opéra National de Paris Bastille *(p102)*, the Cité des Sciences *(pp240–41)* and the Bibliothèque Nationale at Quai de la Gare *(p248)*. With these, and the boldly modern Défense, Grande Arche, Stade de France and Musée du quai Branly building, Paris prepared herself for the 21st century.

Extent Of The City
▢ 1959   ▢ Today

La Grande Arche is taller and wider than Notre-Dame and runs in an axis linking the Arc de Triomphe and the Louvre Pyramid.

Christo's Pont Neuf
To create a work of art, the Bulgarian-born artist Christo wrapped Paris's oldest bridge, the Pont Neuf, in fabric in 1985.

Simone de Beauvoir
Influential philosopher and life-long companion of J-P Sartre, de Beauvoir fought for the liberation of women in the 1950s.

Shopping centre

Citroën Goddess (1956)
With its ultra-modern lines, this became Paris's most prestigious car.

1950 Construction of UNESCO, and the Musée de Radio-France	**1962** André Malraux, Minister of Culture, begins renovation programme of run-down districts and monuments	*Ducting at the Pompidou Centre*	**1977** Pompidou Centre opens. Jacques Chirac is installed as first elected Mayor of Paris since 1871	**1980** Thousands greet Pope John-Paul on his official vis

1945	1950	1955	1960	1965	1970	1975	1980

President de Gaulle

	1958 Establishment of Fifth Republic with de Gaulle as President	**1964** Reorganization of the Ile de France	**1968** Student riots and workers strikes in the Latin Quarter	**1973** Construction of Montparnasse Tower and the Périphérique (ring road)

1969 Les Halles market transfers to Rungis

1985 Christ wraps Pont Ne

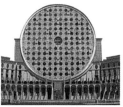

Marne La Vallée
Like a gigantic loud speaker, this residential complex is in one of Paris's dormitory towns near Disneyland® Paris.

Chanel Designs
Paris is the centre of the fashion world with important shows each year.

The Pompidou Centre
The nation's collection of modern art is housed here in this popular building (see pp110–13).

The Fiat Tower
vis one of Europe's tallest buildings.

Opéra National de Paris Bastille (1989)
It marks the bicentenary of the fall of the Bastille.

Students at the Barricades

In May 1968 Paris saw a revolution of a kind. The Latin Quarter was taken over by students and workers. What began as a protest against the war in Vietnam spread to other issues and became an expression of discontent with the government. President de Gaulle rode out the storm but his prestige was severely damaged.

Rioting students clash with police

The Défense Palace, housing the centre for industry, is the oldest tower.

La Défense
This huge business centre was started on the edge of Paris in 1958. Over 150,000 people work here with further expansion due by 2015.

Victorious French football team holding aloft the World Cup trophy in Paris

2002 The Euro replaces the Franc as exclusive legal tender

2007 The Vélib', a public rental bike scheme is launched

2012 Socialist François Hollande elected President

'85 | **1990** | **1995** | **2000** | **2005** | **2010** | **2015** | **2020**

1989 Bicentenary celebrations to mark the French Revolution

1994 Eurostar inaugurated: Paris to London in 3 hrs

1999 December hurricanes hit Paris: Versailles loses 10,000 trees

2007 Centre-right Nicolas Sarkozy elected president

1998 France hosts – and wins – the 1998 football World Cup tournament

PARIS AT A GLANCE

There are nearly 300 places of interest described in the *Area by Area* section of this book. A broad range of sights is covered from the ancient Conciergerie and its grisly associations with the guillotine *(see p87)*, to the modern Opéra National de Paris Bastille *(see p102);* and from the oldest house in Paris, No. 51 Rue de Montmorency *(see p116)*, to the exotic Musée du quai Branly *(see pp194–5)*.

To help make the most of your stay, the following 20 pages are a time-saving guide to the best Paris has to offer. Museums and galleries, historic churches, spacious parks, gardens and squares are all described. There is also a guide to Paris's famous personalities. Each sight has a cross reference to its own full entry. Below are the top tourist attractions to start you off.

Paris's Top Tourist Attractions

Sacré-Coeur
See pp226–7.

Sainte-Chapelle
See pp88–9.

Palace of Versailles
See pp250–55.

Pompidou Centre
See pp110–13.

Jardin du Luxembourg
See p174.

Musée du Louvre
See pp122–9.

Musée d'Orsay
See pp146–9.

Eiffel Tower
See pp196–7.

Bois de Boulogne
See pp256–7.

Notre-Dame
See pp82–5.

Arc de Triomphe
See pp212–13.

◄ Interior of Notre-Dame Cathedral

Remarkable Parisians

By virtue of its strategic position on the Seine, Paris has always been the economic, political and artistic hub of France. Over the centuries, many prominent and influential figures from other parts of the country and abroad have come to the city to absorb her unique spirit. In return, they have left their mark: artists have brought new movements, politicians new schools of thought, musicians and film-makers new trends, and architects a new environment.

Actress Catherine Deneuve

Sacré-Coeur by Utrillo (1934)

Artists

In the early 18th-century, Jean-Antoine Watteau (1684–1721) took the inspiration for his paintings from the Paris theatre. Half a century later, Jean-Honoré Fragonard (1732–1806), popular painter of the Rococo, lived and died here, financially ruined by the Revolution. Later, Paris became the cradle of Impressionism. Its founders Claude Monet (1840–1926), Pierre-Auguste Renoir (1841–1919) and Alfred Sisley (1839–99) met in a Paris studio. In 1907, Pablo

Picasso (1881–1973) painted the seminal work *Les Demoiselles d'Avignon* at the Bateau-Lavoir, *(see p230)* where Georges Braque (1882–1963), Amedeo Modigliani (1884–1920) and Marc Chagall (1887–1985) also lived. Henri de Toulouse-Lautrec (1864–1901) drank and painted in Montmartre. So did Salvador Dalí (1904–89), who frequented the Café Cyrano, centre of the Surrealists. The Paris School eventually moved to Montparnasse, home to sculptors Auguste Rodin (1840–1917), Constantin Brancusi (1876–1957) and Ossip Zadkine (1890–1967).

Political Leaders

Hugh Capet, Count of Paris, became King of France in 987. His palace was on the Ile de la Cité. Louis XIV, XV and XVI lived at Versailles *(see pp250–55)* but Napoleon *(see pp34–5)* preferred the Tuileries. Cardinal Richelieu (1585–1642), the power behind Louis XIII, created the Académie Française and the Palais-Royal *(see p130)*. Today, the President lives in the Palais de l'Elysée *(p211)*.

Portrait of Cardinal Richelieu by Philippe de Champaigne (about 1635)

Films and Film-Makers

Paris has always been at the heart of French cinema. The prewar and immediate post-war classics were usually made on the sets of the Boulogne and Joinville studios, where whole areas of the city were reconstructed, such as the Canal St-Martin for Marcel Carné's *Hôtel du Nord*. Jean-Luc Godard and other New Wave directors preferred to shoot outdoors. Godard's *A Bout de Souffle* (1960) with Jean-Paul Belmondo and Jean Seberg was filmed in and around the Champs-Elysées.

Simone Signoret (1921–85) and Yves Montand (1921–91), the most celebrated couple of French cinema, were long associated with the Ile de la Cité. Actresses, such as Catherine Deneuve (b.1943) and Isabelle Adjani (b.1955), live in the city to be near their couturiers.

Musicians

Jean-Philippe Rameau (1683–1764), organist and pioneer of harmony, is associated with St-Eustache *(see p116)*. Hector Berlioz (1803–69) had his *Te Deum* first performed there in 1855, and Franz Liszt (1811–86) his *Messe Solemnelle* in 1866. A great dynasty of organists, the Couperins, gave recitals in St-Gervais–St-Protais *(see p103)*.

The stage of the Opéra *(see p219)* has seen many talents, but audiences have not always been appreciative. Richard Wagner (1813–83) had his *Tannhäuser* barracked. George Bizet's *Carmen* (1838–75) was booed, as was *Peléas et Mélisande* by Claude Debussy (1862–1918).

Soprano Maria Callas (1923–77) gave triumphal performances here. The composer and conductor Pierre Boulez (b.1925) has devoted his talent to experimental music at IRCAM near the Pompidou Centre (see p338), which he helped to found.

The diminutive *chanteuse* Edith Piaf (1915–63), known for her nostalgic love songs, began singing in the streets of Paris and then went on to tour the world. The acclaimed film about her life, *La Vie en Rose*, was released in 2007.

The Grand Trianon at Versailles, built by Louis Le Vau in 1668

Renée Jeanmaire as Carmen (1948)

Architects

Gothic, Classical, Baroque and Modernist – all co-exist in Paris. The most brilliant medieval architect was Pierre de Montreuil, who built Notre-Dame and Sainte-Chapelle. Louis Le Vau (1612–70) and Jules

Hardouin-Mansart (1646–1708) designed Versailles (see pp250–55). Jacques-Ange Gabriel (1698–1782) built the Petit Trianon (see p251) and Place de la Concorde (see p133). Haussmann (1809–91) gave the city its boulevards (see p36–7). Gustave Eiffel (1832–1923) built his tower in 1889. A century later, I M Pei added the Louvre's glass pyramid (see p129), Jean Nouvel created the Institut du Monde Arabe (see p166–7) and the Musée du Quai Branly (see pp194–5), while Dominique Perrault was behind the Bibliothèque Nationale de France (see p248).

Writers

French has been dubbed "the language of Molière", after playwright Jean-Baptiste Poquelin, alias Molière, (1622–73), who helped create the Comédie-Française, now situated near his home in Rue Richelieu. On the Left Bank, the Odéon Théâtre de l'Europe was home to playwright Jean Racine (1639–99). It is near the statue of Denis Diderot (1713–84), who

published his *L'Encyclopédie* between 1751 and 1776. Marcel Proust (1871–1922), author of the 13-volume *Remembrance of Things Past*, lived on the Boulevard Haussmann. To the existentialists, the district of St-Germain was the only place to be (see pp144–5). Here, Sylvia Beach welcomed James Joyce (1882–1941) to her bookshop on the Rue de l'Odéon. Ernest Hemingway (1899–1961) and F Scott Fitzgerald (1896–1940) wrote novels in Montparnasse.

Proust by J-E Blanche (about 1910)

Scientists

Paris has a Quartier Pasteur, a Boulevard Pasteur, a Pasteur metro and the world-famous Institut Pasteur (see p249), all in honour of Louis Pasteur (1822–95), the great French chemist and biologist. His apartment and laboratory are faithfully preserved. The Institut Pasteur is today home to Professor Luc Montagnier, who first isolated the AIDS virus in 1983. Discoverers of radium, Pierre (1859–1906) and Marie Curie (1867–1934), also worked in Paris. The Curies have been the subject of a long-running play in Paris, *Les Palmes de M. Schutz*.

Exiled in Paris

The Duke and Duchess of Windsor married in France after his abdication in 1936 as King Edward VIII. The city granted them a rent-free mansion in the Bois de Boulogne. Other famous exiles have included Chou En-Lai (1898–1976), Ho Chi Minh (1890–1969), Vladimir Ilyich Lenin (1870–1924), Oscar Wilde (1854–1900) and ballet dancer Rudolf Nureyev (1938–93).

The Duke and Duchess of Windsor

Paris's Best: Churches

The Catholic Church has been the bastion of Parisian society through time. Many of the city's churches are worth visiting. Architectural styles vary and the interiors are often spectacular. Most churches are open during the day and many have services at regular intervals. Paris's tradition of church music is still alive. You can spend an evening enjoying the interiors while listening to an organ recital or classical concert *(see p338)*. A more detailed overview of Paris churches is on pages 50–51.

La Madeleine
Built in the style of a Greco-Roman temple, this church is known for its fine sculptures.

0 kilometres 1

0 miles 0.5

Champs-Elysées

Chaillot Quarter

River Seine

Invalides and Eiffel Tower Quarter

Dôme Church
This memorial to the military engineer Vauban lies in the Dôme Church, where Napoleon's remains were buried in 1840.

Sainte-Chapelle
With its fine stained glass, this chapel is a medieval jewel.

Panthéon
The Neo-Classical Sainte-Geneviève, now the Panthéon, was inspired by Wren's St Paul's Cathedral in London.

Sacré-Coeur
Above the altar in this massive basilica, the chancel vault is decorated with a vast mosaic of Christ by Luc-Olivier Merson.

Montmartre

St-Eustache
With its mixture of Gothic and Renaissance styles, this is one of the finest churches in Paris.

St-Paul–St-Louis
This Christ figure is one of the many rich furnishings in this Jesuit church, built in 1641 for Cardinal Richelieu.

Opéra Quarter

Tuileries Quarter

Beaubourg and Les Halles

The Marais

-Germain-des-Prés

Ile de la Cité

Ile St-Louis

Notre-Dame
The great cathedral was left to rot after the Revolution, until Victor Hugo led a restoration campaign.

Latin Quarter

Luxembourg Quarter

Jardin des Plantes Quarter

ntparnasse

Mosquée de Paris
The minaret of this 1920s mosque is 33 m (100 ft) tall.

St-Séverin
The west door leads to one of the finest medieval churches in the city.

Exploring Paris's Churches

Some of Paris's finest architecture is reflected in the churches. The great era of church building was the medieval period but examples survive from all ages. During the Revolution *(see pp32–3)* churches were used as grain or weapons stores but were later restored to their former glory. Many churches have superb interiors with fine paintings and sculptures.

Facade of Chapelle de la Sorbonne

Tower of St-Germain-des-Prés

Medieval

Both the pointed arch and the rose window were born in a suburb north of Paris at the Basilique-Cathédrale de St-Denis, where most of the French kings and queens are buried. This was the first Gothic building, and it was from here that the Gothic style spread. The finest Gothic church in Paris is the city cathedral, **Notre-Dame**, tallest and most impressive of the early French cathedrals. Begun in 1163 by Bishop Maurice de Sully, it was completed over the next century by architects Jean de Chelles and Pierre de Montreuil, who added the transepts with their fine translucent rose windows. Montreuil's masterpiece is Louis IX's medieval palace chapel, **Sainte-Chapelle**, with its two-tier structure. It was built to house Christ's Crown of Thorns. Other surviving churches in Paris are **St-Germain-des-Prés**, the oldest surviving abbey church in Paris (1050); the tiny, rustic Romanesque **St-Julien-le-Pauvre**; and the Flamboyant Gothic **St-Séverin**, **St-Germain l'Auxerrois** and **St-Merri**.

Renaissance

The effect of the Italian Renaissance swept through Paris in the 16th century. It led to a unique architectural style in which fine Classical detail and immense Gothic proportions resulted in an impure, but attractive cocktail known as "French Renaissance". The best example in Paris is **St-Etienne-du-Mont**, whose interior has the feel of a wide and light basilica. Another is **St-Eustache**, the massive market church in Les Halles, and the nave of **St-Gervais–St-Protais** with its stained glass and carved choir stalls.

St-Gervais–St-Protais

Baroque and Classical

Churches and convents flourished in Paris during the 17th century, as the city expanded under Louis XIII and his son Louis XIV. The Italian Baroque style was first seen on the majestic front of **St-Gervais–St-Protais**, built by Salomon de Brosse in 1616. The style was toned down to suit French tastes and the rational temperament of the Age of Enlightenment *(see pp30–31)*. The result was a harmonious and monumental Classicism in the form of columns and domes. One example is the **Chapelle de la Sorbonne**, completed by Jacques Lemercier in 1642 for Cardinal Richelieu. Grander and more richly decorated, with a painted dome, is the church built by François Mansart to honour the birth of the Sun King at the **Val-de-Grâce** convent. The true gem of the period is Jules Hardouin-Mansart's **Dôme des Invalides**, with its enormous gilded

---

Towers, Domes and Spires

Paris's many churches have dominated her skyline since early Christian times. The Gothic Tour St-Jacques, the only element still extant from a long-gone church, reflects the medieval love of the defensive tower. St-Etienne-du-Mont, with its pointed gable and rounded pediment, shows the transition from Gothic to Renaissance. The dome, a much-used feature of the French Baroque, was used to perfection in the Val-de-Grâce, while St-Sulpice with its severe arrangement of towers and portico is typically Neo-Classical. With its ornate spires, Ste-Clotilde is a Gothic Revival church. Modern landmarks include the mosque, with its minaret.

Gothic

Tour St-Jacques

St-Etienne-du-Mont

Renaissance

dome. Jesuit extravagance can be seen in **St-Paul–St-Louis** built in the style of Il Gesú in Rome. In contrast are Libéral Bruand's chapels, the **Salpêtrière** and **Cathedral of St-Louis-des-Invalides** with their severe geometry and unadorned simplicity. Other fine Classical churches are **St-Joseph-des-Carmes** and the 18th-century bankers' church, **St-Roch**, with its Baroque Marian chapel.

Interior of the Panthéon

Neo-Classical

An obsession with all things Greek and Roman swept France in the mid-18th century and well into the 19th century. The excavations at Pompeii (1738) and the influence of the Italian architect Andrea Palladio produced a generation of architects fascinated by the column, geometry and engineering. The best example of such churches is Jacques-Germain Soufflot's Sainte-Geneviève, now the **Panthéon**. Begun in 1773, its colonnaded dome was also inspired by Christopher Wren's

St Paul's in London. The dome is supported by four pillars, built by Guillaume Rondelet, linking four great arches. The first colonnaded facade was Giovanni Niccolo Servandoni's **St-Sulpice**. Construction of this church began in 1733 and consisted of a two-storey portico, topped by a triangular pediment. **La Madeleine**, Napoleon's grand temple to his victorious army, was constructed on the ground plan of a Greco-Roman temple.

Second Empire and Modern

Franz Christian Gau's **Sainte-Clotilde** of the 1840s is the first and best example in Paris of the Gothic Revival or *style religieux*. Showy churches were built in the new districts created by Haussmann in the Second Empire (pp36–7). One of the most lovely is Victor Baltard's St-Augustin, at the intersection of the Boulevard Malesherbes and the Boulevard de la Madeleine. Here historic detail combines with modern iron columns and girders in a soaring interior space. The great basilica of the late 19th century, **Sacré-Coeur**, was built as a gesture of religious defiance. **St-Jean l'Evangéliste** by Anatole de Baudot is an interesting modern church combining the Art Nouveau style with Islamic arches. The modern gem of Islamic architecture, the **Mosquée de Paris**, is an attractive 1920s building in the Hispanic-Moorish style. It has a grand patio, inspired by the Alhambra, woodwork in cedar and eucalyptus, and a fountain.

The arches of St-Jean L'Evangéliste, reminiscent of Islamic architecture

Finding the Churches

Val-de-Grâce

Baroque and Classical

St-Sulpice

Neo-Classical

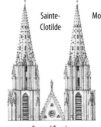

Sainte-Clotilde

Second Empire

Mosquée de Paris

Modern

Paris's Best: Gardens, Parks and Squares

Few cities can boast the infinite variety of styles found in Parisian gardens, parks and squares today. They date from many different periods and have been central to Parisian life for the past 300 years. The Bois de Boulogne and the Bois de Vincennes enclose the city with their lush, green open spaces, while elegant squares and landscaped gardens, such as the Jardin du Luxembourg, brighten the inner city and provide a retreat for those craving a few moments peace from the bustling city.

Parc Monceau
This English-style park features many follies, grottoes, magnificent trees and rare plants.

Champs-Elysées

Chaillot
Quarter

Tuileries
Quarter

River Seine

Invalides and Eiffel
Tower Quarter

Montparnasse

Bois de Boulogne
The Bagatelle gardens, set in this wooded park, have an amazing array of flowers including the spectacular rose garden.

Esplanade des Invalides
From this huge square, lined with lime trees, are some brilliant views over the quays.

Jardin des Tuileries
These gardens are renowned for ornamental ponds, terraces and the collection of bronze figures by Aristide Maillol.

Parc des Buttes-Chaumont
Once a scraggy hilltop, this park was transformed to provide open spaces for the growing city. It is now beautifully landscaped with huge cliffs revealing caves.

Square du Vert-Galant
The square, named after Henri IV's nickname, forms the west point of the Ile de la Cité.

Place des Vosges
Considered one of the most beautiful squares in the world, it was finished in 1612 and is the oldest square in Paris.

Opéra
Quarter

Beaubourg
and Les
Halles

The Marais

Jardin des Plantes
The botanical garden has a vast collection of plants and flowers from around the world.

St-Germain-
des-Prés

Ile de la
Cité

Ile St-Louis

Latin
Quarter

Luxembourg
Quarter

Jardin des Plantes
Quarter

Bois de Vincennes
The flower garden in this charming park is the perfect place to relax.

Jardin du Luxembourg
This park is a favourite with Parisians wanting to escape the bustle of the Latin Quarter.

0 kilometres   1

0 miles   0.5

Exploring Gardens, Parks and Squares

Paris is dotted with many areas of parkland, intimate gardens and attractive tree-lined squares. Each is a reminder of the French capital's illustrious past. Many squares were formed during Napoleon III's transformation of the city, creating a pleasant environment for Parisians to live in (see pp36–7). This aim has been preserved right up to the present day. Paris's parks and gardens have their own character; some are ideal for a stroll, others for romance, while some provide space for sporting activities such as a game of *boules*.

A haven of peace in a busy district is the **Jardin du Palais-Royal**, built by Cardinal Richelieu in the 17th century. An elegant arcade encloses the garden. The 19th-century **Parc Monceau**, in the English picturesque style, has follies and grottoes. The flat **Jardins des Invalides** and the landscaped **Champ-de-Mars** were the grounds of the Hôtel des Invalides and the Ecole Militaire. They were the site of the Paris Universal Exhibition, whose reminder is the Eiffel Tower (pp196–7).

An attractive public garden is attached to the lovely Hôtel Biron, home of the **Musée Rodin**. The 17th-century botanical garden **Jardin des Plantes** is famous for its ancient trees, flowers, alpine garden, hothouses and small zoo.

Engraving of the Jardin du Palais-Royal (1645)

Historic Gardens

The oldest public gardens in Paris were made for queens of France – the **Jardin des Tuileries** for Catherine de Médicis in the 16th century, and the **Jardin du Luxembourg** for Marie de Médicis in the 17th century. The Tuileries form the beginning of the axis running from the Arc de Triomphe du Carrousel through the Arc de Triomphe (pp212–13) to La Défense (p257). These gardens retain the formality devised by landscape architect André Le Nôtre, originally for the **Palace of Versailles**. Many of the Jardin des Tuileries's original sculptures survive, as well as modern pieces, notably the bronze nudes by Aristide Maillol (1861–1944).

The Jardin du Luxembourg also has the traditional formal plan – straight paths, clipped lawns, Classical sculpture and a superb 17th-century fountain. It is shadier and more intimate than the Tuileries, with lots of seats, pony rides and puppet shows to amuse the children.

The **Jardins des Champs-Elysées**, also by Le Nôtre, were reshaped in the English style during the 19th century. The gardens have *Belle Époque* pavilions, three theatres (L'Espace Pierre Cardin, Théâtre Marigny and the Théâtre du Rond Point), smart restaurants – and the ghost of the novelist Marcel Proust, who once played here as a child.

Aquatic Garden, Bois de Vincennes

19th-Century Parks and Squares

The great 19th-century parks and squares owe much to Napoleon III's long exile in London before he came to power. The unregimented planting and rolling lawns of Hyde Park and the leafy squares of Mayfair inspired him to bring

Relaxing in Jardin du Luxembourg

Follies and Rotundas

Dramatic features of Paris's parks and gardens are the many follies and rotundas. Every age of garden design has produced these ornaments. The huge Gloriette de Buffon in the Jardin des Plantes was erected as a memorial to the great naturalist (p168). It is the oldest metal structure in Paris. The pyramid in the Parc Monceau, the oriental temple in the Bois de Boulogne, and the 19th-century temple of love in the Bois de Vincennes reflect a more sentimental age. In contrast are the stark, painted-concrete follies that grace the Parc de la Villette.

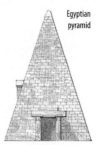

Egyptian pyramid

Parc Monceau

trees, fresh air and park benches to what was then Europe's most congested and dirty capital. Under his direction, landscape gardener Adolphe Alphand turned two woods at opposite ends of the city, the **Bois de Boulogne** (known as the "Bois") and the **Bois de Vincennes**, into English-style parks with duck ponds, lakes and flower gardens. He also added a racecourse to the "Bois". Its most attractive feature is the Bagatelle rose garden and the Jardin d'Acclimatation, a small theme park for families. The "Bois" is best avoided at night.

The two smaller Alphand parks are also pleasant, **Parc Montsouris** in the south and the **Parc des Buttes-Chaumont** in the northeast. The "Buttes" (hills), a favourite with the Surrealists, was a quarry transformed into two craggy mini-mountains with overhanging vegetation, suspended bridge, temple of love and a lake.

Part of the town-planning schemes for the old city included squares and avenues with fountains, sculptures, benches and greenery. One of the best is Ile de la Cité's **Square du Vert-Galant**. The Avenue de l'Observatoire in the **Jardin du Luxembourg** is rich in sculptures made by Jean-Baptiste Carpeaux.

Fountains and sculpture in the Jardins du Trocadéro

Modern Parks and Gardens

The shady **Jardins du Trocadéro** sloping down to the river from the Palais de Chaillot were planted after the 1937 Universal Exhibition. Here is the largest fountain in Paris and fine views of the river and the Eiffel Tower.

More recent Paris gardens eschew formality in favour of wilder planting, multiple levels, maze-like paths, children's gardens and modern sculpture. Typical are the **Parc André-Citroën**, the **Parc de la Villette** and the Jardin Atlantique next to the Gare Montparnasse.

Pleasant strolls may be taken in Paris's waterside gardens: in the modern sculpture park behind Notre-Dame, at the Bassin de l'Arsenal at the Bastille, and along the quays of the Seine between the Louvre and the Place de la Concorde, or on the elegantly residential Ile St-Louis. The planted walkway above the **Viaduc des Arts** is a peaceful way to observe eastern Paris.

Finding the Gardens, Parks and Squares

Parc Montsouris

Jardin des Plantes

Gloriette de Buffon

Bois de Boulogne

Oriental temple

Bois de Vincennes

Temple of love

Parc de la Villette

Modern folly

Paris's Best: Museums and Galleries

Some of the oldest, the newest, and certainly some of the finest museums and galleries are to be found in Paris – many are superb works of art in their own right. They house some of the greatest and strangest collections in the world. Some of the buildings complement their themes, such as the Roman baths and Gothic mansion which form the Musée National du Moyen Age, or the Pompidou Centre, a modern masterpiece. Elsewhere there is pleasing contrast, such as the Picassos in their gracious 17th-century museum, and the Musée d'Orsay housed in its grand old railway station. Together, they make an unrivalled feast for visitors.

Musée des Arts Décoratifs
Decorative and ornamental art like this Paris bathroom by Jeanne Lanvin is displayed here.

Chaillot Quarter

Champs-Elysées

River Seine

Invalides and Eiffel Tower Quarter

Petit Palais
A collection of works by the 19th-century sculptor Jean-Baptiste Carpeaux is housed here, including *The Fisherman and Shell*.

Musée du quai Branly
This wooden sculpture from Papua New Guinea is one of 3,500 artifacts housed in this striking anthropological museum.

Montparnasse

Musée Rodin
The museum brings together works bequeathed to the nation by sculptor Auguste Rodin, like the magnificent *Gates of Hell* doors.

Musée d'Orsay
Carpeaux's *Four Quarters of the World* (1867–72) can be found among this collection of 19th-century art.

Musée du Louvre
The museum boasts one of the world's great collections of paintings and sculpture, from the ancient civilizations to the 19th century. This Babylonian monument, the *Code of Hammurabi,* is the oldest set of laws in existence.

Pompidou Centre
Paris's modern art collection from 1905 to the present day is housed here. The centre also has art libraries and an industrial design centre.

Opéra Quarter

Tuileries Quarter

Beaubourg and Les Halles

The Marais

St-Germain-des-Prés

Ile de la Cité

Ile St-Louis

Latin Quarter

Luxembourg Quarter

Jardin des Plantes Quarter

Musée Picasso Paris
Sculptor and Model (1931) is one of many paintings on display in Picasso's private collection, "inherited" in lieu of tax by the French government after his death in 1973.

Musée Carnavalet
The museum is devoted to the history of Paris. Its historic buildings surround attractive garden courtyards.

Musée de Cluny – Musée National du Moyen Age
The remains of the Gallo-Roman baths are part of this museum of ancient and medieval art.

0 kilometres   1
0 miles   0.5

Exploring Paris's Museums and Galleries

Paris holds great treasures in its museums and art galleries. The major national art collection is to be found at the Musée du Louvre, which began collecting over 400 years ago and is still growing. Other important museums, such as the Musée d'Orsay, the Musée du quai Branly and the Pompidou Centre, have their own treasures, but there are scores of smaller, specialized museums, each with its own interest.

Altar, Musée National du Moyen Age

Greek, Roman and Medieval Art

The **Musée du Louvre** has a fine collection of sculptures from Greek and Roman times, along with medieval sculptures and vestiges of the medieval Louvre under the Sully wing. The **Musée de Cluny–Musée National du Moyen Age**, a superb 15th-century mansion, houses a major medieval collection. Highlights are the Unicorn Tapestries, the Kings' Heads from Notre-Dame and Basel Cathedral's golden altar. Third-century Roman baths adjoin the museum. Remains of houses from Roman and medieval Paris can be seen in the **Crypte Archéologique** near Notre-Dame cathedral.

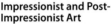

Old Masters

The *Mona Lisa* was one of the **Musée du Louvre's** first paintings, acquired over 400 years ago. It also has other fine Leonardos. They are to be found along with superb Titians, Raphaels and other Italian masters. Other works include Rembrandt's *Pilgrims at Emmäus*, Watteau's *Gilles* and Fragonard's *The Bathers*. The **Musée Cognacq-Jay** has a small, but exquisite, collection of paintings and drawings by 18th-century French painters. The **Musée Jacquemart-André** has works by such masters as Mantegna, Uccello, Canaletto, Rembrandt and Chardin.

Impressionist and Post-Impressionist Art

Installed in a converted 19th-century railway station, the **Musée d'Orsay** boasts the world's largest collection of art from the period 1848–1904. Admired for its fine Impressionist and Post-Impressionist collections,

Dead Poet in Musée Gustave Moreau

it also devotes a lot of space to the earlier Realists and the formerly reviled 19th-century academic and "Salon" masters. There are superb selections of Degas, Manet, Courbet, including his controversial *L'Origine du Monde*, Monet, Renoir, Millet, Cézanne, Bonnard and Vuillard, and some fine Gauguins, Van Goghs and Seurats.

A great ensemble of late Monets is to be found at the **Musée Marmottan Monet** and another at the **Musée de l'Orangerie**, including Monet's last great waterlily murals (1920–25). Here also is a good collection of Cézannes and late Renoirs.

Three artists' studios and homes are now museums of their life and work. The **Musée Rodin**, in an attractive 18th-century mansion and garden, offers a complete survey of the master's sculptures, drawings and paintings. The **Musée Delacroix**, set in a garden near St-Germain-des-Prés, has sketches, prints and oils by the Romantic artist. The **Musée Gustave Moreau**, in an atmospheric 19th-century town house, has an extraordinary collection of intricately painted canvases of legendary *femmes fatales* and dying youths. The **Petit Palais** has an interesting collection of 19th-century paintings with four major Courbets, including *The Sleep*.

Dante and Virgil in the Underworld (1822) by Delacroix, Musée du Louvre

Modern and Contemporary Art

As the international centre of the avant-garde from 1900 to 1940, Paris has a great concentration of modern painting and sculpture. The Pompidou Centre houses the **Musée National d'Art Moderne**, covering 1905 to the present. It has a good selection of Fauvist and Cubist works, particularly by Matisse, Rouault, Braque, Delaunay, and Leger, as well as works by the 1960s' *Nouveaux Réalistes*.

The **Musée d'Art Moderne de la Ville de Paris**, in the elegant 1930s Palais de Tokyo, also has an excellent collection, including Delaunays, Bonnards and Fauvist paintings. The highlight is Matisse's 1932 mural, *The Dance*. In the opposite wing of the same building, the **Palais de Tokyo** showcases some of today's most avant-garde artists.

The **Musée Picasso Paris,** in a lovely 17th-century mansion, has the world's largest Picasso collection, including paintings, drawings and sculptures. Picasso, Matisse, Modigliani, Utrillo and late Derains make up the collection on display at the **Musée de l'Orangerie**. For modern sculpture, the small **Musée Zadkine** has Cubist work by a minor school whose leading light was Ossip Zadkine. The **Musée Antoine Bourdelle** and the **Musée Maillol** house work by these two sculptors.

Penelope by Bourdelle

Furniture, Decorative Arts and Objets d'Art

Pride of place after painting must go to furniture and the decorative arts, contained in a plethora of museums. Fine ensembles of French furnishings and decoration are in the **Louvre** (medieval to Napoleonic) and at the **Palace** of Versailles (17th–18th century). Furniture and *objets d'art* from the Middle Ages to the present century are arranged in period rooms at the **Musée des Arts Décoratifs**. The **Musée d'Orsay** has a large collection of 19th-century furniture, notably Art Nouveau. Louis XV (1715–74) and Louis XVI (1774–93) furniture and decoration can be found in the **Musée Nissim de Camondo**, a mansion from 1912 facing the Parc Monceau. Other notable collections are the **Musée Cognacq-Jay**; the **Musée Carnavalet** (18th-century); the **Musée Jacquemart-André** (French furniture and earthenware); the **Musée Marmottan Monet** (Empire) and **Musée d'Art Moderne de la Ville de Paris** (Art Deco).

Cabinet from Musée des Arts Décoratifs

Jeweller's shop in the Carnavalet

Specialist Museums

Devotees of antique sporting guns, muskets and hounds of the chase should make for the attractive Marais **Hôtel Guénégaud** (Musée de la Chasse et de la Nature). This museum also has some fine 18th-century animal paintings by Jean-Baptiste Oudry and Alexandre-François Desportes, as well as others by Rubens and Brueghel. **The Musée de la Contrefaçon** gives a fascinating insight into the world of counterfeit with examples from every luxury trade, including perfume, wines and spirits, and clothing. Numismatists will find an extensive coin and medallion collection housed in luxurious surroundings at the 18th-century Paris Mint at the **Musée de la Monnaie**. French coins are no longer minted here, but the old Mint still makes medals which are on sale. Stamps are on show at the **Musée de la Poste**. The history of postal services is also covered, as are all aspects of philately old and new, with temporary shows on current philatelic design. Visitors can marvel at the vast national collection of minerals on display at the **Musée de Minéralogie**, which is housed in the Ecole Nationale Supérieure des Mines *(see p175)*. The collection includes 100,000 samples of minerals, rocks, meteorites, gems, ores and artifical minerals from 72 different countries.

Fashion and Costume

The two rival fashion museums in Paris are the **Palais Galliera** and the **Musée de la Mode** within the **Musée des Arts Décoratifs**. Neither has a permanent collection, but both hold regular shows devoted to the great Paris couturiers, such as Saint Laurent and Givenchy. They sometimes display fashion accessories as well and, more rarely but always fascinatingly, historical costumes.

Poster for the Palais Galliera

Asian, African and Oceanian Art

The major collection of Asian art in France is housed at the **Musée National des Arts Asiatiques Guimet**, covering China, Tibet, Japan, Korea, Indochina, Indonesia, India and Central Asia. It includes Chinese bronzes and lacquerware and some of the best Khmer art outside Cambodia. The **Musée Cernuschi** has a smaller but well-chosen Chinese collection, noted for its ancient bronzes and reliefs. France's premier showcase for African, Asian, American tribal and Oceanian arts and cultures is the **Musée du quai Branly**, which displays more than 3,500 objects in truly breathtaking surroundings. The **Musée Dapper** also houses African art and is part of an important ethnographic research centre, housed in an elegant 1901 hôtel particulier with an "African" garden. Its collection of tribal masks is particularly dazzling.

Sri Lankan theatrical mask

Café in Musée de Montmartre

History and Social History

Covering the entire history of the city of Paris, the **Musée Carnavalet** is housed in two historic Marais hôtels. It has period interiors, paintings of the city and old shop signs, a fascinating section covering events and artifacts from the French Revolution, and even Marcel Proust's bedroom. Also in the Marais, the **Musée d'Art et d'Histoire du Judaisme** explores the culture of French Jewry. The **Musée de l'Armée**, in the Hôtel des Invalides, recounts French military history, and the Musée de l'Histoire de France, in the Rococo **Hôtel de Soubise**, has historical documents from the national archives on display. Famous tableaux vivants and characters, both current and historical, await the visitor at the **Grévin** wax museum. The intriguing **Musée de Montmartre**, overlooking Paris's last surviving vineyard, holds exhibitions on the history of Montmartre.

Architecture and Design

The **Cité de l'Architecture et du Patrimoine** (see p202) charts the history of French architecture with scale models of its most iconic buildings. Superb scale models of fortresses built for Louis XIV and later are on display at the **Musée des Plans-Reliefs**. The work of the celebrated Franco-Swiss architect forms the basis of the **Fondation Le Corbusier**. The showpiece is his 1920s villa for his friend, art collector Raoul La Roche. Some of his furniture is also on display.

The French Impressionists

Impression: Sunrise by Monet

Impressionism, the great art revolution of the 19th century, began in Paris in the 1860s, when young painters, influenced in part by the new art of photography, started to break with the academic values of the past. They aimed to capture the "impression" of what the eye sees at a given moment and used brushwork designed to capture the fleeting effects of light falling on a scene. Their favourite subjects were landscapes and scenes from contemporary urban life.

The movement had no founder, though Edouard Manet (1832–83) and the radical Realist painter Gustave Courbet (1819–77) both inspired many of the younger artists. Paintings of scenes of everyday life by Manet and Courbet often offended the academicians who legislated artistic taste. In 1863 Manet's Le Déjeuner sur l'Herbe (see p146) was exhibited at the Salon des Refusés, an exhibition set up for paintings rejected by the official Paris Salon of that year. The first time the term "Impressionist" was used to describe this new artistic movement was at another unofficial exhibition, in 1874. The name came from a painting by Claude Monet, Impression: Sunrise, a view of Le Havre in the mist from 1872. Monet was almost exclusively a landscape artist, influenced by the works of the English artists, Constable and Turner. He always liked to paint out of doors and

Monet's sketchbooks

Harvesting (1876) by Pissarro

The living room of La Roche Villa by Le Corbusier (1923)

Science and Technology

In the Jardin des Plantes, the **Muséum National d'Histoire Naturelle** has sections on palaeontology, minerology, entomology, anatomy and botany, plus a zoo and a botanical garden. In the Palais de Chaillot, the **Musée de l'Homme** is a museum of anthropology and prehistory. It is due

Gabrielle (1910) by Renoir

encouraged others to follow his example.

At the 1874 exhibition, a critic wrote that one should stand well back to see these "impressions" – the further back the better – and that members of the establishment should retreat altogether. Other exhibitors at the show were Pierre-Auguste Renoir, Edgar Degas, Camille Pissarro, Alfred Sisley and Paul Cézanne.

There were seven more Impressionist shows up to 1886. By then the power of the Salon had waned and the whole direction of art had changed. From then on, new movements were defined in terms of their relation to Impressionism. The leading Neo-Impressionist was Georges Seurat, who used thousands of minute dots of colour to build up his paintings. It took later generations to fully appreciate the work of the Impressionists. Cézanne was

rejected all his life, Degas sold only one painting to a museum, and Sisley died unknown. Of the great artists whose genius is now universally recognized, only Renoir and Monet were ever acclaimed in their lifetimes.

Profile of a Model (1887) by Seurat

to reopen in 2015. Next door, the **Musée National de la Marine** covers French naval history from the 17th century onwards, with interesting 18th-century models of ships and sculpted figureheads. The **Musée des Arts et Métiers** displays the world of science and industry, invention and manufacturing. The **Palais de la Découverte** covers the history of science and has a good planetarium, somewhat overshadowed by the spectacular one at the **Cité des Sciences** in the Parc de la Villette. This museum is on several levels, with an IMAX 3D movie screen, the Géode.

Finding the Museums

Artists in Paris

The city first attracted artists during the reign of Louis XIV (1643–1715), and Paris became the most sophisticated artistic centre in Europe; the magnetism has persisted. During the 18th century, all major French artists lived and worked in Paris. In the the latter half of the 19th century and early part of the 20th century, Paris was the European centre of modern and progressive art, and movements such as Impressionism and Post-Impressionism were founded and blossomed in the city.

Rococo Artists

Boucher, François (1703–70)
Chardin, Jean-Baptiste-Siméon (1699–1779)
Falconet, Etienne-Maurice (1716–91)
Fragonard, Jean-Honoré (1732–1806)
Greuze, Jean-Baptiste (1725–1805)
Houdon, Jean-Antoine (1741–1828)
Oudry, Jean-Baptiste (1686–1755)
Pigalle, Jean-Baptiste (1714–85)
Watteau, Jean-Antoine (1684–1721)

Boucher's *Diana Bathing* (1742), typical of the Rococo style (Louvre)

Baroque Artists

Champaigne, Philippe de (1602–74)
Coysevox, Antoine (1640–1720)
Girardon, François (1628–1715)
Le Brun, Charles (1619–90)
Le Sueur, Eustache (1616–55)
Poussin, Nicolas (1594–1665)
Rigaud, Hyacinthe (1659–1743)
Vignon, Claude (1593–1670)
Vouet, Simon (1590–1649)

1600	1650	1700	1750	1800
Baroque			Neo-Classicism	Romanticis
1600	1650	1700	1750	1800

1627 Vouet returns from Italy and is made court painter by Louis XIII. Vouet revived a dismal period in the fortunes of French painting

1667 First Salon, France's official art exhibition; originally held annually, later every two years

Philippe de Champaigne's *Last Supper* (about 1652). His style slowly became more Classical in his later years (Louvre)

1793 Louvre opens as first national public gallery

1819 Géricault paints *The Raft of the Medusa*, one of the greatest works of French Romanticism (see p124)

1648 Foundation of the Académie Royale de Peinture et de Sculpture, which had a virtual monopoly on art teaching

Vouet's *The Presentation in the Temple* (1641) with typically Baroque contrasts of light and shade (Louvre)

Neo-Classical Artists

David, Jacques-Louis (1748–1825)
Gros, Antoine Jean (1771–1835)
Ingres, Jean-Auguste-Dominique (1780–1867)
Vigée-Lebrun, Elizabeth (1755–1842)

David's *The Oath of the Horatii* (1784), in the Neo-Classical style (Louvre)

Romantic and Realist Artists

Courbet, Gustave (1819–77)
Daumier, Honoré (1808–79)
Delacroix, Eugène (1798–1863)
Géricault, Théodore (1791–1824)
Rude, Francois (1784–1855)

Courbet's *The Burial at Ornans* (1850) which showed Courbet to be the foremost exponent of Realism (Musée d'Orsay)

Rude's *Departure of the Volunteers* in 1792 (1836), a tribute to the French Revolution *(see p213)*

Modern Artists

Arp, Jean (1887–1966)
Balthus (1908–2001)
Brancusi, Constantin (1876–1957)
Braque, Georges (1882–1963)
Buffet, Bernard (1928–99)
Chagall, Marc (1887–1985)
Delaunay, Robert (1885–1941)
Derain, André (1880–1954)
Dubuffet, Jean (1901–85)
Duchamp, Marcel (1887–1968)
Epstein, Jacob (1880–1959)
Ernst, Max (1891–1976)
Giacometti, Alberto (1901–66)
Gris, Juan (1887–1927)
Léger, Fernand (1881–1955)
Matisse, Henri (1869–1954)
Miró, Joan (1893–1983)
Modigliani, Amedeo (1884–1920)
Mondrian, Piet (1872–1944)
Picasso, Pablo (1881–1973)
Rouault, Georges (1871–1958)
Saint Phalle, Niki de (1930–2002)
Soutine, Chaim (1893–1943)
Stael, Nicolas de (1914–55)
Tinguely, Jean (1925–91)
Utrillo, Maurice (1883–1955)
Zadkine, Ossip (1890–1967)

Giacometti's *Standing Woman II* (1959), one of his many tall, thin bronze figures *(see p112)*

1874 First Impressionist exhibition

1886 Van Gogh moves to Paris

1904 Picasso settles in Paris

1905 Birth of Fauvism, the first of the "isms" in modern art

m	1850	1900	1950	2000	2050
		Impressionism Modernism			
	1850	1900	1950	2000	2050

1863 Manet's Le *Déjeuner sur l'Herbe* causes a scandalous sensation at the Salon des Refusés, both for "poor moral taste", and for its broad brushstrokes. The artist's *Olympia* was thought just as outrageous, but it was not exhibited until 1865 *(see p147)*

1938 International Surrealist exhibition in Paris

1977 Pompidou Centre opens

2011 Major two-year refurbishment of Musée d'Orsay complete, with new lighting to enhance viewing of Impressionist works of art

Delacroix's *Liberty* Leading the People (1830) romantically celebrates victory in war (Louvre)

Monet's *Impression: Sunrise* (1872), which led to the name Impressionism

Impressionist and Post-Impressionist Artists

Bonnard, Pierre (1867–1947)
Carpeaux, Jean-Baptiste (1827–75)
Cézanne, Paul (1839–1906)
Degas, Edgar (1834–1917)
Gauguin, Paul (1848–1903)
Manet, Edouard (1832–83)
Monet, Claude (1840–1926)
Pissarro, Camille (1830–1903)
Renoir, Pierre-Auguste (1841–1919)
Rodin, Auguste (1840–1917)
Rousseau, Henri (1844–1910)
Seurat, Georges (1859–91)
Sisley, Alfred (1839–99)
Toulouse-Lautrec, Henri de (1864–1901)
Van Gogh, Vincent (1853–90)
Vuillard, Edouard (1868–1940)
Whistler, James Abbott McNeill (1834–1903)

Tinguely and Saint Phalle's *Fontaine Igor Stravinsky* (1980), a modern kinetic sculpture (Pompidou Centre)

PARIS THROUGH THE YEAR

Paris's pulling power is strongest in spring – the season for chestnuts in blossom and sitting at tables under trees. From June, Paris is slowly turned over to tourists; the city almost comes to a standstill for the French Tennis Open, and the major race tracks stage the big summer horse races. Next comes the 14 July Bastille Day parade down the Champs-Elysées; towards the end of the month, the Tour de France usually ends here.

The end of July also sees the end of Paris's three-month Jazz Festival, after which most Parisians abandon the city to visitors until "la rentrée", the return to school and work in September. Dates of events listed on the following pages may vary. For details consult the listings magazines, or contact Paris Infos Mairie. The Office du Tourisme (see p359) also produces an annual calendar of events.

Spring

A good many of the city's annual 20 million visitors arrive in the spring. It is the season for fairs and concerts, when the marathon street race is held and the outdoor temperature is pleasant. Spring is also the time when hoteliers offer weekend packages, often with tickets for jazz concerts and museum passes included.

French Tennis Open, Stade Roland Garros

March
Spring flower shows at Parc Floral (Bois de Vincennes, p237) and Bagatelle Gardens (Bois de Boulogne, pp256–7).
Salon International d'Agriculture (end Feb–early Mar), Paris-Expo, Porte de Versailles. Vast farming fair.
Banlieues Bleues Festival (mid-Mar–early Apr), Paris suburbs. Jazz, blues, soul and funk.
Printemps du Cinema (3 days late Mar). Films can be seen for a very reasonable price at cinemas across Paris and throughout France.

Foire du Trône (late Mar–May), Bois de Vincennes (p237). Large funfair.

April
Paris International Marathon from Place de la Concorde to Avenue Foch.
Chemin de la Croix (Good Friday). Beautiful Stations of the Cross procession, from Montmartre to Sacré Coeur.
Paris Ceramics Festival (mid-Apr), Renowned artists display their wares related to various themes.
Foire de Paris (end Apr–1st week May), Paris Expo, Porte de Versailles. Food, wine, homes and gardens and tourism show.

May
Shakespeare Garden Festival (until Oct), Bois de Boulogne (pp256–7). Classic plays performed outdoors.
Carré Rive Gauche (one week, mid-month). Exhibits at antiques dealers in and around St-Germain-des-Prés (p137).

Grandes Concerts de Versailles (Sep–May), Versailles (p250). Open-air concerts and pyrotechnical displays on Versailles lake.
French Tennis Open (last week May –1st week Jun), Stade Roland Garros (p350). Parisian society meets sport!
Le Printemps des Rues (3rd w/end). Concerts and free street theatre are held in the Bastille/ République area.

Paris International Marathon

Spring colour, Jardin du Luxembourg

Average Daily Hours of Sunshine

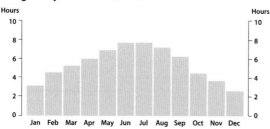

Sunshine Hours
The northerly position of Paris gives it long and light summer evenings, but in winter the daylight recedes with few truly bright days.

Summer

Summer begins with the French Tennis Open, and there are many events and festivities until July. Thereafter, the French begin thinking of their own annual holiday, but there are big celebrations on Bastille Day (14 July) with military displays for the president and his guests.

Jardin du Luxembourg in summer

June

Festival St-Denis, Basilique-Cathédrale de St-Denis. Concerts emphasise large-scale choral works (p338).
Fête du Cinéma, films shown all over Paris for a nominal entry fee (p348).
Flower show, Bois de Boulogne

Final lap of the Champs-Elysées during the Tour de France

(pp256–7). Rose season in the Bagatelle Gardens.
Fête de la Musique (21 Jun), all over Paris. Nightlong summer solstice musical celebrations.
Paris Jazz Festival (May–Jul), Parc Floral de Paris. Jazz musicians come to play in Paris (pp341–2).
Prix de Diane-Longines (mid-Jun), Chantilly. French equivalent of the British Ascot high society horse-racing event.
Les Grandes Eaux Nocturnes (mid-Jun–mid-Aug), Versailles. Son et lumiere in the gardens with music, dance and theatre (p251).
Gay Pride (end Jun). Lively parade around the Bastille.

July

Paris Air and Space Technology Show (Jul, alternate years, next show 2015), Le Bourget Airport.
Festival du cinéma en plein air (mid-Jul–Aug), Parc de la Villette (pp238–9).
Paris Quartier d'Eté (mid- Jul–mid-Aug). Dance, music, theatre, ballet.
Paris-Plage (mid-Jul–mid-Aug). Sand and palm trees deposited on the Right Bank of the Seine create a beach.
Tour de France (late Jul). The world's greatest cycle race comes to a climax in the Champs-Elysées.

March past of troops on Bastille Day (14 July)

Average Monthly Temperature

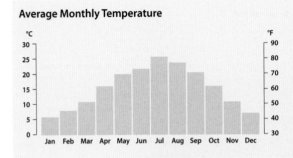

Temperature
The chart shows the average temperatures for each month. It is hottest in July and August and coolest between December and February, though Paris is rarely freezing cold. Temperatures are pleasant in the spring when the number of visitors peaks, and also in autumn.

Autumn

September sees the start of the social season, with gala performances of new films, and parties in big houses on the Ile St-Louis. Paris is the world's largest congress centre and there is a rush of shows in September, ranging from gifts to leisure and music. The pace barely slackens in October and November when Parisians begin to indulge their great love for the cinema. French and Hollywood stars often make appearances at premieres staged on the Champs-Elysées.

September
Festival d'Automne à Paris (mid-Sep –end Dec), throughout Paris. Music, dance, theatre (pp338–9).
La Villette Jazz Festival (mid-Sep). Jazz artists come and blow their horns with gusto throughout the Cité de la Musique (p238).
Journées du Patrimoine (2nd or 3rd week Sep). Historic buildings, monuments and

The Prix de l'Arc de Triomphe (October)

museums are open free to the public for two days, following an all-night party to kick off proceedings.

October
Nuit Blanche (one Sat in Oct). Museums stay open all night and there are art installations around the city.
Prix de l'Arc de Triomphe (1st week), Longchamp. An international field competes for the richest prize in European horse-racing.
Salon de l'Automobile (1st fortnight, alternate years), Paris-Expo, Porte de Versailles. Commercial motor show,

Jazz fusion guitarist Al di Meola playing in Paris

alternated annually with a motorcycle show.
Foire Internationale d'Art Contemporain (FIAC) (last week), Paris-Expo, Porte de Versailles. Paris's biggest international modern and contemporary art fair.

November
BNP Paribas Masters (usually Nov), Palais Omnisports de Paris-Bercy. Prestigious indoor men's tennis tournament. (pp350–51).
Mois de la Photo (Oct–Nov, every two years, next in 2014). Numerous photography shows, film screenings and public discussions.
Beaujolais Nouveau (3rd Thursday Nov). Bars and cafés are crowded on this day, in a race to taste the new vintage.

Autumn in the Bois de Vincennes

Average Monthly Rainfall

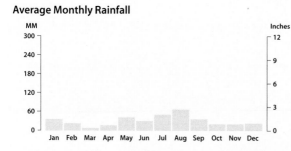

MM
300
240
180
120
60
0

Jan Feb Mar Apr May Jun Jul Aug Sep Oct Nov Dec

Inches
12
9
6
3
0

Rainfall

August is the wettest month in Paris as well as the hottest. In August and September you risk getting caught in storms. Sudden showers, sometimes with hail, can occur between January and April – notoriously in March. There is occasional snow in winter.

Winter

Paris rarely sees snow; winter days tend to be invigorating rather than chilly. There are jazz and dance festivals, candlelit Christmas church services and much celebrating in the streets over the New Year. After New Year, the streets seem to become slightly less congested and on bright days the riverside quays are used as the rendezvous point of strollers and lovers.

December

Christmas illuminations *(until Jan)* in the Grands Boulevards, Opéra, Ave Montaigne, Champs-Elysées and the Rue du Faubourg St-Honoré.
Crèche *(early Dec–early Jan)*, under a canopy in Place de l'Hôtel de Ville, Marais *(p104)*. Lifesize Christmas crib from a different country each year.
Salon du Cheval *(1st fortnight)*, Equestrian trade show, exhibitions and competitions.

Snow in the Tuileries, a rare occurrence

Paris International Boat Show *(1st fortnight)*, Paris-Expo, Porte de Versailles.

January

Fête des Rois (Epiphany). *(6 Jan)*. The *boulangeries* are full of *galettes des rois*.
Prix d'Amérique *(mid-Jan)*. Europe's most famous trotting race, Hippodrome de Vincennes.
Fashion shows, summer collections. *(See Haute Couture p316.)*

February

Carnaval *(weekend before Mardi Gras)*, Quartier de St-Fargeau.
Floraisons *(all month)*, Parc Floral de Paris, Bois de Vincennes *(p237)* and Parc de Bagatelle, Bois de Boulogne *(pp256–7)*. Say farewell to winter with these colourful and impressive displays of crocuses and snowdrops.

Public Holidays

New Year's Day (1 Jan)
Easter Monday varies
Labour Day (1 May)
VE Day (8 May)
Ascension Day (6th Thu after Easter)
Bastille Day (14 Jul)
Assumption (15 Aug)
All Saints' Day (1 Nov)
Remembrance Day (11 Nov)
Christmas (25 Dec)

January fashion show

Eiffel Tower Christmas decorations

A RIVER VIEW OF PARIS

The remarkable French music-hall star Mistinguett described the Seine as a "pretty blonde with laughing eyes". The river most certainly has a beguiling quality, but the relationship that exists between it and the city of Paris is far more than one of flirtation. No other European city defines itself by its river in the same way as Paris. The Seine is the essential point of reference to the city: distances are measured from it, street numbers determined by it, and it divides the capital into two distinct areas, with the Right Bank on the north side of the river and the Left Bank on the south side. These are as well defined as any of the supposedly official boundaries. The city is also divided historically, with the east more closely linked to the city's ancient roots and the west more closely linked to the 19th and 20th centuries.

Practically every building of note in Paris is either along the river or within a stone's throw. The quays are lined by fine bourgeois apartments, magnificent town houses, great museums and striking monuments.

Above all, the river is very much alive. For centuries fleets of small boats used it, but motorized land traffic stifled this once-bustling scene. Today, the river is busy with commercial barges and massive *bateaux mouches* pleasure boats cruising sightseers up and down the river.

The octagonal lake, in the Jardin de Luxembourg, is a favourite spot for children to sail their toy boats. The Seine is host to larger craft, including many pleasure cruisers.

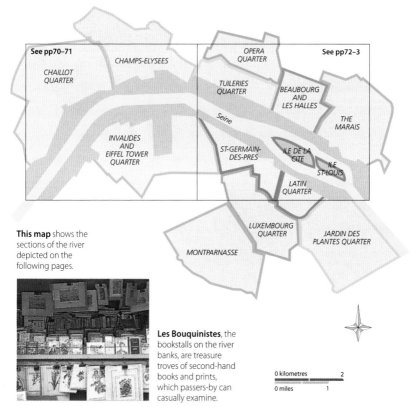

See pp70–71

CHAMPS-ELYSEES

CHAILLOT QUARTER

See pp72–3

OPERA QUARTER

TUILERIES QUARTER

BEAUBOURG AND LES HALLES

THE MARAIS

Seine

INVALIDES AND EIFFEL TOWER QUARTER

ST-GERMAIN-DES-PRES

ILE DE LA CITE

ILE ST-LOUIS

LATIN QUARTER

LUXEMBOURG QUARTER

JARDIN DES PLANTES QUARTER

MONTPARNASSE

This map shows the sections of the river depicted on the following pages.

Les Bouquinistes, the bookstalls on the river banks, are treasure troves of second-hand books and prints, which passers-by can casually examine.

0 kilometres 2

0 miles 1

◀ View of the Seine from Notre-Dame

For keys to symbols *see back flap*

From Pont de Grenelle to Pont de la Concorde

The soaring monuments and grand exhibition halls along this stretch of the river are remnants of the Napoleonic era and the Industrial Revolution with its great exhibitions. The exhilarating self-confidence of the Eiffel Tower, the Petit Palais and the Grand Palais is matched by more recent buildings, such as the Palais de Chaillot, the Maison de Radio-France and the skyscrapers of the Left Bank.

Palais de Chaillot
The curved wings and arching fountains make this a spectacular setting for three museums and a theatre *(p202).*

Palais de Tokyo
Figures by Bourdelle adorn this museum *(p205).*

Bateaux Parisiens
Tour Eiffel
Vedettes de Paris Ile
de France

Trocadéro Ⓜ

Passere
Debil'

The Statue of Liberty was given to the city in 1885. It faces west, towards the original Liberty in New York.

Pont
d'Iéna

Maison de Radio-France
Studios and a radio museum are housed in this circular building *(p204).*

Ⓜ Passy

Musée du
quai Branly

RER Champ de
Mars

Pont de
Bir-Hakeim

Bir-Hakeim
Ⓜ

RER Ave Du Prés.
Kennedy

Eiffel Tower
The tower is the symbol of Paris *(pp196–7).*

The Pont Bir-Hakeim
has a dynamic statue by Wederkinch rising at its north end.

Pont de Grenelle

Grand Palais
Major exhibitions and a science museum are based here *(p210)*.

Petit Palais
Now the Paris museum of fine arts, this was first designed as a companion to the Grand Palais *(p210)*.

Champs-Elysées Clemenceau Ⓜ

Ⓜ Alma Marceau

Pont de l'Alma

Pont des Invalides

Pont Alexandre III

Pont de la Concorde

Ⓜ RER Invalides

RER Pont de l'Alma

Bateaux Mouches

The Zouave is a statue of a soldier on a central pier of the bridge. It is used by Parisians to measure the level of the Seine when it is in flood.

The Liberty Flame, commemorating French Resistance fighters, is also an unofficial memorial to Diana, Princess of Wales.

Pont Alexandre III
Flamboyant statuary decorates Paris's most ornate bridge *(p210)*.

Dôme des Invalides
The majestic gilded dome *(pp188–9)* is here seen from Pont Alexandre III.

Assemblée Nationale Palais-Bourbon
Louis XIV's daughter once owned this palace, which is now used by the Chambre des Députés as the national forum for political debate *(p192)*.

For keys to symbols *see back flap*

From Pont de la Concorde to Pont de Sully

The historic heart of Paris lies on the banks and islands of the east river. At its centre is the Ile de la Cité, a natural stepping stone across the Seine and the cultural core of medieval Paris. Today it is still vital to Parisian life.

Jardin des Tuileries
These gardens are in the formal style (p132).

Musée du Louvre
Before becoming the world's greatest museum and home to the *Mona Lisa*, this was Europe's largest royal palace (pp122–9).

Pont de la Concorde

Assemblée Nationale M

Passerelle Solférino

Quai d'Orsay RER

Pont Royal

Pont du Carrousel

Passerelle des Arts

Musée de l'Orangerie
An important collection of 19th-century paintings is on display here (p133).

The Passerelle des Arts
is a steel reconstruction of Paris's first cast-iron bridge (1804), and was inaugurated in 1984.

Bâteaux Vedettes du Pont Neuf

Musée d'Orsay
Paris's most important collection of Impressionist art is housed in this converted railway station (pp146–9).

Hôtel des Monnaies
Built in 1771–75, this former Mint has a fine coin collection in its old milling halls (p143).

For keys to symbols *see back flap*

Ile de la Cité
The medieval identity of this small island was almost completely erased in the 19th century by Baron Haussmann's grand scheme. Sainte-Chapelle and parts of the Conciergerie are the only buildings of the period that remain today *(pp78–91)*.

Ile St-Louis
This has been a desirable address since the 17th century *(p91)*.

Conciergerie
During the Revolution this building, with its distinctive towers, became notorious as a prison *(p87)*.

The Tour de l'Horloge, a 14th-century clock tower, features the first public clock in Paris. Germain Pilon's fine carvings continue to adorn the clock face.

St-Gervais–St-Protais
The oldest organ in Paris, dating from the early 17th century, is in this church *(p103)*.

Pont Neuf
M
nt Neuf

M Châtelet

Hôtel de Ville
M

Pont au Change

Pont Notre-Dame

Cité
M

Pont d'Arcole

RER M

St-Michel

Petit Pont

Pont au Double

Pont Louis-Philippe

Pont St-Louis

M Pont Marie

Pont Marie

Pont de l'Archevêché

Pont de la Tournelle

Sully Morland M

Pont de Sully

Notre-Dame
This towering cathedral surveys the river *(pp82–5)*.

Bâteaux Parisiens

How to Take a River or Canal Trip

River Seine cruises on a variety of pleasure boats operate along the main sightseeing reaches of the river, taking in many of the city's famous monuments. The Batobus river service operates as a shuttle or bus service, allowing passengers to get on and off anywhere along the route. The main city canal trips operate along the old industrial St-Martin canal in the east of the city, passing through areas of Paris steeped in history.

Pleasure-cruise boat on the River Seine

Types of Boats

Bateaux mouches, *the largest of the pleasure-cruise boats, are a spectacular sight with their passenger areas enclosed in glass for excellent all round viewing. At night, floodlights are used to pick out river bank buildings. A more luxurious version of these is used on the Bateaux Parisien cruises. The* vedettes *are smaller and more intimate boats, with viewing through glass walls. The* Canauxrama canal *boats are flat-bottomed.*

Seine Cruises and Shuttle Services

The Seine cruises and shuttle services information below includes the boarding points, the nearest Metro and RER stations, and the nearest bus routes. Meal cruises must be booked in advance, and passengers must board them 30 minutes before departure. Timings may vary – visitors are advised to check ahead.

Vedettes de Paris Seine Cruise

These superb cruises cover major sights along the river. Some tickets include a snack or champagne. The boarding point is:

Port de Suffren
Map 10 D3. **Tel** 01 44 18 19 50. Ⓜ Bir Hakeim. 🅡🅔🅡 Champs de Mars. 🚌 22, 30, 32, 44, 63, 69, 72, 82, 87. **Departures** mid-Feb–Oct: 10.30am–11pm (mid-Feb–Mar: to 9pm); Nov–mid-Feb: 11.15am–9pm Mon–Fri, 10.30am–10pm Sat & Sun, 10.30am–9pm Christmas hols. Every 30–45 mins. **Duration** 1 hr.
🆆 vedettesdeparis.com

Croisière Dégustation Champagne

Enjoy champagne while a sommelier provides tasting notes. The boarding point is:

Port de Suffren
Map 10 D3. **Tel** 01 44 18 19 50. Ⓜ Bir Hakeim. **Departures** May–Aug: 6.30pm Mon–Sat. **Duration** 1 hr.
🆆 vedettesdeparis.com

Bateaux Parisiens Tour Eiffel Cruise

This company offers sightseeing and meal cruises with a commentary in 13 languages. The boarding point is:

Port de la Bourdonnais
Map 10 D2. **Tel** 08 25 01 01 01. Ⓜ Bir Hakeim. 🅡🅔🅡 Champs de Mars. 🚌 42, 82. **Departures** every 30 mins. Apr–May & Sep: 10am–10pm; Jun–Aug: 10am–11pm; Oct–Mar: 10.30am–9pm (hourly). **Lunch cruise** 12.45pm. **Duration** 2 hr. **Dinner cruise** 6pm, 8.30pm, 9pm. **Duration** 2.5 hr.
🆆 bateauxparisiens.com

Bateaux Parisiens Notre-Dame Cruise

Same route as the Tour Eiffel Cruise, but in the opposite direction. The boarding point is:

Quai de Montebello
Map 13 B4. **Tel** 08 25 01 01 01. Ⓜ Maubert–Mutualité, St-Michel. 🅡🅔🅡 St-Michel. 🚌 24, 27, 47. **Departures** 28 Mar–10 Apr: 2.20–8.15pm; 11 Apr–4 Jul: 12.20–10pm Mon–Thu, 11am–10.45pm Fri–Sun; 5 Jul–23 Aug: 11am–11pm; 24 Aug–21 Sep: 12.20–10pm; 22 Sep–17 Oct: 2.20–6.20pm Sun–Thu; 18 Oct–2 Nov: 2.20–8.15pm. **Duration** 1 hr.

Boarding Points

The boarding points for the river cruises and the Batobus services are easy to find along the river. Here, you can buy tickets, and there are amenities such as snack-bars. Major cruise companies also have foreign exchange booths. There is limited parking around the points, but none near the Pont Neuf.

River boarding point

Batobus Cruises

Shuttle service. 1- and 2-day as well as annual passes available. **Tel** 08 25 05 01 01. **Departures** daily; 8 Sep–10 Apr: 10am–7pm (every 25 min); 11 Apr–7 Sep: 10am–9.30pm (every 20 min). Board at: Eiffel Tower: **Map** 10 D3. M Bir Hakeim. Champs-Elysées: **Map** 11 B1. M Champs-Elysées-Clemenceau. Musée d'Orsay: **Map** 12 D2. M Assemblée Nationale. Louvre: **Map** 12 E2. M Louvre. St-Germain-des-Prés: **Map** 12 E3. M St-Germain-de-Prés. Notre-Dame: **Map** 13 B4. M Saint-Michel. Hôtel de Ville: **Map** 13 B4. M Hôtel de Ville. Jardin des Plantes: **Map** 13 C5. M Jussieu, Cardinal Lemoine. W **batobus.com**

Bateaux Mouches Seine Cruise

One of Paris's best known pleasure boat companies, with a fleet of 14 boats. The boarding point is:

Pont de l'Alma
Map 10 F1. **Tel** 01 42 25 96 10. M Alma-Marceau. RER Pont de l'Alma. 28, 42, 49, 63, 72, 80, 83, 92. **Departure** Apr–Sep: 10.15am–10.30pm daily (every 20–45 min); Oct–Mar: 11am–9pm (from 10.15am Sat & Sun; every 30 min–1 hr; 50 passengers min). **Duration** 1 hr 10 min. **Lunch cruise** 1pm Sat, Sun & bank hols (embark from 12.15pm). **Duration** 1hr 45 min. Under-12s half price. **Dinner cruise** 8.30pm daily (embark from 7.30pm). **Duration** 2 hr 15 min. Formal dress required. W **bateaux-mouches.fr**

Bateaux Vedettes Pont Neuf Cruise

This company runs a fleet of six small boats. The boats are of an older style, for a quainter cruise. Price reductions can be obtained when booking tickets online. The boarding point is:

Square du Vert-Galant (Pont Neuf)
Map 12 F3. **Tel** 01 46 33 98 38. M Pont Neuf. RER Châtelet. 27, 58, 67, 70, 72, 74, 75. **Departures** mid-Mar–Oct: 10.30am, 11.15am, noon; 1.30–10.30pm daily (every 30 min); Nov–mid-Mar: 10.30am, 11.15am, noon, 2–6.30pm (every 45 min), 8pm, 10pm Mon–Thu; 10.30am, 11.15am, noon, 2–6.30pm, 8pm, 9–10pm (every 45 min) Fri–Sun (24 & 31 Dec: last departure 5.45 pm). **Duration** 1 hr. W **vedettesdupontneuf.com**

Canal Trips

The Canauxrama company operates boat cruises along the city's Canal St-Martin and along the banks of the river Marne. The St-Martin journey passes along the tree-lined canal, which has nine locks, two swing bridges and eight romantic footbridges. The Bords de Marne cruise travels well into the suburbs, as far as Bry-sur-Marne. The **Paris Canal Company** (01 42 40 96 97; www.pariscanal.com) also has a St-Martin canal trip, from Parc de la Villette and extending beyond the canal, passing into the River Seine and as far as the Musée d'Orsay.

CANAUXRAMA

Canal St-Martin

The Canauxrama company offers many different trips along this canal, but it has two 125-passenger boats that operate regularly between the Bassin de la Villette and the Port de l'Arsenal. The boarding points are:
Bassin de la Villette: **Map** 8 E1. M Jaurès. Port de l'Arsenal: **Map** 14 E4. M Bastille. **Tel** 01 42 39 15 00. **Departures** Apr–Nov, times may vary so phone to check and to make a reservation: Bassin de la Villette 9.45am and 2.45pm; Port de l'Arsenal 9.45am and 2.30pm daily. On weekday mornings, there are concessions for students, pensioners and children under 12. Children under four travel free (although trip is not recommended for this age). Concert cruises are available on chartered trips on the Canal St-Martin and the Seine. **Duration** 2 hr 30 min. W **canauxrama.fr**

Bords de Marne Croisière

This all-day cruise extends westwards out of Paris down the Marne. The trip includes a commentary, stories and dancing. Bring a picnic or eat lunch in a *guinguette* (open-air café). The boarding point is: Port de l'Arsenal: **Map** 14 E4. M Bastille. **Tel** 01 42 39 15 00. **Departures** Apr–Oct: 9am (reservations only), Jul–Aug: Thu–Sun (arrive 20 min before). Reservations recommended. **Duration** 8 hr.

Canal-cruise boat in the Bassin de la Villette

View of the cityscape of Paris ▶

PARIS
AREA BY AREA

ILE DE LA CITE AND ILE ST-LOUIS

The history of the Ile de la Cité is the history of Paris. This island on the Seine was no more than a primitive village when the conquering Julius Caesar arrived in 52 BC. Ancient kings later made it the centre of political power and in medieval times it became the home of church and law. It no longer has such power, except to draw armies of tourists to the imposing Palais de Justice and to its Gothic masterpiece, Notre-Dame.

The medieval huddles of tiny houses and narrow streets that so characterized the island at one time were swept away by the spacious thoroughfares built in the 19th century. But there are still small areas of charm and relief, among them the colourful bird and flower market, the romantic Square du Vert-Galant and the ancient Place Dauphine.

At the island's eastern end, the St-Louis bridge connects it to the smaller Ile St-Louis. This former swampy pastureland was transformed into an elegant 17th-century residential area, with picturesque, tree-lined quays. More recently, rich artists, doctors, actresses and heiresses have lived here.

Sights at a Glance

Historic Buildings and Streets
2 Ancien Cloître Quartier
6 Hôtel Dieu
8 Conciergerie
10 Palais de Justice
16 Hôtel de Lauzun

Churches and Cathedrals
1 Notre-Dame pp82–5
9 Sainte-Chapelle pp88–9
15 St-Louis-en-l'Ile

Monuments
4 Paris Mémorial des Martyrs de la Déportation

Markets
7 Marché aux Fleurs Reine Elizabeth II

Squares and Gardens
3 Square Jean XXIII
11 Place Dauphine
13 Square du Vert-Galant

Museums and Galleries
5 Crypte Archéologique
14 Société Historique et Littéraire Polonaise

Bridges
12 Pont Neuf

☐ **Restaurants** see p296
1 Au Bougnat

0 metres 400
0 yards 400

See also Street Finder
map 12–13

◀ Statues of apostles that look over the main entrance to Notre-Dame

Street-by-Street: Ile de la Cité

The origins of Paris are here on the Ile de la Cité, the boat-shaped island on the Seine first inhabited over 2,000 years ago by Celtic tribes. One tribe, the Parisii, eventually gave its name to the city. The island offered a convenient river crossing on the route between northern and southern Gaul and was easily defended. In later centuries, the settlement was expanded by the Romans, the Franks and the Capetian kings to form the nucleus of today's city.

There is no older place in Paris, and remains of the first buildings can still be seen today in the archaeological crypt under the square in front of Notre-Dame, the great medieval cathedral and place of pilgrimage for millions of visitors each year. At the other end of the island is another Gothic masterpiece, Sainte-Chapelle – a miracle of light.

The Cour du Mai is the impressive main courtyard of the Palais de Justice.

❼ ★ **Marché aux Fleurs Reine Elizabeth II**
This colourful, lively market is one of Paris's few remaining flower markets. Birds are sold at the Sunday market.

❽ ★ **Conciergerie**
A grisly antechamber to the guillotine, this prison was much used in the Revolution.

The Quai des Orfèvres owes its name to the goldsmiths (orfèvres) who frequented the area from medieval times onward.

❿ **Palais de Justice**
With its ancient towers lining the quays, the old royal palace is today a massive complex of law courts. Its history extends back over 16 centuries.

The Préfecture de Police is the headquarters of the police and was the scene of intense battles during World War II.

To Pont Neuf

QUAI DES ORFÈVRES

PONT ST MICHEL

BLVD DU PALAIS

QUAI DU MARCHE NEUF

PONT AU CHANGE

QUAI LA CO...

RUE DE LUTECE

RUE DE LA CITE

PETIT PONT

❾ ★ **Sainte-Chapelle**
A jewel of Gothic architecture and one of the most magical sights in Paris, Sainte-Chapelle is noted for the magnificence of its stained glass.

CRYPTE DU PARVIS

❺ ★ **Crypte Archéologique**
Deep under the square lie the remains of houses from 2,000 years ago.

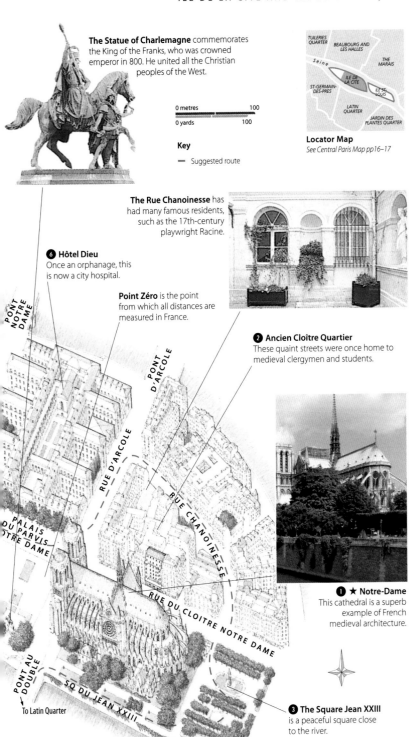

The Statue of Charlemagne commemorates the King of the Franks, who was crowned emperor in 800. He united all the Christian peoples of the West.

0 metres 100
0 yards 100

Key

— Suggested route

Locator Map
See Central Paris Map pp16–17

The Rue Chanoinesse has had many famous residents, such as the 17th-century playwright Racine.

❻ Hôtel Dieu
Once an orphanage, this is now a city hospital.

Point Zéro is the point from which all distances are measured in France.

❷ Ancien Cloître Quartier
These quaint streets were once home to medieval clergymen and students.

❶ ★ Notre-Dame
This cathedral is a superb example of French medieval architecture.

❸ The Square Jean XXIII
is a peaceful square close to the river.

To Latin Quarter

❶ Notre-Dame

No other building is more associated with the history of Paris than Notre-Dame. It stands majestically on the Ile de la Cité, cradle of the city. Pope Alexander III laid the first stone in 1163, marking the start of 170 years of toil by armies of Gothic architects and medieval craftsmen. Ever since, a procession of the famous has passed through the three main doors below the massive towers.

The cathedral is a Gothic masterpiece, standing on the site of a Roman temple. At the time it was finished, in about 1334, it was 130 m (430 ft) long and featured flying buttresses, a large transept, a deep choir and 69-m (228-ft) high towers.

★ **West Front**
Three main doors with superb statuary, a central rose window and an openwork gallery are important details here.

★ **Galerie des Chimères**
The cathedral's legendary gargoyles (chimères) hide behind a large upper gallery between the towers.

KEY

① **Portal of the Virgin** The Virgin surrounded by saints and kings is a fine composition of 13th-century statues.

② **The south tower** houses the cathedral's famous Emmanuel bell.

③ **The spire**, designed by Viollet-le-Duc, soars to a height of 90 m (295 ft).

④ **The treasury** houses the cathedral's religious treasures, including Christ's purported Crown of Thorns.

⑤ **The transept** was built at the start of Philippe-Auguste's reign, in the 13th century.

⑥ **The King's Gallery** features 28 Kings of Judah gazing down on the crowds.

★ **West Rose Window**
This window depicts the Virgin in a medallion of rich reds and blues.

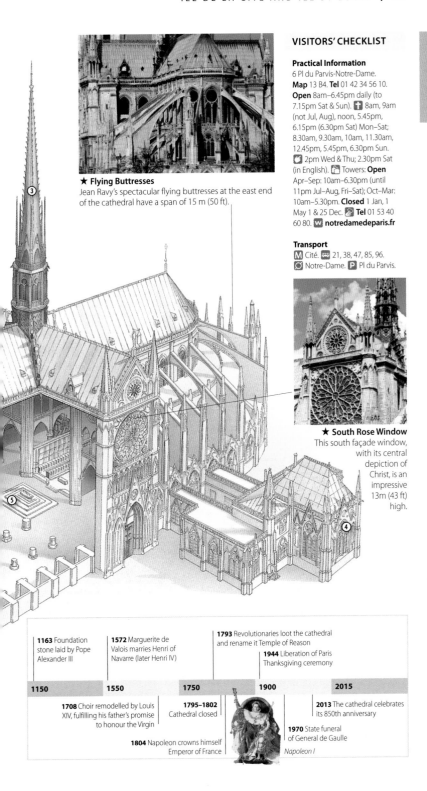

★ **Flying Buttresses**
Jean Ravy's spectacular flying buttresses at the east end of the cathedral have a span of 15 m (50 ft).

VISITORS' CHECKLIST

Practical Information
6 Pl du Parvis-Notre-Dame.
Map 13 B4. **Tel** 01 42 34 56 10.
Open 8am–6.45pm daily (to 7.15pm Sat & Sun). ⊞ 8am, 9am (not Jul, Aug), noon, 5.45pm, 6.15pm (6.30pm Sat) Mon–Sat; 8.30am, 9.30am, 10am, 11.30am, 12.45pm, 5.45pm, 6.30pm Sun. ⊞ 2pm Wed & Thu; 2.30pm Sat (in English). ⊞ Towers: **Open** Apr–Sep: 10am–6.30pm (until 11pm Jul–Aug, Fri–Sat); Oct–Mar: 10am–5.30pm. **Closed** 1 Jan, 1 May 1 & 25 Dec. ⊞ Tel 01 53 40 60 80. W **notredamedeparis.fr**

Transport
Ⓜ Cité. ⊞ 21, 38, 47, 85, 96.
Ⓞ Notre-Dame. Ⓟ Pl du Parvis.

★ **South Rose Window**
This south façade window, with its central depiction of Christ, is an impressive 13m (43 ft) high.

1163 Foundation stone laid by Pope Alexander III

1572 Marguerite de Valois marries Henri of Navarre (later Henri IV)

1793 Revolutionaries loot the cathedral and rename it Temple of Reason

1944 Liberation of Paris Thanksgiving ceremony

1150	1550	1750	1900	2015

1708 Choir remodelled by Louis XIV, fulfilling his father's promise to honour the Virgin

1795–1802 Cathedral closed

2013 The cathedral celebrates its 850th anniversary

1970 State funeral of General de Gaulle

1804 Napoleon crowns himself Emperor of France

Napoleon I

A Guided Tour of Notre-Dame

Notre-Dame's interior grandeur is instantly apparent on seeing the high-vaulted central nave. This is bisected by a huge transept, at either end of which are medieval rose windows, 13 m (43 ft) in diameter. Works by major sculptors adorn the cathedral. Among them are Jean Ravy's old choir screen carvings, Nicolas Coustou's *Pietà* and Antoine Coysevox's Louis XIV statue. In this majestic setting kings and emperors were crowned and royal Crusaders were blessed. But Notre-Dame was also the scene of turmoil. Revolutionaries ransacked it, banished religion, changed it into a temple to the Cult of Reason, and then used it as a wine store. Napoleon restored religion in 1804 and architect Viollet-le-Duc later restored the buildings, replacing missing statues, as well as raising the spire and fixing the gargoyles.

⑨ North Rose Window
This 13th-century stained-glass window depicts the Virgin encircled by figures from the Old Testament.

⑩ View and Gargoyles
The 387 steps up the north tower lead to sights of the famous gargoyles and magnificent views of Paris.

Entrance to the tower

Entrance

① View of Interior
From the main entrance, the view takes in the high-vaulted central nave looking down towards the huge transept, the choir and the high altar.

Key

— Suggested route

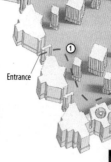

② Le Brun's "May" Paintings
These religious paintings by Charles Le Brun hang in the side chapels. In the 17th and 18th centuries, the Paris guilds presented a painting to the cathedral on May Day each year.

⑦ **Louis XIII Statue**
After many years of childless marriage, Louis XIII pledged to erect a high altar and to redecorate the east chancel to honour the Virgin if an heir was born to him. The future Louis XIV was born in 1638, but it took 60 years before the promises were made good. One of the surviving features from that time is the carved choir stalls.

⑧ **Carved Choir Stalls**
Noted for their early 18th-century carved woodwork, the choir stalls were commissioned by Louis XIII, whose statue stands behind the high altar. Among the details carved in bas-relief on the back of the high stalls are scenes from the life of the Virgin.

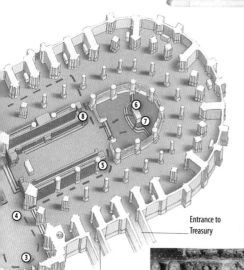

Entrance to Treasury

Entrance to Sacristy

⑥ **Pietà**
Behind the high altar is Nicolas Coustou's *Pietà*, standing on a gilded base sculptured by François Girardon.

⑤ **Chancel Screen**
A 14th-century high stone screen enclosed the chancel and provided canons at prayer with peace and solitude from noisy congregations. Some of it has survived to screen the first three north and south bays.

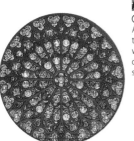

③ **South Rose Window**
Located at the south end of the transept, this window retains some of its original 13th-century stained glass. The window depicts Christ in the centre, surrounded by virgins, saints and the 12 Apostles.

④ **Statue of the Virgin and Child**
Against the southeast pillar of the transept stands the 14th-century statue of the Virgin and Child. It was brought to the cathedral from the chapel of St Aignan, and is known as Notre-Dame de Paris (Our Lady of Paris).

The Square Jean XXIII behind Notre-Dame

❷ Ancien Cloître Quartier

Rue du Cloître-Notre-Dame north to Quai des Fleurs 75004. **Map** 13 B4. Ⓜ Cité. Ⓡ St-Michel.

On the northern side of Notre-Dame cathedral lies a warren of little-explored streets known as the "Old Cloister" quarter. They are all that remains of a once-bustling medieval hub frequented by cathedral seminary students. Today, the narrow streets with well-preserved medieval mansions make for an interesting stroll. The mansions in Rue des Chantres and Rue des Ursins in particular have pretty gardens and cobbled courtyards.

❸ Square Jean XXIII

Rue du Cloître-Notre-Dame 75004. **Map** 13 B4. Ⓜ Cité.

Notre-Dame's St Stephen's door (porte St-Etienne) opens on to this pleasant garden square, dedicated to Pope John XXIII. The garden runs alongside the river and is an excellent place for enjoying the sculptures, rose windows and flying buttresses of the east end of the cathedral.
    From the 17th century, the square was occupied by the archbishop's palace, which was ransacked by rioters in 1831 and later demolished. A square was conceived to replace the Prefect of Paris, Rambuteau. The Gothic-style fountain of the Virgin in the square has been there since 1845.

❹ Paris Mémorial des Martyrs de la Déportation

Sq de l'Ile de France 75004. **Map** 13 B4. **Tel** 01 46 33 87 56. Ⓜ St-Paul, Maubert-Mutualité. Ⓡ St-Michel. **Open** 10am–noon, 2–5pm Tue–Sun (until 7pm Apr–Sep). **Closed** 1 Jan, 1 May, 14 Jul, 15 Aug & 25 Dec.

The memorial to the 200,000 French men, women and children deported to Nazi concentration camps in World War II is covered with the names of the camps to which they were deported. Earth from these camps has been used to form tombs and the interior walls are decorated with poetry. At the far end is the tomb dedicated to the Unknown Deportee.

❺ Crypte Archéologique

7 Pl Jean Paul II, Parvis de Notre-Dame 75004. **Map** 13 A4. **Tel** 01 55 42 50 10. Ⓜ Cité. **Open** 10am–6pm Tue–Sun (last adm: 30 min before closing). **Closed** 1 Jan, 1 May, 8 May, 1 & 11 Nov, 25 Dec. 🎫 free for children under 14. 📷 📱 Ⓦ crypte.paris.fr

Situated on the main square (the *parvis*) in front of

Gallo-Roman ruins in the Crypte Archéologique

Notre-Dame and stretching 120 m (393 ft) underground, this crypt exhibits the remains of foundations and walls that pre-date the cathedral by several hundred years. The foundations of Paris' oldest rampart, dating from the third century BC, are displayed as are the medieval foundations of the Hôtel Dieu. Within the crypt are also traces of a sophisticated underground heating system used for Ancient Roman thermal baths.

Huge variety of colourful flowers for sale at the Marché aux Fleurs Reine Elizabeth II

Arched entrance of Hôtel Dieu, Paris's central hospital

❻ Hôtel Dieu

1 Pl du Parvis Notre-Dame 75004. **Map** 13 A4. **Closed** to the public for visits. Ⓜ Cité.

On the north side of the place du Parvis Notre-Dame is the Hôtel Dieu, the city's oldest hospital serving central Paris. It was built on the site of an orphanage between 1866 and 1878. The original Hôtel Dieu, built in the 12th century and stretching across the island to both banks of the river, was demolished in the 19th century to make way for one of Baron Haussmann's urban-planning schemes. It was here in 1944 that the Paris police courageously resisted the Germans; the battle is commemorated by a monument in Cour de 19-Août. A museum on the hospital's history is planned to open in 2016.

❼ Marché aux Fleurs Reine Elizabeth II

Pl Louis-Lépine 75004. **Map** 13 A3. Ⓜ Cité. **Open** 8am–7.30pm daily; Marché aux Oiseaux: Sun.

The year-round flower market adds colour and scent to an area otherwise dominated by administrative buildings. It is the most famous and, unfortunately, one of the last remaining flower markets in the city of Paris, offering a wide range of specialist varieties such as orchids. Each Sunday, it makes way for an animal market, which is best avoided by sensitive animal lovers.

❽ Conciergerie

2 Bd du Palais 75001. **Map** 13 A3. **Tel** 01 53 40 60 80. Ⓜ Cité. **Open** 9.30am–6pm daily (9am–5pm Nov–end Feb) (last adm: 30 min before closing). **Closed** 1 Jan, 1 May, 25 Dec. 🅿 (combined ticket with Ste-Chapelle, pp88–9, available.) 🅿 phone to check. 🅰 🆆 **conciergerie. monuments-nationaux.fr**

The Conciergerie was under the administration of the palace "concierge", the keeper of the King's mansion. When the King moved to the Marais (in 1417), the palace remained the seat of royal administration and law; and the Conciergerie became a prison, with the "concierge" as its chief gaoler. Henry IV's assassin, Ravaillac, was imprisoned and tortured here.

During the Revolution, it housed over 4,000 prisoners, including Marie-Antoinette, who was held in a tiny cell and Charlotte Corday, who stabbed Revolutionary leader Marat as he lay in his bath. Ironically, the Revolutionary judges Danton and Robespierre also became "tenants" before being sent to the guillotine.

The Conciergerie has a superb four-aisled Gothic Salle des Gens d'Armes (Hall of the Men-at-Arms), the dining hall for the castle's 2,000 members of staff. The building, renovated in the 19th century, retains the 14th-century public clock tower on the Tour de l'Horloge (Palais de Justice). It is the city's oldest and is still operating.

The Conciergerie forms part of the larger Palais du Justice, which is still used by the judicial system.

The Gothic Salle des Gens d'Armes (Hall of the Men-at-Arms) in the Conciergerie

Sainte-Chapelle

Ethereal and magical, Sainte-Chapelle has been hailed as one of the greatest architectural master-pieces of the Western world. In the Middle Ages, the devout likened this church to "a gateway to heaven". Today, no visitor can fail to be transported by the blaze of light created by the 15 magnificent stained-glass windows, separated by the narrowest of columns that soar 15 m (50 ft) to the star-studded, vaulted roof. The windows portray over 1,000 religious scenes in a kaleidoscope of red, gold, green, blue and mauve. The chapel was built in 1248 by Louis IX to house Christ's purported Crown of Thorns (now housed in the Notre-Dame treasury).

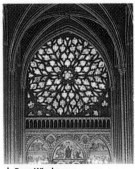

★ Rose Window
Best seen at sunset, the religious story of the Apocalypse is told in 86 panels of stained glass. The window was a gift from Charles VIII in 1485.

Lower Chapel Servants and commoners worshipped here, while the chapel above was reserved for the use of the king and the royal family.

Main Portal
The two-tier structure of the portal, the lower half of which is shown here, echoes that of the chapel.

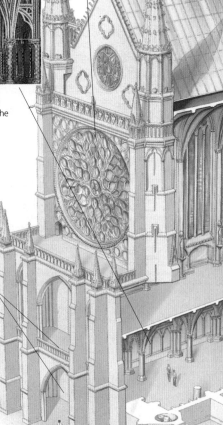

KEY

① **The Crown of Thorns** decorates the pinnacle as a symbol of the first relic bought by Louis IX.

② **The spire** rises 75 m (245 ft) into the air. It was erected in 1853 after four previous spires burned down.

③ **The angel** once revolved so that its cross could be seen from anywhere in Paris.

St Louis' Relics

Louis IX was extremely devout, and was canonized in 1297, not long after his death. In 1239, he acquired the Crown of Thorns from the Emperor of Constantinople and, in 1241, a fragment of Christ's Cross. He built this chapel as a shrine to house them. Louis paid nearly three times more for the relics than for the construction of Sainte-Chapelle. The Crown of Thorns is now kept at Notre-Dame.

VISITORS' CHECKLIST

Practical Information
8 Blvd du Palais.
Map 13 A3. **Tel** 01 53 40 60 80.
Open daily. Mar–Oct: 9.30am–6pm; Nov–Feb: 9am–5pm. Last adm 30 mins before closing.
Closed 1 Jan, 1 May, 25 Dec.
🎫 (combined ticket with Conciergerie, p87, is available.)
📷 📱 🌐 **sainte-chapelle. monuments-nationaux.fr**

Transport
Ⓜ Cité. 🚌 21, 27, 38, 85, 96 to Ile de la Cité. 🚇 St-Michel. 🅾 Notre-Dame. 🅿 Palais de Justice.

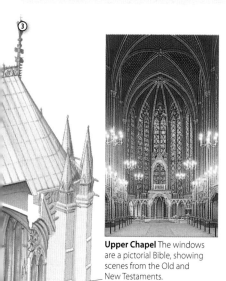

Upper Chapel The windows are a pictorial Bible, showing scenes from the Old and New Testaments.

Upper Chapel Windows

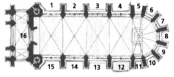

1 Genesis
2 Exodus
3 Numbers
4 Deuteronomy: Joshua
5 Judges
6 *left* Isaiah *right* Rod of Jesse
7 *left* St John the Evangelist *right* Childhood of Christ
8 Christ's Passion
9 *left* St John the Baptist *right* Story of Daniel
10 Ezekiel
11 *left* Jeremiah *right* Tobiah
12 Judith and Job
13 Esther
14 Book of Kings
15 Story of the Relics
16 Rose Window: The Apocalypse

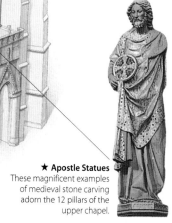

★ Apostle Statues
These magnificent examples of medieval stone carving adorn the 12 pillars of the upper chapel.

★ Window of Christ's Passion
The Last Supper is shown here in one of the most beautiful windows in the upper chapel.

The Pont Neuf, extending to the north and south of the Ile de la Cité

Place Dauphine

⓾ Palais de Justice

4–10 Blvd du Palais (entrance by the Cour de Mai, 8 Blvd du Palais) 75001. **Map** 13 A3. **Tel** 01 44 32 52 52. Ⓜ Cité. **Open** 8.30am–6.30pm Mon–Fri. 🈳

This huge block of buildings making up the law courts stretches the entire width of the Ile de la Cité. It is a splendid sight with its old towers lining the quays. The site has been occupied since Roman times and was the seat of royal power until Charles V moved the court to the Hôtel St-Paul in the Marais during the 14th century. In April 1793, the Revolutionary Tribunal began dispensing justice from the Première Chambre (gilded chamber). Today, the site embodies Napoleon's great legacy – the French judicial system.

⓫ Place Dauphine

75001 (enter by Rue Henri-Robert). **Map** 12 F3. Ⓜ Pont Neuf, Cité.

East of Pont Neuf is this ancient square, laid out in 1607 by Henri IV and named after the Dauphin, the future Louis XIII. No. 14 is one of the few buildings to have avoided any subsequent restoration. This haven of 17th-century charm is popular with *pétanque* (boules) players and employees of the adjoining Palais de Justice.

⓬ Pont Neuf

Quai de la Mégisserie and Quai des Grands Augustins 75001. **Map** 12 F3. Ⓜ Pont Neuf, Cité.

Despite its name (New Bridge), this bridge is the oldest of the modern bridges in Paris and has been immortalized by major literary and artistic figures since it was built. The first stone was laid by Henri III in 1578, but it was Henri IV who inaugurated it and gave it its name in 1607. The bridge has 12 arches and spans 275 m (912 ft). The first stone bridge to be built without houses, it heralded a new era in the relationship between the Cité and the river. Henri IV's statue stands in the central section.

A sculptured relief on the Palais de Justice

Henri IV in Square du Vert-Galant

⓭ Square du Vert-Galant

Ile de la Cité 75001. **Map** 12 F3.
Ⓜ Pont Neuf, Cité.

One of the magical spots of Paris, this square bears the nickname of Henri IV. This amorous and colourful monarch did much to beautify Paris in the early 17th century, and his popularity has lasted to this day. From here, there are splendid views of the Louvre and the Right Bank of the river, where Henri was assassinated in 1610. This is also the point from which the Vedettes du Pont Neuf pleasure boats depart (see pp74–5).

⓮ Société Historique et Littéraire Polonaise

6 Quai d'Orléans 75004. **Map** 13 C4.
Tel 01 55 42 83 83. Ⓜ Pont Marie.
Open 2.15–6pm Tue–Fri. 🖼 🎫
call 01 55 42 83 85 to book.
🖳 **bibliotheque-polonaise-paris-shlp.fr**

The Polish Romantic poet Adam Mickiewicz, who lived in Paris in the 19th century, was a major force in Polish cultural and political life, devoting his writing to helping his country-men who were oppressed at home and abroad. The museum, which was founded in 1903, has exhibition galleries dedicated to not only Mickewicz but also Fryderyk Chopin and Boleslas Biegas. The Society preserves documents and mementos relating to Polish history and culture, develops historical and literary studies, and organizes cultural events.

⓯ St-Louis-en-l'Ile

19 Rue St-Louis-en-l'Ile 75004. **Map** 13 C4. **Tel** 01 46 34 11 60. Ⓜ Pont Marie. **Open** 9.30am–1pm, 2–7.30pm Mon–Sat, 9am–1pm, 2–7pm Sun & public hols. Mass: 6.45pm Mon–Fri, 6.30pm Sat, 11am Sun.

The construction of this church was begun in 1664 from plans by the royal architect Louis Le Vau, who lived on the island. It was completed and consecrated in 1726. Among its outstanding exterior features are the 1741 iron clock at the entrance and the pierced iron spire.

The interior, in the Baroque style, is richly decorated with gilding and marble. There is a statue of Louis holding a crusader's sword. A plaque in the north aisle bears the inscription "in grateful memory of St Louis in whose honour the City of St Louis, Missouri, USA is named". The church is also twinned with Carthage cathedral in Tunisia, where St Louis is buried.

A bust of Adam Mickiewicz

The interior of St-Louis-en-l'Ile

⓰ Hôtel de Lauzun

17 Quai d'Anjou 75004. **Map** 13 C4.
Tel 01 42 76 54 04. Ⓜ Pont Marie.
Closed to the public. 🖳 **paris.fr**

This splendid mansion, also known as Hotel Pimodan, was built by Louis Le Vau in the mid-1650s for Charles Gruyn des Bordes, an arms dealer. It was sold in 1682 to the French military commander Duc de Lauzun, who was a favourite of Louis XIV. It later became a focus for Paris's Bohemian literary and artistic life. It now belongs to the city of Paris, and an establishment dedicated to scientific research is housed here. For those lucky enough to see inside, it offers an unsurpassed insight into wealthy lifestyles in the 17th century. Charles Le Brun worked on the decoration of its magnificent panelling and painted ceilings before moving on to Versailles.

The poet Charles Baudelaire (1821–67) lived on the third floor and wrote most of his controversial masterpiece *Les Fleurs du Mal* in a room packed with antiques and bric-a-brac. The celebrated French Romantic poet, traveller and critic, Théophile Gautier (1811–72), had apartments here in 1848. Meetings of the Club des Haschischines (the Hashish-Eaters' Club) took place here too. Other famous residents were the Austrian poet Rainer Maria Rilke, the English artist Walter Sickert and the German composer Richard Wagner.

THE MARAIS

A place of royal residence in the 17th century, the Marais was all but abandoned during the Revolution, later descending into an architectural wasteland. Sensitive restoration brought the area to life again; some of Paris's most popular museums are now housed in its elegant mansions, while the main streets and narrow passageways bustle with smart boutiques, galleries, and restaurants. Many traders have been driven out by high prices, but enough artisans, bakers, and small cafés survive, as does the ethnic mix of Jews, former Algerian settlers, Asians, and others. Today, the Marais is also the center of the Parisian gay scene.

Sights at a Glance

Historic Buildings and Streets
2 Hôtel de Lamoignon
3 Rue des Francs-Bourgeois
8 Rue des Rosiers
19 Hôtel de Ville
22 Hôtel de Rohan

Churches
15 St-Paul–St-Louis
18 St-Gervais–St-Protais
20 Cloître des Billettes
21 Notre-Dame-des-Blancs-Manteaux

Monuments
13 Colonne de Juillet
17 Mémorial de la Shoah

Opera Houses
12 Opéra National de Paris Bastille

Squares
5 Place des Vosges
14 Place de la Bastille
26 Square du Temple

Museums and Galleries
1 Musée Carnavalet pp96–7
4 Musée Cognacq-Jay
6 Maison de Victor Hugo
7 Hôtel de Bethune-Sully
9 Hôtel de Coulanges
10 Musée Picasso Paris pp100–1
11 Pavillon de l'Arsenal
16 Hôtel des Archevêques Sens
23 Hôtel de Soubise
24 Hôtel de Guénégaud (Musée de la Chasse et de la Nature)
25 Musée des Arts et Métiers
27 Musée d'Art et d'Histoire du Judaïsme

Restaurants see pp296–7
1 Amici Miei
2 L'As du Fallafel
3 Bofinger
4 Le Chemise
5 Chez Hanna
6 Claude Colliot
7 Le Colimaçon
8 Le Dindon en Laisse
9 Les Bonnes Soeurs
10 Le Petit Marché
11 Les Philosophes
12 Qui Plume la Lune
13 Le Trumilou
14 Le Villaret

See also Street Finder maps 13–14

◀ A Jewish patisserie on Rue des Rosiers

For keys to symbols see back flap

Street-by-Street: The Marais

Once an area of marshland as its name suggests (*marais* means swamp), the Marais grew steadily in importance from the 14th century, by virtue of its proximity to the Louvre, the preferred residence of Charles V. Its heyday was in the 17th century, when it became the fashionable area for the monied classes. They built many grand and sumptuous mansions (*hôtels*) that still dot the Marais today. Many of these *hôtels* have been restored and turned into museums. Once again fashionable with the monied classes, designer boutiques, trendy restaurants, art galleries and cafés now line the streets.

To the Pompidou Centre

RUE BARBETTE

RUE ELZEVIR

RUE PAV

RUE DES HOSPITALIERES ST GERVAIS

RUE DES FR

RUE PAVEE

RUE DES ROSIERS

RUE MALHER

❸ Rue des Francs-Bourgeois
This ancient street is lined with intriguing buildings and trendy shops.

❽ Rue des Rosiers
The smell of hot pastrami and borscht wafts from restaurants and shops in the heart of the Jewish area.

❹ Musée Cognacq-Jay
An exquisite collection of 18th-century paintings and furniture is shown in perfect period setting.

0 metres	100
0 yards	100

Key

— Suggested route

❷ Hôtel de Lamoignon
Behind the ornate doorway of this fine mansion is Paris's historical library.

⓫ ★ Musée Picasso Paris
The palatial home of a 17th-century salt-tax collector is the setting for the largest collection of Picassos in the world, the result of a family bequest to the state *(see pp100–101).*

Locator Map
See Central Paris Map pp16–17

The Hôtel le Peletier de St-Fargeau adjoins the Hôtel Carnavalet to form a museum of Paris's history.

❶ ★ Musée Carnavalet
The statue of Louis XIV in Roman dress by Coysevox is in the courtyard of the Hôtel Carnavalet.

❻ Maison de Victor Hugo
Author of *Les Misérables*, Victor Hugo lived at No. 6 Place des Vosges, where his house is now a museum of his life and work.

To Metro
Sully Morland

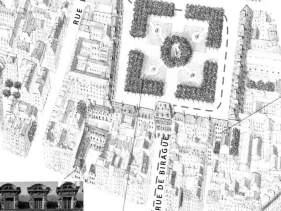

❼ Hôtel de Bethune-Sully
This *hôtel* was built for a notorious gambler.

❺ ★ Place des Vosges
Once the site of jousting and tournaments, the historic Place des Vosges, in the very heart of the Marais, is a square of perfect symmetry.

❶ Musée Carnavalet

Devoted to the history of Paris, this vast museum occupies two adjoining mansions, with entire rooms decorated with panelling, furniture and *objets d'art*; many works of art such as paintings and sculptures of prominent personalities; and engravings showing Paris being built. The main building is the Hôtel Carnavalet, built as a town house in 1548 and transformed in the mid-17th century by François Mansart. The neighbouring 17th-century mansion, Hôtel Le Peletier de Saint-Fargeau, features superb early 20th-century interiors, and the restored Orangery is devoted to Pre-history and Gallo-Roman Paris.

Louis XV Room
This delightful room contains art from the Bouvier collection and panelling from the Hôtel de Broglie.

Memorabilia in this room is dedicated to 18th-century philosophers, in particular Jean-Jacques Rousseau and Voltaire.

★ Charles Le Brun Ceiling
Magnificent works by the 17th-century artist decorate the former study and great hall from the Hôtel de la Rivière.

Sign Gallerie

★ Mme de Sévigné's Gallery
The gallery includes this portrait of Mme de Sévigné, the celebrated letter-writer, whose beloved home this was for the 20 years up to her death.

Entrance

★ Hotel d'Uzès Reception Room
The room was created in 1761 by Claude Nicolas Ledoux. The gold-and-white panelling is from a Rue Montmartre mansion.

Exit

Second floor

Convention Room
Georges Danton's portrait is among the memorabilia of the Revolution.

First floor

VISITORS' CHECKLIST

Practical Information
16 Rue des Francs-Bourgeois 75003. **Map** 14 D3. **Tel** 01 44 59 58 58. **Open** 10am–6pm Tue–Sun (last adm: 5pm for temporary, 5.30pm for permanent exhibitions. Rooms open in rotas; phone to check). **Closed** Mon, public hols. 📷 phone for times. 📷 📶 **carnavalet.paris.fr**

Transport
Ⓜ St-Paul, Chemin Vert. 🚌 29, 69, 76, 96 to St-Paul, Pl des Vosges. 🅿 Hôtel de Ville, Rue St-Antoine.

Marie Antoinette in Mourning (1793)
Alexandre Kucharski painted her at the Temple prison after the execution of Louis XVI.

Fouquet Jewellery Boutique (1900)
The Art Nouveau decor of this shop from Rue Royale is by A Mucha.

Writers' Rooms

Hôtel Le Peletier de Saint-Fargeau

Key to Floorplan

- 🟦 Pre-history to Gallo-Roman
- ⬜ Medieval Paris
- ⬜ Renaissance Paris
- ⬜ 17th-century Paris
- 🟦 Louis XV's Paris
- ⬜ Louis XVI's Paris
- 🟦 Revolutionary Paris
- ⬜ 19th Century
- 🟦 20th Century
- ⬜ Temporary exhibitions
- ⬜ Non-exhibition space
- 🟦 18th-century Paris

★ **Ballroom of the Hôtel de Wendel**
The early 20th-century ballroom interior has been reconstructed. This immense mural depicts the retinue of the Queen of Sheba and is by the Catalan designer and painter José María Sert y Badia.

Gallery Guide

The collection is mainly arranged chronologically. It covers the history of Paris up to 1789. The exhibits covering the 17th century to the Revolution are on the first floor. In the Hôtel Le Peletier de Saint-Fargeau, the ground floor covers the First–Second Empires, with the Pre-history–Gallo-Roman departments in the Orangery; from the Second Empire to the present day is on the first floor, and the second floor is devoted to the Revolution. Some of the rooms are closed due to ongoing renovation and are expected to reopen in 2015.

❷ Hôtel de Lamoignon

24 Rue Pavée 75004. **Map** 14 D3.
Tel 01 44 59 29 40. Ⓜ St-Paul.
Open 10am–6pm Mon–Sat.
Closed public hols. Ⓦ paris.fr

The imposing Hôtel de Lamoignon, one of the oldest mansions in Paris, is home to the Historical Library of the city (BHVP). It was built in 1585 for Diane de France, also known as the Duchesse d'Angoulême, daughter of Henri II. The building is noted for six high Corinthian pilasters topped by a triangular pediment and flourishes of dogs' heads, bows, arrows and quivers – recalling Diane's passion for hunting. The collection includes documents from the French Revolution and 80,000 prints covering the history of Paris.

❸ Rue des Francs-Bourgeois

75003, 75004. **Map** 14 D3.
Ⓜ Rambuteau, Chemin-Vert.

This street is an important thoroughfare in the heart of the Marais, linking the Rue des Archives and the Place des Vosges, with the imposing Hôtel de Soubise at one end and the Musée Carnavalet at the other. The street got its name from the *francs* (free from taxes) –

The exquisite 18th-century works of art and furniture in the Musée Cognacq-Jay

almshouses built for the poor in 1334 at Nos. 34 and 36. These were later closed because of illegal financial activities, although the state kept its pawnshop nearby, still there today.

❹ Musée Cognacq-Jay

Hôtel Donon, 8 Rue Elzévir 75003. **Map** 14 D3. **Tel** 01 40 27 07 21. Ⓜ St-Paul, Chemin Vert. **Open** 10am–6pm Tue–Sun. **Closed** public hols. 📷 by appt. 📱 Ⓦ cognacq-jay.paris.fr

This fine small collection of French 18th-century works of art and furniture was formed by Ernest Cognacq and his wife, Louise Jay, founder of the Art Deco La Samaritaine, which was once Paris's largest department store *(see p117)*. The private collection was bequeathed to the city and

is now housed in the heart of the Marais at the Hôtel Donon – an elegant building dating from 1575 with an 18th-century façade.

❺ Place des Vosges

75003, 75004. **Map** 14 D3.
Ⓜ Bastille, St-Paul.

This square is considered among the most beautiful in the world by Parisians and visitors alike *(see pp26–7)*. Its impressive symmetry – 36 houses, nine on each side, of brick and stone, with deep slate roofs and dormer windows over arcades – is still intact after 400 years. It has been the scene of many historic events over the centuries. A three-day tournament was held here to celebrate the marriage of Louis XIII to Anne of Austria in

The beautiful Place des Vosges with fountains in the central courtyard

1615. The famous literary hostess, Madame de Sévigné, was born here in 1626; Cardinal Richelieu, pillar of the monarchy, stayed here in 1615; and Victor Hugo, the writer, lived here for 16 years.

❻ Maison de Victor Hugo

6 Pl des Vosges 75004. **Map** 14 D3. **Tel** 01 42 72 10 16. Ⓜ Bastille, Chemin Vert. **Open** 10am–6pm Tue–Sun. **Closed** public hols. 🖼 exhibitions only. 🎫 by appt. 🌐 **musee-hugo.paris.fr**

The French poet, dramatist and novelist lived on the second floor of the former Hôtel Rohan-Guéménée from 1832 to 1848. It was here that he wrote most of *Les Misérables* and completed many other famous works. On display are some reconstructions of the rooms in which he lived, pen-and-ink drawings, books and mementos from the crucially important periods in his life, from his childhood to his exile between 1852 and 1870. Temporary exhibitions on Hugo take place regularly.

Marble bust of Victor Hugo by Auguste Rodin

❼ Hôtel de Bethune-Sully

62 Rue St-Antoine 75004. **Map** 14 D4. **Tel** 01 44 54 19 13. Ⓜ Bastille, St-Paul. **Closed** for public visits but the gardens are open from 9am–7pm and the bookstore from 10am–7pm, except public hols. 🎫 🌐 **sully. monuments-nationaux.fr**

This fine 17th-century mansion on one of Paris's oldest streets has been extensively restored, using old engravings and drawings as reference. It was built in 1624 for a notorious gambler, Petit Thomas, who lost his whole fortune in one night. The Duc de Sully, Henri IV's chief minister, purchased the house in 1634 and added some of the interior

Late-Renaissance façade of the Hôtel de Bethune-Sully

decoration as well as the Petit Sully orangery in the gardens. The Hôtel de Bethune-Sully is now the headquarters for the Centre des Monuments Nationaux.

❽ Rue des Rosiers

75004. **Map** 13 C3. Ⓜ St-Paul.

The Jewish quarter in and around this street is one of the most colourful areas of Paris. The street's name refers to the rosebushes within the old city wall. Jews first settled here in the 13th century, with a second significant wave of immigration occurring in the 19th century from Russia, Poland and central Europe. Sephardic Jews arrived from Algeria, Tunisia, Morocco and Egypt in the 1950s and

A bakery on Rue des Rosiers

1960s. Some 165 students were rounded up and deported from the old Jewish Boys' school nearby at 10 rue de Hospitalières-St-Gervais. *N'Oubliez pas* (Lest we forget) is engraved on the wall. Today, this area contains synagogues, bakeries and kosher restaurants *(see p325)*.

❾ Hôtel de Coulanges

35–37 Rue des Francs Bourgeois, 75004. **Map** 13 C3. **Tel** 01 44 61 85 85. Ⓜ St-Paul. **Open** 2–6pm Mon–Fri (until 7pm Apr–Sep). **Closed** public hols. 🌐 **paris-europe.eu**

This *hôtel* is a magnificent example of the architecture of the early 18th century. The right wing of the building, separating the courtyard from the garden, dates from the early 17th century. The *hôtel* was given in 1640 to Philippe II de Coulanges, the King's counsellor. Renamed the *"Petit hôtel Le Tellier"* in 1662 by its new owner Le Tellier, this is where the children of Louis XIV and Madame de Montespan were raised in secrecy. It is home to the Maison de l'Europe, with exhibitions on themes relating to Europe.

⓾ Musée Picasso Paris

On the death of the Spanish-born artist Pablo Picasso (1881–1973), who lived most of his life in France, the French State inherited many of his works in lieu of death duties. It used them to establish the Musée Picasso Paris, which opened in 1985. The museum is housed in a large 17th-century mansion, the Hôtel Salé, in the Marais. The original character of the Hôtel, which was built in 1656 for Aubert de Fontenay, a salt-tax collector (*salé* means "salty"), has been preserved. The breadth of the collection reflects Picasso's development, including his Blue, Pink and Cubist periods. Works include paintings, sculptures, ceramics, drawings and etchings.

★ Self-Portrait
Poverty, loneliness and the onset of winter all made the end of 1901, when this picture was painted, a particularly difficult time for Picasso.

Violin and Sheet Music
This collage (1912) is from the artist's Synthetic Cubist period.

★ The Two Brothers (1906)
During the summer of 1906, Picasso returned to Catalonia in Spain, where he painted this picture.

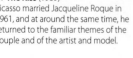

★ The Kiss (1969)
Picasso married Jacqueline Roque in 1961, and at around the same time, he returned to the familiar themes of the couple and of the artist and model.

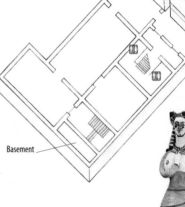

Basement

Gallery Guide

The museum has undergone extensive renovation. The collection of 5,000 works is spread over the entire building, and the space for displays has tripled. Five vaulted rooms in the basement house large-scale sculptures and six rooms are dedicated to Picasso's private collection of works.

Woman with a Mantilla (1949)
Picasso extended his range when he began working in ceramics in 1948.

Painter with Palette and Easel (1928)
This Post-Cubist portrait in oils was painted at a time when Picasso's work was verging on Surrealism.

First floor

Entrance

Ground floor

Entrance

VISITORS' CHECKLIST

Practical Information
Hôtel Salé, 5 Rue de Thorigny.
Map 14 D2.
Tel 01 42 71 25 21.
🅿 ♿ 🎦 groups by appt only.
📷 🎭 Concerts, conferences and performances.
W **museepicassoparis.fr**

Transport
Ⓜ St-Sébastien Froissart, St-Paul.
🚌 29, 69, 75, 96 to St-Paul, Bastille, Pl des Vosges.
🚆 Châtelet-Les-Halles.
🅿 Rue St-Antoine, Bastille.

Picasso and Spain

After 1934, Picasso never returned to his homeland due to his rejection of Franco's regime. However, throughout his life in France he used Spanish themes in his art, such as the bull (often in the form of a minotaur) and the guitar, which he associated with his Andalusian childhood.

Woman Reading (1932)
Purples and yellows were often used by Picasso when painting his model Marie-Thérèse Walter.

★ **Two Women Running on the Beach** (1922)
In 1924, this was used for the stage curtain design for Diaghilev's ballet *The Blue Train*. It proved to be his last major design work for any theatre.

⓫ Pavillon de l'Arsenal

21 Bd Morland 75004. **Map** 14 D5.
Tel 01 42 76 33 97. Ⓜ Sully Morland,
Bastille. **Open** 10.30am–6.30pm Tue–
Sat, 11am–7pm Sun. **Closed** 1 Jan.
📺 📷 ✔ by appointment only.
🌐 **pavillon-arsenal.com**

The Pavillon de l'Arsenal houses a small but fascinating exhibition on the architectural evolution of Paris. Using films, models and panoramic images, this permanent exhibition explores how Paris was built over the centuries, as well as looking at future plans for the city. Up to three temporary exhibitions are also programmed each year.

⓬ Opéra National de Paris Bastille

120 Rue de Lyon 75012. **Map** 14 E4.
Tel 01 40 01 19 70. Ⓜ Bastille.
Open phone for details.
Closed certain public hols. 📷 ♿ ✔
See Entertainment pp337–9.
🌐 **operadeparis.fr**

The controversial "people's opera" was officially opened on 14 July 1989 to coincide with the bicentennial celebrations of the fall of the Bastille. Carlos Ott's imposing building is a notable break with 19th-century opera-house design, epitomized by

The "genius of liberty" on top of the Colonne de Juillet

Garnier's opulent Opéra in the heart of the city *(see pp218–19)*. It is a massive, modern, curved, glass building. The main auditorium seats an audience of 2,700; its design is functional and modern with black upholstered seats contrasting with the granite of the walls and the impressive glass ceiling. With its five moveable stages, this opera house is certainly a masterpiece of technological wizardry.

⓭ Colonne de Juillet

Pl de la Bastille 75004. **Map** 14 E4.
Ⓜ Bastille. **Closed** to the public.

Topped by the statue of the "genius of liberty", this column of hollow bronze reaches 50.5 m (166 ft) into the sky. It is a memorial to those who died in the street battles of July 1830 that led to the overthrow of the monarch *(see pp34–5)*. The crypt contains the remains of 504 victims of the violent fighting and others who died in the 1848 revolution.

⓮ Place de la Bastille

75004. **Map** 14 E4. Ⓜ Bastille.

Nothing is now left of the prison stormed by the revolutionary mob on 14 July 1789 *(see pp32–3)* – an event celebrated annually by the French at home and abroad – although the stones were used for the Pont de la Concorde. A line of paving stones from Nos. 5 to 49 Blvd Henri IV traces the former towers and fortifications. The large, traffic-clogged square which marks the site, was once the border between central Paris and the eastern working-class areas *(faubourgs)*. Gentrification, however, is well underway, with a marina, the Port de Plaisance de l'Arsenal, and attractive cafés and shops.

The glass façade of the Bastille Opéra

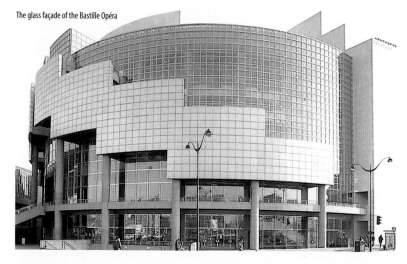

⓯ St-Paul–St-Louis

99 Rue St-Antoine 75004. **Map** 14 D4.
Tel 01 42 72 30 32. Ⓜ St-Paul. **Open**
8am–8pm Mon–Fri, 8am–7.30pm Sat,
9am–8pm Sun. Mass: 6pm Sat,
9.30am, 11am, 7pm Sun. Concerts.

A Jesuit church, St-Paul–St-Louis
was an important symbol of the
influence that the Jesuits held
from 1627, when Louis XIII laid
the first stone, to 1762 when they
were expelled from France. The
Gesù church in Rome served as
the model for the nave, while the
60-m high (180-ft) dome was
the forerunner of those of the
Invalides and the Sorbonne.
Most of the church's treasures
were removed during periods of
turmoil, but Delacroix's masterpiece, *Christ in the Garden of Olives*,
can still be seen. The church is on
one of the main streets of the
Marais, but can also be approach-
ed by the ancient Passage St-Paul.

⓰ Hôtel des Archevêques de Sens

1 Rue du Figuier 75004. **Map** 13 C4.
Tel 01 42 78 14 60. Ⓜ Pont-Marie.
Open 1pm–7.30pm Tue, Fri, Sat;
10am–7.30pm Wed, Thu.
Closed for renovation. 🅿 📷 by
appointment only.

This is one of the few medieval
buildings left in Paris and houses
the Forney fine arts library. In the
16th century, at the time of the
Catholic League, it was occupied
by the Bourbons, the Guises and
Cardinal de Pellevé, whose religious fervour led him to die of rage

The Hôtel des Archevêques de Sens, now
home to a fine arts library

Christ in the Garden of Olives by Delacroix in St-Paul–St-Louis

in 1594 on hearing that the Protestant Henri IV had entered Paris.
Marguerite de Valois, lodged here
by her ex-husband, Henri IV, led a
life of breathtaking debauchery
and scandal, beheading an
ex-lover who had assassinated
her current favourite. The
gardens are open to the public.

The memorial to the unknown Jewish
martyr, dedicated in 1956

⓱ Mémorial de la Shoah

17 Rue Geoffroy-l'Asnier 75004. **Map**
13 C4. **Tel** 01 42 77 44 72. Ⓜ Pont-
Marie, St-Paul. **Open** 10am–6pm
Sun–Fri (10am–10pm Thu). **Closed**
public hols. 🎟 exhibitions. ♿ 📷 🎧
🅆 memorialdelashoah.org

The eternal flame burning in
the crypt here is the memorial
to the unknown Jewish martyr
of the Holocaust. Its striking
feature is a large cylinder that
bears the names of the concentration camps where Jewish
victims of the Holocaust died.
In 2005, a stone wall, engraved
with the names of 76,000 Jews –
11,000 of them children – who
were deported from France to
the Nazi death camps, was
erected here. Artifacts from the
camps are also on display.

⓲ St-Gervais–St-Protais

Pl St-Gervais 75004. **Map** 13 B3.
Tel 01 48 87 32 02. Ⓜ Hôtel de Ville.
Open 5.30am–9pm daily.

Named after Gervase and
Protase, two Roman soldiers
who were martyred by Nero,
this remarkable church dates
from the 6th century. It has
the oldest Classical façade in
Paris, which is formed of a
three-tiered arrangement of
columns: Doric, Ionic and
Corinthian. Behind its façade
lies a beautiful Gothic church
renowned for its association
with religious music. It was for
the church's fine organ that
François Couperin (1668–1733)
composed his two masses.
The church currently has a
Roman Catholic monastic
community whose liturgy
attracts people from all over
the world.

The façade of St-Gervais–St-Protais
with its Classical columns

The elaborate façade of the town hall (Hôtel de Ville), rebuilt in the 19th century according to its original Neo-Renaissance design

⑲ Hôtel de Ville

Pl de l'Hôtel de Ville (visitor entrance 29 Rue de Rivoli) 75004. **Map** 13 B3. **Tel** 01 42 76 40 40. Ⓜ Hôtel-de-Ville. **Open** 10am–7pm Mon–Sat for temporary exhibitions; groups: by arrangement, **Tel** 01 42 76 43 43. **Closed** public hols, official functions. ⚿ 📷 🏠 Ⓦ **rendezvous.paris.fr**

Home of the city council, the town hall is a 19th-century reconstruction of the 17th-century building that was burned down in 1871. It is highly ornate, with elaborate stonework, turrets and statues overlooking a pedestrianized square which is a delight to stroll in, especially at night when the fountains are illuminated.

The square was once the main site for hangings, burnings and other executions. It was here that Ravaillac, Henri IV's assassin, was quartered alive, his body ripped to pieces by four strong horses.

Inside, a notable feature is the long Salle des Fêtes (ballroom), with adjoining salons devoted to science, literature and the arts. The impressive staircase, the decorated ceilings with their chandeliers and the statues and caryatids all add to the air of ceremony and pomp. Whilst these parts are mostly closed to the public (except during some of the Journées du Patrimoine (see p66) and group visits), certain annexes are used for temporary exhibitions on themes related to France (see www.paris.fr for more info).

⑳ Cloître des Billettes

24 Rue des Archives 75004. **Map** 13 B3. **Tel** 01 42 72 38 79 Ⓜ Hôtel-de-Ville. **Open** Cloister 2–7pm daily; church 6.30–8pm Thu, 9.30am–4pm Sun. 🎵 Concerts.

This is the only remaining medieval cloister in Paris. It was built in 1427 for the Brothers of Charity, or *Billettes*, and three of its four original galleries are still standing. The adjoining church is a simple Classical building which replaced the monastic original in 1756.

The oldest cloister in Paris

㉑ Notre-Dame-des-Blancs-Manteaux

12 Rue des Blancs-Manteaux 75004. **Map** 13 C3. **Tel** 01 42 72 09 37. Ⓜ Rambuteau. **Open** 10am–noon, 4.30–7pm Tue–Sat; 10am–noon Sun. 🎵 on request. Concerts.

The name of this church, built in 1685, derives from the white habits worn by the Augustinian friars who founded a convent here in 1258. It has an interesting 18th-century Rococo Flemish pulpit, and its famous organ can be appreciated at one of the church's concerts.

㉒ Hôtel de Rohan

87 Rue Vieille-du-Temple 75003. **Map** 13 C2. **Tel** 01 40 27 60 96. Ⓜ Rambuteau. 🕐 12.30pm 2nd Mon of month. Tel 01 75 47 20 06.

Although not resembling it in appearance, the Hôtel de Rohan forms a pair with the Hôtel de Soubise. It was built by the same architect, Delamair, for Armand de Rohan-Soubise, a cardinal and Bishop of Strasbourg. The *hôtel* has been home to a part of the national archives (one of the largest in the world) since 1927. In the courtyard over the doorway of the stables is the 18th-century sculpture *Horses of Apollo* by Robert Le Lorrain.

Horses of Apollo by Le Lorrain

The Hôtel de Soubise

㉓ Hôtel de Soubise

60 Rue des Francs-Bourgeois 75003.
Map 13 C2. **Tel** 01 40 27 60 96.
Ⓜ Rambuteau. Musée de l'Histoire
de France **Open** 10am–5.30pm Mon,
Wed–Fri, 2–5.30pm Sat & Sun. ⓒ
Tel 06 10 12 62 72. ⓐ Ⓦ **archives-
nationales.culture.gouv.fr**

This imposing mansion, built
from 1705 to 1709 for the
Princesse de Rohan, is one of
two main buildings housing the
national archives. (The other is
the Hôtel de Rohan.) The Hôtel
de Soubise displays a majestic
courtyard and a magnificent
interior decoration dating
from 1735 to 1740 by some
of the most gifted painters
and craftsmen of the day: Carl
Van Loo, Jean Restout, Charles
Natoire and François Boucher.
  Natoire's *rocaille* work on the
Princess's bedroom, the Oval
Salon, forms part of the Musée de
l'Histoire de France. Other exhibits
include Napoleon's will, in which
he asks for his remains to be
returned to France, and letters
by Joan of Arc and Voltaire.

㉔ Hôtel de Guénégaud

62 Rue des Archives 75003. **Map** 13
C2. **Tel** 01 53 01 92 40. Ⓜ Hôtel de
Ville Museum. **Open** 11am–6pm Tue–
Sun (to 9.30pm Thu). **Closed** public
hols. ⓐ ⓕ Ⓦ **chassenature.org**

The celebrated architect François
Mansart built this superb man-
sion in the mid-17th century for
Henri de Guénégaud des Brosses,
who was Secretary of State and
Keeper of the Seals. One wing
now contains the Musée de la
Chasse et de la Nature (Hunting
Museum) inaugurated by André
Malraux in 1967. It holds the
collections of Francois and
Jacqueline Sommer; exhibits
include a fine collection of
hunting weapons. There are also
drawings and paintings by Oudry,
Rubens (including *Diane and her
Nymphs Preparing to Hunt*)
and Rembrandt.

㉕ Musée des Arts et Métiers

60 Rue Réaumur 75003. **Map** 13 B1-C1.
Tel 01 53 01 82 00. Ⓜ Arts et Métiers.
Open 10am–6pm Tue–Sun (to 9.30pm
Thu). **Closed** 1 May & 25 Dec. ⓐ ⓒ
ⓖ 🖥 ⓕ Ⓦ **arts-et-metiers.net**

Housed within the old Abbey of
Saint-Martin-des-Champs, the
Arts and Crafts museum was
founded in 1794 and closed
down two centuries later for
interior restructuring and
renovation. It reopened in 2000
as a high-quality museum of
science and industry displaying
5,000 items (it has 75,000 other
items in store available to
academics and researchers). The
theme is man's ingenuity and
the world of invention and
manufacturing, covering such
topics as textiles, photography
and machines. Among the most
entertaining displays are ones
of musical clocks, mechanical
musical instruments and
automata (mechanical figures),
one of which, the "Joueuse de
Tympanon", is said to represent
Marie-Antoinette.

㉖ Square du Temple

75003. **Map** 13 C1. Ⓜ Temple.

A quiet and pleasant square
today, this was once a fortified
centre of the medieval Knights
Templar. A state within a state,
the area contained a palace, a
church and shops behind high
walls and a drawbridge, making
it a haven for those who were
seeking to escape from royal
jurisdiction. Louis XVI and Marie-
Antoinette were held here after
their arrest in 1792 *(see pp32–3)*.
The king left from here for his
execution by the guillotine.

The exterior of the Musée d'Art et d'Histoire
du Judaïsme

㉗ Musée d'Art et d'Histoire du Judaïsme

Hôtel de St-Aignan, 71 rue du Temple
75003. **Map** 13 C2. **Tel** 01 53 01 86 60.
Ⓜ Rambuteau. **Open** 11am–6pm
Mon–Fri, 10am–6pm Sun (last admission at 5.15pm). **Closed** 1 Jan, 1 May,
Rosh Hashanah & Yom Kippur. ⓐ ⓒ
ⓖ ⓐ ⓕ Ⓦ **mahj.org**

Housed in an elegant Marais
mansion, the museum unites
collections formerly scattered
around the city, and commemorates the culture of French
Jewry from medieval times to
the present. There has been a
sizeable Jewish community in
France since Roman times, and
some of the world's greatest
Jewish scholars were French.
Much exquisite craftsmanship is
displayed, with elaborate silver-
ware and Torah covers. There are
also historical documents, photographs, paintings and cartoons.

BEAUBOURG AND LES HALLES

This Right Bank area is dominated by the modernistic Forum des Halles and the Pompidou Centre. These two spectacular undertakings are thriving public areas of contact for shoppers, art lovers, students and tourists. Literally millions of people flow between the two squares. The Halles is for street fashion, with most of the shops underground, and the clientele strolling under the concrete and glass bubbles is young. Above ground, there are gardens and mini-pavilions. The surrounding streets are coloured by

popular cheap shops and bars, but there are still enough specialist food shops, butchers and small markets to recall what Les Halles must have been like in its prime as the city's thriving market. All roads round Les Halles lead to the Beaubourg area and the Pompidou Centre, an avant-garde assembly of vast pipes, ducts and cables. The adjoining streets, such as Rue St Martin, house small contemporary art galleries. A massive project to renovate Les Halles is currently underway and is scheduled for completion in 2016.

Sights at a Glance

Historic Buildings and Streets
⑩ No. 51 Rue de Montmorency
⑪ Tour Jean Sans Peur
⑬ Bourse du Commerce
⑮ La Samaritaine
⑯ Tour St-Jacques

Churches
❸ St-Merri
⑫ St-Eustache
⑭ St-Germain l'Auxerrois

Modern Architecture
❷ Place Igor Stravinsky
❽ Forum des Halles

Cafés
❻ Café Beaubourg

Fountain
❹ Fontaine des Innocents

Museums and Galleries
❶ *Pompidou Centre pp110–13*
❺ Galerie Marian Goodman
❼ Forum des Images
❾ Musée de la Poupée

☐ **Restaurants** *see pp296–7*
1 L'Ambassade d'Auvergne
2 L'Ange 20
3 Auberge Nicolas Flamel
4 Benoît
5 Blend
6 The Fish Club
7 Frenchie
8 Le Garde Robe
9 Le Hangar
10 Le Pharamond
11 La Régalade St-Honoré
12 Spring
13 Le Tir Bouchon
14 Yam'Tcha

See also Street Finder map 12, 13

0 metres   400
0 yards   400

◄ Large air vents on the exterior of the Pompidou Centre   **For keys to symbols** *see back flap*

Street-by-Street: Beaubourg and Les Halles

When Emile Zola described Les Halles as the "belly of Paris," he was referring to the meat, vegetable and fruit market that had thrived here since 1183. Traffic congestion in the 1960s forced the market to move to the suburbs and Baltard's giant umbrella-like market pavilions were pulled down, despite howls of protest, and replaced by a shopping and leisure complex, the Forum. The conversion worked: today, Les Halles and the Pompidou Centre, which lies in the Beaubourg quarter and has been one of Paris's main tourist attractions ever since it opened in 1977, draw the most mixed crowds in Paris.

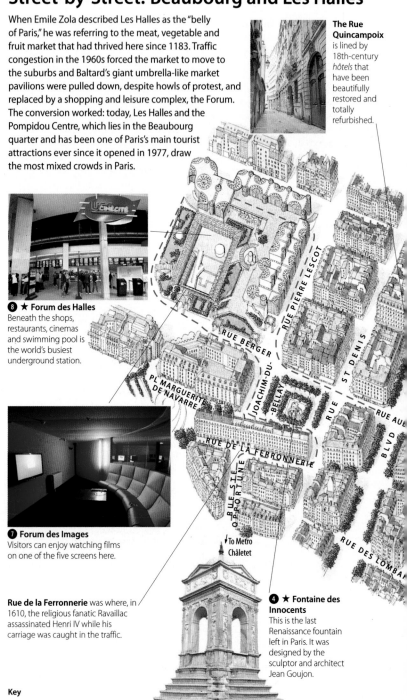

The Rue Quincampoix is lined by 18th-century *hôtels* that have been beautifully restored and totally refurbished.

8 ★ Forum des Halles
Beneath the shops, restaurants, cinemas and swimming pool is the world's busiest underground station.

7 Forum des Images
Visitors can enjoy watching films on one of the five screens here.

Rue de la Ferronnerie was where, in 1610, the religious fanatic Ravaillac assassinated Henri IV while his carriage was caught in the traffic.

↓ To Metro Châletet

4 ★ Fontaine des Innocents
This is the last Renaissance fountain left in Paris. It was designed by the sculptor and architect Jean Goujon.

Key

— Suggested route

Le Défenseur du Temps
This impressive brass-and-steel mechanical clock and sculpture was designed by Jacques Monastier in 1979. It portrays a soldier defending the passage of time against savage beasts which represent the elements.

Locator Map
See Central Paris Map pp16–17

0 metres 100
0 yards 100

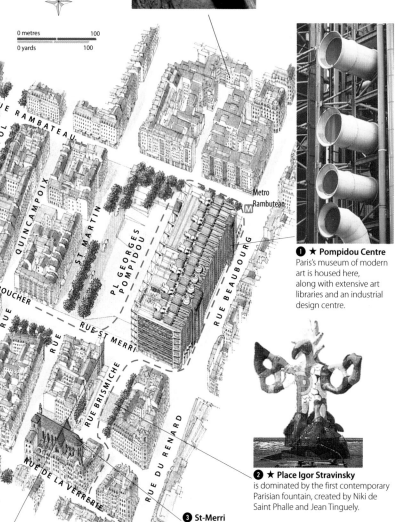

Metro Rambuteau

❶ ★ Pompidou Centre
Paris's museum of modern art is housed here, along with extensive art libraries and an industrial design centre.

❷ ★ Place Igor Stravinsky
is dominated by the first contemporary Parisian fountain, created by Niki de Saint Phalle and Jean Tinguely.

❸ St-Merri
The pulpit of this beautiful church was designed by the Stodtz brothers in the mid-18th century and is supported by a pair of carved palm trees, one on either side.

IRCAM is a research centre dedicated to pioneering new ways of making music.

❶ Pompidou Centre

The Pompidou is like a building turned inside out: escalators, lifts, air and water ducts and even the massive steel struts that are the building's skeleton have all been placed on the outside. This allowed architects Richard Rogers, Renzo Piano and Gianfranco Franchini to create an uncluttered, flexible space within it for the Musée National d'Art Moderne, the world's largest collection of modern art, as well as for the Pompidou's other activities. Schools represented in the museum include Fauvism, Cubism and Surrealism. Outside in the piazza, the street performers attract crowds. The Pompidou also hosts temporary exhibitions that thrust it into the heart of the international art scene.

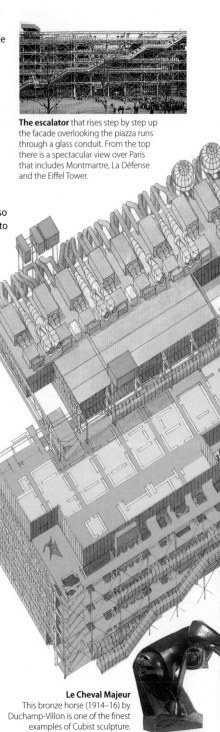

The escalator that rises step by step up the facade overlooking the piazza runs through a glass conduit. From the top there is a spectacular view over Paris that includes Montmartre, La Défense and the Eiffel Tower.

Key to Floorplan

Exhibition space

Non-exhibition space

Gallery Guide

The permanent collections are on Levels 5 & 4: works from 1905 to 1960 are on the former, with the latter reserved for contemporary art from 1960s onwards. Levels 1 & 6 are for major exhibitions, while Levels 1, 2 & 3 house an information library. The lower levels make up "The Forum", the focal public area, which include a performance centre for dance, theatre and music, a cinema and a children's workshop.

Portrait of the Journalist Sylvia von Harden (1926)
The surgical precision of Dix's style makes this a harsh caricature.

Le Cheval Majeur
This bronze horse (1914–16) by Duchamp-Villon is one of the finest examples of Cubist sculpture.

**To Russia, the Asses
and the Others** (1911)
Throughout his life Chagall
drew inspiration from the
small Russian town of Vitebsk,
where he was born.

VISITORS' CHECKLIST

Practical Information
Pl Georges Pompidou.
Map 13 B2. **Tel** 01 44 78 12 33.
🌐 **centrepompidou.fr**
Open MNAM & temp exhibs:
11am–9pm Wed–Mon (to 11pm
Thu); Library: noon–10pm Wed–
Mon (from 11am Sat, Sun & pub
hols); Atelier Brancusi: 2–6pm
Wed–Mon.
🖼 ♿ 🎨 📷 ✏ 🖥 🎭

Transport
Ⓜ Rambuteau, Châtelet,
Hôtel de Ville.
🚌 21, 29, 38, 47, 58, 69, 70, 72,
74, 75, 76, 81, 85, 96.
🚆 Châtelet-Les-Halles.

**The Breakfast
Table** (1915)
Juan Gris'
fragmented objects
with sharp-edges
represent the
synthetic Cubism
style of art.

Le Duo (1937)
Georges Braque, like Picasso,
developed the Cubist technique
of representing different views of
a subject in a single picture.

Basin and
Sculpture
Terrace

Basin and
Sculpture
Terrace

Colour-Coding

The coloured pipes that are the most striking feature at
the back of the Pompidou, on the rue du Renard, moved
one critic to compare the building to an oil refinery. Far
from being merely decorative, the colours serve to
distinguish the pipes' various functions: air-conditioning
ducts are blue, water pipes green and electricity lines are
painted yellow. The areas through which people move
vertically (such as escalators) are red. The white funnels
are ventilation shafts for the underground areas, and
structural beams are clad in stainless steel. The architects'
idea was to help the public understand the way the
dynamics of a building function.

Exploring the Pompidou's Modern Art Collection

With over 60,000 works of art from over 5,000 artists, the Pompidou holds Europe's largest collection of modern and contemporary art. Classic disciplines – painting, sculpture, drawing and photography – are integrated with cinema, architecture, design, and audio-visual archives, to form a complete, chronological overview of modern and contemporary art. The collections, however, keep changing. Works are often loaned out so some pieces may not be on show.

The Two Barges (1906) by André Derain

From 1905–60

The "historical" collections bring together the great artistic movements of the first half of the 20th century, from Fauvism to Abstract Expressionism, to the changing currents of the 1950s. The rich collection of Cubist sculptures, of which the *Cheval Majeur* by Duchamp-Villon (1914–1916) is a fine example, is displayed, as well as examples of the great masters of the 20th century. Matisse, Picasso, Braque, Duchamp, Kandinsky, Léger, Miró, Giacometti and Dubuffet command large areas at the heart of the collection.

Towards the end of his life, Matisse made several collages from cut-up large sheets of gouache-painted paper. Among others, the museum possesses *Jazz* (1943–7). With *Homme à la Guitare* (Man with a Guitar), Braque demonstrates his command of the Cubist technique which he pioneered along with Picasso. Considered as one of the first, if not the first, Abstract painter, Kandinsky transformed works inspired by

nature into constructions of colour and form. The museum has a large collection of the Russian painter's works, of which the Impressions *(Impressions V, Parc, 1911)* mark the end of his Expressionist period before his plunge into Abstract art with *Improvisations XIV* or *Avec l'Arc Noir* (With the Black Arc) both dating from 1912 compositions.

The collection also shows the groups and the movements on which the history of modern art is based, or by which it has been affected, including Dada, Abstract Art and Informal. A pioneer of Informal art, Jean Fautrier is represented in the collections with *Otages* (Hostages), a commemoration of the suffering of the resistance fighters.

At the heart of this chronological progression, various thematic displays are a revelation. One set shows non-figurative art from "Groupe Espace and the Magazine"; a collaboration between painters, sculptors, architects and engineers. Another room recreates the atmosphere of André Breton's workshop in which the works of his Surrealist friends are also shown. Silent pauses have also been allowed for: the room reserved for Miró has vast, moody canvasses such as *La Sieste* that give visitors reason to meditate on the explosion and revolutions of modern art.

With the Black Arc (1912) by Vassily Kandinsky

Brancusi's Studio

The Atelier Brancusi, on the rue Rambuteau side of the piazza, is a reconstruction of the workshop of the Romanian-born artist Constantin Brancusi (1876–1957), who lived and worked in Paris from 1904. He bequeathed his entire collection of works to the French state on condition that his workshop be rebuilt as it was on the day he died. The collection includes sculptures and plinths, photographs and a selection of his tools. Also featured are some of his more personal items such as documents, pieces of furniture and his book collection.

Miss Pogany (1919–20) by Constantin Brancusi

The Good-bye Door (1980) by Joan Mitchell

Art Since 1960

The contemporary art section occupies the fourth floor of the Pompidou Centre and consists of approximately 500 works. Jean-Michel Alberola's exceptional, boldly coloured mural, Vous avez le bonjour de Marcel (2002) welcomes visitors and sets the tone for the contemporary collection.

The collection starts with works by leading French artists of the second half of the twentieth century: artist and sculptor Louise Bourgeois whose work is strongly influenced by the Surrealists, Abstract Expressionism and Minimalism, Pierre Soulages, Jean-Pierre Raynaud, François Morellet and Bertrand Lavier.

Yayoï Kusama's restored masterpiece My Flower Bed (1965–6), made of painted mattress springs and stuffed gloves, is also on view.

The display is organized around a central aisle from which the rooms holding the museum's collections lead off. The central aisle is dotted with sculptures including works by Toni Grand, John Chamberlain and Xavier Veilhan. This hall is, however, dedicated principally to painting with works by Gerhard Richter, Brice Marden, Jean-Michel Basquiat, Philip

Mobile on Two Planes (1955) by Alexander Calder

Guston, Bernard Piffaretti and Katharina Grosse.

Room 3 is an homage to artist, philosopher and art critic Pontus Hulten, chosen by President Georges Pompidou to plan and run the national museum of modern art that was to be one of the four departments of the Pompidou Centre. Pontus Hulten was director of the Musée National

Homogenous Infiltration (1966) by Joseph Beuys

d'Art Moderne from 1973 to 1981, and was responsible for making it the open and cross-disciplinary museum that its founder had intended. Works by Jean Tinguely, Andy Warhol and Niki de Saint Phalle are to be found in this room.

Certain areas in the Pompidou Centre have been designated to bring together different disciplines around a theme such as minimalist painting or conceptual art rather than a school or movement. Other rooms, however, are artist specific with rooms dedicated to New Realist Martial Raysse, Robert Filliou, Christian Botanski, Sarkis, Joseph Beuys and Marcel Broodthaers. These rooms explore installation and photography as well as painting.

The fourth floor allows different aspects of the museum's collections to be

discovered, often reflecting a preference for the more ironic and conceptual forms. German artist Joseph Beuys's Plight (1985), for example, consists of a grand piano in a room where the walls are covered from floor to ceiling with about seven tonnes of thick felt arranged in rolls.

With regards to design and architecture, inflatable structures are explored in an unprecedented way with acidically coloured inflatable pieces on display.

A room is dedicated to French designer Philippe Starck's work with items from the sixties through to the present day on display.

Another room focuses on leading young international architects and designers of the moment, along with a space dedicated to Japanese artists, including Shigeru Ban, the architect behind the construction of the Pompidou Centre's sister gallery in Metz.

Lastly, there is a "global" room bringing together major contemporary pieces by African, Chinese, Japanese, and American artists. Denkifuku (1956), a dress made from light-bulbs, is a key work by Atsuko Tanaka of Japan.

The museum gallery allows temporary exhibitions to be mounted from works held in reserve. A graphic arts exhibition room and a video area complete the arrange-ment. A screening room gives access to the museum's entire collection of videos of a wide range of modern artists.

Le Rhinocéros (1999) by Xavier Veilhan

❷ Place Igor Stravinsky

75004. **Map** 13 B2. Ⓜ Rambuteau.

This lively square on the south side of the Pompidou Centre is filled with modern sculptures and street performers. Since 1983, it has contained the Stravinsky Fountain, which features 16 moving, water-spraying sculptures of skeletons, dragons and a large pair of red lips. The black iron and colourful polyester mechanical sculptures were created by husband-and-wife team Jean Tinguely and Niki de Saint Phalle and pay homage to Igor Stravinsky. Each sculpture represents one of his compositions, including *The Firebird* and *The Rite of Spring*.

Stravinsky's music paved the way for the pioneering work of IRCAM (Institut de la Researche et de la Coordination Acoustique/Musique), which has an entrance on the west side of the square. Founded by the composer Pierre Boulez, it is a research centre dedicated to creating new technologies for contemporary music, as well as a venue for concerts. Much of the Institute is underground, with an overground extension by Renzo Piano, one of the Pompidou Centre's architects. IRCAM runs an annual festival, which usually takes place for up to two weeks in June.

❸ St-Merri

76 Rue de la Verrerie 75004. **Map** 13 B3. **Tel** 01 42 71 93 93. Ⓜ Hôtel-de-Ville. **Open** Apr–Oct: 3–7pm Mon–Sat; Nov–Mar: 2–6pm Mon–Sat. 🎵 8pm Sat & 4pm Sun. Concerts. 🌐 **saintmerry.org**

The site of this church dates back to the 7th century. St Médéric, the abbot of St-Martin d'Autun, was buried here at the beginning of the 8th century after he died while on pilgrimage in Paris. The building of the church – in the Flamboyant Gothic style – was built between 1500 and 1550. The west front is

A Nativity scene from the stained-glass windows in St-Merri

particularly rich in decoration, and the northwest turret contains the oldest bell in Paris, dating from 1331. St-Merri was the wealthy parish church of the Lombard moneylenders, who gave their name to the nearby Rue des Lombards.

❹ Fontaine des Innocents

Place Joachim-du-Bellay 75001. **Map** 13 A2. Ⓜ Les Halles. 🚆 Châtelet-Les-Halles.

This carefully-restored Renaissance fountain stands in the Square des Innocents, the area's main crossroads. Erected in 1549 on the Rue St-Denis, it was moved to its present location in the 18th century, when the square was constructed on the site of a former graveyard. Originally set into a wall, the fountain had only three sides so a fourth had to be constructed. The fountain is a popular meeting place, and is one of the landmarks of Les Halles.

❺ Galerie Marian Goodman

79 Rue du Temple 75003. **Map** 13 C2. **Tel** 01 48 04 70 52. Ⓜ Rambuteau. 🚆 Châtelet-Les-Halles. **Open** 11am–7pm Tue–Sat. **Closed** between exhibitions. 🌐 **mariangoodman.com**

One of many art spaces in the area, this cutting edge gallery is the sister of Marian Goodman Gallery, New York, which has played an important role in presenting European artists to American audiences since the 1970s. Many important contemporary artists, from the continent and the US, have been exhibited in the Paris gallery, including Gerhard Richter, Jeff Wall, Tacita Dean, William Kentridge, Chantal Akerman and Cristina Iglesias.

Housed in a beautiful 17th-century mansion, the contemporary works on display and the Manhattan-style interior contrast in an appealing, if strikingly anachronistic way with the period façade.

❻ Café Beaubourg

43 Rue Saint-Merri, Esplanade du Centre Georges Pompidou 75004. **Map** 13 B2. **Tel** 01 48 87 63 96. Ⓜ Les Halles. 🚆 Châtelet-Les-Halles. **Open** 8–2am daily.

Opened by Gilbert Costes in 1987, this stylish café was designed and decorated by one of France's star architects,

Decoration on the Fontaine des Innocents

The terrace of the Café Beaubourg

Christian de Portzamparc, who created the impressive Cité de la Musique in the Parc de la Villette *(see p238)*. Its vast terrace is lined with comfortable wicker chairs. The spacious and coolly elegant interior is decorated with rows of books, which soften its severely Art Deco ambience. The café is a favourite meeting point for art dealers from the surrounding galleries and Pompidou Centre staff. It serves light meals and brunch. If the crush gets too much around Les Halles, the Café Beaubourg is the ideal place to soothe the nerves.

❼ Forum des Images

2 Rue du Cinéma, Forum des Halles 75001. **Map** 13 A2. **Tel** 01 44 76 63 00. Ⓜ Les Halles. 🄬 Châtelet-Les-Halles. **Open** Collections: 1–10pm Tue–Fri, 2–10pm Sat & Sun; Information & Café: 12.30–9pm Tue–Fri, 2–9pm Sat & Sun. 🅿 ♿ 🄳
🅆 **forumdesimages.fr**

At the forum, you can choose from thousands of cinema, television, and amateur films. Many feature the city of Paris. There is footage on the history of Paris since 1895, including a remarkable news-reel of General de Gaulle avoiding sniper fire during the Liberation of Paris in 1944. There are countless movies such as Truffaut's *Baisers Volés*. On Friday evenings, the forum also hosts "Cours de Cinéma", when classic films are analysed. There are also regular film festivals, "midnight movies" screenings and short film evenings.

❽ Forum des Halles

101 Porte Berger 75001. **Map** 13 A2. Ⓜ Les Halles. 🄬 Châtelet-Les-Halles.

The present Forum des Halles, known simply as Les Halles, was built in 1979, amid much controversy, on the site of the famous old fruit and vegetable market. Emile Zola named the area *Le Ventre de Paris* (The Belly of Paris). The complex is currently being rebuilt, and hence partially closed. Some of the facilities, such as the multi-screen cinema, swimming pool as well as the fantastic Forum des Images film archive centre, continue to remain open. Beneath this complex is a Metro station and major urban railway (RER) hub. Above ground, there

Pygmalion by Julio Silva in the Forum des Halles

is the Nelson Mandela Garden with fountains, ponds and a terraced flower garden.

Sadly, the area can be rather seedy, and is not recommended at night. However, under the direction of architect David Mangin, the major and much-needed remodelling project will hopefully transform the area as well as bring back a food market. The project is expected to take around five years, with work having begun in 2011. Remember to explore the surrounding streets, including the trendy rue Montorgueil to the north.

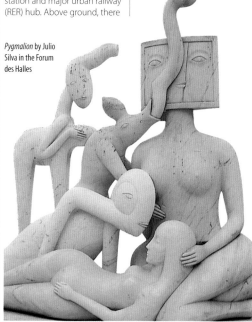

A collection of hand-made dolls in Musée de la Poupée

9 Musée de la Poupée

Impasse Berthaud 75003. **Map** 13 B2. **Tel** 01 42 72 73 11. M Rambuteau. **Open** 1–6pm Tue–Sat. **Closed** public hols. for groups, book in advance. W **museedelapoupeeparis.com**

An impressive collection of hand-made dolls, from the mid-19th century to the present day, are on show in this charming museum. Thirty-six of the displays contain French dolls with porcelain heads ranging from 1850 to 1950. Another 24 display windows are devoted to themed exhibitions of dolls from around the world.

Father and son, Guido and Samy Odin, who own the museum, are at your service. The museum shop stocks everything needed to preserve and maintain these unique works of art, and the "doll hospital" will repair dolls or stuffed animals. There are also workshops for kids on Wednesdays based on themes connected to the current exhibition.

10 No. 51 Rue de Montmorency

75003. **Map** 13 B1. M Réaumur-Sébastopol. **Open** to the public.

This house is considered to be the oldest in Paris. No. 51 was built in 1407 by Nicolas Flamel, a bookkeeper and alchemist. His house was always open to the poor, from whom he asked nothing more than that they should pray for those who were dead. Today, the house is a French restaurant.

11 Tour Jean Sans Peur

20 Rue Etienne-Marcel 75002. **Map** 13 A1. **Tel** 01 40 26 20 28. M Etienne-Marcel. **Open** Apr–early Nov: 1.30pm–6pm Wed–Sun; early Nov–end Mar: 1.30–6pm Wed, Sat, Sun. W **tourjeansanspeur.com**

After the Duc d'Orléans was assassinated on his orders in 1408, the Duc de Bourgogne feared reprisals. To protect himself, he had this 27-m (88-ft) tower built on to his home, the Hôtel de Bourgogne, and moved his bedroom up to the fourth floor (reached by a flight of 140 steps).

12 St-Eustache

Pl du Jour 75001. **Map** 13 A1. **Tel** 01 42 36 31 05. M Les Halles. RER Châtelet-Les-Halles. **Open** 9.30am–7pm Mon–Fri, 10am–7pm Sat, 9am–7pm Sun. P 12.30pm, 6pm Mon–Fri; 6pm Sat; 9.30am, 11am, 6pm Sun. Organ recitals 5.30pm Sun.

With its Gothic plan and Renaissance decoration, St-Eustache is one of the most beautiful churches in Paris. Its interior plan is modelled on Notre-Dame, with five naves and side and radial chapels. The 105 years (1532–1637) it took to complete the church saw the flowering of the Renaissance style, which is evident in the arches, pillars and columns. The stained-glass windows in the chancel are created from cartoons by Philippe de Champaigne.

The church has associations with many famous figures: Molière was buried here; the Marquise de Pompadour, official mistress of Louis XV, was baptized here, as was Cardinal Richelieu.

The Renaissance interior of St-Eustache in the 1830s

Entrance to the Bourse du Commerce, the old corn exchange

⓭ Bourse du Commerce

2 Rue de Viarmes 75001. **Map** 12 F2. **Tel** 08 20 01 21 12. Ⓜ Les Halles. ⓇⒺⓇ Châtelet-Les-Halles. **Open** 8.30am–6.30pm Mon–Fri (ID required). 🖥 groups of up to 10 people by appt. ♿

Compared dismissively by Victor Hugo to a jockey's cap without a peak, the old grain exchange building was France's first iron structure. It was constructed in the 18th century and remodelled in 1889. Today, its huge, domed hall is filled with the hustle and bustle of the Chambre de Commerce et d'Industrie de Paris. It is still worth entering to marvel at the architecture, in particular the beautifully restored cupola and its decor. Also worth a look are the murals depicting French trade and industry through the ages, which were painted in 1889 and have since been restored.

⓮ St-Germain l'Auxerrois

2 Pl du Louvre 75001. **Map** 12 F2. **Tel** 01 42 60 13 96. Ⓜ Louvre, Pont-Neuf. **Open** 1 Sep–30 Jun: 8am–7pm Mon–Sat, 9am–8pm Sun; 1 Jul–1 Sep: 9.30am–7pm Tue–Sat, 9am–7pm Sun. Concerts. Ⓦ **saintgermainauxerrois. cef.fr**

This church has been built in a combination of Renaissance and Gothic styles. The first church on the site was constructed in the 12th century, of which only the foundations of the bell tower remain. The splendid rose stained-glass windows date from the Renaissance period.

After the Valois Court decamped to the Louvre from the Ile de la Cité in the 14th century, this became the favoured church of kings.

The church's many historical associations include the horrific St Bartholomew's Day Massacre on 24 August 1572, the eve of the royal wedding of Henri of Navarre and Marguerite de Valois. Thousands of Huguenots who had been lured to Paris for the wedding were murdered as the church bell tolled. Later, after the Revolution, the church was used as a barn and as a police station. Despite many restorations, it is a jewel of Gothic architecture.

⓯ La Samaritaine

119 Rue de la Monnaie 75001. **Map** 12 F2. Ⓜ Pont-Neuf. **Closed** to the public.

This former department store was founded in 1900 by Ernest Cognacq. Built in 1926 with a framework of iron and wide expanses of glass, La Samaritaine is an outstanding example of the Art Deco style. Cognacq was also a collector of 18th-century art, and his collection is now on display in the Musée Cognacq-Jay in the Marais quarter (see p98).

The building is no longer open to the public and is being redeveloped to create housing, a hotel and shopping complex due for completion in 2016.

The Tour St-Jacques with its ornate decoration

⓰ Tour St-Jacques

Parc de la Tour St-Jacques, corner of Rue de Rivoli and Sebastopol 75004. **Map** 13 A3. Ⓜ Châtelet or Hôtel de Ville. **Open** Gardens: year-round. Tower: visits by appt, call 01 83 96 15 05. 🖥 Gardens: Fri–Sun.

This imposing late Gothic tower, dating from 1523, is all that remains of an ancient church that was a rendezvous for pilgrims setting out on long journeys. The church was destroyed after the Revolution. Earlier, Blaise Pascal, the 17th-century mathematician, physicist, philosopher and writer, used the tower for experiments. Queen Victoria passed by on her state visit in 1854, giving her name to the nearby Avenue Victoria. The tower has recently been extensively renovated and is now open to the public.

The St Bartholomew's Day Massacre (c.1572–84) by François Dubois

TUILERIES QUARTER

The Tuileries area is bounded by the vast expanse of the Concorde square at one end and the Grand Louvre at the other. This was a place for kings and palaces. The Sun King (Louis XIV) lives on in the Place des Victoires, which was designed solely to show off his statue. In Place Vendôme, royal glitter has been replaced by the precious stones of Cartier, Boucheron and Chaumet, and the fine cut of Arab, German and Japanese bankers, not to mention the chic ladies visiting the luxurious Ritz. The area is crossed by two of Paris's most magnificent shopping streets – the long Rue de Rivoli, with its arcades, expensive boutiques, bookshops and luxury hotels, and the Rue St-Honoré, another extensive street, bringing together the richest and humblest in people and commerce.

Sights at a Glance

Historic Buildings and Streets
3 Palais-Royal
18 Banque de France

Churches
7 St-Roch

Theatres
4 Comédie Française

Shops
2 Louvre des Antiquaires
11 Rue de Rivoli

Squares, Parks and Gardens
5 Jardin du Palais-Royal
8 Place des Pyramides
12 Jardin des Tuileries
15 Place de la Concorde
17 Place Vendôme
19 Place des Victoires

Monuments and Fountains
6 Fontaine Molière
10 Arc de Triomphe du Carrousel

Museums and Galleries
1 Musée du Louvre pp122–9
9 Musée des Arts Décoratifs
13 Galerie Nationale du Jeu de Paume
14 Musée de l'Orangerie
16 Village Royal

☐ **Restaurants** see pp298–300
1 Les Ambassadeurs (Hôtel de Crillon)
2 Bistrot Victoires
3 Carré des Feuillants
4 La Cordonnerie
5 Les Fines Gueules
6 Le Grand Véfour
7 Kei
8 Le Meurice
9 Muscade
10 Verjus

See also Street Finder map 5–6, 11–13

0 metres   400
0 yards   400

◀ La Fontaine des Fleuves in Place de la Concorde

For keys to symbols see back flap

Street-by-Street: Tuileries Quarter

Elegant squares, formal gardens, street arcades and courtyards give this part of Paris its special character. Monuments to monarchy and the arts coexist with contemporary luxury: sumptuous hotels, world-famous restaurants, fashion emporiums and jewellers of international renown. Sandblasting and washing have given a fresh glow to the façades of the Louvre and the Palais-Royal square, where Cardinal Richelieu's creation, the royal palace, is now occupied by government offices. From here, the Ministry of Culture surveys the cleaning and restoration of the city's great buildings. The other former royal palace, the Louvre, is now one of the great museums of the world.

❼ St-Roch
The papal statue stands in this remarkably long 17th-century church, unusually set on a north-south axis. St-Roch is a treasure house of religious art.

The Paris Convention and Visitors' Bureau

Metro Pyramides

The Normandy is an elegant hotel in the belle époque style, a form of graceful living that prevailed in Paris at the turn of the 20th century.

❽ Place des Pyramides
Frémiet's gilded statue of Joan of Arc is the focus of pilgrimage for royalists.

↓To the Quai du Louvre

⓬ ★ Jardin des Tuileries
Pony rides are a popular attraction in these formal gardens, which were designed by the royal gardener André Le Nôtre in the 17th century.

❾ Musée des Arts Décoratifs
A highlight of the museum's displays of art and design is the Art Nouveau collection.

6 Fontaine Molière
Louis Visconti's fountain is of the famous playwright, who lived nearby.

Le Grand Véfour's 18th-century decor makes it one of the most beautiful restaurants in Paris. Napoleon Bonaparte and Victor Hugo were two of the many famous people who dined here. (See p299.)

Locator Map
See Central Paris Map pp16–17

5 ★ Jardin du Palais-Royal
The garden is a city haven, bordered by arcades with restaurants and art galleries alongside specialist shops.

4 Comédie Française
France's national theatre is the setting for the works of great dramatists, such as Molière.

3 ★ Palais-Royal
In the 18th century, this former royal palace was a setting for brilliant gatherings, debauchery and gambling. Today, modern sculptures grace the square.

RUE DE RICHELIEU

RUE DE MONTPENSIER

RUE DE VALOIS

PL DU PALAIS-ROYAL

Metro Palais-Royal,
Musée du Louvre

Key

— Suggested route

2 Louvre des Antiquaires
Three floors of a former department store house this chic art and antiques supermarket for the rich collector.

1 ★ Musée du Louvre
Home to French kings for almost four centuries, the Louvre is now a museum with one of the world's great art collections.

0 metres   100
0 yards   100

❶ Musée du Louvre

The Musée du Louvre, containing one of the most important art collections in the world, has a history extending back to medieval times. First constructed as a fortress in 1190 by King Philippe-Auguste to protect Paris against Viking raids, it lost its imposing keep in the reign of François I, who replaced it with a Renaissance-style building. Thereafter, four centuries of French kings and emperors improved and enlarged it. A glass pyramid designed by I M Pei was added to the main courtyard in 1989. All the galleries can be reached from here.

The east façade, facing St-Germain l'Auxerrois

KEY

① **Pavillon des Session**

② **The Jardin du Carrousel**, now part of the Jardin des Tuileries, was once the grand approach to the Tuileries Palace which was burned down in 1871 by the Communards.

③ **The Carrousel du Louvre** underground visitors' complex, with galleries, cloakrooms, lavatories, parking and an information desk, lies beneath the Arc de Triomphe du Carrousel.

④ **The inverted glass pyramid** brings light to the subterranean complex, echoing the museum's main entrance in the Cour Napoléon.

⑤ **Cour Marly** is the glass-roofed courtyard that now houses the Marly Horses (see p125).

⑥ **Richelieu Wing**

⑦ **Cour Puget**

⑧ **Cour Khorsabad**

⑨ **Cour Carrée**

⑩ **The Louvre of Charles V** was transformed from Philippe-Auguste's robust old fortress into a royal residence by Charles V, in about 1360.

⑪ **The Salle des Caryatides** takes its name from the statues of women created by Jean Goujon in 1550 to support the upper gallery.

⑫ **Sully Wing**

⑬ **Cour Napoléon**

⑭ **Cour Visconti-Islamic Art**

⑮ **Denon Wing**

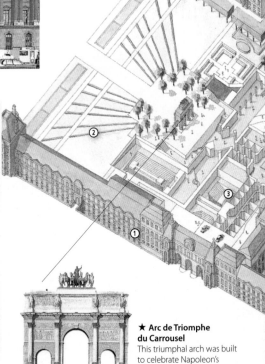

★ **Arc de Triomphe du Carrousel**
This triumphal arch was built to celebrate Napoleon's victories in 1805.

Building the Louvre

Over many centuries, the Louvre was enlarged by a succession of French rulers, shown below with their dates.

Major Alterations

- Reign of François I (1515–47)
- Catherine de' Médici (about 1560)
- Reign of Henri IV (1589–1610)
- Reign of Louis XIII (1610–43)
- Reign of Louis XIV (1643–1715)
- Reign of Napoleon I (1804–15)
- Reign of Napoleon III (1852–70)
- I M Pei (1989) (architect)

Pavillon Richelieu
This imposing 19th-century pavilion is part of the Richelieu Wing, once home to the Ministry of Finance but now converted into magnificent galleries.

VISITORS' CHECKLIST

Practical Information
Map 12 E2. **Tel** 01 40 20 50 50 or 01 40 20 53 17.
Open 9am–5.45pm Wed–Mon (to 9.45pm Wed, Fri).
Closed 1 Jan, 1 May, 25 Dec.
🚫 (free 1st Sun of each month Oct–Mar). Tickets can be purchased at automatic ticket booths located under the Pyramid or online through fnactickets.com, ticketnet.fr or ticketweb.com.
♿ 🔊 ✏ 📷 ⓦ **louvre.fr**

Transport
Ⓜ Palais Royal, Musée du Louvre. 🚌 21, 24, 27, 39, 48, 68, 69, 72, 81, 95. RER Châtelet-Les-Halles. 🅿 Louvre. 🅿 Carrousel du Louvre (entrance via Ave du General Lemonnier); Pl du Louvre, Rue St-Honoré.

★ Pyramid Entrance
The main entrance, designed by the architect I M Pei, was opened in 1989.

★ Perrault's Colonnade
The east façade with its majestic rows of columns was built by Claude Perrault, who worked on the Louvre with Louis Le Vau in the mid-17th century.

★ Medieval Moats
The base of the twin towers and the drawbridge support of Philippe-Auguste's fortress can be seen in the excavated area.

The Louvre's Collection

The Louvre's treasures can be traced back to the collection of François I (1515–47), who purchased many Italian paintings including the Mona Lisa (La Gioconda). In Louis XIV's reign (1643–1715), there were a mere 200 works, but donations and purchases augmented the collection. The Louvre was first opened to the public in 1793 after the Revolution, and has been continually enriched ever since.

The Raft of the Medusa (1819)
Théodore Géricault derived his inspiration for this gigantic and moving work from the shipwreck of a French frigate in 1816. The painting shows the moment when the few survivors sight a sail on the horizon.

The Dying Slave
Michelangelo sculpted this work between 1513 and 1520 as part of a group of statues for the base of the tomb of Pope Julius II in Rome.

Cour Marly

Richelieu Wing

Main entrance

Underground visitors' complex

Pavillon des Sessions

Cour Visconti-Islamic Arts

★ **Mona Lisa**
Leonardo da Vinci painted this small portrait of a Florentine noblewoman, known as *La Gioconda*, in about 1504. It was soon regarded as the prototype of the Renaissance portrait. The sitter's engaging smile has prompted endless commentary ever since. The painting has its own wall in the Salle des Etats (Denon Wing).

Gallery Guide

The main entrance is beneath the glass pyramid. The works are displayed on four floors: the painting and sculpture collections are arranged by country of origin. There are eight departments: Near Eastern antiquities; Egyptian antiquities; Greek, Etruscan and Roman antiquities; Islamic art; sculptures; decorative arts; paintings; and prints and drawings.

The Lacemaker
In this exquisite picture from about 1665, Jan Vermeer gives us a glimpse into everyday domestic life in Holland. The painting came to the Louvre in 1870.

Second floor

★ Marly Horses
Since the 19th century, these wild horses by Guillaume Coustou have stood near the Place de la Concorde. Replicas have replaced them – the originals are now in a glass-covered courtyard in the Louvre.

First floor

Cour Puget

Cour Khorsabad

Cour Napoléon

★ Venus de Milo
Found in 1820 on the island of Milos in Greece, this ideal of feminine beauty was made in the Hellenistic Age at the end of the 2nd century BC.

Sully Wing

Cour Carrée

Ground floor

Key to Floorplan

- Painting
- *Objets d'art* (Decorative Arts)
- Sculpture
- Antiquities
- Non-exhibition space

Exploring the Louvre's Collections

It is important not to underestimate the size of these vast collections and useful to set a few viewing priorities before starting. The collection of European paintings (1400–1850) is comprehensive and 40 per cent of the works are by French artists, while the selection of sculptures is less complete. The museum's antiquities – Oriental, Islamic, Egyptian, Greek, Etruscan and Roman – are of world renown and offer the visitor an unrivalled range of objects. The *objets d'art* on display are very varied and include furniture and jewellery.

The Fortune Teller (c. 1594) by Caravaggio

European Painting: 1200 to 1850

Painting from northern Europe is well covered. One of the earliest Flemish works is Jan van Eyck's *Madonna of Chancellor Rolin* (about 1435) which shows the Chancellor of Burgundy kneeling in prayer before the Virgin and Child. Hieronymus Bosch's *Ship of Fools* (1500) is a fine, satirical account of the

Portrait of Erasmus (1523) by Hans Holbein

futility of human existence. In the Dutch collection, Van Dyck's portrait *King Charles out Hunting* (1635) shows Charles I of England in all his refined elegance. Jacob Jordaens, best known for scenes of gluttony and lust, reveals unusual sensitivity in his *Four Evangelists*. The saucy smile of the *Gipsy Girl* (1628) displays Frans Hals' effortless virtuosity, in sharp contrast to Vermeer's highly-finished *Lacemaker*. Rembrandt's Self-portraits, *Disciples at Emmaus* (1648) and *Bathsheba* (1654) are fine examples of his genius.

There is relatively little German painting, but the three major German painters of the 15th and 16th centuries are represented by important works. There is a *Self-portrait* by Albrecht Dürer as a young artist of 22 (1493), a *Venus by Lucas Cranach (1529) and a portrait of the great humanist scholar Erasmus by Hans Holbein. Works by English artists include Thomas Gainsborough's Conversation in a*

Park (around 1746), Sir Joshua Reynolds' *Master Hare* (1788) and France's only painting by J M W Turner, *Landscape with a River and a Distant Bay* (around 1840).

Many of the master works in the Spanish collection depict the tragic side of life: El Greco's *Christ on the Cross Adored by Donors* (1576) and Francisco de Zurbarán's *Lying-in-State of St Bonaventura* (about 1629) with its dark-faced corpse are two of the Louvre's prize pieces. The subject of José de Ribera's *Club-Footed Boy* (1642) is a poor mute, who carries a scrap of paper requesting alms. Portraits by Goya from the late 18th and early 19th century are in a lighter vein.

The museum's large collection of Italian paintings covers the period 1200 to 1800. The father figures of the early Renaissance, Cimabue and Giotto, are here, as is Fra Angelico, with his *Coronation of the Virgin* (around 1430–1432), and Raphael, with his stately *Portrait of Baldassare Castiglione* (around 1514). There is also a fine portrait in profile of *Sigismondo Malatesta* by Piero della Francesca (around 1450) and an action-packed battle scene by Paolo Uccello. Several paintings by Leonardo da Vinci, for instance the *Virgin with the Infant Jesus and St Anne*, are as enchanting as his *Mona Lisa*.

The collection of French painting ranges from the 14th century to 1848. Paintings after this date are housed in the

Gilles or Pierrot (c. 1717) by Jean-Antoine Watteau

Leonardo da Vinci in France

Leonardo, artist, engineer and scientist, was born in 1452 and became a leading figure in the Italian Renaissance. François I met Leonardo in 1515 and invited him to live and work in France. The painter brought the *Mona Lisa* with him. Already in poor health, he died three years later in the arms of the king.

Self-portrait (early 16th century)

Musée d'Orsay *(see pp146–9).* Outstanding early works are Jean Fouquet's *Portrait of Charles VIII* (around 1450) and *Gabrielle d'Estrée*, mistress of Henri IV, in her bathtub with her sister (1594). From the 16th and 17th centuries there are several splendid works by Georges de la Tour.

That great 18th-century painter of melancholy, Jean Watteau, is represented, as is J H Fragonard, master of the Rococo. His delightfully frivolous subjects are evident in *The Bathers* from 1770. In stark contrast is the Classicism of Nicolas Poussin and the history painting of J L David. Most of J D Ingres' work is in the Musée d'Orsay, but the Louvre kept the erotic *Turkish Bath* of 1862.

European Sculpture: 1100 to 1850

Early Flemish and German sculpture in the collection has many masterpieces such as Tilman Riemenschneider's *Virgin of the Annunciation* from the end of the 15th century and an unusual life-size, nude figure of the penitent *Mary Magdalen* by Gregor Erhart (early 16th century). An ornate gilded-wood altarpiece of the same period exemplifies Flemish church art. Another important work of Flemish sculpture is Adrian de Vries's long-limbed *Mercury and Psyche* from 1593, which was originally made for the court of Rudolph II in Prague. The French section opens with early Romanesque

works, such as the *figure of Christ* by a 12th-century Burgundian sculptor and a *head of St Peter*. With its eight black-hooded mourners, the *tomb of Philippe Pot* (a high-ranking official in Burgundy) is one of the more unusual pieces. *Diane de Poitiers*, mistress of Henri II, had a large figure of her namesake Diana, goddess of the hunt, installed in the courtyard of her castle west of Paris. It is now in the Louvre. The works of Pierre Puget (1620–94), the great sculptor from Marseilles, have been assembled inside a glass-covered courtyard, Cour Puget. They include a figure of *Milo of Crotona*, the Greek athlete who got his hands caught in the cleft of a tree stump and was eaten by a lion. The wild horses of Marly now stand in the glass-roofed Cour Marly, surrounded by other masterpieces of French sculpture, including Houdon's early 19th-century busts of Diderot and Voltaire, and two equestrian pieces by Coysevox.

The Italian sculpture collection includes pre-Renaissance work by Duccio and Donatello, and later masterpieces such as Michelangelo's *Slaves* and Cellini's Fontainebleau *Nymph*.

Tomb of Philippe Pot (late 15th century) by Antoine le Moiturier

Near Eastern, Egyptian, Greek, Etruscan and Roman Antiquities

The range of antiquities in the Louvre is impressive. There are objects from the Neolithic period (about 6000 BC) to the fall of the Roman Empire. Important works of Mesopotamian art include the seated figure of Ebih-il, from 2400 BC, and several portraits of Gudea, Prince of Lagash, from about 2255 BC. A black basalt block bearing the code of the Babylonian King Hammurabi, from about 1700 BC, is one of the world's oldest legal documents.

The warlike Assyrians are represented by delicate carvings and a spectacular reconstruction of part of Sargon II's (722–705 BC) palace with its huge, winged bulls. A fine example of Persian art is the enamelled brickwork depicting the king of Persia's personal guard of archers (5th century BC). It decorated his palace at Susa.

Most Egyptian art was made for the dead, who were provided with the things that they needed for the after-life. It often included vivid images of daily life in ancient Egypt. One example is the tiny funeral chapel built for a high official in about 2500 BC. It is covered with exquisite carvings: men in sailing ships, catching fish, tending cattle and fowl.

It is also possible to gain insights into family life in ancient Egypt through a number of life-like funeral portraits, like the squatting scribe, and several sculptures of married

Winged Bull with Human Head from 8th century BC, found in Khorsabad, Assyria

couples. The earliest sculpture dates from 2500 BC, the latest from 1400 BC.

From the New Kingdom (1555–1080 BC), a special crypt dedicated to the god Osiris contains some colossal sarcophagi, and a large number of mummified animals.

Some smaller objects of considerable charm include a 29-cm (11-inch) headless body of a woman, sensually outlined by the transparent veil of her dress and thought to be Queen Nefertiti (about 1365–1349 BC).

The department of Greek, Roman and Etruscan antiquities contains a vast array of fragments, among them some exceptional pieces. There is a large, geometric head from the Cyclades (2700 BC) and an elegant, swan-necked bowl, quite modern in its unadorned simplicity. It is hammered out of a single gold sheet and dates from about 2500 BC. The Archaic Greek period, from the 7th to the 5th century BC, is represented by the *Auxerre Goddess*, one of the earliest-known pieces of Greek sculpture, and the *Hera of Samos* from the Ionian Islands. From the height of the Classical Greek period (about the 5th

Winged Victory of Samothrace (Greece, late 3rd–early 2nd century BC)

century BC), there are several fine male torsos and heads such as the *Laborde Head*. This head has been identified as part of the sculpture that once decorated the west pediment of the Parthenon in Athens.

The two most famous Greek statues in the Louvre, the *Winged Victory of Samothrace* and the *Venus de Milo (see p125)*, belong to the Hellenistic period (late 3rd to 2nd century BC) when more natural-looking human forms were beginning to be produced.

The undisputed star of the Etruscan collection is the terracotta *Sarcophagus of the*

Etruscan sarcophagus (6th century BC)

Cenestian Couple, who appear as though they are attending an eternal banquet.

The sculptures in the Roman section demonstrate the great debt owed to the art of ancient Greece. There are many fine pieces: a bust of Agrippa, a basalt head of Livia, the wife of Augustus, and a splendid, powerful bronze head of Emperor Hadrian from the 2nd century AD. This has the look of a true portrait, unlike so many Imperial heads which are uninspired and impersonal.

Squatting Scribe (Egyptian, about 2500 BC)

Decorative Arts

The term *objets d'art* (art objects) covers a vast range of "decorative art" objects: from jewellery, silver and glassware, to French and Italian bronzes, porcelain, snuffboxes and armour. The Louvre has well over 8,000 items, from many ages and regions.

Many of these precious objects were in the Abbey of St-Denis, where the kings of France were crowned. Long before the Revolution, a regular flow of visitors had made it something of a museum. After the Revolution, all the objects were removed and presented to the nation. Much was lost or stolen during the move but what remains is still outstanding.

The treasures include a serpentine stone plate from the 1st century AD with a 9th-century border of gold and precious stones. (The plate itself is inlaid with eight golden dolphins.) There is also a porphyry vase which Suger, Abbot of St-Denis, had mounted in gold in the shape of an eagle, and the golden sceptre made for King Charles V in about 1380.

The French crown jewels include the coronation crowns of Louis XV and Napoleon, sceptres, swords and other accessories of the coronation ceremonies. On view is also the Regent, one of the purest diamonds in the world. It was bought in 1717 and worn by Louis XV at his coronation in 1722.

One whole room is taken up with a series of tapestries called the *Hunts of Maximilian*, which were originally executed for Emperor Charles V in 1530 after drawings by Bernard Van Orley.

The large collection of French furniture ranges from the 16th to the 19th centuries and is assembled by period, or in rooms devoted to donations by distinguished collectors such as

The Eagle of Suger (mid-12th century)

Isaac de Camondo. On display are important pieces by exceptionally prominent furniture-makers such as André-Charles Boulle, cabinet-maker to Louis XIV, who worked at the Louvre in the late 17th to mid-18th centuries. He is noted for his technique of inlaying copper and tortoiseshell. From a later date, the curious inlaid steel and bronze writing desk, created by Adam Weisweiler for Queen Marie-Antoinette in 1784, is one of the more unusual pieces in the museum's collection.

In 2012, the Islamic Art Department opened in the Cour Visconti I with around 18,000 objects on display covering 3,000 years of history from three continents. The museum also recently installed decorative art galleries dedicated to art objects from the reign of Louis XIV and the 18th century.

The Glass Pyramid

Plans for the modernization and expansion of the Louvre were first conceived in 1981. They included the transfer of the Ministry of Finance from the Richelieu wing of the Louvre to offices elsewhere, and a new main entrance to the museum. A Chinese-American architect, I M Pei, was chosen to design the changes. He designed the pyramid as both the focal point and entrance to the Louvre. Made out of glass, it enables the visitor to see the historic buildings that surround it while allowing light down into the underground visitors' reception area.

❷ Louvre des Antiquaires

2 Pl du Palais-Royal 75001. **Map** 12 F2. **Tel** 01 42 97 27 27. Ⓜ Palais-Royal. **Closed** for renovations. 🚻 📱 *See Shopping pp328–9.* ⓦ **louvre-antiquaires.com**

A large department store – the Grands Magasins du Louvre – was converted at the end of the 1970s into this three-floor collection of art galleries and antique shops. Few bargains are found here, but the 250 shops of this chic market provide clues about what *nouveaux riches* collectors are seeking.

❸ Palais-Royal

Pl du Palais-Royal 75001. **Map** 12 E1. Ⓜ Palais-Royal. **Closed** to public.

This former royal palace has had a turbulent history. Starting out in the early 17th century as Richelieu's Palais Cardinale, it passed to the Crown on his death and became the child-hood home of Louis XIV. Under the control of the 18th-century royal dukes of Orléans, it was the scene of brilliant gatherings, interspersed with periods of debauchery and gambling. The cardinal's theatre, where Molière had performed, burned down in 1763, but was replaced by the Comédie Française. After the Revolution, the palace became a gambling house. It was reclaimed in 1815 by the future King Louis-Philippe, one

Colonnaded façade of the Comédie Française

of whose librarians was Alexandre Dumas. The building narrowly escaped the flames of the 1871 uprising.

After being restored again, between 1872 and 1876, the palace reverted to the state, and it now houses both the Council of State, the supreme legal body for administrative matters, and its more recent "partner", the Constitutional Council. Another wing of the palace is occupied by the Ministry of Culture.

❹ Comédie Française

1 Place Colette 75001. **Map** 12 E1. **Tel** 0825 101 680. Ⓜ Palais-Royal. **Open** for performances. ♿ 📱 📷 📹 *See Entertainment pp334–6.* ⓦ **comedie-francaise.fr**

Overlooking two charming, if traffic-choked, squares named after the writers Colette and

André Malraux, sits France's national theatre. The company has its roots partly in Molière's 17th-century players. In the foyer is the armchair in which Molière collapsed, dying, on stage in 1673 (ironically while he was performing *Le Malade Imaginaire – The Hypochon-driac*). Since the company's founding in 1680 by Louis XIV, the theatre has enjoyed state patronage as a centre of national culture, and it has been based in the present building since 1799. The repertoire includes works of Racine, Molière, Corneille, and Shakespeare, as well as those of modern playwrights.

A stone plaque to Pierre Corneille

Palais-Royal courtyard lined with columns

❺ Jardin du Palais-Royal

6 Rue de Montpensier, Pl du Palais-Royal 75001. **Map** 12 F1. Ⓜ Palais-Royal.

The present garden is about a third smaller than the original one, laid out by the royal gardener for Cardinal Richelieu in the 1630s. This is due to the construction, between 1781 and 1784, of 60 uniform houses bordering three sides of the square. Today, restaurants, art galleries and specialist shops line the square, which maintains a strong literary history – Jean Cocteau, Colette and Jean Marais are among its famous former residents.

The courtyard contains the controversial black-and-white striped stone columns that form conceptual artist Daniel Buren's *Les Deux Plateaux*. The columns were installed in the pedestrianized Palais-Royal courtyard in 1986, in the face of strong opposition. These columns are now beloved of children and skateboarders alike.

Statue in the Jardin du Palais-Royal

❻ Fontaine Molière

Rue de Richelieu 75001. **Map** 12 E1. Ⓜ Palais-Royal.

France's most famous playwright lived near here, in a house on the site of No. 40 Rue de Richelieu. The 19th-century fountain is by Louis Visconti, who also designed Napoleon's tomb at Les Invalides *(see pp188–9)*.

Vien's *St Denis Preaching to the Gauls* (1767) in St-Roch

❼ St-Roch

296 Rue St-Honoré 75001. **Map** 12 E1. **Tel** 01 42 44 13 20. Ⓜ Tuileries, Pyramides. **Open** 2 Sep–30 Jun: 8am–7pm daily; 1 Jul–1 Sep: 9am–7pm Tue–Sun. **Closed** non-religious public hols. ✚ Daily, times vary. Concerts.

This huge church was designed by Lemercier, architect of the Louvre, and its foundation stone was laid by Louis XIV in

Seated statue of Molière

1653. Jules Hardouin-Mansart added the large Lady Chapel with its richly decorated dome and ceiling in the 18th century and two further chapels extended the church to 126 m (413 ft), just short of Notre-Dame. It is a treasure house of religious art, much of it from now-vanished churches and monasteries. It also contains the tombs of the playwright Pierre Corneille, the royal gardener André Le Nôtre and the philosopher Denis Diderot. The façades reveal marks of Napoleon's attack, in 1795, on royalist troops who were defending the church steps.

❽ Place des Pyramides

75001. **Map** 12 E1. Ⓜ Tuileries, Pyramides.

Joan of Arc, wounded nearby fighting the English in 1429, is honoured by a 19th-century equestrian statue by the sculptor Emmanuel Frémiet. The statue is a rallying point for royalists.

❾ Musée des Arts Décoratifs

Palais du Louvre, 107–111 Rue de Rivoli 75001. **Map** 12 E2. **Tel** 01 44 55 57 50. Ⓜ Palais-Royal, Tuileries. **Open** 11am–6pm Tue–Sun (until 9pm Thu for temporary exhibitions); last adm 30 mins before closing. Library: 1–7pm Mon, 10am–7pm Tue, 10am– 6pm Wed–Fri. 🎨 🚻 ♿ 📷 🎬 🏛
Ⓦ lesartsdecoratifs.fr

With five floors and over 100 rooms, this museum offers an eclectic display of decorative and ornamental art and design from the Middle Ages to the present. Among the highlights are the Art Nouveau and Art Deco rooms, jewellery and Gallé glass. The doll collection is remarkable.

The Galerie des Bijoux is particularly interesting, with a huge collection of more than 1,300 pieces, from medieval brooches to Cartier designs.

The restaurant offers lovely views over the Tuileries Gardens.

Also open for temporary exhibitions are the adjoining Musée de la Mode and the Musée de la Publicité. The former often shows parts of its haute couture collections. Past exhibitions have included a tribute to Christian Lacroix with a retrospective of his designs.

With a catalogue of over 40,000 historic posters dating from the 18th century to 1949, the Musée de la Publicité brings together thousands of objects linked to advertising as well as films. The entry fee includes access to all three museums. Dual tickets can also be purchased that allow access

Lemot's Restoration group of statues with the gilded figure of Victory

to the Musée Nissim de Camondo too (see p234).

❿ Arc de Triomphe du Carrousel

Pl du Carrousel 75001. **Map** 12 E2. Ⓜ Palais-Royal.

Built by Napoleon in 1806–8 as an entrance to the former Palais des Tuileries, this vast arch's marble columns are topped by Grande Armée soldiers. They replaced the Horses of St Mark's which were returned to Venice in 1815.

⓫ Rue de Rivoli

75001. **Map** 11 C1 & 13 A2. Ⓜ Louvre, Palais-Royal, Tuileries, Concorde.

The long arcades with their shops, topped by Neo-Classical apartments, date back to the early 18th century, though they were only finished in the 1850s. Commissioned by Napoleon after his victory at Rivoli, in 1797, the street completed the link between the Louvre and the

Arcades along the Rue de Rivoli

Champs-Elysées, and became an important artery as well as an elegant centre for commerce. The Tuileries walls were replaced by railings and the whole area opened up.

Today, along the Rue de Rivoli, there are makers of expensive men's shirts and bookshops towards the Place de la Concorde, and popular department stores near the Châtelet and Hôtel de Ville. Angélina's, at No. 226, is said to serve the best hot chocolate in Paris (see p310).

⓬ Jardin des Tuileries

Place de la Concorde 75001. **Map** 12 D1. **Tel** 01 40 20 90 43. Ⓜ Tuileries, Concorde. **Open** Apr–May & Sep: 7am–9pm; Jun–Aug: 7am–11pm; Oct–Mar: 7.30am–7.30pm.

These formal gardens were once the gardens of the old Palais des Tuileries. They are an integral part of the landscaped area running parallel to the Seine from the Louvre to the Champs-Elysées and the Arc de Triomphe.

The gardens were laid out in the 17th century by André Le Nôtre, royal gardener to Louis XIV. Restoration created an additional garden as well as filling the entire gardens with striking sculptures.

The formal gardens of Jardin des Tuileries

❸ Galerie Nationale du Jeu de Paume

Jardin des Tuileries, 1 Pl de la Concorde 75008. **Map** 11 C1. **Tel** 01 47 03 12 50. Ⓜ Concorde. **Open** 11am–7pm Tue–Sun (to 9pm Tue). **Closed** 1 Jan, 1 May & 25 Dec as well as in between exhibitions. 🖼🖼♿ 🖼🖼🖼🖼 Ⓦ **jeudepaume.org**

The Jeu de Paume – or réal tennis court – was built by Napoleon III in 1851. When réal (royal) tennis was replaced in popularity by lawn tennis, the court was used to exhibit art. Eventually, an Impressionist museum was founded here. In 1986, the collection moved to the Musée d'Orsay *(see pp146–9)*. The Jeu de Paume now houses the Centre National de la Photographie, and shows exhibitions of contemporary art.

Entrance to the Jeu de Paume

❹ Musée de l'Orangerie

Jardin des Tuileries, Pl de la Concorde 75001. **Map** 11 C1. **Tel** 01 44 77 80 07. Ⓜ Concorde. **Open** 9am–6pm Wed–Mon (last adm: 5.15pm). **Closed** 1 May, 14 Jul morning & 25 Dec. 🖼♿🖼 by appt. 🖼🖼 Ⓦ **musee-orangerie.fr**

Claude Monet's crowning work, the water lily series, or *Nymphéas*, can be found here. The series was painted in his garden at Giverny, near Paris, and presented to the public in 1927. This superb work is complemented well by the outstanding Walter-Guillaume collection of artists of the Ecole de Paris, from the late Impressionist era to the inter-

Monet's water lilies, on display in the Musée de l'Orangerie

war period. This is a remarkable concentration of masterpieces, including a room of dramatic works by Soutine and some 14 works by Cézanne – still lifes, portraits *(Madame Cézanne)* and landscapes, such as *Dans le Parc du Château Noir*.

Renoir is represented by 27 canvases, including *Les Fillettes au Piano (Young Girls at the Piano)*. There are early Picassos, works by Henri Rousseau – notably *La Carriole du Père Junier (Old Junier's Cart)* – Matisse and a portrait of Paul Guillaume by Modigliani. All are bathed in the natural light that flows through the window. Temporary exhibitions are shown on the lower ground floor.

❺ Place de la Concorde

75008. **Map** 11 C1. Ⓜ Concorde.

This is one of Europe's most magnificent and historic squares, covering more than 8 ha (20 acres) in the middle of Paris. Starting out as Place Louis XV, for displaying a statue of the king, it was built in the mid-18th century by architect Jacques-Ange Gabriel, who chose to make it an open octagon with only the north side containing mansions. In

The 3,200-year-old obelisk from Luxor

the square's next incarnation, as the Place de la Révolution, the statue was replaced by the guillotine. The death toll in the square in two and a half years was 1,119, including Louis XVI, Marie-Antoinette (who died in view of the small, secret apartment she kept at No. 2 Rue Royale) and the revolutionary leaders Danton and Robespierre.

Renamed Concorde (originally by chastened Revolutionaries) in a spirit of reconciliation, the grandeur of the square was enhanced in the 19th century by the 3,200-year-old Luxor obelisk, two fountains and eight statues personifying French cities. It has become the culminating point of triumphal parades down the Champs-Elysées each 14 July, most notably on the memorable Bastille Day of 1989 when the Revolution's bicentenary was celebrated by a million people, and many world leaders.

Colonnaded entrance to the Village Royale

ⓖ Village Royal

75008. **Map** 5 C5. Ⓜ Madeleine.
Galerie Royale: **Open** 8am–8.30pm,
boutiques 10am–7pm Mon–Sat.
Closed public hols.

This delightful enclave of
18th-century town houses sits
discreetly between the Rue
Royale and the Rue Boissy
d'Anglas. The Galerie Royale is
the former home of the
Duchess d'Abrantès. It was
converted in 1994 by architect
Laurent Bourgois who has
combined both classical and
modern elements in superb
style. The village was formerly
the home of glassworkers and
silversmiths, and for a while,

examples of antique glass and
silverware were on display.
Nowadays, chic shoppers flock in
droves to the designer boutiques
that are here, such as Chanel, Dior
and Eric Bompard Cashmere, or
they stop by for a coffee break
in the up-market café, Le Village.

ⓗ Place Vendôme

75001. **Map** 6 D5. Ⓜ Tuileries.

Perhaps the best example of
18th-century elegance in the
city, the architect Jules
Hardouin-Mansart's royal
square was begun in 1698. The
original plan was to house
academies and embassies
behind the arcaded façades.
However, bankers moved in
and created opulent homes.
Miraculously, the square has
remained virtually intact, and is
home to jewellers and bankers.
Among the famous, Frédéric
Chopin died here in 1848 at
No. 12 and César Ritz
established his famous hotel
at the turn of the 20th century
at No. 15.

ⓘ Banque de France

31 Rue Croix des Petits Champs
75001. **Map** 12 F1. Ⓜ Palais Royal.
Closed Galerie Dorée closed for
restoration until autumn 2015. Visits
by appt only; book at least a year in
advance. Call 01 42 92 26 33.

Founded by Napoleon in 1800,
France's central bank is housed in
a building intended for quite
different purposes. The 17th-
century architect François

Napoleon's statue in
Place Vendôme

Formal Gardens in Paris

The South Parterre at Versailles *(see pp250–51)*

For the past 300 years, the main
formal gardens in Paris have been
open to the public and are a firm
fixture in the city's life. The Jardin
des Tuileries *(see p132)* is gradually
being renovated, with ongoing
replanting; the Jardin du
Luxembourg *(see p174)*, the private
garden of the French Senate, is still
beloved of Left Bankers; and the
Jardin du Palais-Royal *(see p131)* is
enjoyed by those who seek peace
and privacy.

French landscaping was raised to
an art form in the 17th century,
thanks to Louis XIV's talented
landscaper André Le Nôtre, who
created the gardens of Versailles
(see pp250–51). He achieved a
brilliant marriage between the
traditional Italian Renaissance
garden and the French love of
rational design.

The role of the French garden
architect was not to tend nature
but to transform it, pruning and
planting to create leafy sculptures
out of trees, bushes and hedges.
Complicated geometrical designs
that were created in beds and
paths were interspersed with

The long Galerie Dorée in the Banque de France

Mansart designed this mansion for Louis XIII's Secretary of State, Louis de la Vrillière, with the splendid 50-m (164-ft) long Galerie Dorée specially created for hanging his great collection of historical paintings. The house was later sold to the Comte de Toulouse, son of Louis XIV and Madame de Montespan. It was reconstructed in the 19th century after the Revolution. The bank's most famous alumnus is Jacques Delors, president of the European Commission 1985–94.

⓳ Place des Victoires

75002. **Map** 12 F1. Ⓜ Palais-Royal.

This circle of elegant mansions was built in 1685 solely to offset the statue of Louis XIV by Desjardins, which was placed in the middle, with torches burning day and night. The proportions of the buildings and even the arrangement of the surrounding streets were all designed by the architect and courtier Jules Hardouin-Mansart to display the statue to its best advantage.

Unfortunately, the 1792 mobs were less sycophantic and tore down the statue. A replacement, of a different style, was erected in 1822, to the detriment of the whole system of proportions of buildings to statue. Yet the square retains much of the original design, and today, it is the address of major names in the fashion business, most notably Thierry Mugler and Kenzo.

Louis XIV on Place des Victoires

A Bagatelle garden with floral colour *(see p257)*

pebbles and carefully thought-out splashes of floral colour. Symmetry and harmony were the landscaper's watchwords, a sense of grandeur and magnificence his ultimate goal. In the 17th century, as now, French formal gardens served two purposes: as a setting or backdrop for a château or palace, and for enjoyment. The best view of a formal garden was from the first floor of the château, from which the combination of boxwood hedges, flowers and gravel came together in an intricate, abstract pattern, a blossoming tapestry which complemented the château's interior. Paths of trees drew the eye into infinity, reminding the onlooker of how much land belonged to his host, and therefore establishing his undoubted wealth. So, early on the formal garden became a status symbol, and it still is. This is obvious in both private gardens and in grand public projects. Napoleon Bonaparte completed his vista from the Jardin des Tuileries with a triumphal arch. The late President Mitterrand applied the principle in building his Grand Arche de la Défense *(see pp42–3, 257)* along the same axis as the Tuileries and Arc de Triomphe.

But formal gardens were also made to be enjoyed. People in the 17th century believed that walking in the fresh air kept them in good health. What more perfect spot than a formal garden bedecked with statues and fountains for additional entertainment. The old and infirm could be carried around in sedan chairs and people could meet one another around a boxwood hedge or on a stone bench under the marble gaze of the goddess Diana.

ST-GERMAIN-DES-PRES

This Left Bank area is fuller and livelier, its streets and cafés more crowded than when it was at the forefront of the city's intellectual life in the 1950s. The leading figures of the time have now gone, and the rebellious disciples have returned to their bourgeois roots. But the new philosophers are there, the radical young thinkers who emerged from the 1960s upheavals, and the area still has its major publishing houses, whose executives entertain treasured writers and agents at the celebrated cafés. They now share the area with the smart set, those who patronize Yves St-Laurent's opulent premises and the elegant Rue Jacob's chic interior designers. On the south side of Boulevard St-Germain, the streets are quiet and quaint, with lots of good restaurants, and at the Odéon end, there are brassy cafés and a profusion of cinemas.

Sights at a Glance

Historic Buildings and Streets
2 Palais Abbatial
7 Boulevard St-Germain
8 Rue du Dragon
10 Rue de l'Odéon
12 Cour de Rohan
13 Cour du Commerce St-André
15 Académie Française
16 Ecole Nationale Supérieure des Beaux-Arts
17 Hôtel Feydeau de Brou
18 Quai Voltaire

Churches
1 St-Germain-des-Prés

Theatres
11 Odéon Théâtre de L'Europe

Cafés and Restaurants
4 Les Deux Magots
5 Café de Flore
6 Brasserie Lipp
9 Le Procope

Museums and Galleries
3 Musée Eugène Delacroix
14 Musée de la Monnaie
19 *Musée d'Orsay pp146–9*
20 Musée Nationale de la Légion d'Honneur

Restaurants *see pp302–4*
1 Agapé Substance
2 Alcazar
3 Bistrot de Paris
4 Les Bouquinistes
5 Comme à Savonnières
6 Le Comptoir du Relais
7 L'Epigramme
8 Kitchen Galerie Bis
9 Le Procope
10 Shu
11 Ze Kitchen Galerie

See also Street Finder map 11–12

0 metres 400
0 yards 400

◀ The clock in the main hall of the Musée d'Orsay

For additional keys to symbols *see back flap*

Street-by-Street: St-Germain-des-Prés

After World War II, St-Germain-des-Prés became synonymous with intellectual life centred on bars and cafés. Philosophers, writers, actors and musicians mingled in the cellar nightspots and brasseries, where existentialist philosophy co-existed with American jazz. The area is now smarter than in the heyday of Jean-Paul Sartre and Simone de Beauvoir, the haunting singer Juliette Greco and the New Wave film-makers. The writers are still around, enjoying the pleasures of sitting in Les Deux Magots, Café de Flore and other haunts. The 17th-century buildings have survived, but signs of change are evident in the plethora of affluent shops dealing in antiques, books and fashion.

④ Les Deux Magots
The café is famous for the patronage of celebrities such as Hemingway.

⑤ Café de Flore
In the 1950s, French intellectuals wrestled with new philosophical ideas in the Art Deco interior of the café.

⑥ Brasserie Lipp
Colourful ceramics decorate this famous brasserie once frequented by politicians.

RUE DU DRAGON

RUE DU SABOT

RUE DE RENNES

RUE BONAPARTE

RUE DU FOUR

① ★ St-Germain-des-Prés
Descartes and the king of Poland are among the notables buried here in Paris's oldest church.

⑦ ★ Boulevard St-Germain
Café terraces, boutiques, cinemas, restaurants and bookshops characterize the central section of the Left Bank's main street.

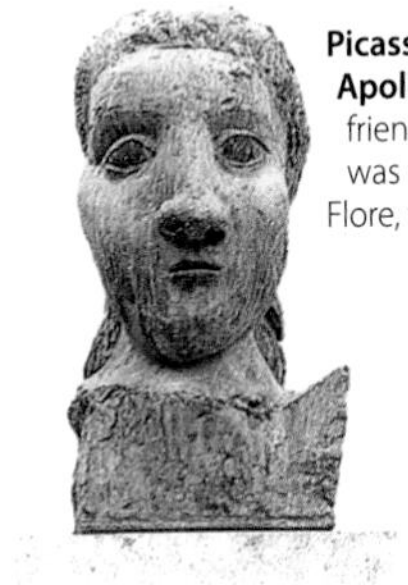

Picasso's sculpture Homage to Apollinaire is a tribute to the artist's friend, the poet Guillaume Apollinaire. It was erected in 1959, near the Café de Flore, where the poet held court.

3 ★ Musée Delacroix
Here, Delacroix created the splendid mural, *Jacob Wrestling*, for St-Sulpice *(see p174)*.

TUILERIES QUARTER
BEAUBOURG AND LES HALLES
Seine
ST-GERMAIN-DES-PRES
ILE DE LA CITE
INVALIDES AND EIFFEL TOWER QUARTER
LUXEMBOURG QUARTER
LATIN QUARTER

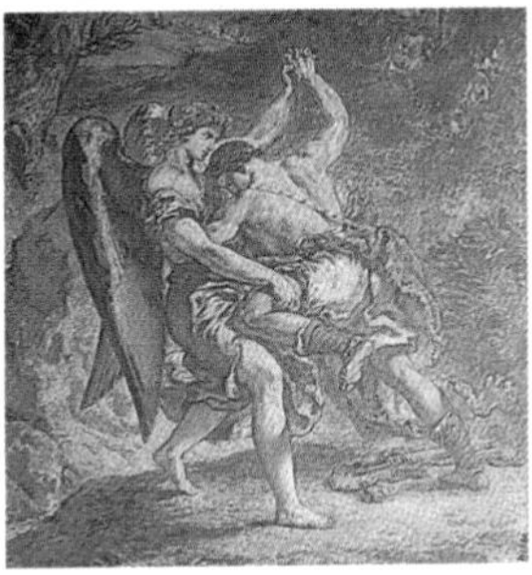

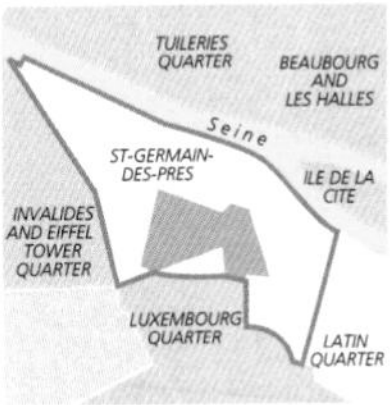

Locator Map
See Central Paris Map pp16–17

Key
– Suggested route

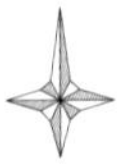

0 metres 100
0 yards 100

Rue de Fürstenberg is a tiny square with old-fashioned street lamps and shady trees. It is often used as a film setting.

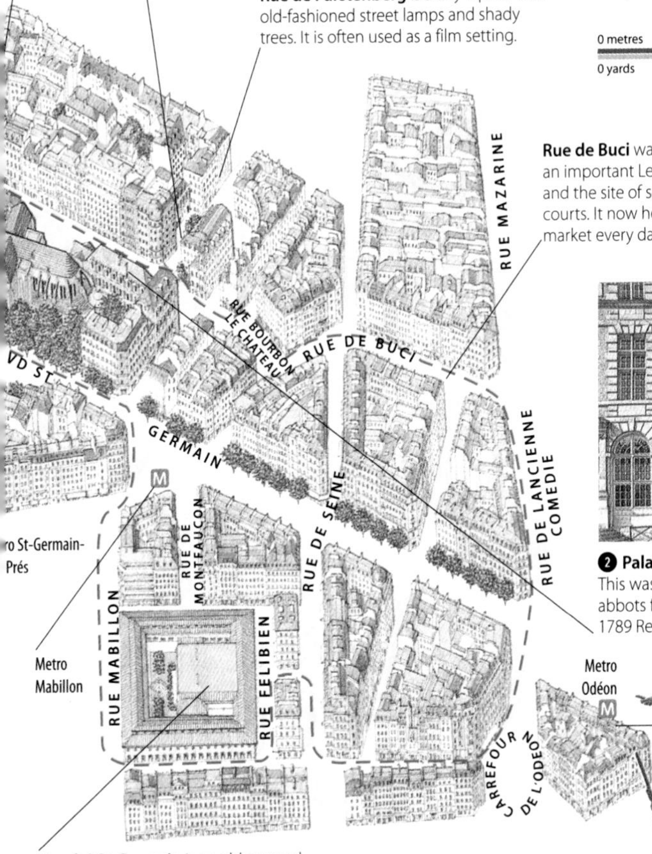

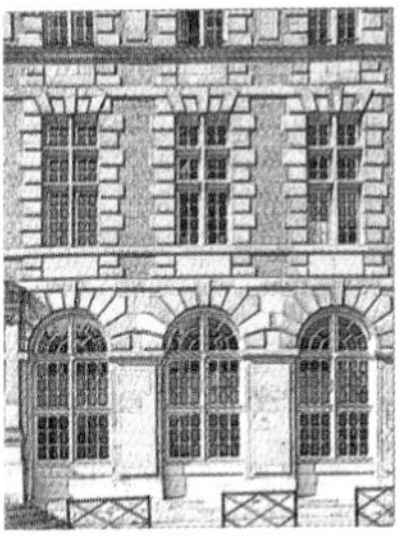

RUE MAZARINE
RUE BOURBON LE CHATEAU
RUE DE BUCI
VD ST
GERMAIN
RUE DE L'ANCIENNE COMEDIE
RUE DE SEINE
RUE DE MONTFAUCON
RUE MABILLON
RUE FELIBIEN
CARREFOUR DE L'ODEON
M
ro St-Germain-
Prés
Metro Mabillon
Metro Odéon

Rue de Buci was for centuries an important Left Bank street and the site of some réal tennis courts. It now holds a lively market every day.

2 Palais Abbatial
This was the residence of abbots from 1586 till the 1789 Revolution.

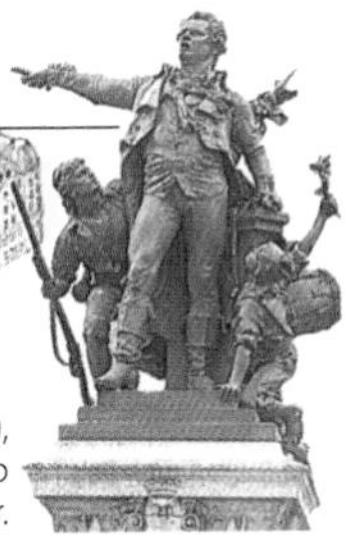

Marché St-Germain is an old covered food market which was opened in 1818, taking over the site of a former fairground *(see p331)*.

Danton's statue (1889), by Auguste Paris, is a tribute to the Revolutionary leader.

❶ St-Germain-des-Prés

3 Pl St-Germain-des-Prés 75006. **Map** 12 E4. **Tel** 01 55 42 81 10. Ⓜ St-Germain-des-Prés. **Open** 8am–7.45pm daily. Concerts (call ahead for times). 🕇 7pm Mon–Fri; 12.15pm, 7pm Sat; 11am, 5pm (in Spanish), 7pm Sun. 🖼 Ⓦ eglise-sgp.org

This is the oldest church in Paris, originating in 542 when King Childebert built a basilica to house holy relics. This became an immensely powerful Benedictine abbey, which was suppressed during the Revolution, when most of the buildings were destroyed by a fire in 1794. One of the Revolution's most horrific episodes took place in a nearby

Our Lady of Consolation statue in St-Germain- des-Prés

monastery when 318 priests were hacked to death by the mob on 3 September 1792. The present church dates from about the 11th century and was heavily restored in the 19th century. One of the three original towers survives, housing one of the oldest belfries in France. The interior is an interesting mix of architectural styles, with some 6th-century marble columns,

Gothic vaulting and Romanesque arches. Famous tombs include those of René Descartes, the poet Nicolas Boileau, and John Casimir, king of Poland, who later became abbot of St-Germain-des-Prés in 1669.

❷ Palais Abbatial

1–5 Rue de l'Abbaye 75006. **Map** 12 E4. Ⓜ St-Germain-des-Prés. **Closed** to the public.

This brick and stone palace was built in 1586 for Charles of Bourbon who was cardinal-abbot of St-Germain and, very briefly, king of France. Ten more abbots lived here until the Revolution, when the building

An ironwork detail from the façade of the Palais Abbatial

was sold. James Pradier, the 19th-century sculptor who was famous for his female figures, established a studio here. The palace is now noted for its mixture of building materials and its vertical windows.

Eugène Delacroix

❸ Musée Eugène Delacroix

6 Rue de Fürstenberg 75006. **Map** 12 E4. **Tel** 01 44 41 86 50. Ⓜ St-Germain-des-Prés, Mabillon. **Open** 9.30am–5pm Wed–Mon (last adm: 4.30pm). **Closed** 1 Jan, 1 May, 25 Dec. 📷 🖼 🏠 Ⓦ musee-delacroix.fr

The leading non-conformist Romantic painter, Eugène Delacroix, known for his passionate and highly-coloured canvases, lived and worked here from 1857 to his death in 1863. Here, he painted *The Entombment of Christ* and *The Way to Calvary* (which now hang in the museum). He also created superb murals for the Chapel of the Holy Angels in the nearby St-Sulpice church, which is part of the reason why he moved to this area. The

first-floor apartment and garden studio now form a national museum, where regular exhibitions of Delacroix's work are held. The apartment has a portrait of George Sand, self-portraits, studies for future works and artistic memorabilia.

The charm of Delacroix's garden is reflected in the tiny Fürstenberg square. With its pair of rare catalpa trees and old-fashioned street lamps, the square is one of Paris's most romantic corners.

❹ Les Deux Magots

6 Pl St-Germain-des-Prés 75006. **Map** 12 E4. **Tel** 01 45 48 55 25. Ⓜ St-Germain-des-Prés. **Open** 7.30am–1am daily. **Closed** for one week in Jan. Ⓦ lesdeuxmagots.com

The café still trades on its reputation as the meeting place of the city's literary and intellectual elite. This derives from the patronage of Surrealist artists and writers including Ernest Hemingway in the 1920s and 1930s, and existentialist philosophers and writers in the 1950s.

The present clientele is more likely to be publishers or people-watchers than the new Hemingway. The café's name comes from the two wooden statues of Chinese commercial agents *(magots)* that adorn one of the pillars. This is a good place for enjoying an old-fashioned hot chocolate and watching the world go by.

The interior of Les Deux Magots

Façade of the Café de Flore, former meeting-place of existentialists

❺ Café de Flore

172 Blvd St-Germain 75006. **Map** 12
E4. **Tel** 01 45 48 55 26. Ⓜ St-Germain-
des-Prés. **Open** 7am–2am daily.
♿ restricted. 🆆 **cafedeflore.fr**

The classic Art Deco interior
of this café, all-red seating,
mahogany and mirrors, has
changed little since the
war. Like its rival Les Deux
Magots, Café de Flore has
hosted most of the French
intellectuals during the
post-war years. Jean-Paul Sartre
and Simone de Beauvoir
developed their philosophy
of existentialism here.

A waiter at the Brasserie Lipp

❻ Brasserie Lipp

151 Blvd St-Germain 75006. **Map** 12
E4. **Tel** 01 45 48 53 91. Ⓜ St-Germain-
des-Prés. **Open** 9am–1am daily.
🆆 **groupe-bertrand.com/lipp**

Third of the famous cafés around
St-Germain-des-Prés, Brasserie
Lipp combines Alsatian beer,
sauerkraut and sausages (it was
founded by a refugee from
Alsace) with excellent coffee.
This has produced a Left Bank
fixture once popular with French
politicians and fashion gurus,
which is now popular with
visitors. Originally opened in the
late 19th century, it is regarded
by many as the quintessential
Parisian brasserie, although the
experience is more atmospheric
than culinary these days. The
interior is bright with ceramic
tiles of parrots and cranes.

❼ Boulevard St-Germain

75006, 75007. **Map** 11 C2 & 12 D4.
Ⓜ Solférino, Rue du Bac, St-Germain-
des-Prés, Mabillon, Odéon.

The left bank's most celebrated
thoroughfare, over 3 km (2
miles) long, curves across three
districts from the Ile St-Louis to
the Pont de la Concorde. The
architecture is homogeneous
because the boulevard was
another of Baron Haussmann's
bold strokes of 19th-century
urban planning, but it
encompasses a wide range of
different lifestyles as well as a
number of religious and cultural
institutions. From the east (the
low street numbers), the
boulevard passes the late
François Mitterrand's private
town residence in the Rue de
Bièvre, as well as the Maubert-
Mutualité market square, the
Musée de Cluny and the
Sorbonne university, before
crossing the lively Boulevard
St-Michel.

It continues past the Ecole
de Médecine and the Place de
l'Odéon to St-Germain-des-Prés,
with its historic church and café
terraces. Fashion boutiques,
cinemas, restaurants and
bookshops give this central
portion its distinctive character.
It is also here that one is most
likely to see a celebrity. The area
is active from midday to the
early morning hours.

Continuing further, beyond
this section the boulevard
becomes more exclusively
residential and then distinctly
political with the Ministry of
Defence and the National
Assembly buildings.

❽ Rue du Dragon

75006. **Map** 12 D4. Ⓜ St-Germain-
des-Prés.

This short street, between the
Boulevard St-Germain and the
Carrefour de la Croix Rouge,
dates back to the Middle Ages
and still has houses from the
17th and 18th centuries. Notice
their large doors, tall windows
and ironwork balconies. A group
of Flemish painters lived at No.
37 before the Revolution. The
novelist Victor Hugo rented a
garret at No. 30 when he was a
19-year-old bachelor.

VICTOR HUGO
HABITA CETTE MAISON
EN 1821

26 FÉVRIER 1907
LES HUGOPHILES

A plaque at No. 30 Rue du Dragon commemorating Victor Hugo's house

9 Le Procope

13 Rue de l'Ancienne-Comédie 75006.
Map12 F4. **Tel** 01 40 46 79 00.
Ⓜ Odéon. **Open** 11.30am–midnight
daily. *See The History of Paris pp28–9.*
Ⓦ **procope.com**

Founded in 1686 by the Sicilian
Francesco Procopio dei Coltelli,
this claims to be the world's first
coffee house. It quickly became
popular with the city's political
and cultural elite.

Its patrons have included the
philosopher Voltaire – who
supposedly drank 40 cups of his
favourite mixture of coffee and
chocolate every day – and the
young Napoleon, who would
leave his hat as security while he
went searching for the money
to pay the bill. Le Procope is
now an 18th-century-style
restaurant run by the famous
Frères Blanc group.

Odéon Théâtre de l'Europe, former home of
the Comédie-Française

10 Rue de l'Odéon

75006. **Map** 12 F5. Ⓜ Odéon.

Sylvia Beach's bookshop
Shakespeare & Company
(see pp323–4) stood at No. 12
from 1921 to 1940. She
befriended many struggling
American and British writers,
such as Ezra Pound, T S Eliot,
Scott Fitzgerald and Ernest
Hemingway. It was largely due
to her support – as secretary,
editor, agent and banker – that
James Joyce's *Ulysses* was first
published in English. Adrianne
Monnier's French equivalent at
No. 7 opposite, Les Amis des
Livres, was frequented by André
Gide and Paul Valéry.

Opened in 1779 to improve
access to the Odéon theatre,
this was the first street in
Paris to have pavements with
gutters and it still has many
attractive houses and shops,
most of them dating from the
18th century.

The rear façade of Le Procope restaurant

11 Odéon Théâtre de l'Europe

Place de l'Odéon 75006. **Map** 12
F5. **Tel** 01 44 85 40 40. Ⓜ Odéon,
Luxembourg. **Open** for performances
only. Visits on request; check
website for details. ⚙ ♿ 🎭 *See
Entertainment pp334–6.* Ⓦ **theatre-odeon.fr**

This Neo-Classical theatre was
built in 1779 in the grounds of
the former Hôtel de Condé. The
site had been purchased by the
king and given to the city to
house the Comédie Française.
The premiere of *The Marriage of
Figaro*, by Beaumarchais, took
place here in 1784. With the arrival
of a new company in 1797, the
name of the theatre was changed
to Odéon. In 1807, the theatre
was consumed by fire. It was
rebuilt later the same year by the
architect Jean-François Chalgrin.

Following World War II, the
theatre specialized in modern
drama. Today, plays are often
performed in foreign languages,
including English. The auditorium
is very impressive, not least for
its ceiling, painted by André
Masson in 1965.

A young Hemingway in the 1920s

The unusual middle courtyard in the
Cour de Rohan

12 Cour de Rohan

75006. **Map** 12 F4. Ⓜ Odéon. Access
from the Rue du Jardinet until 8pm;
8pm–8am access from the Blvd
St-Germain.

This picturesque series of three
courtyards was originally part
of the 15th-century pied-à-
terre of the archbishops of
Rouen (corrupted to "Rohan").
The middle courtyard is the
most unusual. Its three-legged
wrought-iron mounting block,
known as a *pas-de-mule*, was
used at one time by elderly
women and overweight
prelates to mount their mules.
It is probably the last
mounting block left in Paris.
Overlooking the yard is the
façade of a fine Renaissance
building, dating from the
beginning of the 17th century.
One of its important former
residents was Henri II's
mistress, Diane de Poitiers.

The third courtyard opens on
to the tiny Rue du Jardinet,
where the composer Saint-
Saëns was born in 1835.

⓮ Cour du Commerce St-André

75006. **Map** 12 F4. Ⓜ Odéon.

No. 9 has a particularly grisly past, because it was here that Dr Guillotin is supposed to have perfected his "philanthropic decapitating machine". In fact, although the idea was Guillotin's, it was Dr Louis, a Parisian surgeon, who was responsible for putting the "humane" plan into action. When the guillotine was first used for execution in 1792, it was known as a *Louisette*.

A print of a Revolutionary mob at a guillotine execution

⓯ Musée de la Monnaie

11 Quai de Conti 75006. **Map** 12 F3. **Tel** 01 40 46 56 66. Ⓜ Pont-Neuf, Odéon. **Open** call for opening times. 📷 🎥 📽 Films. 🌐 **monnaiedeparis.fr**

When Louis XV decided to rehouse the Mint in the late 18th century, he hit upon the idea of launching a design competition for the new building. The present Hôtel des Monnaies is the result

of this competition. It was completed in 1777, and the architect, Jacques Antoine, lived here until his death.

Coins were minted in the mansion until 1973, when the process was moved to Pessac in the Gironde. The minting and milling halls now contain the coin and medallion museum.

The museum has undergone an extensive renovation designed to showcase Monnaie de Paris's cultural offerings. Centred around a tranquil public space and surrounded by artist workshops, the permanent gallery focuses on the history of coins and minting. There are also shops, in which work by resident artisans is available to buy, a gastronomic restaurant run by chef Guy Savoy, and a more casual café.

⓯ Académie Française

23 Quai de Conti 75006. **Map** 12 E3. **Tel** 01 44 41 43 00. Ⓜ Pont-Neuf, St-Germain-des-Prés. **Open** 2nd Sun of the month. 📷 Reserve in advance at www.institut-de-france.fr 📷 entry by guided tours only for 30 people or more as part of a conference. 🌐 **academie-francaise.fr**

This striking Baroque building was built as a school in 1688 and was given over to the Institut de France in 1805. Its cupola was designed by the palace's architect, Louis Le Vau, to harmonize with the Palais du Louvre.

The Académie Française is the oldest of the five academies of the institute. It was founded in 1635 by Cardinal Richelieu and charged with the compilation of an official dictionary of the French language. From the beginning,

A sign to the former Mint, which is now a museum

membership has been limited to 40, who are entrusted with working on the dictionary.

⓰ Ecole Nationale Supérieure des Beaux-Arts

13 Quai Malaquais 75006. **Map** 12 E3. **Tel** 01 47 03 50 00. Ⓜ St-Germain-des-Prés. **Open** Mon; groups by appt only (phone 01 42 46 92 02 or book online on www.cultival.fr). 📷 Temporary exhibitions: Tue–Fri (check website for opening hours). 📷 10am Mon–Fri. Reserve in advance. 📚 Library. 🌐 **ensba.fr**

The main French school of fine arts occupies an enviable position at the corner of the Rue Bonaparte and the riverside Quai Malaquais. The school is housed in several buildings, the most imposing being the 19th-century Palais des Etudes.

A host of budding French and foreign painters and architects have crossed the large courtyard to study in the ateliers of the school, young American architects in particular have frequented the halls over the past century.

The façade of the Ecole Nationale Supérieure des Beaux-Arts

The Celebrated Cafés of Paris

Outdoor seating at the busy Café de Flore

One of the most enduring images of Paris is the café scene. For the visitor, it is the romantic vision of great artists, writers or eminent intellectuals consorting in one of the Left Bank's celebrated cafés. For the Parisian, the café is one of life's constants, an everyday experience, providing people with a place to tryst, drink and meet friends, or to conclude business deals, or to simply watch the world go by.

The first café anywhere can be traced back to 1686, when the café Le Procope (see p142) was opened. In the following century, cafés became a vital part of Paris's social life. And with the widening of the city's streets, particularly during the 19th century and the building of Haussmann's Grands Boulevards, the cafés spread out on to the pavements, evoking Emile Zola's comment as to the "great silent crowds watching the street live".

The nature of a café was sometimes determined by the interests of its patrons. Some were the gathering places for those interested in playing chess, dominoes or billiards. Literary gents gathered in Le Procope

⓱ Hôtel Feydeau de Brou

13 Rue de l'Université 75007. **Map** 12 D3. Ⓜ Rue du Bac. **Closed** to the public.

This fine 18th-century mansion was originally built as two houses in 1643 by Briçonnet. In 1713, they were replaced by a *hôtel*, built by Thomas Gobert for the widow of Denis Feydeau de Brou. It was passed on to her son, Paul-Espirit Feydeau de Brou, until his death in 1767. The *hôtel* then became the residence of the Venetian ambassador. It was occupied by Belzunce in 1787 and became a munitions depot during the Revolution until the restoration of the monarchy in 1815.

It once housed the Ecole Nationale d'Administration (now in Strasbourg), where many of the elite in politics, economics and science were once students. Today, the building is used by France's famous Science Po University.

⓲ Quai Voltaire

75006 and 75007. **Map** 12 D3. Ⓜ Rue du Bac.

Formerly part of the Quai Malaquais, then later known as the Quai des Théatins, the Quai Voltaire is now home to some of the most important antiques dealers in Paris. It is also noted for its attractive 18th-century

Plaque marking the house in Quai Voltaire where Voltaire died

houses and for the famous people who lived in many of them, making it an especially interesting and pleasant street to walk along.

The 18th-century Swedish ambassador Count Tessin lived at No. 1, as did the sculptor James Pradier, famed for his statues and for his wife, who swam naked across the Seine. Louise de Kéroualle, spy for Louis XIV and created Duchess of Portsmouth by the infatuated Charles II of England, lived at Nos. 3–5.

Famous past residents of No. 19 included the composers Richard Wagner and Jean Sibelius, the novelist Charles Baudelaire and the exiled Irish writer and wit Oscar Wilde.

The French philosopher Voltaire died at No. 27, the Hôtel de la Villette. St- Sulpice, the local church, refused to accept his corpse (on the grounds of his atheism) and his body was rushed into the countryside to avoid a pauper's grave.

Entertainment in the Claude Alain café in the Rue de Seine during the 1950s

during Molière's time in the 17th century. In the 19th century, First Empire Imperial guards officers were drawn to the Café d'Orsay and Second Empire financiers gathered in the cafés along the Rue de la Chaussée d'Antin. The smart set patronized the Café de Paris and Café Tortini, and theatre-goers met at the cafés around the Opéra, including the Café de la Paix (see p217). The most famous cafés are on the Left Bank, in St-Germain

and Montparnasse, where the literati of old used to gather and where the glitterati of today love to be seen. Before World War I, Montparnasse was haunted by hordes of Russian revolutionaries, most eminently Lenin and Trotsky, who whiled away their days in the cafés, grappling with the problems of Russia and the world over a *petit café*. Cultural life flourished in the 1920s, when Surrealists, like Salvador Dalí and Jean Cocteau, dominated café life, and later when American writers led by Ernest Hemingway and Scott Fitzgerald talked, drank and worked in various cafés, among them La Coupole (see p180), Le Sélect and La Closerie des Lilas (see p181).

After the end of World War II, the cultural scene shifted northwards to St-Germain. Existentialism had

become the dominant creed and Jean-Paul Sartre its tiny charismatic leader. Sartre and his intellectual peers and followers, among them the writers Simone de Beauvoir and Albert Camus, the poet Boris Vian and the enigmatic singer Juliette Greco, gathered to work and discuss their ideas in Les Deux Magots (see p140) and the nearby rival Café de Flore (see p141). The traditional habitué of these cafés is still to be seen, albeit mixing with the international jet-set and with self-publicizing intellectuals hunched over their notebooks.

Works by one of St-Germain's elite, Albert Camus (1913–60)

⑲ Musée d'Orsay

See pp146–9.

⑳ Musée Nationale de la Légion d'Honneur

2 Rue de la Légion d'Honneur (Parvis du Musée d'Orsay) 75007. **Map** 11 C2. **Tel** 01 40 62 84 25. **Ⓜ** Solférino. **Ⓡ** Musée d'Orsay. **Open** 1–6pm Wed–Sun. Group visits by appt on Tue. **Closed** 1 Jan, 1 May, 15 Aug, 1 Nov, 25 Dec. **♿ ⬛ ⬛ ⬛ musee-legiondhonneur.fr**

Next to the Musée d'Orsay is the truly massive Hôtel de Salm. It was

The Musée d'Orsay, converted from a railway station into a museum

Napoleon III's Great Cross of the Legion of Honour

one of the last great mansions to be built in the area (1782). The first owner was a German count, Prince de Salm-Kyrbourg, who was guillotined in 1794.

Today, the building contains a museum where one can learn all about the Legion of Honour, a decoration launched by Napoleon I. Those awarded the

honour wear a small red rosette in their buttonhole. The impressive displays of medals and insignia are complemented by paintings. In one of the rooms, Napoleon's Legion of Honour is on display with his sword and breastplate.

The museum also covers decorations from most parts of the world, among them the British Victoria Cross and the American Purple Heart.

⑲ Musée d'Orsay

In 1986, 47 years after it had closed as a mainline railway station, Victor Laloux's superb late 19th-century building was reopened as the Musée d'Orsay. Commissioned by the Orléans railway company to be its Paris terminus, it avoided demolition in the 1970s. During the conversion, much of the original architecture was retained. The museum, which has undergone extensive renovation, was set up to present each of the arts of the period from 1848 to 1914 in the context of contemporary society and the other forms of creative activity happening at the time. Renovations to the upper levels have expanded exhibition spaces to improve the display of works.

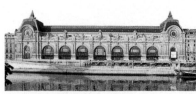

The Museum, from the Right Bank
Victor Laloux designed the building for the Universal Exhibition in 1900.

Chair by Charles Rennie Mackintosh
The style developed by Mackintosh was an attempt to express ideas in a framework of vertical and horizontal forms, as in this tearoom chair (1900).

★ The Gates of Hell (1880–1917)
Rodin included figures that he had already created, such as *The Thinker* and *The Kiss*, in this famous gateway.

Key to Floorplan

- Architecture & Decorative Arts
- Sculpture
- Painting before 1880
- Impressionism
- Neo- and Post-Impressionism
- Naturalism and Symbolism
- Art Nouveau
- Symbolism (small formats)
- Temporary exhibitions
- Non-exhibition space

Gallery Guide

The collection occupies three levels. On the ground floor, there are works from the mid to late 19th century. The middle level features Art Nouveau decorative art and a range of paintings and sculptures from the second half of the 19th century to the early 20th century, as well as Neo Impressionist art. The upper level has an outstanding collection of Impressionist art.

The Dance (1867–8)
Carpeaux's sculpture caused a scandal when first exhibited.

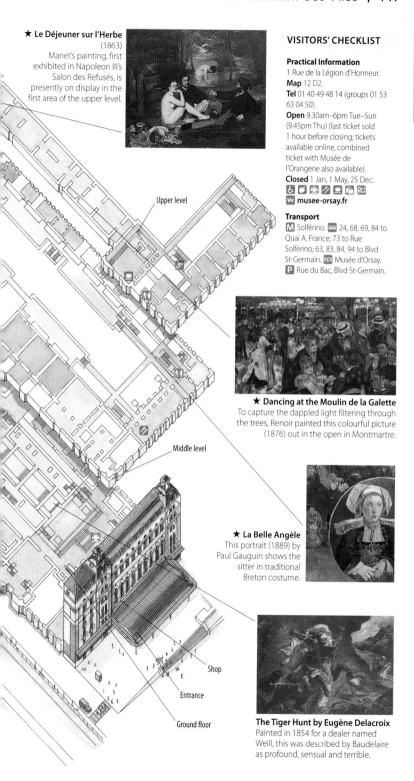

★ **Le Déjeuner sur l'Herbe**
(1863)
Manet's painting, first exhibited in Napoleon III's Salon des Refusés, is presently on display in the first area of the upper level.

Upper level

Middle level

Shop

Entrance

Ground floor

VISITORS' CHECKLIST

Practical Information
1 Rue de la Légion d'Honneur.
Map 12 D2.
Tel 01 40 49 48 14 (groups 01 53 63 04 50).
Open 9.30am–6pm Tue–Sun (9.45pm Thu) (last ticket sold 1 hour before closing; tickets available online, combined ticket with Musée de l'Orangerie also available).
Closed 1 Jan, 1 May, 25 Dec.
♿ 🚻 🅿 🧥 📷 📙 🍴 🚭
w **musee-orsay.fr**

Transport
Ⓜ Solférino. 🚌 24, 68, 69, 84 to Quai A. France; 73 to Rue Solférino; 63, 83, 84, 94 to Blvd St-Germain. 🚆 Musée d'Orsay. 🅿 Rue du Bac, Blvd St-Germain.

★ **Dancing at the Moulin de la Galette**
To capture the dappled light filtering through the trees, Renoir painted this colourful picture (1876) out in the open in Montmartre.

★ **La Belle Angèle**
This portrait (1889) by Paul Gauguin shows the sitter in traditional Breton costume.

The Tiger Hunt by Eugène Delacroix
Painted in 1854 for a dealer named Weill, this was described by Baudelaire as profound, sensual and terrible.

Exploring the Musée d'Orsay

The Musée d'Orsay picks up where the Louvre ends, showing a variety of art forms from 1848 to 1914. Its star attraction is a superb collection of Impressionist art, which includes famous works by Monet, Renoir, Manet and Degas as well as Neo-Impressionist works by pointillist Georges Seurat and Post-Impressionist works by Gauguin and Van Gogh. The museum also holds world-class temporary exhibitions and excellent lunchtime and evening concerts.

Ceiling design (1911) by the artist and designer Maurice Denis

Art Nouveau

The Belgian architect and designer Victor Horta was among the first to give free rein to the sinuous line that gave Art Nouveau its French sobriquet of *Style Nouille* (noodle style). Taking its name from a gallery of modern design that opened in Paris in 1895, Art Nouveau flourished throughout Europe until World War I.

In Vienna, Otto Wagner, Koloman Moser and Josef Hoffmann combined high craft with the new design, while the School of Glasgow, under the impetus of Charles Rennie Mackintosh, developed a more rectilinear approach which anticipated the work of Frank Lloyd Wright in the United States.

René Lalique introduced the aesthetics of Art Nouveau into jewellery and glassware, while Hector Guimard, inspired by Horta, is most famous today for his once-ubiquitous Art Nouveau entrances to the Paris metro.

One exhibit not to be missed is the carved wooden bookcase by Rupert Carabin (1890), with

its proliferation of allegorical seated female nudes, bronze palm fronds and severed bearded heads.

Sculpture

The museum's central aisle overflows with an oddly-assorted selection of sculptures. These illustrate the eclectic mood around the middle of the 19th century when the Classicism of Eugène Guillaume's *Cenotaph of the Gracchi* (1848–53) co-existed with the Romanticism of François Rude. Rude created the relief on the Arc de Triomphe (1836), often referred to as *La Marseillaise (see p213)*.

There is a wonderful series of 36 busts of members of parliament (1832) – bloated, ugly, unscrupulous and self-important – by the satirist Honoré Daumier, and work by the vital but short-lived genius Jean-Baptiste Carpeaux, whose first major bronze, *Count Ugolino* (1862), was a character from Dante. In 1868, he produced his Dionysian delight, *The Dance*, which caused a storm of protest: it was "an insult to public morals". This contrasts with the derivative and mannered work of such sculptors as Alexandre Falguière and Hyppolyte Moulin.

Edgar Degas' famous *Young Dancer of Fourteen* (1881) was displayed during his lifetime, but

the many bronzes on show were made from wax sculptures found in his studio after his death. In contrast, the sculpture of Auguste Rodin was very much in the public eye, and his sensuous and forceful work makes him pre-eminent among 19th-century sculptors. The museum contains many of his works, including the original plaster of *Balzac* (1897). Rodin's talented companion, Camille Claudel, who spent much of her life in an asylum, is represented by a grim allegory of mortality, *Maturity* (1899–1903).

The turn of the 20th century is marked by the work of Emile-Antoine Bourdelle and Aristide Maillol.

Painting Before 1880

The surprising diversity of styles in 19th-century painting is emphasized by the close juxtaposition on the ground floor of all paintings prior to 1870 – the crucial year in which Impressionism first made a name for itself. The raging colour and almost Expressionistic vigour of Eugène Delacroix's *Lion Hunt* (1854) stands next to Jean-Dominique Ingres' cool Classical *The Spring* (1820–56). As a reminder of the academic manner that dominated the century up to that point, the uninspired waxwork style of Thomas Couture's monumental *The Romans in the Age of Decadence* (1847) dominates the central aisle. In a class of their own are Edouard Manet's provocative *Olympia* and *Le Déjeuner sur l'Herbe* (1863), while works painted around the same time by his friends, Claude Monet, Pierre-Auguste Renoir, Frédéric Bazille and Alfred Sisley, give a glimpse of the Impressionists before the Impressionist movement began.

Young Dancer of Fourteen (1881) by Edgar Degas

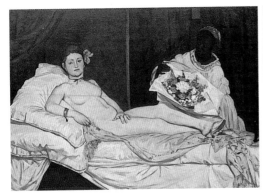

Olympia (1863) by Edouard Manet

Impressionism

Rouen Cathedral caught at various moments of the day (1892–3) is one of the many works on show by Claude Monet, the leading figure of the Impressionist movement. Pierre-Auguste Renoir's plump nudes and his young people *Dancing at the Moulin de la Galette* (1876) were painted at the high point of his Impressionist period. Other artists on display include Camille Pissarro, Alfred Sisley and Mary Cassatt.

Edgar Degas and Paul Cézanne are included here, although their techniques differed from those of the Impressionists. Degas often favoured crisp Realism, though he was quite capable of using the sketchy manner of the Impressionists, as, for instance, in *L'Absinthe* (1876). Cézanne was more concerned with substance than light, as can be seen in his *Apples and Oranges* (1895–1900). Van Gogh was momentarily influenced by the movement but then went his own way, illustrated here by works from the collection of Dr Gachet.

Breton Peasant Women (1894) by Paul Gauguin

Neo-Impressionism

Although labelled Neo-Impressionism, the work of Georges Seurat (which includes *The Circus* from 1891) was quite unrelated to the older movement. He, along with Maximilien Luce and Paul Signac, painted by applying small dots of colour that blended together when viewed from a distance. *Jane Avril Dancing* (1892) is just one of many pictures by Henri de Toulouse-Lautrec on display. The work Paul Gauguin made at Pont-Aven in Brittany is shown next to that of younger artists who knew him at the time, such as Emile Bernard and the Nabis group. There are also a number of paintings from his Tahitian period. Works by Vincent Van Gogh are also included here.

The Nabis (which included Pierre Bonnard) tended to treat the canvas as a flat surface out of which a sense of depth emerged as the viewer gazed upon it.

The dream-like visions of Odilon Redon are in the Symbolist vein, while the naïve art of Henri (Douanier) Rousseau is represented by *War* (1894) and *The Snake Charmer* (1907).

Naturalism and Symbolism

Three large rooms are devoted to paintings that filled the Salons from 1880 to 1900. The work of the Naturalists was sanctioned by the Third Republic and widely reproduced at the time. Fernand Cormon's figure of *Cain* was highly acclaimed when it first appeared in the 1880 Salon. Jules Bastien-Lepage's interest lay in illustrating peasant life, and in 1877 he painted *Haymaking*, which established him as one of the leading Naturalists. His fairly free handling of paint was influenced by what he had learned from Manet and his friends. More sombrely (and effectively) naturalistic is Lionel Walden's view of *The Docks of Cardiff* (1894).

Symbolism developed as a reaction against Realism and Impressionism and tended to be dominated by images of dreams and thoughts. This resulted in a wide variety of subjects and modes of expression. There is the over-sweet vision of levitating harpists, *Serenity* by Henri Martin (1899), Edward Burne-Jones' monumental work *Wheel of Fortune* (1883) and Jean Delville's *School of Plato* (1898). One of the most evocative paintings in this section is Winslow Homer's lyrical *Summer Night* (1890).

Blue Water Lilies (1919) by Claude Monet

LATIN QUARTER

Student book shops, cafés, cinemas and jazz clubs fill this ancient riverside quarter between the Seine and the Luxembourg Gardens. Famous institutes of learning abound, among them the two most prestigious lycées, Henri IV and Louis le Grand, through which passes a large percentage of the future French elite.

As the leaders of the 1968 revolt *(see pp42–3)* disappeared into the mainstream of French life, so the Boulevard St-Michel, the area's spine, turned increasingly to commerce, not demonstrations. Today, there are cheap shops and fast-food outlets, and the maze of narrow, cobbled streets off the boulevard is full of inexpensive ethnic shops, quirky boutiques and avant-garde theatres and cinemas. But the area's 800 years of history are difficult to erase. The Sorbonne retains much of its old character and the eastern half of the area has streets dating back to the 13th century. The long Rue St-Jacques, stretching out of the city, is on the site of a road built by the Romans and is probably the oldest street in Paris.

Sights at a Glance

Historic Buildings and Streets
2 Boulevard St-Michel
7 La Sorbonne
8 Collège de France

Churches
3 St-Séverin
4 St-Julien-le-Pauvre
9 Chapelle de la Sorbonne
10 St-Etienne-du-Mont
11 Panthéon pp160–61

Squares
5 Place Maubert

Museums and Galleries
1 Musée de Cluny – Musée National du Moyen Age pp154–7
6 Musée de la Préfecture de Police

Restaurants *see pp302–4*
1 58 Qualité Street
2 Anahuacalli
3 L'Atlas
4 Bistrot Terroir Parisien
5 Brasserie Balzar
6 Breakfast in America
7 El Loubnane
8 Itinéraires
9 Perraudin
10 Le Petit Châtelet
11 Le Petit Pontoise
12 Le Pré Verre
13 Sola
14 La Tour d'Argent

0 metres 200
0 yards 200

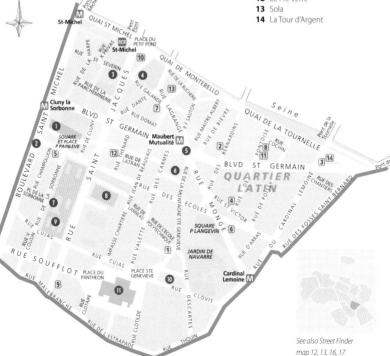

See also Street Finder
map 12, 13, 16, 17

◀ Interior view of the Panthéon's dome

For keys to symbols *see back flap*

Street-by-Street: Latin Quarter

Since the Middle Ages this riverside quarter has been dominated by the Sorbonne, and acquired its name from the early Latin-speaking students. It dates back to the Roman town across from the Ile de la Cité; at that time the Rue St-Jacques was one of the main roads out of Paris. The area is generally associated with artists, intellectuals and the bohemian way of life; it also has a history of political unrest. In 1871, the Place St-Michel became the centre of the Paris Commune, and in May 1968 it was the site of the student uprisings. Today the eastern half has become sufficiently chic, however, to contain the homes of some of the establishment.

Place St-Michel contains a fountain by Davioud. The bronze statue by Duret shows St Michael killing the dragon.

Metro St-Michel

Metro Cluny La Sorbonne

❷ ★ **Boulevard St-Michel**
The northern end of the Boul'Mich, as it is affectionately known, is a lively mélange of cafés, book and clothes shops, with bars and experimental cinemas nearby.

❶ ★ **Musée National du Moyen Age**
One of the finest collections of medieval art in the world is kept here in a superb late 15th-century building.

No. 22 Rue St-Séverin is the narrowest house in Paris and used to be the residence of Abbé Prévost, author of *Manon Lescaut*.

❸ ★ St-Séverin
Begun in the 13th century, this beautiful church took three centuries to build and is a fine example of the flamboyant Gothic style.

Rue du Chat qui Pêche (meaning "street of the fishing cat") is the narrowest street in Paris at just 1.8 m (6 ft) wide.

Little Athens is a lively place in the evening, especially at the weekend, when the Greek restaurants situated in the touristy streets around St-Séverin are at their busiest.

Locator Map
See Central Paris Map pp16–17

Shakespeare & Co (see pp323–4) at No.37 Rue de la Bûcherie is a delightful, if chaotic, bookshop. Any books purchased here are stamped with Shakespeare & Co Kilomètre Zéro Paris.

Rue du Fouarre used to host lectures in the Middle Ages. The students sat on straw (fouarre) in the street.

❹ ★ St-Julien-le-Pauvre
Rebuilt in the 17th century, this church was used to store animal feed during the Revolution.

Metro
Maubert
Mutualité

Rue Galande was home to the rich and chic in the 17th century, but subsequently became notorious for its taverns.

| 0 metres | 100 |
| 0 yards | 100 |

Key
— Suggested route

❶ Musée de Cluny – Musée National du Moyen Ag‹

The museum is housed in the former town house of the Abbots of Cluny, l'Hotel de Cluny. Surrounded by imaginatively recreated medieval gardens, the museum is a unique combination of Gallo-Roman ruins, incorporated into a medieval mansion, and one of the world's finest collections of medieval art.

Medieval Mansion
The museum building was completed in 1500 during the abbacy of Jacques d'Amboise, Abbot of Cluny.

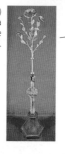

★ Golden Rose (1330)
The goldsmith Minucchio da Siena made this rose for the Avignon Pope John XXII.

★ Lady with the Unicorn
This outstanding series of six tapestries is a fine example of the *millefleurs* style, which was developed in the 15th and early 16th centuries. The style is noted for its graceful depiction of plants, animals and people.

Gallo-Roman Baths
Built in AD 100, the baths lasted for about 100 years before being abandoned.

Caldarium
(hot bath room)

Gallo-Roman Frigidarium
The arches of this cold bath room date from the 1st and 2nd centuries. They are thought to have been decorated with pairs of carved ship's prows, symbolizing the association of Paris boatmen.

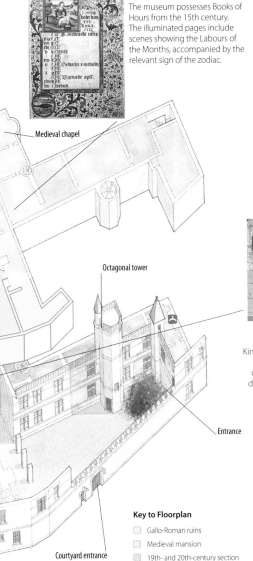

Books of Hours

The museum possesses Books of Hours from the 15th century. The illuminated pages include scenes showing the Labours of the Months, accompanied by the relevant sign of the zodiac.

Medieval chapel

Octagonal tower

Entrance

Courtyard entrance

Key to Floorplan

- Gallo-Roman ruins
- Medieval mansion
- 19th- and 20th-century section

VISITORS' CHECKLIST

Practical Information

6 Pl Paul-Painlevé.
Map 13 A5.
Tel 01 53 73 78 16/00.
Open 9.15am–5.45pm
Wed–Mon. **Closed** 1 Jan, 1 May,
25 Dec. 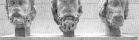 Concerts.
Workshops.
w musee-moyenage.fr

Transport

M Cluny-La-Sorbonne,
St-Michel, Odéon. 21, 27, 38,
63, 86, 87 to Rue Soufflot, Rue
des Ecoles. St-Michel, Cluny-
La Sorbonne. **P** Blvd
St-Germain, Pl Edmond Rostand.

★ **Gallery of the Kings**
In 1977, 22 of the 27 stone heads of the Kings of Judah (carved around 1220 during the reign of Philippe Auguste) were unearthed during excavations in the Rue de la Chaussée-d'Antin behind the Opéra.

Gallery Guide

The collection is spread throughout the two floors of the building. It is mainly medieval and covers a wide range of items, including illuminated manuscripts, tapestries, textiles, precious metals, alabaster, ceramics, sculpture and church furnishings. A number of Gallo-Roman artifacts are displayed around the sides of the frigidarium, and the small circular room nearby contains some capitals.

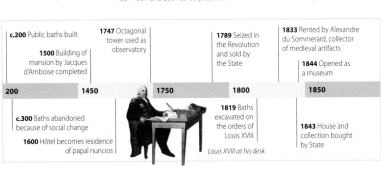

200	1450	1750	1800	1850

c.200 Public baths built

1500 Building of mansion by Jacques d'Amboise completed

1747 Octagonal tower used as observatory

1789 Seized in the Revolution and sold by the State

1833 Rented by Alexandre du Sommerard, collector of medieval artifacts

1844 Opened as a museum

c.300 Baths abandoned because of social change

1600 Hôtel becomes residence of papal nuncios

1819 Baths excavated on the orders of Louis XVIII

1843 House and collection bought by State

Louis XVIII at his desk

Exploring the Moyen Age's Collection

Alexandre du Sommerard took over the Hôtel de Cluny in 1833 and installed his art collection with great sensitivity to the surroundings and a strong sense of the dramatic. After his death the Hôtel and its contents were sold to the State and turned into a museum.

The Arithmetic tapestry

Tapestries

The tapestries are remarkable for their quality, age and state of preservation. In *The Arithmetic*, one of the liberal arts of the Quadrivium alongside geometry, astronomy and music is personified by an elegant female figure in period dress, counting tokens while consulting the book given as a present by one of the surrounding men. More everyday scenes are shown in the magnificent series *The Noble Life* (about 1500). Upstairs is the *Lady with the Unicorn* series.

Carvings

The diverse techniques of medieval European wood-carvers are well represented. From the Nottingham work-shops in England, there are wood as well as alabaster works which were widely used as altarpieces all over Europe. Among the smaller works of this genre are *The School*, which is touchingly realistic and dates from the early 16th century.

Upstairs there are some fine Flemish and south German woodcarvings. The multi-coloured figure of St John is typical. Two notable altar-pieces on display are the intricately carved and painted *Lamentation of Christ* (about 1485) from the Duchy of Clèves, and the Averbode altarpiece, which was made in 1523 in Antwerp, and depicts three scenes including the Last Supper. Not to be missed is a beautiful full-length figure of Mary Magdalene.

Stained Glass

Most of the Cluny's glass from the 12th and 13th centuries is French. The oldest examples were originally installed in the Basilique-Cathédrale de St-Denis in 1144. There are also three fragments from the Troyes Cathedral, destroyed by fire, two of which illustrate the life of St Nicholas while the third depicts that of Christ.

Numerous panels came to the Cluny from Sainte-Chapelle *(see pp88–9)*, during its mid-19th-century restoration, and were never returned, including five scenes from the story of Samson dating from 1248.

The technique of contrasting coloured glass with surround-ing grisaille (grey-and-white panels) developed in the latter half of the 13th century. Four panels from the royal château at Rouen illustrate this.

Stained-glass scene from Brittany (1400)

The School woodcarving (English, early 16th century)

La Reine de Saba, the head of a queen from St-Denis from before 1120

Sculpture

The highlight here is the Gallery of the Kings, a display of heads and decapitated figures from Notre-Dame. There is also a very graceful statue of Adam, sculpted in the 1260s.

In the vaulted room opposite are displays of fine Romanesque sculpture retrieved from French churches. Among the earliest are the 12 capitals from the nave of St-Germain-des-Prés, from the early 11th century. Retrieved from the portal of St-Denis is a boldly sculpted head of a queen, *Le Reine de Saba* (c.1140) which, though badly mutilated, is still compelling.

Other Romanesque and early Gothic capitals include six finely sculpted works from Catalonia and four of the museum's most famous statues, early 13th-century apostles made for Sainte-Chapelle.

Everyday Objects

Household goods show another side to medieval life, and this large collection is grouped in a sensitive way to illustrate their use – from wallhangings and caskets to kitchenware and clothing. Children's toys bring a very human aspect to the display, while travel cases and religious emblems evoke journeys of exploration and pilgrimage.

Precious Metalwork

The museum has a fine collection of jewellery, coins, metal and enamelwork from Gallic times to the Middle Ages. The showcase of Gallic jewellery includes gold torques, bracelets and rings, all of a simple design. In between these is one of the Cluny's most precious exhibits, the Golden Rose, a delicately wrought piece commissioned by Pope John XXII in 1330 and the oldest known of its kind.

The earliest enamelwork on display is the late Roman and Byzantine *cloisonné* pieces, culminating in the remarkable Limoges enamels, which flourished in the late 12th century. There are also two exceptional altarpieces, the Golden Altar of Basel and the Stavelot altarpiece.

Cross from Italy (late 15th century)

Lady with the Unicorn Tapestries

This series of six tapestries was woven in the late 15th century in the southern Netherlands. It is valued for its fresh harmonious colours and the poetic elegance of the central figure. Allegories of the senses are illustrated in the first five: sight (gazing into a mirror), hearing (playing a portable organ), taste (sampling sweets), smell (sniffing carnations) and touch (the lady holding the unicorn's horn). The enigmatic sixth tapestry (showing jewels being placed in a box) includes the words "to my only desire" and is now thought to represent the principle of free choice.

The Pillar of the Nautes

Gallo-Roman Ruins

One of the main reasons for visiting the Musée de Cluny – Musée National du Moyen Age is to see the scale and layout of its earliest function, the Gallo-Roman baths. The vaulted *frigidarium* (cold bath room) was the largest of its kind in France. Here there is another of the museum's highlights, the restored Pillar of the Nautes (boatmen), unearthed during excavations beneath Notre-Dame in 1711. Composed of five carved stone blocks representing Gallic and Roman divinities, its crowning element is presumed to depict the Seine's boatmen. There are also the ruins of the *caldarium* and *tepidarium* (hot and tepid baths), and visitors can tour the underground vaults.

Unicorn on the sixth tapestry

❷ Boulevard St-Michel

75005 & 75006. **Map** 12 F5 & 16 F1.
Ⓜ St-Michel, Cluny-La Sorbonne.
ⓇⒺⓇ Luxembourg.

Cut through the area in 1869, the boulevard initially gained fame from its many literary cafés, but nowadays many have been replaced by clothes shops. Nos. 60–64 house the Ecole Nationale Supérieure des Mines, one of France's leading engineering schools (see p175). In the Place St-Michel, marble plaques commemorate the many students who died here in 1944 fighting the Nazis.

Door of St-Séverin church decorated with carved stone arches

❸ St-Séverin

3 Rue-des-Prêtres-St-Séverin 75005.
Map 13 A4. **Tel** 01 42 34 93 50.
Ⓜ St-Michel. **Open** 11am–7.30pm Mon–Sat, 9am–8.30pm Sun. 🕇 daily. Concerts. 🖥 **saint-severin.com**

One of the most beautiful churches in Paris, St-Séverin is a perfect example of the Flamboyant Gothic style. It is named after a 6th-century hermit who lived in the area and persuaded the future St Cloud, grandson of King Clovis, to take holy orders. Construction finished during the early 16th century and included a remarkable double

Inside St-Julien-le-Pauvre

ambulatory circling the chancel. In 1684, the Grande Mademoiselle, cousin to Louis XIV, adopted St-Séverin after breaking with St-Suplice and had the chancel modernized.

The burial ground here, which is now a garden, was the site of the first operation for gall stones in 1474. An archer who had been condemned to death was offered his freedom by Louis XI if he consented to the operation and lived. (It was a success, and the archer went free.) In the garden stands the church's medieval gable-roofed charnel house.

❹ St-Julien-le-Pauvre

1 Rue St-Julien-le-Pauvre 75005.
Map 13 A4. **Tel** 01 43 54 52 16. Ⓜ St-Michel. ⓇⒺⓇ St Michel-Notre-Dame.
Open 9.30am–1.30pm, 3–6.30pm daily. 🕇 12.15pm Tue & Thu, 11am Sun. Concerts. See Entertainment p338.

At least three saints can claim to be patron of this church, but the most likely is St Julian the Hospitaller. The church, together with St-Germain-des-Prés, is one of the oldest in Paris, dating from between 1165 and 1220. The university held its official meetings in the church until 1524, when a student protest created so much damage that university meetings were barred from the church by parliament. Since 1889, it has belonged to the Melchite sect of the Greek Orthodox Church, and it is now the setting for chamber and religious music concerts.

❺ Place Maubert

75005. **Map** 13 A5. Ⓜ Maubert-Mutualité.

From the 12th to the middle of the 13th century, "La Maub" was one of Paris's scholastic centres, with lectures given in the open air. After the scholars moved to the new colleges of the Montagne St-Geneviève, the square became a place of torture and execution, including that of the philosopher Etienne Dolet, who was burnt at the stake in 1546.

So many Protestants were burnt here in the 16th century that it became a place of pilgrimage for the followers of the new faith. Its dark reputation has been replaced by respectability and a notable street market.

❻ Musée de la Préfecture de Police

4 Rue de la Montagne Ste-Geneviève 75005. **Map** 13 A5. **Tel** 01 44 41 52 50.
Ⓜ Maubert-Mutualité. **Open** 9.30am–5pm Mon–Fri. **Closed** Sat & public hols. 📷 by appt.

A darker side to Paris's history is illustrated in this small, rather old-fashioned museum. Created in 1909, the collection traces the development of the police in Paris from the Middle Ages to the 20th century. Curiosities on show include arrest warrants for figures such as the famous revolutionary Danton, and a rather sobering display of weapons and tools used by famous criminals. There is also a section on the part the police played in the Resistance and subsequent liberation of Paris.

Weapons in the police museum

❼ La Sorbonne

1 Rue Victor Cousin 75005. **Map** 13 A5. **Tel** 01 40 46 22 11. Ⓜ Cluny-La Sorbonne, Maubert-Mutualité. **Open** by appt only: by appt only: write to visites.sorbonne@ac-paris.fr. Ⓦ **english.paris-sorbonne.fr**

The Sorbonne, seat of the University of Paris, was established in 1253 by Robert de Sorbon, confessor to Louis IX, for 16 poor students to study theology. From these modest beginnings, the college soon became the centre of scholastic theology. In 1469, the rector had three printing machines brought over from Mainz, thereby founding the first printing house in France. The college's opposition to liberal 18th-century philosophy led to its suppression during the Revolution. It was re-established by Napoleon in 1806. The buildings built by Richelieu in the early 17th century were replaced by the ones seen today, with the exception of the chapel.

Statues outside the college

❽ Collège de France

11 Pl Marcelin-Berthelot 75005. **Map** 13 A5. **Tel** 01 44 27 12 11. Ⓜ Maubert-Mutualité. **Open** Oct–Jun: 9am–6pm Mon–Fri. Ⓦ **college-de-france.fr**

One of Paris's great institutes of research and learning, the college was established in 1530 by François I. Guided by the great humanist Guillaume Budé, the king aimed to counteract the intolerance and dogmatism of the Sorbonne. A statue of Budé stands in the west courtyard, and the unbiased approach to learning is reflected in the inscription on the old college entrance: *docet omnia* (all are taught here). Lectures are free and open to the public, depending on availability.

16th-century belfry tower

St-Etienne-du-Mont

Medieval window

Rood screen

❾ Chapelle de la Sorbonne

Pl de la Sorbonne 75005. **Map** 13 A5. **Tel** 01 40 46 22 11. Ⓜ Cluny-La Sorbonne, Maubert-Mutualité. 🆁 Luxembourg. **Open** for guided tours only (one Sat every month), by appt.

Designed by Lemercier and built between 1635 and 1642, this chapel is, in effect, a monument to Richelieu, with his coat of arms on the dome supports and his white marble tomb, carved by Girardon in 1694, in the chancel. The chapel's attractive lateral façade looks on to the main courtyard of the Sorbonne.

Chapelle de la Sorbonne clock

❿ St-Etienne-du-Mont

Pl Ste-Geneviève 75005. **Map** 17 A1. **Tel** 01 43 54 11 79. Ⓜ Cardinal Lemoine. **Open** 8.45am–7.45pm Tue–Fri, 8.45am–noon, 2–7.45pm Sat, 2.30–7pm Sun (school holidays: 10am–noon, 4–7.45pm Tue–Sat). daily.

This remarkable church houses not only the shrine of Sainte Geneviève, patron saint of Paris, but also the remains of the great literary figures Racine and Pascal. Some parts are in the Gothic style and others date from the Renaissance, including a magnificent rood screen which crosses the nave like a bridge. The stained-glass windows are also of note.

⑪ Panthéon

When Louis XV recovered from desperate illness in 1744, he was so grateful to be alive that he conceived a magnificent church to honour Sainte Geneviève. The design was entrusted to the French architect Jacques-Germain Soufflot, who planned the church in Neo-Classical style. Work began in 1764 and was completed in 1790, ten years after Soufflot's death, under the control of Guillaume Rondelet. But with the Revolution underway, the church was soon turned into a pantheon – a location for the tombs of France's great and good. Napoleon returned it to the Church in 1806, but it was secularized and then desecularized once more before finally being made a civic building in 1885.

The Façade
Inspired by the Rome Pantheon, the temple portico has 22 Corinthian columns.

Pediment Relief
David d'Angers' pediment bas-relief depicts the mother country (France) granting laurels to her great men.

The Panthéon Interior
The interior has four aisles arranged in the shape of a Greek cross, from the centre of which the great dome rises.

KEY

① **The arches of the dome** show a renewed interest in the lightness of Gothic architecture and were designed by Rondelet. They link four pillars supporting the dome, which weighs 10,000 tonnes and is 83 m (272 ft) high.

② **The dome galleries** afford a magnificent panoramic view of France's capital.

③ **The dome lantern** allows only a little light to filter into the church's centre. Intense light was thought inappropriate for the place where France's heroes rested.

Entrance

★ **Frescoes of Sainte Geneviève**
Murals along the south wall of the nave depict the life of Sainte Geneviève. They are by Pierre Puvis de Chavannes, the 19th-century fresco painter.

VISITORS' CHECKLIST

Practical Information
Pl du Panthéon. **Map** 17 A1. **Tel** 01 44 32 18 00. **Open** Apr–Sep: 10am–6:30pm daily; Oct-Mar: 10am–6pm daily (last adm 45 mins before). **Closed** 1 Jan, 1 May, 25 Dec. Renovations underway; call ahead of visit 🛗 ♿ 🎫 🖥 **pantheon. monuments-nationaux.fr**

Transport
Ⓜ Jussieu, Cardinal-Lemoine.
🚌 84 to Panthéon; 21, 27, 38, 82, 84, 85, 89 to Gare du Luxembourg.
RER Luxembourg Ⓟ Pl E Rostand.

★ Iron-Framed Dome
The tall dome, with its stone cupolas and three layers of shells, was inspired by St Paul's in London and the Dôme des Invalides *(see pp188–9)*.

Colonnade
The colonnade encircling the dome is both decorative and part of an ingenious supporting system.

Monument to Diderot
This is Alphonse Terroir's statue (1925) to the political writer Denis Diderot.

The Panthéon's Enshrined

The first of France's great men to be entombed was the popular orator Honoré Mirabeau. (Later, under the revolutionary leadership of Maximilien Robespierre, he fell from grace and his body was removed.) Voltaire followed. A statue of Voltaire by Jean-Antoine Houdon stands in front of his tomb. In the 1970s, the remains of the wartime Resistance leader Jean Moulin were reburied here. Pierre and Marie Curie's remains were transferred here in 1995, followed by Alexandre Dumas in 2002. Others here include Jean-Jacques Rousseau, Victor Hugo and Emile Zola.

★ Crypt
Covering the entire area under the building, the crypt divides into galleries flanked by Doric columns. Many French notables rest here.

JARDIN DES PLANTES QUARTER

This area, traditionally, has been one of the most tranquil corners of Paris. It takes its character from the 17th-century botanical gardens where the kings of the ancien régime grew medicinal herbs and where the National Natural History Institute stands today.

The many hospitals in the area, notably Paris's largest, Pitié-Salpêtrière, add to the atmosphere. A market takes over the lower part of Rue Mouffetard every day, and the streets off Mouffetard are redolent of life in medieval times.

Sights at a Glance

Historic Buildings and Streets
5 Arènes de Lutèce
7 Rue Mouffetard
12 Groupe Hospitalier Pitié-Salpêtrière

Churches
8 St-Médard
9 Mosquée de Paris

Modern Architecture
1 Institut du Monde Arabe

Squares, Parks and Gardens
3 Ménagerie
6 Place de la Contrescarpe
11 Jardin des Plantes

Museums and Galleries
1 Musée de la Sculpture en Plein Air
4 Collection des Minéraux de l'Université
10 Muséum National d'Histoire Naturelle
13 La Manufacture des Gobelins

Restaurants see pp302–4
1 L'Agrume
2 Chez Gladines
3 Dans les Landes
4 Marty
5 Mavrommatis

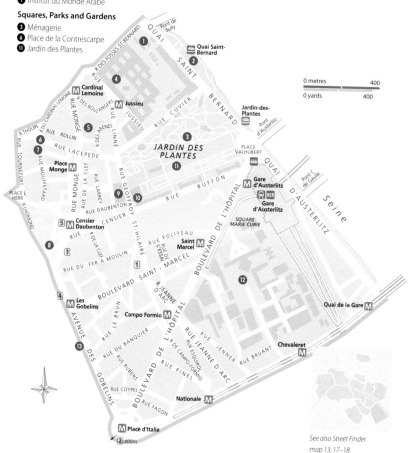

0 metres 400
0 yards 400

See also Street Finder map 13, 17–18

◀ Pedestrians strolling in the Jardin des Plantes

For keys to symbols see back flap

Street-by-Street: Jardin des Plantes Quarter

Two physicians to Louis XIII, Jean Hérouard and Guy de la Brosse, obtained permission to establish the royal medicinal herb garden in the sparsely populated St-Victor suburb in 1626. The herb garden and gardens of various religious houses gave the region a rural character. In the 19th century the population and thus the area expanded and it became more built up, until it gradually assumed the character it has today: a well-to-do residential patchwork of 19th- and early 20th-century buildings interspersed with much older and some more recent buildings.

Metro Cardinal Lemoine

6 Place de la Contrescarpe
This village-like square filled with restaurants and cafés buzzes with student life after dusk.

7 ★ Rue Mouffetard
Locals flock to the daily open-air market here which is one of the oldest Paris street markets. A hoard of *louis d'or gold* coins from the 18th century was found at No. 53 during its demolition in 1938.

Pot de Fer fountain is one of 14 that Marie de Médicis had built on the Left Bank in 1624 as a source of water for her palace in the Jardin du Luxembourg.
The fountain was rebuilt in 1671.

Metro Place Monge

Passage des Postes
is an ancient alley which was opened in 1830. Its entrance is in the Rue Mouffetard.

8 St-Médard
This church was started in the mid-15th century and completed by 1655. In 1784 the choir was made Classical in style, and the nave's 16th-century windows were replaced with contemporary stained glass.

RUE DU CARDINAL LEMOINE

RUE ROLLIN

RUE ST MÉDARD

RUE ORTOLAN

RUE GRACIE

RUE MOUFFETARD

RUE DE L'EPEE DE B

RUE DES PATRIARCHES

RUE DE L'ARBALETE

RUE DE CANDOLLE

★ Arènes de Lutèce
The Roman amphitheatre of Lutetia was used for burials in the 4th century.

Locator Map
See Central Paris Map pp16–17

Rue des Arènes is round the corner from the Arènes de Lutèce. No. 5 is an interesting Gothic Revival house in which the writer Jean Paulhan lived from 1940.

Cuvier Fountain is a memorial to naturalist Georges Cuvier. It was erected in 1840 by P Vigouroux, with figure carving by Jean-Jacques Feuchère.

Metro Censier-Daubenton

★ Mosquée de Paris
This Hispano-Moorish mosque, the centre of Paris's Muslim community, includes within its walls a Turkish bath, a Moorish café and restaurant, and an oriental bazaar.

Key

— Suggested route

0 metres   100
0 yards   100

❶ Institut du Monde Arabe

1 Rue des Fossées St-Bernard, Pl Mohammed V 75005. **Map** 13 C5. **Tel** 01 40 51 38 38. **M** Jussieu, Cardinal-Lemoine. **Open** Museum & temp exhibs: 10am–6pm Tue–Thu (until 9.30pm Fri, 7pm Sat & Sun and public hols). Library: closed for renovations. 🅰 ♿ 🅲 Lectures. 🅰 📺 **W** imarabe.org

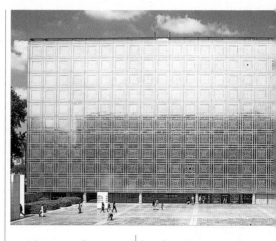

This cultural institute was founded in 1980 by France and 20 Arab countries with the intention of fostering cultural links between the Arab world and the West. It is housed in a magnificent building designed by Jean Nouvel (also responsible for the Musée du quai Branly, *see pp194–5*), combining modern materials with the spirit of traditional Arab architecture. The white marble book tower, which can be seen through the glass of the west wall, spirals upwards bringing to mind the minaret of a mosque. The emphasis that is traditionally placed on interior space in Arab architecture has been used here to create an enclosed courtyard reached by a narrow gap splitting the building in two.

From floors four to seven, there's a fascinating display of Islamic works of art from the 9th to the 19th centuries, including ceramics, sculpture, carpets and astrolabes. There is also a library and media archive.

❷ Musée de la Sculpture en Plein Air

Quai St-Bernard, Square Tino Rossi 75005. **Map** 13 C5. **M** Gare d'Austerlitz, Sully-Morland.

Butting up to the left-hand corner of the Institut du Monde Arabe, the Pont de Sully links the Ile St Louis with both banks of the Seine. Opened in 1877 and built of cast iron, the Pont de Sully is not an especially beautiful structure. Despite this, it is well worth pausing for a moment on the bridge for a fabulous view of Notre-Dame rising dramatically behind the graceful Pont de la Tournelle.

Running along the river from the Pont de Sully as far as the Pont d'Austerlitz is the peaceful Quai St-Bernard. Not always so sedate, Quai St-Bernard was famous during the 17th century as a spot for nude bathing, until scandalized public opinion made it illegal. The grassy slopes adjoining the quai make a perfect spot to enjoy a picnic. Opened in 1975, they are known as the Jardin Tino Rossi in honour of the celebrated Corsican singer. The garden has a display of open-air sculpture known as the Musée de la Sculpture en Plein Air. Vandalism and other problems have unfortunately necessitated the removal of some of the exhibits.

❸ Ménagerie

57 Rue Cuvier/Rue Buffon 75005. **Map** 17 C1. **Tel** 01 40 79 37 94. **M** Jussieu, Austerlitz. **Open** 9am–6pm Mon–Sat (to 6.30pm Sun & public hols). Last adm 30 mins before. 🅰 🅲 📺 🅿 🅰 🅲 for groups, by appt. **W** mnhn.fr

France's oldest public zoo is situated in the lovely surroundings of the Jardin des Plantes. It was set up during the Revolution to house survivors from the Royal menagerie at Versailles – all four of them. The state then rounded up animals from circuses and exotic creatures were sent from abroad. Unfortunately, during the Prussian siege of Paris (1870–71), most of them were slaughtered to feed the hungry citizens *(see p226)*. Today, the zoo specializes in small mammals, insects, birds, primates and reptiles. It is a great favourite with children as it allows them to get quite close to the animals, either in the petting enclosure, or during feeding times. The lion house contains panthers from China and other attractions include a large monkey house, a waterfowl aviary, and wild sheep and goats.

The displays in the vivarium (enclosures of live animals in their natural habitat) are changed at regular intervals and there is a permanent exhibition of micro-arthropods (also known as creepy-crawlies!)

Child playing at the zoo

Light Screens

The south elevation is made up of 1,600 high-tech metal screens which filter the light entering the building. Their design is based on *moucharabiyahs* (carved wooden screens found on the outsides of buildings from Morocco to Southeast Asia).

Each screen contains 21 irises which are controlled electronically, opening and closing in response to the amount of sunlight falling on photosensitive screens.

The central iris is made up of interlocking metal blades which move to adjust the size of the central opening.

The peripheral irises are linked to one another and to the central iris. They open and close in unison forming a delicate pattern of light and shade inside the institute.

❹ Collection des Minéraux de l'Université

Université Pierre et Marie Curie, 75005. **Map** 17 B1. **Tel** 01 44 27 52 88. Ⓜ Jussieu. **Open** 1pm–6pm Wed–Mon. **Closed** 1 Jan, Easter, 1 May, 14 Jul, 1 Nov, 25 Dec. 🚫 🔲 🏠 📷 💷 groups Tue pm. 🚫 **Closed** to public. Scheduled to move to Rue de Fossés Saint Bernard.

This fascinating small museum is housed in the main university building, named after the distinguished scientists. The collection comprises cut and uncut gemstones and rock crystal from all over the world, shown to maximum advantage through the expert use of specialized lighting.

❺ Arènes de Lutèce

49–59 Rue Monge/4 Rue des Arenes 75005. **Map** 17 B1. **Tel** 01 45 35 02 56. Ⓜ Jussieu. *See p23.* **Open** hours vary

The remains of this vast Roman arena (Lutetia was the Roman name for Paris) date from the late 1st century. Its destruction began towards the end of the 3rd century at the hands of the Barbarians, and later, parts of it were used to build the walls of the Ile de la Cité. The arena was then gradually buried and its exact location preserved only in old documents and the local name Clos des Arènes. It was rediscovered in 1869 during the construction of the Rue Monge and the allocation of building plots nearby. Action towards its restoration began with the campaigning of Victor Hugo (among others) in the 19th century but work did not get really underway until 1918.

With a seating capacity of 15,000, arranged in 35 tiers, the original arena was used both for theatrical performances and as an amphitheatre for gladiator fights. This type of combined use was peculiar to Gaul (France), and the arena is similar to the other ones in Nîmes and Arles.

The public park at the Arènes de Lutèce

Buffon and the Jardin des Plantes

At the age of 32, Georges Louis Leclerc, Comte de Buffon (1707–88), became the curator of the Jardin des Plantes at a time when the study of natural history was at the forefront of contemporary thought – Charles Darwin's *The Origin of Species* was to be published 120 years later. Buffon masterminded the reorganization of the Jardin, propelling it to a pre-eminent position within the scientific world. He was elected to the Académie Française in 1752 following the publication of his two main works, *Natural History* and *The Epoques of Nature*. He died in his house in the Jardin.

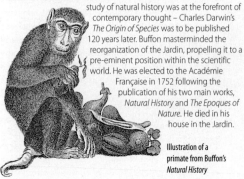

Illustration of a primate from Buffon's *Natural History*

❻ Place de la Contrescarpe

75005. **Map** 17 B1. Ⓜ Place Monge.

At one time, this site lay outside the city walls. It gets its name from the backfilling of the moat that ran along Philippe-Auguste's wall. The present square was laid out in 1852. At No. 1, there is a memorial plaque to the old "pine-cone club" immortalized in the writings of Rabelais; here, a group of writers known as *La Pléiade* (named after the constellation of The Pleiades) used to meet in the 16th century.

The area has always been used for meetings and festivals. Today, it is extremely lively at weekends, and on Bastille Day *(see p67)*, a delightful ball is held here.

Part of the medieval city wall

❼ Rue Mouffetard

75005. **Map** 17 B2. Ⓜ Censier-Daubenton, Place Monge.
Open Market Place Maubert: 7am–2.30pm Tue, Thu, Sat (to 3pm Sat); Place Monge: 7am– 2.30pm Wed, Fri, Sun (to 3pm Sun). *See Shops and Markets p331.*

A major thoroughfare since Roman times, when it linked Lutetia (Paris) and Rome, this street is one of the oldest in the city. In the 17th and 18th centuries, it was known as the Grande Rue du Faubourg St-Marcel, and many of its buildings date from that time. Some of the small shops still have ancient painted signs, and some houses have mansard roofs. No. 125 has an attractive, restored Louis XIII façade, and the entire front of No. 134 has beautiful decoration of wild beasts, flowers and plants. At No. 60, the *Fontaine de Pot-de-Fer* is a small fountain dating from Roman times. Later on, it was connected to an aqueduct used by Marie de Médicis to take water to the Palais du Luxembourg and its gardens.

The area is known for its open-air markets, especially those in Place Maubert, Place Monge, and Rue Daubenton, a side street where a lively African market takes place.

At night, the street bustles with people enjoying the Greek, Italian, Argentinian and other cuisines on offer at the many small restaurants.

❽ St-Médard

141 Rue Mouffetard 75005. **Map** 17 B2. **Tel** 01 44 08 87 00. Ⓜ Censier-Daubenton. **Open** Times vary; check website ahead of visit. 🚻 ♿
🌐 **saintmedard.org**

The origins of this charming church go back to the 9th century. St Médard, counsellor to the Merovingian kings, was known for giving a wreath of white roses to young girls noted for their virtue. The churchyard became notorious in the 18th century as the centre of the cult of the Convulsionnaires, whose hysterical fits were brought on by the contemplation of miracle cures. The interior has many fine paintings, including the 17th-century *St Joseph Walking with the Christ Child* by Francisco de Zurbarán.

Decoration inside the mosque

❾ Mosquée de Paris

2 bis Pl du Puits de l'Ermite 75005 (Turkish baths/tearoom: 39 Rue Geoffrey Saint-Hilaire). **Map** 17 C2. **Tel** 01 45 35 97 33; 01 43 31 38 20 (tearoom, baths). Ⓜ Place Monge. **Open** Baths: 10am–9pm Wed–Mon; tearoom: 9am–midnight daily. **Closed** Muslim hols. 🚫 ☐ 🛍 Library. 🌐 **mosqueedeparis.net** Café & baths: 🌐 **la-mosquee.com**

Built in the 1920s in the Hispano-Moorish style, this group of buildings is the spiritual centre for Paris's Muslim community and the home of the Grand Imam. The complex comprises religious, educational and commercial sections; at its heart is a mosque. Each of the mosque's domes is decorated differently, and the minaret stands nearly 33 m (100 ft) high. Inside is a grand patio with mosaics on the walls and tracery on the arches.

Once used only by scholars, the mosque's place in Parisian life has grown over the years. The Turkish baths are strictly for women only. A tearoom and restaurant serve Moorish specialities.

Skull of the reptile dimetrodon

❿ Muséum National d'Histoire Naturelle

2 Rue Buffon 75005. **Map** 17 C2. **Tel** 01 40 79 54 79. Ⓜ Jussieu, Austerlitz. **Open** Grande Galerie: 10am–6pm Wed–Mon. **Closed** 1 May. 🅿 ♿ restricted. 🖥 📷 Library. Ⓦ mnhn.fr

The highlight of the museum is the Grande Galerie de l'Evolution. There are also four other departments: palaeontology, featuring skeletons, casts of various animals and an exhibition showing the evolution of the vertebrate skeleton; palaeo-botany, devoted to plant fossils; mineralogy (closed for reno-vation), including gemstones; and entomology, with some of the oldest fossilized insects on earth. The bookshop is in the house that was occupied by the naturalist Buffon, from 1772 until his death in 1788.

⓫ Jardin des Plantes

57 Rue Cuvier/2 Rue Buffon 75005. **Map** 17 C1. **Tel** 01 40 79 56 01. Ⓜ Jussieu, Austerlitz. **Open** 7.30am–8pm (8am–5.30pm winter) daily. 🅿 📷

The botanical gardens were established in 1626, when Jean Hérouard and Guy de la Brosse, Louis XIII's physicians, obtained permission to found a royal medicinal herb garden here and then a school of botany, natural

history and pharmacy. The garden was opened to the public in 1640 and flourished under Buffon's direction. Now one of Paris's great parks, it includes a natural history museum, botanical school and zoo.

As well as beautiful vistas and walkways flanked by ancient trees and punctuated with statues, the park has a remarkable alpine garden with plants from Corsica, Morocco, the Alps and the Himalayas and an unrivalled display of herbaceous and wild plants. It also has the first Cedar of Lebanon to be planted in France, originally from Britain's Kew Gardens.

The Cedar of Lebanon, Jardin des Plantes

⓬ Groupe Hospitalier Pitié-Salpêtrière

47–83 Blvd de l'Hôpital 75013. **Map** 18 D3. **Tel** 01 42 16 00 00/17 60 60. Ⓜ St-Marcel, Austerlitz. 🚇 Gare d'Austerlitz. **Open** Chapel 9am– 6pm daily. ✝ 3.30pm daily. ♿

The vast Salpêtrière Hospital stands on the site of an old gunpowder factory and derives its name from the saltpetre used in the making of explosives. It was founded by Louis XIV in 1656 to help sick or socially-disadvantaged women and children and later became renowned for its pioneering humane treatment of the insane. Princess Diana died here in 1997, following an automobile accident in a Paris underpass.

Outside the Hôpital Salpêtrière

⓭ Mobilier National et La Manufacture des Gobelins

42 Ave des Gobelins 75013. **Map** 17 B3. **Tel** 01 44 08 53 49. Ⓜ Gobelins. **Open** 11am–6pm Tue–Sun (for temp exhibitions only). Groups by appt. 🅿 **Closed** 1 Jan, 1 May, 25 Dec. Ⓦ mobiliernational.culture.gouv.fr

Originally a dyeing workshop set up in about 1440 by the Gobelin brothers, the building became a tapestry factory early in the 17th century. Louis XIV took it over in 1662 and gathered together the greatest craftsmen of the day – carpet weavers, cabinet makers and silversmiths – to furnish his new palace at Versailles *(see pp250–55)*. Working under the direction of court painter Charles Le Brun, 250 Flemish weavers laid the foundations for the factory's international reputation. Today, weavers continue to work in the traditional way but with modern designs, including those of Picasso and Matisse.

Versailles tapestry by Le Brun, La Mobilier National et La Manufacture des Gobelins

LUXEMBOURG QUARTER

Many a Parisian dreams of living in the vicinity of the Luxembourg Gardens, a quieter, greener and more reflective place than its neighbouring areas. Luxembourg is one of the most captivating places in the capital. Its charm is in its old gateways and streets, its bookshops, and in the sumptuous yet intimate gardens. Though eminent writers such as Paul Verlaine and André Gide no longer stroll in its groves, the paths, lawns and avenues are still full of charm, drawing in numerous students from the nearby *grandes écoles* and *lycées*. On warm days, old men meet under the chestnut trees to play chess or the traditional game of boules. To the west, the buildings are public and official, and to the east, the houses are shaded by the tall chestnut trees of the Boulevard St-Michel.

Sights at a Glance

Historic Buildings and Streets
3 Palais du Luxembourg
6 Institut Catholique de Paris

Churches
2 St-Sulpice
7 St-Joseph-des-Carmes
10 Val-de-Grâce

Fountains
4 Fontaine Médicis
9 Fontaine de l'Observatoire

Squares, Parks and Gardens
1 Place St-Sulpice
5 Jardin du Luxembourg

Museums and Galleries
8 Musée du Luxembourg
11 Ecole Nationale Supérieure des Mines

☐ Restaurants see pp304–5
1 L'Auberge du 15
2 L'Ourcine
3 Les Papilles

See also Street Finder maps 12, 16

0 metres 400
0 yards 400

◀ Fontaine Médicis, Jardin du Luxembourg

For keys to symbols *see back flap*

Street-by-Street: Luxembourg Quarter

Situated only a few steps from the bustle of St-Germain-des-Prés, this graceful and historic area offers a peaceful haven in the heart of a modern city. The Jardin du Luxembourg and Palais du Luxembourg dominate the quarter. The gardens became fully open to the public in the 19th century under the ownership of the Comte de Provence (later Louis XVIII), when for a small fee visitors could come in and feast on fruit from the orchard. Today the gardens, palace and old houses on the streets to the north remain unspoilt and attract many visitors.

To St-Germain-des-Prés

❶ Place St-Sulpice
The Fontaine des Quatre Points Cardinaux depicts four church leaders at the cardinal points of the compass. Point also means "never": the leaders were never made cardinals.

❷ ★ St-Sulpice
This Classical church was built over 134 years to Daniel Gittard's plans. It has a facade by the Italian architect Giovanni Servandoni.

RUE HENRI DE JOUVENEL

RUE SERVANDONI

RUE GARANCIÈRE

RUE FEROU

RUE DE VAUGIRARD

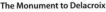

The Monument to Delacroix (1890) by Jules Dalou is situated near the private gardens of the French Senate. Beneath the bust of the leading Romantic painter Eugène Delacroix are the allegorical figures of Art, Time and Glory.

❺ ★ Jardin du Luxembourg
Many fine statues were erected in the Luxembourg gardens in the 19th century during the reign of Louis-Philippe.

The Rue de Tournon is full of elegant architecture, boutiques and old bookshops. At No. 12 is the Grand Hôtel d'Entragues, reconstructed by Neveu in the 18th century during Louis XVI's reign.

Locator Map
See Central Paris Map pp16–17

Key

— Suggested route

| 0 metres | 100 |
| 0 yards | 100 |

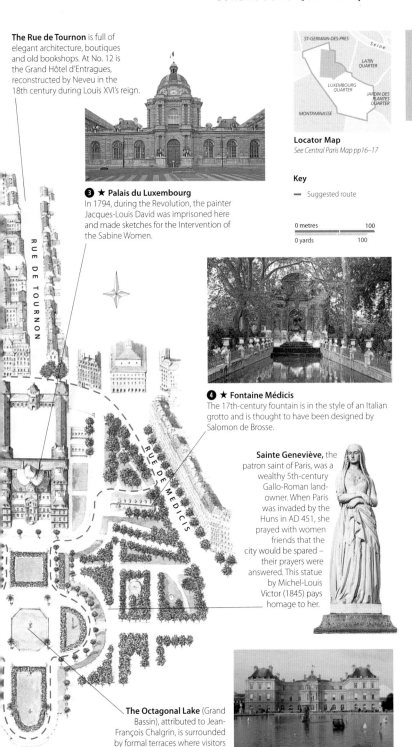

❸ ★ **Palais du Luxembourg**
In 1794, during the Revolution, the painter Jacques-Louis David was imprisoned here and made sketches for the Intervention of the Sabine Women.

RUE DE TOURNON

RUE DE MÉDICIS

❹ ★ **Fontaine Médicis**
The 17th-century fountain is in the style of an Italian grotto and is thought to have been designed by Salomon de Brosse.

Sainte Geneviève, the patron saint of Paris, was a wealthy 5th-century Gallo-Roman landowner. When Paris was invaded by the Huns in AD 451, she prayed with women friends that the city would be spared – their prayers were answered. This statue by Michel-Louis Victor (1845) pays homage to her.

The Octagonal Lake (Grand Bassin), attributed to Jean-François Chalgrin, is surrounded by formal terraces where visitors to the gardens often sunbathe.

❶ Place St-Sulpice

75006. **Map** 12 E4. Ⓜ St-Sulpice.

This large square, which is dominated on the east side by the enormous church from which it takes its name, was built in the last half of the 18th century.

Two main features of the square are the Fountain of the Four Bishops by Joachim Visconti (1844) and the pink-flowering chestnut trees. There is also the Café de la Mairie, a rendezvous of writers and students, which is often featured in French films.

Stained-glass window of St-Sulpice

❷ St-Sulpice

2 Rue Palatine, Pl St-Sulpice 75006. **Map** 12 E5. **Tel** 01 46 33 21 78. Ⓜ St-Sulpice. **Open** 7.30am–7.30pm daily. ✝ daily. 📷 (Tel 01 43 25 03 10).

It took more than a century, from 1646, for this huge and imposing church to be built. The result is a simple two-storey west front with two tiers of elegant columns. The overall harmony of the building is marred only by the towers, one at each end, which do not match.

Large arched windows fill the vast interior with light. By the front door are two huge shells given to François I by the Venetian Republic – they rest on rock-like bases sculpted by Jean-Baptiste Pigalle.

In the side chapel to the right of the main door are three magnificent murals by Eugène Delacroix: *Jacob Wrestling with the Angel (see p139), Heliodorus Driven from the Temple* and *St-Michael Killing the Dragon.* If you are lucky, you can catch an organ recital.

❸ Palais du Luxembourg

15 Rue de Vaugirard 75006. **Map** 12 E5. **Tel** 01 42 34 20 60 (groups, apply three months in advance); 01 44 54 19 30 (individuals). Ⓜ Odéon. 🅁🅔🅡 Luxembourg. 📷 one Sat each month. ✉ 🅦 **senat.fr**

Now the home of the French Senate, this palace was designed by Salomon de Brosse in the style of Florence's Pitti Palace to remind Marie de Médicis, widow of Henri IV, of her native town. By the time it was finished (1631), Marie had been banished, but it remained a royal palace until the Revolution, when it temporarily served as a prison. In World War II, it was the headquarters of the Luftwaffe, with air-raid shelters built under its gardens. The Musée du Luxembourg, in the east gallery, hosts renowned art exhibitions *(see p175).*

Figures on the Fontaine Médicis

❹ Fontaine Médicis

Jardin du Luxembourg, Rue de Vaugirard 75006. **Map** 12 F5. 🅁🅔🅡 Luxembourg.

Built in 1624 for Marie de Médicis by an unknown architect, this vigorous Baroque fountain stands at the end of a long pond filled with goldfish. The mythological figures were added much later by Auguste Ottin (1866).

❺ Jardin du Luxembourg

Blvd St-Michel/Rue de Vaugirard/Rue Guynemer 75006. **Map** 12 E5. **Tel** 01 42 34 23 89. Ⓜ Odéon. 🅁🅔🅡 Luxembourg. **Open** dawn–dusk daily. 🖥 🅦 **senat.fr/visite**

A green oasis covering 25 ha (60 acres) in the heart of the Left Bank, this is the most popular park in Paris. The layout is centred around the Luxembourg Palace and is dominated by a splendid octagonal pool – usually full of toy sailing boats.

Apart from the aesthetic attraction of its formal terraces and broad avenues, statues of various queens of France are also dotted throughout the park, as well as an impressive figure of Saint Genevieve, the patron of Paris, and, by way of contrast, a Cyclops.

The park also includes an open-air café, a puppet theatre, a large children's play area, tennis courts, a bandstand, a bee-keeping school and a gardening school.

Sculptures on Palais du Luxembourg

⑥ Institut Catholique de Paris

21 Rue d'Assas 75006. **Map** 12 D5. **Tel** 01 44 39 52 00. Ⓜ St-Placide, Rennes. Musée Bible et Terre Sainte **Closed** to the public. Tel 01 45 44 09 55. Ⓦ **icp.fr**

Founded in 1875, this is one of the most distinguished teaching institutions in France with some 23,000 students. It also houses a small museum: the Musée Bible et Terre Sainte which displays numerous objects excavated in the Holy Land. They give an interesting insight into daily life in Palestine through out the ages.

⑦ St-Joseph-des-Carmes

70 Rue de Vaugirard 75006. **Map** 12 D5. **Tel** 01 45 44 89 77. Ⓜ St-Placide. **Open** 7am–7pm Mon–Sat, 9am–7pm Sun. **Closed** Easter Mon, Pentecost. ⬆ ♿ restricted. 📷 3pm Sat. Ⓦ **sjdc.fr**

Completed in 1620, this church was built as the chapel for a Carmelite convent but was used as a prison during the Revolution. In 1792, more than a hundred priests met a grisly end in the church's courtyard as part of the September Massacres *(see pp32–3)*. Their remains are now in the crypt.

Façade of St-Joseph-des-Carmes, a site of the September Massacres in 1792

Carpeaux's fountain sculpture

⑧ Musée du Luxembourg

19 Rue de Vaugirard 75006. **Map** 12 E5. **Tel** 01 40 13 62 00. Ⓜ St-Sulpice. ⓇⒺⓇ Luxembourg. **Open** 10am–7.30pm daily (to 10pm Mon & Fri). Times vary depending on exhibitions; check website ahead of visit. **Closed** 1 May & 25 Dec. ♿ 🎧 📷 🛒 ✉ 🍴 Ⓦ **museeduluxembourg.fr**

In 1615, under the orders of Marie de Médicis, architect Salomon de Brosse built the Palais du Luxembourg. The two adjoining galleries were designed to hang the Queen's collection of paintings by Rubens. In 1750, the east wing became France's first public gallery, housing works by artists such as Leonardo da Vinci, Rembrandt and Van Dyck. Following extensive renovations, today it hosts impressive temporary exhibitions.

⑨ Fontaine de l'Observatoire

Ave de l'Observatoire/Rue d'Assas. **Map** 16 E2. ⓇⒺⓇ Port Royal.

Situated at the southern tip of the Jardin du Luxembourg, this is one of the liveliest fountains in Paris. Made of bronze, it has four women holding aloft a globe representing four continents –

the fifth, Oceania, was left out for reasons of symmetry. There are some subsidiary figures, including dolphins, horses and a turtle. The sculpture was erected in 1873 by Jean-Baptiste Carpeaux.

⑩ Val-de-Grâce

1 Pl Alphonse-Laveran 75005. **Map** 16 F2. **Tel** 01 40 51 51 92. Ⓜ Gobelins. ⓇⒺⓇ Port Royal. **Open** noon–6pm Tue–Thu, 1am–7.30pm. 🎧 🍴 frequent, pm; 11am Sun (except Aug). 📷 by appt. Museum **Open** as church. **Closed** 1 Jan, 1 May, 25 Dec. Concerts. Ⓦ **valdegrace.org**

One of the most beautiful churches in France, Val-de-Grâce was built for Anne of Austria (wife of Louis XIII) in thanks for the birth of her son. Young Louis XIV laid the first stone in 1645. François Mansart is the great architect behind it.

The church is noted for its imposing lead-and-gilt dome, which stands at an impressive 41 m (135 ft). In the cupola is Pierre Mignard's fresco, with over 200 triple-life-size figures. The six huge marble columns that frame the altar are similar to those at St Peter's in Rome. Henrietta of France (wife of Charles I) is buried here, along with 26 members of the French royal family.

Today, the church is part of a military hospital complex, which also houses a museum of military medicine.

⑪ Ecole Nationale Supérieure des Mines

60 Blvd St-Michel. **Map** 16 F1. **Tel** 01 40 51 91 39. ⓇⒺⓇ Luxembourg. Museum **Open** 1.30–6pm Tue–Fri; 10am–12.30pm, 2–5pm Sat. Times vary in Jul & Aug. **Closed** public hols. 🎧 📷 Ⓦ **musee.mines-paristech.fr**

Louis XIV set up the School of Mines in 1783 to train mining engineers. Today, it is one of the most prestigious *grandes écoles* – schools that provide the élite for the civil service and professions. It also houses the national collection of minerals – the *Musée de Minéralogie*.

MONTPARNASSE

In the first three decades of the 20th century, Montparnasse was a thriving artistic and literary centre. Many modern painters and sculptors, new novelists and poets, the great and the young were drawn to this area. Its ateliers, conviviality and renowned Bohemian lifestyle made it a magnet for genius, some of it French, much of it foreign. The great epoch ended with World War II, and change continued with the destruction of many ateliers and the construction of the soaring Tour Montparnasse, Paris's tallest office tower, which heralded the more modern *quartier*. But Montparnasse has not lost its appeal. The great cafés remain and attract a lively international crowd. There are small café-theatres, and the area springs to life at the weekends with movie-going crowds.

Sights at a Glance

Historic Buildings and Streets
3 Rue Campagne-Première
10 Catacombes de Paris
11 Observatoire de Paris

Modern Architecture
5 Tour Montparnasse

Cafés and Restaurants
1 La Coupole
12 La Closerie des Lilas

Cemeteries
4 Cimetière du Montparnasse pp182–3

Museums and Galleries
2 Musée Zadkine
6 Musée Antoine Bourdelle
7 Musée de la Poste
8 Musée du Montparnasse
9 Fondation Cartier

☐ **Restaurants** see pp304–5
1 L'Arbre de Sel
2 L'Assiette
3 La Cantine du Troquet
4 La Cerisaie
5 La Closerie des Lilas
6 La Coupole
7 Le Dôme
8 L'Epicuriste
9 Le Jeu de Quilles
10 Moustache
11 Le Parc aux Cerfs
12 Tavola di Gio
13 Le Timbre
14 Les Zazous

See also Street Finder maps 15–16

0 metres 400
0 yards 400

◄ Bronze angel statue at the Cimetière du Montparnasse

For keys to symbols *seen back flap*

Street-by-Street: Montparnasse

Renowned for its mix of art and high living,
Montparnasse continues to live up to its
name: Mount Parnassus was the mountain
dedicated by the ancient Greeks to Apollo,
god of poetry, music and beauty. That mix
was especially potent in the 1920s and 1930s,
when such artists and writers as Picasso,
Hemingway, Cocteau, Giacometti, Matisse
and Modigliani were to be seen in the local
bars, cafés and cabarets.

5 ★ **Tour Montparnasse**
One of Europe's tallest tower blocks rests on 56
piles that extend 62 m (203 ft) below the surface.

4 ★ **Cimetière du Montparnasse**
This fine sculpture, *The Separation of a Couple* by de Max, stands in the smallest of the city's major cemeteries.

Metro Edgar Quinet

RUE DU DEPART

RUE D'ODESSA

RUE DU MONTPARNASSE

BLV

RUE DE LA GAITE

BLVD EDGAR QUINE

The Théâtre Montparnasse at
No. 31, with its fully-restored
original 1880s decor.

Académie de la Grande-Chaumière at no. 14 offers tuition in painting and sculpture. Former students of note include Alberto Giacometti and Amedeo Modigliani.

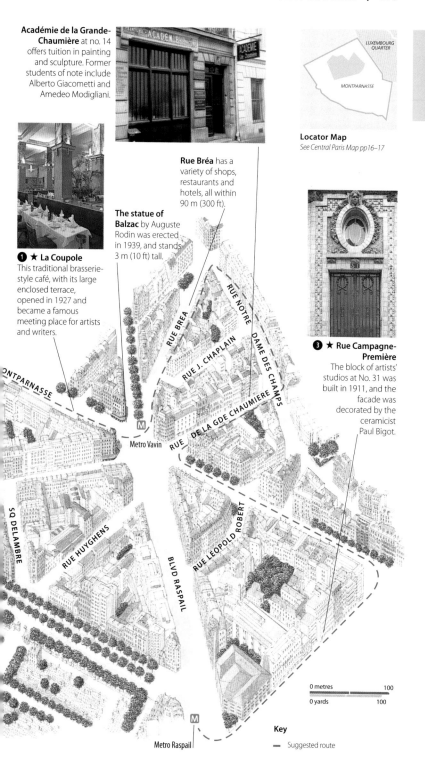

Locator Map
See Central Paris Map pp16–17

Rue Bréa has a variety of shops, restaurants and hotels, all within 90 m (300 ft).

The statue of Balzac by Auguste Rodin was erected in 1939, and stands 3 m (10 ft) tall.

❶ ★ La Coupole
This traditional brasserie-style café, with its large enclosed terrace, opened in 1927 and became a famous meeting place for artists and writers.

❸ ★ Rue Campagne-Première
The block of artists' studios at No. 31 was built in 1911, and the facade was decorated by the ceramicist Paul Bigot.

RUE BRÉA

RUE NOTRE DAME DES CHAMPS

RUE J. CHAPLAIN

RUE DE LA GDE CHAUMIERE

MONTPARNASSE

Metro Vavin

SQ DELAMBRE

RUE HUYGHENS

BLVD RASPAIL

RUE LEOPOLD ROBERT

Metro Raspail

0 metres 100
0 yards 100

Key

— Suggested route

❶ La Coupole

102 Blvd du Montparnasse 75014. **Map** 16 D2. **Tel** 01 43 20 14 20. Ⓜ Vavin, Montparnasse. **Open** 8.30am–midnight daily (from 8am Mon–Fri and to 11pm Sun & Mon). *See Restaurants & Cafés p311*

Established in 1927, this historic café-restaurant and dance hall underwent a face-lift in the 1980s. Its red velvet seats and famous columns, decorated by various artists, have survived. Among its clientele have been Jean-Paul Sartre, Josephine Baker and Roman Polanski.

Art Deco murals adorning the cavernous interiors of La Coupole

❷ Musée Zadkine

100 bis Rue d'Assas 75116. **Map** 16 E1. **Tel** 01 55 42 77 20. Ⓜ Notre-Dame-des-Champs. **Open** 10am–6pm Tue–Sun. **Closed** public hols. 🅿 🅲 by appt, Tel 01 49 54 75 92. ♿ limited. Ⓦ **zadkine.paris.fr**

The Russian-born sculptor Ossip Zadkine lived here from 1928 until his death in 1967. The small house, studio and garden contain his works. Here he produced his great commemorative sculpture, *Ville Détruite*, commissioned by Rotter-dam after World War II, and two monuments to Vincent Van Gogh, one for Holland and one for Auvers-sur-Oise, where Van Gogh died. The museum's works span the development of Zadkine's style, from his Cubist beginnings to Expressionism and Abstractionism.

❸ Rue Campagne-Première

75014. **Map** 16 E2. Ⓜ Raspail.

This street has some interesting Art Deco buildings and a long artistic tradition. Modigliani, ravaged by opium and tuberculosis, lived at No. 3 during his last years. Between the wars many artists resided here, including Picasso, Joan Miró and Kandinsky.

❹ Cimetière du Montparnasse

See pp182–3.

❺ Tour Montparnasse

33 Ave du Maine 75014. **Map** 15 C2. Ⓜ Montparnasse-Bienvenüe. **Tel** 01 45 38 52 56. **Open** Apr–Sep: 9.30am–11.30pm daily (last lift 11pm); Oct–Mar: 9.30am–10.30pm daily (to 11pm Fri & Sat). 🅿 🅲 🅳 🅵 Ⓦ **tourmontparnasse56.com**

This was Europe's largest office block when it was built in 1973 as the focal point of a new business sector. At 210 m (690 ft) high, it totally dominates the area's skyline.

The views from the 59th floor are spectacular (up to 40 km on a clear day). The tower also boasts Europe's fastest lift (56 floors in 38 seconds) and a panoramic bar.

Panoramic view of Paris from the 59th floor of Tour Montparnasse

Sculptures in the Great Hall of the Musée Antoine Bourdelle

❻ Musée Antoine Bourdelle

18 Rue Antoine Bourdelle 75015. **Map** 15 B1. **Tel** 01 49 54 73 73. Ⓜ Montparnasse-Bienvenüe. **Open** 10am–6pm Tue–Sun. **Closed** public hols. 🅿 ♿ limited. Ⓦ **bourdelle.paris.fr**

The prolific sculptor, Antoine Bourdelle, lived and worked in the studio here from 1884 until his death in 1929. The house, studio and garden are now a museum devoted to his life and work. Among the 900 sculptures on display are the original plaster casts of his monumental works planned for wide public squares. They are housed in the Great Hall in an extension and include the group of sculptures for the relief decoration of the Théâtre des Champs-Elysées.

❼ Musée de la Poste

34 Blvd de Vaugirard 75015. **Map** 15 B2. **Tel** 01 42 79 24 24. Ⓜ Montparnasse-Bienvenüe. **Open** 10am–6pm Mon–Sat (to 8pm 1st Thu of month). **Closed** public hols. 🅿 🅲 by appt. Library. Ⓦ **museede laposte.fr**

Every conceivable aspect of the history of the French postal service and methods of transportation is covered in this well laid out collection. There is even a room devoted to mail delivery in times of war – carrier pigeons were used during the Franco-Prussian War with postmarks stamped on their wings. Postage stamp art is displayed in the gallery.

Post boxes on display at Musée de la Poste

❽ Musée du Montparnasse

21 Ave du Maine 75015. **Map** 15 C1. **Tel** 01 42 22 91 96. Ⓜ Montparnasse-Bienvenüe, Falguière. **Closed** Temporarily closed to the public; check website for further details. Ⓦ **museedumont parnasse.net**

During World War I, this was a canteen for needy artists which, by its status as a private club, was not subject to curfew, and so the likes of Picasso, Braque, Modigliani and Léger could eat for 65 centimes and then party until late at night. This symbolic place is now dedicated to temporary art exhibitions, usually of an African theme, and also hosts evenings of music and poetry recitals.

❾ Fondation Cartier

261 Blvd Raspail 75014. **Map** 16 E3. **Tel** 01 42 18 56 50. Ⓜ Raspail. **Open** 11am–8pm Tue–Sun (to 10pm Tue). **Closed** 1 Jan, 25 Dec. 🅿 ♿ ✉ 📷 Ⓦ **fondation.cartier.com**

This foundation for contemporary art is housed in a building designed by architect Jean Nouvel. He has created an air of transparency and light, as well as incorporating a cedar of Lebanon planted in 1823 by François-René de Chateaubriand. The structure complements the nature of the exhibitions of progressive art, which showcase personal, group or thematic displays, often including works by young unknowns.

❿ Catacombes de Paris

1 Ave du Colonel Henri Rol-Tanguy 75014. **Map** 16 E4. **Tel** 01 43 22 47 63. Ⓜ Denfert-Rochereau. **Open** 10am–5pm Tue–Sun (last adm: 4pm). **Closed** public hols. 🎧 📷 Ⓦ **catacombes.paris.fr**

In 1786 a monumental project began here: the removal of the millions of skulls and bones from the unsanitary city cemetery in Les Halles to the ancient quarries formed by excavations at the base of the three "mountains": Montparnasse, Montrouge and Montsouris. It took 15 months to transport the bones and corpses across the city in huge carts to their new resting place at night.

It is believed that the Comte d'Artois (later Charles X) threw wild parties in the catacombs, and during World War II the French Resistance set up its headquarters here. Above the door outside are the words "Stop! This is the empire of death."

⓫ Observatoire de Paris

61 Ave de l'Observatoire 75014. **Map** 16 E3. **Tel** 01 40 51 22 21 (2–4pm Mon–Fri). Ⓜ Denfert-Rochereau. **Open** Guided tours only: 1st Wed each month at 2pm; groups: Mon, Wed, Fri 2–4pm. **Closed** Aug. 🎧 📷 Booking is essential: visite.paris@obspm.fr Ⓦ **obspm.fr**

In 1667 Louis XIV was persuaded by his scientists and astronomers that France needed a royal observatory. Building began on 21

June, the day of summer solstice, and took five years to complete. One of the leading centres in the world, research undertaken here included the calculation of the exact dimensions of the solar system in 1672, calculations of the dimensions of longitude, the mapping of the moon in 1679 and the discovery of the planet Neptune in 1846.

The facade of the Observatoire

⓬ La Closerie des Lilas

171 Blvd du Montparnasse 75014. **Map** 16 E2. **Tel** 01 40 51 34 50. Ⓜ Vavin. Ⓡ Port Royal. **Open** Bar: 11–1.30am, brasserie: noon–2.30pm & 7–10.30pm. Ⓦ **closeriedeslilas.fr**

Lenin, Trotsky, Hemingway and Scott Fitzgerald all frequented the Montparnasse bars, but the Closerie was their favourite. Much of Hemingway's novel *The Sun Also Rises* takes place here which he wrote on the terrace in just six weeks. Today the terrace is ringed with trees and the area more elegant, but much of the original decor remains (see pp40–41).

Skulls and bones stored in the catacombs

❹ Cimetière du Montparnasse

The Montparnasse Cemetery was planned by Napoleon outside the city walls to replace the numerous, congested small cemeteries within the old city, viewed as a health hazard at the turn of the 19th century. It was opened in 1824 and became the resting place of many illustrious Parisians, particularly Left Bank personalities. Like all French cemeteries, it is divided into rigidly aligned paths forming blocks or divisions. The Rue Emile Richard cuts it into two parts, the Grand Cimetière and the Petit Cimetière.

★ Charles Baudelaire Cenotaph
This is a monument to the great poet and critic (1821–67), author of *The Flowers of Evil.*

★ Charles Pigeon Family Tomb
This wonderfully pompous belle époque tomb depicts the French industrialist and inventor in bed with his wife.

KEY

① **Charles-Augustin Sainte-Beuve** was a critic of the French Romantic generation, and is generally described as the "father of modern criticism".

② **André Citroën**, an engineer and industrialist who died in 1935, founded the famous French car firm.

③ **Frédéric Auguste Bartholdi** was the sculptor of the Statue of Liberty (1886) in New York.

④ **Alfred Dreyfus** was a Jewish army officer whose unjust trial for treason in 1894 provoked a political and social scandal.

⑤ **The Pétain family tomb** contains the wife of the marshal who collaborated with the Germans during World War II. Pétain himself is buried on Ile d'Yeu, where he was imprisoned.

⑥ **Guy de Maupassant** was a 19th-century novelist.

⑦ **Samuel Beckett**, the great Irish playwright renowned for *Waiting for Godot*, spent most of his life in Paris. He died in 1989.

⑧ **The Tower** is all that remains of a 17th-century windmill. It was part of the old property of the Brothers of Charity on which the cemetery was built.

⑨ **Tristen Tzara**, the Romanian writer, was leader of the literary and artistic Dada movement in Paris in the 1920s.

⑩ **Man Ray** was an American photographer who immortalized the Montparnasse artistic and café scene in the 1920s and 1930s.

⑪ **Charles Baudelaire**, the 19th-century poet, is buried here in his detested stepfather's family tomb, along with his beloved mother.

⑫ **Chaïm Soutine**, a poor Jewish Lithuanian, was a Montparnasse Bohemian painter of the 1920s. He was a friend of the Italian artist Modigliani.

⑬ **Camille Saint-Saëns**, the pianist, organist and composer who died in 1921, was one of France's great post-Romantic musicians.

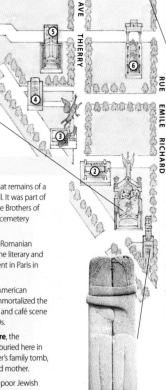

The Kiss by Brancusi
This is the famous Primitivo-Cubist sculpture (a response to Rodin's *Kiss*) by the great Romanian artist, who died in 1957 and is buried just off the Rue Emile Richard.

★ Serge Gainsbourg
The French singer, composer and pop icon of the 1970s and 1980s, is best known for his wistful and irreverent songs. He was married to the actress Jane Birkin.

VISITORS' CHECKLIST

Practical Information
3 Blvd Edgar Quinet.
Map 16 D3.
Tel 01 44 10 86 50.
Open Mid-Mar–mid-Nov:
8am–6pm Mon–Fri, 8.30am–6pm
Sat, 9am–6pm Sun; mid-Nov–
mid-Mar closes 5.30pm. 🅿 ♿

Transport
Ⓜ Edgar Quinet. 🚌 28, 58,
68, 82, 83, 88, 91 to Port Royal.
🚇 Port Royal. 🅿 Rue Campagne-
Première, Blvd St-Jacques

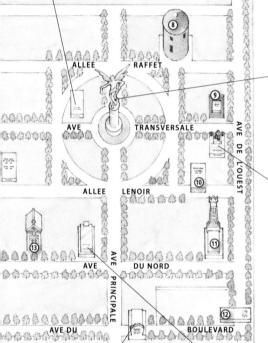

Génie du Sommeil Eternel
Horace Daillion's wistful bronze angel of Eternal Sleep (1902) is the cemetery's centrepiece.

Henri Laurens
The French sculptor (1885–1954) was a leading figure in the Cubist movement.

Jean Seberg
The Hollywood actress, chosen by Jean-Luc Godard as the star for his film *A Bout de Souffle,* was the epitome of American blonde beauty, youth and candour.

★ Jean-Paul Sartre and Simone de Beauvoir
The famous existentialist couple, undisputed leaders of the post-war literary scene, lie here close to their Left Bank haunts.

INVALIDES AND EIFFEL TOWER QUARTER

Everything in the area of Invalides is on a monumental scale. Starting from the sprawling 18th-century buildings of the Ecole Militaire on the corner of the Avenue de la Motte Picquet, the Parc du Champ de Mars stretches down to the Eiffel Tower and the Seine. The avenues around the Tower are lined with luxurious buildings, some in the Art Nouveau style, and numerous embassies. The area was already highly prized between the World Wars when the noted actor Sacha Guitry lived there. Even earlier, in the 18th century, wealthy residents of the Marais moved to this part of the city, building the aristocratic town houses that line the Rue de Varenne and Rue de Grenelle.

Sights at a Glance

Historic Buildings and Streets
⑥ Hôtel des Invalides
⑧ Hôtel Matignon
⑪ Assemblée Nationale Palais-Bourbon
⑫ Rue Cler
⑬ Les Egouts
⑮ Champ-de-Mars
⑰ No. 29 Avenue Rapp
⑲ Ecole Militaire

Church and Temples
① *Dôme des Invalides pp188–9*
② St-Louis-des-Invalides
⑩ Sainte-Clotilde

Modern Architecture
⑱ Village Suisse
⑳ UNESCO

Monuments and Fountains
⑯ *Eiffel Tower pp196–7*

Museums and Galleries
③ Musée de l'Ordre de la Libération
④ Musée de l'Armée
⑤ Musée des Plans-Reliefs
⑦ Musée Rodin
⑨ Musée Maillol
⑭ *Musée du quai Branly pp194–5*

Restaurants *see pp301–2*
1 L'Affable
2 L'Affriolé
3 L'Ami Jean
4 L'Arpège
5 Au Bon Accueil
6 Au Petit Sud Ouest
7 La Billebaude
8 Café Constant
9 Les Cocottes de Christian Constant
10 Coutume
11 Le Florimond
12 La Fontaine de Mars
13 Giallo Oro
14 Le Jules Verne
15 Pasco
16 Le Troquet
17 La Villa Corse

See also Street Finder maps 9–10, 11

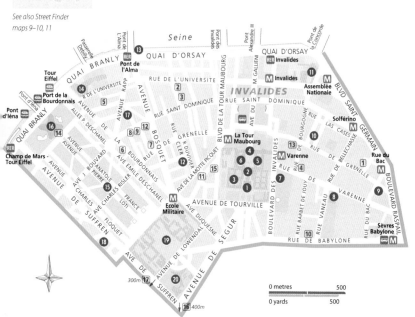

◀ View of the Eiffel Tower

For keys to symbols *see back flap*

Street-by-Street: Invalides

The imposing Hôtel des Invalides, from which the area takes its name, was built from 1671 to 1676 by Louis XIV for his wounded and homeless veterans and as a monument to his own glory. At its centre, the glittering golden roof of the Sun King's Dôme des Invalides marks the final resting place of Napoleon Bonaparte. The emperor's body was brought here from St Helena in 1840, 19 years after he died, and placed inside the majestic red sarcophagus, designed by Joachim Visconti, that lies at the centre of the Dôme's circular glass-topped crypt. Just to the east of the Hôtel on the corner of the Boulevard des Invalides, the superb Musée Rodin offers artistic relief from the pomp and circumstance of the surrounding area.

General de Gaulle's Liberation Order and compass

Metro La Tour Maubourg

The façade of the Hôtel is 196 m (645 ft) long and is topped by dormer windows, each decorated in the shape of a different trophy. A head of Hercules sits above the central entrance.

❹ ★ Musée de l'Armée
This vast museum covers military history from the Stone Age to World War II. It contains the third-largest collection of armoury in the world.

❸ Musée de l'Ordre de la Libération
The Order was set up to honour feats of heroism during World War II.

❷ ★ Cathedral of St-Louis-des-Invalides
From St-Louis, the soldier's chapel, it is possible to see into the Dôme, which was built as Louis XIV's private chapel.

AVE DE TOURVILLE

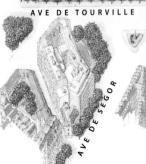

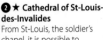

| 0 metres | 100 |
| 0 yards | 100 |

❻ Hôtel des Invalides
After the two World Wars, Louis XIV's Hôtel was returned to its original use as a hospital for veterans.

Locator Map
See Central Paris Map pp16–17

Key

— Suggested route

Metro Varenne

The Invalides gardens were designed by de Cotte in 1704 and are lined by bronze cannons from the 17th and 18th centuries.

❺ Musées des Plans-Reliefs
This museum contains military models of forts and towns, as well as a display on model-making.

❼ ★ Musée Rodin
By the time he died in 1917, Auguste Rodin had revolutionized the art of sculpture. All his key works, including *The Thinker* (c. 1880), are on display.

The Cour d'Honneur is still used for military parades. Seurre's statue of Napoleon, known as the Little Corporal, stands above the south side.

❶ ★ Dôme des Invalides and Napoleon's Tomb
The Dôme took 27 years to build. In the crypt lies Napoleon, whose final wish was to have his ashes "rest on the banks of the Seine".

❶ Dôme des Invalides

Jules Hardouin-Mansart was asked in 1676 by the Sun King, Louis XIV, to build the Dôme des Invalides among the existing buildings of the Invalides military complex. A soldiers' church had already been built, but the Dôme was to be reserved for the exclusive use of the Sun King and for the location of royal tombs. The resulting masterpiece complements the surrounding buildings and is one of the greatest examples of 17th-century French architecture.

After Louis XIV's death, plans to bury the royal family in the church were abandoned, and it became a monument to Bourbon glory. In 1840 Louis-Philippe decided to install Napoleon's remains in the crypt, and the addition of the tombs of Vauban, Marshal Foch and other figures of military prominence have since turned this church into a French military memorial.

Gilded Dome
The cupola was first gilded in 1706.

① **Tomb of Joseph Bonaparte**
The sarcophagus of Napoleon's older brother, the King of Naples and later of Spain, is in the side chapel to the right as visitors enter.

Key

━ Tour route

Main entrance

② **Memorial to Vauban**
Commissioned by Napoleon I in 1808, this contains an urn with Sébastien le Prestre de Vauban's heart. He was Louis XIV's great military architect and engineer who died in 1707. His long military career culminated in his appointment as Marshal of France in 1703. He revolutionized siege warfare when he introduced his ricochet-batteries. His reclining figure by Antoine Etex lies on top of the memorial, mourned by Science and War.

⑥ Glass Gallery
Access to the glass-topped crypt containing Napoleon's tomb is by the curved stairs in front of the altar. The glass partition behind the altar separates the Dôme from the older Invalides chapel beyond.

VISITORS' CHECKLIST

Practical Information
Esplanade des Invalides.
Map 11 A4. **Tel** 08 10 11 33 99
Hôtel National des Invalides:
Open Apr– Oct: 10am–6pm
daily (Jul & Aug: to 7pm; Apr–Sep:
to 9pm Tue), Nov–Mar: 10am–
5pm daily. **Closed** 1st Mon of
month, 1 Jan, 1 May, 25 Dec. 🅿️
♿ restricted (01 47 05 36 47).
📷 groups. 📱 📸

Transport
Ⓜ La Tour- Maubourg, Varenne.
🚌 28, 63, 69, 80, 82, 83, 87, 92, 93
to Les Invalides. Ⓡ Invalides. 🅾️
Tour Eiffel. 🅿️ Rue de Constantine.

⑤ St Jérôme's Chapel
Passing across the centre of the church, the side chapel to the right of the main entrance contains the tomb of Napoleon's younger brother, Jérôme, King of Westphalia presenting his sword to Christ.

Stairs to crypt

③

④ Dôme Ceiling
Looking upwards, Charles de la Fosse's circular painting (1692) on the ceiling shows the Glory of Paradise, with Saint Louis presenting his sword to Christ.

Napoleon's Return

King Louis-Philippe decided to bring the Emperor Napoleon's body back from St Helena (see pp34–5) as a gesture of reconciliation to the Republican and Bonapartist parties contesting his regime. The Dôme des Invalides, with its historical and military associations, was an obvious choice for Napoleon's final resting place. His body was encased in six coffins and finally placed in the crypt in 1861, in the culmination of a grand ceremony which was attended by Napoleon III.

③ Tomb of Marshal Foch
Ferdinand Foch's imposing bronze tomb was built by Paul Landowski in 1937.

The impressive altar of St-Louis-des-Invalides

❷ Cathedral of St-Louis-des-Invalides

Hôtel des Invalides, Esplanade des Invalides/129 Rue de Grenelle 75007. **Map** 11 A3. Ⓜ Varenne, La Tour-Maubourg. Ⓡ Invalides. **Tel** 08 10 11 33 99/01 44 42 38 77. **Open** Apr–Oct: 10am–6pm daily; Nov–Mar: 10am–5pm daily. **Closed** 1 Jan, 1 May, 25 Dec.

The "soldiers' church" was built from 1679 to 1708 by Jules Hardouin-Mansart from the original designs by Libéral Bruand. The imposing, but stark, interior is decorated with banners seized in battle.

The fine 17th-century organ was built by Alexandre Thierry. The first performance of Berlioz's *Requiem* was given on it in 1837, with an orchestra accompanied by a battery of outside artillery.

❸ Musée de l'Ordre de la Libération

Hôtel des Invalides, 51 bis Blvd de La Tour-Maubourg, 75007. **Map** 11 A3. **Tel** 01 47 05 04 10. Ⓜ La Tour-Maubourg. **Closed** for renovations until June 2015. 📷 🖼

This museum is devoted to the wartime Free French and their

leader, General Charles de Gaulle. The Order of Liberation was created by de Gaulle in 1940. It is France's highest honour and was bestowed on those who made an outstanding contribution to the final victory in World War II.

Those who received the honour were French civilians and members of the armed forces, plus some famous overseas leaders, including King George VI, Winston Churchill and General Dwight Eisenhower.

❹ Musée de l'Armée

Hôtel des Invalides, Esplanade des Invalides/Place Vauban 75007. **Map** 11 A3. **Tel** 08 10 11 33 99. Ⓜ La Tour-Maubourg, Varenne. Ⓡ Invalides. **Open** 10am–6pm (Nov–Mar: 5pm) daily (last adm: 30 mins before closing time). Times may vary; check website ahead of visit. **Closed** 1st Mon of month (except Jul, Aug, Sep), 1 Jan, 1 May, 25 Dec. 📷 (Ticket includes entry to the Musée de l'Ordre de la Libération and the Musée des Plans-Reliefs.) ♿ ground floor only. 📷 🖼 📷 Film. 🌐 **musee-armee.fr**

This is one of the most comprehensive museums of military history in the world, with exhibits ranging from the Stone Age to the final days of World War II. The third-largest collection of armoury in the world is housed here.

Situated in the northeast refectory, the Ancient Armoury department is worth visiting for the collection on display as much as for the 17th-century murals by Joseph Parrocel adorning the walls. These celebrate Louis XIV's military conquests.

The life of Charles de Gaulle and his role in World War II are documented in the *Historial de Gaulle*, a film and multi-media attraction (closed

on Mondays). The Département Moderne is in two parts: the first (1648–1792) covers the reign of Louis XIV, while the second (1792–1871) displays a collection of Napoleon's mementoes. Items include his famous frock coat and felt hats, as well as his stuffed dog.

A map of Alessandria, Italy (1813)

❺ Musée des Plans-Reliefs

Hôtel des Invalides 75007. **Map** 11 A3. **Tel** 01 45 51 92 45. Ⓜ La Tour-Maubourg, Varenne. Ⓡ Invalides. **Open** 10am–6pm (Nov–Mar: 5pm) daily. **Closed** 1st Mon of month (except Jul, Aug, Sep), 1 Jan, 1 May, 1 Nov, 25 Dec. 📷 🖼 🌐 **museedesplans reliefs.culture.fr**

The detailed models of French forts and fortified towns, some dating back to Louis XIV's reign, were considered top secret until the 1950s, when they were put on public display. The oldest model is that of Perpignan, dating to 1686. It shows the fortifications drawn up by the legendary 17th-century military architect Vauban, who built the defences around several French towns, including Briançon.

The façade of the Musée de l'Ordre de la Libération

The Invalides main entrance

❻ Hôtel des Invalides

Esplanade des Invalides 75007. **Map** 11 A3. **Tel** 08 10 11 33 99. La Tour-Maubourg, Varenne. **Open** 7.30am–7pm daily (Apr–Sep: to 9pm Tue). Last adm: 15 mins before closing time. **Closed** 1 Jan, 1 May, 25 Dec. 🚻 🛒 **musee-armee.fr**

Founded by Louis XIV, this was the first military hospital and home for French war veterans and disabled soldiers who had hitherto been reduced to begging. The decree for building this vast complex was signed in 1670, and construction, following the designs of Libéral Bruand, was finished five years later.

Today, the Classical façade is one of the most impressive sights in Paris, with its four storeys, cannon in the forecourt, garden and tree-lined esplanade stretching to the Seine. The south side leads to the Cathedral of St-Louis-des-Invalides, the soldiers' church, which backs on to the magnificent Dôme des Invalides of Jules Hardouin-Mansart. The dome was regilded in 1989 and now glitters anew.

❼ Musée Rodin

79 Rue de Varenne 75007. **Map** 11 B3. **Tel** 01 44 18 61 10. Varenne. **Open** 10am–5.45pm Tue–Sun (to 8.45pm Wed). **Closed** 1 Jan, 1 May, 25 Dec. 🚻 🛒 restricted. 🛒 🛒 occas. **musee-rodin.fr**

Auguste Rodin, widely regarded as the greatest 19th-century French

sculptor, lived and worked in the elegant Hôtel Biron from 1908 until his death in 1917.

In return for a state-owned flat and studio, Rodin left his work to the nation, and it is now exhibited here. Some of his most celebrated sculptures are on display in the garden: *The Burghers of Calais*, *The Thinker*, *The Gates of Hell* and *Balzac*. Inside, exhibits span the whole of Rodin's career.

Between 2012 and 2014, the museum underwent extensive renovation of Hôtel Biron which resulted in a more accessible and effective layout of the permanent collection.

❽ Hôtel Matignon

57 Rue de Varenne 75007. **Map** 11 C4. **Tel** 01 42 75 80 00. Solférino, Rue du Bac. **Closed** to the public, but garden open to public 1st Sat of each month.

One of the most beautiful mansions in the Faubourg area, this was built by Jean Courtonne in 1721 and has been substantially remodelled since. Former owners include Talleyrand, the statesman and diplomat who held legendary parties here, and several members of the nobility. It has been the official residence of the French Prime Minister since 1958 and has the largest private garden in Paris.

Rodin's *The Kiss* (1886) at the Musée Rodin

❾ Musée Maillol

59/61 Rue de Grenelle 75007. **Map** 11 C4. **Tel** 01 42 22 59 58. Sèvres-Babylone, Rue du Bac. **Open** 10.30am–7pm Wed–Mon (to 9.30pm Fri & Mon; last adm 45 mins before). **Closed** 1 Jan, 25 Dec. 🛒 🛒 🛒 🛒 **museemaillol.com**

Once the home of novelist Alfred de Musset, this museum was created by Dina Vierny, former model of Aristide Maillol. All aspects of the artist's work are here: drawings, engravings, paintings, sculpture and decorative objects. Also displayed is Vierny's private collection, including works by Matisse, Picasso and Rodin.

Large allegorical figures of the city of Paris and the four seasons decorate Bouchardon's fountain in front of the house.

Sculptured figures at Ste-Clotilde

❿ Sainte-Clotilde

12 Rue de Martignac 75007. **Map** 11 B3. **Tel** 01 44 18 62 60. Solférino, Varenne, Invalides. **Open** 9am–7.30pm Mon–Fri, 10am–8pm Sat & Sun. Times vary for Jul & Aug; check website. **Closed** non-religious public hols. 🛒 🛒 **sainte-clothilde.com**

Designed by the German-born architect François-Christian Gau and the first of its kind to be built in Paris, this Neo-Gothic church was inspired by the mid-19th-century enthusiasm for the Middle Ages, made fashionable by such writers as Victor Hugo. The church is noted for its imposing twin towers, visible from across the Seine. The interior includes sculpted stations of the cross by James Pradier and stained-glass windows. The composer César Franck was the organist here for 32 years.

Neo-Classical façade of the Assemblée Nationale Palais-Bourbon

⓫ Assemblée Nationale Palais-Bourbon

126 Rue de l'Université 75007. **Map** 11 B2. **Tel** 01 40 63 60 00. Ⓜ Assemblée-Nationale. Ⓡ Invalides. **Open** during sessions: guided visits on Sat at 10am, 11am, 2pm & 3pm. Outside sessions: reserve about 2 months in advance; call 01 40 63 56 00 for details 10am–noon Mon–Fri. 📷 🎧 🌐 **assemblee-nationale.fr**

Built in 1722 for the Duchesse de Bourbon, daughter of Louis XIV, the Palais-Bourbon was confiscated during the Revolution. It has been home to the lower house of the French Parliament since 1830.

During World War II, the palace became the Nazi administration's seat of government. The public can enter to watch parliament in action. The grand Neo-Classical façade with its fine columns was added in 1806, partly to mirror the facade of La Madeleine church facing it across the Seine. The adjacent Hôtel de Lassay is the residence of the president of the National Assembly.

⓬ Rue Cler

75007. **Map** 10 F3. Ⓜ Ecole-Militaire, La Tour-Maubourg. Market: **Open** Tue–Sat, Sun am. *See Shops and Markets p330*

This is the street market of the seventh arrondissement, the richest in Paris, for here live the bulk of senior civil servants, captains of industry and many diplomats. The market area occupies a pedestrian precinct stretching south from the Rue de Grenelle. It is colourful, but very much an exclusive market, with the best-dressed shoppers in town. The produce is excellent, the pâtisserie and cheese shops in particular.

⓭ Les Egouts

Pont Alma, Right Bank, opposite 93 Quai d'Orsay 75007. **Map** 10 F2. **Tel** 01 53 68 27 81. Ⓜ Alma-Marceau. Ⓡ Pont de l'Alma. **Open** Oct–Apr: 11am–5pm Sat–Wed (until 6pm from May–Sep). Last adm 1 hr before closing. **Closed** 1 Jan, 2 wks Jan, 25 Dec. 🎧 📷

One of Baron Haussmann's finest achievements, the majority of Paris's sewers (*égouts*) date from the Second Empire (*see pp34–5*). If laid end to end, the 2,100 km (1,300 miles) of sewers would stretch from Paris to Istanbul. In the 20th century, the sewers became a popular attraction. All tours are limited to a small area around the Quai d'Orsay entrance and are on foot (the sewers may close after heavy rain). Be aware that they can be dangerous to explore on your own, instead discover the mysteries of underground Paris at the Sewer Museum.

⓮ Musée du quai Branly

See pp194–5.

⓯ Champ-de-Mars

75007. **Map** 10 E3. Ⓜ Ecole-Militaire. Ⓡ Champ-de-Mars–Tour-Eiffel.

The gardens stretching from the Eiffel Tower to the Ecole Militaire were originally a parade ground for the officer cadets of the Ecole Militaire. The area has since been used for horse-racing, balloon ascents and the mass celebrations for 14 July, the anniversary of the Revolution. The first ceremony was held in 1790 in the presence of a glum, captive Louis XVI.

An illustration of a balloon

Vast exhibitions were held here in the late 19th century, including the 1889 World Fair for which the Eiffel Tower was erected. *Le Mur de la Paix*, Jean-Michel Wilmotte's monument to world peace, stands at one end.

The fruit and vegetable market in the Rue Cler

Doorway at No. 29 Avenue Rapp

⑯ Eiffel Tower

See pp196–7.

⑰ No. 29 Avenue Rapp

75007. **Map** 10 E2. M Pont-de-l'Alma.

A prime example of Art Nouveau architecture is No. 29 and it won its designer, Jules Lavirotte, first prize at the Concours des Facades de la Ville de Paris in 1901. Its ceramics and brickwork are decorated with animal and flower motifs intermingling with female figures. These are superimposed on a multi-coloured sandstone base to produce a façade that is deliberately erotic, and was certainly subversive in its day. Also worth visiting is Lavirotte's building, complete with watchtower, which can be found in the Square Rapp.

⑱ Village Suisse

38-78 Ave de Suffren/54 Ave de la Motte-Piquet. **Map** 10 E4. **Tel** 01 73 79 15 41. M Dupleix. **Open** 10.30am–7pm Thu–Mon.

The Swiss government built a mock-Alpine village for the 1900 Universal Exhibition held in the Champ-de-Mars nearby. It was later used as a centre for dealing in secondhand goods. In the 1950s and 1960s, antique dealers moved in, and everything became more fashionable and expensive.

⑲ Ecole Militaire

1 Pl Joffre 75007. **Map** 10 F4. **Tel** 01 80 50 14 00. M Ecole-Militaire. **Open** by special permission only – contact the Commandant in writing at Ecole de Guerre, Case 46, 75700 Paris SP07.

The Royal Military Academy of Louis XV was founded in 1751 to educate 500 sons of impoverished officers. It was designed by architect Jacques-Ange Gabriel, and one of the features is the central pavilion. This is a magnificent example of the French Classical style, with eight Corinthian pillars and a quadrangular dome. The interior is decorated in Louis XVI style; of main interest are the chapel and a Gabriel-designed wrought-iron banister on the main staircase. An early cadet was Napoleon, whose passing-out report stated that "he could go far if the circumstances are right".

⑳ UNESCO

7 Pl de Fontenoy 75007. **Map** 10 F5. **Tel** 01 45 68 10 00, 01 45 68 10 60 (in English). M Ségur, Cambronne. **Open** by guided visits only: 10am & 3pm Tue–Fri, duration 30 min. **Closed** public hols; Sat & Sun. Closed every 6 months for 3 weeks for official sessions. Booking essential: visits@unesco.org by reservation. Exhibitions, films. **w** unesco.org

This is the headquarters of the United Nations Educational, Scientific and Cultural Organization (UNESCO). The organization's stated aim is to contribute to international peace and security through education, science and culture.

It is a trove of modern art, notably a huge mural by Picasso and sculptures by Henry Moore.

Moore's *Reclining Figure* at UNESCO (erected 1958)

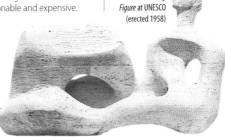

⑭ Musée du quai Branly

Widely regarded as former President Jacques Chirac's legacy to Paris's cultural scene, quai Branly has proved a major tourist pull since it opened in 2006. The stylish Jean Nouvel building displays 3,500 exhibits from the French state's vast non-western art collection, one of the world's most prolific. Outside, the grounds offer visitors breathing space and in summer, the museum's 500-seat auditorium opens onto an outdoor theatre for music and dance. The rooftop restaurant boasts breathtaking views.

Interior
Subdued natural light creates intimacy, while an undulating open-plan design reflects the diversity and convergence of different cultures.

Scarecrow (Vietnam)
This bamboo scarecrow is used by hill minorities in South East Asia to protect the rice fields. It is adorned with powerful and protective designs like the central "solar" symbol.

Musical instrument tower

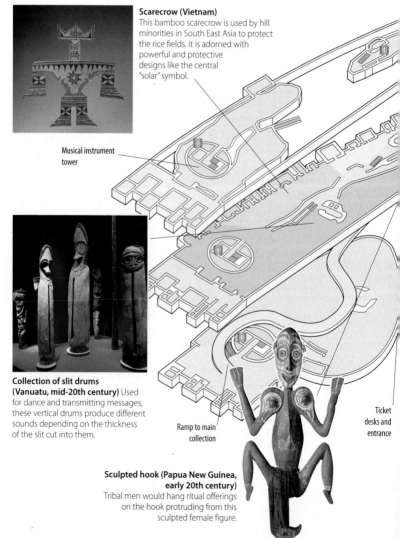

Collection of slit drums (Vanuatu, mid-20th century) Used for dance and transmitting messages, these vertical drums produce different sounds depending on the thickness of the slit cut into them.

Ramp to main collection

Ticket desks and entrance

Sculpted hook (Papua New Guinea, early 20th century)
Tribal men would hang ritual offerings on the hook protruding from this sculpted female figure.

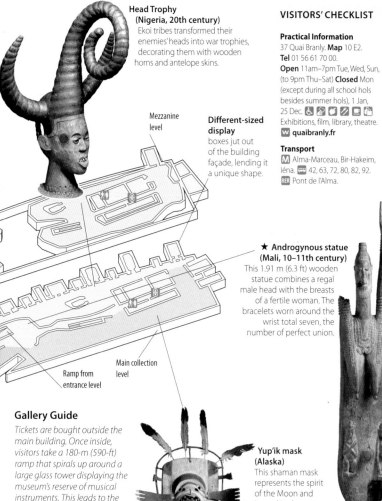

**Head Trophy
(Nigeria, 20th century)**
Ekoi tribes transformed their
enemies' heads into war trophies,
decorating them with wooden
horns and antelope skins.

Mezzanine
level

**Different-sized
display**
boxes jut out
of the building
façade, lending it
a unique shape.

★ **Androgynous statue
(Mali, 10–11th century)**
This 1.91 m (6.3 ft) wooden
statue combines a regal
male head with the breasts
of a fertile woman. The
bracelets worn around the
wrist total seven, the
number of perfect union.

Main collection
level

Ramp from
entrance level

Gallery Guide

*Tickets are bought outside the
main building. Once inside,
visitors take a 180-m (590-ft)
ramp that spirals up around a
large glass tower displaying the
museum's reserve of musical
instruments. This leads to the
main collection level, where
a suggested route passes
through four colour-coded
zones of Oceania, Asia, Africa
and the Americas. There are
stairs from the main collection
level to the three mezzanine
galleries, all of which house
temporary exhibitions.*

**Yup'ik mask
(Alaska)**
This shaman mask
represents the spirit
of the Moon and
is used in dances
performed inside
the communal
men's house.

Key to Floorplan

- 🟦 Asia
- ⬜ Africa
- 🟦 The Americas
- 🟩 Oceania
- ⬜ Temporary exhibition space
- 🟨 Musical instrument tower
- ⬜ Non-exhibition space

★ **Museum architecture**
Set on pillars above the verdant museum gardens, architect Jean
Nouvel's elegant building resembles the elongated shadow of the
nearby Eiffel Tower. An exterior glass wall and thickets of trees help
shield the museum from the outside world.

⓰ Eiffel Tower

Originally built to impress visitors to the 1889 Universal Exhibition, the Eiffel Tower (Tour Eiffel) was meant to be a temporary addition to the Paris skyline. Built by the engineer Gustave Eiffel, it was fiercely decried by 19th-century aesthetes. The author Guy de Maupassant lunched there to avoid seeing it. The world's tallest building until 1931, when New York's Empire State Building was completed, the tower is now the symbol of Paris. During the 2014 renovations, a glass floor was installed on the first level, in addition to an interactive museum chronicling the past and present of the tower.

Lift Engine Room
Eiffel emphasized safety over speed when choosing the lifts for the tower.

Ironwork Pattern
According to Eiffel, the complex pattern of wrought-iron girders came from the need to stabilize the tower in strong winds. But Eiffel's design quickly won admirers for its pleasing symmetry.

The Daring and the Deluded

The tower has inspired many crazy stunts. It has been climbed by mountaineers, cycled down by a journalist, and used by trapeze artists and as a launch pad by parachutists. In 1912, an Austrian tailor, Franz Reichelt, attempted to fly from the parapet with only a modified cape for wings. He plunged to his death in front of a large crowd. According to the autopsy, he died of a heart attack before even touching the ground.

Birdman Reichelt

★ **Hydraulic Lift Mechanism**
Still in working order, this part of the original 1900 mechanism was automated in 1986.

KEY

① **The third level**, 276 m (905 ft) above the ground, can hold 400 people at a time.

② **Le Jules Verne Restaurant** is one of the best restaurants in Paris, offering superb food and panoramic views *(see p302)*.

③ **The second level** is at 115 m (376 ft), separated from the first level by 359 steps, or a few minutes in the lift.

④ **The first level**, at 57 m (187 ft) high, can be reached by lift or by 345 steps.

Champ-de-Mars
The gardens of this former parade ground stretch from the base of the tower to the Ecole Militaire.

★ Viewing Gallery
On a clear day, it is possible to see for
72 km (45 miles), including a distant
view of Chartres Cathedral.

Double-Decker Lifts
During the tourist season, the limited
capacity of the lifts means that it can take
up to a couple of hours to reach the top.
Queuing for the lifts requires patience
and a good head for heights.

The Tower in Figures

- The top (including the antennae) is 324 m
  (1,063 ft) high
- The top can move in a curve of 18 cm (7 in)
  under the effect of heat
- 1,665 steps to the third level
- 2.5 million rivets hold the tower together
- Never sways more than 7 cm (2.5 in)
- 10,100 tonnes in weight
- 60 tonnes of paint are used every
  seven years

A workman building the tower

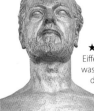

★ Eiffel Bust
Eiffel's (1832–1923) achievement
was crowned with the Légion
d'Honneur in 1889. Another
honour was the bust by
Antoine Bourdelle,
placed beneath the
tower in 1929.

CHAILLOT QUARTER

The village of Chaillot was absorbed into Paris in the 19th century and transformed into an area rich in grand Second Empire avenues (*see pp36–7*) and opulent mansions. Some of the avenues converge on the Place du Trocadéro, once renowned for its elegant cafés, which leads to the Avenue du Président Wilson, with a greater concentration of museums than any other street in Paris. Many of the area's private mansions are occupied by embassies, including the imposing Vatican embassy, and by major company headquarters. To the west is the territory of the *haute bourgeoisie*, one of Paris's most exclusive, if staid, residential neighbourhoods.

Sights at a Glance

Gardens
6 Jardins du Trocadéro

Modern Architecture
1 Palais de Chaillot

Aquarium
2 Aquarium de Paris – Cinéaqua

Cemeteries
10 Cimetière de Passy

Museums and Galleries
3 Cité de l'Architecture et du Patrimoine
4 Musée de l'Homme
5 Musée National de la Marine
7 Musée du Vin
8 Maison de Balzac
9 Maison de Radio-France
11 Musée de la Contrefaçon
12 Musée Dapper

13 Galerie-Musée Baccarat
14 Musée National des Arts Asiatiques Guimet
15 Musée Galliera
16 Musée d'Art Moderne de la Ville de Paris
17 Palais de Tokyo

See also Street Finder maps 3–4, 9–10

Restaurants *see pp300–301*

1 6 New York
2 Antoine
3 L'Astrance
4 Chez Géraud
5 Hiramatsu
6 Paul Chêne
7 Prunier

◀ Gilded bronze statues outside the Palais de Chaillot, with the Eiffel Tower in the background   **For keys to symbols** *see back flap*

Street-by-Street: Chaillot

The Chaillot hill, with its superb position overlooking the Seine, was the site chosen by Napoleon for "the biggest and most extraordinary" palace that was to be built for his son – but by the time of his downfall only a few ramparts had been completed. Today, the monumental Palais de Chaillot, with its two massive curved wings, stands on the site. From the terrace in front of the Palais there is a magnificent view over the Trocadéro gardens and the Seine to the Eiffel Tower.

The statue of Marshal Ferdinand Foch, who led the Allies to victory in 1918, was unveiled on 11 November 1951. The monument was built by Robert Wlérick and Raymond Martin to commemorate the centenary of Foch's birth and the 33rd anniversary of the 1918 Armistice.

Metro Trocadéro

PL DU TROCADERO

The Place du Trocadéro was created for the Universal Exhibition of 1878. Initially it was known as the Place du Roi-de-Rome, in honour of Napoleon's son.

PL J MARTI

AVE PAUL DOUMER

RUE FRANKLIN

BLVD DELESSERT

RUE LE NO...

5 ★ Musée de la Marine
With a focus on France's maritime history, this museum includes exhibits of navigational instruments.

0 metres	100
0 yards	100

1 ★ Palais de Chaillot
This Neo-Classical building was created for the World Fair of 1937. It replaced the Palais du Trocadéro, which was originally built in 1878.

4 Musée de l'Homme
The main collection is due to reopen late in 2015. Until then enjoy the interesting temporary exhibitions held here.

The Théâtre National de Chaillot, beneath the terrace, includes a multi-purpose cultural centre and a modern 1,200-seat theatre. *(See pp334–6).*

Locator Map
See Central Paris Map pp16–17

❸ **Cité de l'Architecture et du Patrimoine**
This vast complex houses an architecture museum, a school, library and archive, and various heritage organizations.

❻ **Jardins du Trocadéro**
The present layout of the gardens was created by R Lardat after the World Fair of 1937.

❷ **Aquarium de Paris – Cinéaqua**
Built to blend in with the Chaillot hillside, this aquarium also has a cinema complex.

The Pont d'Iéna was built by Napoleon to celebrate his victory in 1806 over the Prussians at Jena (Iéna) in Prussia. It was widened in 1937 to complement the building of the Palais de Chaillot.

The Trocadéro fountains are operated in sequence, culminating in the massive water cannons in the centre firing towards the Eiffel Tower. They are illuminated at night.

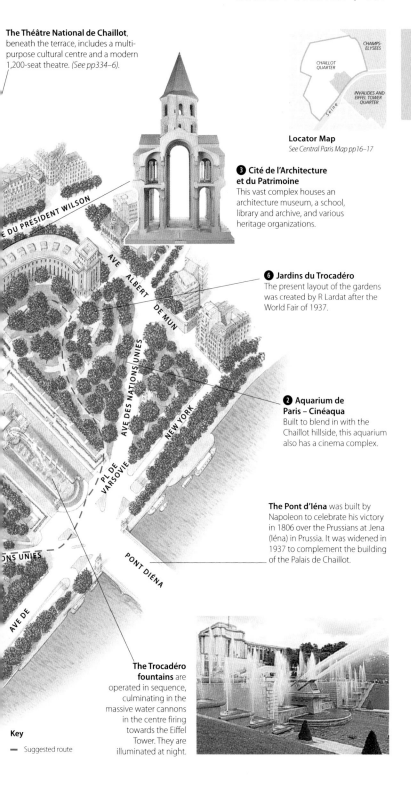

Key

— Suggested route

Trocadéro fountains in front of the Palais de Chaillot

❶ Palais de Chaillot

17 Pl du Trocadéro 75016. **Map** 9 C2.
Tel 01 53 65 30 00. Ⓜ Trocadéro.
🚻 🖥 🏛

The Palais, with its huge, curved colonnaded wings each culminating in an immense pavilion, was designed in Neo-Classical style for the 1937 Paris Exhibition by Léon Azéma, Louis-Hippolyte Boileau and Jacques Carlu. It is adorned with sculptures and bas-reliefs. On the walls of the pavilions, there are gold inscriptions by the poet and essayist Paul Valéry.

The *parvis* or square, situated between the two pavilions, is decorated with large bronze sculptures and ornamental pools. On the terrace in front of the *parvis* stand two bronzes, *Apollo* by Henri Bouchard and *Hercules* by Albert Pommier. Stairways lead from the terrace to the Théâtre National de Chaillot *(see pp334–5)*, which, since World War II, has enjoyed huge fame for its avant-garde productions.

❷ Aquarium de Paris – Cinéaqua

5 Ave Albert de Mun 75016. **Map** 10 D2. **Tel** 01 40 69 23 23. Ⓜ Trocadéro, Iéna. **Open** 10am–7pm daily (last adm: 6pm). **Closed** 14 Jul. 🚻 ♿ Ⓦ cineaqua.com

Originally built in 1878 for the Universal Exhibition, this is now a state-of-the-art aquarium which is home to over 500 species of sea creatures, including seahorses, clownfish, stonefish and some spectacular sharks and rays.

The building is located in a former quarry and has been designed to blend in entirely with the Chaillot hillside.

Cinema screens showing cartoons and animal documentaries are interspersed with the aquariums. There are also art exhibitions and shows for children in the theatre.

Church model from Bagneux, Cité de l'Architecture et du Patrimoine

❸ Cité de l'Architecture et du Patrimoine

Palais de Chaillot, Pl du Trocadéro 75016. **Map** 9 C2. **Tel** 01 58 51 52 00. Ⓜ Trocadéro. **Open** 11am–7pm Wed–Mon (to 9pm Thu). 🚻 🖥 🏛 Ⓦ citechaillot.fr

In the east wing of the Palais de Chaillot, this museum charts the development of French architecture through the ages. Among the unmissable displays is the Galerie des Moulages, which covers the period from the Middle Ages to the Renaissance. Here, you will find three-dimensional models of great French cathedrals, such as Chartres. Also worth a look is the Galerie Moderne et Contemporaine, with a reconstruction of a Le Corbusier-designed apartment.

Shark basin, one of the 43 tanks at the Aquarium de Paris – Cinéaqua

❹ Musée de l'Homme

Palais de Chaillot, 17 Pl du Trocadéro 75016. **Map** 9 C2. **Tel** 01 44 05 72 72. Ⓜ Trocadéro. **Closed** until late 2015. 🗺 Exhibitions, films. 📷 💻 📱 🌐 **museedehomme.fr**

Situated in the west wing of the Chaillot palace, this museum traces the process of human evolution, from prehistoric times to the present, through a series of anthropological exhibits from around the world.

The museum is currently undergoing extensive renovations that will lead to its housing one of the most comprehensive prehistoric collections in the world. It is currently closed and is scheduled to reopen in 2015.

Gabon mask at Musée de l'Homme

Relief outside the Musée de la Marine

❺ Musée National de la Marine

Palais de Chaillot, 17 Pl du Trocadéro 75016. **Map** 9 C2. **Tel** 01 53 65 69 69. Ⓜ Trocadéro. **Open** 11am–6pm Wed–Mon (to 7pm Sat & Sun). **Closed** 1 Jan, 1 May, 25 Dec. 🗺 📷 ✏ by appt; 01 53 65 69 53. 📱 Films, videos. 🌐 **musee-marine.fr**

French maritime history from the days of the royal wooden warships to today's aircraft carriers and nuclear submarines is told through wonderfully exact scale models (most of them two centuries old), mementos of naval heroes, paintings and navigational instruments. The museum was set up by Charles X in 1827, and was then moved to the Chaillot palace in 1943. Exhibits include Napoleon's barge, models of the fleet he assembled at Boulogne-

sur-Mer in 1805 for his planned invasion of Britain, and displays on underwater exploration and fishing vessels.

❻ Jardins du Trocadéro

75016. **Map** 10 D2. Ⓜ Trocadéro.

These lovely gardens cover 10 ha (25 acres). Their centrepiece is a long rectangular ornamental pool, bordered by stone and bronze-gilt statues, which look spectacular at night when the fountains are illuminated. The statues include *Man* by P Traverse and *Woman* by G Braque, *Bull* by P Jouve and *Horse* by G Guyot. On either side of the pool, the slopes of the Chaillot hill lead down to the Seine and the Pont d'Iéna. There is a freshwater aquarium in the northeast corner of the gardens, which are laid out with trees, small streams and bridges.

❼ Musée du Vin

Rue des Eaux, 5 Sq Charles Dickens 75016. **Map** 9 C3. **Tel** 01 45 25 63 26. Ⓜ Passy. **Open** 10am–6pm Tue–Sat. **Closed** 1 Jan, 25 Dec. 🗺 ✉ 📷 ✏ tours with wine tasting available for groups. Reserve in advance. ✏ lunchtime only Tue–Sat. 🌐 **museeduvinparis.com**

Waxwork figures and cardboard cut-outs graphically illustrate the history of wine making in

Wax figure on display in the vaulted cellar of Musée du Vin

these atmospheric vaulted medieval cellars, which were once used by the monks of Passy. The exhibits include a collection of old wine bottles, glasses and corkscrews, as well as an array of scientific instruments that were used in the wine-making and bottling processes. There is also an atmospheric restaurant, wine for sale and tours which include a wine-tasting session.

Balzac's modest house

❽ Maison de Balzac

47 Rue Raynouard 75016. **Map** 9 B3. **Tel** 01 55 74 41 80. Ⓜ Passy, La Muette. **Open** 10am–6pm Tue–Sun (last adm: 5.30pm). **Closed** public hols. Reference library: Tue & Thu. 📷 ✏ 📱 🌐 **balzac.paris.fr**

The novelist Honoré de Balzac lived here from 1840 to 1847 under a false name, Monsieur de Brugnol, to avoid his numerous creditors. During this time, he wrote many of his most famous novels, among them *La Cousine Bette* (1846).

The house now contains a reference library, with first editions and manuscripts, and a museum with memorabilia from his life. Many of the rooms have drawings and paintings portraying Balzac's family and close friends. The Madame Hanska room is devoted to the memory of the Russian woman who corresponded with Balzac for 18 years and was his wife for the five months before his death in 1850.

The house has a back entrance leading into Rue Berton, which was used to evade unwelcome callers. Rue Berton, with its ivy-covered walls, has retained much of its old, rustic charm.

Debussy's grave in the Cimetière de Passy, in the shadow of the Eiffel Tower

❾ Maison de Radio-France

116 Ave du Président-Kennedy 75016.
Map 9 B4. **Tel** 01 56 40 22 22.
Ⓜ Ranelagh. **Open** for concerts,
check website for details. ♿
Ⓦ **radiofrance.fr**

Maison de Radio-France is an impressive building designed by Henri Bernard in 1963 as the headquarters of France's public radio network. The largest single structure in France, it is made up of three concentric circular buildings with a rectangular tower and covers 2 ha (5 acres).

The 70-odd studios and main public auditorium are the home of French national public radio. Radio France sponsors more than 100 concerts each year, including performances by the Orchestre National de France – several of these concerts are held at the Maison de Radio-France.

❿ Cimetière de Passy

2 Rue du Commandant-Shloesing
75016. **Map** 9 C2. Ⓜ Trocadéro.
Open 8.30am–5.30pm Mon–Sat, 9am–
5.30pm Sun (to 6pm 16 Mar–5 Nov).

Located in the elegant 16th arrondissement, this small cemetery, which opened in 1820, is packed with the graves of eminent Parisians, including the composers Claude Debussy and Gabriel Fauré and painter Edouard Manet, as well as many politicians and aristocrats, such as Ghislaine Dommanget, Princess of Monaco.

⓫ Musée de la Contrefaçon

16 Rue de la Faisanderie 75016.
Map 3 A5. **Tel** 01 56 26 14 03.
Ⓜ Porte Dauphine. **Open** 2–5.30pm
Tue–Sun, ring doorbell. Morning visits
by appt. **Closed** public hols, 2 weeks
and weekends in Aug. 🎨 📷 📱

French cognac and perfume producers, and the luxury trade in general, have been plagued for years by counterfeiters operating around the world. This museum was set up by the manufacturers' union and illustrates the history of this type of fraud, which has been going on since Roman times. Among the impressive display of forgeries are copies of Louis Vuitton luggage, Cartier watches and fake wine.

⓬ Musée Dapper

35 bis Rue Paul-Valéry, 75116.
Map 3 C4. **Tel** 01 45 00 91 75.
Ⓜ Victor-Hugo. **Open** Temporary
exhibitions: 11am–7pm Wed, Fri–
Mon. **Closed** 1 Jan, 25 Dec. 🎨
📱 by appt. 📷 🖥 Ⓦ **dapper.fr**

Not just a museum, but a world-class ethnographic research centre called the Dapper Foundation, this lively centre showcases African art and culture. Located in an attractive building with an "African" garden, it is a treasure house of vibrant colour and powerful, evocative work from sub-Saharan Africa. The emphasis is on pre-colonial folk arts, with sculpture, carvings, and tribal work, but

there is later art too. Displays include a collection of tribal masks, with a dazzling array of richly carved religious, ritual and funerary masks, as well as theatrical masks used for comic, magical or symbolic performances, some dating back to the 12th century.

⓭ Galerie-Musée Baccarat

11 Place des Etats-Unis 75016.
Map 4 D5. **Tel** 01 40 22 11 00.
Ⓜ Boissière, Iéna. **Open** 10am–6pm
Mon, Wed–Sat. **Closed** public hols.
🎨 📷 by appt. 🖥 Ⓦ **baccarat.fr**

The Galerie-Musée Baccarat shows off some 1,200 articles made by the Baccarat crystal glass company, which was founded in Lorraine. These include services created for the royal and imperial courts of Europe and one-off pieces created in the workshops.

Khmer art in the Musée National des Arts Asiatiques Guimet

⓮ Musée National des Arts Asiatiques Guimet

6 Pl d'Iéna 75116. **Map** 10 D1. **Tel** 01
56 52 53 00. Ⓜ Iéna. **Open** 10am–
6pm Wed–Mon (last adm: 5.15pm).
Closed 1 Jan, 1 May, 25 Dec. 🎨 📱
♿ 📷 🖥 Panthéon
Bouddhique (additional galleries) at
19 Ave d'Iéna. **Tel** 01 40 73 88 00.
Open Call ahead; 10am–5.45pm
(garden open to 5pm). Ⓦ **guimet.fr**

The Musée Guimet has the finest collection of Khmer (Cambodian) art in the West. It was originally set up in Lyon in

1879 by the industrialist and orientalist Emile Guimet. Moved to Paris in 1884, it meticulously represents every artistic tradition from Afghanistan to India, China, Japan and the rest of southeast Asia. With over 45,000 artworks, the museum is acclaimed for some especially unusual collections, including the Cambodian Angkor Wat sculptures and 1600 artworks from the Himalayas. Other highlights include Chinese bronzes and lacquerware, and many statues of Buddha. Seasonal tea ceremonies are held in the Panthéon Bouddhique. Call for details.

⓯ Palais Galliera

10 Ave Pierre 1er de Serbie 75116. **Map** 10 E1. **Tel** 01 56 52 86 00. Ⓜ Iéna, Alma Marceau. Museum: **Open** for exhibitions only. 10am–6pm Tue–Sun (to 9pm Thu). Library & documentation centre: by appt, call 01 56 52 86 46. **Closed** public hols and in between expos. ♿ Children's workshops. Ⓦ **palaisgalliera.paris.fr**

Devoted to the evolution of fashion, this museum is housed in the Renaissance-style palace built for the Duchesse Maria de Ferrari Galliera in 1892. The collection comprises more than 100,000 outfits, from the 18th century to the

present day. Some have been donated by such fashionable women as Baronne Hélène de Rothschild and Princess Grace of Monaco. The museum holds around three temporary exhibitions every year.

Gabriel Forestier's sculpted doors, Musée d'Art Moderne

⓰ Musée d'Art Moderne de la Ville de Paris

11 Ave du Président-Wilson 75116. **Map** 10 E1. **Tel** 01 53 67 40 00. Ⓜ Iéna, Alma Marceau. **Open** 10am–6pm Tue–Sun (to 10pm Thu). **Closed** public hols. ♿ temporary exhibitions. ♿ 📷 🖥 🖼 🎞 Films. Ⓦ **mam.paris.fr**

This large lively museum houses the city of Paris's own renowned collection of modern art, covering all major 20th-century movements and artists (the 21st century will be included).

Established in 1961, the museum occupies the vast east wing of the Palais de Tokyo, which was built for the 1937 World Fair.

One of the museum's highlights is Raoul Dufy's gigantic mural *La Fée Electricité* (*The Spirit of Electricity*), which traces the history of electricity through the ages. One of the largest paintings in the world, measuring 600 sq metres (6,500 sq ft), this curved mural takes up a whole room at the museum. Also notable are the Cubists, Amadeo Modigliani, Georges Rouault and the Fauves. This group of avant-garde artists was dominated by Henri Matisse, whose celebrated mural, *La Danse*, is on display here in both versions.

Bas-relief on the walls of Palais de Tokyo

⓱ Palais de Tokyo

Palais de Tokyo, 13 Ave du Président-Wilson 75116. **Map** 10 E1. **Tel** 01 81 97 35 88. Ⓜ Iéna, Alma Marceau. **Open** noon–midnight Wed–Mon. **Closed** 1 Jan, 1 May, 25 Dec. ♿ ♿ 📷 🖥 🖼 Ⓦ **palaisdetokyo.com**

This open-space modern art museum is located in an adjacent wing to the Musée d'Art Moderne de la Ville de Paris, within the imposing 1937 Palais de Tokyo building. It presents an innovative, ever-changing programme of contemporary art exhibitions, fashion shows and avant-garde performances. Quirky installations, by artists such as Pierre Joseph, Wang Du and Frank Scurti have earned the Palais de Tokyo a reputation as one of the most cutting-edge art houses in Europe.

Garden and rear façade of the Musée Galliera

CHAMPS-ELYSEES

Two great streets dominate this area – the Avenue des Champs-Elysées and the Rue St-Honoré. The former is the capital's most famous thoroughfare. Its breadth is spectacular. The pavements are wide and their cafés, cinemas and shops attract throngs of people, who come to eat and shop, but also to see and to be seen. Rond Point des Champs-Elysées is the pretty end, with shady chestnut trees and pavements colourfully bordered by flower beds. Luxury and political power are nearby. Five-star hotels, fine restaurants and upmarket shops line the nearby streets and avenues. And along Rue St-Honoré are the heavily guarded presidential Palais de l'Elysée, the sumptuous town mansions of business chiefs, and the many embassies and consulates.

Sights at a Glance

Historical Buildings and Streets
5 Palais de l'Elysée
6 Avenue Montaigne
8 Avenue des Champs-Elysées
9 Place Charles de Gaulle (l'Etoile)

Monuments
10 Arc de Triomphe pp212–13

Bridges
1 Pont Alexandre III

Museums and Galleries
2 Grand Palais
3 Palais de la Découverte
4 Petit Palais
7 Musée Jacquemart- André

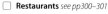

☐ **Restaurants** *see pp300–301*
1 Apicius
2 Café Lenôtre
3 Chez Diep
4 Le Cinq (Four Seasons George V)
5 Copenhague
6 L'Epicure (Hotel Bristol)
7 Graindorge
8 Le Hide
9 L'Huîtrier
10 Korean Barbecue Champs-Elysées
11 Lasserre
12 Minipalais
13 Pierre Gagnaire
14 Relais de l'Entrecôte
15 Le Timgad
16 Relais Plaza
17 Taillevent

| 0 metres | 500 |
| 0 yards | 500 |

See also Street Finder map 3–4, 5, 11

◄ Detail of a sculpture on the main facade of the Arc de Triomphe

For keys to symbols *see back flap*

Street-by-Street: Champs-Elysées

The formal gardens that line the Champs-Elysées from the Place de la Concorde to the Rond-Point have changed little since they were laid out by the architect Jacques Hittorff in 1838. They were used as the setting for the World Fair of 1855, which included the Palais de l'Industrie, Paris's answer to London's Crystal Palace. The Palais was later replaced by the Grand Palais and Petit Palais, which were created as a showpiece of the Third Republic for the Universal Exhibition of 1900. They sit on either side of an impressive vista that stretches from Place Clémenceau across the elegant curve of the Pont Alexandre III to the Invalides.

The Théâtre du Rond-Point was the home of the Renaud-Barrault Company. There are plaques on the back door of the theatre representing Napoleon's campaigns.

Metro Franklin D Roosevelt Ⓜ

❻ Avenue Montaigne
Christian Dior and other *haute couture* houses are based on this chic avenue.

❷ ★ Grand Palais
Designed by Charles Girault, this grand 19th-century building is still used for major exhibitions.

AVE DES CH

AVE G. EISENHOWER

AVE FRANKLIN D ROOSEVELT

RUE JEAN GOUJON

RUE FRANÇOIS PREMIER

LASSERRE

The Lasserre restaurant is decorated in the style of a luxurious ocean liner from the 1930s.

PL DU CANADA

COURS LA REINE

PONT DES INVALIDES

❸ Palais de la Découverte
Outside this museum of scientific discoveries is a pair of equestrian statues.

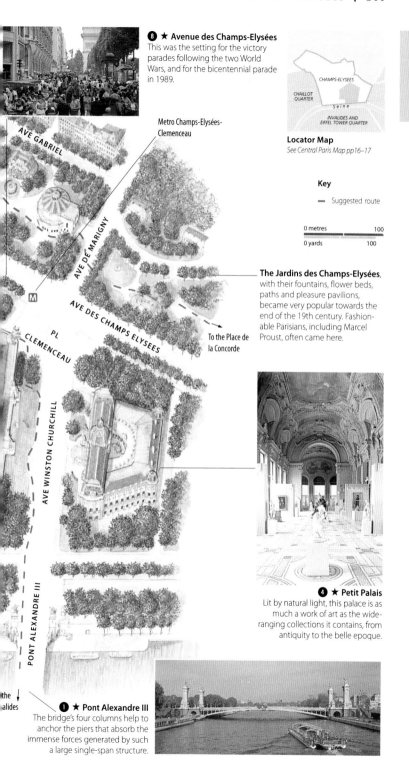

❽ ★ Avenue des Champs-Elysées
This was the setting for the victory parades following the two World Wars, and for the bicentennial parade in 1989.

Metro Champs-Elysées-Clemenceau

AVE GABRIEL

AVE DE MARIGNY

M

AVE DES CHAMPS ELYSEES

PL CLEMENCEAU

AVE WINSTON CHURCHILL

PONT ALEXANDRE III

Locator Map
See Central Paris Map pp16–17

Key

— Suggested route

0 metres   100
0 yards   100

The Jardins des Champs-Elysées, with their fountains, flower beds, paths and pleasure pavilions, became very popular towards the end of the 19th century. Fashionable Parisians, including Marcel Proust, often came here.

To the Place de la Concorde

❹ ★ Petit Palais
Lit by natural light, this palace is as much a work of art as the wide-ranging collections it contains, from antiquity to the belle epoque.

To the Invalides

❶ ★ Pont Alexandre III
The bridge's four columns help to anchor the piers that absorb the immense forces generated by such a large single-span structure.

Pont Alexandre III

❶ Pont Alexandre III

75008. **Map** 11 A1. Ⓜ Champs-Elysées-Clemenceau.

This is Paris's prettiest bridge with its exuberant Art Nouveau decoration of lamps, cherubs, nymphs and winged horses at either end. It was built between 1896 and 1900, in time for the Universal Exhibition, and it was named after Tsar Alexander III, whose son Nicholas II laid the foundation stone in October 1896.

The style of the bridge reflects that of the Grand Palais, to which it leads on the Right Bank. The construction of the bridge is a marvel of 19th-century engineering, consisting of a 6-m (18-ft) high single-span steel arch across the Seine. The design was subject to strict controls that prevented the bridge from obscuring the view of the Champs-Elysées or the Invalides. So today you can still enjoy magnificent views from here.

❷ Grand Palais

Porte A, Ave Général Eisenhower 75008. **Map** 11 A1. **Tel** 01 44 13 17 17. Ⓜ Champs-Elysées-Clemenceau. **Open** for temporary exhibitions (check website for opening hours). **Closed** 1 May, 25 Dec. 🎫 🎦 ♿ 🎦 usually 6pm Wed–Fri, 11am & 4.45pm Sat but call to check. 🎧 🖥 🏛 Ⓦ grandpalais.fr

Built at the same time as the Petit Palais and the Pont Alexandre III, the exterior of this massive palace combines an imposing Classical stone facade with a riot of Art Nouveau ironwork. The enormous glass roof (15,000 sq metres/160,000 sq ft) has Récipon's colossal bronze statues of flying horses and chariots at its four corners. The metal structure supporting the glass weighs 8,500 tonnes, some 500 tonnes more than the Eiffel Tower. Today, the restored Grand Palais hosts contemporary art exhibitions and other events; major temporary and touring exhibitions are held at the Galeries Nationales in the same building.

❸ Palais de la Découverte

Ave Franklin D Roosevelt 75008. **Map** 11 A1. **Tel** 01 44 43 20 20. Ⓜ Franklin D Roosevelt. **Open** 9.30am– 6pm Tue–Sat, 10am–7pm Sun. **Closed** 1 Jan, 1 May, 14 Jul, 15 Aug, 25 Dec. 🎫 by permission. 📷 🖥 Ⓦ palais-decouverte.fr

Opened in a wing of the Grand Palais for the World Fair of 1937, this science museum is a much-loved Paris institution. Demonstrations and displays, including a planetarium, cover many subjects and explain such phenomena as electromagnetism.

Palais de la Découverte

Grand Palais

Entrance to the Petit Palais

❹ Petit Palais

Ave Winston Churchill 75008. **Map** 11 B1. **Tel** 01 53 43 40 00. Ⓜ Champs-Elysées-Clemenceau. **Open** 10am–6pm Tue–Sun (to 8pm Thu). **Closed** public hols. 🎫 🎦 for exhibitions. 🖥 Ⓦ petitpalais.paris.fr

Built for the Universal Exhibition in 1900, to stage a major display of French art, this jewel of a building now houses the Musée des Beaux-Arts de la Ville de Paris. Arranged around a pretty semi-circular courtyard and garden, the palace is similar in style to the Grand Palais, and has Ionic columns, a grand porch and a dome, which echoes that of the Invalides (see p191).

The Cours de la Reine wing, nearest the river, is used for temporary exhibitions, while the Champs-Elysées side of the palace houses the permanent collections. These are divided into sections: Greek and Roman; medieval and Renaissance ivories and sculptures; Renaissance

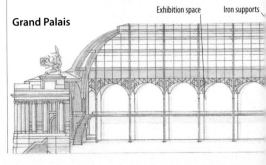

Exhibition space   Iron supports

clocks and jewellery; and 17th-, 18th- and 19th-century art and furniture. There are also many works by the Impressionists.

❺ Palais de l'Elysée

55 Rue du Faubourg-St-Honoré 75008. **Map** 5 B5. Ⓜ St-Philippe-du-Roule. **Closed** to the public.

Backing onto splendid English-style gardens, the Elysée Palace was built in 1718 for the Comte d'Evreux and has been the official residence of the President of the Republic since 1873. From 1805 to 1808 it was occupied by Napoleon's sister, Caroline, and her husband, Murat. Two charming rooms have been preserved from this period: the Salon Murat and the Salon d'Argent. General de Gaulle used to give press conferences in the Hall of Mirrors. Today, the President's modernized apartments can be found on the first floor opposite the Rue de l'Elysée.

❻ Avenue Montaigne

75008. **Map** 10 F1. Ⓜ Franklin D Roosevelt.

In the 19th century this avenue was famous for its dance halls and its Winter Garden, where Parisians went to hear Adolphe Sax play his newly-invented saxophone. Today it is still one of Paris's most fashionable streets, bustling with restaurants, cafés, hotels and designer boutiques.

The Second-Empire Smoking Room in the Musée Jacquemart-André

❼ Musée Jacquemart-André

158 Blvd Haussmann 75008. **Map** 5 A4. **Tel** 01 45 62 11 59. Ⓜ Miromesnil, St-Philippe-du-Roule. **Open** 10am–6pm daily (to 8.30pm Mon & Sat). ♿🚻🔒📷🛍♿ restricted. 🆆 **musee-jacquemart-andre.com**

This museum is known for its fine collection of Italian Renaissance and French 18th-century works of art, as well as its beautiful frescoes by Tiepolo. Highlights include works by Mantegna, Uccello's masterpiece *St George and the Dragon* (circa 1435), paintings by Boucher and Fragonard and 18th-century tapestries.

❽ Avenue des Champs-Elysées

75008. **Map** 5 A5. Ⓜ Franklin D Roosevelt, George V.

Paris's most famous and popular thoroughfare had its beginnings in about 1667, when the landscape garden designer, André Le Nôtre, extended the royal view from the Tuileries by creating a tree-lined avenue which eventually became known as the Champs-Elysées (Elysian Fields). It has been France's national "triumphal way" ever since the home-coming of Napoleon's body from St Helena in 1840. With the addition of cafés and restaurants in the second half of the 19th century, the Champs-Elysées became the place in which to be seen.

❾ Place Charles de Gaulle (l'Etoile)

75008. **Map** 4 D4. Ⓜ Charles de Gaulle-Etoile.

Known as the Place de l'Etoile until the death of Charles de Gaulle in 1969, the area is still referred to simply as l'Etoile, the star. The present *place* was laid out in accordance with Baron Haussmann's plans of 1854 (*see pp36–7*). For motorists, it is the ultimate challenge.

Glass cupola

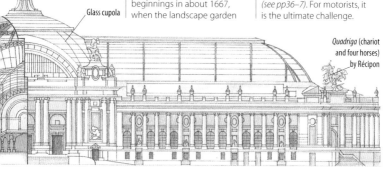

Quadriga (chariot and four horses) by Récipon

⑩ Arc de Triomphe

After his greatest victory, the Battle of Austerlitz in 1805, Napoleon promised his men, "You shall go home beneath triumphal arches." The first stone of what was to become the world's most famous triumphal arch was laid the following year. But disruptions to architect Jean Chalgrin's plans and the demise of Napoleonic power delayed the completion of this monumental building until 1836. Standing 50 m (164 ft) high, the Arc is now the customary starting point for victory celebrations and parades.

★ **Tomb of the Unknown Soldier**
An unknown French soldier from World War I is buried here.

KEY

① **The Battle of Aboukir**, a bas-relief by Seurre the Elder, depicts a scene of Napoleon's victory over the Turkish army in 1799.

② **The frieze** was executed by Rude, Brun, Jacquet, Laitié, Caillouette and Seurre the Elder. This east façade shows the departure of the French armies for new campaigns. The west side shows their return.

③ **Thirty shields** just below the Arc's roof each bear the name of a victorious Napoleonic battle fought in either Europe or Africa.

④ **East façade**

⑤ **The viewing platform** affords one of the best views in Paris, overlooking the Champs-Elysées on one side, and the Grande Arche de la Défense on the other.

⑥ **The Battle of Austerlitz** by Gechter shows Napoleon's army breaking up the ice on the Satschan lake in order to drown thousands of enemy troops.

⑦ **Officers** of the Imperial Army are listed on the walls of the smaller arches.

⑧ **Entrance to museum**

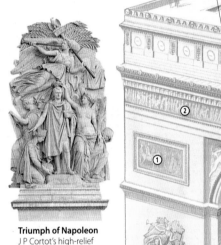

Triumph of Napoleon
J P Cortot's high-relief celebrates the Treaty of Vienna peace agreement of 1810.

1806 Napoleon commissions Chalgrin to build triumphal Arc

1836 Louis-Philippe completes the Arc

1885 Victor Hugo's body lies in state under the Arc

1944 Liberation of Paris. De Gaulle leads the crowd from the Arc

1800	1850	1900

1840 Napoleon's cortège passes under the Arc

1919 Victory parade of Allied armies through the Arc

1815 Downfall of Napoleon. Work on Arc ceases

Napoleon's Nuptial Parade

Napoleon divorced Josephine in 1809 because she was unable to bear him children. A diplomatic marriage was arranged in 1810 with Marie-Louise, daughter of the Austrian emperor. Napoleon was determined to impress his bride by going through the Arc on their way to the wedding at the Louvre, but work had barely been started. So Chalgrin built a full-scale mock-up of the arch on the site for the couple to pass beneath.

VISITORS' CHECKLIST

Practical Information
Pl Charles de Gaulle.
Map 4 D4.
Tel 01 55 37 73 77.
Open Apr–Sep: 10am–11pm daily; Oct–Mar: 10am–10.30pm daily (last adm: 45 mins earlier).
Closed am only 8 May, 14 Jul, 11 Nov; daily 1 Jan, 1 May, 25 Dec. 🛃 🎦 🏠 ♿

Transport
Ⓜ RER Charles de Gaulle–Etoile. 🚌 22, 30, 31, 52, 73, 92 to Pl C de Gaulle. 🅿 off Pl C de Gaulle.

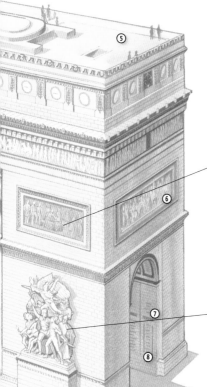

General Marceau's Funeral
Marceau defeated the Austrians in 1795, only to be killed the following year, still fighting them.

★ Departure of the Volunteers in 1792
François Rude's work shows citizens leaving to defend the nation.

Place Charles de Gaulle
Twelve avenues radiate from the Arc at the centre. Some bear the names of important French military leaders, such as Avenues Marceau and Foch. *(See pp36–7)*.

OPERA QUARTER

The Opéra quarter bustles with bankers and stockbrokers, newspapermen and shoppers, theatre-goers and sightseers. Much of its 19th-century grandeur survives in the Grands Boulevards of Baron Haussmann's urban design. These are still a favourite with thousands of Parisian and foreign promenaders, drawn by the profusion of stores, which range from the exclusively expensive to the popular.

Much more of the area's older character is found in the many passages – delightful narrow shopping arcades with steel and glass roofs. Fashion's bad boy, Jean-Paul Gaultier, has a shop adjoining one of the smartest,

Galerie Vivienne. But more authentically old-style Parisian are the Passage des Panoramas and the Passage Jouffroy, the Passage Verdeau, with its old cameras and comics, and the tiny Passage des Princes. Two of Paris's finest food shops are in the area. Fauchon and Hédiard are noted for mouthwatering mustards, jams, pâtés and sauces. The area still has a reputation as a press centre, although *Le Monde* has moved out, and it has a place in the history of cinema and theatre – the Lumière brothers held the world's first public film show here in 1895. The Opéra National de Paris Garnier is famous for its dazzling belle epoque interior.

Sights at a Glance

Historical Buildings and Streets
2 Place de la Madeleine
3 Les Grands Boulevards
10 Palais Brongniart
12 Avenue de l'Opéra

Churches
1 La Madeleine

Shops
7 Drouot (Hôtel des Ventes)
9 Les Passages

Opera Houses
4 Opéra National de Paris Garnier

Museums and Galleries
5 Bibliothèque-Musée de l'Opéra
6 Paris Story
8 Musée Grévin
11 Bibliothèque Nationale Richelieu

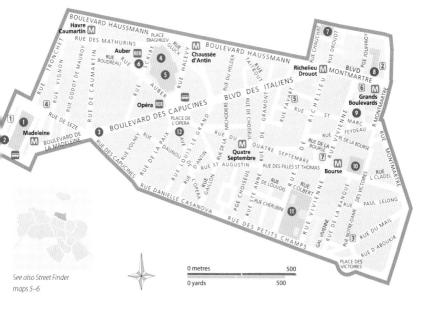

See also Street Finder maps 5–6

◀ The ceiling of the foyer of the Opéra National de Paris Garnier   For keys to symbols *see back flap*

Street-by-Street: Opéra Quarter

It has been said that if you sit for long enough at the Café de la Paix (opposite the Opéra National de Paris Garnier) the whole world will pass by. During the day, the area is a mixture of commerce – France's top three banks are based here – and tourism. A profusion of shops, ranging from the chic, exclusive and expensive to popular department stores, draw the crowds. In the evening, the theatres and cinemas attract a totally different clientele, and the cafés along the Boulevard des Capucines throb with life.

Statue by Gumery on the Opéra

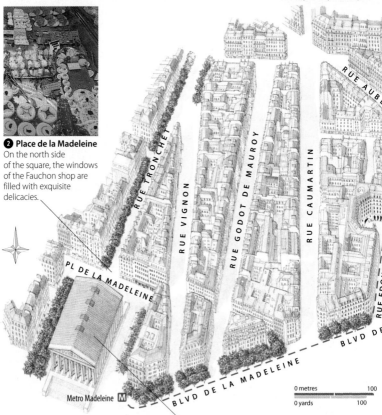

❷ Place de la Madeleine
On the north side of the square, the windows of the Fauchon shop are filled with exquisite delicacies.

Metro Madeleine Ⓜ

| 0 metres | 100 |
| 0 yards | 100 |

Key

— Suggested route

❶ ★ La Madeleine
The final design of this church, which is dedicated to Mary Magdalene, differs from this original model, now in the Musée Carnavalet (*see pp96–7*).

❹ ★ Opéra National de Paris Garnier
With a mixture of styles ranging from Classical to
Baroque, this building from 1875 has come to
symbolize the opulence of the Second Empire.

Locator Map
See Central Paris Map pp16–17

**❺ Bibliothèque-Musée
de l'Opéra**
The world of opera is
celebrated here.

The Place de l'Opéra
was designed by
Baron Haussmann and
is one of Paris's busiest
intersections.

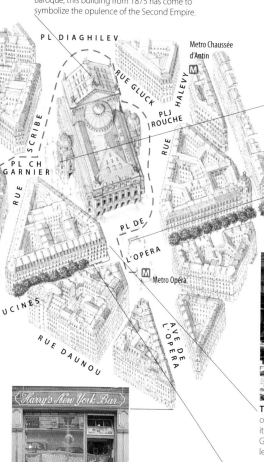

The Café de la Paix maintains its
old-fashioned ways and still has
its 19th-century decor, designed by
Garnier. Their vanilla slices are
legendary *(see p311)*.

Harry's Bar was named
after Harry MacElhone, a
bartender who bought the bar
in 1913. Past regulars have
included F Scott Fitzgerald and
Ernest Hemingway.

**❸ ★ Boulevard des
Capucines**
At No. 14 a plaque tells
of the world's first public
screening of a movie, by
the Lumière brothers in
1895; it took place in the
Salon Indien, a room in
the Grand Café.

Charles Marochetti's *Mary Magdalene Ascending to Heaven* (1837) behind the high altar of La Madeleine

❶ La Madeleine

Pl de la Madeleine 75008. **Map** 5 C5.
Tel 01 44 51 69 00. Ⓜ Madeleine.
Open 9.30am–7pm daily.
✝ frequent. Concerts. 🎭 *See
Entertainment pp338–9.*

This church, which is dedicated
to Mary Magdalene,
is one of the best-
known buildings in
Paris because of its
prominent location
and great size. It
stands facing south to
Place de la Concorde
and is the architectural
counterpoint of the
Palais-Bourbon (home
of the Assemblée
Nationale, the French
parliament) across the
river. It was started in 1764
but not consecrated until
1845. There were proposals to
convert it into a parliament, a
stock exchange or the city's
first train station.

Napoleon decided to build
a temple dedicated to military
glory and he commissioned
Pierre Vignon to design it, after
the battle of Jena (Iéna) in 1806.
A colonnade of 20 m high (64 ft)
Corinthian columns encircles
the building and supports a
sculptured frieze. The bas-reliefs
on the bronze doors are by
Henri de Triqueti and show the
Ten Commandments. The inside
is decorated with marble and
gilt, and has some fine
sculpture, notably François
Rude's *Baptism of Christ.*

❷ Place de la Madeleine

75008. **Map** 5 C5. Ⓜ Madeleine.
Flower market **Open**
8am–7.30pm Mon–Sat.

The place de la
Madeleine was
created at the
same time as the
Madeleine church.
It is a food lover's
paradise, with many
shops specializing
in luxuries such as
truffles, champagne,
caviar and handmade

Fauchon tin

chocolates. Fauchon, the
millionaires' supermarket, is
situated at No. 26 and stocks
more than 20,000 items *(see
pp325–7).* The large house at
No. 9 is where Marcel Proust
spent his childhood. To the
east of La Madeleine is a small
flower market *(see p330)* and
some excellently preserved
19th-century public toilets.

Opéra National de Paris Garnier

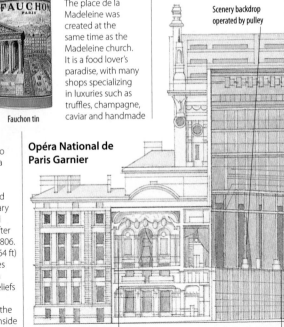

Scenery backdrop
operated by pulley

Backstage area

Stage

❸ Les Grands Boulevards

75002 & 75009. **Map** 6 D5–7 C5.
Ⓜ Madeleine, Opéra, Richelieu-Drouot, Grands Boulevards.

A broad thoroughfare divided into eight boulevards – Madeleine, Capucines, Italiens, Montmartre, Poissonnière, Bonne Nouvelle, St-Denis and St-Martin – runs from La Madeleine to the Place de la République. The route was constructed in the 17th century to turn obsolete city fortifications into fashionable promenades – *boulevard* came from the Middle Dutch *bulwerc*, which means bulwark or rampart. The boulevards became so famous in the 19th century that the name *boulevardier* was coined for someone who cuts a figure on the boulevards.

Around the Madeleine church and the Opéra, it is still possible to gain an impression of what the Grands Boulevards looked like in their heyday, lined with cafés and chic shops. Elsewhere, most of the cafés and restaurants have long since gone, and the old façades are now hidden by neon advertising. However, the

Boulevard de la Madeleine

Grands Boulevards and the nearby department stores on the Boulevard Haussmann still attract large crowds.

❹ Opéra National de Paris Garnier

Pl de l'Opéra 75009. **Map** 6 D4–E4.
Tel 08 92 89 90 90. Ⓜ Opéra. **Open** 10am–5pm daily (1pm on matinée days); mid-Jul–late Aug: 10am–6pm. Reservations for guided tours 01 42 46 92 04. **Closed** public hols. 🅿 🎫 ♿
See Entertainment pp337–9.
🆆 **operadeparis.fr**

Sometimes compared to a giant wedding cake, this building was designed by Charles Garnier for Napoleon III; construction started in 1862. Its unique appearance is due to a mixture of materials (including stone, marble and bronze) and styles, ranging from Classical to Baroque,

with a number of columns, friezes and sculptures on the exterior. The building was not completed until 1875; work was interrupted by the Prussian War and 1871 uprising.

In 1858, Count Orsini had attempted to assassinate the emperor outside the old opera house. This prompted Garnier to include a pavilion on the east side of the building, with a curved ramp leading up to it so that the sovereign could safely step out of his carriage into the suite of rooms adjoining the royal box.

The functions performed by each part of the building are reflected in the structure. Behind the flat-topped foyer, the cupola sits above the auditorium, while the triangular pediment that rises up behind the cupola marks the front of the stage. Underneath the building is a small lake, which provided inspiration for the phantom's hiding place in Paul Leroux's *Phantom of the Opera*, and is used by firemen for water rescue safety training.

Don't miss the magnificent Grand Staircase, made of white marble with a balustrade of red and green marble, and the Grand Foyer, with its domed ceiling covered with mosaics. The five-tiered auditorium is a riot of red velvet, plaster cherubs and gold leaf, which contrast with the false ceiling painted by Marc Chagall in 1964.

Most operas are performed at the Opéra Nationale de Paris Bastille *(see p102)*, but the ballet remains here.

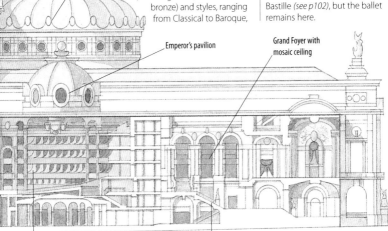
Statue by Millet

Green copper roofed cupola

Emperor's pavilion

Grand Foyer with mosaic ceiling

Auditorium with seating for about 2,000

Grand Staircase

Sign outside the Grévin waxwork museum

❺ Bibliothèque-Musée de l'Opéra

Pl de l'Opéra 75009. **Map** 6 E5.
Tel 01 53 79 37 40. Ⓜ Opéra.
Open 10am–5pm daily. **Closed** 1 Jan,
1 May. 🎫 🎫 🎫

The way in to this small,
charming museum was once
the emperor's private entrance
to the Opéra. The museum
tells the history of opera
and ballet through a large
collection of scores, manuscripts, photographs and
artists' memorabilia. Other
exhibits include paintings,
models of stage sets and
busts of major composers.
There is also a superb library,
containing books and manuscripts on theatre, dance and
music. The museum organizes
two special exhibitions
every year.

❻ Paris Story

11 bis Rue Scribe 75009. **Map** 6 D4.
Tel 01 42 66 62 06. Ⓜ Opéra.
Open 10am–6pm daily; show every
hour. 🎫 🎫 🎫 Ⓦ **paris-story.com**

Especially useful for the first-
time visitor, this small museum
covers everything you need to
know about the history and
architecture of Paris in an hour-
long film and interactive display.
The film covers 2,000 years of
history from Lutèce (the Roman
name for Paris) to the Paris of
today. The show is narrated by a
holographic figure of Victor Hugo
and visitors can listen to it in
English via headphones. A 3-D
model of the city allows you to
pin-point and learn about various
monuments with a description
of the 156 most important and
interesting sites. Plasma screens
show a sequence shot by the
Lumière Brothers in 1898.

❼ Drouot (Hôtel des Ventes)

9 Rue Drouot 75009. **Map** 6 F4. **Tel** 01
48 00 20 20. Ⓜ Richelieu Drouot.
Open 11am–6pm Mon–Sat, sales
from 2pm. **Closed** Jul: Sat & Sun. Ⓟ
🎫 🎫 🎫 *See Shops and Markets
pp328–9.* Ⓦ **drouot.com**

This is the leading French
auction house (Hôtel des
Ventes) and it takes its name
from the Comte de Drouot who
was Napoleon's aide-de-camp.
There has been an auction
house on the site since 1858,
and in 1860, Napoleon III visited
the Hôtel and purchased a
couple of earthenware pots.

It has been known as the
Nouveau Drouot ever since
the 1970s, when the existing
building was demolished and
replaced with today's rather
dull structure.

Although overshadowed
internationally by Christie's and
Sotheby's, auctions at the
Nouveau Drouot nevertheless
provide a lively spectacle and
involve a fascinating range of
rare objects. Its presence in the
area has attracted many antique
and stamp shops.

❽ Musée Grévin

10 Blvd Montmartre 75009. **Map** 6 F4.
Tel 01 47 70 85 05. Ⓜ Grands
Boulevards. **Open** 10am–6:30pm
Mon–Fri, 10am–7pm Sat & Sun (times
can vary, call ahead to check). 🚻 🖥
🎫 🎫 Ⓦ **grevin.com**

This waxwork museum was
founded in 1882 and is now a
Paris landmark, on a par with
Madame Tussauds in London.
It contains tableaux of vivid
historical scenes (such as Louis
XIV at Versailles and the arrest of
Louis XVI), the Palais des Mirages
– a giant walk-in kaleidoscope,
and the Cabinet Fantastique,
which includes regular
conjuring shows given by a live
magician. Famous figures from
the worlds of art, sport and
politics are also on show, with
new celebrities replacing faded
and forgotten stars.

❾ Les Passages

75002. **Map** 6 F5. Ⓜ Bourse.

The early 19th-century Parisian
shopping arcades (known as
passages or *galeries*) are located
between the Boulevard
Montmartre and the Rue
St-Marc (the extensive Passage
des Panoramas). Other arcades
are found between the Rue du
Quatre Septembre and the Rue
des Petits Champs.

At the time of their
construction, the Passages
represented a new traffic-free
area for commerce, work-
shops and apartments. They
fell into disuse, but were
dramatically revamped in the

Model of a set for *Les Huguenots* (1875) in the Musée de l'Opéra

The colonnaded Neo-Classical façade of the Palais de la Bourse

1970s and now house an eclectic mixture of small shops selling anything from designer jewellery to rare books. They have high, vaulted roofs of iron and glass. Many have seen better days, but one of the most charming is the Galerie Vivienne (off the Rue Vivienne or the Rue des Petits Champs) with its mosaic floor and excellent tearoom.

Galerie Vivienne

⓾ Palais Brongniart

(Bourse des Valeurs) 4 Pl de la Bourse 75002. **Map** 6 F5. **Tel** 01 83 92 20 20. Ⓜ Bourse. **Closed** to the public. Ⓦ palaisbrongniart.com

This Neo-Classical temple of commerce was commissioned by Napoleon and was home to the French Stock Exchange from 1826 to 1987. It earlier housed the trading floor of the Palais de la Bourse.

Today, the French stock market is located at 29 Rue Cambon (not open to visits). This building is now used as a conference centre.

⓫ Bibliothèque Nationale Richelieu

58 Rue de Richelieu and 5 Rue Vivienne 75002. **Map** 6 F5. **Tel** 01 53 79 59 59. Ⓜ Bourse. **Open** 10am–6pm Mon–Fri, 9am–5pm Sat. **Closed** public hols, 2 weeks in Sep. 🖱 by appt; 01 53 79 49 49. Ⓦ bnf.fr

The Bibliotheque Nationale (National Library) originated with the manuscript collections of medieval kings, to which, by law, a copy of every French book printed since 1537 has been added. The collection, which includes two Gutenberg bibles, is partially housed in this complex. Despite the removal of the printed books, periodicals and CD-Roms to the Bibliothèque Nationale François Mitterand (see p248) at Tolbiac, the rue Richelieu buildings still contain a huge variety of items, including original manuscripts by Victor Hugo and Marcel Proust. The library also has the richest collection of engravings and photographs in the world. Sadly, the 19th-century reading room is not open to the public.

The library is undergoing renovation until 2019, however it is still open to the public.

⓬ Avenue de l'Opéra

75001 & 75002. **Map** 6 E5. Ⓜ Opéra, Pyramides.

This broad avenue is a notable example of Baron Haussmann's dramatic modernization of Paris in the 1860s and 1870s (see pp36–7), and is the city's only tree-less avenue. Much of the medieval city (including a mound from which Joan of Arc began her crusade against the English) was cleared to make way for the wide thoroughfares. The Avenue de l'Opéra, running from the Palais-Royal to the Opéra National de Paris Garnier, was completed in 1876. The uniformity of the five-storey buildings that line it contrast with those found in nearby streets, which date from the 17th and 18th centuries. Nearby, in Place Gaillon, is the bar and restaurant Drouant where the Goncourt Prize for literature is decided. The avenue is dominated by travel and luxury shops. The Institut d'Etudes Supérieures des Arts is at No. 5.

Avenue de l'Opéra

MONTMARTRE

Montmartre and art are inseparable. By the end of the 19th century, the area was a mecca for artists, writers, poets and their disciples, who gathered to sample the bordellos, cabarets, revues and other exotica that gave Montmartre its reputation as a place of depravity in the eyes of the city's more sober, upstanding citizens. Many of the artists and writers have long since left the area, but the lively night life remains, though it has taken on a seedier character. The hill of Montmartre (the Butte) still has its physical charms and the village atmosphere remains intact despite many visitors. Mobs of eager tourists ascend the hill, mostly congregating on the old village square, the Place du Tertre, which is packed with easel painters, and also in front of the Sacré-Coeur church. Elsewhere, there are tiny, exquisite squares, winding streets, small terraces, long stairways, plus the Butte's famous vineyard where the few grapes are harvested in early autumn. And there are spectacular views of the city from various points, most especially from the monumental Sacré-Coeur.

Sights at a Glance

Historic Buildings and Streets
11 Bateau-Lavoir
14 Moulin de la Galette
15 Avenue Junot

Churches
1 Sacré-Coeur pp226–7
2 St-Pierre de Montmartre
8 Chapelle du Martyre
10 St-Jean l'Evangéliste de Montmartre

Cemeteries
13 Cimetière de Montmartre

Squares
3 Place du Tertre
9 Place des Abbesses

Theatres and Nightclubs
6 Au Lapin Agile
12 Moulin Rouge

Museums and Galleries
4 Espace Dalí Montmartre
5 Musée de Montmartre
7 Halle Saint Pierre

Restaurants see pp 298–300
1 Babalou
2 La Balançoire
3 Le Chamarré de Montmartre
4 Chez Toinette
5 Churrasqueira Galo
6 Crêperie Broceliande
7 Le Cul de Poule
8 La Famille
9 Le Grand 8
10 Guilo Guilo
11 Le Lamarck
12 Le Miroir
13 Le Pantruche
14 Tentazioni
15 Un Zèbre à Montmartre

See also Street Finder maps 2, 6, 7

0 metres 400
0 yards 400

◀ Display of vintage posters in Montmartre

For map symbols *see back flap*

Street-by-Street: Montmartre

The steep *butte* (hill) of Montmartre has been associated with artists for over 200 years. Théodore Géricault and Camille Corot came here at the start of the 19th century, and in the 20th century Maurice Utrillo immortalized the streets in his works. Today street painters thrive on a lively tourist trade as visitors flock to this picturesque district which in places still preserves the atmosphere of pre-war Paris. The name of the area is ascribed to local martyrs tortured in Paris around AD 250, hence *mons martyrium*.

Clos Montmartre is one of the last surviving vineyards in Paris. The grape harvest is celebrated on the first Saturday in October.

Metro Lamarck Caulaincourt

❻ ★ Au Lapin Agile
This rustic café and cabaret was a popular meeting point for artists including Picasso.

❺ ★ Musée de Montmartre
The museum features the work of artists who lived in the area: this Portrait of a Woman (1918) is by the Italian painter and sculptor Amedeo Modigliani.

❹ Espace Dalí Montmartre
This is France's only permanent collection of the Surrealist master's sculptures, paintings and graphic works.

❸ ★ Place du Tertre
The bustling square is the tourist centre of Montmartre and is full of portraitists and other easel artists. Cafés and bars surround the square.

A La Mère Catherine was a favourite eating place of Russian Cossacks in 1814. They would bang on the table and shout *"Bistro!"* (Russian for "quick") – hence the Paris bistro was born.

0 metres 100
0 yards 100

MONTMARTRE

OPERA
QUARTER

TUILERIES QUARTER | BEAUBOURG AND LES HALLES

Locator Map
See Central Paris Map pp16–17

Key

— Suggested route

❶ ★ Sacré-Coeur
This Romano-Byzantine church, started in the 1870s and completed in 1914, has many treasures, such as this figure of Christ by Eugène Benet (1911).

❷ St-Pierre de Montmartre
This church became the Temple of Reason during the Revolution.

❼ La Halle Saint Pierre
The museum hosts exhibitions of Art Brut and Naïve Art. This oil painting, L'Opéra de Paris (1986), is by L Milinkov.

Square Willette lies below the parvis (forecourt) of the Sacré-Coeur. It is laid out on the side of the hill in a series of descending terraces with lawns, shrubs, trees and flowerbeds.

The funiculaire, or cable railway, at the end of the Rue Foyatier takes you to the foot of the basilica of the Sacré-Coeur. Metro tickets are valid on it.

❶ Sacré-Coeur

At the outbreak of the Franco Prussian War in 1870, two Catholic businessmen made a private religious vow to build a church dedicated to the Sacred Heart of Christ, should France be spared the impending Prussian onslaught. The two men, Alexandre Legentil and Hubert Rohault de Fleury, lived to see Paris saved from invasion despite the war and a lengthy siege – and the start of work on the Sacré-Coeur basilica. The project was taken up by Archbishop Guibert of Paris. Work began in 1875 to Paul Abadie's designs. They were inspired by the Romano-Byzantine church of St-Front in Périgueux. The basilica was completed in 1914, but its consecration was forestalled by the Great War until 1919, when France was victorious.

The Principal Façade
The best view of the domed and turreted Sacré-Coeur is from the gardens below.

★ Great Mosaic of Christ
The colossal mosaic (1912–22) dominating the chancel vault was designed by Luc Olivier Merson and Marcel Magne.

Virgin Mary and Child (1896)
This Renaissance-style silver statue is one of two in the ambulatory by P Brunet.

KEY

① **The bell tower** (1895) is 83 m (252 ft) high and contains one of the heaviest bells in the world. The bell itself weighs 18.5 tonnes and the clapper 850 kg (1,900 lb).

② **Spiral staircase**

③ **The inner structure** supporting the dome is made from stone.

④ **The stained-glass gallery** affords a view of the whole of the interior.

★ Crypt Vaults
A chapel in the basilica's crypt contains Legentil's heart in a stone urn.

The Siege of Paris

Prussia invaded France in 1870. During the four-month siege of Paris, instigated by the Prusso-German statesman Otto von Bismarck, hungry Parisians were forced to eat the city's horses and other animals.

★ **Ovoid Dome**
This is the second-highest point in Paris, after the Eiffel Tower.

Statue of Christ
The basilica's most important statue is symbolically placed above the two bronze saints.

Equestrian Statues
The statue of Joan of Arc is one of a pair by H Lefèbvre. The other is of Saint Louis.

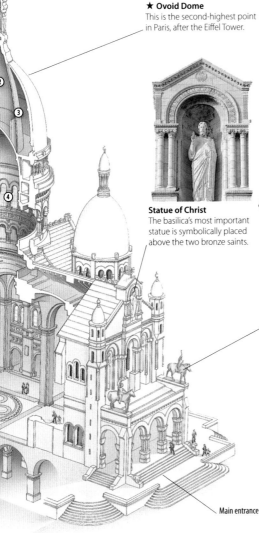

Main entrance

★ **Bronze Doors**
Relief sculptures on the doors in the portico entrance illustrate scenes from the life of Christ, such as the Last Supper.

VISITORS' CHECKLIST

Practical Information
33 Rue du Chevalier-de-la-Barre 75018. **Map** 6 F1. **Tel** 01 53 41 89 00. Basilica: **Open** 6am–10.30pm daily. Dome and crypt: **Open** May–Sep: 8.30am–8pm daily; Oct–Apr: 9am–5pm daily. Crypt: **Closed** Oct–Apr: Tue. 🔗 for crypt and dome. 🕇 7am, 11.15am, 6.30pm, 10pm Mon–Fri (processional at 3pm Fri); 7am, 11.15am, 10pm Sat; 7am, 11am, 6pm, 10pm Sun. ✉ ♿ restricted. 🏠 🌐 **sacre-coeur-montmartre.com**

Transport
Ⓜ Abbesses (then take the funiculaire to the steps of the Sacré-Coeur), Anvers, Barbès-Rochechouart, Lamarck-Caulaincourt. 🚌 30, 31, 54, 80, 85. Ⓟ Blvd de Clichy, Rue Custine.

Montmartre streetside paintings

❷ St-Pierre de Montmartre

2 Rue du Mont-Cenis 75018. **Map** 6 F1. **Tel** 01 46 06 57 63. **M** Abbesses. **Open** 8.45am–7pm daily. **various** times. **Concerts.** **W** saintpierrede montmartre.net

Situated in the shadow of Sacré-Coeur, St-Pierre de Montmartre is one of the oldest churches in Paris. It is all that remains of the great Benedictine Abbey of Montmartre, founded in 1133 by Louis VI and his wife, Adelaide of Savoy, who, as its first abbess, is buried here.

Inside are four marble columns supposedly from a Roman temple which once stood on the site. The vaulted choir dates from the 12th century, the nave was remodelled in the 15th century and the west front in the 18th. During the Revolution, the abbess was guillotined, and the church fell into disuse. It was reconsecrated in 1908. Gothic-style stained glass windows replace those destroyed by a bomb in World War II. The tiny cemetery opens to the public only on 1 November.

Doors to St-Pierre church

❸ Place du Tertre

75018. **Map** 6 F1. **M** Abbesses.

Tertre means "hillock", or mound, and this picturesque square is the highest point in Paris at some 130 m (430 ft). It was once the site of the abbey gallows but is associated with artists, who began exhibiting paintings here in the 19th century. It is lined with colourful restaurants – La Mère Catherine dates back to 1793. The house at No. 21 was formerly the home of the irreverent "Free Commune", founded in 1920 to perpetuate the Bohemian spirit of the area. The Old Montmartre information office is now here.

Surrealist artist Salvador Dalí

❹ Espace Dalí Montmartre

11 Rue Poulbot 75018. **Map** 6 F1. **Tel** 01 42 64 40 10. **M** Abbesses. **Open** 10am–6pm daily (to 8pm Jul–Aug). **W** daliparis.com

A permanent exhibition of 330 works by the prolific painter and sculptor Salvador Dalí is displayed here at the heart of Montmartre. Inside, the vast, dark setting reflects the dramatic character of this 20th-century genius as moving lights grace first one, then another, of his Surrealist works to a soundtrack of Dalí's recorded voice. This fascinating museum also houses a commercial art gallery, a library and a shop selling books, prints and postcards.

❺ Musée de Montmartre

12 Rue Cortot 75018. **Map** 2 F5. **Tel** 01 49 25 89 37. **M** Abbesses, Anvers, Blanche, Lamarck-Caulaincourt. **Open** 10am–6pm daily (Jun–Sep: to 7pm). **Closed** 1 Jan, 25 Dec. **W** museedemontmartre.fr

During the 17th century, this charming home belonged to the actor Roze de Rosimond (Claude de la Rose), a member of Molière's theatre company who, like his mentor Molière, died during a performance of Molière's play *Le Malade Imaginaire*. From 1875, the big white house, undoubtedly the finest in Montmartre, provided living and studio space for artists, including Maurice Utrillo and his mother, Suzanne Valadon, a former acrobat and model who became a talented painter, as well as Raoul Dufy and Auguste Renoir.

The museum recounts the history of Montmartre from the days of the abbesses to the present, through artifacts, drawings and photographs. It is particularly rich in memorabilia of Bohemian life, and has a reconstruction of the Café de l'Abreuvoir, Utrillo's favourite watering hole.

Café de l'Abreuvoir reconstructed

The deceptively rustic exterior of Au Lapin Agile, in the heart of Montmartre

❻ Au Lapin Agile

22 Rue des Saules 75018. **Map** 2 F5.
Tel 01 46 06 85 87. Ⓜ Lamarck-
Caulaincourt. **Open** 9pm–1am
Tue–Sun. *See Entertainment pp334–5.*
Ⓦ au-lapin-agile.com

The former Cabaret des Assassins
derived its current name from a
sign painted by the humorist
André Gill. His picture of a rabbit
escaping from a cooking pot *(Le
Lapin à Gill)* is a pun on his own
name. The club enjoyed popularity with intellectuals and artists
at the start of the 20th century.
Here in 1911, the novelist Roland
Dorgelès and a group of other
regulars staged one of the
modern art world's most
celebrated hoaxes, with the help
of the café owner's donkey, Lolo.
A paintbrush was tied to Lolo's
tail, and the resulting daub was
shown to critical acclaim at the
Salon des Indépendants, under
the enlightening title *Sunset
over the Adriatic*, before the joke
was revealed.
   In 1903, the premises were
bought by the cabaret
entrepreneur Aristide Bruand
(painted in a series of posters by
Toulouse-Lautrec). The venue
was depicted by Pablo Picasso
in an oil painting which was
sold for $20 by the cabaret's
owner in 1912. In 1989, the

painting was sold at auction
for $67.5 million.
   Today, the cabaret venue
manages to retain much of its
original atmosphere.

❼ Halle Saint Pierre

Halle St-Pierre, 2 Rue Ronsard 75018.
Map 7 A1. **Tel** 01 42 58 72 89.
Ⓜ Anvers. **Open** 10am–6pm Mon–
Fri, 11am–7pm Sat, noon–6pm Sun
(Aug: noon–6pm Mon–Fri). **Closed**
some public hols. 🎟 ✉ ♿ 🖥 📷
Ⓦ hallesaintpierre.org

In 1945, the French painter Jean
Dubuffet developed the concept
of *Art Brut* (Outsider or Marginal
Art) to describe works created
outside the boundaries of
"official" culture, often by insane
asylum inmates or the mentally
handicapped. The Halle Saint
Pierre, at the foot of the Butte, is

Art Brut at Halle Saint Pierre

a museum and gallery devoted
to these "raw" art forms. It also
hosts avant-garde theatre and
musical productions, holds
regular literary evenings and
debates and runs children's
workshops. The permanent
collection includes more than
500 works of Naïve art collected
by the publisher Max Fourny in
the 1970s. There is also a
specialist bookshop and café.

❽ Chapelle du Martyre

9 Rue Yvonne-Le-Tac 75018. **Map** 6 F1.
Ⓜ Pigalle. **Open** 3pm–5pm Fri, 1st
Sat & Sun of each month.

This 19th-century chapel stands
on the site of a medieval
convent chapel, which was said
to mark the place where the
early Christian martyr and first
bishop of Paris, Saint Denis,
was beheaded by the Romans
in AD 250. It remained a major
pilgrimage site throughout the
Middle Ages. In 1534, in the
crypt of the original chapel,
Ignatius de Loyola, founder of
the Society of Jesus (the mighty
Jesuit order designed to save
the Catholic Church from the
onslaught of the Protestant
Reformation), took his Jesuit
vows with six companions.

The famous silhouette of the Moulin Rouge nightclub

❾ Place des Abbesses

75018. **Map** 6 F1. Ⓜ Abbesses.

This is one of Paris's most picturesque squares. It is sandwiched between the rather dubious attractions of Place Pigalle with its strip clubs and the Place du Tertre which is mobbed by hundreds of tourists. Be sure not to miss the Abbesses metro station with its unusual green wrought-iron arches and amber lights.

Entrance to the Abbesses metro

Designed by the architect Hector Guimard, it is one of the few original Art Nouveau stations.

❿ St-Jean l'Evangéliste de Montmartre

19 Rue des Abbesses 75018. **Map** 6 F1. **Tel** 01 46 06 43 96. Ⓜ Abbesses. **Open** 9am–7pm Mon–Sat; 9.30am–6pm Sun (to 7pm summer). 🕇 frequent. 📷

Designed by Anatole de Baudot and completed in 1904, this church was the first to be built from reinforced concrete. The flower motifs on the interior are typical of Art Nouveau, while its interlocking arches suggest Islamic architecture. The red-brick facing has earned it the nickname St-Jean-des-Briques.

Detail of St-Jean l'Evangéliste facade

⓫ Bateau-Lavoir

13 Pl Emile-Goudeau 75018. **Map** 6 F1. Ⓜ Abbesses. **Closed** to public.

This ramshackle tenement building took its name from its resemblance to the laundry boats that used to operate along the River Seine. Between 1890 and 1920 it was home to some of the most talented artists and poets of the day. They lived in squalid conditions with only one tap and took it in turns to sleep in the beds. Picasso, Raoul Dufy, Van Dongen, Marie Laurencin, Juan Gris, Modigliani and Jean Cocteau were just a few of the residents. It was here that Picasso painted *Les Demoiselles d'Avignon* in 1907, usually regarded as the painting that inspired Cubism. The original building burned down in 1970, but a concrete replica has been built – with studio space for up-and-coming artists.

⓬ Moulin Rouge

82 Blvd de Clichy 75018. **Map** 6 E1. **Tel** 01 53 09 82 82. Ⓜ Blanche. **Open** Dinner: 7pm; shows: 9pm and 11pm daily. 📷 📺 *See Entertainment pp335–6.* 🖥 moulinrouge.fr

Built in 1885, the Moulin Rouge was turned into a dance hall as early as 1900. The cancan originated in Montparnasse, in the polka gardens of the Rue de la Grande-Chaumière, but it will always be associated with the Moulin Rouge where the wild and colourful dance shows were immortalized in the posters and drawings of Henri de Toulouse-Lautrec. The high-kicking routines of famous "Dorriss girls" such as Yvette Guilbert and Jane Avril continue today in a glittering, Las Vegas-style revue that includes sophisticated light shows and displays of magic.

⑬ Cimetière de Montmartre

20 Ave Rachel 75018. **Map** 2 D5. **Tel** 01 53 42 36 30. Ⓜ Place de Clichy, Blanche. **Open** 8am–6pm daily (opens 8.30am Sat, 9am Sun). ♿ 📷 call 01 53 42 36 30.

This has been the resting place for many artistic luminaries since the beginning of the 19th century. The composers Hector Berlioz and Jacques Offenbach (who wrote the famous cancan tune) are buried here, alongside many other celebrities such as La Goulue (stage name of Louise Weber, the high-kicking *danseuse* who was the cancan's first star performer and Toulouse-Lautrec's model), the painter Edgar Degas, writer Alexandre Dumas *fils*, German poet Heinrich Heine, Russian dancer Vaslav Nijinsky, and film director François Truffaut. It's an evocative, atmospheric place, conveying some of the heated energy and artistic creativity of Montmartre a century ago.

Nearby, close to Square Roland Dorgelès, there is another, smaller, often overlooked Montmartre cemetery – **Cimetière St-Vincent**. Here lie more of the great artistic names of the district, including the Swiss composer Arthur Honegger and the writer Marcel Aymé. Most notable of all at St-Vincent is the grave of the great French painter Maurice Utrillo, the quintessential Montmartre artist, many of whose works are

Moulin de la Galette

now some of the most enduring images of the area.

⑭ Moulin de la Galette

T-junction at Rue Tholoze and Rue Lepic 75018. **Map** 2 E5. Ⓜ Lamarck-Caulaincourt, Abbesses.

Once some 14 windmills dotted the Montmartre skyline and were used for grinding wheat and pressing grapes. Today only two remain: the Radet, now a restaurant confusingly named Moulin de la Galette which stands further along the Rue Lepic, and the rebuilt Moulin de la Galette, originally built in 1622 and formerly known as the Blute-fin. One of its mill owners, Debray, was supposedly crucified on the windmill's sails during the 1814 Siege of Paris. He had been trying to repulse the invading Cossacks. At the end of the

19th century both mills became famous dance halls providing inspiration for many artists, notably Pierre-Auguste Renoir and Vincent Van Gogh.

The steep Rue Lepic is a busy shopping area. The Impressionist painter Armand Guillaumin once lived on the first floor of No. 54. Van Gogh inhabited its third floor, and painted the view from there.

⑮ Avenue Junot

75018. **Map** 2 E5. Ⓜ Lamarck-Caulaincourt.

Opened in 1910, this broad, peaceful street includes many painters' studios and beautiful Art Deco houses. No. 13 has mosaics designed by its former resident, illustrator Francisque Poulbot, who was famous for his drawings of children and street urchins. At No. 15 is Maison Tristan Tzara, named after its previous owner, the Romanian Dadaist poet. Its eccentric design by the Austrian architect Adolf Loos aimed to complement the poet's character. No. 23 is Villa Léandre, with its quaint Anglo-Norman style houses.

Just off the Avenue Junot up the steps of the Allée des Brouillards is an 18th-century architectural folly, the Château des Brouillards. In the 19th century it was the home of the French Symbolist writer Gérard de Nerval, who took his pet lobster for walks in the Palais-Royal gardens.

Cimetière de Montmartre, the final resting place of many famous people

FURTHER AFIELD

Many of the châteaux outside Paris originally built as country retreats for the aristocracy and post-Revolutionary bourgeoisie are now preserved as museums. Versailles is without doubt the finest, but if your tastes are Modernist, there's also Le Corbusier architecture to see. Disneyland® Paris and Parc de la Villette offer plenty to amuse adults and children alike, and there are delightful parks to relax in when the bustle of the city gets too much.

Sights at a Glance

Historic Buildings and Streets
18 Bercy
19 Bibliothèque Nationale de France
20 13th Arrondissement
22 Cité Universitaire
24 Institut Pasteur
26 *Versailles pp250–55*
27 Rue de la Fontaine
28 Fondation Le Corbusier
32 La Défense
33 Château de Malmaison

Churches
1 St-Alexandre-Nevsky Cathedral
7 Basilique-Cathédrale de Saint-Denis
23 Notre-Dame du Travail

Markets
6 Marché aux Puces de St-Ouen
8 Portes St-Denis et St-Martin
15 Marché d'Aligre

Leisure Parks
11 *Parc de la Villette pp238–41*
14 *Disneyland® Paris pp244–7*

Parks, Gardens and Canals
2 Parc Monceau
9 Canal St-Martin
10 Parc des Buttes-Chaumont
17 Château et Bois de Vincennes
21 Parc Montsouris
25 Parc André Citroën
30 Bois de Boulogne

Cemeteries
13 *Cimetière du Père Lachaise pp242–3*

Museums and Galleries
3 Musée Nissim de Camondo
4 Musée Cernuschi
5 Musée Gustave Moreau
12 Musée du Fumeur
16 Cité Nationale de l'Histoire de l'Immigration
29 Musée Marmottan- Monet
31 Musée des Années 30

Key
Main sightseeing areas
Motorways
Major Roads

0 km — 5
0 miles — 3

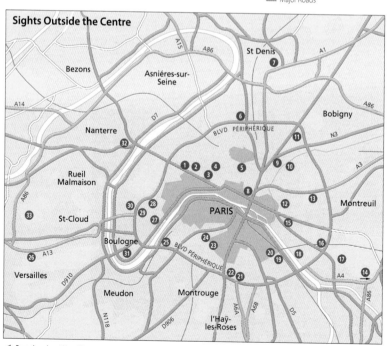

Sights Outside the Centre

◄ Formal garden at Versailles

For additional keys to symbols *see back flap*

North of the City

St-Alexandre-Nevsky Cathedral

❶ St-Alexandre-Nevsky Cathedral

12 Rue Daru 75008. **Map** 4 F3. **Tel** 01 42 27 37 34. Ⓜ Courcelles. **Open** 3pm–5pm Tue, Fri, Sun. 🕆 6pm Sat, 10am Sun. 🎧 📷 by appt.

This imposing Russian Orthodox cathedral with its five golden-copper domes signals the presence of a large Russian community in Paris. Designed by members of the St Petersburg Fine Arts Academy and financed jointly by Tzar Alexander II and the local Russian community, the cathedral was completed in 1861. Inside, a wall of icons divides the church in two. The Greek-cross plan and the rich interior mosaics and frescoes are Neo-Byzantine in style, while the exterior and gilt domes are traditional Russian Orthodox.

The Russian population in the city increased dramatically following the Bolshevik Revolution of 1917, when thousands of Russians fled to Paris for safety. The Rue Daru, in which the cathedral stands, and the surrounding area form "Little Russia", with its Russian schools and the many dance academies, and delightful tea shops and bookshops where visitors can browse.

❷ Parc Monceau

35 Blvd de Courcelles 75017. **Map** 5 A3. **Tel** 01 42 27 39 56. Ⓜ Monceau. **Open** 7am–8pm daily (to 10pm summer). *See Eight Guided Walks pp260–61.*

This green haven dates back to 1778 when the Duc de Chartres (later Duc d'Orléans) commissioned the painter-writer and amateur landscape designer Louis Carmontelle to create a magnificent garden. Also a theatre designer, Carmontelle created a "garden of dreams", an exotic landscape full of architectural follies in imitation of English and German fashion of the time. In 1783, the Scottish landscape gardener Thomas Blaikie laid out an area of the garden in English style. The park was the scene of the first recorded parachute landing, made by André-Jacques Garnerin on 22 October 1797.

Over the years, the park changed hands and in 1852 it was acquired by the state and half the land sold off for property development. The remaining 9 ha (22 acres) were made into public gardens. These were restored and new buildings erected by Adolphe Alphand, architect of the Bois de Boulogne and the Bois de Vincennes.

Today, the park remains one of the most chic in the capital but has lost many of its early features. A *naumachia* basin flanked by Corinthian columns remains. This is an ornamental version of a Roman pool used for simulating naval battles. There are also a Renaissance arcade, pyramids, a river and the Pavillon de Chartres, a charming rotunda designed by Nicolas Ledoux which was once used as a tollhouse. Just south of here is a huge red pagoda, which now houses a gallery devoted to Asian art.

❸ Musée Nissim de Camondo

63 Rue de Monceau 75008. **Map** 5 A3. **Tel** 01 53 89 06 40, 01 53 89 06 50. Ⓜ Monceau, Villiers. **Open** 10am–5.30pm Wed–Sun (last adm: 4.30pm). **Closed** public hols. 🎧 ♿ restricted. 🖥 lesartsdecoratifs.fr

Comte Moïse de Camondo, a leading Jewish financier during the belle epoque, commissioned this mansion in 1914. It was built in the style of the Petit Trianon, at Versailles (*see pp250–55*), to house a rare collection of 18th-century furniture, tapestries, paintings and other precious objects. The museum has been faithfully and lovingly restored to recreate an aristocratic town house of the Louis XV and XVI eras. In the museum, there are Savonnerie carpets, Beauvais tapestries and the Buffon service (Sèvres

Colonnade beside the *naumachia* basin in Parc Monceau

Musée Nissim de Camondo

porcelain). The very latest gadgets, for the period, are now displayed in the restored kitchen and service quarters, equipped with the utmost efficiency, taste and forethought by their owner.

❹ Musée Cernuschi

7 Ave Vélasquez 75008. **Map** 5 A3. **Tel** 01 53 96 21 50. **M** Villiers, Monceau. **Open** 10am–6pm Tue–Sun (last adm: 5.30pm). **Closed** public hols. 🖼 🗆 🖼 **w** cernuschi.paris.fr

This mansion near Parc Monceau contains an intriguing private collection of late East Asian art which was amassed by the Milanese-born politician and banker Enrico Cernuschi (1821–96). The original bequest of 5,000 lacquered, ceramic, bronze and ivory items has been augmented by donations and acquisitions over the years. The wide-ranging collection, now about ten thousand items, includes a 5th-century seated Bodhisattva (Buddhist divine being) from Yunkang; *La Tigresse* (a 12th- century BC bronze vase); and *Horses and Grooms*, an 8th-century T'ang painting on silk attributed to the era's greatest horse painter, court artist Han Kan.

Bodhisattva in the Musée Cernuschi

❺ Musée Gustave Moreau

14 Rue de la Rochefoucauld 75009. **Map** 6 E3. **Tel** 01 48 74 38 50. **M** Trinité. **Open** 10am–12.45pm, 2–5.15pm Mon, Wed, Thu, 10am–5.15pm Fri–Sun. **Closed** 1 Jan, 1 May, 25 Dec. 🖼 🖼 **w** musee-moreau.fr

The Symbolist painter Gustave Moreau (1825–98), known for his vivid, imaginative works depicting biblical and mythological fantasies, left to the French state a vast collection of more than 1,000 oils, watercolours and some 4,000 drawings in his town house. One of Moreau's best-known and most outstanding works, *Jupiter and Semele*, can be seen here. There is also a superb collection of his unfinished sketches.

Angel Traveller by Gustave Moreau, in the Musée Gustave Moreau

❻ Marché aux Puces de St-Ouen

Rue des Rosiers, St-Ouen 75018. **Map** 2 F2. **M** Porte-de-Clignancourt, Garibaldi. **Open** 9am–6pm Sat, 10am–6pm Sun, 11am–5pm Mon; reduced hours during summer. 🗆 call 01 40 11 77 36. See Markets p331. **w** marcheaux puces-saintouen.com

This is the oldest, most expensive and largest of the Paris flea markets, covering 6 ha (15 acres). In the 19th century, rag merchants and tramps would gather outside the city limits and offer their wares for sale. By

Marché aux Puces du St-Ouen, an antiques and bric-a-brac market

the 1920s, there was a proper market here, where masterpieces could sometimes be purchased cheaply from the often uniformed sellers. Today, it is divided into specialist markets. Known especially for its profusion of furniture and ornaments from the Second Empire (1852–70), few bargains are to be found these days, yet some 150,000 bargain-hunters, tourists and dealers still flock here to browse among more than 2,000 stalls *(see p331)*.

❼ Basilique-Cathédrale de Saint-Denis

1 Rue de la Légion D'Honneur, 93200 St-Denis. **Tel** 01 48 09 83 54. **M** St-Denis-Basilique. **RER** St-Denis. **Open** Apr–Sep: 10am–6.15pm Mon–Sat, noon–6.15pm Sun; Oct–Mar: 10am–5.15pm Mon–Sat, noon–5.15pm Sun (last adm: 30 mins before closing). **Closed** 1 Jan, 1 May, 25 Dec. 🕀 8.30am, 10am Sun. 🖼 🖼 🗆 🖼

Constructed between 1137 and 1281, the cathedral is on the site of the tomb of St Denis, the first bishop of Paris, who was beheaded in AD 250. The building was the original influence for Gothic art. From Merovingian times, it was a burial place for rulers of France. During the Revolution, many tombs were desecrated and scattered, but the best were stored, and now represent a collection of funerary art. Memorials include those of Dagobert (died 638), Henri II (died 1559) and Catherine de' Medici (died 1589), and Louis XVI and Marie-Antoinette (died 1793).

❽ Portes St-Denis et St-Martin

Blvds St-Denis & St-Martin 75010.
Map 7 B5. Ⓜ Strasbourg-St-Denis.

These gates give access to the two ancient and important north–south thoroughfares whose names they bear. They once marked the entrance to the city. The Porte St-Denis is 23 m (76 ft) high and was built in 1672 by François Blondel. It is decorated with figures by Louis XIV's sculptor, François Girardon. The gates commemorate victories of the king's armies in Flanders and the Rhine that year. Porte St-Martin is 17 m (56 ft) tall and was built in 1674 by Pierre Bullet. It celebrates Besançon's capture and the defeat of the Triple Alliance of Spain, Holland and Germany.

East of the City

Boats berthed at Port de l'Arsenal

❾ Canal St-Martin

Map 8 E2. Ⓜ Jaurès, J Bonsergent, Goncourt. *See pp262–3.*

The 5-kilometre (3-mile) canal, opened in 1825, provides a shortcut for river traffic between loops of the Seine. It has long been loved by novelists, film directors and tourists alike. It is dotted with barges and pleasure boats that leave from the Port de l'Arsenal. At the north end of the canal is the Bassin de la Villette waterway and the elegant Neo-Classical Rotonde de la Villette, spectacularly floodlit at night.

Western arch of the Porte St-Denis, once the entrance to the city

❿ Parc des Buttes-Chaumont

Rue Manin 75019 (main access from Rue Armand Carrel). Ⓜ Botzaris, Buttes-Chaumont. **Open** 7am–8pm daily (until 10pm in summer). **Closed** Some areas will be closed for renovation until 2016.
🚗 🚲 *See pp270–71.*

For many, this is the most pleasant and unexpected park in Paris. The panoramic hilly site was converted in the 1860s by Baron Haussmann from a rubbish dump and quarry with a gallows below. Haussmann worked with the landscape architect/designer Adolphe Alphand, who organized a vast programme to furnish the new pavement-lined avenues with benches and lampposts. Others involved in the creation of this park were the engineer Darcel and the landscape gardener Barillet-Deschamps. They created a lake, made an island with real and artificial rocks, gave it a Roman-style temple and added a waterfall, streams, foot-bridges leading to the island and beaches. Today, visitors will also find boating facilities and donkey rides.

⓫ Parc de la Villette

See pp238–41.

⓬ Musée du Fumeur

7 Rue Pache 75011. **Tel** 01 46 59 05 51.
Ⓜ Voltaire. **Open** 12.30–7pm Mon–Sat. **Closed** 1st week of Jan, 1 May, 8 May, 25 Dec. 🚗 🏠

As France's public spaces are all tobacco free, this quaint museum nostalgically documents the history of tobacco and smoking through the ages. Objects used by smokers across the world, including 17th-century clay pipes, rare snuff boxes, and period engravings, sit alongside modern works of art dedicated

Parc des Buttes-Chaumont

to smoking. Aficionados can consult the library which offers essays and articles from tobacco magazines, plus regular film-showings covering subjects such as how tobacco is cultivated and how to roll a cigar. A "vapor lounge" caters for those fond of electronic cigarettes.

⑬ Cimetière du Père Lachaise

See pp242–3.

⑭ Disneyland® Paris

See pp244–7.

⑮ Marché d'Aligre

Place d'Aligre 75012. **Map** 14 F5. Ⓜ Ledru-Rollin. **Open** 7.30am–1pm Mon–Sat (outdoor market closed Mon), 7.30am–2pm Sun.

On Sunday mornings, this lively market offers one of the most colourful sights in Paris. French, Arab and African traders hawk fruit, vegetables, flowers and clothing on the streets, while the adjoining covered market, the Beauveau St-Antoine, offers fruit, vegetables and many intriguing international delicacies.

Aligre is where old and new Paris meet. Here, the established community of this old artisan quarter coexists with a more recently established group of hip urban professionals, who have been lured here by the transformation of the nearby Bastille area (see p102).

⑯ Cité Nationale de l'Histoire de l'Immigration

293 Ave Daumesnil 75012. **Tel** 01 53 59 58 60. Ⓜ Porte Dorée. **Open** 10am–5.30pm Tue–Fri, 10am–7pm Sat, Sun. **Closed** 1 Jan, 1 May, 25 Dec. ✉ 🎥 ⚠ ♿ restricted. 📷 🌐 **histoire-immigration.fr**

This museum and aquarium is housed in a beautiful Art Deco building that was designed especially for the 1931 Colonial Exhibition. The impressive façade has a vast frieze by

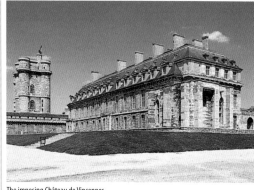
The imposing Château de Vincennes

A Janniot, depicting the contributions of France's overseas territories.

Formerly the home of the Musée National des Arts d'Afrique et d'Océanie (whose collection was moved to the Musée du quai Branly in 2003, see pp194–5), the Palais de la Porte Dorée now houses the Cité Nationale de l'Histoire de l'Immigration. This acts as both a museum and a cultural centre, with regular live performances and films on the subject of the history of immigration in France.

The magnificent 1930s Hall d'Honneur and the Salle des Fêtes (ballroom) are also open to the public. In the basement, there is a magnificent tropical aquarium filled with colourful fish, as well as terrariums containing tortoises and crocodiles.

Exterior relief on the Cité Nationale de l'Histoire de l'Immigration

⑰ Château et Bois de Vincennes

Ⓜ Château de Vincennes. Ⓡ Vincennes. Château Ave de Paris 94300 Vincennes. **Tel** 01 48 08 31 20. **Open** Mid-May–end Sep: 10am–6pm daily; end Sep–mid-May: 10am–5pm daily; options available for guided visits), last adm 45 mins before closing. **Closed** public hols. 🎥 ✉ 📷 Bois de Vincennes: **Open** dawn to dusk daily. 🌐 **chateau-vincennes.fr**

The Château de Vincennes, enclosed by a defensive wall and a moat, was once a royal residence. It was here that Henry V of England died painfully of dysentery in 1422. His body was boiled in the Château's kitchen to prepare it for shipping back to England. Abandoned when Versailles was completed, the château was converted into an arsenal by Napoleon.

The 14th-century *donjon*, or keep, is the tallest in Europe and is a fine example of medieval military architecture. It houses the Château's museum. Building work on the Gothic chapel started in 1380, but was not finished until around 1550. The chapel has beautiful stone rose windows and a single aisle. Two 17th-century pavilions house a museum of army insignia.

Once a royal hunting ground, the forest of Vincennes was given to the City of Paris by Napoleon III in 1860. Baron Haussmann's landscape architect added ornamental lakes and cascades. Among its main attractions is the largest funfair in France (open from Palm Sunday to end of May).

⓫ Parc de la Villette

The old slaughterhouses and livestock market of Paris have been transformed into this Bernard Tschumi-designed urban park. Its vast facilities stretch across 55 ha (136 acres) of a previously run-down part of the city. The plan is to revive the tradition of parks for meetings and activities and to stimulate interest in the arts and sciences. Work began in 1984, and the park has grown to include a science museum, a concert hall, an exhibition pavilion, a spherical cinema, a circus and a music centre. Linking them all is the park itself, with its *folies*, walkways, gardens and playgrounds. In the summer the park holds an open-air film festival.

The Folies
These red cubes punctuate the park and provide a variety of services, such as a café and a children's workshop.

Children's Playground
The maze-like setting, complete with sand pits and colourful play equipment makes this playground a paradise for young children.

★ Grande Halle
The old cattle hall has been transformed into a flexible exhibition space with mobile floors and auditorium.

Entrance

★ Cité de la Musique
This quirky but elegant all-white complex holds the music conservatory, a concert hall, library, studios and a museum.

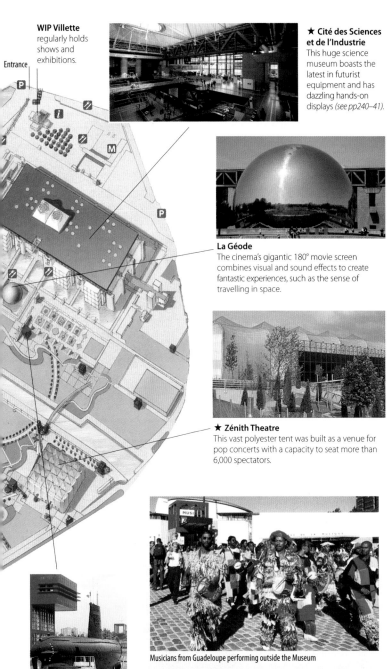

WIP Villette regularly holds shows and exhibitions.

Entrance

★ Cité des Sciences et de l'Industrie
This huge science museum boasts the latest in futurist equipment and has dazzling hands-on displays *(see pp240–41)*.

La Géode
The cinema's gigantic 180° movie screen combines visual and sound effects to create fantastic experiences, such as the sense of travelling in space.

★ Zénith Theatre
This vast polyester tent was built as a venue for pop concerts with a capacity to seat more than 6,000 spectators.

Musicians from Guadeloupe performing outside the Museum

Le Musée de la Musique

This museum brings together a collection of over 4,500 instruments, objects, tools and works of art covering the history of music since the Renaissance. The permanent collection of over 900 items is displayed chronologically and can be traced using infrared audio headphones.

L'Argonaute
The exhibit consists of a 1950s submarine and a nearby navigation museum.

Cité des Sciences et de l'Industrie

This hugely popular science and technology museum occupies the largest of the old Villette slaughterhouses, which now form part of a massive urban park. Architect Adrien Fainsilber has created an imaginative interplay of light, vegetation and water in the high-tech, five-storey building, which soars 40 m (133 ft) high, stretching over 3 ha (7 acres). At the museum's heart is the Explora exhibit, a fascinating guide to the worlds of science and technology. Visitors can take part in computerized games on space, the earth, transport, energy, design and sound. On other levels there is a children's science city, a library and shops.

The Main Hall
With a soaring network of shafts, bridges, escalators and balconies, the vast Main Hall has a cathedral-like atmosphere.

★ The Story of the Universe
An exploration of the birth of the universe, this exhibit takes you back 13.7 billion years to the creation of the first atom.

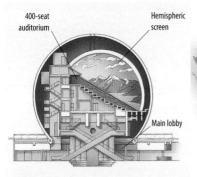

400-seat auditorium

Hemispheric screen

Main lobby

La Géode

This vast sphere houses a hemispherical cinema screen, 1,000 sq m (11,000 sq ft), showing IMAX and 3D films. The Géode is prohibited for women more than six-months pregnant.

KEY

① **The moat** was designed by Fainsilber so that natural light could penetrate into the lower levels of the building.

② **The Globalo-Scope** is a 3D projection on a globe, which shows climate change and several other phenomena on a global scale.

③ **The greenhouse** is a square hothouse, 32 m (105 ft) high and wide, linking the park to the building.

Planetarium
Explore our solar system in immersive films and sessions with astronomy specialists.

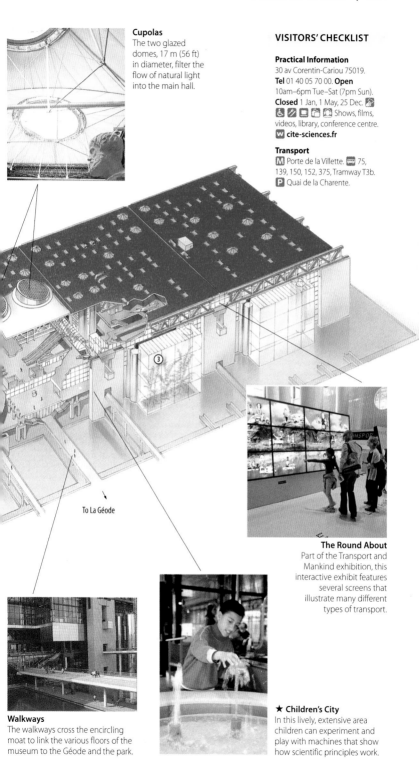

Cupolas
The two glazed domes, 17 m (56 ft) in diameter, filter the flow of natural light into the main hall.

VISITORS' CHECKLIST

Practical Information
30 av Corentin-Cariou 75019.
Tel 01 40 05 70 00. **Open**
10am–6pm Tue–Sat (7pm Sun).
Closed 1 Jan, 1 May, 25 Dec. Shows, films, videos, library, conference centre.
W cite-sciences.fr

Transport
M Porte de la Villette. 75, 139, 150, 152, 375, Tramway T3b.
P Quai de la Charente.

③

To La Géode

The Round About
Part of the Transport and Mankind exhibition, this interactive exhibit features several screens that illustrate many different types of transport.

Walkways
The walkways cross the encircling moat to link the various floors of the museum to the Géode and the park.

★ Children's City
In this lively, extensive area children can experiment and play with machines that show how scientific principles work.

⓭ Cimetière du Père Lachaise

Paris's most prestigious cemetery is set on a wooded hill overlooking the city. The land was once owned by Père de la Chaise, Louis XIV's confessor, but it was bought by order of Napoleon in 1803 to create a new cemetery. The cemetery became so popular with the Paris bourgeoisie that it was expanded six times during the century. Here were buried celebrities such as the writer Honoré de Balzac and the composer Frédéric Chopin, and more recently, the singer Jim Morrison and the actor Yves Montand. Famous graves and striking funerary sculpture make this a pleasant place for a leisurely, nostalgic stroll.

The Columbarium was built at the end of the 19th century. The American dancer Isadora Duncan is one of the many celebrities whose ashes are housed here.

★ **Simone Signoret and Yves Montand**
France's most famous post-war cinema couple were renowned for their left-wing views and long turbulent relationship.

KEY

① **Marcel Proust** brilliantly chronicled the *Belle Époque* in his novel *Remembrance of Things Past*.

② **Allan Kardec** was the founder of a 19th-century spiritual cult, which still has a strong following. His tomb is forever covered in pilgrims' flowers.

③ **Mur des Fédérés** is the wall against which the last Communard rebels were shot by government forces in 1871. It is now a place of pilgrimage for left-wing sympathizers.

④ **George Rodenbach**, the 19th-century poet, is depicted as rising out of his tomb with a rose in the hand of his outstretched arm.

⑤ **Elizabeth Demidoff**, a Russian princess who died in 1818, is honoured by a three-storey Classical temple by Quaglia.

⑥ **The remains of Molière**, the great 17th-century actor and dramatist, were transferred here in 1817 to add historic glamour to the new cemetery.

⑦ **Frédéric Chopin**, the great Polish composer, belonged to the French Romantic generation.

⑧ **Monument aux Morts** by Paul Albert Bartholomé is one of the best monumental sculptures in the cemetery. It dominates the central avenue.

Entrance

Théodore Géricault
The French Romantic painter's masterpiece, *The Raft of the Medusa* (*see p124*), is depicted on his tomb.

★ Oscar Wilde
The Irish dramatist, aesthete and great wit was cast away from virtuous Britain to die of drink and dissipation in Paris in 1900. Jacob Epstein sculpted the monument.

VISITORS' CHECKLIST

Practical Information
16 Rue du Repos.
Tel 01 55 25 82 10.
Open 8am–5.30pm daily (from 8.30am Sat, 9am Sun; mid-Mar– early Nov: to 6pm). 🗓 ℹ

Transport
Ⓜ Père Lachaise, Alexandre Dumas. 🚌 60, 61, 64, 69, 26 to Pl Gambetta. 🅿 Pl Gambetta.

★ Edith Piaf
Known as "the little sparrow" because of her size, Piaf was the 20th century's greatest French popular singer. In her tragic voice, she sang of the sorrows and love woes of the Paris working class.

Victor Noir
The life-size statue of this 19th-century journalist shot by Pierre Bonaparte, a cousin of Napoleon III, is said to have fertility powers.

Sarah Bernhardt
The great French tragedienne, who died in 1923 aged 78, was famous for her portrayal of Racine heroines.

François Raspail
The tomb of this much-imprisoned partisan of the 1830 and 1840 revolutions is in the form of a prison.

★ Jim Morrison
The death of *The Doors'* lead singer in Paris in 1971 is still a mystery.

⓮ Disneyland® Paris

Disneyland® Paris is built on a massive scale – the 2,230-ha (5,510-acre) site encompasses two theme parks; seven hotels (several with swimming pools); a shopping, dining and entertainment village; an ice skating rink; a lake; two convention centres; and a golf course. One stop down the line from their very own train station lies Val d'Europe, a huge shopping mall with more than 180 shopping outlets, including 60 discount stores, and a SEA LIFE Aquarium.

Unbeatable for complete escapism, combined with vibrant excitement and sheer energy, the Parks offer extreme rides and gentle experiences accompanied by phenomenal visual effects.

The Queen of Hearts' Castle, in Alice's Curious Labyrinth

The Parks

Disneyland® Paris consists of Disneyland® Park and Walt Disney Studios® Park. Disneyland® Park is based on the Magic Kingdom of California and has more than 60 rides or attractions. The most recent is Walt Disney Studios® Park, where interactive exhibits and live shows bring alive the wizardry of the movie and television industry. Find out more at: www.disneylandparis.com or call 0844 800 8898 (UK), 0825 30 60 30 or 30 05 00 (France).

Getting There

By Car
Disneyland® Paris lies 32 km (20 miles) east of Paris, and has its own link (exit 14) from the A4 east-bound from Paris and the A4 west-bound, from Strasbourg. Follow the signs to Marne la Vallée (Val d'Europe) until you see the Disneyland signs. (Disney's Davy Crockett Ranch is exit 13.)

By Air
Both Orly and Charles de Gaulle Airports have a shuttle bus (VEA) which runs every 30 minutes (45 in low season). No booking is necessary. The fare is about €13–17 per person.

By Train
The Paris RER A runs directly to the parks at Marne la Vallée, as does the TGV with connections throughout Europe, including with the Eurostar.

Parking

There is space for over 12,000 vehicles, and an efficient moving sidewalk conveys you to the exit. Parking costs €15 per day for cars, and €20 for campers and coaches. Parking at Disneyland® Paris hotels is free to guests, and the Disneyland® Hotel and Disney's Hotel New York offer valet parking.

Opening Hours

The Parks tend to open at 10am all year round. Disneyland® Park closes at 11pm in high season and earlier in low season. The Walt Disney Studios® Park closes at 8pm in high season and 6pm in low season. Special events, such as Hallowe'en and New Year's eve, can mean extended hours; check the website for details.

When to Visit

The busiest times are Christmas and New Year, mid-February to early April and July to early September, and mid-October. Busiest days are Saturday– Monday; Tuesday and Wednesday are quietest.

Length of Visit

To experience everything Disneyland® Paris has to offer, you really need to spend three or four days at the resort. Although it is possible to tour the Parks in one day each, to enjoy them at less than break-neck pace you need at least two days for Disneyland® Park alone, and if you want to include Buffalo Bill's Wild West show or

Eating and Drinking

There's no need to leave the park to eat during the day. **Au Chalet de la Marionnette** (Fantasyland®) is excellent for kids (and almost deserted at 3pm), as is the **Cowboy Cook-out Barbecue** (Frontierland®), which tends to be rather more crowded. **Colonel Hathi's Pizza Outpost** (Adventureland®) is worth a visit just to see the authentic colonial gear, whilst **Café Hyperion – Videopolis** (Discoveryland®) offers good food plus excellent entertainment, but service is very slow.

You pay a premium for full-service restaurants but the experience of eating in **Blue Lagoon Restaurant** (Adventureland®) is one you will remember. You dine on the "shore" of a Caribbean Pirate hideaway while the boats from Pirates of the Caribbean glide past. **Walt's**, on Main Street, USA®, is also a good but pricey restaurant offering American fare. If you're lucky, they'll seat you so that you can watch the afternoon Main Street parade in comfort from an upstairs window.

In Disney Village® **Annette's Diner** is staffed by roller-skating waitresses against a background of 1950s records. **Planet Hollywood®** is another good option, and the **Rainforest Café®** provides an interestingly animated meal. Bavarian specialities are on the menu in **King Ludwig's Castle**, while a giant **McDonald's®** serves the usual fare. The hotel restaurants are more expensive the nearer they are located to the park.

visit all of the attractions in Disney Village®, then you'll be pushed to manage it all in under four days. Locals turn up on a daily basis from Paris, which is only 35 minutes away on the RER, but most guests from further afield will stay in hotels. Disney offer several packages for those who wish to stay on site. These include passes for the Parks, and accommodation with continental breakfast included. All-inclusive packages can also be booked.

Tickets

Tickets can be bought online, as part of a package or from any Disney Store before you leave home, or at the Park upon arrival – though this means queuing. One-, two- or three-day tickets are available. Hopper tickets allow same day entry to both Parks. The Paris transport system RATP also sells tickets combining RER travel and entry to the Parks. Once inside, you can use your ticket to get a fast pass for certain rides with a specific time slot to enable entry without queuing.

Getting Around

Disney provides an efficient transport system between the Parks and the hotels (excluding Disney's Davy Crockett Ranch), with buses on the half hour. In summer, a fleet of little open-top buses drives slowly around Lake Disney, ferrying guests between the three lakeside hotels and Disney Village®. If you're staying at any of the on-site hotels it's only a short

Sleeping Beauty Castle, the centrepiece of the Park

Which Hotel?

There are six hotels on site, and one in woodland 2 km (3 miles) away. The best hotels are the closest to the Parks.

Hotel Santa Fe®: basic, small and reasonably inexpensive. The only hotel offering parking immediately outside your room.
Hotel Cheyenne®: a Wild West theme hotel, about 17 minutes' walk from the park. Small rooms (with bunks for the kids), a Native American village play area. Inexpensive and a great experience. Kids love this hotel.
Sequoia Lodge®: a lakeside "hunter's lodge", moderately priced with more than 1,000 rooms. Ask for a room in the main building. Rooms at the front have great views.
Newport Bay Club®: a huge, nautically-themed, hotel on the lakeside. Moderately priced, this massive hotel has a huge convention centre, magnificent swimming pool and three floors offering extra services for a supplement.
Disney's Hotel New York: expensive and business-oriented with a large convention centre. An ice-skating rink is available Oct–Mar.
Disneyland® Hotel: the jewel in the crown. Expensive, but right at the entrance to the Disneyland® Park. Full of delightful touches, such as grandfather clocks and ever-present Disney characters. The Castle Club is a 50-room hotel-within-a-hotel. If you can afford it, a week of decadent fawning and unrestrained hedonism can be yours!
Disney's Davy Crockett Ranch: log cabins sleeping 4–6 are grouped around a woodland trail, as well as traditional camping facilities. The best choice for family activities with some excellent facilities: the pool ranks as one of the best in Disneyland® Paris.

walk (20 minutes at most) to the Park gates.

Money

Credit cards are accepted everywhere within the resort. ATMs and commission-free foreign exchange are available immediately inside the Park entrances and at reception in all the hotels.

Disabled Travellers

City Hall (immediately within Disneyland® Park) has a brochure outlining the facilities for the disabled, and a Disabled Guest Guide can be pre-ordered (free) from the website. The complex is designed very much with the disabled in mind and wheelchairs can be hired, but note that cast members are not allowed to assist with lifting people or moving wheelchairs.

Staying in a Disney Hotel

The on-site hotels offer rooms at a wide range of prices; generally, those closest to the Parks are the most expensive. Advantages include virtually no

The runaway mine-train track of Big Thunder Mountain

travelling to reach the Parks, fast passes (ask at reception about restrictions) and "early bird" entry to the parks on selected dates (usually at peak times).

If you stay at a Disney hotel, you will be given a hotel ID card which is very important. As well as being used to charge anything you buy back to your hotel room (and have it delivered there), it also allows you entry to the Disneyland hotel grounds early in the morning while they're still shut to day trippers (the grounds also act as an entrance to the Park).

For children (of any age), one of the most exciting bonuses of staying in an on-site hotel is the chance to dine with Disney characters.

Exploring Disneyland® Paris

The resort consists of two large entertainment areas, Disneyland® Park and the Walt Disney Studios® Park. The former celebrates Hollywood folklore and fantasies, both past and future, while the latter highlights the ingenuity of the production processes involved in cinema, animation and television. The resort offers a plethora of attractions and themed parades chosen from the wonderful world of Disney.

Disneyland® Park

Main Street, USA®

Main Street represents a fantasy small-town America, right down to the traffic, which includes horse-drawn rail cars, a paddy wagon and other vintage transport in a system that runs between Town Square and Central Plaza. The Victorian façades offer a wealth of detail, and front interesting stores. The Emporium is the place for gifts. Further along, you can snack at Casey's Corner or succumb to the aromas from Cookie Kitchen or the Cable Car Bake Shop. Either side of the shops are the Discovery and Liberty Arcades, offering a covered route to the Central Plaza and hosting displays and small stalls.

On certain nights, thousands of lights set Main Street's paving aglow. Disney's Fantillusion, a fantasy of music, live action and illuminated floats, begins at Town Square. From Main Street you can ride a 19th-century "steam" engine. Do note that boarding elsewhere than Main Street, is not always possible before noon.

Frontierland®

This homage to America's Wild West hosts some of the Park's most popular attractions. Big Thunder Mountain, a rollercoaster ride, is circled by the Thunder Mesa river boat that takes a musical cruise around America's finest natural monuments. Phantom Manor is an excellent ghost ride with realistic special effects. Pocahontas Indian Village and Legends of the Wild West are both popular with younger children.

Adventureland®

Enjoy the wild rides and Audio-Animatronics of Adventureland®. Indiana Jones™ and the Temple of Peril hurtles you through a derelict mine. The ride has torches, steep drops and tight 360º loops.

Pirates of the Caribbean is a great boat ride through underground prisons and past fighting galleons. La Cabane des Robinson, based on Jonathan Wyss's *Swiss Family Robinson*, starts with a shaky climb up a 27-m (88-ft) Banyan Tree. From here, you explore the rest of the island, including the caves of Ben Gunn from *Treasure Island* and the awe-inspiring suspension bridge near Spyglass Hill. The children's playground, Pirates' Beach, and Aladdin's Enchanted Passage are also well worth a visit.

Fantasyland®

The buildings here are modelled on those in animated movies. Many attractions are for younger children, such as Snow White and the Seven Dwarfs, and Pinocchio's Fantastic Journey. The very young will love Dumbo the Flying Elephant. Peter Pan's Flight is a triumph of imagination and technology, flying you high over the streets of London. A popular diversion is Alice's Curious Labyrinth.

Hourly, there's a musical parade of clockwork figures at "It's a small world". Aboard a boat, you meander through lands of animated models to the strains of the eponymous song. Le Pays des Contes de Fées (Storybook Land) is another boat ride. Next, hop aboard Casey Jr for a train ride circling the boats.

Discoveryland

Science fiction and the future are the themes here. The multi-loop ride Space Mountain®: Mission 2 draws crowds from the outset, but at the end of the day, you can often walk straight on. Les Mystères du Nautilus takes you right into the submarine from *20,000 Leagues Under the Sea*. Autopia, where you can drive a real, petrol-engined car, is a magnet for youngsters. Orbitron® features spaceships, whilst Star Tours takes you on a breathtaking journey in a star shuttle. Buzz Lightyear Laser Blast takes you into the world of toys where you have to shoot Emperor Zurg's electronic army.

The best shows are in Videopolis. Captain EO is a masterpiece of total sensory stimulation.

Walt Disney Studios® Park

Front lot

Inside the giant studio gates, you can't miss Mickey Mouse as he appears in *The Sorcerer's Apprentice*. Also hard to miss is the "Earful Tower", a massive studio icon based on the water tower at the Disney Studios in California. Disney Studio 1 houses a film set boulevard, complete with stylised street façades and venues such as the 1930's-style Club Swankedero, the Liki Tiki tropical bar and the ultra cool rat-packesque Hep Cat Club. Also behind the façades is the Legends of Hollywood store.

Toon Studio®

A huge *Sorcerer's Apprentice* hat marks the entrance to the Art of Disney Animation®, an interactive attraction tracing the history of moving imagery. Animagique® brings together some of the greatest moments from the Disney corpus. In Flying Carpets over Agrabah®, the genie from *Aladdin* invites spectators to take part in an astonishing magic carpet ride. Crush's Coaster® takes you into the underwater animated world of Nemo where you face sharks. Toy Story Playland, which opened in 2010, takes visitors to "Andy's Back-Yard" for a simulated parachute dive.

Production Courtyard®

At the interactive attraction, Stitch Live!, an animated Stitch talks to the audience while CinéMagique is a must for film buffs, as it covers the history of both American and European cinema. Must dos include the

Studio Tram Tour and a go on the latest ride Twilight Zone Tower of Terror™ where you plunge 13 floors inside a haunted hotel.

Backlot

This area focuses on special effects, film music recording and dare-devil stunts. Armageddon Special Effects presents a tour of film trickery, while Rock 'n' Roller Coaster is a high-speed attraction (in fact, it is the fastest ride in any Disney theme park) that

combines a once-in-a-lifetime ride with neon lights and pulsating Aerosmith music.

La Place de Rémy

This new themed area plays host to the park's 60th attraction, Ratatouille : L'Aventure Totalement Toquée de Rémy. The six-seater "ratmobile" whisks visitors off on a culinary adventure through the cold storage and dining room of Chef Gusteau's famous Paris restaurant.

Rides and Attractions

This chart is designed to help you make the best use of your time at Disneyland.

Rides and Attractions	Queues	Height / Age Restriction	Best Time to Ride or Visit	Fastpass®	Scary Rating	May Cause Motion Sickness	Rating Overall
Phantom Manor	▶		Any		❷		★
Big Thunder Mountain	●	1.2m	FT	✔	❷		★
Pocahontas Indian Village	○		Any		❶		▼
Indiana Jones™ & the Temple of Peril	●	1.4m	LT	✔	❸	✔	★
Adventure Isle	○		Any		❶		▼
La Cabane des Robinson	○		Any		❶		▼
Pirates of the Caribbean	○		Any		❶		★
Peter Pan's Flight	●		FT	✔	❶		◆
Snow White & the Seven Dwarfs	●		▶11		❶		◆
Pinocchio's Fantastic Journey	●		▶11		❶		▼
Dumbo the Flying Elephant	●		FT		❶		▼
Mad Hatter's Teacups	▶		▶12		❶		▼
Alice's Curious Labyrinth	○		Any		❶		▼
"It's a Small World"	○		Any		❶		◆
Casey Jr – Le Petit Train du Cirque	○		▶11		❶		◆
Le Pays des Contes de Fées	○		Any		❶		◆
Buzz Lightyear Laser Blast	▶		Any	✔	❶	✔	◆
Star Tours	○	1.32m	Any	✔	❶		★
Space Mountain®: Mission 2	●	1.32m	LT	✔	❸	✔	★
Captain EO	○		Any		❶		★
Autopia	●		FT		❶		▼
Orbitron®	●	1.2m	FT		❶		▼
Disney Studio 1	▶		Any		❶		◆
Art of Disney Animation®	▶		Any		❶		▼
Animagique®	●		Any		❶		◆
Crush's Coaster®	○	1.07m	Any		❶	✔	★
Flying Carpets Over Agrabah®	●	1.2m	FT		❶	✔	◆
Playhouse Disney Live on Stage!	○		Any		❶		★
CinéMagique	▶		Any		❶		◆
Stitch Live!	▶		FT		❶		◆
Studio Tram Tour®	●		FT		❶		★
Twilight Zone Tower of Terror™	●	1.02m	Any	✔	❸	✔	★
Armageddon Special Effects	●		Any		❶		▼
Rock 'n' Roller Coaster	●	1.2m	Any	✔	❸	✔	★
L'Aventure Totalement Toquée de Rémy	●	1.07m	Any	✔	❶		▼

Short - ○ Medium - ▶ Long - ● Anytime - Any Before 11 - ▶11 First thing -FT Last thing- LT
Not Scary - ❶ Slightly - ❷ Very - ❸ Quite good - ▼ Very good - ◆ Outstanding - ★

⓲ Bercy

75012. **Map** 18 F3. Ⓜ Bercy, Cour St-Emilion.

This former wine-trading quarter east of the city centre, with its once-grim warehouses, pavilions and slum housing, has been transformed into a modern district. An automatic metro line (Line 14) links it to the heart of the city.

The centrepiece of Bercy is the Palais Omnisports de Paris-Bercy, now the city centre's principal venue. The vast pyramidal structure has become a contemporary landmark. Many sports events are held here, as well as classical operas and rock concerts (see pp337 and 341).

Other architecturally adventurous buildings dominate Bercy, notably Chemetov's building for the Ministry of Finance, and Frank Gehry's American Center. This houses the Cinémathèque Française, a wonderful cinema museum that hosts frequent retrospectives on famous directors.

At the foot of these structures, the imaginatively designed 70-ha (173-acre) Parc de Bercy provides a welcome green space for this part of the city. The park's attractions for children include a traditional carousel.

Former wine stores and cellars along Cours St Emilion have been restored as bars, restaurants and shops, and one of the warehouses now contains the Musée des Arts Forains (Fairground Museum), which is

Bibliothèque Nationale de France

open only for private tours. There is also a multiscreen cinema and numerous hotels.

⓳ Bibliothèque Nationale de France

Quai François-Mauriac 75013. **Map** 18 F4. **Tel** 01 53 79 59 59. Ⓜ Bibliothèque F Mitterrand, Quai de la Gare. **Open** Exhibitions: 10am–8pm Tue–Sat, 1–7pm Sun. **Closed** pub hols & 2 wks Sep. 🖼 🖬 for groups by appt. 🛗 🖉 🖾 🖾 **bnf.fr**

Dominique Perrault's 1996 land-mark national library is the most striking of all the Grands Projets with which President Mitterrand revitalized this area. Four towers house 12,000,000 volumes, with reference and research libraries in the central podium. Resources include 50,000 digitized illustrations, sound archives and CD-ROMs. Exhibitions on its hidden collections are often held.

South of the City

⓴ 13th Arrondissement

Zac Paris Rive Gauche, 75013. **Map** 18 F5. Ⓜ Bibliotheque F Mitterrand.

Following a ten-year redevelopment project, the Zac Paris Rive Gauche, Paris's 13th arrondissement has become an area of startling urban regeneration. The once-disused area of land between Gare d'Austerlitz and Ivry-sur-Seine has now been revived to house a university with some 30,000 students. The area also boasts the MK2 Bibliothèque, a vast cinema complex with 14 screens, cafés and exhibition areas. Connected to Bercy by a bridge, the area also offers new housing, schools and business opportunities.

㉑ Parc Montsouris

2 Rue Gazan, Blvd Jourdan 75014. Ⓜ Porte d'Orléans. 🅁🅴🆁 Cité Universitaire, Glaciere. **Open** 8am–5.30pm Mon–Fri (to 9:30pm in summer); 9am–dusk weekends. Times may vary. 🖾

This English-style park was laid out by the landscape architect Adophe Alphand between 1865 and 1878. It has a restaurant, lawns, slopes and a lake that is home to many species of birds. Children will enjoy the play-grounds, pony rides and puppet theatre. The park is the second largest in central Paris and is also home to a weather station.

Bercy's striking American Center, designed by Frank Gehry

㉒ Cité Universitaire

17–21 Blvd Jourdan 75014. **Tel** 01 44 16 64 00. Ⓜ Porte d'Orléans. ⒭ Cité Universitaire. Ⓦ **ciup.fr**

This is an international city in miniature for more than 5,000 foreign students attending university in Paris. Created in the 1920s, it now contains 40 houses and, fascinatingly, each is in an architectural style linked to different countries. The Swiss House and the Franco-Brazilian House were designed by the Modernist architect Le Corbusier. The International House, donated by John D Rockefeller in 1936, has a library, restaurant, swimming pool and theatre. The student community makes this a lively and stimulating area of the city to visit.

Japan House at Cité Universitaire

㉓ Notre-Dame du Travail

36 Rue Guilleminot 75014. **Map** 15 B3. **Tel** 01 44 10 72 92. Ⓜ Pernety. **Open** 7.30am–7.45pm Mon–Fri, 9am–7.30pm Sat, 8.30am–7:30pm Sun. ✝ 9am, 12.15pm, 7pm Mon–Fri (only at 7pm on Wed during school hols), 6.30pm Sat, 9am (in Portuguese), 10.45am, 6pm Sun (in Latin).

This church dates from 1901 and is made of an unusual mix of materials: stone, rubble and bricks over a riveted steel and iron framework. It was the creation of Father Soulange-Boudin, a priest who organized cooperatives and sought to

The Sebastopol Bell in Notre-Dame du Travail

reconcile labour and capitalism. Local parishioners raised the money for its construction, but lack of funds meant that many features, such as the bell towers, were never built. On the façade hangs the Sebastopol Bell, a trophy from the Crimean War given to the people of the Plaisance district by Napoleon III. The Art Nouveau interior has been completely restored, and features paintings of saints.

㉔ Institut Pasteur

Musée Pasteur: 25–28 Rue du Docteur Roux 75015. **Map** 15 A2. **Tel** 01 45 68 80 00. Ⓜ Pasteur. **Open** 2pm–5.30pm Mon–Fri (visits 2pm, 3pm, 4pm). **Closed** Aug, public hols. ▣ ▤ Films, videos. ▣ compulsory, tours at 2pm, 3pm & 4pm; ID required. ▣ Ⓦ **pasteur.fr**

The Institut Pasteur is France's leading medical research centre and was founded by the world-renowned scientist Louis Pasteur in 1888–9. He discovered the process of milk pasteurization as well as vaccines against rabies and anthrax. The centre houses a museum which includes a reconstruction of Pasteur's apartment and laboratory. It was designed by his grandchildren (also scientists) and is faithful to the original down to the last detail. Pasteur's tomb is in a basement crypt built in the style of a small Byzantine chapel. The tomb of

Dr Emile Roux, the inventor of the treatment of diphtheria by serum injection, lies in the garden. The institute has laboratories for pure and applied research, lecture theatres, a reference section, and a hospital founded to apply Pasteur's theories.

There is also a library – the institute's original building from 1888 – where research into AIDS is carried out, led by pioneering Professor Luc Montagnier who discovered the HIV virus in 1983.

Garden in the Parc André Citroën

㉕ Parc André Citroën

Rue Balard 75015. **Tel** 01 56 56 11 56. Ⓜ Javel, Balard. **Open** 8am–dusk Mon–Fri (9am Sat, Sun & public hols). ▣ ▣ reservation 01 40 71 75 60.

Louis Pasteur

Opened in 1992, this park offers the city's third large-scale vista on the Seine, along with Les Invalides and the Champ-de-Mars. Designed by both landscapers and architects, it is a blend of styles, ranging from a wildflower meadow in the north to the sophisticated monochrome mineral and sculpture gardens of the southern section. Water sculptures dot the park, and glasshouses nurture a range of environments. During the summer, there is a tethered hot-air balloon from which visitors can enjoy great views of the city.

㉖ The Palace and Gardens of Versailles

Visitors passing through the rich interior of this colossal palace, or strolling in its vast gardens, will understand why it was the glory of the Sun King's reign. Starting in 1668 with his father's modest hunting lodge, Louis XIV built the largest palace in Europe, housing 20,000 people at a time. Architects Louis Le Vau and Jules Hardouin-Mansart designed the buildings, Charles Le Brun did the interiors, and André Le Nôtre, the great landscaper, redesigned the gardens. The gardens are formally styled into regular patterns of paths and groves, hedges and flowerbeds, pools of water and fountains.

★ **Formal Gardens**
Geometric paths and shrubberies are features of the formal gardens.

★ **The Château**
Louis XIV made the château into the centre of political power in France (see pp252–5).

KEY

① **The Water Parterre's** vast pools of water are decorated with superb bronze statues.

② **The Fountain of Latona** features marble basins topped with Balthazar Marsy's statue of the goddess Latona.

③ **The South Parterre's** shrubbery and ornate flowerbeds overlook the Swiss pond.

④ **The Orangery** was built beneath the Parterre du Midi to house exotic plants in winter.

⑤ **The King's Garden with Mirror Pool** are a 19th-century English garden and pool created by Louis XVIII.

⑥ **The Grand Canal** was the setting for Louis XIV's many boating parties.

Fountain of Neptune

Dragon Fountain
The fountain's centrepiece is a winged monster.

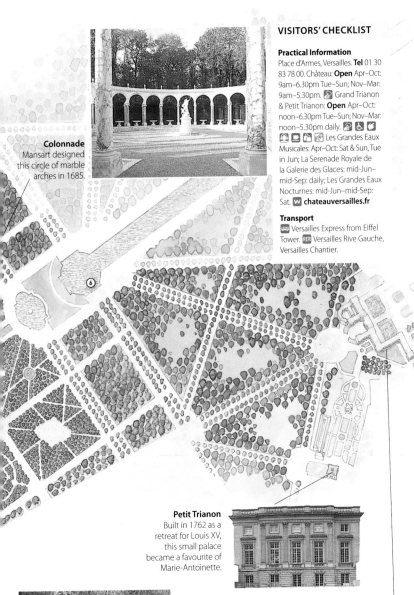

Colonnade
Mansart designed this circle of marble arches in 1685.

Petit Trianon
Built in 1762 as a retreat for Louis XV, this small palace became a favourite of Marie-Antoinette.

Fountain of Neptune
Groups of sculptures spray spectacular jets of water in Le Nôtre and Mansart's 17th-century fountain.

★ Grand Trianon
Louis XIV built this small palace of stone and pink marble in 1687 to escape the rigours of court life, and to enjoy the company of his mistress, Madame de Maintenon.

The Main Palace Buildings of Versailles

The present palace grew as a series of "envelopes" enfolding the original hunting lodge, whose low brick front is still visible in the centre. In the 1660s, Louis Le Vau built the first envelope, a series of wings which expanded into an enlarged courtyard. It was decorated with marble busts, antique trophies and gilded roofs. On the garden side, columns were added to the west façade and a great terrace was created on the first floor. Mansart took over in 1678 and added the two immense north and south wings and filled Le Vau's terrace to form the Hall of Mirrors. He designed the chapel, which was finished in 1710. The Opera House (L'Opéra) was added by Louis XV in 1770.

Main Gate

South Wing
The wing's original apartments for great nobles were replaced by Louis-Philippe's museum of French history.

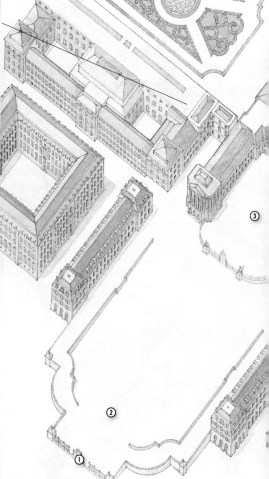

KEY

① **The Main Gate of Honour,** Mansart's original gateway grille, is surmounted by the royal arms and is the entrance to the Courtyard of Honour.

② **Courtyard of Honour**

③ **The Royal Courtyard** was separated from the Courtyard of Honour by elaborate grillwork during Louis XIV's reign. It was accessible only to royal carriages.

④ **The Clock** overlooking the Marble Courtyard is flanked by Hercules and Mars.

⑤ **Versailles History Gallery** has a permanent exhibition detailing the construction of Versailles from Louis XIII's hunting lodge to modern times.

Louis XV

| 1661 Louis XIV enlarges château | 1722 12-year-old Louis XV occupies Versailles | 1793 Louis XVI and Marie-Antoinette executed | 1837 Inauguration of the Museum of the History of France |

1667 Grand Canal begun

1668 Construction of new château by Le Vau

| 1650 | 1700 | 1750 | 1800 | 1850 | 1900 |

1682 Louis XIV and Marie-Thérèse move to Versailles

1715 Death of Louis XIV. Versailles abandoned by court

1789 King and queen forced to leave Versailles for Paris

1919 Treaty of Versailles signed on 28 June

1671 Interior decoration by Le Brun begun

1774 Louis XVI and Marie-Antoinette live at Versailles

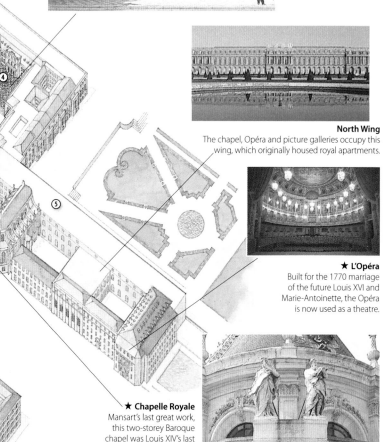

★ Marble Courtyard
The courtyard is decorated with marble paving, urns, busts and a gilded balcony.

North Wing
The chapel, Opéra and picture galleries occupy this wing, which originally housed royal apartments.

★ L'Opéra
Built for the 1770 marriage of the future Louis XVI and Marie-Antoinette, the Opéra is now used as a theatre.

★ Chapelle Royale
Mansart's last great work, this two-storey Baroque chapel was Louis XIV's last addition to Versailles.

Inside the Château of Versailles

The sumptuous main apartments are on the first floor of the vast château complex. Around the Marble Courtyard are the private apartments of the king and the queen. On the garden side are the state apartments where official court life took place. These were richly decorated by Charles Le Brun with coloured marbles, stone and wood carvings, murals, velvet, silver and gilded furniture. Beginning with the Salon d'Hercule, each state room is dedicated to an Olympian deity. The climax is the Hall of Mirrors, where 357 great mirrors face 17 tall arched windows.

★ Queen's Bedroom
In this room, the queens of France gave birth to the royal children in full public view.

Key to Floorplan

- South wing
- Coronation room
- Madame de Maintenon's apartments
- Queen's apartments and private suite
- State apartments
- King's apartments and private suite
- North wing
- Non-exhibition space

The Salon du Sacre is adorned with huge paintings of Napoleon by Jacques-Louis David.

Exit to gardens

Entrance

Entrance

Stairs to ground floor reception area

Pursuit of the Queen

On 6 October 1789, a Parisian mob invaded the palace seeking the despised Marie-Antoinette. The queen, roused in alarm from her bed, fled towards the king's rooms through the anteroom known as the Oeil-de-Boeuf. As the mob tried to break into the room, the queen beat on the door of the king's bedroom. Once admitted, she was safe, at least until morning, when she and the king were removed to Paris by the cheering and triumphant mob.

★ Chapelle Royale
The chapel's first floor was reserved for the royal family and the ground floor for the court. The interior is richly decorated in white marble, gilding and Baroque murals.

★ Hall of Mirrors
Great state occasions were held in this multi-mirrored room stretching 73 m (240 ft) along the west façade. The Treaty of Versailles was ratified here in 1919, ending World War I.

Oeil-de-Boeuf

The King's Bedroom is where Louis XIV died in 1715, aged 77.

Salon de la Guerre
The room's theme of war is dramatically reinforced by Antoine Coysevox's stuccoed relief of Louis XIV riding to victory.

Salon d'Apollon
Designed by Le Brun and dedicated to the god Apollo, this was Louis XIV's throne room. A copy of Hyacinthe Rigaud's famous portrait of the king (1701) hangs here.

The Cabinet du Conseil is where the king received his ministers and his family.

Louis XVI's library features Neo-Classical panelling and the king's terrestrial globe.

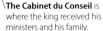

Access to gardens

★ Salon de Vénus
A Louis XIV statue stands amidst the rich marble decor of this room.

West of the City

An Art Nouveau window in the Rue la Fontaine

㉗ Rue la Fontaine

75016. **Map** 9 A4. **M** Jasmin, Michel-Ange Auteuil.

The Rue la Fontaine and surrounding streets act as a showcase for some of the most exciting architecture of the early 20th century. At No. 14 stands the Castel Béranger, a stunning apartment block made from cheap building materials to keep costs low, yet featuring stained glass, convoluted ironwork, balconies and mosaics. It established the reputation of Art Nouveau architect Hector Guimard, who went on to design the entrances for the Paris Metro. Several more examples of his work can be seen further along the street, such as the Hôtel Mezzara at No. 60.

㉘ Fondation Le Corbusier

10 Square du Docteur Blanche 75016. **Tel** 01 42 88 75 72. **M** Jasmin. **Open** Villa La Roche only: 1.30–6pm Mon, 10am–6pm Tue–Sat. Library open by appt, 1.30–6pm Mon–Thu, to 5pm Fri, Tel 01 42 88 41 53. **Closed** public hols, 1 week in Aug, 24 Dec–2 Jan. 🎬 Films. 🎥 Tue at 2pm (Tue & Fri in summer). 📷 See *History of Paris pp40–41*. **W** fondationlecorbusier.asso.fr

In a quiet corner of Auteuil are the villas La Roche *(see p267)* and Jeanneret, the first two Parisian houses built by the 20th-century architect Charles-Edouard Jeanneret, known as Le Corbusier. Built in the 1920s, they show his revolutionary use of white concrete in Cubist forms. Rooms flow into each other allowing maximum light, and the houses stand on stilts with windows along their entire length. Villa La Roche was owned by the art patron Raoul La Roche and today serves as a documentation centre on Le Corbusier. Villa Jeanneret is closed to the public. Note that the façades of both the houses are currently undergoing renovation.

㉙ Musée Marmottan-Monet

2 Rue Louis Boilly 75016. **Tel** 01 44 96 50 33. **M** Muette. **Open** 10am–6pm Tue–Sun (to 8pm Thu). **Closed** 1 Jan, 1 May, 25 Dec. 📷 👥 📷 **W** marmottan.fr

The museum was created in 1934 in the 19th-century mansion of the art historian Paul Marmottan. In 1932, he bequeathed his house and his Renaissance, Consular and First Empire collections of paintings and furniture to the Institut de France. The focus of the museum changed after the bequest by Michel Monet of 65 paintings by his father, the Impressionist Claude Monet. Some of his most famous paintings are here, including *Impression – Sunrise*, a beautiful canvas from the Rouen Cathedral series, and several *Water Lilies*.

Part of Monet's personal art collection also passed to the museum, including paintings by Camille Pissarro and the Impressionists Pierre Auguste Renoir and Alfred Sisley. The museum also displays medieval illuminated manuscripts.

La Barque (1887) by Claude Monet, in the Musée Marmottan

㉚ Bois de Boulogne

75016. **M** Porte Maillot, Porte Dauphine, Porte d'Auteuil, Sablons. **Open** 24 hrs daily. 🌳 to specialist gardens and museum. 👥 Shakespeare garden: **Open** 9.30am–dusk daily. 🎭 Open-air theatre: **Open** May–Sep. Bagatelle & Rose gardens: **Open** 9.30am. Closing times vary from 4.30pm to 8pm according to season. Jardin d'Acclimatation: **Tel** 01 40 67 90 82. **Open** 10am–7pm daily (Oct–Mar: 6pm). 📷 📷 📷

Between the western edges of Paris and the River Seine, this 865-ha (2,137-acre) park offers greenery for strolling, boating, picnicking or spending a day at the races. The Bois de Boulogne is all that remains of the vast Forêt du Rouvre. In the

Villa La Roche, home of the Fondation Le Corbusier

Kiosque de l'Empereur, on an island in the Grand Lac, Bois de Boulogne

mid-19th century, Napoleon III had it redesigned and landscaped by Haussmann along the lines of London's Hyde Park.

There are many beautiful areas within the Bois. The Pré Catelan is a self-contained park with the widest beech tree in Paris, and the charming Bagatelle gardens feature architectural follies and an 18th-century villa famous for its rose garden, where an international rose competition is held in June.

The villa was built in 64 days as a bet between the Comte d'Artois and Marie-Antoinette. The Bois de Boulogne has a reputation as a seedy area after dark so is best avoided at night.

③ Musée des Années 30

28 Ave André Morizet, Boulogne-Billancourt 92100. **Tel** 01 55 18 53 00/ 01 55 18 46 42. M Marcel Sembat. **Open** 11am–6pm Tue–Sun. **Closed** 1 Jan, 1 May, 25 Dec. & annees30.com

Inaugurated in 1998, this museum of the 1930s forms part of an arts complex, the Espace Landowski, named after Paul Landowski, a sculptor who lived in Boulogne-Billancourt from 1905 until his death in 1961, and his musician brother, Marcel. Several of Paul's works are on show here among the collection of some 800 sculptures, 2,000 paintings, furniture and ceramics.

The museum gives a vivid impression of the aesthetic mood of the era and its decorative arts through the work of artists such as Juan Gris and Robert Mallet-Stevens, classics of industrial design, and film-makers such as Renoir and Pagnol. The museum organizes temporary exhibitions, as well as themed tours of the architectural and industrial heritage of Boulogne-Billancourt.

La Grande Arche in La Défense

② La Défense

1 Parvis de la Défense. M RER La Défense. **Closed** to the public. See History of Paris pp42–3. grandearche.com

This skyscraper business district on the western edge of Paris is one of Europe's largest modern office developments and covers 80 ha (198 acres). It was launched in the 1960s to create a new home for leading French and multi-national companies. Since then, a major artistic scheme has transformed many of the squares into fascinating open-air museums.

In 1989, La Grande Arche was added to the complex, an enormous hollow cube large enough to contain Notre-Dame cathedral. This was designed by Danish architect Otto von Spreckelsen as part of major construction works, or *Grands Travaux*, which were initiated by (and are now a memorial to) the late President François Mitterrand.

The arch is currently closed to the public. A date for when it is scheduled to reopen has not yet been fixed.

③ Château de Malmaison

Ave du Château de Malmaison 92500 Rueil-Malmaison. **Tel** 01 41 29 05 55. RER La Défense then bus 258. **Open** Apr–Sep: 10am–12.30pm, 1.30–5.45pm Wed–Mon (6.15pm Sat, Sun); Oct–Mar: 10am–12.30pm, 1.30–5.15pm Wed–Mon (5.45pm Sat, Sun). **Closed** 1 Jan, 25 Dec. *See History of Paris pp34–5.* chateau-malmaison.fr

This 17th-century château was bought in 1799 by Josephine de Beauharnais, wife of Napoleon I. A magnificent veranda, Classical statues and a small theatre were added. After his campaigns, Napoleon and his entourage would come here to relax. The Château became Josephine's main residence after their divorce. Today, it is an important Napoleonic museum, together with the nearby Château de Bois-Préau. Furniture, portraits, artifacts and mementos of the imperial family are displayed in rooms reconstructed in the style of the First Empire. Part of the original grounds still exists, including Josephine's famous pretty rose garden.

The Empress Josephine's bed in the Château de Malmaison

EIGHT GUIDED WALKS

Paris is a city for walking. It is more compact and easier to get around than many other great capitals. Most of its great sights are within walking distance of one another and they are close to the heart of the city, the Ile de la Cité.

There are 14 classic tourist areas described in the *Area by Area* section of this book, each with a short walk marked on its *Street-by-Street map*, taking you past many of the most interesting sights. Yet Paris offers a wealth of lesser-known but equally remarkable areas, whose special history, architecture and local customs reveal other facets of the city.

The eight walks around the following neighbourhoods take in the main sights and also introduce visitors to their subtle details, such as street markets, quirky churches, canals, gardens, old village streets and bridges. And the literary, artistic and historical associations allow the past and present to blend into the changing and vibrant life of the modern city. Auteuil is renowned for its luxury modern residential architecture, Monceau for its sumptuous Second Empire mansions and Ile St-Louis for its *ancien régime* town houses and narrow streets. The old-fashioned charm of the iron footbridges survives along Canal St-Martin, and steep village streets that were once home to famous artists still enrich Montmartre. A tranquil village atmosphere also pervades two lesser-known hilltop districts – Buttes-Chaumont, with one of Paris's loveliest parks, and Buttes-aux-Cailles, whose quaint, cobbled alleyways belie its association with the ill-fated Paris Commune of 1871, while the once working-class area of Faubourg St-Antoine has been given a new lease of life as an artisans' quarter with a pleasure-boat harbour.

All the walk areas are readily accessible by public transport and the nearest metro stations and bus routes are listed in the *Tips for Walkers* boxes. For each walk there are suggestions on convenient resting points, such as cafés and squares, along the route.

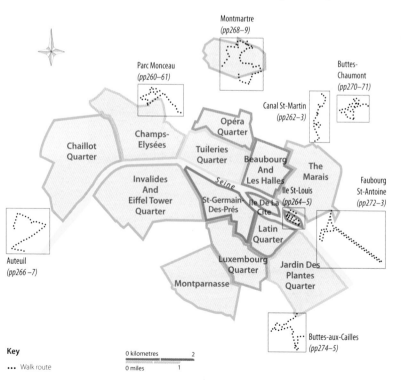

Montmartre
(pp268–9)

Buttes-Chaumont
(pp270–71)

Parc Monceau
(pp260–61)

Canal St-Martin
(pp262–3)

Opéra
Quarter

Chaillot
Quarter

Champs-
Elysées

Tuileries
Quarter

Beaubourg
And
Les Halles

The
Marais

Faubourg
St-Antoine
(pp272–3)

Invalides
And
Eiffel Tower
Quarter

Seine

St-Germain-
Des-Prés

Ile De La
Cité

Ile St-Louis
(pp264–5)

Latin
Quarter

Auteuil
(pp266–7)

Luxembourg
Quarter

Jardin Des
Plantes
Quarter

Montparnasse

Buttes-aux-Cailles
(pp274–5)

Key

••• Walk route

0 kilometres   2

0 miles   1

◀ Paintings for sale at the bustling Place du Tertre

A 90-Minute Walk around Parc Monceau

This leisurely walk passes through the exquisite late-18th-century Parc Monceau, the centrepiece of a smart Second Empire district. It then follows a route along surrounding streets, where groups of opulent mansions stunningly convey the magnificence in which some Parisians live, before ending at Place St-Augustin. For details on Monceau sights, see pages 234–5.

Ruysdaël gate

Parc Monceau to Avenue Velasquez

The walk starts at the Monceau Metro station ① on the Boulevard de Courcelles. Enter the park where Nicolas Ledoux's 18th-century

Parc Monceau's tollhouse ②

lined street with 19th-century Neo-Classical mansions. At No. 7 is the splendid Cernuschi museum ⑥, which houses a collection of Far Eastern art.

tollhouse ② stands. On either side are sumptuously gilded 19th-century wrought-iron gates which support ornate lampposts.

Take the second path on the left past the monument to Guy de Maupassant ③ (1897). This is only one of a series of six belle époque monuments of prominent French writers and musicians which are picturesquely scattered throughout the park. Most of them feature a solemn bust of a great man who is accompanied by a swooning muse.

Straight ahead is the most important remaining folly, a moss-covered Corinthian colonnade ④ running around the edge of a charming tiny lake with the requisite island in the centre. Walk around the colonnade and under a 16th-century arch ⑤ transplanted from the old Paris Hôtel de Ville (see p104), which burned down in 1871.

Turn left on the Allée de la Comtesse de Ségur and go into Avenue Velasquez, a wide tree-

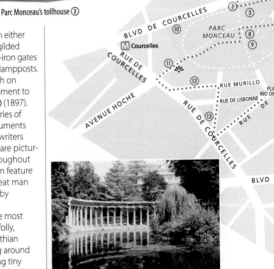

Colonnade in Parc Monceau ④

Avenue Velasquez to Avenue Van Dyck

Re-enter the park and turn left into the second small winding path, which is bordered by an 18th-century mossy pyramid ⑦, antique tombs, a stone arcade, an obelisk and a small Chinese stone pagoda. The romantically melancholy tone of these follies suits the spirit of the late 18th century.

Turn right on the first path past the pyramid and walk back to the central avenue. Straight ahead, a Renaissance bridge fords the little stream running from the lake. Turn left and walk

past the monument (1902) to the musician Ambroise Thomas ⑧. Immediately behind, there is a lovely artificial mountain with cascade. Turn left on the next avenue and walk to the monument (1897) to the composer Charles Gounod ⑨ on the left. From here, follow the first winding path to the right towards the Avenue Van Dyck exit. Ahead to the right, in the corner of the park, is the Chopin monument ⑩ (1906), and looking along the Allée de la Comtesse de Ségur, the monument to the 19th-century French poet Alfred de Musset.

Ambroise Thomas statue ⑧

Avenue Van Dyck to Rue de Monceau

Leave the park and pass into Avenue Van Dyck. No. 5 on the right is an impressive Parc Monceau mansion ⑪, a Neo-Baroque structure built by chocolate manufacturer Emile Menier; No. 6 is in the French Renaissance style that came back into favour in the 1860s. Straight ahead, beyond the ornate grille, there is a fine view of Avenue Hoche and in the distance, the Arc de Triomphe.

The mountain cascade ⑧

Walk past the gate and turn left into Rue de Courcelles and left again into Rue Murillo, bordered by more elaborate town houses in 18th-century and French Renaissance styles ⑫. At the crossing of Rue Rembrandt, on the left, is another gate into the park and on the right, a massive apartment building from 1900 (No. 7) and an elegant French Renaissance house with an elaborately carved wooden front door (No. 1). At the corner of the Rue Rembrandt and the Rue de Courcelles is the oddest of all the neighbourhood buildings, a striking five-storey red Chinese pagoda ⑬. It is an exclusive emporium of Chinese art.

Turn left on to the Rue de Monceau, walk past Avenue Ruysdaël and continue to the Musée Nissim de Camondo at No. 63 Rue de Monceau ⑭. Some nearby buildings worth having a look at are Nos. 52, 60 and 61 ⑮.

Boulevard Malesherbes

At the junction of Rue de Monceau and Boulevard Malesherbes, turn right. This long boulevard with dignified six-storey apartment buildings is typical of the great avenues cut through Paris by Baron Haussmann, Prefect of the Seine during the Second Empire *(see pp36–7)*. They greatly pleased the Industrial Age bourgeoisie, but horrified sensitive souls and writers who compared them with the buildings of New York.

No. 75 is the posh marble front of Benneton, the most fashionable Paris card and stationery engraver ⑯. On the left, approaching the Boulevard Haussmann, looms the greatest 19th-century Paris church, St-Augustin ⑰, built by Victor-Louis Baltard. Enter the church through the back door on Rue de la Bienfaisance. Walk through the church and leave by the main door. On the left is the massive stone building of the French Officers' club, the Cercle Militaire ⑱. Straight ahead is a bronze statue of Joan of Arc ⑲. Continue on to Place St-Augustin to St-Augustin Metro station.

Key

••• Walk route

| 0 metres | 250 |
| 0 yards | 250 |

Joan of Arc statue ⑲

Five-storey Chinese pagoda ⑬

Tips for Walkers

Starting point: Blvd de Courcelles.

Length: 3 km (2 miles).

Getting there: The nearest Metro is Monceau, reached by bus No. 30; No. 84 goes to Metro Courcelles and No. 94 stops between Monceau & Villiers Metros.

St Augustin church: Open 8.30am–7pm Mon–Fri, 8.30am–noon, 2.30–7.30pm Sat, 8.30am–12.30pm, 4–7.30pm Sun.

Stopping off points: Near the Renaissance bridge in the Parc Monceau, a kiosk serves coffee and sandwiches (summer only). There is a brasserie at Place de Rio de Janeiro and several cafés around Place St-Augustin. The Square M Pagnol off Ave C Claire is a pleasant place to take in the beauty of the park.

For additional keys to symbols *see back flap*

A 90-Minute Walk along the Canal St-Martin

The walk along the quays on either side of the Canal St-Martin is an experience of Paris very different from that of smarter districts. Here, the older surviving landmarks of the neighbourhood – the factories, warehouses, dwellings, taverns and cafés – hint at life in a thriving 19th-century industrial, working-class world. But there are also the gentler charms of the old iron footbridges, the tree-lined quays, the inevitable fishermen, the river barges, and the still waters of the broad canal basins. A walk along the canal, which connects the Bassin de la Villette with the Seine, will evoke images of the Pernod-drinking, working-class Paris of Jean Gabin and Edith Piaf.

The 18th-century Rotonde de la Villette ②

Bassin de la Villette looking north ③

Place de Stalingrad to Avenue Jean-Jaurès

From the Stalingrad metro station ①, follow Boulevard de la Villette to the square in front of the Rotonde de la Villette ②. This is one of the few remaining 18th-century tollhouses in Paris, designed by the celebrated Neo-Classical architect Nicolas Ledoux in the 1780s. The fountains, square and terraces were designed in the 1980s to provide an attractive setting and fine views of the Bassin de la Villette ③ to the north.

Walk towards Avenue Jean-Jaurès. On the left is the first lock ④ leading down to the canal, as well as the art-house cinema chain MK2's landmark complexes, which are linked together by a boat.

Tips for Walkers

Starting point: Place de Stalingrad.
Length: 3.5 km (2 miles).
Getting there: The nearest metro is Stalingrad: bus No.54 stops there, and No.26 at metro Jaurès.
Hôpital St-Louis: Chapel open 2–5pm Fri–Sun; the courtyard is open daily.
Stopping off points: Ethnic food shops and restaurants abound in the lively Rue du Faubourg du Temple and nearby streets. The Quai de Valmy and Rue Beaupaire offer plenty of modish restaurants and bars (Le Point Ephémère, The Hôtel Du Nord, Chez Prune). There is a shady public garden on Boulevard Jules Ferry.

View from Rue E Varlin bridge ⑦

Key

••• Walk route

0 metres	500
0 yards	500

EIGHT GUIDED WALKS | 263

Courtyard garden of Hôpital St-Louis ⑭

Party headquarters ⑨ on Place du Colonel Fabien, with its curving glazed tower.

Return to the Quai de Jemmapes, where at No. 134 ⑩ stands one of the few surviving brick-and-iron industrial buildings that used to line the canal in the 19th century. At No. 126 ⑪ is another notable modern building, a residence for the aged, with monumental concrete arches and glazed bay windows. Further along, at No. 112 ⑫, is an Art Deco apartment building with bay windows, decorative iron balconies and tiles. On the ground floor is a modernized former 1930s proletarian café. Here the canal curves gracefully into the third lock, spanned by a charming transparent iron footbridge ⑬.

Hôpital St-Louis to Rue Léon-Jouhaux

Turn left into Rue Bichat, which leads to the remarkable 17th-century Hôpital St-Louis ⑭. Enter through the hospital's old main gate with its high-pitched roof and massive stone arch. Pass into the courtyard. The hospital was founded in 1607 by Henri IV, the first Bourbon king, to care for the victims of the plague. Leave the courtyard from the central gate on the wing on your left. Here you pass by the 17th-century hospital chapel ⑮ and out into the Rue de la Grange aux Belles.

Turn left and walk back to the canal. At the junction of Rue de la Grange Batelière and the Quai de Jemmapes stood, until 1627, the notorious Montfaucon gallows ⑯, one of the chief public execution spots of medieval Paris. Turn into the Quai de Jemmapes. At No. 101 ⑰ is the original front of the Hôtel du Nord, made famous in the eponymous 1930s film. In front is another iron footbridge and a drawbridge ⑱ for traffic, providing a charming setting with views of the canal on either side. Cross over and continue down the Quai de Valmy until the last footbridge ⑲ at the corner of the Rue Léon-Jouhaux. From here the canal can be seen disappearing under the surface of Paris, to continue its journey through a great stone arch.

Square Frédéric Lemaître to Place de la République

Walk along Square Frédéric Lemaître ⑳ to the start of Boulevard Jules Ferry, which has a public garden stretching down its centre. The garden was built over the canal in the 1860s. At its head stands a charmingly nostalgic statue of a flower girl of the 1830s, *La Grisette* ㉑. This is the crossroads of a busy working-class street, Rue du Faubourg du Temple ㉒, with flourishing ethnic shops and restaurants. Follow the street to the right and on to the metro station in the Place de la République.

Iron footbridges over the canal ⑤

Quai de Valmy to Rue Bichat

Cross over to the Quai de Jemmapes, which runs the length of the east side of the canal and down to the first bridge on Rue Louis Blanc ⑤. Cross the bridge to the Quai de Valmy. From the corner there is a glimpse of the oblique granite and glass front of the Paris Industrial Tribunal ⑥ on the Rue Louis Blanc.

Continue along Quai de Valmy. At Rue E Varlin cross the bridge ⑦, from where there is an attractive view of the second canal lock, lockkeeper's house, public gardens and old lampposts. At the other side of the bridge and slightly to the left, go along the pedestrianized Rue Haendel, which provides a good view of the towering buildings of a social housing estate ⑧. Nearby is the French Communist

Shop, Rue du Faubourg du Temple ㉒

For additional keys to symbols *see back flap*

A 90-Minute Walk around the Ile St-Louis

The walk around this tiny island passes along the picturesque tree-lined quays from Pont Louis-Philippe to Quai d'Anjou, taking in the 17th-century *hôtels* that infuse the area with such a powerful sense of period. It then penetrates into the heart of the island along the main street, Rue St-Louis-en-l'Ile, enlivened by chic restaurants, cafés, art galleries and boutiques, before returning to the north side of the island and back to Pont Marie. For more information on the main sights, see pages 79 and 91.

Left Bank view of the Ile St-Louis

Fishing on a St-Louis quayside

Metro Pont Marie to Rue Jean-du-Bellay

From the Pont Marie Metro station ①, walk down Quai des Celestins and Quai de l'Hôtel de Ville, lined with bookstands, with views of Ile St-Louis. Turn left at Pont Louis-Philippe ② and, having crossed it, take the steps down to the lower quay immediately to the right. Walk around the tree-shaded west point of the island ③, then up the other side to the Pont St-Louis ④. Opposite the bridge, on the corner of Rue Jean-du-Bellay, is Le Flore en l'Ile ⑤, the smartest café-cum-tea salon on the island.

Quai d'Orléans

From the corner of the Quai d'Orléans and the Rue Jean-du-Bellay, there are fine views of the Panthéon's dome and Notre-Dame. Along the quay, Nos. 18–20, the Hôtel Rolland, has unusual Hispano-Moorish windows. No. 12 ⑥ is one of several stately 17th-century houses with handsome wrought-iron

balconies. At No. 6, the former Polish library, founded in 1838, now houses the Société Historique et Littéraire Polonaise *(see p91)*, focusing on the life of Polish poet Adam Mickiewicz ⑦; it also contains some Chopin scores and autographs by George Sand and Victor Hugo. On the right, the Pont de la Tournelle ⑧ links the island to the Left Bank.

Windows of the Hôtel Rolland ⑥

Key

••• Walk route

0 metres	250
0 yards	250

Quai de Béthune to Pont Marie

Continue beyond the bridge and into Quai de Béthune, where the Nobel-laureate Marie Curie lived at No. 36 ⑨, and where beautiful wrought-iron balconies gracefully decorate Nos. 34 and 30. The

St-Louis church door ⑰

19th-century bridge joining the river banks. Ahead is the charming 19th-century Square Barye ⑬, a shady public garden at the east point of the island, from where there are fine river views.

From here, travel towards the Quai d'Anjou as far as the corner of Rue St-Louis-en-l'Ile to see the most famous house on the island, the Hôtel Lambert ⑭ *(see pp28–9)*. Continue into the Quai d'Anjou, where Hôtel de Lauzun ⑮ at No. 17 has a severe Classical front and a beautiful gilded balcony. Now turn left into Rue Poulletier and note the convent of the Daughters of Charity ⑯ at No. 5 bis. Further on, at the corner of Rue Poulletier and Rue St-Louis-en-l'Ile, is the island church, St-Louis ⑰ *(see p91)*, with its unusual tower, projecting clock and carved main door.

Proceed along Rue St-Louis-en-l'Ile, which abounds in small, chic, bistro-style restaurants with pleasantly old-fashioned decors. No. 31 is the original Berthillon ice cream shop ⑱, No. 60 an art gallery ⑲ with an original 19th-century window front, and at No. 51 is one of the few 18th-century *hôtels* on the island, Hôtel Chernizot ⑳, with a superb Rococo balcony resting on leering gargoyles.

Turn right into Rue Jean-du-Bellay and along to Pont Louis-Philippe. Turn right again into the Quai de Bourbon, lined by

Gargoyle at No. 51 Rue St-Louis-en-l'Ile ⑳

one of the island's finest rows of *hôtels*, the most notable being Hôtel Jassaud at No. 19 ㉑. Continue to the 17th-century Pont Marie ㉒ and cross it to the Pont Marie Metro on the other side.

Tips for Walkers

Starting point: Pont Marie Metro.
Length: 2.6 km (1.6 miles).
Getting there: The walk starts from the Pont Marie metro. However, bus route 67 takes you to Rue du Pont Louis-Philippe and also crosses the island along Rue des Deux Ponts and Blvd Pont de Sully; routes 86 and 87 also cross the island along Blvd Pont de Sully.
Stopping off points: There are cafés, such as Flore en l'Ile and the Berthillon shops for ice cream *(see p310)*. Restaurants on the Rue St-Louis-en-l'Ile include Auberge de la Reine Blanche (No. 30) and Le Fin Gourmet (No. 42), as well as a pâtisserie and a cheese shop. Good resting-points are the tree-shaded quays and Square Barye to the eastern end of the island.

Hôtel Richelieu ⑩ at No. 18 is one of the island's most beautiful houses. It features a fine garden where it has retained its original Classical blind arcades.

If you turn left down Rue Bretonvilliers, there is an imposing 17th-century house ⑪, with a high-pitched roof resting on a great Classical arch spanning the street. Back on the Quai de Béthune, proceed to the Pont de Sully ⑫, a late

The 17th-century Pont Marie ㉒

For additional keys to symbols *see back flap*

A 90-Minute Walk in Auteuil

Part of the fascination of the walk around this bastion of
bourgeois life in westernmost Paris lies in the contrasting
nature of the area's streets. The old village provincialism of
Rue d'Auteuil, where the walk begins, leads on to masterpieces
of luxurious modern architecture along Rue La Fontaine and
Rue du Docteur Blanche. The walk ends at the Jasmin Metro
station. For more on the sights of Auteuil, see page 256.

Rue d'Auteuil

The walk begins at Place d'Auteuil
①, a leafy village square with
a striking Guimard-designed
Metro station entrance,
an 18th-century funerary
obelisk, and the
19th-century Neo-
Romanesque Notre
Dame d'Auteuil. Walk
down Rue d'Auteuil,
the main street of the
old village, and take in
the sense of a past
provincial world. The
Auberge du Mouton
Blanc brasserie at No. 40
② now occupies the
premises of the area's
oldest tavern, favoured
by Molière and his

Wallace fountain ④

actors in the 1600s. The house at
Nos. 45–47 ③ was the residence
of American presidents John
Adams and his son John Quincy
Adams. Move on to the
pleasantly shaded Place Jean
Lorrain ④, the site of the local
market. Here, there is a Wallace

drinking fountain, donated by
the English millionaire, Richard
Wallace in the 19th century. Turn
left down Rue Poussin and
right into Rue Donizetti to see
the Villa Montmorency ⑤, a
private enclave of luxury
villas, built on the former
country estate of the
Comtesse de Boufflers.

Rue La Fontaine

Return to Rue La
Fontaine, renowned for
its many Hector Guimard
buildings. Marcel Proust
was born at No.96. Henri
Sauvage's ensemble of
artists' studios at No. 65
⑥ is one of the most
original Art Deco
buildings in Paris. No. 60 is a
Guimard Art Nouveau house
⑦ with elegant cast-iron
balconies. Further along, there
is a small Neo-Gothic chapel at
No. 40 ⑧ and Art Nouveau
apartment buildings at Nos.
19 and 21 ⑨. No. 14 is
Guimard's most
spectacular building,
the Castel Béranger
⑩, with a superb
iron gate.

**Obelisk, Place
d'Auteuil ①**

Tips for Walkers

Starting point: Place d'Auteuil.
Length: 3 km (2 miles).
Getting there: The nearest Metro
station to the starting point is
Eglise d'Auteuil, and buses that
take you there are Nos. 22, 52
and 62.
Stopping off points: At No. 40
Rue d'Auteuil is the inexpensive
trendy brasserie, L'Auberge du
Mouton Blanc, with 1930s decor.
At No. 35bis Rue La Fontaine is
Acajou, serving innovative cuisine
and owned by a young chef.
Place Jean Lorrain is a pleasantly
shaded square where walkers can
rest, and on Rue La Fontaine,
there is a small park in front of the
Neo-Gothic chapel at No. 40.
Further on at Place Rodin, there is
a pleasant public garden.

Doorway of No. 28 Rue d'Auteuil

RUE DU DOCTEUR BLANCHE
RUE DE L'YV
RUE H. HEINE
RUE
RUE JA
RUE
RAFFET
RUE DE LA SOURCE
*Villa
Montmorency*
AVENUE
⑤
RUE LA FONT
RUE POUSSIN
RUE D'AUTEUIL
PLACE J
LORRAIN ④ RUE ② D'AUT
Ⓜ ③
Michel
Ange
Auteuil
RUE MICHEL ANGE
RUE BOILEAU
⑯
⑱
⑰

Key

••• Walk route

0 metres   250
0 yards   250

Pointillist painter Georges Seurat lived at No. 39 ⑩. Continue along Rue des Abbesses and turn right at Rue Ravignan.

Rue Ravignan

From here there is a sweeping view of Paris. Climb the steps straight ahead to the deeply shaded Place Emile Goudeau ⑪. To the left, at No. 13, is the original entrance to the Bateau-Lavoir, the most important cluster of artists' studios in Montmartre. Here Picasso lived and worked in the early 1900s.

Walking past Montmartre Vineyard ⑱

Further up, at the corner of Rue Orchampt and Rue Ravignan, there is a row of picturesque 19th-century artists' studios ⑫.

Rue Ravignan to Rue Lepic

Continue up the hill along the small public garden, Place Jean-Baptiste Clément ⑬. At the top, cross Rue Norvins. Opposite is an old Monmar-tois restaurant, Auberge de la Bonne Franquette ⑭, which used to be a favourite gathering place for 19th-century artists. Continue along the narrow Rue St-Rustique, from where Sacré-Coeur can be seen. At the end and to the right is Place du Tertre ⑮, the main village square. From here go north on Rue du Mont Cenis and turn left to Rue Cortot. Erik Satie, the eccentric composer, lived in No. 6 ⑯, and at No. 12 is the Musée de Montmartre ⑰. Turn right on Rue des Saules and walk past the very pretty Montmartre vineyard ⑱ to the Au Lapin Agile ⑲ at the corner of Rue St-Vincent. Go back down Rue des Saules and right on Rue de l'Abreuvoir, an attractive street of late 19th-century villas and gardens. Continue into l'Allée des Brouillards, a leafy pedestrian alley. No. 6 ⑳ was Renoir's last house in Montmartre. Take the steps down into the Rue Simon Dereure and immediately turn left into a small park, which can be crossed to reach Avenue Junot. Here, No. 15 ㉑ was the house of Dadaist Tristan Tzara in the early 1920s. Continue up Avenue Junot, turn right on Rue Girardon and right again on Rue Lepic.

Au Lapin Agile cabaret ⑲

Rue Lepic to Place Blanche

At the corner is one of the area's few surviving windmills, the Moulin du Radet ㉒, now a restaurant confusingly called Moulin de la Galette. Continue along Rue Lepic: to the right at the top of a slope is another windmill, the original Moulin de la Galette ㉓, now a private home. Turn left on Rue de l'Armée d'Orient, with its quaint artists' studios ㉔, and left again into Rue Lepic. Van Gogh lived at No. 54 ㉕ in June 1886. Continue to Place Blanche, and on Boulevard de Clichy to the right is the Moulin Rouge ㉖.

Key

••• Walk route

| 0 metres | 250 |
| 0 yards | 250 |

Moulin Rouge cabaret near the Place Blanche ㉖

For additional keys to symbols *see back flap*

A 90-Minute Walk in Buttes-Chaumont

This area in the east of the city is little known to many visitors, yet it contains one of Paris's biggest and most beautiful parks and some fascinating architecture. The walk is quite strenuous with many steps, and takes in a charming micro-village, the Butte Bergeyre, which is perched high above the city and has unusual houses in contrasting styles. After descending from the village, the walk continues in Buttes-Chaumont park, a vast hill complete with a lake with a huge island and folly, rocky outcrops and a wonderful variety of trees and plants.

small garden ⑩. This is owned by the city but tended by local residents who can often be found working here.

Head back down the Rue Georges Lardennois to the Rue Michel Tagrine and take the ivy-draped steps back down to the main road ⑪. Continue straight and then turn right onto the Avenue Mathurin-Moreau, noting the fine Art Deco building ⑫ at 42 with its glittering gold-coloured tile detail. At the end of the road, cross the Rue Manin to the entrance to the park.

View across city towards Sacré-Coeur ⑧

The Butte Bergeyre

From the metro Buttes-Chaumont ① take the Rue Botzaris, turning right onto the Avenue Simon Bolivar until you reach the stairs at 54 ②, which lead up into the Butte Bergeyre. At the top of the stairs pause to absorb the enchanting atmosphere of this micro-village of five little streets. Construction started in the 1920s but there are also some modern buildings. Carry on into the Rue Barrelet de Ricou ③ to admire the ivycovered house at 13 ④, then continue to the end of the road to take a left into the Rue Philippe Hecht ⑤ where the chalet-style house at 7 ⑥ is an interesting contrast to the creeper-covered Art Deco gem at 13 ⑦. At the end of the street take a left up to the corner of the Rue Georges Lardennois and the Rue Rémy-de-Gourmont for a wonderful view across the city ⑧ of Montmartre with its wedding-cake Sacré-Coeur on top. Be sure to admire the tiny patch of grapevines ⑨ in the residents' garden below. Close to this mini-vineyard is a

Some of the lovely mature trees in the park

The suspension bridge, for the best view of the park ⑱

Key

••• Walk route

| 0 metres | 200 |
| 0 yards | 200 |

⊕ Botzaris ㉓

Tips for Walkers

Starting point: Metro Buttes-Chaumont.
Length: 2.5 km (1.5 miles).
Note: Very steep walk in parts, with many steps.
Getting there: Go to Buttes-Chaumont metro station, on line 7bis. Or take buses Nos. 26, 60 and 75 to the stop for Buttes Chaumont park.
Stopping off points: The park is full of lovely spots to rest, and the benches near the lake are good if bringing your own refreshments. La Kaskad café opposite the park (at 2 Place Armand-Carrel) is a fashionable spot for snacks and drinks with a terrace that is ideal on a sunny day.

Clifftop folly, the park's summit ⑰

The Buttes-Chaumont Park

Commissioned by Napoleon III and Baron Haussman in 1864, the park covers 25 ha (61 acres) and took four years to complete. It was built by the engineer Adolphe Alphand and the architect Gabriel Davioud. It is packed with mature trees including planes, poplars, ash, maples, chestnuts, sequoias and beautiful magnolias. At the entrance to the park there is a man-made rock structure ⑬

with steps carved out of the facade; climb them to the top. Go on along a tree-lined path to join the Avenue du General Puebla Liniers and follow this until reaching the Carrefour de la Colonne ⑭ where there is a red brick mansion house. With your back to this go ahead to a little bridge lined with terracotta tiles. Cross the bridge ⑮. Take the right branch of steps and head up to the top of the cliff. Cross a tiny bridge ⑯ and turn left up some steps to the folly ⑰, a copy of the Temple of Sibyl near Rome. This is the highest point in the park, providing views across the city all the way to the Sacré-Coeur. Now take the path on the right back to the first bridge. Then branch right down the steps within man-made rock to an impressive 63-m (206-ft) long bridge ⑱. Towering over the lake, this provides wonderful views of the park. The bridge may be closed for repairs, so in that instance use the terracotta-tiled bridge as before. Cross the bridge and follow the path down to the lake. The lake ⑲ is encircled by weeping willows and benches for breaks to

admire the 50-m (164-ft) high man-made island ⑳. Follow the lake round until you hear rushing water. One of the park's most impressive features is the 32-m (105-ft) high waterfall ㉑ hidden inside a grotto. Walk right up to the waterfall looking up to see a patch of sky and some glorious man-made stalactites. Take a stepping-stone to the other side of the cave and then exit and rejoin the path round the lake, heading left. Ascend the few steps, then veer to the left and up the hill ㉒. Follow the path around to the Carrefour de la Colonne and continue along the Avenue de la Cascade to the exit ㉓. From here you can take the metro from Botzaris.

Man-made waterfall, inside the grotto ㉑

For additional keys to symbols see back flap

A 90-Minute Walk in Faubourg St-Antoine

In the east of the city, a few steps away from the bustle of the Bastille, lies the Faubourg St-Antoine district, traditionally a working-class neighbourhood full of furniture designers, carpenters and artisans whose legacy can still be seen today. From the Place de la Bastille, the walk takes in Paris's pleasure-boat port, the artisan area around the Viaduc des Arts – a former viaduct with arts and crafts studios nestling in the arches – and onto the Promenade Plantée for a fascinating tree-filled stroll.

Les Grandes Marches, Place de la Bastille

The Port de Plaisance, with many pleasure boats ④

Port de Plaisance

Tucked away near the traffic of Place de La Bastille ① lies an area of tranquillity that's of interest to boat-lovers and landlubbers alike. The Port de Plaisance and Paris-Arsenal garden ② was inaugurated in 1983 to provide a harbour for pleasure craft. Linking the Seine to the Canal St-Martin, the harbour was previously where commercial barges loaded and unloaded cargo. Today, it's a pretty spot full of yachts, dinghies and Parisians out for a stroll. The cobbled stones on the quayside and old-fashioned lamp-posts add to the port's atmosphere. The lawns are perfect for a picnic and the children's play areas, while small, are well stocked with rocking chairs, slides and climbing apparatus ③. Continue to the end of the marina to the lock ④. Cross over the lock bridge, observing the pedestrian crossing sign, and head down on the other quayside turning back towards the Place de La Bastille. Just before the grey steel bridge ⑤, take the stairs up and then

the bridge over to the Boulevard de la Bastille ⑥. Cross the Boulevard and take a right and then left onto the Rue Jules César ⑦ all the way to the end of the street, turn left and then cross the Rue de Lyon turning right onto the Avenue Daumesnil and the start of the Viaduc des Arts ⑧.

Viaduc des Arts

In 1859 the Paris Viaduct was built to take a railway line that linked the Faubourg St-Antoine district with the suburbs. In 1994 the restored and revamped Viaduc des Arts opened with 50 shops and studios nestling in the bridge's rose stone archways.

In keeping with the tradition of the area, the ateliers are all linked to the arts, and some of the city's master craftsmen call the arches home. The superb window

Place de la Bastille with the impressive Opéra de Paris Bastille ①

displays at the first studio "Maison Guillet"  **9** give a hint of the quality of craftsmanship to come. Guillet specializes in providing silk flowers for Paris's top theatre and fashion houses. The "Ateliers du Temps Passé" **10** at 5 is a restorer of paintings, while Lorenove at 11 restores period glass. Number 13 is the base for hot interior designer Cherif, and the whimsical "Le Bonheur des Dames" **11** at 17 provides all sorts of materials for embroidery fans. For refreshment, stop at the Viaduc Café at 43 **12**, which dishes up simple meals and hearty salads to the area's hip creatives. Vertical at 63 **13** mixes art and nature with

One of the arts and crafts shop fronts under the Viaduc des Arts **8**

twisting "botanical sculptures". Moving on past the metal furnituremaker Baguès at 73, the antique lace restorers Marie Lavande at 83, the Atelier Le Tallec 93/95, which specializes in hand-painted porcelain, it is clear that the spirit of the old artisans' area is alive and well. For those of a musical bent, Allain Cadinot repairs and sells Boehm flutes at 99, while Roger Lanne is a violin- and cello-maker at 103 **14**. With the coppersmith at 111, the terracotta tile specialist at 113 and the frame-maker at 117, you are close to the end of the viaduct, where the last atelier Jean-Charles

woods. For a longer walk, turn right along the Promenade and follow it to the city's edge. Or turn left and head back towards the Bastille. This narrow walkway offers wonderful views of the rooftops, and you can see into some apartments. With roses, lavender and maples, the walkway is a delight. At the end **17**, take the steps down to the Rue de Lyon **18** leading to the Bastille metro, pausing only to ponder the modern architecture of the Opéra de Paris Bastille **19** *(see p102)*.

Promenade Plantée, a lovely rooftop walkway **16**

Tips for Walkers

Starting point: Bastille Metro.
Length: 2.6 km (1.6 miles).
Getting there: Bastille Metro is served by lines 1, 8 and 5. Bus Nos. 29, 65, 69, 76, 86, 87, 91 and more. Get off at "Place de la Bastille" stop.
Stopping off points: The area is full of great cafés, bars and restaurants. Les Grandes Marches (Place de la Bastille) is a chic place for lunch, dinner or just coffee before you start or afterwards. Nearby Rue de Charonne is lined with some fun bars. During the walk, take a break at the Viaduc Café (43 Viaduc des Arts).

Brosseau **15** perhaps sums up the street's diversity specializing in making hats, scent and cutlery.

Promenade Plantée

Turn left, follow the signs and take the steps up to the Promenade Plantée **16**, a walk-way on top of the viaduct. It is 4.5km (2.8 miles) long and goes all the way to the Vincennes

Montgallet Ⓜ
300 metres / 330 yards

Bois de Vincennes
3 km / 2 miles

Dugommier Ⓜ
450 metres / 500 yards

Key

••• Walk route
••• Detour route

| 0 metres | 200 |
| 0 yards | 200 |

For additional keys to symbols *see back flap*

A 90-Minute Walk in Butte-aux-Cailles

This walk takes place in and around the Butte-aux-Cailles, a lovely "village" set on a hill that is all quiet streets, leafy squares and buzzy local bistros. The area made history in 1783 when the first manned balloon flight touched down here. In the 1800s it was home to many workers from the small factories in the area and was one of the first areas to fight during the Paris Commune. However, it only really developed after 1910 and the architecture reflects the social ideals of the day – that individual houses and green spaces aid health.

Quiet, cobbled streets typify the Butte-aux-Cailles ⑪

Buttes-aux-Cailles

Take the "Auguste Blanqui" exit out of the Place d'Italie metro station ①, noting the Guimard decoration. Follow the bustling Rue Bobillot until you reach the Rue Paulin-Méry ② and take your first steps into the peace of the Butte-aux-Cailles. The contrast is surprising as you walk the quiet, narrow, cobbled streets with their old-fashioned street lamps. Note the painted shutters on 5 ③ and the trees in the small garden in front of the house opposite. Continue straight ahead, cross over the Rue du Moulin-des-Prés and turn left into the Rue Gérard past the red brick terraces and plant-decked villas ④. Keep on into the Rue Samson and then turn right onto the Rue Jonas and left onto the Rue des Cinq Diamants ⑤. At 43 ⑥ there is a hip Franco-Thai restaurant, Le 43. Those interested in history may appreciate the Association des Amis de la Commune de Paris at 46 ⑦, which sells T-shirts, books

Road sign in the Butte-aux-Cailles area

and pamphlets on that bloody episode in Parisian history. Turn right into the Passage Barrault, a cobbled alleyway with ivy-covered walls and a countryside feel ⑧. At the end of the passage, turn left onto the Rue Barrault and continue up the street until the right turn into the Rue Daviel. At 10 Rue Daviel the row of cottages known as "Little Alsace" ⑨ because of their chalet style are, in fact, one of the first public housing schemes in Paris. The public can visit their intimate courtyards during the day. Opposite, walk down the Villa Daviel ⑩, a tiny street of terraces with small front gardens overflowing with greenery. Retrace your steps back up to the Rue Barrault, turn left and then right onto the artery of the area, the Rue de la Butte-aux-Cailles ⑪. Head up the street to the Place de la Commune de Paris ⑫, which

today looks unremarkable yet was the site of a major street battle in May 1871. Continue up the Rue de la Butte-aux-Cailles. Les Abeilles at 21 ⑬ is a curious store dedicated to bee-keeping and a delight for honey lovers. Pancakes in the old-fashioned crêperie Des Crêpes et des Cailles at 13 may satisfy if you are just peckish, but further down at 18 is the area's best-known restaurant Le Temps de Cerises ⑭. Fittingly, as it's only a few minutes' walk from the Place de la Commune, it's run as a co-operative and is also the unofficial neighbourhood HQ.

Les Abeilles, for honey enthusiasts ⑬

Le Temps des Cerises, full of bohemian atmosphere ⑭

Tips for Walkers

Starting point: Place de l'Italie metro.
Length: 2.6 km (1.6 miles).
Getting there: Start from the Place D'Italie metro via lines 5, 6 and 7. Or take buses Nos 27, 47, 57, 67 and 83 and get off at the stop "Place d'Italie".
Stopping off points: The Rue de la Butte-aux-Cailles is full of great cafés and restaurants. Le Temps des Cerises (No. 18) is very atmospheric, while Fusion (No. 12) is devoted to fusion cuisine. On Rue des Cinq Diamants, Chez Gladines (No. 30) is a great bet for a good lunch, while Les Cailloux (No. 58) is a chic option.

Key

••• Walk route

| 0 metres | 200 |
| 0 yards | 200 |

At the end of the road is the Place Paul Verlaine ⑮. On the other side of the square is the red brick Art Nouveau swimming pool ⑯. Built in 1924, it houses one indoor pool and two lovely outdoor swimming areas. Take the steps in front of the building to find the modern fountain on the Place ⑰. This is supplied by le puits artésien, a local well 580 m (1,902 ft) deep, dating from 1863. You may see locals queuing to fill plastic bottles here. Exit the square, take a right and then another right past the chic restaurant Chez Nathalie with its flowery terrace, which is always packed in summer, into the Rue Vandrezanne, continuing down this pedestrianized street into the passage Vandrezanne, a steep cobbled alleyway with antiquated lampposts ⑱. Cross over the Rue Moulinet and take the Rue Moulin des Prés until you come to the Rue Tolbiac. Cross this busy road then take a right stepping back into another time at the Square des Peupliers ⑲. Built in 1926, each house is different, reflecting the ideals of the time. All have pretty little gardens, most have lovely Art Nouveau porches and the ornate gilded lamp posts are very special. Leave the Square des Peupliers and take a right back onto the Rue du Moulin-des-Prés. Head

Crêpes from Des Crêpes et des Cailles

down the street, noting the interesting rough stone houses ⑳, straight past an unusual purple Art Nouveau-style house at 104 ㉑. Take a right onto the Rue Damesme, turn right into the Rue du Docteur Leray and then right again onto Rue Dieulafoy ㉒. Here are several unique, colourful cottages with flower-filled front gardens behind railings. At the end of the row, take a right onto the Rue Henri Pape, a left onto the Rue Damesme, walk up to the Rue Tolbiac and back out into modern, busy, Paris. Turn right and walk up to the metro Tolbiac ㉓.

Square des Peupliers, with its unique houses ⑲

For additional keys to symbols see back flap

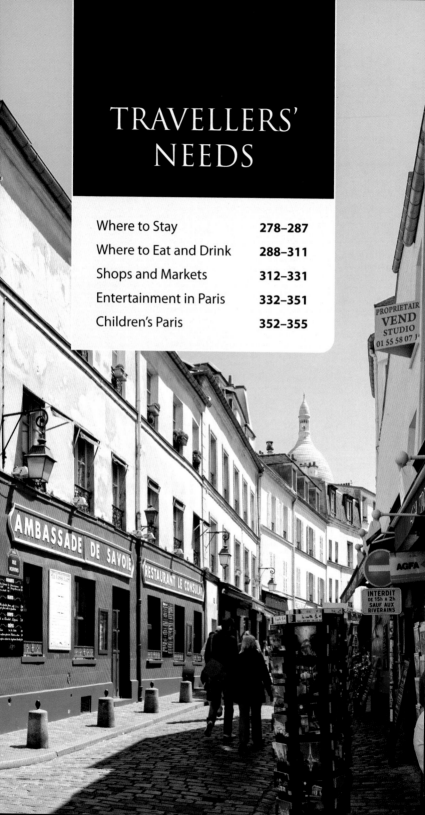

TRAVELLERS'
NEEDS

WHERE TO STAY

Paris has more guest rooms than almost any other city in Europe. Its hotels vary from magnificent luxury operations like Le Meurice and Four Seasons George V (the French call them *palaces*) to much simpler hotels that are nevertheless full of charm. It is worth noting that *hôtel* does not always mean "hotel". It can also mean a town hall (*hôtel de ville*), hospital (*Hôtel-Dieu*) or mansion. A wide range of hotels, listed under five themes – luxury, charming (*hôtels de charme*), design, romantic, self-catering and bed-and-breakfasts – and in three price brackets are reviewed on pages 284–7. All offer good value for money.

Where to Look

Hotels in Paris tend to cluster by type in particular areas. As a very broad generalization, luxury and big-business hotels tend to be on the Right Bank and *hôtels de charme* are on the Left Bank.

In the fashionable districts near the Champs-Elysées and the Opéra Garnier lie many of the city's grandest hotels, including Le Bristol, the Four Seasons George V and Le Meurice (*see p284*). Several less well known but elegant hotels can be found in the residential and ambassadorial quarter near the Palais de Chaillot.

To the east, still on the Right Bank, in the Marais, a number of old mansions have been converted into exceptionally attractive boutique hotels, such as Le Pavillon de la Reine (*see p284*). The nearby areas around Les Halles and the Rue St-Denis, however, tend to be seedy and attract prostitutes and drug addicts. Just south of the Marais across the Seine, the Ile St-Louis and

Ile de la Cité have several lovely hotels.

The Left Bank covers some of the most popular tourist areas and has an excellent range of small hotels of great character. The atmosphere subtly changes from the much upgraded Latin Quarter and the chic and arty areas north and south of Boulevard St-Germain to the rather tatty Boulevard itself and the staid institutional area towards Les Invalides and the Eiffel Tower. The hotels tend to reflect this.

Further from the centre, Montparnasse has several large business hotels in high-rise blocks, and the Porte de Versailles area to the south is usually packed with trade fair participants. The station areas around Gare du Nord and Gare de Lyon offer a number of basic hotels (choose carefully). Montmartre has some pleasant hotels if you don't mind the hilly location, but beware of hotels allegedly in Montmartre but actually in the seedier parts of

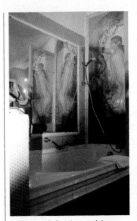

Bathroom with charming murals in Degrés de Notre-Dame (*see p285*)

the red-light, sex-show district of Pigalle. If you are looking for a hotel in person, the best times for inspecting are late morning or mid-afternoon. If the hotels are fully booked, try again after 6pm, when unclaimed provisional bookings become free. Don't rely on the impression of a hotel given by the reception desk; ask to see the room offered. For airport hotels, see p369.

Hotel Prices

Hotel prices aren't always cheaper in low season (mid-November to March or July and August), because fashion shows and other major events throughout the year can pack rooms, raising prices. However, in the older hotels, differences in the size and position of rooms can have a marked effect on cost.

Twin rooms are slightly more expensive than double rooms; single occupancy rates are as high or nearly as high as

Facade of the chic Hôtel D'Aubusson (*see p284*)

◄ Le Consulat restaurant on Rue Norvins, Montmartre

for two people sharing (tariffs are almost always quoted per room, not per person). Rooms without a bath tend to be about 20 per cent cheaper than those with. You might find a half-board arrangement unnecessary when Paris has such a wide choice of good restaurants to suit all budgets.

It is always worth trying to negotiate a discount. In some hotels, special deals are offered, especially for students, families or senior citizens. Discounts are often available when booking online or when booking a package trip.

Hidden Extras

By law, tax and service must be included in the price quoted or displayed at the reception desk or in the rooms. Tips are unnecessary other than for exceptional service, such as if the concierge books you a show, or if the maid does some washing for you. Before you make a reservation, you should always establish whether breakfast is included in the price or not. Beware of extras such as drinks or snacks in your room, especially from a mini-bar, which will probably be pricey, as will laundry services, garage parking and telephone calls from your room – especially telephone calls made through the switchboard.

Check the hotel's cancellation policy – some hotels charge a

A suite at the historic Lancaster *(see p287)*

fee for cancellation less than 24 or 48 hours before the start of the booking.

Hotel Gradings

French hotels are classified by the tourist authorities into five broad categories: one to four stars, plus a five-star rating which was introduced in 2009. Some very simple types of accommodation are unclassified. Star ratings serve to provide an indication of the level of facilities you can expect (for example, any hotel with more than three stars should have a lift). Increasingly, the French rating system also tries to take account of such factors as room size, service, attentiveness of the staff, cleanliness, dining options and decor.

Facilities

Few Parisian hotels below a four-star rating have a restaurant,

Statue in the Relais Christine *(see p284)*

although there is nearly always a breakfast room. Many hotel restaurants close in August. Older hotels may also lack a public lounge area. More modern or expensive hotels have correspondingly better facilities and usually some kind of bar.

Inexpensive hotels may not have a lift – this can be a significant drawback when you are dragging suitcases upstairs. Usually only the more expensive hotels have parking facilities. If you are driving, you may prefer to stay in one of the peripheral motel-style chains *(see pp281 & 283)*.

All but the very simplest city hotels will have a telephone in the bedroom; most also have a television. Business facilities such as conference rooms and equipment are available in grander hotels, and Wi-Fi is commonplace.

Two people who are sharing can specify whether they want a double bed *(grand lit)* or twin beds *(lits jumeaux)*.

Four Seasons George V *(see p284)*

Le Meurice in the Tuileries Quarter *(see p284)*

What to Expect

Some hotel beds still use the time-honoured French bolster, a sausage-shaped headrest that can be uncomfortable if you are unused to it. If you prefer pillows, first check in the wardrobe as they may be kept there, or ask for *oreillers*. Most hotels offer en suite bathrooms, but be sure to check if you want a bath *(baignoire)* rather than a shower *(douche)*. Simpler places, such as hostels, may offer shared facilities on the landing *(au palier)*. A duplex room is a suite on two floors.

In Paris, the traditional French hotel breakfast of fresh coffee, croissants, jam and orange juice has in many places become an elaborate buffet breakfast with cold meats and cheeses and a range of fruits, yoghurts and pastries. Some of the luxury hotels are now such popular venues for breakfast that it is worth reserving a place in the breakfast area if you don't want to eat in your room. A pleasant alternative is to head for the nearest café, where French workers enjoy breakfast over a newspaper.

Check-out time is usually noon and if you stay in your room longer you may be charged for an extra day.

Special Breaks

Because Paris is such a popular destination with leisure as well as business travellers, weekend packages are often available via travel agents or the Internet. Providing there are no major events taking place, you can reduce costs by visiting in low season and negotiating a discount, or by seeking out an all-inclusive package.

Travelling with Children

Families with young children will often find they can share a room at no or very little extra cost, and some operators offer packages with this in mind. Few hotels refuse to accept children, though facilities specifically for children are not universal. Some hotels will arrange babysitting.

Travellers with Special Needs

A limited number of hotels are well geared for use by disabled visitors. **Groupement pour l'Insertion des Personnes Handicapées Physiques (GIHP)** *(see p361)* gives advice regarding where to find information about accessible places to stay. **J'accede** *(see p361)* has details of accessible hotels on its website.

Self-Catering

Self-catering accommodation is a popular alternative for visitors staying in Paris. The **Citadines Apart'hotel** chain offers fully furnished studios and apartments with kitchens in several central Paris locations (as well as in many other major European cities). These are a good self-catering option for either a short break or an extended stay. Some hotel-type facilities are available, including laundry services, babysitting and grocery delivery, but you pay extra for them.

The **Office du Tourisme et des Congrès de Paris** provides a full list of self-catering accommodation agencies. The better known ones include **Allo Logement Temporaire**, **At Home In Paris**, **Haven in Paris**, **Paris Appartements Services** and **Holiday France Rentals**. **Good Morning Paris** and **France-Lodge** also arrange self-catering apartments, as well as acting as B&B agencies *(see Directory p283)*. All provide furnished apartments for stays from one week to six months, sometimes in the apartment of a Parisian who is abroad. Prices are comparable to other apartment accommodation, sometimes slightly cheaper for the larger apartments.

The quiet and stylish Hôtel des Grands Hommes *(see p287)*

The courtyard of the Relais Christine *(see p284)*

Staying in Private Homes

The bed-and-breakfast, that typically British phenomenon, is known as *chambre d'hôte* or *café-couette* ("coffee and a quilt") in France. B&B accommodation is generally available at moderate prices, between €45 and €100 for a double room per night. **Alcôve & Agapes** offers rooms in some enviable districts of Paris, all within walking distance of a metro station. It is worth enquiring about suites and rooms with a private lounge, kitchen or terrace. All homes are routinely inspected.

France-Lodge is a good-value agency specializing in long-stay room rentals and apartments. A registration fee of €15 a year is payable but rentals are generally cheaper than with other agencies. **Good Morning Paris** provides guest rooms and tourist information. A two-night minimum stay is required when booking *(for details of all of these see Directory p283).*

Chain Hotels

A mushroom crop of motel-style establishments on the outskirts of Paris accommodates large numbers of both business and leisure visitors. The very cheapest chains such as Formule 1, Première Classe and Fasthôtel really have nothing except price to recommend them. Further up the ladder are **Campanile**, **Ibis** and **Choice Hotels**. These establishments are practical, relatively inexpensive and useful if you have a car, but lack any real Parisian atmosphere or character. Many are in drab locations on busy roads and may suffer from traffic noise. The newer motels of these chains are smarter and better equipped than the older ones.

Several chains – **Sofitel**, **Novotel** and **Mercure** – are geared to business travellers, providing better facilities at higher prices; indeed some of the more central ones are positively luxurious. Reductions can make these hotels good value at weekends. Many of the hotels have restaurants attached. Most of the chains produce their own brochures, often with useful maps detailing the motel's precise location. For a list of chain hotels, see the Directory on page 283.

Hostels and Dormitory Accommodation

There are several hostel organizations in Paris. **Maisons Internationales de la Jeunesse et des Etudiants (MIJE)** provides dormitory rooms for those aged from 18 to their early 30s in three splendid 17th-century mansions in the Marais – the residences have all been renovated. There is no advance booking (except for groups) – call at the central offices on the day.

The **Bureau Voyage Jeunesse (BVJ)** has two hostels with double rooms (€35–€49 per night) and dormitory accommodation (€30 per night), with breakfast and luggage room facilities. Bookings cannot be made more than a fortnight in advance.

Ethic Etapes has six centres in and around Paris with individual, shared and dormitory rooms.

Fédération Unie des Auberges de Jeunesse (FUAJ) is a member of the International Youth Hostels Federation. There is no age limit at their three Paris area hostels.

St Christopher's Paris, on the Canal St Martin, provides excellent facilities and offers tours of Paris.

The early-17th-century, wooden-beamed dining area inside Jeu de Paume *(see p284)*

Camping

The only campsite in Paris itself is the **Camping Indigo Paris** (around €20–€40 per night). This well-equipped site next to the Seine is open all year round but is usually fully booked during the summer. Pitches for tents, caravans as well as rental of mobile homes are available. There are many other campsites in the surrounding region, some close to an RER line. The **Camping International de Jablines** (around €26 per night) is conveniently located just 9 km (5.5 miles) from Disneyland® Paris and a 25-minute RER train ride from central Paris. **Camping International Maisons-Laffitte** (around €30 per night) is located in a pleasant suburb on the River Seine and is open from April to October. The local RER station is a 10-minute walk away. Trains from here take 20 minutes to the city centre and 50 minutes to Disneyland® Paris. Versailles is 20 minutes from the campsite by car. Details of other sites can be obtained from the Paris tourist office or from a booklet produced by the **Fédération Française de Camping-Caravaning (FFCC)** *(see Directory p283).*

How to Book

Paris is busiest at Christmas and New Year, and during France's school breaks around Easter and October. Tourists pour in from May to September, but Parisians pour out *en masse* in August, when many shops and restaurants close. Disneyland® Paris has further increased the pressure to find accommodation, as many visitors choose to stay in the capital and commute to the park on the RER.

If you have decided on a hotel, it is vital to book ahead by at least a month. The hotels listed on pages 284–7 are among the best in their category and will fill particularly quickly. Make a reservation six weeks in advance between May and October. The best way is to book directly with the hotel. If you make your initial inquiry by

Tourist information desk, Charles de Gaulle airport

telephone, ring during the day if possible – you are more likely to find staff authorized to take bookings. You should send confirmation of your reservation (email addresses can be found on hotel websites, which are provided in the listings in this guide); credit card details are often required to guarantee your booking.

It is usually possible to make a reservation through your hotel's website. It can be worth doing this as some hotels offer special deals for visitors who book online.

If you prefer to use an agency, **Ely 12 12** can book hotels and other kinds of accommodation, as well as excursions such as boat trips along the Seine.

If you aren't too fussy about where you stay, or if all the hotels are full, you can book via the **Office du Tourisme et des Congrès de Paris**, which offers an on-the-spot booking service for a reasonable fee.

Deposits

If you make a reservation by telephone, you will be asked for either your credit card number (from which any cancellation fee may be deducted) or a deposit *(arrhes)*, which can be as much as the price of a night's stay. It's quite acceptable in France to specify your choice of room when you book. Try to arrive at your hotel by 6pm on the day you have booked, or at least telephone to say you will be late, otherwise you may lose the room. If you have any problems, consult the Office du Tourisme et des Congrès de Paris.

Tourist Information Desks

You can book hotels at all airport information desks but only in person and for the same day. Information desks at train stations, such as the Gare de Lyon, Gare du Nord and Pyramides, provide a similar booking arrangement for all forms of accommodation. Many Paris information desks also keep a complete list of city hotels and some book entertainment and excursions *(see pp358 & 359).*

Recommended Hotels

The hotels on pages 284–7 of this guide are a selection of the best luxury, romantic, design and charming hotels in Paris. They are first listed according to type, and then by area and by price. Most of the hotels are spread across the main tourist areas, although some that are further afield have been included if they offer particularly good value for money, facilities, service or charm. The selection is not confined to hotels. There are also B&Bs and self-catering apartments, which tend to be cheaper than hotels, for visitors on a tight budget. What they all have in common is that they are more than just a bed for the night – they have something extra that makes it worth seeking them out. Throughout the listings, certain hotels have been marked DK Choice – these offer an exceptional experience, such as beautiful rooms, a historic setting, superlative service, spectacular views, a fabulous spa, family-friendly amenities or a combination of these.

Caravans at Camping International Maisons-Laffitte

DIRECTORY

Office du Tourisme et des Congrès de Paris

25 Rue des Pyramides 75001.
Tel 01 49 52 42 63. *See also p359.*
W parisinfo.com

Agencies

Ely 12 12
182 Rue du Faubourg
St-Honoré 75008.
Tel 01 43 59 12 12.
W ely1212.com

Self-Catering

**Allo Logement
Temporaire**
38 Rue Legendre 75017.
Tel 09 51 24 87 42.
W allo-logement-temporaire.asso.fr

At Home in Paris
15 Ave de Friedland 75008.
Tel 01 42 12 40 40.
W athomeinparis.fr

Citadines Apart'hotel
Tel 01 41 05 79 05.
W citadines.com

Haven In Paris
Tel +1 61 7395 4243 (US).
W haveninparis.com

**Holiday France
Rentals**
Tel 01 55 37 97 36, 06 08
07 46 98.
W holidays-france-rentals.com

**Paris Appartements
Services**
20 Rue Bachaumont
75002. **Tel** 01 40 28 01 28.
W paris-appartements-services.com

Residences de Tourisme

Pierre et Vacances
Tel 0892 70 21 80 (France),
0870 0267 145 (UK), +33 1
58 21 55 50 (international).
W pierreetvacances.com

Résidence du Roy
8 Rue François-1er 75008.
Tel 01 42 89 59 59.
W leshotelsduroy.com/en/la-residence-du-roy

Bed & Breakfast

Alcôve & Agapes
Tel 01 44 85 06 05.
W bed-and-breakfast-in-paris.com

France-Lodge
2 Rue Meissonier 75017.
Tel 01 56 33 85 85.
W francelodge.fr

Good Morning Paris
43 Rue Lacépède, 75005.
Tel 01 47 07 28 29.
W goodmorningparis.fr

Chain Hotels

Campanile
Tel 0207 519 50 45 (UK).
W campanile.com

Choice Hotels
Tel 08 00 91 24 24 (central
reservations);
877 424 6425 (US and
Canada).
W choicehotels.com

**Crowne Plaza
République**
10 Pl de la République
75011.
Tel 01 43 14 43 50.
W ihg.com

**Hilton Paris
La Defense**
2 Place de la Défense
92053.
Tel 01 46 92 10 10.
W 3.hilton.com

**Holiday Inn
St-Germain-des-Prés**
92 Rue de Vaugirard.
Tel 01 49 54 87 00.
W holidayinn.com

**Hotel Warwick
Champs-Elysées**
5 Rue de Berri 75008.
Tel 01 45 63 14 11.
W warwickparis.com

Ibis Styles Paris Bercy
77 Rue de Bercy 75012.
Tel 0825 88 00 00.
W accorhotels.com

Ibis Paris Bastille
15 Rue Breguet 75011.
Tel 01 49 29 20 20.
W ibishotel.com

**Mercure Paris Bercy
Bibliotheque**
6 Blvd Vincent Auriol
75013. **Tel** 01 45 82 48 00.
W mercure.com

**Mercure Paris Gare
Montparnasse**
20 Rue de la Gaîté 75014.
Tel 08 25 80 29 29.
W mercure.com

**Mercure Paris
Vaugirard Porte
de Versailles**
69 Blvd Victor 75015.
Tel 01 44 19 03 03.
W mercure.com

**Mercure Paris
Tour-Eiffel Grenelle**
64 Blvd de Grenelle 75015.
Tel 01 45 78 90 90.
W mercure.com

Méridien Etoile
81 Blvd Gouvion
Saint-Cyr 75017.
Tel 01 40 68 34 34.
W lemeridienetoile.com

Novotel Paris Bercy
85 Rue de Bercy 75012.
Tel 01 43 42 30 00.
W novotel.com

**Novotel Paris
Les Halles**
8 Pl Marguerite de
Navarre 75001.
Tel 01 42 21 31 31.
W novotel.com

Novotel Tour Eiffel
61 Quai de Grenelle
75015. **Tel** 01 40 58 20 00.
W novotel.com

**Paris Rive Gauche
Hotel and
Conference Centre**
17 Blvd St-Jacques 75014.
Tel 01 40 78 79 80.
W marriott.com/paris

**Royal Garden
Champs-Elysées**
218-220 Rue du Faubourg
St-Honoré 75008.
Tel 01 49 53 03 03.
W royalgardenparis.com

Sofitel Le Faubourg
15 Rue Boissy d'Anglas
75008.
Tel 01 44 94 14 14.
W sofitel.com

**Sofitel Paris La
Défense**
33 Voie des Sculpteurs
92800.
Tel 01 47 76 44 43.
W sofitel.com

Sofitel Scribe
1 Rue Scribe 75009.
Tel 01 44 71 24 24.
W sofitel.com

Hostels

BVJ
20 Rue Jean-Jacques
Rousseau 75001.
Tel 01 53 00 90 90.
W bvj-hotel.com

Ethic Etapes
27 Rue de Turbigo 75002.
Tel 01 40 26 57 64.
W ethic-etapes.fr

FUAJ – Le d'Artagnan
80 Rue Vitruve 75020.
Tel 01 40 32 34 56.
W fuaj.org

MIJE
13 Boulevard
Beaumarchais 75004.
Tel 01 42 74 23 45.
W mije.com

St Christopher's Paris
159 Rue de Crimée 75019.
Tel 01 40 34 34 40.
W st-christophers.co.uk

Camping

Camping Indigo Paris
2 Allée du Bord de l'Eau
75016. **Tel** 01 45 24 30 00.
W campingparis.fr

Camping Inter-national de Jablines
Jablines-Annet 77450.
Tel 01 60 26 09 37 (closed
Nov–mid-Apr).
W camping-jablines.com

Camping Inter-national Maisons-Laffitte
1 Rue Johnson 78600.
Tel 01 39 12 21 91.
W sandaya.fr/web/FR/
Campings/France/Paris/
Maisons-Laffitte/
Apercu.htm

FFCC
78 Rue de Rivoli 75004.
Tel 01 42 72 84 08.
W ffcc.fr

Where to Stay

Luxury

Ile de la Cité and Ile St-Louis

Jeu de Paume €€€
54 Rue St-Louis en l'Ile, 75004
Tel *01 43 26 14 18*   **Map** 13 C4
W jeudepaumehotel.com
A beamed building dating from the early 17th century has been transformed into a rustic-chic hotel with luxurious rooms.

Beaubourg and The Marais

DK Choice

Le Pavillon de la Reine €€€
28 Place des Vosges, 75003
Tel *01 40 29 19 19*   **Map** 14 D3
W pavillon-de-la-reine.com
Overlooking the city's most beautiful square, this hotel has an unrivalled setting. The 17th-century mansion, once home to Anne of Austria, has been modernized in elegant country-house style, with plush, romantic bedrooms and a pampering spa. It also has a peaceful small garden.

Tuileries, Opéra and Montmartre

Le Meurice €€€
228 Rue de Rivoli, 75001
Tel *01 44 58 10 10*   **Map** 12 D1
W lemeurice.com
The last word in Empire-style luxury, this is the most stylish of the city's *grande dame* hotels: a palace with glitzy rooms, glorious views and a luxurious spa.

Mandarin Oriental €€€
251 Rue St-Honoré, 75001
Tel *01 70 98 78 88*   **Map** 12 D1
W mandarinoriental.com/Paris
The rooms here are very comfortable, with Art Deco and Oriental details. Eastern service and Parisian style provide a winning combination.

W Paris – Opéra €€€
4 Rue Meyerbeer, 75009
Tel *01 77 48 94 94*   **Map** 6 E4
W wparisopera.com
France's first W has a cool, young vibe. It's a combination of 1870s features and witty modern furnishings, with comfortable beds and excellent cocktails.

Champs-Elysées and Chaillot Quarter

Keppler €€
10 Rue Keppler, 75116
Tel *01 47 20 65 05*   **Map** 4 E5
W keppler.fr
A super-chic hotel, with bold black-and-white decor, offering classic comfort. The rooms contain beautiful antiques.

Four Seasons George V €€€
31 Avenue George V, 75008
Tel *01 49 52 71 00*   **Map** 4 E5
W fourseasons.com/paris
An icon. The glamour and glitz of the original George V is enhanced by modern Four Seasons luxury.

Le Bristol €€€
112 Rue du Faubourg St-Honoré, 75008
Tel *01 53 43 43 00*   **Map** 5 A4
W lebristolparis.com
Antiques, Flemish tapestries and chandeliers fill this elegant hotel. Don't miss a dip in the pool.

St-Germain and Latin Quarter

Hôtel d'Aubusson €€€
33 Rue Dauphine, 75006
Tel *01 43 29 43 43*   **Map** 12 F4
W hoteldaubusson.com
Four-star comfort in a 17th-century stone house with a courtyard.

Relais Christine €€€
3 Rue Christine, 75006
Tel *01 40 51 60 80*   **Map** 12 F4
W relais-christine.com
A luxurious and intimate haven of calm with a panelled salon and a private garden.

The Caron de Beaumarchais, with its delightful 18th-century decor

Hôtels de Charme

Beaubourg and The Marais

Hôtel du 7e Art €
20 Rue St-Paul, 75004
Tel *01 44 54 85 00*   **Map** 14 D4
W paris-hotel-7art.com
An homage to old movies, with framed film posters everywhere. Snug bar and modest bedrooms.

Britannique €€
20 Avenue Victoria, 75001
Tel *01 42 33 74 59*   **Map** 13 A3
W hotel-britannique.fr
Seascapes and other naval details adorn this hotel with a British feel.

Caron de Beaumarchais €€
12 Rue Vieille du Temple, 75004
Tel *01 42 72 34 12*   **Map** 13 C3
W carondebeaumarchais.com
The 18th-century theme here comes alive with colourful fabrics and dainty upholstered furniture.

Tuileries, Opéra and Montmartre

Hôtel Chopin €
46 Passage Jouffroy, 75009
Tel *01 47 70 58 10*   **Map** 6 F4
W hotelchopin.fr
A popular hotel, located in a 19th-century glass-roofed arcade.

Brighton €€
218 Rue de Rivoli, 75001
Tel *01 47 03 61 61*   **Map** 12 D1
W paris-hotel-brighton.com
Enjoy views of the Tuileries amid faux marble columns and chandeliers. Family-friendly.

L'Ermitage Sacre-Coeur €€
24 Rue Lamarck, 75018
Tel *01 42 64 79 22*   **Map** 7 A1
W ermitagesacrecoeur.fr
Murals by the artist Roland Dubuc decorate this delightful hotel.

Mansart €€
5 Rue des Capucines, 75001
Tel *01 42 61 50 28*   **Map** 6 D5
W paris-hotel-mansart.com
The antique-filled bedrooms here have plenty of character.

The tranquil summer garden at Le Bristol

Champs-Elysées and Chaillot Quarter

Nicolo   €€
3 Rue Nicolo, 75116
Tel *01 42 88 83 40*   **Map** 9 A2
W hotel-nicolo.fr
A blissfully quiet hotel crammed
with antique furniture, Oriental
rugs and huge wildlife prints.

St-Germain and Latin Quarter

Degrés de Notre Dame   €€
10 Rue des Grands Degrés, 75005
Tel *01 55 42 88 88*   **Map** 13 B4
W lesdegreshotel.com
A vintage charmer: attractive
beamed bedrooms lead off a
frescoed staircase.

Hôtel de Fleurie   €€
32–34 Rue Grégoire-de-Tours, 75006
Tel *01 53 73 70 00*   **Map** 12 F4
W hoteldefleurie.fr
The statue-adorned façade draws
you into this hotel, and its
modern comforts keep you there.

Hôtel des Grandes Ecoles   €€
75 Rue Cardinal Lemoine, 75005
Tel *01 43 26 79 23*   **Map** 17 B1
W hotel-grandes-ecoles.com
A hotel that exudes old-fashioned
charm. The garden is perfect for
summer breakfasts.

Hôtel St-Paul Rive Gauche €€
43 Rue Monsieur le Prince, 75006
Tel *01 43 26 98 64*   **Map** 12 F5
W hotelsaintpaulparis.com
Stone walls and beams at this
hotel offer a country vibe. Stylish
rooms, some with four-poster beds.

Verneuil   €€
8 Rue de Verneuil, 75007
Tel *01 42 60 82 14*   **Map** 12 D3
W hotel-verneuil-saint-germain.com
Cosy rooms, antiques, books and
objets d'art, at this homely hotel.

Luxembourg and Montparnasse

DK Choice

**Hôtel des Académies et
des Arts**   €€
*15 Rue de la Grande Chaumière,
75006*
Tel *01 43 26 66 44*   **Map** 16 D2
W hotel-des-academies.com
Two artists have created an
original look for this
captivating hotel. Jérôme
Mesnager's joyful painted
silhouettes of dancers and
acrobats decorate the walls,
while sculptor Sophie de
Watrigant's equally charming
figures adorn the hotel
staircase. The bedrooms,
tearoom and spa have a
refined feel.

Hôtel Ste-Beuve   €€
9 Rue Ste-Beuve, 75006
Tel *01 45 48 20 07*   **Map** 16 D1
W hotelsaintebeuve.com
Low-key but with an inherent
sense of style, this hotel has
colourful bedrooms. A log fire
burns in the lovely salon in winter.

Récamier   €€
3 bis Place St-Sulpice, 75006
Tel *01 43 26 04 89*   **Map** 12 E5
W hotelrecamier.com
A small but perfectly
formed hotel in a very quiet
location. Neat rooms and
impeccable service.

Further Afield

Hôtel de la Porte Dorée   €
273 Avenue Daumesnil, 75012
Tel *01 43 07 56 97*
W hoteldelaportedoree.com
Traditional elegance:
cosy rooms with beautiful
furniture, antiques and
trompe-l'oeil murals.

Hôtel du Nord   €
47 Rue Albert Thomas, 75010
Tel *01 42 01 66 00*   **Map** 8 D5
W hoteldunord-leparivelo.com
A cosy, modest hotel with
pretty, distinctive rooms
and bicycles for guests
to use.

La Manufacture   €€
8 Rue Philippe de Champagne, 75013
Tel *01 45 35 45 25*   **Map** 17 C4
W hotel-la-manufacture.com
A smart, modern hotel
in a 19th-century building,
with warm wood floors and
attractive decor.

La Villa Paris   €€
33 Rue de la Fontaine à Mulard, 75013
Tel *01 43 47 15 66*
W la-villa-paris.com
Enjoy all the comforts of home
at this B&B in a 1920s house.
Rooms are luxurious with
refined decor.

Langlois   €€
63 Rue St-Lazare, 75009
Tel *01 48 74 78 24*   **Map** 6 D3
W hotel-langlois.com
Housed in a former 19th-
century bank, this traditional
hotel offers bags of character
and belle époque and Art
Nouveau decor.

Manoir de Beauregard   €€
43 Rue des Lilas, 75019
Tel *01 42 03 10 20*
W manoir-de-beauregard-paris.com
A B&B in a fine 18th-century
manor with a formal garden.

Résidence Foch   €€
10 Rue Marbeau, 75116
Tel *01 45 00 46 50*   **Map** 3 B4
W foch-paris-hotel.com
Historical prints decorate
the walls and fabrics at this
intimate hotel.

Design

Champs-Elysées and Chaillot Quarter

Hotel Fouquet's Barrière   €€€
46 Avenue George V, 75008
Tel *01 40 69 60 00*   **Map** 4 E5
W lucienbarriere.com
A very hip, modern hotel with
Surrealist design touches.

Le A   €€€
4 Rue d'Artois, 75008
Tel *01 42 56 99 99*   **Map** 5 A4
W paris-hotel-a.com
Bold murals and a monochromatic
theme feature in this stylish,
cutting-edge hotel.

For more information on types of hotels *see page 282*

Refined elegance at the Duc de St-Simon

Invalides and Eiffel Tower Quarter

Mayet   €€
3 Rue Mayet, 75006
Tel *01 47 83 21 35*   **Map** 15 B1
W mayet.com
Colourful painted tables and
abstract murals jazz up the decor
at this smart hotel.

Valadon Colors   €€
16 Rue Valadon, 75007
Tel *01 47 53 89 85*   **Map** 10 F3
W hotelvaladon.com
Superb beds, bold colours and
funky furniture – a three-star hotel
that stands out from the crowd.

7 Eiffel   €€€
17 bis Rue Amélie, 75007
Tel *01 45 55 10 01*   **Map** 10 F3
W hotel-7eiffel-paris.com
Subdued, stylish decoration with
dashes of colour make up this
elegant hotel. Great roof terrace.

St-Germain and Latin Quarter

Bel Ami   €€
7–11 Rue St-Benoît, 75006
Tel *01 42 61 53 51*   **Map** 12 E3
W hotel-bel-ami.com
In a former 19th-century printing
works, this hip, minimalist hotel is
where the media crowd hangs out.

Le Bellechasse   €€
8 Rue de Bellechasse, 75007
Tel *01 45 50 22 31*   **Map** 11 C3
W lebellechasse.com
Vibrant frescoes, zany patterns
and brilliant colours fill this fun,
Christian Lacroix-designed gem.

Seven   €€
20 Rue Berthollet, 75005
Tel *01 43 31 47 52*   **Map** 17 A2
W sevenhotelparis.com
With a space-age design, this
chic hotel has fibre-optic lighting
and themed rooms.

Luxembourg and Montparnasse

La Maison Montparnasse   €
53 Rue de Gergovie, 75014
Tel *01 45 42 11 39*   **Map** 15 B4
W lamaisonmontparnasse.com
A simple hotel painted in
rainbow colours – a different
hue for each storey.

Apostrophe   €€
3 Rue de Chevreuse, 75006
Tel *01 56 54 31 31*   **Map** 16 E2
W apostrophe-hotel.com
A quirky, family-run hotel that will
appeal to people with an artistic
or literary bent. Rooms have
been decorated by local artists.

Le Six   €€€
14 Rue Stanislas, 75006
Tel *01 42 22 00 75*   **Map** 16 D1
W hotel-le-six.com
Decorated in understated coffee
and cream, this is a chic, modern
hotel. The spa and hammam are
an added luxury.

Further Afield

Mama Shelter   €
109 Rue de Bagnolet, 75020
Tel *01 43 48 48 48*
W mamashelter.com/en/paris
Classy and hip, yet good value.
The Philippe Starck-designed
rooms at this hotel have iMacs,
microwaves and mood lighting.

Romantic

Ile de la Cité and Ile St-Louis

St-Louis en l'Isle   €€
75 Rue St-Louis en l'Ile, 75004
Tel *01 46 34 04 80*   **Map** 13 C4
W saintlouisenlisle.com
A superb location without sky-high
prices. Stylish and intimate, with
rooms in neutral shades.

Beaubourg and The Marais

DK Choice

Le Petit Moulin   €€
29–31 Rue du Poitou, 75003
Tel *01 42 74 10 10*   **Map** 14 D2
W hotelpetitmoulinparis.com
The oldest *boulangerie* in Paris
now houses a tiny, eccentric
hotel designed by Christian
Lacroix. The 17 distinctive
rooms display the same love
of colour and opulence that
shapes his fashion designs.
All are wildly romantic, with
audacious murals.

Tuileries, Opéra and Montmartre

Le Relais Montmartre   €€
6 Rue Constance, 75018
Tel *01 70 64 25 25*   **Map** 6 E1
W hotel-relais-montmartre.com
Arranged around a diminutive
courtyard, this welcoming hotel's
rooms have dainty period
furniture and painted beams.

Hotel Particulier Montmartre €€€
23 Avenue Junot, Pavillon D, 75018
Tel *01 53 41 81 40*   **Map** 2 E5
W hotel-particulier-montmartre.com
The five intimate suites here
feature cutting-edge design and
are the size of small apartments.
There is also a pretty garden.

DK Choice

Terrass   €€€
*12–14 Rue Joseph de Maistre,
75018*
Tel *01 46 06 72 85*   **Map** 6 E1
W terrass-hotel.com
A relaxed four-star hotel with
elegant rooms, Terrass has the
seasons covered. In winter,
there's a cosy piano bar with an
open fire and armchairs to sink
into. In summer, the roof terrace
comes into its own. The top
floor affords spectacular views
across the rooftops to the Eiffel
Tower and beyond.

Champs-Elysées and Chaillot Quarter

Daniel   €€€
8 Rue Frédéric Bastiat, 75008
Tel *01 42 56 17 00*   **Map** 4 F4
W hoteldanielparis.com
A Chinese jewel box, this hotel
is filled with Oriental fabrics,
wallpapers, carpets and objects.
Flamboyant and uplifting.

Lancaster €€€
7 Rue de Berri, 75008
Tel *01 40 76 40 76* **Map** 4 F4
W hotel-lancaster.com
Marlene Dietrich's favourite
hotel exudes understated luxury.

Shangri La €€€
10 Avenue d'Iéna, 75116
Tel *01 53 67 19 98* **Map** 10 D1
W shangri-la.com/paris/shangrila
A madly romantic hotel in a belle
époque palace, the former home
of Napoleon's grandnephew.

Invalides and Eiffel
Tower Quarter

Hôtel de la Tour Maubourg €€
150 Rue de Grenelle, 75007
Tel *01 47 05 16 16* **Map** 11 A3
W hoteltourmaubourgparis.com
A gracious and homely hotel
with harmonious bedrooms.

Hôtel de Varenne €€
44 Rue de Bourgogne, 75007
Tel *01 45 51 45 55* **Map** 11 B3
W varenne-hotel-paris.com
A lovely garden is the main asset
of this hotel, which offers Louis
XVI- and Empire-style bedrooms.

DK Choice

Duc de St-Simon €€€
14 Rue de St-Simon, 75007
Tel *01 44 39 20 20* **Map** 11 C3
W hotelducdesaintsimon.com
In an 18th-century town house,
this alluring, quiet hotel has
traditional decor. Upholstered
furniture, antiques, skillful paint
effects and bedrooms in
sumptuous colours lend it a
smart but homely feel. Relax in
the cellar bar, so glorious you'll
never want to leave. Since
standard rooms are on the
small side, it's worth upgrading.

St-Germain and
Latin Quarter

Hôtel de Buci €€
22 Rue de Buci, 75006
Tel *01 55 42 74 74* **Map** 12 E4
W buci-hotel.com
Travel back to the 18th century at
this hotel with antiques, rich
colours and luxurious fabrics.

Relais St-Germain €€
9 Carrefour de l'Odéon, 75006
Tel *01 44 27 07 97* **Map** 12 F4
W hotel-paris-relais-saint-
germain.com
Irresistible and typically Parisian,
this hotel has an upmarket bistro
and large, luxurious bedrooms.

Hôtel des Grands Hommes €€€
17 Place du Panthéon, 75005
Tel *01 46 34 19 60* **Map** 17 A1
W hoteldesgrandshommes.com
Enjoy views of the Panthéon at
this glossy hotel. Housed in an
18th-century building, it has
sumptuous Baroque-style decor.

Villa d'Estrées €€€
17 Rue Gît le Cœur, 75006
Tel *01 55 42 71 11* **Map** 12 F4
W villadestrees.com
An elegant hideaway, this family-
run establishment offers rooms,
suites and apartments.

Luxembourg and
Montparnasse

Louis II €€
2 Rue St-Sulpice, 75006
Tel *01 46 33 13 80* **Map** 12 E4
W hotel-louis2.com
The rooms in this friendly hotel are
full of character, with handmade
mattresses and pretty fabrics.

Hôtel de L'Abbaye €€€
10 Rue Cassette, 75006
Tel *01 45 44 38 11* **Map** 12 D5
W hotelabbayeparis.com
Fresh flowers, deep sofas and
picture-covered walls set the
scene at this elegant hotel.

Further Afield

Hôtel de Banville €€
166 Boulevard Berthier, 75017
Tel *01 42 67 70 16* **Map** 4 D1
W hotelbanville.fr
Comfort and refinement are key
at this Art Deco hotel.

Self-Catering
and B&B
Ile de la Cité and
Ile St-Louis

Hospitel €
1 Place du Parvis Notre-Dame, 75004
Tel *01 44 32 01 00* **Map** 13 A4
W hotel-hospitel.fr
A bright, comfortable B&B with
welcoming staff above a hospital.

Tuileries, Opéra and
Montmartre

Loft Paris €
7 Cité Véron, 75018
Tel *06 14 48 47 48* **Map** 6 E1
W loft-paris.fr
Five homely self-catering apart-
ments offer plenty of character.
There are great views from the
top-floor apartment.

Champs-Elysées and
Chaillot Quarter

Palais de Chaillot €
35 Avenue Raymond Poincaré, 75116
Tel *01 53 70 09 09* **Map** 9 C1
W hotelpalaisdechaillot.com
A simple, modern B&B decorated
in bright colours.

St-Germain and
Latin Quarter

Marignan €
13 Rue du Sommerard, 75005
Tel *01 43 54 63 81* **Map** 13 A5
W hotel-marignan.com
Pristine bedrooms and a quaint
breakfast room are a feature of
this family-run B&B.

Further Afield

DK Choice

Arvor St-Georges €€
8 Rue Laferrière, 75009
Tel *01 48 78 60 92* **Map** 6 F3
W hotelarvor.com
Behind a subdued façade,
this welcoming, family-friendly
B&B offers retro-modern style.
The open-plan reception, which
includes a bar and breakfast
area, is decorated with
conceptual artist Daniel Buren's
striped posters. A single wall
of bold colour enlivens the
otherwise white and minimalist,
though comfortable, bedrooms.

HotelHome Paris 16 €€€
36 Rue George Sand, 75016
Tel *01 45 20 61 38*
W hotelhome.fr
Seventeen cheerfully decorated
apartments of various sizes make
up this apartment-hotel
complex. Good for families.

The colourful Christian Lacroix-designed
Le Petit Moulin

For more information on types of hotels *see page 282*

WHERE TO EAT AND DRINK

The French national passion for good cuisine makes eating out one of the greatest pleasures of a visit to Paris. Everywhere in the city, you see people eating – in restaurants, bistros, tea salons, cafés and wine bars.

Most restaurants serve French food but there is a range of Chinese, Vietnamese, Thai, Korean and North African eateries in many areas as well as Italian, Greek, Middle Eastern and Indian ones. Most places serve lunch from noon to about 2pm, and the menu often includes fixed-price meals. Parisians usually start to fill restaurants for dinner around 8.30pm and most places serve from around 7.30pm until 11pm. Many restaurants are closed in August. *(See also Cafés, Tea Salons and Bars pp308–11.)*

What to Eat

A tremendous range of food is available in Paris, from the rich meat dishes and perfect pâtisserie for which France is most famous to simpler French regional cuisines *(see pp292–3).* The latter are available in brasseries and bistros – the type usually depends on the birthplace of the chef. Simple, small meals can be enjoyed in cafés, wine bars and pâtisseries, while more substantial meals can be had in the numerous brasseries and bistros.

The best ethnic food comes from France's former colonies: Vietnam and North Africa. North African eateries are known as couscous restaurants and serve filling, somewhat spicy, inexpensive food that varies in quality. Vietnamese restaurants are also good value and provide a light alternative to rich French food. Paris also has some good Japanese restaurants, notably around Rue Monsieur le Prince (6th arrondissement), as well as Rue Ste-Anne (2nd) and Avenue de Choisy (13th arrondissement).

Where to find good Restaurants and Cafés

You can eat well in almost any part of Paris. Wherever you are, as a rule of thumb you will find that the most outstanding restaurants and cafés are those that cater predominantly to a French clientele.

The Left Bank probably has the greatest concentration of restaurants, especially in tourist areas like St-Germain-des-Prés and the Latin Quarter. The quality of food varies, but there are some commendable bistros, outdoor cafés and wine bars – see pages 308–11 for a selection of the best places to go in Paris for light meals and snacks. The Latin Quarter also has a high concentration of Greek and Turkish restaurants centred chiefly around Rue de la Huchette.

Le Pré Verre restaurant *(see p303)*

In the Marais and Bastille areas, small bistros, tea salons and cafés are plentiful, some modern and fashionable. These areas also have many traditional long-established bistros and brasseries that are good.

The Champs-Elysées and Madeleine area offer everything from smart, traditional cafés to fast-food outlets and a scattering of delectable tea rooms. There are some very good expensive restaurants here too.

Montparnasse still has some great cafés from the 1920s, including Le Sélect and La Rotonde, on the Boulevard du Montparnasse *(see p311).* Sensitive renovation has recaptured much of their old splendour. This area is also well known for its many pancake restaurants *(crêperies).* Rue de Montparnasse, for example, is lined with *crêperies* serving *galettes,* sweet *crêpes* and Normandy cider.

Le Verre Volé bistrot and wine shop *(see p307)*

There are many noteworthy restaurants, bistros and cafés in the Louvre-Rivoli area, competing with tourist-oriented, overpriced cafés. Just to the east, Les Halles is choc-a-bloc with fast food joints and mediocre restaurants but there are a few places of note.

Good Japanese food can be found near the Opéra together with some fine brasseries, but otherwise, the area around the Opéra and Grands Boulevards is not the best for restaurants. Near the Bourse are some reputable restaurants and bistros, often frequented by stockbrokers.

Montmartre has a predictable number of tourist restaurants, but it also has a few very pleasant small bistros. One traditional bistro, complete with a zinc bar, is Un Zèbre à Montmartre (see p298), which serves delicious, inexpensive food.

Quiet neighbourhoods in the evening, the Invalides, Eiffel Tower and Palais de Chaillot tend to have less noisy, more serious restaurants than areas with lively nightlife. Prices can be high.

Two Chinatowns, one in the area south of the Place d'Italie, the other in the traditionally working-class, hill-top area of Belleville, have concentrations of ethnic food but few French restaurants of note. There are a number of Vietnamese eateries as well as large, inexpensive Chinese ones, and Belleville is also packed with small North African restaurants.

La Tour d'Argent decoration (see p304)

Le Grand Véfour next to the Palais-Royal gardens (see p299)

Types of Restaurants and Cafés

One of the most enjoyable aspects of eating in Paris is the diversity of places to eat. Bistros are small, often moderately priced restaurants with a limited selection of dishes. Those from the belle époque era are particularly beautiful, with zinc bars, mirrors and attractive tiles. The food is generally, but not always, regional and traditional. Many chefs from the smartest restaurants have also opened bistros and these can be very good value.

Brasseries are mostly large bustling eateries, many with an Alsatian character serving carafes of Alsatian wine and platters of sauerkraut and sausage. They have immense menus, and most serve food throughout the day and are open late. Outside, you may well see impressive pavement displays of shellfish, with apron-clad oyster shuckers working late into the night.

Cafés open early in the morning, and apart from the large tourist cafés, most close by around 10pm. They serve drinks and food all day long from a short menu of salads, sandwiches, omelettes and grills. At lunch, most also offer a small choice of hot daily specials.

A typical bistro menu

Café prices vary from area to area, in direct proportion to the number of tourists. Smarter cafés, like Café de Flore and Les Deux Magots, serve food until late at night. Those cafés specializing in beer almost always include onion tarts, French fries and hearty bowls of steamed mussels on the menu. Brunch is served in many places at weekends, from around €17.

Wine bars are informal. They usually have a moderately priced, simple lunch menu and serve wine by the glass. Some serve snacks at any time of day – such as marvellous open sandwiches (tartines) made with sourdough Poilâne bread topped with cheese, sausage or pâté. A few stay open for dinner.

Tea salons open for breakfast or mid-morning until the early evening. Many offer lunch, as well as a selection of sweet pastries for afternoon tea. They are best visited in the middle of the afternoon and offer coffee and hot chocolate as well as fine teas. Some, like Le Loir dans la Théière, are casual with sofas, while Mariage Frères is more formal. Angélina on the Rue de Rivoli is famous for its hot chocolate, and Ladurée has excellent macaroons. (For addresses see pp310–11.)

Bofinger, a traditional brasserie in Bastille *(see p296)*

Vegetarian Food

Wholly vegetarian restaurants in Paris are still relatively few, and standard restaurant menus typically offer only a few vegetarian options. You can often fare well by ordering two courses from the list of *entrées* (first courses). North African restaurants will serve couscous with vegetables only, but these may have come out of the meat pot.

Never be timid about asking for a change in a dish. If you see a salad with ham, bacon or foie gras, ask the waiter for it without the meat. If you are going to a smart restaurant, telephone ahead and ask the manager if it is possible to prepare a special meal for you. Most restaurants will be happy to oblige.

Organic produce is increasingly used in French cuisine – look out for *biologique* or *bio* on the menu. Some places can also provide gluten-free dishes.

How Much to Pay

Prices for meals in Paris range from the extremely economic to the astronomical. You can still enjoy a hearty restaurant or café lunch for €25, but a typical good bistro, brasserie or restaurant meal in central Paris will average €40–€55 with wine. Remember that the better French wines will increase the size of your bill significantly.

More expensive restaurants begin at about €60 with wine and go up to €210 for the top establishments. Many places offer a *formule* or *prix-fixe* (fixed price) menu, especially at lunch, and this will almost always offer the best value. Some restaurants feature two course menus for under €20 – a few at this price include wine. Coffee usually carries an extra charge.

All French restaurants are obliged by law to display their menu outside. The posted rates include service but a tip for particularly good service will always be appreciated (any amount from one Euro to five per cent of the total).

The most widely accepted credit card is Visa. Few restaurants accept American Express, and some bistros do not accept credit cards at all, so it is wise to enquire when you book. Travellers' cheques are not accepted either, and many cafés require cash.

The Menu

Menu boards in small restaurants and bistros, and even in big brasseries, are often handwritten and can be difficult to decipher, so ask for help if necessary. The first course generally includes a choice of seasonal salads or vegetables, pâté and small hot or cold vegetable dishes or tarts. Small fish dishes like smoked salmon, grilled sardines, herring, fish salads and tartares are also often on the menu. Brasseries have shellfish such as oysters, which can also be eaten as a main course.

Main dishes usually include a selection of meat, poultry and fish. Game often features in the autumn. Most restaurants also offer fresh, good-value daily specials *(plats du jour)*.

Eating at the classy Benoît, run by Alain Ducasse *(see p297)*

Cheese is eaten either as a dessert or as a pre-dessert course. Coffee is served after, not with, dessert. You will need to ask specifically if you want it *au lait* (with milk). Decaffeinated coffee *(décaféiné)* and herbal teas *(tisanes)* are also popular.

In most restaurants, you will be asked if you would like a drink before ordering food. A typical apéritif is kir (white wine with a drop of *crème de cassis*, a black currant liqueur) or *kir royal* (champagne with crème de cassis). Beer is rarely drunk before a meal in France *(see What to Drink in Paris pp294–5)*.

Bistros and brasseries usually include the wine list with the menu. The more expensive restaurants have separate wine lists, which are generally brought to the table by the wine waiter *(sommelier)*, who can help with choosing the wine.

Qui Plume la Lune, a chic modern restaurant *(see p297)*

The lavish interior of Le Train Bleu restaurant in the Gare de Lyon *(see p307)*

Service

The lunchtime service in popular Paris eateries is generally very brisk, if sometimes a little brusque, due to the sheer pressure of numbers. Evening meals can usually be enjoyed at a more leisurely pace.

Children

French children are introduced early to eating in restaurants and as a rule are well-behaved. Consequently, children are usually very welcome. However, there may be little room inside a busy restaurant to bring in push-chairs or prams, and relatively few restaurants provide special facilities such as high-chairs or baby seats.

Terminus Nord brasserie *(see p307)*, opposite the Gare du Nord

Smoking

There are strict anti-tobacco laws in France. It is illegal to smoke inside bars and restaurants. Smoking is permitted, however, on restaurant, café and pub terraces provided they are not enclosed.

Wheelchair Access

Parisian restaurants are generally accommodating, and a word when you book should ensure that you are given a more conveniently situated table when you arrive. It is always worth checking that toilets can also be used by wheelchair users, since access can be restricted.

Picnics

Picnicking is the best way to enjoy the wonderful fresh produce, local bread, cheeses, charcuterie and pastries from the markets and enticing shops to be found all over the city. For more details, see pages 325–7. It is also a good way of enjoying the many parks that Paris has to offer.

Recommended Restaurants

The restaurants on pages 296–307 of this guide cover a spectrum of cuisine styles and prices, and are the best of their kind in Paris. They are listed by area, mostly in the main tourist districts, although there are a number slightly further afield that merit a special trip.

Many Paris restaurants are still firmly rooted in the past, serving traditional French bistro and brasserie specialities such as *steak-frites*, snails and seafood, as well as regional dishes such as cassoulet and *confit* of duck. However, there are also those that embrace new trends in a modern bistro style of high-calibre cooking – *"cuisine bistronomique"*. These bistros offer an inventive, market-driven reworking of classic recipes, served in homely surroundings at reasonable prices. Another development in the Paris restaurant scene, especially at haute cuisine establishments, is the influx of foreign chefs. Many of them come from Japan, and they are refreshing and invigorating Parisian dining.

Throughout the listings, certain restaurants have been highlighted as DK Choice. These offer a particularly special quality, such as outstanding food, excellent value, a romantic ambience, a uniquely Parisian dining experience or a combination of these.

The Flavours of Paris

From the glittering temples of haute cuisine to the humblest neighbourhood bistro, Paris is a paradise for food lovers, whether you dine on foie gras and truffles or steak-frites, a seafood platter or a perfumed Moroccan couscous. France is immensely proud of its food, from classic haute cuisine to the most rustic of regional dishes. All are available in the capital and, though the French themselves will debate endlessly about the ideal sauce to complement meat or fish, or the right wine to accompany them, they will always be in total agreement that theirs is the best food in the world.

Girolles (chanterelles) on a stall in rue Mouffetard market

prize ingredients of the season. Even if you are not shopping for food to cook, the markets are worth browsing and, after an hour or so in the crowded, narrow streets of the rue de Buci or rue Moufettard you will be more than ready for lunch.

The food of the French provinces, once despised for its rusticity, is now celebrated and almost every region is

represented in the capital, from the rich, bourgeois cuisines of Burgundy and Lyon to the celebrated healthy Mediterranean diet of Provence. Paris itself is surrounded by top quality market gardens which supply young peas, carrots and potatoes. Salmon, asparagus, and wild mushrooms come from the Loire; Normandy brings

What all French chefs agree on is the importance of using the finest quality ingredients, and there is no better place to appreciate the quality of French produce than in the markets of Paris. Here, top chefs may be spied early in the morning, alongside local shoppers, seeking inspiration and the

Selection of fine French cheeses in perfect condition

Comté

Brie

Tomme de chevre

Ami du Chambertin

Roquefort

Classic French Cuisine

What is usually thought of as classic French cuisine was developed in royal palaces and noble châteaux, with the emphasis on luxury and display, not frugality or health. Dishes are often bathed in rich sauces of butter or cream, enhanced with luxurious ingredients like truffles, foie gras, rare mushrooms and alcohol. Meat is treated with reverence, and you will usually be asked how you want your beef, lamb or duck cooked; the French tend to like their beef rare or medium rare (*bleu* or *saignant*) and their lamb and duck pink (*rose*). For well-cooked meat, ask for "*bien cuit*" but still expect at least a tinge of pinkness. The most famous country classics include slowly cooked casseroles like *coq au vin* and *boeuf bourguignonne*, as well as the bean, sausage and baked duck dish *cassoulet*, from the southwest.

Escargots à la Bourguignonne are plump Burgundy snails served in their shells with garlic, butter and parsley.

salt-marsh lamb, apples and Camembert. Salers beef and lentils come from the Auvergne; beef and Bresse chickens from Burgundy; not forgetting Basque ham, Collioure anchovies, lamb from the Pyrenees, or fragrant Provençal melons.

The New Style

In recent years, innovative chefs have developed new styles of cooking, reacting against the richness of trad-itional cookery, and using fresh ingredients, lightly cooked to retain their flavour. Sauces are made of light reductions to enhance, not obscure, the main ingredient of a dish. A wave of invention and originality has resulted in a plethora of unusual ingredients, fresh twists on the classics, and sometimes

Mouthwatering display in a Parisian patisserie

wonderful new combinations and flavours, such as sea bass with bean purée and red wine sauce, or with fermented grape juice; sole with quince juice and tarragon; tempura of langoustines with cinnamon beurre blanc; rabbit with Indian spices and tomato polenta; and rosemary ice cream or lavender sorbet.

Foreign Food

Paris can also offer diners an amazing selection of world flavours, especially those of France's former colonies – for example, Moroccan tajines and Cambodian fish with coconut milk. Most fascinating of all is to observe how these cuisines are developing, as young chefs adapt and com-bine traditional ingredients and culinary styles with those of France.

Sealed jars of whole duck-liver foie gras, a luxury item

ON THE MENU

Andouillettes Sausages made from pork intestines

Blanquette de veau Veal stew with a creamy sauce

Confit de canard Cured duck leg with garlic and herbs

Crottin chaud en salade Goat's cheese on toast with salad

Cuisses de grenouille Frogs' legs in garlic butter

Iles flottantes Meringues floating in a custard sauce

Plateau de fruits de mer Platter of raw and cooked seafood

Ris de veau Veal sweetbreads

Rognons à la moutarde Kidneys in mustard sauce

Salade frisée aux lardons Endive salad with fried bacon

Sole meunière Fried sole with melted butter

Moules marinière are mussels steamed in a fragrant sauce of white wine, garlic, parsley and sometimes cream.

Coq au vin is a male chicken braised with red wine, herbs, garlic, baby onions and button mushrooms.

Tarte tatin is a caramelized upside-down buttery apple tart, created at the hotel Tatin in the Loire Valley.

What to Drink in Paris

Paris is the best place in France to sample a wide range of the country's many different wines. It's cheapest to order wine by the carafe, normally referred to by size: 25cl *(quart)*, 33cl *(fillette)*, 50cl *(demi)* or 75cl *(pichet,* equivalent to a bottle). Cafés and wine bars usually offer wine by the glass – *un petit blanc* is a small glass of white, a larger glass of red is *un ballon de rouge*. House wine is nearly always reliable.

Paris's last vineyard, near Sacré-Coeur *(see p224)*

Red Wine

Distinctive bottle shapes for Bordeaux and Burgundy

Some of the world's finest red wines come from the Bordeaux and Burgundy regions, but for everyday drinking, choose from the vast range of basic southern French or Côtes du Rhône wines. Or try one of the Beaujolais *crus*, such as Morgon or Fleurie from southern Burgundy, or lighter reds from the Loire, such as Chinon or Saumur-Champigny.

Bordeaux châteaux include Margaux, which makes some of the world's most elegant red wines.

Burgundy includes some big, strong red wines from the village of Gevrey-Chambertin in the Côte de Nuits.

Beaujolais Nouveau, the fruity first taste of the year's new wine, is released on the third Thursday of November.

The Loire has very good red wines from the area around Chinon. They are usually quite light and very dry.

Southern Rhône is famous for its dark, rich red wines from Châteauneuf-du-Pape, north of Avignon.

Northern Rhône has some dark, spicy red wines, best aged for at least ten years, from Côte-Rôtie near Vienne.

Fine Wine Vintage Chart

	2009	2008	2007	2006	2005	2004	2003	2002	2001
Bordeaux									
Margaux, St-Julien, Pauillac, St-Estèphe	10	8	7	8	9	7	8	6	7
Graves, Pessac-Léognan (red)	9	8	7	8	9	7	6	6	7
Graves, Pessac-Léognan (white)	7	8	7	8	9	8	7	6	7
St-Emilion, Pomerol	9	8	7	8	9	7	6	5	8
Burgundy									
Chablis	9	8	9	8	9	8	7	8	8
Côte de Nuits (red)	9	7	6	7	9	7	7	6	7
Côte de Beaune (white)	9	7	7	8	9	8	7	8	8
Loire									
Bourgueil, Chinon	9	8	8	7	9	7	7	8	7
Sancerre (white)	9	8	7	8	9	8	7	7	8
Rhone									
Hermitage (red)	9	7	10	7	9	7	7	4	7
Hermitage (white)	9	8	10	7	9	7	6	4	8
Côte-Rôtie	8	7	8	7	9	7	6	4	7
Châteauneuf-du-Pape	9	8	9	8	9	7	6	3	7

The quality scale from 1 to 10 represents an overall rating for the year and is only a guideline

White Wine

The finest white Bordeaux and Burgundies are best with food, but for everyday drinking, try a light dry wine such as Entre-Deux-Mers from Bordeaux, or Anjou Blanc or Sauvignon de Touraine from the Loire. Alsace makes some reliable white wines. Sweet wines such as Sauternes, Barsac or Coteaux du Layon are delicious with *foie gras*.

Alsace wines are usually labelled by grape variety. Gewürztraminer is one of the most distinctive.

Loire wines include Puilly-Fumé. It is very dry, often with a slightly smoky perfume.

Alsace Riesling and Burgundy

Sparkling Wine

In France, champagne is the first choice for a celebration drink, and styles range from non-vintage to deluxe. Many other wine regions make sparkling wines by the champagne method which tend to be a lot cheaper. Look out for Crémant de Loire, Crémant de Bourgogne, Vouvray Mousseux, Saumur Mousseux and Blanquette de Limoux.

Burgundy wines include Chablis, a fresh, full-flavoured dry wine from the northernmost vineyards.

The Loire has the perfect partner to seafood dishes in Muscadet, a dry white wine from the Atlantic Coast.

Champagne

Champagne vineyards east of Paris produce the famous sparkling wine. Billecart-Salmon is a light, pink Champagne.

Sweet Bordeaux are luscious, golden-coloured dessert wines, the most famous being Barsac and Sauternes.

Aperitifs and Digestifs

Kir, white wine mixed with a small amount of black currant liqueur or *crème de cassis*, is the ubiquitous *apéritif*. Also common is aniseed-flavoured *pastis* which is served with ice and a pitcher of water and can be very refreshing. Vermouths, especially Noilly-Prat, are also common apéritifs. *Digestifs*, or after-dinner drinks, are often ordered with coffee and include *eaux-de-vie*, the strong colourless spirits infused with fruit, and brandies such as Cognac, Armagnac and Calvados.

Kir: white wine with cassis

Other Drinks

The brightly coloured drinks consumed in cafés all over Paris are mixtures of flavoured syrups and mineral waters, called *sirops à l'eau*. The emerald-green drinks use mint syrup, the red ones grenadine. Fruit juices and tomato juice are sold in bottles unless you specify *citron pressé* or *orange pressée* (freshly squeezed lemon or orange), which is served with a pitcher of water and with sugar or sugar syrup for you to dilute and sweeten to taste. If you ask for water, you will be served mineral water, sparkling (*gazeuse*) or still (*naturelle*); if you don't want to be charged, ask for tap water (*eau de robinet*).

Beers

Beer in France is sold either by the bottle or, more cheaply, on tap by the glass – *un demi*. The cheapest is lager-style *bière française*, and the best brands are Meteor and Mutzig, followed by "33", "1664" and Kronenbourg. Pelforth makes very good dark beer and lager. Some bars and cafés specialize in foreign beers, especially from Belgium, and these are very malty and strong – Leffe, for example, comes as *brune* (dark, fully flavoured) or as a lighter *blonde* (lager). There are bars that brew their own beer. (For beer bars *see p309*).

Fresh lemon juice is served with water and sugar

Where to Eat and Drink

Ile de la Cité and Ile St-Louis

Au Bougnat   €€
Traditional French   **Map** 13 B4
26 Rue Chanoinesse, 75004
Tel *01 43 54 50 74*
The modest decor at this bistro echoes its simple, traditional cuisine – delicious frogs' legs, veal stew, *entrecôte* and pear tart.

Beaubourg and The Marais

Amici Miei   €
Sardinian   **Map** 14 E3
44 Rue St-Sabin, 75011
Tel *01 42 71 82 62*   **Closed** *Mon & Sun*
Fans claim that this rustic, unpretentious trattoria makes the best thin-crust pizzas in Paris. Follow a pizza with the strawberry and basil panna cotta.

Blend   €
American   **Map** 13 A1
44 Rue d'Argout, 75002
Tel *01 40 26 84 57*
A no-nonsense restaurant where the chef blends different cuts of the top-quality beef and fresh produce to make the perfect burger.

Chez Hanna   €
Moroccan and Israeli   **Map** 13 C3
54 Rue des Rosiers, 75004
Tel *01 42 74 74 99*   **Closed** *Mon*
A favourite with locals who come here for the hummus and falafel sandwiches: golden outside, moist within, and crammed with crisp vegetables, juicy aubergine and chilli and tahini sauce.

DK Choice

L'As du Fallafel   €
Israeli   **Map** 13 C3
34 Rue des Rosiers, 75004
Tel *01 48 87 63 60*   **Closed** *Sat*
What draws the crowds here are the best falafel sandwiches you're likely to taste: warm pitta bread packed with crunchy cabbage, melting aubergine and velvety hummus, with a deliciously piquant sauce. At lunchtime, you'll find a queue snaking down the street for the falafel stand. Later, you might be able to get a table inside.

Le Dindon en Laisse   €
Traditional French   **Map** 14 D4
18 Rue Beautreillis, 75004
Tel *01 48 04 06 24*
"The Turkey on a Leash" is a cheerful eatery with stellar food: risottos, flavoursome meat and game dishes, as well as good wines. In summer, dine alfresco.

Le Garde Robe   €
French tapas   **Map** 12 F2
41 Rue de l'Arbre Sec, 75001
Tel *01 49 26 90 60*   **Closed** *Sun*
This narrow space serves tapas – oysters, cheeses and charcuterie – accompanied by wonderful wines.

Bofinger   €€
Alsatian   **Map** 14 E4
5–7 Rue de la Bastille, 75004
Tel *01 42 72 87 82*
A perfectly preserved belle époque interior with a stained-glass cupola makes this one of the city's most beautiful brasseries. The menu of classic dishes includes great shellfish.

Claude Colliot   €€
Modern French   **Map** 13 B2
40 Rue des Blancs Manteaux, 75004
Tel *01 42 71 55 45* **Closed** *Sun & Mon*
Innovative seasonal cooking by this self-taught chef in a sleek setting, frequented by the stars. .

DK Choice

Auberge Nicolas Flamel   €€
Traditional French   **Map** 13 C2
51 Rue de Montmorency, 75003
Tel *01 42 71 77 78*   **Closed** *Sun*
Nicolas Flamel, said to have been an alchemist, built this house in 1407, which makes it the oldest in Paris. The interior, set over two floors, is charmingly haphazard, and candlelit dinners among the stone walls and beams have a romantic ambience. The traditional dishes are well executed.

Frenchie   €€
Modern French   **Map** 7 A5
5–6 Rue du Nil, 75002
Tel *01 40 39 96 19*   **Closed** *lunch daily; Sat & Sun*
One of Paris's hottest bistros. The intensely flavoured dishes, on fixed-price menus, are an irresistible draw. Book months ahead, or try your luck at the wine bar opposite, which also serves his food.

L'Ambassade d'Auvergne   €€
Auvergnat   **Map** 13 B2
22 Rue du Grenier St-Lazare, 75003
Tel *01 42 72 31 22*
With the atmosphere of a rustic inn, this restaurant transports you to rural Auvergne. A menu highlight is *aligot* (potatoes with cheese and garlic).

L'Ange 20   €€
Traditional French   **Map** 13 B2
8 Rue Geoffroy L'Angevin, 75004
Tel *01 40 27 93 67*   **Closed** *Mon*
Choose between seven-hour cooked lamb and duck with orange at this snug bistro. Both are deliciously tender.

The elegant interior of Qui Plume La Lune

The belle époque decor at Bofinger

La Régalade St-Honoré €€
Traditional French   Map 12 F2
123 Rue St-Honoré, 75001
Tel *01 42 21 92 40*   **Closed** *Sat & Sun*
Make sure you're hungry when you get here: Bruno Doucet's glorious, complex country cooking is served in generous portions.

Le Chemise €€
Modern French   Map 14 E1
42 Rue de Malte, 75011
Tel *01 49 29 98 77* **Closed** *Sun & Mon*
A sleek, chic, neo-bistro: wooden floors, super-comfortable leather chairs and cooking that puts an innovative spin on the traditional.

Le Colimaçon €€
Modern French   Map 13 C3
44 Rue Vieille du Temple, 75004
Tel *01 48 87 12 01*
Traditional recipes are interpreted in a modern way, and prepared with seasonal ingredients, at this restaurant with rustic-style decor. The signature dish is melt-in-the-mouth snails.

Le Hangar €€
Traditional French   Map 13 B2
12 Impasse Berthaud, 75003
Tel *01 42 74 55 44*   **Closed** *Mon & Sun*
Dishes here include pan-fried foie gras on puréed potatoes, and creamy risotto, as well as great desserts. No credit cards are accepted.

Le Petit Marché €€
Modern French   Map 14 D3
9 Rue de Béarn, 75003
Tel *01 42 72 06 67*
Highlights of the short Asian-inspired menu here include enticing sesame-seared tuna and decadent chocolate fondant with praline *crème anglaise*.

Le Pharamond €€
Traditional French   Map 13 A1
24 Rue de la Grande Truanderie, 75001
Tel *01 40 28 45 18* **Closed** *Mon & Sun*
Norman specialities, including tripe cooked in cider and Calvados, feature strongly on the menu at this restaurant inside a belle époque building.

Les Bonnes Soeurs €€
Modern French   Map 14 D3
8 Rue du Pas de la Mule, 75003
Tel *01 42 74 55 80*
This small modern bistro, close to the fashionable Place des Vosges, is known for good value brunches (reservations recommended).

Les Philosophes €€
Traditional French   Map 13 C3
28 Rue Vieille du Temple, 75004
Tel *01 48 87 49 64*
Try this popular all-day café for first-rate onion soup, *steak-frites*, omelettes and the house speciality: tomato *tarte tatin*. The puddings are truly memorable.

Le Tir Bouchon €€
Traditional French   Map 13 A1
22 Rue Tiquetonne, 75002
Tel *01 42 21 95 51*
An endearingly old-fashioned restaurant where the chef adds a gourmet touch to classic regional dishes. The honey-roasted duck is very popular.

Le Trumilou €€
Traditional French   Map 13 B4
84 Quai de l'Hôtel de Ville, 75004
Tel *01 42 77 63 98*
Sit out in summer and enjoy the river views at this legendary bistro. With few frills, the fare is as traditional as the decor. House specialities include *canard aux pruneaux* (duck with prunes).

Le Villaret €€
Traditional French   Map 14 E2
13 Rue Ternaux, 75011
Tel *01 43 57 89 76* **Closed** *Sat lunch & Sun*
This snug eatery, all exposed brick walls and beams, is renowned for using ingredients fresh from the morning market. There is also a great cheeseboard.

The Fish Club €€
Seafood   Map 13 A1
58 Rue Jean-Jacques Rousseau, 75001
Tel *01 40 26 68 75* **Closed** *Sun & Mon*
Dig into small sharing plates centered around fish and seafood, including ceviche and oysters, accompanied by cocktails such as the refreshing Pisco Sour.

Benoît €€€
Lyonnaise   Map 13 B2
20 Rue St-Martin, 75004
Tel *01 42 72 25 76*
A Paris institution, run by chef Alain Ducasse. Choose from a menu of hearty standards such as veal sweetbreads and cassoulet. Outstanding wine list.

Qui Plume La Lune €€€
Modern French   Map 14 D1
50 Rue Amelot, 75011
Tel *01 48 07 45 48*   **Closed** *Mon, Tue & Sun*
Splash out on the five-course menu: each dish is a sparkling fusion of Breton and Japanese cuisines. The spare, stylish decor includes an illuminated tree.

DK Choice

Spring €€€
Modern French   Map 12 F2
6 Rue Bailleul, 75001
Tel *01 45 96 05 72*   **Closed** *Mon & Sun*
A magician in the kitchen, Chicago-born Daniel Rose produces a fixed-price tasting menu that is created around what's fresh in the market. There's no choice, but his unique versions of French classics, paired with outstanding wines, are inspired. If you can't get a table, try his wine bar, Buvette, in the basement.

Yam'Tcha €€€
Asian fusion   Map 12 F2
4 Rue Sauval, 75001
Tel *01 40 26 08 07*   **Closed** *Mon & Sun; Tue lunch*
The name means "drink tea", and tea pairings are recommended with Adeline Grattard's Chinese-influenced dishes with subtle French notes. Advance booking is recommended.

For more information on types of restaurants *see page 291*

Tuileries, Opéra and Montmartre

Babalou €
Italian **Map** 7 A1
4 Rue Lamarck, 75018
Tel 01 42 51 37 32 **Closed** mid-Jan–mid-Feb
A restaurant with a big heart and smiling staff. Home-made pasta, pizza, risotto and other Italian staples are all perfectly cooked.

Chartier €
Traditional French **Map** 6 F4
7 Rue du Faubourg Montmartre, 75009
Tel 01 47 70 86 29
Leap back to the 1890s at this iconic brasserie. Traditionally dressed waiters deliver simple, inexpensive food in glorious belle époque surroundings.

Churrasqueira Galo €
Portuguese **Map** 7 B2
69 Rue de Dunkerque, 75009
Tel 01 48 74 49 40
The kind of restaurant that locals would rather keep to themselves. Try the delectable chicken, hot off the rôtisserie. Family-friendly.

Crêperie Broceliande €
Crêperie **Map** 6 F1
15 Rue des Trois Frères, 75018
Tel 01 42 23 31 34 **Closed** Mon & Tue lunch; 3 wks in summer
A little slice of Brittany, complete with a carved dresser and checked tablecloths. The crêpes are utter perfection: paper-thin and with a range of delicious fillings, both savoury and sweet.

Le Cul de Poule €
Traditional French **Map** 6 F3
53 Rue des Martyrs, 75009
Tel 01 53 16 13 07 **Closed** Sun
A modest, fun eatery where unpretentious but excellent daily specials and good-quality wines are served inside or al fresco.

Les Fines Gueules €€
Traditional French **Map** 12 F1
43 Rue Croix des Petits Champs, 75001
Tel 01 42 61 35 41
Part wine bar, part bistro, this spot is renowned for its charcuterie, and steak tartare with sautéed potatoes. Large wine list.

Tentazioni €
Sicilian **Map** 6 E1
26 Rue Tholozé, 75018
Tel 01 53 28 45 20 **Closed** Mon
A cosy, rustic trattoria run by the welcoming Leopardi family. All the traditional dishes are tempting, but be sure to leave some room for the rich, decadent tiramisu.

Un Zèbre à Montmartre €
Lyonnaise **Map** 6 E1
38 Rue Lepic, 75018
Tel 01 42 23 97 80
Enjoy a bargain set-price meal at this colourful, bustling bistro. Highlights include slow-cooked beef, and chocolate fondant.

Bistrot Victoires €
Traditional French **Map** 12 F1
6 Rue la Vrillière, 75001
Tel 01 42 61 43 78
Entrecôte, roast chicken and other classic dishes are served at this busy bistro. The vintage interior features a zinc bar and banquette seating.

Chez Georges €€
Traditional French **Map** 12 F1
1 Rue du Mail, 75002
Tel 01 42 60 07 11 **Closed** Sat & Sun
A vintage treasure, beloved of US cookery writer Julia Child. The traditional bistro fare is sublime, and includes steak au poivre.

Chez Toinette €€
Traditional French **Map** 6 E1
20 Rue Germain Pilon, 75018
Tel 01 42 54 44 36 **Closed** Mon & Sun; Aug
Behind an unprepossessing façade, this small restaurant

bursts with charm. Among the best dishes are the delicious duck foie gras, roast pigeon (in winter), snails, lamb shank and sea bass.

Fauchon Le Café €€
Traditional French **Map** 5 C5
30 Place de la Madeleine, 75008
Tel 01 70 39 38 39 **Closed** Sun
Part of an upmarket delicatessen, this eatery serves food that is as elegant as the surroundings. For a cheaper menu, try La Cantine, the informal basement eatery.

Guilo Guilo €€
Asian **Map** 6 E1
8 Rue Garreau, 75018
Tel 01 42 54 23 92 **Closed** Mon & Sun
Palate-popping "New Wave" Japanese cuisine. Watching chef Eichi Edakuni at work in his open kitchen is not unlike witnessing a theatrical performance.

DK Choice

La Cordonnerie €€
Traditional French **Map** 12 E1
20 Rue St-Roch, 75001
Tel 01 42 60 17 42
For a typical French bistro experience, try this friendly eatery decorated with shiny copper pans and a grandfather clock. The owner/chef, who was taught to cook by his father, uses market-fresh produce, prepared in an open kitchen, and discusses the menu with every customer. An experience not to be missed.

La Famille €€
Modern French **Map** 6 F1
41 Rue des Trois Frères, 75018
Tel 01 42 52 11 12 **Closed** Mon & Sun; Aug
Chef Iñaki Aizpitarte first drew attention to this hotspot. Although he has gone, his fusion menu remains, as do the fashionistas.

Le Grand 8 €€
Traditional French **Map** 7 A1
8 Rue Lamarck, 75018
Tel 01 42 55 04 55 **Closed** Mon & Tue
A tiny restaurant with a touch of class, often frequented by locals. The perfect beef, lamb and vegetable risottos are a highlight, not to mention the terrific caramelized apple millefeuille.

Le Lamarck €€
Corsican **Map** 7 A1
8 Rue Lamarck, 75018
Tel 01 53 41 01 60 **Closed** Mon, Tue & Sun
Owner François Grimaldi plays guitar and sings while diners

Chartier, a belle époque brasserie in Montmartre

Key to prices see page 296

The bar at Carré des Feuillants, a temple of haute cuisine

enjoy his tasty traditional dishes. A restaurant full of real warmth and charm.

Le Miroir €€
Traditional French Map 6 F3
94 Rue des Martyrs, 75018
Tel *01 46 06 50 73* **Closed** *Sun & Mon*
Bistro-style comfort food is served here, cooked by an haute cuisine-trained trio of chefs. This airy restaurant is a magnet for locals.

Le Nansouty €€
Traditional French Map 7 A1
35 Rue Ramey, 75018
Tel *01 42 52 58 87* **Closed** *lunch & Sun*
Traditional, hearty French fare, off the beaten track in Montmartre. Excellent wine list.

Le Pantruche €€
Modern French Map 6 E2
3 Rue Victor Massé, 75009
Tel *01 48 78 55 60* **Closed** *Sat & Sun; 3 wks Aug*
A retro-chic bistro where chef Franck Baranger wows the crowds with seasonal specialities such as celery root soup. The fixed-price menu offers great value.

Les Noces de Jeannette €€
Traditional French Map 6 F5
14 Rue Favart, 75002
Tel *01 42 96 36 89*
Named after an opera by Victor Massé, this restaurant has two intimate rooms, superbly decorated with opera and cinema posters. Excellent brasserie-style cuisine.

Le Vaudeville €€
Traditional French Map 6 F5
29 Rue Vivienne, 75002
Tel *01 40 20 04 62*
A boisterous, marble-clad brasserie with a delightful Art Deco interior. You can't go wrong

by ordering the seafood platter or smoked salmon.

Muscade €€
European Map 12 E1
36 Rue de Montpensier, 75001
Tel *01 42 97 51 36* **Closed** *Mon*
The essence of French Classicism: a restaurant/tearoom with a covered terrace in the glorious Palais-Royal gardens. Great for people-watching.

DK Choice

Racines €€
Bistro/Wine bar Map 6 F5
8 Passage des Panoramas, 75002
Tel *01 40 13 06 41* **Closed** *Sat & Sun; 3 wks Aug*
Its setting in a gorgeous 19th-century shopping arcade makes this charming *bistrot à vins* a favourite with shoppers and locals alike. The short menu features French and Italian dishes, excellent charcuterie, ratatouille, lamb and pork, and seductive desserts. Serious wines, many from bio-dynamic producers, are a bonus.

Carré des Feuillants €€€
French fine dining Map 12 D1
14 Rue de Castiglione, 75001
Tel *01 42 86 82 82* **Closed** *Sun*
Legendary chef Alain Dutournier prepares exquisite dishes from his native Gascony with sheer genius. Accompany them with a wine from an extensive list.

Caviar Kaspia €€€
Russian Map 5 C5
17 Place de la Madeleine, 75008
Tel *01 42 65 33 32* **Closed** *Sun*
Enjoy caviar and smoked salmon, accompanied by chilled vodka, in plush surroundings with honey-coloured panelling, heavy curtains and marvellous views.

DK Choice

Kei €€€
Modern French Map 12 F1
5 Rue Coq Héron, 75001
Tel *01 42 33 14 74* **Closed** *Mon & Sun, Thu lunch*
A practitioner of the exciting fusion of French and Japanese cuisines, Kei Kobayashi is at the helm of this sophisticated restaurant. Decorated in elegant silver and grey, Kei is a showcase for imaginative and delicious dishes that skillfully balance flavours and textures. A top sommelier advises on the best wines to pair with the food.

La Balançoire €€€
Traditional French Map 6 E1
6 Rue Aristide Bruant, 75018
Tel *01 42 23 70 83*
"The Swing" is a child-friendly restaurant dotted with jars of sweets. The menu is seasonal and imaginative.

Le Chamarré de Montmartre €€€
Fusion Map 2 F5
52 Rue Lamarck, 75018
Tel *01 42 55 05 42*
Creative fare from Mauritian chef Antoine Heerah includes Seychelles-style sea bass. The airy dining room has striped furnishings and a flower-filled terrace.

Le Grand Véfour €€€
Modern French fine dining
Map 12 F1
17 Rue de Beaujolais, 75001
Tel *01 42 96 56 27* **Closed** *Sat & Sun; Aug*
Savour Guy Martin's astonishing cuisine in an 18th-century, jewel-like restaurant next to the Palais-Royal gardens. Many famous people have dined here, including Napoleon and Josephine.

The enchanting Louis XVI decor at the historic Le Grand Véfour

For more information on types of restaurants *see page 291*

The dining room of Le Meurice

Le Meurice €€€
Modern French fine dining
Map 12 D1
228 Rue de Rivoli, 75001
Tel *01 44 58 10 55* **Closed** *Sat &*
Sun
Enjoy Yannick Alléno's subtle,
varied cooking in Philippe
Starck's reinterpretation of
a Versailles salon. Service is
formal, but not stiff. Menus
change seasonally.

Verjus €€€
American **Map** 12 E1
52 Rue de Richelieu, 75001
Tel *01 42 97 54 40* **Closed** *Sat & Sun*
Intensely flavoured, tapas-style
dishes are served in this casual,
white-walled dining room.
Less expensive fare is available
in the cellar wine bar and
sandwich bar.

Champs-Elysées and Chaillot Quarter

Chez Diep €
Asian **Map** 5 A5
22 Rue de Ponthieu, 75008
Tel *01 42 56 23 96* **Closed** *Sun*
Appetizing specialities from China,
Thailand and Vietnam pepper the
menu at this modest restaurant
with decor that evokes Thailand.
Attentive service.

Korean Barbecue
Champs-Elysées €
Korean **Map** 5 A5
7 Rue de Ponthieu, 75008
Tel *01 42 25 35 41* **Closed** *Sun;*
3 wks Aug
Paper-thin beef from the
barbecue, so tender it melts
in your mouth, and fresh, crisp
vegetables are a highlight at this
friendly, family-run restaurant.

Chez Géraud €€
Traditional French **Map** 9 B3
31 Rue Vital, 75016
Tel *01 45 20 33 00* **Closed** *Sat & Sun*

An enduring neighbourhood
fixture, where dishes made from
fresh produce are served in an
appealing, traditional setting.

Graindorge €€
Belgian **Map** 4 D3
15 Rue de l'Arc de Triomphe, 75017
Tel *01 47 54 00 28* **Closed** *Sun*
A splendid selection of
beers on tap accompanies
Belgian national treasures such
as *waterzooi de homard* (lobster
broth) and *potjevleesch*
(meat terrine).

DK Choice

Café Lenôtre €€
Modern French **Map** 5 B5
Le Pavillon Elysée Lenôtre, 10 Ave-
nue des Champs-Elysées, 75008
Tel *01 42 65 85 10* **Closed** *Nov–*
Mar: Sun & Mon
An elegant pavilion built for
the 1900 Exposition Universelle
is now occupied by an outpost
of the Lenôtre catering company. The decor is smart and
modern, complementing the
creative, contemporary food;
the desserts, in particular,
are show-stealers. In summer,
diners can enjoy lunch on
the terrace. The food is reasonably priced and the staff is
very attentive.

Le Hide €€
Traditional French **Map** 4 D3
10 Rue du Général Lanrezac, 75017
Tel *01 45 74 15 81* **Closed** *lunch & Sun*
Japanese chef Hide Kobayashi
prepares generous, no-nonsense
bistro food. Good-value fixed-
price menu.

Le Mini Palais €€
Modern French **Map** 11 A1
Grand Palais, 3 Avenue Winston
Churchill, 75008
Tel *01 42 56 42 42*
A gastronomic treat in an
elegant, fashionable setting with
a lovely colonnaded terrace.

Le Timgad €€
Moroccan **Map** 3 C3
21 Rue Brunel, 75017
Tel *01 45 74 23 70*
Terrific Moroccan food in an
ornate setting. *Briks* (thin pastry
with a deep-fried filling), tagines
and couscous are imaginatively
spiced and impeccably cooked.

L'Huîtrier €€
Seafood **Map** 4 E2
16 Rue Saussier-Leroy, 75017
Tel *01 40 54 83 44* **Closed** *Jul: Sun &*
Mon; Aug
Oysters – ordered by the dozen
or half-dozen – are the stars of the
show at this modern restaurant.

DK Choice

Relais de l'Entrecôte €€
Steakhouse **Map** 4 F5
15 Rue Marbeuf, 75008
Tel *01 49 52 07 17*
Established in 1959, this family-
run restaurant offers a warm
atmosphere and fantastic
steaks. Once you get in – the
queues can be long – your
hardest decision will be how to
have your steak cooked. The
high-quality beef is cut thin, the
frites are done to perfection and
the secret-recipe sauce is something to write home about. A
great place for a family outing.

The lavish interiors of Lasserre

6 New York   €€€
Modern French   **Map** 10 E1
6 Avenue de New York, 75016
Tel *01 40 70 03 30*   **Closed** *Sun*
Taste fabulous dishes from
talented chef Jérôme Gangneux,
prepared with ingredients fresh
from the market, at this modern,
welcoming restaurant.

DK Choice

Antoine   €€€
Seafood   **Map** 10 E1
10 Avenue de New York, 75116
Tel *01 40 70 19 28*   **Closed** *3 wks
Aug*
Enjoy sensational seafood
while admiring the view at this
restaurant by the river – you can
see across the Seine to the Eiffel
Tower. Fresh ingredients are at
the heart of Antoine Vigneron's
cuisine. Produce is imported
from the Basque country, the
Mediterraean, Brittany and even
Norway. Try the bouillabaisse or
the signature sea bass, grilled
on fennel wood and served
with steamed vegetables.

Apicius   €€€
Modern French fine dining
Map 4 F4
20 Rue d'Artois, 75008
Tel *01 43 80 19 66*   **Closed** *Sat & Sun*
Jean-Pierre Vigato produces
culinary fireworks in this 18th-
century mansion set in glorious
gardens. Book ahead – and bring
a plump wallet.

Copenhague   €€€
Danish   **Map** 4 E4
*142 Avenue des Champs-Elysées,
75008*
Tel *01 44 13 86 26*
If you crave a change from
French cooking, this restaurant
could be ideal. Fish is the star
attraction here, along with the
spectacular views over the
Champs-Elysées.

Hiramatsu   €€€
Modern French fine dining
Map 9 C1
52 Rue de Longchamp, 75116
Tel *01 56 81 08 80*   **Closed** *Sat & Sun*
Hiroyuki Hiramatsu's cooking is
a flawless blend of French and
Japanese styles. Splash out
on the wonderful nine-course
tasting menu.

Lasserre   €€€
Traditional French fine dining
Map 11 A1
*17 Avenue Franklin D Roosevelt,
75008*
Tel *01 43 59 02 13*   **Closed** *Sun
& Mon; 3 wks Aug*

The lavish orchid-filled interior
is a fitting background for
Christophe Moret's refined
cooking. A retractable roof
opens to the stars. Great
selection of desserts.

L'Astrance   €€€
Modern French fine dining
Map 9 C3
4 Rue Beethoven, 75016
Tel *01 40 50 84 40*   **Closed** *Mon,
Sat & Sun*
Book months in advance to
secure a table at this celebrated
three-Michelin starred 26-seater,
and sample Pascal Barbot's
inspired tasting menu.

Le Cinq   €€€
Modern French fine dining
Map 4 E5
*Four Seasons George V, 31 Avenue
George V, 75008*
Tel *01 49 52 71 54*
Hotel dining at its sublime
best. Chef Eric Briffard produces
faultless, original cuisine in a
sumptuous grey-and-gold
dining room.

L'Epicure   €€€
Traditional French fine dining
Map 5 B4
*Le Bristol, 112 Rue du Faubourg
St-Honoré, 75008*
Tel *01 53 43 43 40*
A lovely room, with windows
overlooking the garden, is the
ideal backdrop to Eric Fréchon's
triple-Michelin-starred cooking
at this restaurant.

Paul Chêne   €€€
Traditional French fine dining
Map 9 C1
123 Rue Lauriston, 75116
Tel *01 47 27 63 17*   **Closed** *Sun*
Step back in time at this
classic restaurant, founded
in 1959 by Paul Chêne, linchpin
of traditional cuisine, and little
changed since. Wide choice of
superb desserts.

Pierre Gagnaire   €€€
Modern French fine dining
Map 4 E4
6 Rue Balzac, 75008
Tel *01 58 36 12 50*   **Closed** *Sat & Sun;
Aug*
Pierre Gagnaire, an advocate of
molecular gastronomy, provides
groundbreaking cuisine at this
three-Michelin-starred restaurant.

Prunier   €€€
Seafood   **Map** 4 D4
16 Avenue Victor Hugo, 75116
Tel *01 44 17 35 85*   **Closed** *Sun; Aug*
This pretty Art Deco jewel has a
seasonal menu, along with an
impressive variety of caviars.

Relais Plaza   €€€
Modern French   **Map** 10 F1
*Le Plaza Athénée, 25 Avenue
Montaigne, 75008*
Tel *01 53 67 64 00*
This fashionable brasserie with
Art Deco touches is to see and
be seen in. The imaginative menu
is inspired by Alain Ducasse.

Taillevent   €€€
Traditional French fine dining
Map 4 F4
15 Rue Lamennais, 75008
Tel *01 44 95 15 01*   **Closed** *Sat & Sun;
Aug*
Exquisite haute cuisine in a 19th-
century mansion. Alain Solivérès's
incomparable cooking is paired
with a remarkable wine list.

Invalides and Eiffel
Tower Quarter

Café Constant   €
Traditional French   **Map** 10 E3
139 Rue St-Dominique, 75007
Tel *01 47 53 73 34*
Arrive early to be sure of a table
at Christian Constant's no-frills
but ever popular café. Brilliantly
conceived comfort food, such as
beef stew, is on the menu.

The façade of seafood restaurant Prunier

For more information on types of restaurants *see page 291*

Coutume €
Modern French   Map 11 B4
47 Rue de Babylone, 75007
Tel *01 45 51 50 47*
Bright and airy café serving
superb coffee and healthy
sandwiches as well as salads
for lunch. Good brunch option.

Pasco €
Mediterranean   Map 11 A3
*74 Boulevard de la Tour Maubourg,
75007*
Tel *01 44 18 33 26*
You will find dishes with simple,
seasonal ingredients – such as
fish, fresh vegetables, herbs, spices
and lashings of olive oil – at this
contemporary, rustic restaurant.

Au Bon Accueil €€
Modern French   Map 10 E2
14 Rue de Monttessuy, 75007
Tel *01 47 05 46 11* **Closed** *Sat & Sun;
3 wks Aug*
The good-value *prix-fixe* menus
at this upmarket bistro never
skimp on quality ingredients. Sit
at the pavement tables for a
great view of the Eiffel Tower.

Au Petit Sud Ouest €€
Southwestern French   Map 10 E3
46 Avenue de la Bourdonnais, 75007
Tel *01 45 55 59 59* **Closed** *Sun
& Mon; Aug*
Enjoy authentic specialities from
the Landes, many of them duck-
based, at this friendly restaurant.
Individual toasters ensure piping-
hot bread for the foie gras.

Giallo Oro €€
Italian   Map 11 B3
38 Rue de Bourgogne, 75007
Tel *01 45 50 14 57* **Closed** *Sun*
A tiny, friendly restaurant, Giallo
Oro offers hearty home-cooked
food. The menu consists mainly
of pasta, but there are also
seafood and meat dishes.

L'Affable €€
Modern French   Map 11 C3
10 Rue de St-Simon, 75007
Tel *01 42 22 01 60* **Closed** *Sat & Sun;
Aug*
This enticing bistro has an excellent *prix-fixe* lunch and attentive
waiters. The menu is French with
hearty classics such as *ris de veau*
(sweetbreads).

L'Affriolé €€
Traditional French   Map 10 F2
17 Rue Malar, 75007
Tel *01 44 18 31 33* **Closed** *Sun
& Mon; Aug*
A local fixture, this colourful bistro
is usually packed. Dishes such as
caramelised lamb sweetbreads
with aubergine caviar and mustard
are cooked with finesse.

L'Ami Jean €€
Basque   Map 10 F2
27 Rue Malar, 75007
Tel *01 47 05 86 89* **Closed** *Sun
& Mon; Aug*
Stéphane Jego puts an avant-
garde spin on Basque cooking –
with dishes such as lamb sweetbreads with paper-thin chorizo –
at this lively eatery. Book ahead.

La Billebaude €€
Burgundian   Map 10 F3
29 Rue Exposition, 75007
Tel *01 45 55 20 96* **Closed** *Sun
& Mon; Aug*
Melt-in-the-mouth scallops, sea
bream with sorrel sauce, wild
boar stew and foie gras are just
some of this cheerful restaurant's
standard regional dishes.

La Fontaine de Mars €€
Southwestern French   Map 10 F3
129 Rue St-Dominique, 75007
Tel *01 47 05 46 44*
Complete with lace curtains,
gingham tablecloths, efficient
waiters and fantastic food, this
is an archetypcal bistro. Duck
cassoulet is the signature dish
when in season (Sep–May).

La Villa Corse €€
Corsican   Map 10 E5
164 Boulevard de Grenelle, 75015
Tel *01 53 86 70 81* **Closed** *Sun*
Tastes and aromas transport you
to the Mediterranean island of
Corsica. Delicious, strongly
flavoured dishes such as olive
veal and wild boar stew are
served in warm surroundings.

Le Florimond €€
Traditional French   Map 10 F3
19 Avenue de la Motte-Picquet, 75007
Tel *01 45 55 40 38* **Closed** *Sun & first
Sat of the month; 1 wk Aug*
Pascal Guillaumin's authentic
menu includes his grandmother's

recipe for stuffed cabbage, and
delectable lobster ravioli, plus
vanilla *millefeuille* and other
tempting desserts.

**Les Cocottes de Christian
Constant** €€
Modern French   Map 10 E3
135 Rue St-Dominique, 75007
Tel *01 45 50 10 31*
The clue is in the name – *cocottes*
(dishes served in cast-iron
casseroles) are the speciality
here. Service is very efficient.

Le Troquet €€
Basque   Map 10 F5
21 Rue François Bonvin, 75015
Tel *01 45 66 89 00* **Closed** *Sun & Mon;
Aug; 1 wk Christmas; 1st wk May*
A favourite with serious foodies.
Chef Marc Mouton's dishes are
full of surprises and forthright
flavours. The six-course tasting
menu is fabulous.

L'Arpège €€€
Traditional French fine dining
Map 11 B3
84 Rue de Varenne, 75007
Tel *01 47 05 09 06* **Closed** *Sat & Sun*
A paradise for vegetable lovers:
Alain Passard grows his own
produce for this glossy three-
Michelin-starred restaurant. Try
his superb signature apple tart.

Le Jules Verne €€€
Modern French fine dining
Map 10 D3
5 Avenue Gustave Eiffel, 75007
Tel *01 45 55 61 44*
Dine in the sky, on the Eiffel
Tower's second platform. Alain
Ducasse's destination restaurant
has breathtaking 360-degree
views and stylish cuisine.

St-Germain, Latin Quarter and Jardin des Plantes Quarter

DK Choice

58 Qualité Street €
Tapas   Map 13 A5
*58 Rue de la Montagne-Sainte-
Geneviève, 75005*
Tel *01 43 26 70 43* **Closed** *Sun*
This small spot just behind the
Panthéon is a deli, sandwich
shop, tearoom, wine bar
and bistro all in one. Small
plates to share – including
oysters, Iberian ham and
burrata – are washed down
with wines by the glass
or bottle. Warm, friendly
atmosphere.

The rustic and cosy interior of L'Ami Jean,
a Basque bistro

The view from Le Jules Verne, on the second platform of the Eiffel Tower

Breakfast in America €
American **Map** 13 B5
17 Rue des Ecoles, 75005
Tel *01 43 54 50 28*
All-day breakfast is served at
this authentic American diner:
crispy bacon, pancakes with
maple syrup, burgers, fries,
veggie wraps and much more.

Chez Gladines €
Basque **Map** 17 B5
30 Rue des Cinq Diamants, 75013
Tel *01 45 80 70 10*
A haven of satisfying, no-frills
cooking. The house speciality –
gigantic salads, served in
earthenware bowls and
smothered with sautéed
potatoes – are not to be missed.

Comme à Savonnières €
Traditional French **Map** 12 E4
18 Rue Guisarde, 75006
Tel *01 43 29 52 18* **Closed** *Mon
& Sun*
A friendly bistro, frequented
mostly by locals, whose name
and menu give a nod to the
chef's Loire Valley roots. The
main draws are bean and
pig's trotter salad and the
generous profiteroles.

Alcazar €€
Modern French **Map** 12 F4
62 Rue Mazarine, 75006
Tel *01 53 10 19 99* **Closed** *Aug*
British style-guru Terence
Conran's contemporary take
on a Parisian brasserie. Seafood,
Mediterranean cuisine and
English-inspired dishes are
on the menu.

Anahuacalli €€
Mexican **Map** 13 B5
30 Rue des Bernardins, 75005
Tel *01 43 26 10 20*
A cheerful cantina serving typical
Mexican dishes – guacamole,
corn tortillas and *queso* (melted
cheese) with chorizo.

Bistrot de Paris €€
Traditional French **Map** 12 D3
33 Rue de Lille, 75007
Tel *01 42 61 16 83* **Closed** *Sun & Mon;
26 & 27 Jul; Christmas; New Year*
Tables are always packed at this
Art Nouveau gem, a former haunt
of the Left Bank literati. The menu
features superior bistro classics.

DK Choice

Brasserie Balzar €€
Traditional French **Map** 13 B5
49 Rue des Ecoles, 75005
Tel *01 43 54 13 67*
Highly skilled waiters in long
aprons and waistcoats serve solid
brasserie fare at this venerable
institution. It certainly looks the
part, with its smoked mirrors
and globe lights. You're likely to
rub shoulders with an academic
crowd from La Sorbonne. There's
a café section as well.

Dans Les Landes €€
Southwestern French tapas
Map 17 B2
119 bis Rue Monge, 75005
Tel *01 45 87 06 00*
A fun place for sharing dishes.
Choose from a long list of tapas-
style dishes or try a *plat du jour*.

El Loubnane €€
Lebanese **Map** 13 A4
29 Rue Galande, 75005
Tel *01 43 26 70 60* **Closed** *Mon*
Enjoy delicious meze at this
family-run restaurant. Don't miss
the *makanik* sausages and the
katayef – miniature crêpes stuffed
with rosewater and pistachio nuts.

Itinéraires €€
Modern French **Map** 13 B5
5 Rue de Pontoise, 75005
Tel *01 46 33 60 11* **Closed** *Sun & Mon;
2 wks Aug; 2 wks Dec*
The calm, contemporary decor
here is as stylish as Sylvain

Sendra's cooking. With a young
vibe and a shared-table policy,
this is a perfect place for singles.

Kitchen Galerie Bis €€
Modern French **Map** 12 F4
25 Rue des Grands Augustins, 75006
Tel *01 46 33 00 85* **Closed** *Sun
& Mon; 2 wks Aug*
Doubling up as a modern art
gallery, this restaurant with mini-
malist decor serves contemporary
French cuisine with an Asian twist.
Try the fabulous tapas-style dishes.

L'Agrume €€
Modern French **Map** 17 C2
15 Rue des Fossés St-Marcel, 75005
Tel *01 43 31 86 48* **Closed** *Sun,
Mon & Tue; Aug; 2 wks Dec*
Foodies roll up here to sample
the five-course tasting menu. The
presentation is simple, but the
flavours are fabulous.

L'Atlas €€
Moroccan **Map** 13 B5
12 Boulevard St-Germain, 75005
Tel *01 44 07 23 66* **Closed** *Mon*
With its Moorish decor and tasty
tagines, you will feel like you're in
Marrakech in this restaurant. Try
the monkfish with cinnamon.

L'Epigramme €€
Traditional French **Map** 12 F4
9 Rue de l'Éperon, 75006
Tel *01 44 41 00 09* **Closed** *Mon
& Sun; Aug; 1 wk Dec*
Impeccable bistro dishes are
served at this inviting restaurant
with contemporary country-inn-
style decor. Try the Basque pork
with turnip *choucroute*.

Le Petit Châtelet €€
Traditional French **Map** 13 A4
39 Rue de la Bûcherie, 75005
Tel *01 46 33 53 40* **Closed** *Sun & Mon;
Christmas*
A small restaurant renowned for
its enchanting pitched roof, and
a terrace with magnificent views
of Notre Dame. Great bistro dishes.

Le Petit Pontoise €€
Traditional French **Map** 13 B5
9 Rue de Pontoise, 75005
Tel *01 43 29 25 20* **Closed** *Christmas*
A picture-postcard bistro. Black-
boards display tempting specials
such as duck *parmentier* and pan-
fried foie gras. Book ahead.

Le Pré Verre €€
Modern French **Map** 13 A5
8 Rue Thénard, 75005
Tel *01 43 54 59 47* **Closed** *Mon
& Sun*
Asian accents are evident in the
dishes at this snug, buzzing
eatery. Wines come from small
producers. Outstanding value.

For more information on types of restaurants *see page 291*

Le Procope €€
Traditional French **Map** 12 F4
13 Rue de l'Ancienne Comédie, 75006
Tel 01 40 46 79 00
The city's oldest café – a magnet for writers, politicians and artists since 1686 – still has its original ambience. Specialities include *coq au vin* and shellfish platters.

Marty €€
Traditional French **Map** 17 B3
20 Avenue des Gobelins, 75005
Tel 01 43 31 39 51 **Closed** Aug
The Art Deco interior of this venerable institution is lovely, but it is the robust dishes, such as roast duck and steak-frites, that steal the show. Still in the hands of the founder's family.

Mavrommatis €€
Greek **Map** 17 B2
42 Rue Daubenton, 75005
Tel 01 43 31 17 17 **Closed** Mon
Take a Greek culinary cruise at the Mavrommatis brothers' gem, with its stylish decor and elegant clientele. Superb food, including grilled octopus and moussaka.

Perraudin €€
Traditional French **Map** 16 F1
157 Rue St-Jacques, 75005
Tel 01 46 33 15 75
Checked tablecloths and hearty fare characterize this restaurant, which brims with old-fashioned charm. Bookings are accepted only from 7pm to 8pm.

Shu €€
Japanese **Map** 12 F4
8 Rue Suger, 75006
Tel 01 46 34 25 88 **Closed** Sun; 1 wk Easter; 3 wks Aug
The owner/chef Osamu Ukai constructs ravishing skewers (*kushiage*) for *omakase* dining, which means leaving the choice up to him. Staff are charming and attentive.

Terroir Parisien €€
Traditional French **Map** 13 B5
20 Rue St-Victor, 75005
Tel 01 44 31 54 54
The classic dishes here are made from locally grown produce supplied by small farmers. This latest venture of Yannick Alléno (of Le Meurice fame, *see p300*) is in a beautiful modern space with a vaulted wooden ceiling.

Agapé Substance €€€
Modern French **Map** 12 F4
66 Rue Mazarine, 75006
Tel 01 43 29 33 83 **Closed** Sun & Mon
From his open kitchen, prodigy David Toutain impresses with his tapas-style cuisine. Cool and modern, with counter seating.

DK Choice

La Tour d'Argent €€€
Traditional French fine dining
Map 13 B5
15 Quai de la Tournelle, 75005
Tel 01 43 54 23 31 **Closed** Sun & Mon; 3 wks Aug
Established in 1582 and showing no signs of age, this world-famous Parisian institution has a fabulously romantic sixth-floor dining room complete with spectacular views. The service is formal and elegant. Chef Laurent Delabre has rejuvenated the menu of classic French dishes with great panache. The ground-floor bar doubles up as a gastronomic museum.

Le Comptoir du Relais €€€
Traditional French **Map** 12 F4
9 Carrefour de l'Odéon, 75006
Tel 01 44 27 07 97
Devotees have been known to wait hours for a table at Yves Camdeborde's celebrated temple to bistro cuisine. Try the signature pig's trotters.

Les Bouquinistes €€€
Modern French **Map** 12 F3
53 Quai des Grands Augustins, 75006
Tel 01 43 25 45 94 **Closed** 2 wks Aug
Overlooking the Seine, this is an offshoot of Guy Savoy's gastronomic empire. It serves relatively simple dishes based on exquisite seasonal produce.

Sola €€€
Japanese fusion **Map** 13 A4
12 Rue de l'Hôtel Colbert, 75005
Tel 09 65 01 73 68 (lunch)/01 43 29 59 04 (dinner) **Closed** Sun & Mon; 3 wks Aug
Hiroki Yoshitake's wonderfully subtle dishes blend the best of Japanese and French cuisines. Well-stocked sake bar.

Ze Kitchen Galerie €€€
International fusion **Map** 12 F4
4 Rue des Grands Augustins, 75006
Tel 01 44 32 00 32 **Closed** Sun; 2 wks Aug
Inventive cooking, informed by chef William Ledeuil's travels in Southeast Asia, is offered in this eatery with displays of modern art.

Luxembourg and Montparnasse

L'Arbre de Sel €€
Korean **Map** 15 B1
138 Rue de Vaugirard, 75015
Tel 01 47 83 29 52 **Closed** Sun; Aug
Mouthwatering dishes – spicy, very spicy and vegetarian – are beautifully presented at this pleasant restaurant with efficient service.

L'Assiette €€
Southwestern French **Map** 15 C4
181 Rue du Château, 75014
Tel 01 43 22 64 86 **Closed** Mon & Tue; late Jul–late Aug
David Rathgeber, who trained under Alain Ducasse, brings style to the earthy regional cuisine here.

L'Auberge du 15 €€
Modern French **Map** 16 F3
15 Rue de la Santé, 75013
Tel 01 47 07 07 45 **Closed** Sun & Mon; Aug
A contemporary spin on classic bistro fare is served at this eatery with modern rustic decor.

La Cantine du Troquet €€
Basque **Map** 15 B3
101 Rue de l'Ouest, 75014
Tel 01 45 40 04 98 **Closed** Sat & Sun
Savour dishes prepared with flair by Christian Etchebest at this lively bistro with long, shared tables. No reservations are taken, so arrive when it opens, at 7pm.

The 18th-century-style dining room of Le Procope, the oldest café in Paris

The long dining counter at Agapé Substance

La Cerisaie €€
Southwestern French   **Map** 16 C2
70 Boulevard Edgar Quinet, 75014
Tel *01 43 20 98 98* **Closed** *Sat & Sun;*
mid-Jul–mid-Aug
Regional specialities come in
generous portions at this tiny,
friendly bistro. The first-class wine
list includes a number of talented
small producers.

La Coupole €€
Traditional French   **Map** 16 D2
102 Boulevard du Montparnasse, 75014
Tel *01 43 20 14 20*
Visit this historic 600-seat brasserie,
dating from 1927, for the bustling
ambience and fabulous Art Deco
furnishings. Seafood platters top
the bill. Great for people-watching.

L'Epicuriste €€
Traditional French   **Map** 15 A1
41 Boulevard Pasteur, 75015
Tel *01 47 34 15 50* **Closed** *Sun*
& Mon; Aug
Enjoy specialities created with
ingredients fresh from the market
in this bistro with a modern
interior. The signature dish is
braised lamb shanks in red wine
sauce with caramelized fennel
with orange and capers

Le Jeu de Quilles €€
Traditional French   **Map** 16 D4
45 Rue Boulard, 75014
Tel *01 53 90 76 22* **Closed** *Mon & Sun;*
Tue lunch; 2 wks Aug
Top-quality ingredients (some
available from the *épicerie* at the
front) make up the timeless dishes
in this eatery with a simple interior.

L'Ourcine €€
Southwestern French   **Map** 17 A3
92 Rue Broca, 75013
Tel *01 47 07 13 65* **Closed** *Mon & Sun;*
Jul–Aug
Sylvain Danière has lighted upon
a recipe for success at this simple
bistro. The menu changes all the
time. Expect superb dishes from

the Basque and Béarn regions,
such as piquillo peppers stuffed
with puréed cod and potato.

Les Papilles €€
Traditional French   **Map** 16 F1
30 Rue Gay Lussac, 75005
Tel *01 43 25 20 79* **Closed** *Sun*
A charming multi-tasker: deli,
coffee bar, wine shop and bistro
all in one. The set, fixed-price
dinners are unforgettable.

Le Parc aux Cerfs €€
Traditional French   **Map** 16 D2
50 Rue Vavin, 75006
Tel *01 43 54 87 83* **Closed** *2 wks Aug*
Good-value prices and a pretty
courtyard make "The Deer Park" a
winner. The menu features new
variations on old classics.

DK Choice

Le Timbre €€
Traditional French   **Map** 16 D1
3 Rue Ste-Beuve, 75006
Tel *01 45 49 10 40* **Closed** *Sun &*
Mon; mid-Jul–mid-Aug
This is what it says: a "postage
stamp" of a restaurant, the realm
of British chef Chris Wright. For
his short but considered menu,
he chooses the finest, freshest
ingredients and prepares them
in full view of the diners. Don't
miss his *terrine de campagne*.

Moustache €€
Modern French   **Map** 16 D1
3 Rue Ste-Beuve, 75006
Tel *01 42 22 56 65* **Closed** *Mon & Sun;*
1 wk Aug
Exposed brick walls and crisp
tablecloths create a stylish setting
for Fabien Chivot's sensational
dishes, injected with Asian flavours.

Les Zazous €€
Traditional French   **Map** 15 C1
46 Blvd du Montparnasse 75015
Tel *01 45 49 32 88* **Closed** *Mon*

Classic bistro, with creative menus
and reasonably fixed-priced
meals, plus a terrace for al fresco
dining in the warmer months.

Tavola di Gio €€
Italian   **Map** 16 D2
210 Boulevard Raspail, 75014
Tel *01 43 35 47 17* **Closed** *Christmas &*
New Year
A genial trattoria with a pristine
modern look, but traditional
specialities. The pasta and
seafood are recommended.

DK Choice

La Closerie des Lilas €€€
Traditional French   **Map** 16 E2
171 Boulevard du Montparnasse,
75006
Tel *01 40 51 34 50*
The acclaimed writer Ernest
Hemingway was a regular at
this long-lived, little-changed
establishment, also favoured
by other literati and artists. If
you're feeling flush, splash out
on classic cuisine in the
restaurant proper. Prices are
kinder in the brasserie and bar,
where a pianist plays every
evening. The summer terrace is
also a treat.

Le Dôme €€€
Seafood   **Map** 16 D2
108 Boulevard du Montparnasse,
75014
Tel *01 43 35 25 81* **Closed** *mid-Jul–*
mid-Aug: Sun & Mon
A rendezvous for US intellectuals
in the early 1900s, and
nicknamed "the Anglo-American
café," Le Dôme is known for its
seafood. You can't go wrong
with the oysters or mixed
seafood platters.

Adding the finishing touches to a seafood
platter at La Coupole

For more information on types of restaurants *see page 291*

Further Afield

Chez Prune €
European   **Map** 8 D4
36 Rue Beaurepaire, 75010
Tel 01 42 41 30 47 **Closed** *Christmas & New Year*
A top spot for Sunday brunch, or for more satisfying dishes prepared with ingredients fresh from the market. Sit outside and lap up the canal view.

La Marine €
Seafood   **Map** 8 D5
55 bis Quai de Valmy, 75010
Tel 01 42 39 69 81
Unsurprisingly, fish is this buzzing restaurant's speciality: served in a stew or in pastry, or as a steak with nettle sauce. Advance booking recommended.

DK Choice

Le Baron Rouge €
Wine bar/tapas & platters
Map 14 F5
1 Rue Théophile Roussel, 75012
Tel 01 43 43 14 32
Sample divine oysters direct from the Atlantic coast, or platters of cheeses and charcuterie, inside this tiny, lively bar. At peak times, the crowd spills out onto the pavement. There is a great selection of wines to be enjoyed by the glass, or you can fill an empty bottle from one of the barrels bulging in the doorway.

L'Encrier €
Traditional French   **Map** 14 F5
55 Rue Traversière, 75012
Tel 01 44 68 08 16 **Closed** *Sun; 3 wks Aug–Sep*
An inviting, homely restaurant, jam-packed with locals. Try the Rocquefort, and Jurançon wine.

Pizza e Fichi €
Pizzeria   **Map** 2 D1
17 Rue Alexandre Dumas, 75011
Tel 01 43 67 50 11 **Closed** *Sat & Sun; Aug*
Bright and family-friendly, this pizzeria offers an impressive variety of toppings – Gorgonzola, sundried tomatoes, anchovies, artichokes, potatoes and *chèvre*.

Rose Bakery €
British vegetarian   **Map** 6 F3
46 Rue des Martyrs, 75009
Tel 01 42 82 12 80 **Closed** *2 wks Aug*
The haunt of expats homesick for scones, as well as a growing crowd of Anglophile Parisians, this café serves quiches, salads, soup and English cakes. It also has fabulous coffee and Neal's Yard cheeses.

A La Biche au Bois €€
Traditional French   **Map** 14 E5
45 Avenue Ledru-Rollin, 75012
Tel 01 43 43 34 38 **Closed** *Sat & Sun; late Jul–end Aug; Christmas; New Year*
Popular for its exemplary home cooking, this bistro comes into its own in the game season, with grouse, venison and wild boar dishes. The *prix fixe* menu includes a platter of cheeses and desserts.

Albion €€
Mediterranean   **Map** 7 A3
80 Rue du Faubourg Poissonnière, 75010
Tel 01 42 46 02 44 **Closed** *Mon & Sun; 3 wks Aug; 2 wks Christmas*
A wine-focused bistro, bar and shop in one. Eat simple, delicious fare in the dining area at the back, and soak up the genial ambience.

DK Choice

Auberge Etchegorry €€
Basque   **Map** 17 B4
41 Rue de Croulebarbe, 75013
Tel 01 44 08 83 51 **Closed** *Sun & Mon, 3 weeks in Aug*
In the early 19th century, this was the site of a rural tavern frequented by Victor Hugo. Today, the old, rustic interior of this restaurant, with copper pans on the walls and salamis hanging from wooden beams, evokes those days. The food is as comforting as the decor – dishes include *confits* and scallops and black pudding with caramelized apples

DK Choice

Brasserie Flo €€
Alsatian   **Map** 7 B4
7 Cour des Petites-Ecuries, 75010
Tel 01 47 70 13 59
This captivating brasserie has striking decoration from the early 1900s: rich wood wall panels, stained-glass windows, leather-covered bench seats and brass luggage racks. The fare reflects its Alsatian origins, with a straightforward brasserie menu that includes superb shellfish and sauerkraut, and beer drawn from the barrel.

Chatomat €€
Modern French
6 Rue Victor Letalle, 75020
Tel 01 47 97 25 77 **Closed** *Sun & Mon; mid-Aug–early Sep*
In an airy, industrial-looking building with exposed brick walls, this lively restaurant has a limited menu, but the food is astonishingly original.

Chez Grenouille €€
Traditional French   **Map** 6 D2
52 Rue Blanche, 75009
Tel 01 42 81 34 07
Country cuisine is at the core of gifted chef Alexis Blanchard's bistro menu. The offal and game dishes are exceptional.

Julien €€
Alsatian   **Map** 7 B5
16 Rue du Faubourg Saint-Denis, 75010
Tel 01 47 70 12 06
Inside a splendid Art Nouveau building, with Alphonse Mucha murals and huge mirrors, this historic brasserie serves appetizing classic dishes.

Khun Akorn €€
Thai
8 Avenue de Taillebourg, 75011
Tel 01 43 56 20 03
In warm weather, head straight for the pretty roof terrace here. The interior, decorated in Eastern style, is also attractive. The cuisine is beautifully flavoured.

Le Bistrot Lorette €€
Modern French   **Map** 6 E3
43 Rue Notre-Dame de Lorette, 75009
Tel 01 42 81 13 87 **Closed** *Sun & Mon; first 3 wks Aug*
Locals love this restaurant for its fantastic food and cosy, laid-back atmosphere. Specialities include prawns with avocado tartare, tender veal with *chèvre* and basil sauce, and lamb *en croûte* with a Provençal lasagne..

Le Bistrot Paul Bert €€
Traditional French   **Map** 2 F2
18 Rue Paul Bert, 75011
Tel 01 43 72 24 01 **Closed** *Sun & Mon; Aug*
Superb food, a great wine list and charming 1930s decor ensure this bistro never falls out of fashion.

Alfresco dining at Chez Prune, in the Canal Saint-Martin area

Terminus Nord, a historic brasserie near the Eurostar terminal

Le Verre Volé €€
Modern French Map 8 D4
67 Rue de Lancry, 75010
Tel *01 48 03 17 34* **Closed** *Aug*
Booking is essential at this tiny,
easy-going wine shop-cum-
bistro, with a kitchen that
punches well above its weight.

Le Volant Basque €€
Basque Map 10 D5
13 Rue Béatrix Dussane, 75015
Tel *01 45 75 27 67* **Closed** *Sun; last
wk Jul; 3 wks Aug*
Cosy restaurant serving traditional
cuisine at its best: staples include
the signature *boeuf bourguignon*,
veal stew, home-made fruit tarts
and chocolate mousse.

Les Zygomates €€
Modern French
7 Rue de Capri, 75012
Tel *01 40 19 93 04* **Closed** *Sun
& Mon; Aug*
Wonderfully innovative food is
served in this charming former
delicatessen. Dishes include
turkey in a salted rosemary crust
and snail and mushroom ravioli.

Mama Shelter €€
Traditional French
109 Rue de Bagnolet, 75020
Tel *01 43 48 48 48*
Philippe Starck's on-trend decor
sets the scene for this lively
brasserie. The food from chef
Alain Senderens's kitchen is firmly
rooted in tradition, featuring
classics such as duck *parmentier*.

Neva Cuisine €€
Modern French Map 5 C2
2 Rue de Berne, 75008
Tel *01 45 22 18 91* **Closed** *Sat & Sun;
3 wks Aug*
A 1930s café is home to Mexican-
born Beatriz Gonzalez's stylish restaurant. The innovative cooking
includes pea soup and cod steak
with aubergine caviar. Don't miss
chef Yannick Tranchant's desserts.

Septime €€
Modern French
80 Rue de Charonne, 75011
Tel *01 43 67 38 29* **Closed** *Sat & Sun;
Aug*
The elegant, minimalist decor
and an open kitchen complement
Bertrand Grébaut's avant-garde
cooking at this bistro.

Terminus Nord €€
Traditional French Map 7 B2
23 Rue de Dunkerque, 75010
Tel *01 42 85 05 15*
A great Parisian institution dating
from 1925, this Art Nouveau and
Art Deco gem serves delicious
classic food. Always bustling and
fun for people-watching.

Villa Pereire €€
Modern French Map 4 E1
116 Boulevard Pereire, 75017
Tel *01 43 80 88 68* **Closed** *Aug*
Popular with locals, this eatery has
plush, Empire-style decor. The
fusion menu includes crayfish
and vegetable spring rolls.

Au Trou Gascon €€€
Southwestern French
40 Rue Taine, 75012
Tel *01 43 44 34 26* **Closed** *Sat & Sun*
Exquisite cuisine is served at
Alain Dutournier's restaurant. Try
the signature *cassoulet*, or lamb
from the Pyrenees. There is an
astonishing Armagnac selection,
and the wines range from
prestigious Bordeaux to little-
known *crus*.

La Grande Cascade €€€
Traditional French fine dining
Map 3 A3
*Bois de Boulogne, Allée de
Longchamp, 75016*
Tel *01 45 27 33 51*
Savour superb cuisine in this
crescent-shaped dining room,
the epitome of belle époque
elegance. There are stunning
views from the romantic terrace.

Le Grand Venise €€€
Italian
171 Rue de la Convention, 75015
Tel *01 45 32 49 71* **Closed** *Sun
& Mon; Aug; Christmas*
A restaurant that is generous in
every respect: from the owner's
hospitality to the huge portions
of pasta, meat and fish dishes. Be
sure to try the caramel ice cream.

Le Pavillon Montsouris €€€
Traditional French
20 Rue Gazan, 75014
Tel *01 43 13 29 00* **Closed** *mid-Feb–
mid-Mar*
Enjoy classic dishes in the
conservatory or on the terrace in
this belle époque pavilion with a
magical park setting. The fixed-
price menu is good value.

Le Quinzième €€€
Modern French
14 Rue Cauchy, 75015
Tel *01 45 54 43 43* **Closed** *Sat & Sun*
There is a happy marriage of
tradition and innovation in TV
chef Cyril Lignac's exquisite
cuisine. The service is seamless.

DK Choice

Le Train Bleu €€€
Traditional French Map 18 E1
*Gare de Lyon, 1 Place Louis
Armand, 75012*
Tel *01 43 43 09 06*
Named after the express train
that once whisked the in-crowd
to the Riviera, this isn't just a
station restaurant. Its early-
19th-century decor is ravishing
and wildly romantic, with
flamboyantly gilded ceilings
and enchanting frescoes. The
menu consists of upmarket
brasserie classics. The pastries
are a highlight.

The cosy Le Baron Rouge bar, serving
charcuterie, cheese platters and oysters

For more information on types of restaurants *see page 291*

Cafés, Tea Salons and Bars

Good food and drink is so much a part of everyday life in Paris that you can eat and drink well without ever going to a restaurant. Whether you want to enjoy a meal or casual drink at a café, wine bar or tearoom, buy a crêpe from a street stand or a quiche or crusty *baguette* sandwich from a bakery, or buy a market picnic of cheeses, breads, salads and *pâtés*, informal eating is one of the city's great gastronomic strengths.

Paris is also a wonderful city for drinking. Wine bars in every quarter offer various wines by the glass. Beer bars have astounding selections, and Irish pubs are much-loved spots serving Guinness in a relaxed, sometimes rowdy atmosphere. Alternatively, choose from chic hotel bars or fun late-night bars *(see also pp294–5)*.

Cafés

Paris is famous for its cafés, and rightly so. You can't walk far in this city without passing one. They range in size from tiny to huge, some with pinball machines, a tobacconist and betting stations, some with elegant belle époque decorations and immaculately attired waiters. Every Parisian has their favourite local café and these establishments function as the heart of any neighbour-hood. The life of a café changes throughout the day and it's always fascinating to check out the locals at leisure, sipping their morning espresso, tucking into a hearty lunch or drinking an *apéritif* after work. Most cafés will serve you light food and drink at any time of day.

Breakfast definitely is one of the busiest times and fresh croissants and *pains au chocolat* (chocolate-filled pastries) sell fast. The French often eat these dipped in a bowl or large cup of milky coffee or hot chocolate. Eating breakfast out at a café, or at least grabbing a quick caffeine fix in the morning, is a fundamental part of the French lifestyle.

The café lunch usually includes *plats du jour* (daily specials) and, in the smaller cafés, these are great Parisian bargains, rarely costing more than €16 for two courses. The specials are often substantial meat dishes such as *sauté d'agneau* (sautéed lamb) or *blanquette de veau* (veal with a white sauce), with fruit tarts for dessert. For a simpler lunch, salads, sandwiches and omelettes are usually available at any time of day. One of the best places for this kind of food is **Le Petit Saint-Benoît** in St-Germain-des-Prés. **Le Rostand** by the Luxembourg Gardens is also an excellent place to eat as is **Café Constant** *(see p301)* in the Invalides district.

Most museums have reliable cafés, but those at the Pompidou Centre *(see pp110–11)* and the Musée d'Orsay *(see pp146–7)* are especially good. When visiting the Louvre, it is worth waiting till you re-emerge from the galleries and stopping at the upmarket **Café Marly** in front of the glass pyramid under the arcades for an expensive, yet memorable drink or meal. Should you find yourself in the department store **Galeries Lafayette** *(see p313)*, it's worth going to the café for the fabulous views over Paris.

Cafés in the main tourist and nightlife areas (Boulevard St-Germain, Les Halles, Avenue des Champs-Elysées, Boulevard Montparnasse, the Opéra and Bastille) generally stay open late – some not closing their doors until 2am.

It is important to note that prices change depending on where in the café you choose to enjoy your drink. Standing at the bar is usually a little cheaper than sitting at one of the tables, and heading outside to the terrace will normally cost you more again.

Tea Salons

Tearooms have become increasingly popular in Paris over the last few years and the selection of teas is normally impressive. Some tea salons also offer light lunches, as well as breakfast and afternoon tea, including **Angélina**, with its belle époque decor. **Mariage Frères** in the Marais is well known for its exhaustive drink list and also sells loose tea and lovely teapots to take home. **Ladurée** on the Champs Elysées is a Parisian institution where well-heeled ladies sip tea and nibble the house speciality macaroons. For a more exotic atmosphere, visit the mosaic-tiled **Café de la Mosquée**, at Paris's mosque in the Jardin des Plantes area, for sticky pastries and excellent mint tea.

Wine Bars

Most Parisian wine bars are small, convivial neighbourhood places. They open early, many doubling as cafés for breakfast, and offer a small, good-quality lunch menu. It's best to get there early or after 1.30pm if you want to avoid the crowds. Most wine bars are usually closed by 9pm.

Wine bar owners tend to be passionate about wine, most of them buying directly from producers. Young Bordeaux wines and those from the Loire, the Rhône and the Jura can be surprisingly good, and wine bar owners usually seek out interesting tipples. The **L'Ecluse** chain specializes in Bordeaux, but for the most part, you will find delicious lesser-known wines at very reasonable prices. Serious oenophiles might like to visit wine bars attached to leading wine shops so that any interesting vintages tasted can be ordered by the case-load and enjoyed at home. There are several examples of this type of place in Paris – **Juvenile's**, **Lavinia** and **Legrand Filles et Fils** in the Opéra district are among the finest. Juveniles is a small shop with a zinc bar run by a Scotsman. The selection is very good, especially for wines from the New World, and great food is also served here. Lavinia is Europe's largest wine store, the choice is vast, there are regular tastings and the sleek bar serves many wines by the glass. Legrand is an old-fashioned vintner whose bar is extremely popular with Parisian wine buffs. Another fashionable wine bar of this type is **Willi's Wine Bar** in the Beaubourg and Les Halles district. The delightful **Rouge Passion**, situated below Montmartre, is a great place to spend a whole evening. Wine-tasting classes with guest *sommeliers* are a regular feature in this bar.

Beer Bars and Pubs

Paris has both pubs and beer bars. Whereas pubs are simply for drinking, beer bars also serve a particular style of food and are larger. *Moules-frites* (a generous bowl of steamed mussels served with French fries), *tarte aux poireaux* (leek tart) and *tarte aux oignons* (onion tart) are classic examples of the food they serve. The chief reason for going to a beer bar, however, is for the beer. The lists are often vast: some specialize in Belgian *gueuze* (heavy, malty, very alcoholic beer), others have beers from all around the world.

Some beer bars are open from noon, whereas pubs may open later in the afternoon. Pubs are usually open every day, often until 1 or 2am. The pubs in Paris have a good mix of expatriate and French clients. Some pubs are also micro-breweries serving beer brewed on the premises. The **Frog and Princess** and the **Frog and Rosbif** are good examples of this type of pub, serving several types of home-brewed beer. The bar staff are very friendly and will happily help you choose the beer that's right for you. Aside from traditionally English pubs such as **The Bombardier** in the Latin Quarter, Paris has dozens of Irish pubs and a few Scottish pubs. The

best Irish pubs include **Coolin** and **Corcoran's** in St-Germain-des-Prés, **Kitty O'Sheas** and **Carr's** in the Tuileries district and **O'Sullivans by the Mill** in Montmartre. A Highland fling and good whisky can be found in the **Highlander** in St-Germain-des-Prés and **The Auld Alliance** in the Marais.

Bars

Being such an elegant city, it's no surprise that Paris has more than its share of cocktail and late-night bars too. Some pretty Paris brasseries, such as **La Coupole**, **La Rotonde** and **La Closerie des Lilas**, have long wooden or zinc bars, accomplished bartenders, a glamorous ambience and a sense of distinguished times past. Hotel bars are some of the loveliest places for cocktails in Paris. Bar 228 at **Le Meurice Hotel** *(see p284)* has a cosy atmosphere and lavish decor. It serves a wide range of cocktails and there is live jazz every evening. Other hotel bars of note include Le V at **Four Seasons George V** *(see p284)*, where the bartenders will shake your martini at your table and present it in an individual silver shaker, the perennially popular bar in the hotel **Balzac** and the fashionable **Le Bar du Plaza at the Plaza Athénée**.

La Mezzanine de l'Alcazar is one of Paris's most fashionable bars, while **Yono** is very young and trendy. Other hip bars include **Le Fumoir** next to the Louvre with its long elegant bar, happy hour between 6 and 8pm and excellent cocktails, **Andy Wahloo**, which is tiny with a Moroccan design, **De LaVille** café, which is popular as a pre-club destination, **Le China**, which has a wonderful cocktail menu and **The Lizard Lounge**, which attracts a noisy, young crowd. The modern Philippe Starck-designed bar and restaurant **Kong**, on top of the Kenzo store near the Pont Neuf, is one of Paris's trendiest places for drinks.

Bars which are less trendy but great for a relaxing drink include the tiny, stone-clad **Stolly's** in the Marais and legendary **Harry's Bar**, which claims to have invented the Bloody Mary.

Take-Away Food

Crêpes are the traditional Parisian street food. Although there are fewer good crêpe stands than there used to be, they still exist. Sandwich bars provide *baguettes* with a wide range of fillings; a Parisien – a type of *baguette* – is normally Emmental cheese with ham. Camembert-filled sandwiches are delicious to taste, but vegetarians should be aware that *crudités* (raw vegetables) may include non-vegetarian ingredients too. The best fast food in Paris is freshly-baked flat *fougasse* (foccacia) bread sprinkled with savoury flavourings. It is sold fresh from a wood-burning oven and filled with one or more fillings of your choice. You can buy it at **Cosi** in Rue de Seine. Busy tourist areas also have their share of kebab shops for a speedy snack.

Ice-cream stands open around noon, and stay open late in summer. It's worth queuing for the city's best ice cream at **Maison Berthillon**. Seasoned gourmets come from across the city to queue around the block for a scoop or two of their delicious concoctions. Chocoholics will be delighted with their intense cocoa ice cream, whilst fruit fans can expect sorbets packed with flavour. There are several branches of Berthillon in the city but the Ile St Louis store is particularly recommended: nothing beats strolling along the Seine catching the drips from a divine ice-cream cone. Ice-cream obsessives might also like to head to **Amorino**, which makes Italian-style *gelati*. Don't miss the *amaretto gelato* which comes sprinkled with crushed *amaretti* biscuits.

DIRECTORY

Ile De La Cité and Ile St-Louis

TEA SALONS

Le Flore en l'Ile
42 Quai d'Orléans 75004.
Map 13 B4.

ICE–CREAM PARLOURS

Amorino
47 Rue St-Louis-en-l'Ile
75004. **Map** 13 C4.
One of several branches.

Maison Berthillon
29–31 Rue St-Louis-en-
l'Ile 75004.
Map 13 C4.

Tuileries Quarter

CAFÉS

Café Marly
93 Rue de Rivoli, Palais du
Louvre 75001. **Map** 12 F2.

WINE BARS

La Cloche des Halles
28 Rue Coquillière 75001.
Map 12 E2.

Le Rubis
10 Rue du Marché
St-Honoré 75001.
Map 12 D1.

Juvenile's
47 Rue de Richelieu
75001. **Map** 12 E1.

TEA SALONS

Angélina
226 Rue de Rivoli 75001.
Map 12 D1.

Ladurée
16 Rue Royale 75008.
Map 5 C5.

PUBS

Carr's
1 Rue du Mont-Thabor
75001. **Map** 12 D1.

Kitty O'Sheas
10 Rue des Capucines
75002. **Map** 6 D5.

BARS

Bars du Ritz
15 Pl Vendôme 75001.
Map 6 D5.

Harry's Bar
5 Rue Daunou 75002.
Map 6 E5.

The Marais

CAFÉS

Au Petit Fer à Cheval
30 Rue Vieille du Temple
75004. **Map** 13 C3.

L'Etoile Manquante
34 Rue Vieille du Temple
75004. **Map** 13 C3.

Ma Bourgogne
19 Pl des Vosges 75004.
Map 14 D3.

Le Trésor
7 Rue du Trésor 75004.
Map 13 C3.

TEA SALONS

Le Loir dans la Théière
3 Rue des Rosiers 75004.
Map 13 C3.

Mariage Frères
30–32 Rue du Bourg-
Tibourg 75004.
Map 13 C3.

BEER BARS

Café des Musées
49 Rue de Turenne 75003.
Map 14 D3.

WINE BARS

La Belle Hortense
31 Rue Vieille du Temple
75004. **Map** 13 C3.

La Trinquette
67 Rue des Gravilliers
75003. **Map** 13 C1.

Le Coude Fou
12 Rue du Bourg-Tibourg
75004. **Map** 13 C3.

PUBS

The Auld Alliance
80 Rue François Miron
75004. **Map** 13 C3.

Stolly's
16 Rue Cloche Perce
75004. **Map** 13 C3.

BARS

L'Apparement Café
18 Rue des Coutures
St-Gervais 75003.
Map 14 D2.

Les Philosophes
28 Rue Vieille du Temple
75004. **Map** 13 C3.

The Lizard Lounge
18 Rue du Bourg-Tibourg
75004. **Map** 13 C3.

Yono
37 Rue Vieille du Temple
75004. **Map** 13 C3.

Beaubourg and Les Halles

CAFÉS

Café Beaubourg
43 Rue Saint-Merri,
Esplanade du Centre
Georges Pompidou
75004. **Map** 13 B2.
(see p108).

WINE BARS

La Garde Robe
41 Rue de l'Arbre Sec
75001. **Map** 12 E2.

Willi's Wine Bar
13 Rue des Petits Champs
75001. **Map** 12 F1.

PUBS

Frog and Rosbif
116 Rue Saint-Denis
75002. **Map** 13 B1.

Quigley's Point
5 Rue du Jour 75001.
Map 13 A1.

BARS

Andy Wahloo
69 Rue des Gravilliers
75003. **Map** 13 B1.

Experimental Cocktail Club
37 Rue Saint-Sauveur
75002. **Map** 13 A1.

Kong
1 Rue du Pont Neuf
75001. **Map** 13 A2.

Le Fumoir
6 Rue de l'Amiral-de-
Coligny 75001. **Map** 12 F2.

St-Germain-des-Prés

CAFÉS

Café de Flore
(See p141).

Café de la Mairie
8 Place St-Sulpice 75006.
Map 12 E4.

Les Deux Magots
(See p140).

La Palette
43 Rue de Seine 75006.
Map 12 E4.

Le Petit Saint-Benoit
4 Rue Saint-Benoit, 75006.
Map 12 E3.

Sandwich Bars

Cosi
54 Rue de Seine 75006.
Map 12 E4.

WINE BARS

Au Sauvignon
80 Rue des Sts-Pères
75007. **Map** 12 D4.

Bistro des Augustins
39 Quai des Grands-
Augustins 75006.
Map 12 F4.

PUBS

Coolin
15 Rue Clément 75006.
Map 12 E4.

Corcoran's
28 Rue Saint-André des
Arts 75006. **Map** 12 F4.
One of four other pubs.

Frog and Princess
9 Rue Princesse 75006.
Map 12 E4.

Highlander
8 Rue de Nevers 75006.
Map 12 F3.

The Moose
16 Rue des Quatre-Vents
75006. **Map** 12 F4.

BARS

Le Bar Dix
10 Rue de l'Odéon
75006. **Map** 12 F4.

Birdland
8 Rue Guisarde 75006.
Map 12 E4.

Café Mabillon
164 Blvd St-Germain
75006. **Map** 12 E4.

Fubar
5 Rue St Sulpice 75006.
Map 12 F4.

La Mezzanine de l'Alcazar
62 Rue Mazarine 75006.
Map 12 F4.

Prescription Cocktail Club
23 Rue Mazarine 75006.
Map 12 F4.

DIRECTORY

Zéro de Conduite
14 Rue Jacob 75006.
Map 12 E3.

Latin Quarter

CAFÉS

Panis
21 Quai Montebello
75005. **Map** 13 A4.

WINE BARS

Les Pipos
2 Rue de l'Ecole Polytech-
nique 75005. **Map** 13 A5.

Le Vin qui Danse
4 Rue des Fossés-
St-Jacques 75005.
Map 17 A1.

BEER BARS

La Gueuze
19 Rue Soufflot 75005.
Map 12 F5.

PUBS

The Bombardier
2 Place du Panthéon
75005. **Map** 17 A1.

BARS

**Le Caveau des
Oubliettes**
52 Rue Galande 75005.
Map 13 A4.

Jardin des
Plantes

CAFÉS

**Café Littéraire de
l'Institut du Monde
Arabe**
1 Rue des Fossés-St-
Bernard 75005.
Map 13 C5.

TEA SALONS

Café de la Mosquée
39 Rue Geoffroy St-Hilaire
75005.
Map 17 C2.

PUBS

Bière Academy
7 Rue des Ecoles 75005.
Map 13 B5.

ICE-CREAM
PARLOURS

Gelati d'Alberto
45 Rue Mouffetard
75005. **Map** 17 B1.

Luxembourg
Quarter

CAFÉS

Au Petit Suisse
16 Rue de Vaugirard
75006. **Map** 12 F5.

Le Rostand
6 Place Edmond Rostand
75006.
Map 12 F5.

BEER BARS

**L'Académie de
la Bière**
88 Blvd de Port-Royal
75005. **Map** 17 B3.

Montparnasse

CAFÉS

Café de la Place
23 Rue d'Odessa 75014.
Map 15 C2.

La Rotonde
7 Pl 25 Août 1944 75014.
Map 16 D2.

**Le Sélect
Montparnasse**
99 Blvd du Montparnasse
75006.
Map 16 D2.

WINE BARS

Le Rallye Peret
6 Rue Daguerre 75014.
Map 16 D4.

TEA SALONS

Justine
96 Rue Oberkampf 75011.
Map 14 E1.

BARS

La Closerie des Lilas
171 Blvd du
Montparnasse 75006.
Map 16 D2.

La Coupole (Café Bar)
102 Blvd du
Montparnasse 75014.
Map 16 D2.
(see p178).

Cubana Café
45 Rue Vavin 75006.
Map 16 E1.

Le Café Tournesol
9 Rue de la Gaîté 75014.
Map 2 E2.

Invalides and
Eiffel Tower
Quarter

CAFÉS

Café Constant
139 Rue St-Dominique
75007. **Map** 11 B2.

PUBS

O'Brien's
77 Rue Saint-Dominique
75007. **Map** 10 F3.

BARS

Comptoir du 7
39 Ave de la Motte-
Picquet 75007.
Map 10 F4.

ICE-CREAM
PARLOURS

Häagen-Dazs
64 Ave de la Motte-Picquet
75015. **Map** 10 F4.

Champs-Elysées

WINE BARS

L'Ecluse
64 Rue François 1er
75008. **Map** 4 F5.

Wine by One
27 Rue de Marignan
75008. **Map** 4 F1.

TEA SALONS

Ladurée
75 Ave des Champs-
Elysées 75008. **Map** 4 F5.

BARS

**Le Bar du Plaza at the
Plaza Athénée**
25 Ave Montaigne 75008.
Map 10 F1.

Hotel Balzac Bar
6 Rue Balzac 75008.
Map 4 F4.

Opéra Quarter

CAFÉS

Café de la Paix
Intercontinental Paris Le
Grand, 12 Blvd des
Capucines 75009.
Map 6 E5. *(see p217).*

WINE BARS

Bistro du Sommelier
97 Blvd Haussmann
75008. **Map** 5 C4.

Lavinia
3-5 Blvd de la Madeleine
75001.
Map 6 D5.

Legrand Filles et Fils
1 Rue de la Banque
75002. **Map** 12 F1.
Tel 01 42 60 07 12.

Montmartre

CAFÉS

Le Saint Jean
16 Place des Abbesses
75018. **Map** 6 F1.

Le Sancerre
35 Rue des Abbesses
75018. **Map** 6 E1.

WINE BARS

Rouge Passion
14 Rue Jean Baptiste
Pigalle 75009.
Map 6 D2.

PUBS

**O'Sullivans by
the Mill**
92 Blvd de Clichy 75018.
Map 6 E21.

Further Afield

WINE BARS

Le Verre Volé
67 Rue de Lancry 75010.
Map 8 D4.

BARS

L'Autre Café
62 Rue Jean-Pierre
Timbaud 75011.
Map 8 F5.

Café Charbon
109 Rue Oberkampf
75011. **Map** 14 E1.

Chez Prune
36 Rue Beaurepaire
75010. **Map** 8 D4.

Le China
50 Rue de Charenton
75012. **Map** 14 F5.

Pause Café
41 Rue de Charonne
75011. **Map** 14 F4.

GLUTEN-FREE

BioSphere Cafe
47 Rue Laborde 75008.
Map 5 B3.

SHOPS AND MARKETS

Paris seems to be the very definition of luxury and good living. Beautifully dressed people sip wine by the banks of the Seine against a backdrop of splendid architecture, or hurry down gallery-lined streets carrying parcels from specialist shops. The least expensive way of joining the chic set is to create French style with accessories or costume jewellery. Alternatively, splash out on the fashion, or the wonderful food and related items from kitchen gadgets to tableware. Remember too that Parisian shops and markets are the ideal place to indulge in the French custom of strolling through the streets, seeing and being seen. For high fashion there are the exquisite *couture* house window displays on Avenue Montaigne, or you can browse at the bookstalls along the Seine. A survey of some of the most famous places to shop follows.

Opening Hours

Shops are usually open from 10am to 7pm, Monday to Saturday, but hours can vary. Many department stores stay open late on Thursday, while boutiques may shut for an hour or two at midday. Markets and local neighbourhood shops close on Mondays. Some smaller shops shut for the summer, usually in August, but they may leave a note on the door suggesting an open equivalent nearby.

How to Pay

Cash is readily available from the ATMs in most banks, which accept both credit and bank debit cards. Visa and MasterCard are the most widely accepted credit cards.

VAT Exemption

A sales tax (TVA) of 5.5–19.6 per cent is imposed on most goods and services in EU countries.

Non-EU residents shopping in France are entitled to a refund of this if they spend a minimum of €175 in one shop in one day. You must have been resident in France for less than six months and either carry the goods with you out of the country within three months of purchase or get the shop to forward them to you. If shopping in a group, you can usually buy goods together in order to reach the minimum.

Larger shops will generally supply a form *(bordereau de détaxe* or *bordereau de vente)* and help you to fill it in. When you leave France or the EU you present the form to Customs, who either permit you to be reimbursed straight away, or forward your claim to the place where you bought the merchandise; the shop eventually sends you a refund. If you know someone in Paris it may be quicker if they can pick up the refund for you at the shop. Alternatively at

Shopping in Avenue Montaigne

large airports such as Orly and Roissy some banks may have the facilities to refund you on the spot. Though the process involves a lot of paperwork, it can be worth it. There is no refund on food, drink, tobacco, cars and motorbikes. Bicycles, however, can be reimbursed.

Sales

The best sales *(soldes)* are held in January and July, although you can find sale items before Christmas. If you see goods labelled *Stock*, it means that they are stock items. *Dégriffé* means designer labels marked down, frequently from the previous year's collections. *Fripes* indicates that the clothes are second-hand. The sales tend to occupy prime floor space for the first month and are then relegated to the back of the store.

Printemps, the *grande dame* of Parisian department stores

Department Stores

Much of the pleasure of shopping in Paris is derived from going to the small specialist shops. But if time is short, try the *grands magasins* (department stores). Some still operate a ticket system for selling goods. The shop assistant writes up a ticket for goods from their own boutique which you take to one of the cashiers. You then return with your validated ticket to pick up your purchase. This can be time-consuming, so go early in the morning and don't shop on Saturdays. The French don't pay much attention to queues, so be assertive! One peculiarity of a visit is that the security guards may ask to inspect your bags as you leave. These are random checks and should not be taken as an implication of theft.

Department stores vary in style and content, but all have places to eat. **Printemps** is noted for its exciting and innovative household goods section, and large menswear store. The clothes departments for women and children are well-stocked. The lovely domed restaurant in the cupola often hosts chic after-hours parties; these are private, but do visit the restaurant during shopping hours.

Kenzo designerwear in the Place des Victoires *(see pp316–17)*

Snails from the *charcuterie*

Apollonia Poilâne's bread bearing her trademark "P" *(see pp325–7)*

BHV (Le Bazar de l'Hôtel de Ville) is a DIY enthusiast's paradise. It also sells a host of other items related to home decor. The Left Bank **Le Bon Marché** was Paris's first department store and today is its most chic. The designer clothing sections are well-sourced, the high-end accessories are excellent and the own-brand linen has a good quality to price ratio. The prepared food sections serve restaurant-quality fare to take away.

Galeries Lafayette is perhaps the best-known department store and has a wide range of clothes available at all price levels. Its first-floor trends section plays host to lots of innovative designers. Having taken over part of the old Marks & Spencer, Galeries Lafayette boasts a wonderful food hall, Lafayette Gourmet, which offers a vast array of mouthwatering goodies.

FNAC is the largest retailer in France of books, music and electronic equipment. There are numerous shops around Paris, but the branch on the Champs-Elysées specializes in music, DVDs and concert tickets and is open until 11.45pm daily. All of their products are available online, too, along with tickets for concerts, sporting events and theatrical events.

Bookstall, Vanves market *(see p331)*

DIRECTORY

Addresses

BHV
52–64 Rue de Rivoli 75004.
Map 13 B3. **Tel** 09 77 40 14 00.

Le Bon Marché
24 Rue de Sèvres 75007.
Map 11 C5. **Tel** 01 44 39 80 00.

FNAC
Forum des Halles, 1/7 Rue Pierre Lescot 75001.
Map 13 A2.
Tel 0825 020 020.
74 Ave des Champs-Elysées 75008.
Map 4 F5.
Tel 0825 020 020.
136 Rue de Rennes 75006.
Map 16 D1.
Tel 08 25 02 00 20.
W fnac.com

Galeries Lafayette
40 Blvd Haussmann 75009.
Map 6 E4. **Tel** 01 42 82 34 56.

Printemps
64 Blvd Haussman 75009.
Map 6 D4. **Tel** 01 42 82 50 00.

Paris's Best: Shops and Markets

By turns ultra-conservative and wackily avant-garde, Paris is a treasure trove of quality shops and boutiques. Time-honoured emporia mix with modern precincts in a city that buzzes with life in its inner quarters, not least in the markets. Here you can buy everything from exotic fruit and vegetables to fine china and vintage treasures. Whether you're shopping for handmade shoes, perfectly-cut clothes or traditionally-made cheeses, or simply soaking up the atmosphere, you won't be disappointed.

Place de la Madeleine
Top-class groceries and delicacies are sold on the north side of this square. *(See p216.)*

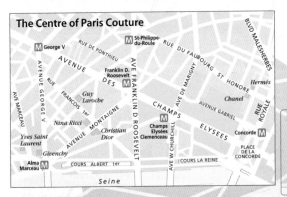

The Centre of Paris Couture

George V · RUE DE PONTHIEU · St-Philippe-du-Roule · RUE DU FAUBOURG ST HONORE · BLVD MALESHERBES · AVENUE · RUE FRANCOIS 1er · AVENUE GEORGE V · AVE MARCEAU · Franklin D. Roosevelt · AVE DE MARIGNY · Hermès · Guy Laroche · AVENUE MONTAIGNE · AVE FRANKLIN D ROOSEVELT · CHAMPS ELYSEES · AVENUE GABRIEL · Chanel · RUE ROYALE · Nina Ricci · Christian Dior · Champs Elysées Clemenceau · Concorde · Yves Saint Laurent · Givenchy · PLACE DE LA CONCORDE · Alma Marceau · COURS ALBERT 1er · AVE W CHURCHILL · COURS LA REINE · Seine

See inset map

Champs-Elysées

Chanel
Coco Chanel (1883–1971) reigned over the fashion world from No. 31 Rue Cambon. The main boutique is in the Avenue Montaigne. *(See p317.)*

Invalides and Eiffel Tower Quarter

Rue de Rivoli
Inexpensive mementos like this Paris snow globe can be found in the shops on the Rue de Rivoli. *(See p132.)*

Marché de la Porte de Vanves
This charming and relaxed market sells old books, linen, postcards, china and musical instruments. *(Weekends only – see p331.)*

| 0 kilometres | 1 |
| 0 miles | 0.5 |

Kenzo
The Japanese designer has colourful apparel for men, women and children in his clothes shops. *(See p317.)*

Cartier
The early Cartier jewellery designs with their beautifully-cut stones are still highly sought after. This shop in the Rue de la Paix sells all the Cartier lines. *(See p321.)*

Rue de Paradis
Here you can buy porcelain and crystal at reduced prices at the company showrooms. Look out for Lumicristal which stocks Baccarat and Bernardaud. *(See pp322–4.)*

Passage des Panoramas
This once-prosperous covered arcade is home to the historic Stem print shop. *(See p220.)*

Opéra Quarter

Kenzo

Tuileries Quarter

Beaubourg and Les Halles

The Marais

er **Seine**

St-Germain-des-Prés

Ile de la Cité

Ile St-Louis

Rue des Francs-Bourgeois
Stylish fashion stores see *(pp316–17)* line this thoroughfare in the Marais.

Latin Quarter

Luxembourg Quarter

Jardin des Plantes Quarter

ontparnasse

Marché de la Porte de Vanves

Rue Mouffetard
The market sells cheeses and other quality foods. *(See p331.)*

Forum des Halles
This modern glass arcade has many shops. *(See p115.)*

Clothes and Accessories

For many people, Paris is synonymous with fashion and Parisian style is the ultimate in chic. More than anywhere else in the world, women in Paris seem to be in tune with current trends and when a new season arrives they rush, as one, to don the look. Though less trend-conscious generally, Parisian men are aware of style and mix and match patterns and colours with élan. Finding the right clothes at the right price means knowing where to shop. For every luxury boutique on the Avenue Montaigne, there are ten shops by young designers waiting to become the next Jean-Paul Gaultier – and hundreds more selling imitations.

Haute Couture

Paris is the home of *haute couture*. Original *couture* garments, as opposed to imitations and adaptations, are one-off creations, designed by one of the *haute couture* houses listed with the Fédération Française de la Couture. The rules for being classified by the Fédération are fairly strict, and some top brands are not included. Astronomical prices put *haute couture* beyond the reach of all but a few immensely deep pockets, but it's still the lifeblood of the fashion industry providing inspiration for the mass market.

The fashion seasons are launched with the *couture* shows in January and July. Many shows are held in the Carrousel du Louvre (see p123). If you want to see a show, you stand a much better chance of getting a seat at the private *couture* shows (the main shows are for buyers and the press). To do this, call the press offices of the *haute couture* houses a month in advance. You can only be sure you have a place when you receive the ticket. Alternatively, telephone the fashion house or, if you're in Paris, try going to the boutique and asking if there's a show – and do remember to dress the part.

Most *couture* houses make *prêt-à-porter* clothes as well – ready-to-wear clothes fitted on a standard model. They're still not cheap, but give you an idea of some of the designer elegance and creativity at a fraction of the cost.

Women's Clothes

The highest concentration of *couture* houses is on the Right Bank. Most are on or near the Rue du Faubourg-St-Honoré and the classier Avenue Montaigne: **Christian Dior**, **Pierre Cardin**, **Chanel**, **Gianni Versace**, **Givenchy**, **Nina Ricci** and **Saint Laurent**. This is where you will rub shoulders with the rich and famous.

Hermès offers timeless chic. **MaxMara's** Italian elegance is quite popular in France and no one can resist a **Giorgio Armani** suit. **Karl Lagerfeld** has a shop where the latest creations from his own line, Lagerfeld Gallery, are exhibited.

The theatrical **Paco Rabanne** and chic **Prada** have also stuck to the Right Bank, but many other fine fashion houses prefer the Left Bank. Try **Sonia Rykiel** for knitwear, **Junko Shimada** for sporty casuals and **Barbara Bui** for soft, feminine clothes.

Many designers have a Left Bank branch in addition to their Right Bank bastions, and there are many ready-to-wear shops here. For sheer quality, there's **Georges Rech**, but don't forget Saint Laurent or **Jil Sander** for their exquisite tailoring. Try Armani's St-Germain temple of fashion, or Prada's more affordable diffusion line, **Miu Miu**, in the Rue du Faubourg St Honoré. **Joseph** has its cult following for well-cut clothes, and **Irié** is the place for reasonably-priced clothes which are trendy but will stand the test of time. Also in the Saint-Germain-des-Prés district, the **Comptoir des Cotonniers** stocks excellent basics, **Maje** has everything from boho chic to stylish cuts, and **Vanessa Bruno** is extremely popular for feminine flair. Simple cuts with quirky details can be found at **Zadig et Voltaire**, which has a following amongst French fashionistas.

Ready-to-wear shops blanket Paris, and in the beautiful Place des Victoires, they thrive off shoppers looking to escape the crowds on Rue du Faubourg-St-Honoré. The **Victoire** boutique offers one of the best collections of current designer labels with Michael Klein, Helmut Lang and Thierry Mugler among many others.

Kenzo is here (its flagship store is on Place des Victoires), along with fellow Japanese designers **Comme des Garçons**, with its avant-garde, quirky fashion for both sexes, and **Claudie Pierlot** just down the street, near Ventilo. The nearby Rue Jean-Jacques-Rousseau has now become one of the city's prime shopping spots.

Moving east to the Rue du Jour, **Agnès B** presents the latest French fashions. There are also many shops selling inexpensive copies of new designs in the centre. **Maison Martin Margiela** carries excellent quality basics with a twist.

The Marais is a haven for up-and-coming designers and is always busy on Saturdays. One of the best streets is the Rue des Rosiers, which includes the wonderful **Zadig et Voltaire**, **L'Eclaireur** and a branch of **Tehen** for clothes. **Nina Jacob** is on the neighbouring Rue des Francs-Bourgeois, and daring designer **Azzedine Alaïa's** shop is just around the corner. **Abou d'Abi Bazar** stocks a range of designers, and Japanese company **Muji** sells stylishly-simple staple garments and accessories.

The Bastille area has trendy boutiques, as well as some more established names. Designer **Jean-Paul Gaultier** has a boutique in the

DIRECTORY

Women's Clothes

Abou d'Abi Bazar
125 Rue Vielle du Temple
75003. **Map** 13 C3.
Tel 01 42 71 13 26.

Agnès B
6 Rue du Jour 75001.
Map 13 A1. **Tel** 01 45 08
56 56. **W** agnesb.com
One of several branches.

Azzedine Alaïa
7 Rue de Moussy & 18 Rue
de la Verrerie 75004. **Map**
13 C3 & B3. **Tel** 01 42 72
19 19.

Barbara Bui
23 Rue Etienne-Marcel
75001. **Map** 13 A1.
Tel 01 40 26 43 65.
W barbarabui.com
One of several branches.

Chanel
42 & 51 Ave Montaigne
75008. **Map** 5 A5. **Tel** 01 44
50 73 00. **W** chanel.com
One of several branches.

Christian Dior
30 Ave Montaigne 75008.
Map 10 F1. **Tel** 01 40 73
73 73. **W** dior.com

Claudie Pierlot
1 bis des Victoires 75002.
Map 12 F1. **Tel** 01 44 82 55
38. **W** claudiepierlot.com
One of several branches.

Colette
213 Rue St-Honoré 75001.
Map 12 D1. **Tel** 01 55 35
33 90. **W** colette.fr

Comme des Garçons
54 Rue du Faubourg
St-Honoré 75008.
Map 4 E3. **Tel** 01 53 30
27 27. **W** comme-des-
garcons.com

**Comptoir des
Cotonniers**
33 Rue des Francs
Bourgeois 75004. **Map** 13
C3. **Tel** 01 42 76 95 33.
W comptoirdes
cotonniers.com
One of several branches.

L'Eclaireur
40 rue de Sévigné 75003.
Map 14 D3.
Tel 01 48 87 10 22.
W leclaireur.com
One of several branches.

Eres
2 Rue Tronchet 75008.
Map 5 C5.
Tel 01 47 42 28 82.
W eresparis.com
One of several branches.

Gaëlle Barré
17 Rue Keller 75011.
Map 14 F4.
Tel 01 43 14 63 02.
W gaellebarre.com

Georges Rech
181 Blvd Saint Germain
75007. **Map** 12 D4.
Tel 01 45 48 31 77.
W georges-rech.fr

Giorgio Armani
18 Ave Montaigne 75008.
Map 10 F1.
Tel 01 42 61 55 09.
W armani.com

Givenchy
28 Rue du Faubourg-St-
Honoré 75008.
Map 5 C5.
Tel 01 42 68 31 00.
W givenchy.com
One of several branches.

H&M
15 Rue du Commerce
75015. **Map** 10 E5.
Tel 01 40 57 24 60.
One of several branches.

Hermès
24 Rue du Faubourg-St-
Honoré 75008. **Map** 5 C5.
Tel 01 40 17 46 00.
W hermes.com
One of several branches.

Irié
8 Rue du Pré-aux-Clercs
75007. **Map** 12 D3.
Tel 01 42 61 18 28.

Isabel Marant
16 Rue de Charonne
75011. **Map** 14 F4.
Tel 01 49 29 71 55.
W isabelmarant.com

Jay Ahr
2 Rue du 29 Juillet 75001.
Map 12 D1.
Tel 01 42 96 95 23.

Jean-Paul Gaultier
6 Rue Vivienne 75002.
Map 12 F1.
Tel 01 42 86 05 05.
W jeanpaulgaultier.com
One of several branches.

Jil Sander
56 Ave Montaigne 75008.
Map 10 F1. **Tel** 01 44 95
06 70. **W** jilsander.com

Joseph
147 Blvd St-Germain
75006. **Map** 12 E4.
Tel 01 55 42 77 56.

Junko Shimada
13 Rue St-Florentin 75008.
Map 11 C1.
Tel 01 42 77 67 00.

Kenzo
3 Pl des Victoires 75001.
Map 12 F1. **Tel** 01 40 39
72 03. **W** kenzo.com
One of several branches.

Kookaï
82 Rue Reaumur 75002.
Map 13 B1. **Tel** 01 45 08
93 69. **W** kookai.fr
One of several branches.

The Kooples
22 Rue Royale 70008.
Map 5 C5.
Tel 01 40 15 98 23.
W thekooples.com
One of several branches.

La City
92 Ave des Champs
Elysees 75008. **Map** 4 F5.
Tel 01 58 56 21 49.
W lacity.fr

Les Petites
10 Rue du Four 75006.
Map 13 A1.
Tel 01 55 42 98 78.
W lespetites.fr
One of several branches.

Mac Douglas
9 Rue de Sèvres 75006.
Map 12 D4.
Tel 01 45 48 14 09.
One of several branches.

Maje
9 Rue du Cherche-Midi
75006. **Map** 12 D4. **Tel** 01
45 44 21 20.**W** maje.com

**Maison Martin
Margiela**
25 bis Rue de Mont-
pensier 75001. **Map** 12
E1.**Tel** 01 40 15 07 55.
One of several branches.

Mango
6 Blvd des Capucines
75009. **Map** 6 E5.
Tel 01 53 30 82 70.
One of several branches.

MaxMara
31 Ave Montaigne 75008.
Map 5 A5. **Tel** 01 47 20 61
13.**W** maxmara.com
One of several branches.

Miu Miu
92 Rue du Fbg St-Honoré
75008. **Map** 5 C5.
Tel 01 58 62 53 20.
W miumiu.com

Muji
47 Rue des Francs-
Bourgeois 75004. **Map** 14
D3. **Tel** 01 49 96 41 41.

Nina Jacob
23 Rue des Francs-
Bourgeois 75004.
Map 14 D3.
Tel 01 42 77 41 20.

Nina Ricci
39 Ave Montaigne 75008.
Map 10 F1.
Tel 01 83 97 72 12.
W ninaricci.fr

Pierre Cardin
59 Rue du Faubourg-St-
Honoré 75008. **Map** 5 B5.
Tel 01 42 66 68 98.
W pierrecardin.com

Prada
10 Ave Montaigne 75008.
Map 3 C5. **Tel** 01 53 23 99
40. **W** prada.com
One of two branches.

Promod
60 Rue Caumartin 75009.
Map 6 D4.**Tel** 01 45 26 01
11.One of several branches.

Ragtime
23 Rue de l'Echaudé
75006. **Map** 12 E4.
Tel 01 56 24 00 36.

Saint Laurent
38 Rue du Faubourg-
St-Honoré 75008.
Map 5 C5. **Tel** 01 42 65
74 59. **W** ysl.com One
of several branches.

Sandro
42 Rue Etienne Marcel
75002. **Map** 12 F1.
Tel 01 44 82 58 87.
W sandro-paris.com
One of several branches.

Sinéquanone
16 Rue du Four 75006.
Map 12 E4.
Tel 01 56 24 2774.
One of several branches.

Rue du Faubourg St-Antoine. His "senior" and "junior" collections reflect price and attitude. **Isabel Marant's** boutique is renowned for its originality, and **Gaëlle Barré** is a stylist with a fast-growing reputation. *The* swimsuit store is **Eres**, while for leather, it's **Mac Douglas**.

Young designers' clothes are found at **Colette**, **Stella Cadente** and **Jay Ahr** (where you will find great evening dresses), while **Sandro** has several boutiques. For fabulous, if somewhat pricey, clothes from the 1920s to the 1950s, try **Ragtime**.

Not all Parisians have pocketbooks that allow them to shop on the Avenue Montaigne, but those on smaller budgets still manage to look chic in clothes from high street stores. There are many large chain stores here which have branches in other European cities. Chain stores tend to stock each store differently, depending on the desires and buying patterns of the local clientele. Because of this, it is possible to find quintessentially French fashion in large chains such as **Zara**, particularly at the branches on Rue de Rennes and near the Opera.

Mighty Swedish retailer **H&M** has an exciting concept store for young fashion in Paris's 15th arrondissement and stocks designs by Sonia Rykiel in some of its larger shops. French high street stores are also numerous. Well-known names such as **Kookaï** and **Mango** stock fresh and funky items. **Sinéquanone** and **LA City**, on the other hand, are rather classic in their designs, while **Promod** is a very cheap store for fun merchandise.

Children's clothes

Lots of options for children exist in various styles and many price ranges. Many top designers of adult clothes also have boutiques for children. These include **Kenzo**, **Baby Dior**, **Agnès B**, **Sonia Rykiel** and **Teddy's**. Ready-to-wear shops such as **Jacadi** and **Du Pareil au Même** are serviceable

and wide-ranging; **Tartine et Chocolat** offer delectable classics with a contemporary twist. **Bonpoint** stocks adorably chic clothing for mini-Parisians. **Petit Bateau** is coveted as much by grown-ups as it is by children. The inevitable has finally happened – children now have their own concept store in **Bonton**, which stocks baby toiletries, stylish clothing, toys and furniture for children's rooms.

For little feet, **Froment-Leroyer** probably offers the best all-round classics. **Six Pieds Trois Pouces** has a vast choice of styles.

Men's Clothes

Men's fashions are a mix of bespoke tailoring and ready-to-wear, with menswear collections by the top designers every bit as coveted as their feminine counterparts.

On the Right Bank, there's **Giorgio Armani**, **Pierre Cardin**, **Kenzo**, **Lanvin** (also good for accessories) and **Saint Laurent**. On the Left Bank, **Michel Axel** and **Jean-Charles de Castelbajac** are known for their ties and **Francesco Smalto's** elegant creations are worn by some of the world's leading movie stars. Multi-brand boutique **French Trotters** stocks several labels for those who like to make a fashion statement, while **Versace** offers classic, suave Italian style. **APC**, **Paul Smith** and **Sandro** garments are rather more contemporary, and **Polo by Ralph Lauren** and **Loft Design By** are chic without being overtly trendy, and thus are likely to have a longer shelf-life.

The ultimate in Parisian elegance for men is a suit, custom-made shirt or silk tie from **Charvet**. A trip to the Place Vendôme store is a pleasure in itself. Be sure to ask the charming and friendly staff for a tour around their atelier for an insight into how such exquisite creations are crafted. **Printemps Homme** is a great department store for men which mixes designer and high-street brands.

Lifestyle Stores

Since **Colette** first burst on to the Parisian shopping scene in the late 1990s, the fad for lifestyle shops has shown no sign of slowing down.

Concept stores tend to be high-end affairs crammed with designer labels, some obscure, some household names, all grouped together to kit you out with everything you could possibly need. From fashionable books to shoes, beauty products, household goods, music and furniture via designer mineral water, handbags, trainers and evening gowns, the one-stop shopping experience provides the ultimate in retail therapy.

Spree in Montmartre mixes fashion, art and design so that you can buy a great outfit and some interesting art at the same time, while **Montaigne Market** brings together the best of *haute couture* and new designers.

Vintage and Second-Hand Stores

The vintage craze hit Paris some time back and there are some wonderful shops to plunder for a retro look. The best of the bunch is **Didier Ludot**, where an Aladdin's Cave of chic *haute couture* is elegantly displayed. From vintage Courrèges dresses to excellent condition Chanel suits, this is the place for top of the range retro.

The **Depôt-Vente de Buci-Bourbon** is another good place to bargain hunt.

A cheaper option and a way to access more recent looks is to head for one of the many second-hand or consignment stores in the city. Chic Parisians discard their outfits with the seasons, so it is easy to pick up some quality items which are normally in top condition from places such as **Réciproque** in Passy or **Alternatives** in the Marais. Sample pieces, sale stock and last season's collection pieces can be found at **Le Mouton à Cinq Pattes**.

DIRECTORY

Sonia Rykiel
175 Blvd St-Germain
75006. **Map** 12 D4.
Tel 01 49 54 60 60.
w soniarykiel.com
One of several branches.

Stella Cadente
102 Blvd Beaumarchais
75011. **Map** 14 E2.
Tel 09 50 90 25 55.
w stella-cadente.com

Vanessa Bruno
25 Rue St-Sulpice
75006. **Map** 12 E4.
Tel 01 43 54 41 04.
w vanessabruno.com

Ventilo
27 bis Rue du Louvre
75002. **Map** 12 F2.
Tel 01 44 76 82 95.
w ventilo.fr
One of several branches.

Versace
45 Ave Montaigne
75008. **Map** 10 F1.
Tel 01 47 42 88 02.
w versace.com

Victoire
10 Place des Victoires
75002. **Map** 12 F1.
Tel 01 49 27 94 76.
w monvictoire.fr
One of several branches.

Yohji Yamamoto
25 Rue du Louvre 75001.
Map 12 F1.
Tel 01 42 21 42 93.

Zadig et Voltaire
3 Rue des Rosiers
75004. **Map** 13 C3.
Tel 01 44 59 39 06.
One of several branches.

Zara
45 Rue de Rennes
75006. **Map** 16 D1.
Tel 01 44 39 03 50.
w zara.fr
One of several branches.

Children's Clothes

Agnès B
(See p317).

Baby Dior
(See p317 Christian Dior).

Bonpoint
320 Rue St-Honoré 75001.
Map 13 A2.**Tel** 01 49 27
94 82. **w** bonpoint.com
One of several branches.

Bonton
82 rue de Grenelle
75007. **Map** 10 F3.
Tel 01 44 39 09 20.
w bonton.com
One of several branches.

Du Pareil au Même
1 Rue St-Denis 75001.
Map 13 B3. **Tel** 01 42 36
07 57. **w** dpam.fr
One of several branches.

Froment-Leroyer
7 Rue Vavin 75006.
Map 16 E1.
Tel 01 43 54 33 15.
w froment-leroyer.fr
One of several branches.

Jacadi
17 Rue Tronchet
75008. **Map** 5 C5.
Tel 01 42 65 84 98.
w jacadi.fr
One of several branches.

Kenzo
(See p317).

Petit Bateau
116 Ave des Champs
Elysées 75008. **Map** 4 E4.
Tel 01 40 74 02 03.
w petit-bateau.com
One of several branches.

Six Pieds Trois Pouces
78 Ave de Wagram
75017. **Map** 4 E2.
Tel 01 46 22 81 64.
One of several branches.

Tartine et Chocolat
84 Rue du Faubourg-St-
Honoré 75008.
Map 5 B5.
Tel 01 45 62 44 04.
w tartine-et-chocolat.fr

Teddy's
38 Rue François-1er
75008. **Map** 10 F1.
Tel 01 47 20 79 79.

Men's Clothes

APC
38 Rue Madame 75006.
Map 12 E5.
Tel 01 42 22 12 77.
w apc.fr
One of several branches.

Celio
26 Rue du Faubourg
St-Antoine 75012.
Map 14 E4.
Tel 01 43 42 31 68.
One of several branches.

Charvet
28 Place Vendôme 75001.
Map 6 D5. **Tel** 01 42 60 30
70. **w** charvet.com

Francesco Smalto
44 Rue François-1er
75008. **Map** 4 F5.
Tel 01 47 20 96 04.
w smalto.com

French Trotters
128 Rue Vieille du Temple
75003. **Map** 13 C3. **Tel** 01
44 61 00 14.

Giorgio Armani
(See p317).

Jean-Charles de Castelbajac
61 Rue des St Peres
75006. **Tel** 09 64 48 48 54.
w jc-de-castelbajac.
com

Kenzo
(See p317).

Lanvin
15 Rue du Faubourg
St-Honoré 75008.
Map 14 F4. **Tel** 01 44 71
31 25. **w** lanvin.com
One of several branches.

Loft Design By
18 Ave Franklin
Roosevelt 75008. **Map** 5
A5. **Tel** 01 45 61 12 37.
One of several branches.

Michel Axel
44 Rue du Dragon 75006.
Map 12 D4.
Tel 01 42 84 13 86.
w michelaxel.com

Paul Smith
22 Blvd Raspail 75007.
Map 12 D4.
Tel 01 53 63 08 74.

Pierre Cardin
(See p317).

Printemps Homme
64 Blvd Haussmann
75009. **Map** 5 A4.
Tel 01 42 82 50 00.

Saint Laurent
6 Pl St-Sulpice
75006. **Map** 12 D4.
Tel 01 43 29 43 00.
w ysl.com

Sandro
30 Pl du Marché St-
Honoré 75001. **Map** 12
E1. **Tel** 01 58 62 49 00.

Versace
45 Ave Montaigne
75008. **Map** 10 F1.
Tel 01 47 42 88 02.
w versace.com

Lifestyle Stores

Colette
(See p317).

Montaigne Market
57 Ave Montaigne
75008. **Map** 5 A5.
Tel 01 42 56 58 58.
w montaigne
market.com

Spree
16 Rue de La Vieuville
75018. **Map** 6 F1.
Tel 01 42 23 41 40.
w spree.fr

Vintage and Second-Hand Stores

Alternatives
18 Rue du Roi-de-Sicile
75004. **Map** 13 C3.
Tel 01 42 78 31 50.

Depôt-Vente de Buci-Bourbon
4 Rue de Bourbon-le-
Château 75006.
Map 12 E4.
Tel 01 46 34 28 28.

Didier Ludot
24 Galerie Montpensier
75001. **Map** 12 E1.
Tel 01 42 96 06 56.
w didierludot.fr

Le Mouton à Cinq Pattes
8/18 Rue St-Placide
75006. **Map** 11 C5.
Tel 01 45 48 86 26.
One of several branches.

Réciproque
89-92-95 & 101 Rue de la
Pompe 75016. **Map** 9 A1.
Tel 01 47 04 30 28.

Jewellery

The *couture* houses probably stock some of the best jewellery and scarves. **Chanel's** jewels are classics, while **Hermès** offers elegant designs in natural materials. **Yves Saint Laurent** is a great place for accessories.

Among the main expensive Paris jewellery outlets are **Boucheron**, **Mauboussin** and **Poiray**. They are for the serious jewellery buyer. Other top retailers include **Harry Winston** and **Cartier**. **Dinh Van** has some quirky pieces, whilst **Mikimoto** is a must for pearls and **H Stern** has some innovative designs using semi-precious and precious stones. For a range of more unusual jewellery and accessories, try the **Swarovski Boutique**, which is owned by the Swarovksi crystal family.

Trends and imitations can be found around the Marais, the Bastille and Les Halles, in that order for quality. Those of note include **Scooter**, where chic young Parisians shop, **Métal Pointu's**, which sells great fantasy jewellery, and **Agatha** for copies of Chanel designs and basics.

Exquisite silver pieces and fine jewellery are available at the famous **Tiffany and Co's** Parisian outlets, which are located on the chic Rue de la Paix.

Another Parisian jeweller, **Monsieur**, creates fine hand-made jewellery. These are available at their Marais atelier-boutique.

Shoes, Bags and Belts

Fairtrade trainers (organic cotton and natural Amazonian rubber) by Veja can be found in **Le Bon Marché**. Go to **Repetto** for cult pumps in a host of colours, or **Sidonie Larizzi**, who will make up shoes from one of numerous leather swatches. Current favourites with the fashion set include **Michel Perry**, **Jérôme Dreyfuss** and **Robert Clergerie**. **Christian Louboutin** and **Rodolphe Ménudier** are mainstays for sexy stilettos. **Carel** stocks smart basics, **Cosmo Paris** and

Vivaldi sell trendy models and **Jonak** is a must for good imitations of designer footwear. **Bowen** has a selection of traditional men's shoes and **Berluti** is the last word in elegance for many Parisian men.

Beautifully made leather goods can be found at **Longchamp**, **Gucci** and **Hermès**, who still make special orders in their Paris workshops. For luxe Italian leather, **Prada's** products are of the highest quality. For ladies' hand-bags, nothing beats **Chanel** or **Dior** at the top end of the scale, although **Goyard** comes close. Mid-range bags from **Furla** are a great compromise, as are the colourful bags from **Karine Dupont**. Fabric bags from **Jamin Puech**, **Vanessa Bruno** or **Hervé Chapelier** are a feature in every chic Parisian closet. For a great range of shoes, accessories and bags at reasonable prices, **Lollipops** boutiques can be found across Paris.

Hats

One of Paris's favourite milliners is **Marie Mercié**. **Anthony Peto** now creates men's hats at her old shop in Rue Tiquetonne. For quirky creations in wool, try **Grevi** who sell matching scarves and gloves.

Lingerie

For a delightful selection of beautiful, modern lingerie go to **Fifi Chachnil**. La Boîte à Bas sells fine French stockings, whereas **Princesse Tam Tam** offers trendy, quality items at reasonable prices, whilst divine designer underwear can be found at cult store **Sabbia Rosa**. The ultimate in magnificent Parisian lingerie can be bought off the peg or made to order at **Cadolle**, the store which invented the bra. **Aubade**, known for its sophisticated and sensual lingerie, is a trusted brand amongst French women.

Size Chart

For Australian sizes, follow the British and American conversions.

Children's clothing

French	2–3	4–5	6–7	8–9	10–11	12	14	14+ (years)	
British	2–3	4–5	6–7	8–9	10–11	12	14	14+ (years)	
American	2–3	4–5	6–6x	7–8	10–11	12	14	16 (size)	

Children's shoes

French	24	25½	27	28	29	30	32	33	34
British	7	8	9	10	11	12	13	1	2
American	7½	8½	9½	10½	11½	12½	13½	1½	2½

Women's dresses coats and skirts

French	34	36	38	40	42	44	46
British	6	8	10	12	14	16	18
American	2	4	6	8	10	12	14

Women's blouses and sweaters

French	81	84	87	90	93	96	99 (cms)
British	31	32	34	36	38	40	42 (inches)
American	6	8	10	12	14	16	18 (size)

Women's shoes

French	36	37	38	39	40	41
British	3	4	5	6	7	8
American	5	6	7	8	9	10

Men's suits

French	44	46	48	50	52	54	56	58
British	34	36	38	40	42	44	46	48
American	34	36	38	40	42	44	46	48

Men's shirts

French	36	38	39	41	42	43	44	45
British	14	15	15½	16	16½	17	17½	18
American	14	15	15½	16	16½	17	17½	18

Men's shoes

French	39	40	41	42	43	44	45	46
British	6	7	7½	8	9	10	11	12
American	7	7½	8	8½	9½	10½	11	11½

DIRECTORY

Jewellery

Agatha
97 Rue de Rennes 75006.
Map 12 D5.
Tel 01 45 48 92 57.
W agatha.fr
One of several branches.

Boucheron
26 Pl Vendôme 75001.
Map 6 D5. **Tel** 01 42 61 58
16. W boucheron.com
One of several branches.

Cartier
13 Rue de la Paix 75002.
Map 6 D5. **Tel** 01 58 18
23 00. W cartier.fr
One of several branches.

Chanel
(See p317).

Dinh Van
16 Rue de la Paix 75002.
Map 6 D5. **Tel** 01 42 61
74 49. W dinhvan.com
One of several branches.

H Stern
Westin Hotel, 3 Rue
Castiglione 75001.
Map 12 D1. **Tel** 01 42 60
22 27. W hstern.net
One of several branches.

Harry Winston
6 Rue de la Paix,
75002. **Map** 6 D5.
Tel 01 47 20 03 09.
W harrywinston.com

Mauboussin
20 Pl Vendôme 75001.
Map 6 D5.
Tel 01 44 55 10 00.
W mauboussin.fr

Métal Pointu's
19 Rue des Francs-
Bourgeois 75004. **Map** 14
D3. **Tel** 01 40 29 44 34.
W metalpointus.com

Mikimoto
8 Pl Vendôme 75001.
Map 6 D5. **Tel** 01 42 60 33
55. W mikimoto.fr

Monsieur
53 Rue Charlot 75003.
Map 14 D2.
Tel 01 42 71 12 65.
W monsieur-paris.com

Poiray
8 Rue de la Paix 75002.
Map 6 D5. **Tel** 01 42 97
99 00. W poiray.com

Saint Laurent
32 Rue du Faubourg-St-
Honoré 75008. **Map** 5 C5.
Tel 01 42 65 74 59.

Scooter
19 Rue du Dragon 75006.
Map 12 D4.
Tel 01 45 49 48 28.
One of several branches.

Swarovski Boutique
146 Ave des Champs
Elysees 75008. **Map** 4 E4.
Tel 01 45 61 13 80.
W swarovski.com

Tiffany & Co
6 Rue de la Paix 75002.
Map 6 D5.
Tel 01 40 20 20 20.
One of two branches.

Shoes, Bags and Belts

Berluti
26 Rue Marbeuf 75008.
Map 4 F5. **Tel** 01 53 93
97 97. W berluti.com

Bowen
12 Rue Marbeuf 75008.
Map 4 F5.
Tel 01 47 20 45 90.

Carel
2 Rue Tronchet 75008.
Map 6 D4.
Tel 01 43 66 21 58.
One of several branches.

Christian Louboutin
38-40 Rue de Grenelle
75007. **Map** 10 F3.
Tel 0800 10 19 19 19.
One of two branches.

Cosmo Paris
25 Rue du Four 75006.
Map 12 E4.
Tel 01 56 24 15 49.

Furla
281 Rue St-Honoré 75008.
Map 5 C5. **Tel** 01 42 97
50 47. W furla.com
One of several branches.

Goyard
233 Rue St-Honoré
75001. **Map** 5 C5.
Tel 01 42 60 57 04.
W goyard.com

Gucci
350 Rue Saint Honoré
75001. **Map** 12 D1.
Tel 01 42 66 21 58.
W gucci.com

Hermès
(See p317).

Hervé Chapelier
1bis Rue du Vieux-
Colombier 75006.
Map 12 D4.
Tel 01 44 07 06 50.

Jamin Puech
61 Rue de Hauteville
75010. **Map** 7 B4.
Tel 01 40 22 08 32.

Jérôme Dreyfuss
1 Rue Jacob 75006.
Map 12 E4.
Tel 01 43 54 70 93.

Jonak
70 Rue de Rennes
75006. **Map** 16 D1.
Tel 01 45 48 27 11.
One of several branches.

Karine Dupont
16 Rue du Cherche-Midi
75006. **Map** 12 D4.
Tel 01 42 74 20 20.

Le Bon Marché
24 Rue de Sèvres 75007.
Map 11 C5.
Tel 01 44 39 80 00.

Lollipops
326 Rue Vaugirard 75015.
Tel 01 56 08 11 11.
W lollipopsparis.fr

Longchamp
21 Rue du Vieux
Colombier 75006.
Map 12 D4.
Tel 01 42 22 74 75.
W longchamp.com

Michel Perry
42 Rue de Grenelle
75007. **Map** 10 F3.
Tel 01 42 22 99 12.

Prada
6 Rue du Faubourg Saint-
Honoré 75008.
Map 5 C5.
Tel 01 58 18 63 30.
W prada.com

Repetto
22 Rue de la Paix 75002.
Map 6 D5.
Tel 01 44 71 83 12.
One of several branches.

Robert Clergerie
5 Rue du Cherche-Midi
75006.
Map 12 D4.
Tel 01 45 48 75 47.

Rodolphe Ménudier
14 Rue de Castiglione
75001. **Map** 12 D1.
Tel 06 07 02 81 91.

Vanessa Bruno
(See p319).

Vivaldi
38 Rue de Rivoli 75001.
Map 13 A2.
Tel 01 44 54 08 56.

Hats

Anthony Peto
56 Rue Tiquetonne 75002.
Map 13 A1.
Tel 01 40 26 60 68.

Grevi
1 Place Alphonse-Deville
75006. **Map** 14 D3.
Tel 01 42 22 05 69.
W grevi.com

Marie Mercié
23 Rue St-Sulpice 75006.
Map 12 E4.
Tel 01 43 26 45 83.

Lingerie

Aubade
22 Rue du Vieux
Colombier 75006.
Map 12 D4.
Tel 01 45 48 16 62.

La Boîte à Bas
27 Rue Boissy-d'Anglas
75008. **Map** 5 C5.
Tel 01 42 66 26 85.

Cadolle
4 Rue Cambon 75001.
Map 6 D5.
Tel 01 42 60 94 22.

Fifi Chachnil
68 Rue Jean-Jacques
Rousseau 75001.
Map 12 F2.
Tel 01 42 21 19 93.
W fifichachnil.com

Princesse Tam Tam
5 Rue Montmartre
75001. **Map** 13 A1.
Tel 01 45 08 47 52.
One of several branches.

Sabbia Rosa
73 Rue des Sts-Pères
75006. **Map** 12 D4.
Tel 01 45 48 88 37.

Gifts and Souvenirs

Paris has a wealth of stylish gifts and typical souvenirs, from designer accessories and perfume to French foods and Eiffel Tower paperweights. Shops on the Rue de Rivoli and around major tourist attractions such as Nôtre Dame or Sacré Coeur offer a range of cheap holiday trinkets. Les Drapeaux de France sells historic uniformed and costumed figurines. For upscale mementos, try quality reproductions of artwork and jewellery in museum boutiques – Le Musée du Louvre, Musée d'Orsay, Les Arts Décoratifs or Musée Carnavalet.

Gifts

Printemps has excellent own-brand accessories, especially ladies' handbags. The luxury floor is ideal for window-shopping or high-end purchases such as Tiffany jewellery or Cartier watches. It also stocks small, reasonably-priced items.

For those looking to take home gastronomic tasters, the famed food hall at **Le Bon Marché**, La Grande Epicerie, offers anything and everything you might need for a gourmet feast or quick snack.

Galeries Lafayette now boasts the world's biggest lingerie department.

Perfume and Cosmetics

Many shops advertise discounted perfume and cosmetics. Some even offer duty-free perfume to shoppers from outside the EU, with discounts on the marked prices when you show your passport. They include **Eiffel Shopping** near the Eiffel Tower. The **Sephora** chain has a big selection, or try the department stores for a range of designers' perfumes. In particular, the beauty department at **Printemps** is one of Europe's biggest with one of the world's largest perfume selections. It stocks many beauty brands that are hard to find elsewhere.

If you fancy stepping back in time, **Detaille 1905** is the place for you. This old-fashioned perfumery filled to the brim with fragrant goodies personifies belle époque style and charm. The shop's own range of six main fragrances for women and for men is still made from

original recipes. **Parfums Caron** also has many scents created over 100 years ago, which are unavailable elsewhere, so this is the place to find exclusive presents that you will almost certainly decide to keep for yourself. Beautifully packaged perfumes made from natural essences are available from **Annick Goutal**. **Guerlain** has the ultimate in beauty care, while the elegant shops of **L'Artisan Parfumeur** specialize in exquisitely packaged scents that evoke specific memories. They have also reissued favourites from the past, including perfume made to exactly the same formula as one that was worn at the court of Versailles. Famed perfume-maker **Fragonard** sells an array of scents, soaps and candles from the South of France. **Frédéric Malle** is another big name in top-of-the-range scent. Exclusive perfumes can also be found in the beautiful surroundings of the gardens of the Palais Royal at **Serge Lutens**. Lutens, the company's creative director and a renowned parfumier, creates exquisite and exotic scents which can only be bought in this particular store.

Paris is also home to several *haute* cosmetics designers. One of the most renowned is Terry de Gunzberg, whose store **By Terry** stocks fantastic products. Personalize your gift by having a message inscribed on the sleek, silver packaging.

Household Goods

Though certain items are obviously rather delicate to carry home, it is difficult to ignore some of the world's most elegant tableware, found in Paris's chic shops. If you are wary of loading up your holdall with breakable pieces, many shops will arrange to ship crockery overseas. Luxury household goods can be found on the Rue Royale, where many of the best shops are located. They sell items such as rustic china and reproduction and modern silver-ware. **Lalique's** Art Nouveau and Art Deco glass sculptures are collected all over the world. Impeccable silverware, including fine photograph frames and even chopsticks, comes from **Christofle**.

For a great variety of porcelain and crystal, try **La Cristallerie Paradis**, which stocks Baccarat, Daum and Limoges crystal, or go to **Baccarat** itself. Baccarat also has a boutique on the Place de la Madeleine. The interior designer **Pierre Frey** has a showroom displaying fabrics which have been made into a fabulous array of cushions, bedspreads and tablecloths. Excellent quality bed linen can also be found at **Yves Delorme**.

Eiffel Tower cheese graters, porcelain doll umbrellas and dog-shaped pie-cutters add just the right amount of kitsch to any gift from design shop **Pylones**. **La Chaise Longue** has a selection of well-designed *objets*, along with fun gift ideas. **Sengtai** sells stylish, ethically and ecologically produced tableware and decorative items. **Storie Shop** and **Muskhane** stock hip and ethnic accessories for funky flats. The extensive interior design store at **Galeries Lafayette** has everything a proud home-owner could need from fancy mops to cutting-edge three-piece suites. **Sentou** stores are full of chic designer pieces for Parisian living. Sentou Raspail, on the Left Bank, offers the store's complete range while Sentou Marais focuses on lighting and furniture.

Kitchen equipment which can't be beaten, including copper pans, comes from **E. Dehillerin**. A must-have item in many Parisian homes is a scented candle from **Diptyque**. *Figuier* is their most popular fragrance. The basement at **BHV** *(see p313)* is full of all sorts of tools and equipment for doing up your house and sprucing up the garden.

Books, Magazines and Newspapers

Many English and American publications can be found at large magazine stands or at some of the bookshops listed. If French is no obstacle, the weeklies *Pariscope*, *L'Officiel des Spectacles* and *Télérama*'s Paris supplement *Sortir* have the most comprehensive listings for the city.

The *International Herald Tribune*, an English-language daily newspaper, is published in Paris and contains good American news coverage. The *Paris Voice* webzine and the bi-weekly FUSAC (*France–USA Contacts* small ads magazine) are also published in English.

Some of the large department stores have a book section *(see* Department Stores *p313)*. There is a large branch of **WHSmith**, and **Galignani** was the first English bookshop to be established in Europe in 1801. The **San Francisco Book Company** offers English-language books at good prices and **Shakespeare & Co** is a Left Bank legend facing Notre-Dame. The **Abbey Bookshop** has a good selection of literary and

academic second-hand books. **Agora Presse** stocks a vast range of magazines, including a many titles from abroad.

French-language bookshops include **Librarie La Hune**, specializing in art, design, architecture, photography, fashion and cinema; **Gibert Joseph**, selling general and educational books; and **Le Divan**, which has social science, psychology, literature and poetry sections. **I Love My Blender** on Rue du Temple is dedicated to English-language authors and sells wonderful gifts.

Flowers

Some Parisian florists such as **Pascal Mutel** are very well known, so be sure to buy one of their signature vases. **Monceau Fleurs** offers a good selection at reasonable prices; **Mille Feuilles** and **Jacques Semer** in Montmartre. is the place to go to in the Marais. *(See also* Specialist Shops *p324)*. Stunning silk flowers can be found at **Sia**, a chic store that brims over with beautiful artifical blooms.

Specialist Shops

For cigars, **A La Civette** is perhaps Paris's most beautiful tobacconist. It is also probably the most devoted to its wares and has humidified shop windows to keep its merchandise in top condition.

Go to **A L'Olivier** in the Rue de Rivoli for a wonderful selection of exotic oils and vinegar. Or, if honey is your favourite condiment, try **La Maison du Miel**, where you can buy all sorts of fine honeys, including varieties made from lavender and acacia flowers. You can also buy refreshing beeswax soap and a variety of candles here.

Mariage Frères has become a cult favourite for its 350 varieties of tea; it also sells a number of teapots and its tea shop serves up many tempting treats *(see p310)*.

Couture fabrics can be purchased from a range at **Wolff et Descourtis**. For an unusual gift of traditional French card games or tarot cards, go to **Jeux Descartes**.

Le Grand Recré is a chain of toyshops, while the name **Armorial** is synonymous with high-quality stationery and paper products. **Calligrane** sells a tempting range of high-quality desk accessories and paper products.

Hidden away down an atmospheric passage, **Pep's** repairs all broken umbrellas and parasols in France's only brolly hospital.

For the ultimate in eccentric shopping, visit **Deyrolle**, Paris's famous taxidermist. Where else could you find the right gift for the person who has everything.

DIRECTORY

Souvenir and Museum Shops

Les Arts Décoratifs
107 Rue de Rivoli 75001.
Map 12 D1.
Tel 01 44 55 57 50.

Les Drapeaux de France
1 Place Colette 75001.
Map 12 E2.
Tel 01 40 20 00 11.

Musée Carnavalet
(See p97).

Le Musée du Louvre
(See p123).

Musée d'Orsay
(See p147).

Gifts

Le Bon Marché
24 Rue de Sèvres 75007.
Map 11 C5.
Tel 01 44 39 80 00.

Galeries Lafayette
40 Blvd Haussmann
75009. **Map** 6 E4.
Tel 01 42 82 34 56.
One of two branches.

Printemps
64 Blvd Haussmann

75009. **Map** 6 D4.
Tel 01 42 82 50 00.

Perfume and Cosmetics

Annick Goutal
16 Rue de Bellechasse
75007.
Map 11 C3.
Tel 01 45 51 36 13.
One of several branches.

L'Artisan Parfumeur
24 Blvd Raspail 75007.
Map 16 D1.
Tel 01 42 22 23 32.
One of several branches.

By Terry
36 Passage Vérot-Dodat
75001.
Map 12 F2.
Tel 01 44 76 00 76.

Detaille 1905
10 Rue St-Lazare
75009.
Map 6 D3.
Tel 01 48 78 68 50.

Eiffel Shopping
9 Ave de Suffren
75007.
Map 10 D3.
Tel 01 45 66 55 30.

DIRECTORY

Fragonard
203 Rue St Honoré 75001.
Map 12 D1.
Tel 01 47 03 07 07.
W fragonard.com

Frédéric Malle
21 Rue du Mont
Thabor 75001.
Map 12 D1.
Tel 01 42 22 16 89.

Guerlain
68 Ave des Champs-
Elysées 75008.
Map 4 F5.
Tel 01 45 62 52 57.
W guerlain.com
One of several branches.

Parfums Caron
34 Ave Montaigne
75008. **Map** 10 F1.
Tel 01 47 23 40 82.

Sephora
70-72 Ave des Champs-
Elysées 75008.
Map 11 B1. **Tel** 01 53 93
22 50. W sephora.fr
One of several branches.

Serge Lutens
142 Galerie de Valois
75001. **Map** 12 F1.
Tel 01 49 27 09 09.

Household Goods

Baccarat
11 Pl de la Madeleine
75008. **Map** 5 C5.
Tel 01 42 65 36 26.
W baccarat.fr
(See also p204).

La Chaise Longue
30 Rue Croix-des-Petits-
Champs 75001. **Map** 12
F1. **Tel** 01 42 96 32 14.
One of several branches.

Christofle
24 Rue de la Paix 75002.
Map 6 D5.
Tel 01 42 65 62 43.
W christofle.com
One of several branches.

Cire Trudon
78 Rue de Seine 75006.
Map 12 E4.
Tel 01 43 26 46 50.

La Cristallerie Paradis
17 bis Rue de Paradis
75010. **Map** 7 B4.
Tel 01 48 24 72 15.

Diptyque
34 Blvd St Germain 75006.
Map 13 B5.
Tel 01 43 26 77 44.
W diptyqueparis.com
One of several branches.

E. Dehillerin
18-20 Rue Coquillière
75001.
Map 12 F1.
Tel 01 42 36 53 13.
W e-dehillerin.fr

Lalique
11 Rue Royale 75008.
Map 5 C5.
Tel 01 53 05 12 81.

Muskhane
3 Rue Pastourelle 75003.
Map 13 C2.
Tel 09 77 06 53 47.

Pierre Frey
1 & 2 Rue Furstenberg
75006. **Map** 12 E4.
Tel 01 46 33 73 00.
W pierrefrey.com

Pylones
57 Rue St Louis en L'Ile
75004. **Map** 13 B4.
Tel 01 46 34 05 02.
W pylones.com

Sengtai
6 Rue du Pont aux Choux,
75003.
Map 14 D2.
Tel 09 82 38 43 58.

Sentou
26 Blvd Raspail 75007.
Map 12 D4.
Tel 01 45 49 00 05.
29 Rue François Miron
75004.
Map 13 C3.
Tel 01 42 78 50 60.

Storie Shop
20 Rue Delambre 75014.
Map 16 D2.
Tel 01 83 56 01 98.
W storieshop.com

Yves Delorme
8 Rue Vavin 75006.
Map 16 D1.
Tel 01 44 07 23 14.

Books, Magazines and Newspapers

Abbey Bookshop
29 Rue de la
Parcheminerie 75005.
Map 13 A4.
Tel 01 46 33 16 24.

Agora Presse
19 Rue des Archives 75004.
Map 13 C3.
Tel 01 42 74 47 24.

Le Divan
203 Rue de la Convention
75015. **Map** 12 E3.
Tel 01 53 68 90 68.

Galignani
224 Rue de Rivoli 75001.
Map 13 A2.
Tel 01 42 60 76 07.

Gibert Joseph
26-34 Blvd St-Michel
75006. **Map** 12 F5.
Tel 01 44 41 88 88.

Librarie La Hune
18 Rue de l'Abbaye 75006.
Map 12 E4.
Tel 01 45 48 35 85.

I Love My Blender
36 Rue du Temple 75004.
Map 13 C2. **Tel** 01 42 77 50
32. W ilovemyblender.fr

San Francisco Book Company
17 Rue M le Prince 75006.
Map 12 F5.
Tel 01 43 29 15 70.

Shakespeare & Co
37 Rue de la Bûcherie
75005. **Map** 13 A4.
Tel 01 43 25 40 93.

WHSmith
248 Rue de Rivoli 75001.
Map 11 C1.
Tel 01 44 77 88 99.
W whsmith.fr

Flowers

Jacques Semer
56 Rue Caulaincourt
75018. **Map** 2 E5.
Tel 01 42 23 53 04.

Monceau Fleurs
104 Rue Monge 75005.
Map 17 B2. **Tel** 01 47 07
17 94. W monceau
fleurs.com

Pascal Mutel
95 Rue de Courcelles
75017. **Map** 4 E2.
Tel 01 47 63 40 78.
W pascalmutel.com

Sia
3-5 Blvd Malesherbes
75008. **Map** 5 5C.
Tel 01 42 66 11 73.

Specialist Shops

A La Civette
157 Rue St-Honoré 75001.
Map 12 F2. **Tel** 01 42 96
04 99. W alacivette.fr

A L'Olivier
23 Rue de Rivoli 75004.
Map 13 C3. **Tel** 01 48 04
86 59. W alolivier.com

Armorial
109 Bd Hausmann 75008.
Map 5 B4. **Tel** 01 42 60 20
08. W armorial.fr

Calligrane
6 Rue du Pont-Louis-
Philippe 75004. **Map** 13
B4. **Tel** 01 48 04 09 00.

Deyrolle
46 Rue du Bac 75007.
Map 12 D3.
Tel 01 42 22 30 07.

Jeux Descartes
52 Rues des Écoles 75005.
Map 13 A5.
Tel 01 43 26 79 83.

La Maison du Miel
24 Rue Vignon 75009.
Map 6 D5.
Tel 01 47 42 26 70.
W maisondumiel.com

Le Grand Recré
8-12 Rue d'Amsterdam
75009. **Map** 6 D3.
Tel 01 42 93 24 41.
One of several branches.

Mariage Frères
30 Rue du Bourg-Tibourg
75004. **Map** 13 C3.
Tel 01 42 72 28 11.
W mariagefreres.com
One of several branches.

Pep's
223 Rue St-Martin 75003.
Map 8 E4. **Tel** 01 42 78 11
67. W peps-paris.com.fr

Wolff et Descourtis
18 Galerie Vivienne
75002. **Map** 12 F1.
Tel 01 42 61 80 84.

Food and Drink

Paris is as famous for food as it is for fashion. Gastronomic treats include *foie gras*, cold meats from the *charcuterie*, cheese and wine. Certain streets are so overflowing with food shops that you can put together a picnic for 20 in no time: try the Rue Montorgueil (*see p331*). The Rue Rambuteau, running either side of the Pompidou Centre, has a marvellous row of fishmongers, cheese delicatessens and shops selling prepared foods. (*See also* What to Eat and Drink in Paris *pp292–5* and Cafés, Tea Salons and Bars *pp308–9*.)

Bread and Cakes

There is a vast range of breads and pastries in France's capital. The *baguette* is often translated as "French bread"; a *bâtard* is similar but thicker, while a *ficelle* is thinner. A *fougasse* is a crusty, flat loaf made from *baguette* dough, often filled with onions, cheese, herbs or spices. Since most French bread contains no fat, it goes stale quickly: the sooner you eat it, the better. The French would never eat day-old bread so be sure to be up in time to make it to the bakery for breakfast!

Croissants can be bought *ordinaire* or *au beurre* – the latter is flakier and more buttery. *Pain au chocolat* is a chocolate-filled pastry eaten for breakfast and *chausson aux pommes* is filled with apples. There are also pear, plum and rhubarb variations. A *pain aux raisins* is a bread-like wheel filled with custard and raisins.

Poilâne sells perhaps the only bread in Paris known by the name of its baker (the late Lionel, brother of Max), and his hearty wholewheat bread is tremendously popular, with freshly baked loaves being jetted around the world to satisfy the cravings of certain film stars. There are always big queues at the weekend and around 4pm when a fresh batch comes out of the oven.

Many think **Ganachaud** bakes the best bread in Paris. Thirty different kinds, including ingredients such as walnuts and fruit, are made in old-fashioned ovens.

Maison Kayser, a high-end chain bakery, produces a variety of artisan breads and baguettes including *pain au cèrèale* (multi-grain bread) and *pain d'amande* (almond bread), the owner's favourite.

It is very important to remember that every Parisian has a favourite neighbourhood bakery, so when you are buying bread locally, simply plump for the shop with the longest queues.

Many of the Jewish delicatessens have the best ryes and the only pumpernickels in town. One of the best known is **Sacha Finkelsztajn**.

Le Moulin de la Vierge uses a wood fire to bake organic breads and rich pound cakes. **Boulangerie de l'Ouest** is second only to **Max Poilâne** in the Montparnasse area with *baguettes*, *fougasses*, cakes and pastries. **Pâtisserie Secco** sells a good selection of filled *baguettes*, salads and excellent cakes. **Pierre Hermé** is to cakes what Chanel is to fashion, while **Ladurée** macaroons are legendary.

Chocolate

Like all food in France, chocolate is to be savoured. **Christian Constant**'s low-sugar creations are made with pure cocoa and are known to connoisseurs. **Dalloyau** makes all types of chocolate and is not too expensive (it's also known for its pâtisserie and cold meats). **Fauchon** is world famous for its luxury food products. Its chocolates are excellent, as is the pâtisserie. **Lenôtre** makes classic truffles and pralines. Robert Linxe at **La Maison du Chocolat** is constantly inventing fresh, rich chocolates with mouthwatering exotic ingredients. **Richart** boasts beautifully presented and hugely-expensive chocolates, which are usually coated with dark chocolate or liqueur-filled. **Debauve & Gallais** are best known for their wonderful and delicious glacé chestnut treats (*marron glacés*).

Charcuterie and Foie Gras

Charcuteries often sell cheese, snails, truffles, smoked salmon, caviar and wine as well as cold meats. **Fauchon** has a good grocery, as does the department store **Le Bon Marché**. **Hédiard** is a luxury shop similar to Fauchon, and **Maison de la Truffe** sells *foie gras* and cured salami sausages as well as truffles. For Beluga caviar, Georgian tea and Russian vodka, go to **Boutique Petrossian**.

Award-winning **Gilles Verot** is known for his *charcuterie* delicacies, which are also available in London and New York.

Aux Vrais Produits d'Auvergne has a number of outlets where you can stock up on dried and fresh sausages and delicious Cantal cheese (rather like Cheddar). **Maison Pou** is a sparklingly clean and popular shop selling *pâté en croute* (pâté baked in pastry), *boudins* (black and white puddings), Lyonnais sausages, ham and *foie gras*. Just off the Champs-Elysées, **Vignon** has superb *foie gras* and Lyonnais sausages as well as popular prepared foods.

Together with truffles and caviar, *foie gras* is the ultimate in gourmet food, from cheaper *paté de foie gras* to the more expensive whole liver itself. Though most specialist food shops sell *foie gras*, you can be sure of quality at **Comtesse du Barry**, which has six outlets in Paris. **Divay** is relatively inexpensive and will ship overseas. **Comptoir de la Gastronomie** has a range of excellent *foie gras*.

Cheese

Although Camembert is undoubtedly a favourite, there is an overwhelming range of cheeses available.

A friendly *fromager* will help you choose. **Marie-Anne Cantin** is one of the leading figures in the fight to protect traditional production methods, and her fine cheeses are available at the shop that she inherited from her father. Some say that **Alléosse** is the best cheese delicatessen in Paris. It is an Aladdin's cave of cheeses made according to traditional methods and matured in the shop's own cellars. **Fromagerie Quatrehomme** sells farm-made cheeses, many of which are in danger of becoming extinct; these include a rare and delicious truffle Brie (when in season). **Le Jardin Fromager** is one of the best shops in Paris for all types of cheese – the *chèvre* (goat's cheese) is particularly good, and outside on the pavement, the daily specials are offered at remarkably reasonable prices. **Laurent Dubois**, a cheesemaker on the Blvd Saint Germain, is known for his speciality, marinated goat cheese. **Androuet** is a Parisian institution with several branches across the city. Try a pungent Munster or a really ripe Brie. A charming cheese shop on the bustling Rue Montorgueil market street, **La Fermette**, offers a dazzling array of dairy products, which the helpful and friendly staff will happily vacuum-pack for the journey home. This is imperative when bringing cheese through customs, so don't forget to ask your *fromager* to wrap it for you. Well-heeled locals queue in the street to buy oozing *livarot* and sharp *chèvre* from **La Fromagerie d'Auteuil**.

Wine

The chain store which has practically cornered the everyday tippling market is **Nicolas** – there's a branch in every neighbourhood with a range of wines to suit all pockets. As a rule, the salespeople are knowledgeable and helpful. Try the charming **Legrand Filles et Fils** *(see p311)* for a carefully chosen selection. **Caves Taillevent** on the Rue du Faubourg-St-Honoré is worth a sightseeing tour. It is an enormous, overwhelming cellar with some of the most expensive wines. **Cave Péret** on the Rue Daguerre has a vast selection of wines and can offer personal advice. The beautiful **Ryst-Dupeyron**, in the St-Germain quarter, displays whiskies, wines, ports, and Monsieur Ryst's own Armagnac. He will even personalize a bottle for that special occasion.

Other great wine stores include **Lavinia** *(see p311)*, which is the largest in Europe, and **La Cave des Papilles**, one of the best suppliers of organic wines in the capital. The staff in **Les Caves Augé** are also very knowledgeable and friendly.

Champagne

Fabulous fizz can be found at most wine stores, but some know their bubbles better than others. The **Nicolas** chain, mentioned above, frequently has great offers on well-known brands, so this is a good place to come and stock up on your favourite famous tipple. **La Cave des Martyrs**, on the Rue des Martyrs, is a friendly and well-stocked wine shop with charming staff to help you with your selection. The **De Verre en Vers**, on the Rue d'Auteuil, is a good place to go for hard-to-find vintages. The *sommelier* here is very knowledgeable and able to provide excellent alternative advice if your preferred brand is out of stock. **Legrand Filles et Fils**, on the Rue de la Banque, is one of the few shops in Paris to stock Salon, a rare high-end champagne. They also sell champagne by Jacques Selosse which is little-known but well-loved by champagne connoisseurs. **Les Caves du Panthéon**, on the Rue Saint Jacques, is a small but lovely wine shop which has a particularly interesting selection of champagnes. **Le Repaire du Bacchus** is a Parisian chain reputed for the quality of its wines, including champagnes, and its knowledgeable staff. The climate-controlled section of **Hédiard** at Place de la Madeleine is a good place to find rare, fine sparkling wines. The upscale foodhall **La Grande Epicerie** has a wine cellar with a fine selection of champagnes. A stroll along the Boulevard St-Germain can be enhanced with a visit to **La Maison des Millésimes**, a wonderful store carrying excellent vintages of household-name champagnes.

Oysters

The ultimate aphrodisac for some, a slippery sea creature for others, there is no doubt that the once humble oyster can cause heated debate. In Paris, the argument tends to be over the best place to purchase the gourmet mollusc, with every seafood fan worth his platter claiming a favourite spot. It is, of course, important to get it right. A deciding factor for some is the grace with which your fishmonger will agree to open them for you. In general, a polite request will be honoured, although sometimes you may have to wait a while before being presented with a platter perfect for a picnic. The fishmonger on the Rue Cler market street, **La Sablaise Poissonnerie**, has an excellent reputation as does the **Poissonnerie du Dôme** in the city's 14th arrondissement. Over in the traditionally rough-and-ready area around the Rue Oberkampf, you can find excellent oysters at the **Poissonnerie Lacroix**. If you prefer to eat your oysters on the spot, then head to an *huitrerie* (oyster bar) such as **L'Ecume Saint-Honoré** near chic Rue St-Honoré, where you can tuck into your oysters and a wide range of other shellfish straight away at the few tables tucked into the corner of the store.

DIRECTORY

Bread and Cakes

Boulangerie de l'Ouest
4 Pl Constantin Brancusi 75014. **Map** 15 C3.
Tel 01 43 21 76 18.

Ganachaud
226 Rue des Pyrénées 75020.
Tel 09 51 41 11 61.

Maison Kayser
14 Rue Monge 75005.
Map 13 B5.
Tel 01 44 07 17 81.
W **maison-kayser.com**

Max Poilâne
87 Rue Brancion 75015.
Tel 01 48 28 45 90.

Le Moulin de la Vierge
105 Rue Vercingétorix 75014. **Map** 15 A4.
Tel 01 45 43 09 84

Pâtisserie Secco
20 Rue Jean-Nicot 75007.
Map 10 F2.
Tel 01 43 17 35 20.

Pierre Hermé
72 Rue Bonaparte 75006.
Map 12 E4.
Tel 01 43 54 47 77.

Poilâne
8 Rue du Cherche-Midi 75006. **Map** 12 D4.
Tel 01 45 48 42 59.

Sacha Finkelsztajn
27 Rue des Rosiers 75004.
Map 13 C3.
Tel 01 42 72 78 91.

Chocolate

Christian Constant
37 Rue d'Assas 75006.
Map 16 E1.
Tel 01 53 63 15 15.

Dalloyau
101 Rue du Faubourg-St-Honoré 75008. **Map** 5 B5.
Tel 01 42 99 90 00.

Debauve & Gallais
30 Rue des Saints-Pères 75007. **Map** 12 D4.
Tel 01 45 48 54 67
One of two branches.

Fauchon
24–26 Pl de la Madeleine 75008. **Map** 5 C5.
Tel 01 70 39 38 00.
W **fauchon.com**

Lenôtre
36 Ave de la Motte Picquet 75007. **Map** 10 F4. **Tel** 01 45 55 71 25.
One of several branches.

La Maison du Chocolat
225 Rue du Faubourg-St-Honoré 75008. **Map** 4 E3.
Tel 01 42 27 39 44.

Richart
258 Blvd St-Germain 75007. **Map** 11 C2.
Tel 01 45 55 66 00.

Charcuterie and Foie Gras

Boutique Petrossian
18 Blvd La tour-Maubourg 75007. **Map** 11 A2.
Tel 01 44 11 32 22.

Comptoir de la Gastronomie
34 Rue Montmartre 75001. **Map** 13 A1.
Tel 01 42 33 31 32.

Comtesse du Barry
1 Rue de Sèvres 75006.
Map 12 D4. **Tel** 01 45 48 32 04. W **comtesse dubarry.com**
One of several branches.

Divay
4 Rue Bayen 75017. **Map** 4 D2. **Tel** 01 43 80 16 97.

Fauchon
26 Pl de la Madeleine 75008. **Map** 5 C5.
Tel 01 70 39 38 00.

Gilles Verot
7 Rue Lecourbe 75015.
Tel 01 47 34 01 03.
W **verot-charcuterie.fr**

Hédiard
21 Pl de la Madeleine 75008. **Map** 5 C5.
Tel 01 43 12 88 88.

Maison de la Truffe
19 Pl de la Madeleine 75008. **Map** 5 C5.
Tel 01 42 65 53 22.

Maison Pou
16 Ave des Ternes 75017. **Map** 4 D3.
Tel 01 43 80 19 24.

Vignon
13 Rue Clement Marot 75008.
Map 4 F5.
Tel 01 47 20 10 01.

Cheese

Alléosse
13 Rue Poncelet 75017.
Map 4 E3.
Tel 01 46 22 50 45.

Androuet
134 Rue Mouffetard 75005. **Map** 17 B1.
Tel 01 45 87 85 05.
W **androuet.com**

Fromagerie Quatrehomme
62 Rue de Sèvres 75007.
Map 11 C5.
Tel 01 47 34 33 45.

La Fermette
86 Rue Montorgueil 75002. **Map** 13 A1.
Tel 01 42 36 70 96.

La Fromagerie d'Auteuil
58 Rue d'Auteuil 75016.
Tel 01 45 25 07 10.

Le Jardin Fromager
53 Rue Oberkampf 75011. **Map** 14 E1.
Tel 01 48 05 19 96.

Laurent Dubois
47 Blvd Saint Germain 75005. **Map** 13 A5.
Tel 01 43 54 50 93.

Marie-Anne Cantin
12 Rue du Champ-de-Mars 75007. **Map** 10 F3.
Tel 01 45 50 43 94.

Wine

Cave Péret
6 Rue Daguerre 75014.
Map 16 D4.
Tel 01 43 22 57 05.

Les Caves Augé
116 Blvd Haussmann 75008. **Map** 5 C4.
Tel 01 45 22 16 97.

La Cave des Papilles
5 Rue Daguerre 75014.
Map 16 D4.
Tel 01 43 20 05 74.

Caves Taillevent
199 Rue du Faubourg-St-Honoré 75008. **Map** 4 F3. **Tel** 01 45 61 14 09.

Nicolas
35 Blvd Malesherbes 75008. **Map** 5 C5.
Tel 01 42 65 00 85.
W **nicolas.com**

Ryst-Dupeyron
79 Rue du Bac 75007.
Map 12 D3.
Tel 01 45 48 80 93.

Champagne

La Cave de la Grande Epicerie
38 Rue de Sèvres 75007.
Map 11 C5.
Tel 01 44 39 81 17.

La Cave des Martyrs
39 Rue des Martyrs 75009. **Map** 6 F3.
Tel 01 40 16 80 27.

Les Caves du Panthéon
174 Rue St-Jacques 75005. **Map** 13 A5.
Tel 01 46 33 90 35.

De Verre en Vers
1 Rue de Joseph de Maistre 75018.
Tel 01 46 06 80 84.

Hédiard
21 Place de la Madeleine 75008. **Map** 5 C5.
Tel 01 43 12 88 88.

La Maison des Millésimes
137 Boulevard St-Germain 75006. **Map** 12 F4.
Tel 01 40 46 80 01.

Le Repaire du Bacchus
112 rue de Mouffetard 75005. **Map** 17 B2. **Tel** 01 47 07 39 40. W **lerepaire debacchus.com**
One of several branches.

Oysters

L'Ecume Saint-Honoré
6 Rue du Marché St-Honoré 75001. **Map** 12 D1. **Tel** 01 42 61 93 87.

Poissonnerie du Dôme
4 Rue Delambre 75014.
Map 16 D2.
Tel 01 43 35 23 95.

Poissonnerie Lacroix
44 Rue Oberkampf 75011.
Map 14 E1.
Tel 01 47 00 93 13.

La Sablaise
28 Rue Cler 75007.
Map 10 F3.
Tel 01 45 51 61 78.

Art and Antiques

In Paris, you can buy art and antiques either from shops and galleries with established reputations, or from flea markets and avant-garde galleries. Many of the prestigious antiques shops and galleries are located around the Rue du Faubourg-St-Honoré and are worth a visit even if you can't afford to buy. On the Left Bank is Le Carré Rive Gauche, an organization of 30 antiques dealers. *Objets d'art* over 50 years old, worth more than a given amount (values vary for all categories of art object), will require a *Certificat pour un bien culturel* to be exported anywhere in the world (provided by the vendor), plus a *licence d'exportation* for non-EU countries. Seek professional advice from the large antique shops.

Exporting

The Ministry of Culture designates *objets d'art*. Export licences are available from the **Comité National des Conseillers du Commerce Extérieur de la France**. The **Centre des Renseignements des Douanes** has a booklet, *Bulletin Officiel des Douanes*, with all the details.

Modern Crafts and Furniture

One of the best places for furniture and *objets d'art* is **Sentou**, where you can find objects and textiles, as well as furniture by contemporary designers. Another essential venue is the showroom of the Italian designer, **Giulio Cappellini**. **Le Viaduc des Arts** (see pp272–3) is a railway viaduct, each arch of which has been transformed into a shop front and workshop space. A great place for contemporary metalwork, tapestry, sculpture, ceramics and much more.

Antiques and Objets d'Art

If you wish to buy antiques, you might like to stroll around the areas that boast many galleries – in Le Carré Rive Gauche around Quai Malaquais, try **L'Arc en Seine** and **Anne-Sophie Duval** for Art Nouveau and Art Deco. Rue Jacob is still one of the best places to seek beautiful objects, antique or modern. Close to the Louvre, the **Louvre**

des Antiquaires (see p130) sells expensive, quality furniture. On the Rue du Faubourg-St-Honoré, you will find **Didier Aaron**, expert on furniture from the 17th and 18th centuries. **Village St-Paul**, between the Quai des Célestins, the Rue Saint Paul and the Rue Charlemagne, is the most charming group of antiques shops and is also open on Sundays.

Philippe de Beauvais focuses on antique lighting fixtures, especially chandeliers. **Le Village Suisse** in the south of the city also groups many art and antiques dealers. Located in Le Village Suisse, **Ghislaine Chaplier** carries an eclectic inventory of small antiques and rare glass objects.

Reproductions, Posters and Prints

A beautiful, contemporary art gallery called **Artcurial** on the Place des Champs-Elysées has one of the best selections of international art periodicals, books and prints. On the Boulevard Saint Germain, **Librarie La Hune** is a popular bookshop, particularly for art publications. The museum bookshops, especially those in the Palais de Tokyo (see p205), Louvre (see p123), Musée d'Orsay (see p147) and Pompidou Centre (see p111) are good places to buy art books, posters and postcards.

Galerie Documents on the Rue de Seine sells original antique posters. Or leaf through

the second-hand book stalls along the banks of the Seine.

Art Galleries

Established art galleries are located on or around the Avenue Montaigne. The **Louise Leiris** gallery on Rue de Téhran was founded in 1920 by D H Kahnweiler, the dealer who "discovered" both Georges Braque and Pablo Picasso.

Artcurial Gallery, located on the ground floor of the Hôtel Dassault, holds regular exhibitions and specializes in limited editions of contemporary sculpture, photography, prints and multiples. **Galerie Lelong** is devoted to contemporary artists.

On the Left Bank, **Adrien Maeght** has a tremendous stock of paintings at prices to suit most budgets; he also publishes fine art books. **Galerie 1900–2000** specializes in works by Surrealist and Dada artists, and **Galerie Jeanne Bucher** represents post-war Abstraction with artists like Nicolas de Staël and Vieira da Silva. **Dina Vierny** is a bastion of Modernism, founded by sculptor Aristide Maillol's famous model of the same name. **Rue Louise-Weiss**, in the east of Paris, is home to the **Air de Paris** gallery. In the Marais, try **Yvon Lambert**, **Galerie Daniel Templon** – specializing in American art, **Galerie Sit Down**, **Galerie Bernard Jordan** and **Galerie du Jour Agnès B**. In the same area, **Galerie Florence Loewy** is a fashionable place to buy catalogues on new artists, if not their actual works.

Auctions and Auction Houses

The great Paris auction centre, in operation since 1858, is **Drouot-Richelieu** (see p220). Bidding can be intimidating since most of it is done by dealers. Beware of the auctioneer's high-speed patter. *La Gazette de L'Hôtel Drouot* tells you what auctions are coming up when.

Drouot-Richelieu has its own auction catalogue as well. The house only accepts cash and French cheques, but there is an exchange desk on site. A 10–15 per cent commission to the house is charged, so add it on to any price you hear. You may view from 11am to 6pm on the day before the sale, and from 11am to noon on the morning of the sale. Items

considered not good enough for the main house are sold at **Drouot-Nord**. Here, auctions take place from 9am to noon and viewing is just five minutes before the sales begin. Exhibits and events are held at their **12-Drouot** space.

The **Crédit Municipal** holds around 12 auctions a month, and almost all the items on sale are small objects and furs offloaded by rich Parisians. The rules follow

those at Drouot. Information can also be found in *La Gazette de L'Hôtel Drouot.*

Service des Domaines sells all sorts of odds and ends, and here you can still find bargains. Many of the wares come from bailiffs and from Customs and Excise *(see p358)* confiscations. Viewing is from 10am to 11.30am on the day of the sale in St-Maurice, southeast of the city.

DIRECTORY

Exporting

Centre des Renseignements des Douanes
Tel 08 11 20 44 44.
W douane.gouv.fr

Comité National des Conseillers du Commerce Extérieur de la France
22 Ave Franklin Roosevelt 75008. **Map** 5 A4.
Tel 01 53 83 92 92.
W cnccef.org

Modern Crafts and Furniture

Cappellini
242 Bis Blvd St-Germain 75007. **Map** 12 D3.
Tel 01 42 84 03 78.
W cappellini.it

Sentou
26 Blvd Raspail 75007.
Map 12 D4.
Tel 01 45 49 00 05.

Le Viaduc des Arts
1–129 Ave Daumesnil 750012. **Map** 14 F5.
Tel 01 44 75 80 66.
This comprises a series of shops on the Avenue.

Antiques and Objets d'Art

Anne-Sophie Duval
5 Quai Malaquais 75006.
Map 12 E3.
Tel 01 43 54 51 16.
W annesophie
duval.com

L'Arc en Seine
31 Rue de Seine 75006.
Map 12 E3.
Tel 01 43 29 11 02.

Didier Aaron
152 Blvd Haussmann 75008. **Map** 5 B4.
Tel 01 47 42 47 34.
W didieraaron.com

Ghislaine Chaplier
Le Village Suisse, Gallery No 65 Place de Zurich, 10 Ave de Champaubert 75015. **Map** 10 E5.
Tel 01 45 67 30 55.

Louvre des Antiquaires
2 Pl du Palais-Royal 75001.
Map 12 E2.
Tel 01 42 97 27 27.

Philippe de Beauvais
43–45 Ave Bosquet 75007. **Map** 10 F3.
Tel 01 47 63 20 72.

Village St-Paul
Between the Quai des Célestins, the Rue St-Paul and the Rue Charlemagne 75004. **Map** 13 C4.

Le Village Suisse
54 Ave de la Motte-Picquet and 78 Ave de Suffren 75015.
Map 10 E4.
Tel 01 73 79 15 41.
W levillagesuisseparis.com

Reproductions, Posters & Prints

Galerie Documents
53 Rue de Seine 75006.
Map 12 E4.
Tel 01 43 54 50 68.

Librarie La Hune
16–18 Rue de l'Abbaye 75006. **Map** 12 E4.
Tel 01 45 48 35 85.

Art Galleries

Adrien Maeght
42 Rue du Bac 75007. **Map** 12 D3. Tel 01 45 48 45 15.

Air de Paris
28–32 Rue Louise Weiss 75013. **Map** 18 E4.
Tel 01 44 23 02 77.

Dina Vierny
36 Rue Jacob 75006.
Map 12 E3.
Tel 01 42 60 23 18.

Galerie 1900–2000
8 Rue Bonaparte 75006.
Map 12 E3.
Tel 01 43 25 84 20.

Galerie Bernard Jordan
77 Rue Charlot 75003.
Map 14 D1. Tel 01 42 77 19 61. W galeriebernard jordan.com

Galerie Florence Loewy
9 rue de Thorigny 75003.
Map 14 D2.
Tel 01 44 78 98 45.

Galerie Jeanne Bucher
53 Rue de Seine 75006.
Map 12 E4.
Tel 01 44 41 69 65.

Galerie du Jour Agnès B
44 Rue Quincampoix 75004. **Map** 13 B2.
Tel 01 44 54 55 90.

Galerie Lelong
13 Rue de Téhéran 75008. **Map** 5 A3.
Tel 01 45 63 13 19.

Galerie Sit Down
4 Rue Ste-Anastase 75003. **Map** 14 D2.
Tel 01 42 78 08 07.

Galerie Daniel Templon
30 Rue Beaubourg 75003. **Map** 13 B1.
Tel 01 42 72 14 10.

Louise Leiris
47 Rue de Monceau 75008. **Map** 5 A3.
Tel 01 45 63 28 85.

Yvon Lambert
108 Rue Vieille du Temple 75003. **Map** 14 D2.
Tel 01 42 71 09 33.

Auction Houses

12-Drouot
12 Rue Drouot 75009.
Map 6 F4.
Tel 01 48 00 20 00.
W drouot.fr

Artcurial Gallery
7 Rond Point des Champs-Elysées 75008.
Map 5 A5.
Tel 01 42 99 20 20.

Crédit Municipal
55 Rue des Francs-Bourgeois 75004.
Map 13 C3.
Tel 01 44 61 64 00.
W creditmunicipal.fr

Drouot-Nord
64 Rue Doudeauville 75018.
Tel 01 48 00 20 99.

Drouot-Richelieu
9 Rue Drouot 75009.
Map 6 F4.
Tel 01 48 00 20 20.

Service des Domaines
Tel 01 45 11 62 62.

Markets

For eye-catching displays of wonderful food and a lively atmosphere, there is no better place to shop than a Paris market. There are large covered food markets; markets where stalls change regularly; and permanent street markets with a mixture of shops and stalls which are open on a daily basis. Each has its own personality reflecting the area in which it is located. A list of some of the more famous markets, with approximate opening times, follows. For a complete list of markets, contact the Paris Office du Tourisme (see p282). And while you're enjoying browsing round the stalls, remember to keep an eye on your purse. Bargaining is not automatic, but you might be able to negotiate near closing time.

Fruit and Vegetable Markets

The French treat food with the kind of reverence usually reserved for religion. Many still shop on a daily basis to be sure of buying the freshest produce possible, so food markets tend to be busy. The majority of fruit and vegetable markets are open from around 8am to 1pm and from 4pm to 7pm Tuesday to Saturday, and from 9am to 1pm Sunday.

Buy produce loose rather than in boxes, but keep a close eye on what the stallholder puts in your bag. Most outdoor stalls prefer to serve you rather than allow you to handle the produce yourself, but don't be afraid to point to the individual fruit and vegetables of your choice. Your connoisseurship will be respected. A little language is useful for specifying *pas trop mur* (not too ripe), or *pour manger ce soir* (to be eaten tonight). If you go to the same market every day, you'll become familiar to the stall holders and will be less likely to be fobbed off with the occasional "reject" fruit or vegetable. You will also get to know the stalls worth buying from and the produce worth buying. Seasonal fruit and vegetables are, of course, usually a good buy, tending to be fresher and cheaper than at other times of the year. Finally, it is best to shop at markets early in the day when the food is freshest and the queues are shortest.

Flea Markets

It's often said that you can no longer find bargains at the Paris flea markets. Though this may be true, it's still worth going to one for the sheer fun of browsing. And bear in mind that the price quoted is not the one that you are expected to pay – it is generally assumed that you will bargain. Most flea markets are located on the city's boundaries. Whether you pick up any real bargains has as much to do with luck as with judgement, and may depend on whether the seller knows the true value of their goods. The biggest, busiest and most famous market, incorporating several smaller specialist ones, is the Marché aux Puces de St-Ouen. Be sure to keep your eye on your wallet, as pickpockets frequent these markets.

Specialist Markets

Try the Marché aux Fleurs Madeleine, the Marché aux Fleurs Reine Elizabeth II (see p87) or the Marché aux Fleurs Ternes in the Champs-Elysées district for fresh flowers. On the Ile de la Cité on Sundays, the Marché aux Oiseaux bird market replaces the flower market. Stamp collectors will enjoy the permanent Marché aux Timbres where you can buy old postcards. In Montmartre, the Marché St-Pierre, famous for cheap fabrics, is patronized by professional designers.

Marché d'Aligre

(See p237.)
Built in 1779, this lively covered market is one of the cheapest in the city. Here, traders hawk ingredients such as North African olives, groundnuts and hot peppers and there are even a few halal butchers. The noise reaches a crescendo at weekends when the cries of the market boys mingle with those of militants of all political persuasions as the latter petition and protest in the Place d'Aligre. The stalls on the square sell mostly second-hand clothes and bric-à-brac. This is a trendy, Bohemian area of town with few tourists and many Parisians.

Rue Cler

(See p192.)
This high-class, pedestrianized food market is patronized mainly by the politicians and captains of industry who live and work in the vicinity, so it's good for people-spotting! The produce is excellent – there's a Breton delicatessen and some good *fromageries*.

Marché des Enfant Rouges

39 Rue de Bretagne 75003. **Map** 14 D2.
Ⓜ Temple, Filles-du-Calvaire.
Open 8.30am–1pm, 4–7.30pm Tue–Sat (to 8pm Fri, Sat); 8.30am–2pm Sun.
This long-established, charming fruit and vegetable market on the Rue de Bretagne is part covered, part outdoors and dates from 1620. The produce is famous for its freshness, and there are cheap eateries too. On Sunday mornings, there are sometimes street performers and accordionists.

Marché aux Fleurs Madeleine

Pl de la Madeleine 75008.
Map 5 C5. Ⓜ Madeleine.
Open 8am–7.30pm Mon–Sat.

Marché aux Fleurs Ternes

Pl des Ternes 75017. **Map** 4 E3.
Ⓜ Ternes. **Open** 8am–7.30pm Tue–Sun.

Marché St-Pierre

Pl St-Pierre 75018. **Map** 6 F1.
Ⓜ Anvers. **Open** 2–7pm Mon, 9am–7pm Tue–Sat.

Marché aux Timbres

Ave Marigny 75008. **Map** 5 B5.
Ⓜ Champs-Elysées–Clemenceau.
Open 9am–7pm Thu, Sat, Sun & public hols.

Marché Joinville

Corner of Rue Jomard and Rue de Joinville 75019. Ⓜ *Crimée.*
Open *7am–2.30pm Thu & Sun.*

This lively canalside market is known for its cheap fruit and vegetables. It is situated on the Canal d'Ourcq, near the Parc de la Villette, and is always teeming with shoppers.

Marché St-Germain

4–6 Rue Lobineau 75006. **Map** *12 E4.* Ⓜ *Mabillon.* **Open** *8.30am–1pm, 4–8pm Tue–Fri; 8.30am–1.30pm, 3.30–8pm Sat; 8am–1.30pm Sun.*

St-Germain is one of the few covered markets left in Paris and has been enhanced by renovation. Here, you can buy Italian, Mexican, Greek, Asian and organic produce and other goods.

Rue de Lévis

75017. **Map** *5 B2.* Ⓜ *Villiers.* **Open** *10am–7.30pm Tue–Sat; 10am–1pm Sun.*

Rue de Lévis is a bustling, popular food market near the Parc Monceau with a number of good pâtisseries, an excellent cheese delicatessen and a *charcuterie* which is known for its savoury pies. The part of the street that leads to Rue Legendre sells haberdashery and fabrics. The shops on this pedestrianized street also have stalls outside selling their wares.

Rue Montorgueil

75001 & 75002. **Map** *13 A1.* Ⓜ *Les Halles.* **Open** *usually 9am–7pm Tue–Sun.*

The Rue Montorgueil is what remains of the old Les Halles market. The street has been repaved and restored to its former glory. Here, you can buy expensive, exotic fruit and vegetables like green bananas and yams from the market gardeners' stalls. You can also sample the delicious offerings from the delicatessens or from the Stohrer pastry shop.

Rue Mouffetard

(See p168.)

Rue Mouffetard is one of the oldest market streets in Paris. Although it has become touristy and somewhat overpriced, it's still a charming winding street full of quality food products and street musicians. There is also a lively African market down the nearby side street of Rue Daubenton, and a number of fashion boutiques and bars in the area.

Rue Poncelet

75017. **Map** *4 E3.* Ⓜ *Ternes.* **Open** *8am–1pm, 4–7.30pm Tue–Sat; 8am–1pm Sun.*

The Rue Poncelet food market is situated away from the main tourist areas of Paris but is worth visiting for its authentic French atmosphere. Choose from the many bakeries, pâtisseries and *charcuteries* or enjoy authentic Auvergne specialities from Aux Fermes d'Auvergnes.

Marché aux Puces de la Porte de Vanves

Ave Georges-Lafenestre & Ave Marc-Sangnier 75014. Ⓜ *Porte-de-Vanves.* **Open** *7am–2pm Sat & Sun.*

Porte de Vanves is a small market selling good-quality bric-à-brac and junk as well as some second-hand furniture. It's best to get to the market early on Saturday morning for the best choice of wares. Artists exhibit nearby in the Place des Artistes.

Marché Président-Wilson

Situated in Ave du Président-Wilson, between Pl d'Iéna & Rue Debrousse 75016. **Map** *10 D1.* Ⓜ *Alma-Marceau.* **Open** *7am–2.30pm Wed, 7am–3pm Sat.*

This very chic food market on Avenue Président-Wilson is close to the Musée d'Art Moderne and the Palais Galliera fashion museum. It has become important because there are no other food shops nearby. It is best for meat.

Marché aux Puces de Montreuil

Porte de Montreuil, 93 Montreuil 75020. Ⓜ *Mairie de Montreuil.* **Open** *7am–7.30pm Mon, Sat & Sun.*

Go early to the Porte de Montreuil flea market, where you'll have a better chance of picking up a bargain. The substantial second-hand clothes section attracts many young people. There's also a wide variety of items including used bicycles, bric-à-brac and an exotic spices stand.

Marché aux Puces de St-Ouen

(See p235.)

This is the best known, the most crowded and the most expensive of all the flea markets, situated on the northern outskirts of the city. Here, you'll find a range of markets, locals dealing from their car boots and a number of extremely large buildings

packed with stalls. Some of them are very upmarket, others sell junk. The flea market is a 10–15-minute walk from Clignancourt Metro – don't be put off by the somewhat sleazy Marché Malik which you have to pass through on your way from the metro. A *Guide des Puces* (guide to the flea markets) can be obtained from the information kiosk in the Marché Biron on the Rue des Rosiers. The more exclusive markets will take credit cards and arrange for goods to be shipped home. New stock arrives on Friday, the day when professionals come from all over the world to sweep up the best buys.

Among the markets here, the Marché Jules Vallès is good for turn-of-the-19th century *objets d'art.* Marché Paul-Bert is more expensive, but charming. Items on sale include furniture, books and prints. Both markets deal in second-hand goods rather than antiques.

In a different league, Marché Biron sells elegant, expensive antique furniture of very high quality. Marché Vernaison is the oldest and biggest market, good for collectables such as jewellery as well as lamps and clothes. No information about the Marché aux Puces is complete without mentioning Chez Louisette in the Vernaison market. This café is always full of locals enjoying the home cooking and the well-intentioned renditions of Edith Piaf songs. Marché Cambo is a fairly small market with beautifully-displayed antique furniture. Marché Serpette is popular with the dealers: everything sold here is in mint condition.

Marché Raspail

Situated on Blvd Raspail between Rue du Cherche-Midi & Rue de Rennes 75006. **Map** *12 D5.* Ⓜ *Rennes.* **Open** *7am–2.30pm Tue, Fri; 9am–2pm Sun.*

The Raspail market sells typical French groceries as well as Portuguese produce on Tuesdays and Fridays. But Sunday is the day for which it's famous, when health-conscious Parisians turn up in droves for the organically-grown produce. Marché Raspail is not a cheap market, but it is very good.

Rue de Seine and Rue de Buci

75006. **Map** *12 E4.* Ⓜ *Odéon.* **Open** *8am–1pm, 4–7pm Tue–Sat; 9am–1pm Sun.*

The stalls here are expensive and crowded but sell quality fruit and vegetables. There are also a large florist's and two excellent pâtisseries.

ENTERTAINMENT IN PARIS

Whether you prefer classical drama or cabaret, showgirls or ballet, opera or jazz, cinema or dancing the night away, Paris has it all. Free entertainment is aplenty as well, from the street performers outside the Pompidou Centre to musicians busking in the Metro. Parisians themselves enjoy strolling along the boulevards or sitting at a pavement café, and nursing a drink. Of course, for the ultimate "oh-la-la!" experience, showgirls await you at celebrated cabarets while bright young things pose in nightclubs. For fans of spectator sports, there is tennis, the Tour de France, horse racing, football or rugby. Recreation centres and gyms cater to the more active, while the municipal swimming pools delight waterbabies. You can also catch a game of *boules* (or *pétanque*) in Paris's squares and parks.

Practical Information

For the visitor in Paris, there is no shortage of information about what's on offer.

The **Office du Tourisme**, near the Tuileries and Opéra is the city's main tourism distribution point for leaflets and schedules of events. It has a recorded information telephone service giving details of free concerts and exhibitions along with information on transport to the venues. Its website is also extremely useful. Your hotel reception desk or concierge should also be able to help you with any such information. They usually keep a wide range of brochures and leaflets for guests, and will generally be more than happy to make reservations for you.

Ballerina of the Ballet de l'Opéra

Booking Tickets

Depending on the event, tickets can be bought at the door, but for blockbuster concerts it is necessary to book well in advance. For most major events, including some classical music concerts and museum shows, tickets can be purchased online or at the **FNAC** chain. For popular events book well ahead, Parisians can be very quick off the mark for hot tickets. However, for theatre, opera and dance performances you can often buy inexpensive tickets at the last minute. If the tickets are marked *sans visibilité*, you will be able to see the stage only partially, or perhaps not at all.

Nightclubbing in Paris

Often, obliging ushers will put you in a better seat, depending on availability, but don't forget to tip.

Theatre box offices are open daily from approximately 11am–7pm. Most box offices accept credit card bookings made by phone or in person, but you may have to arrive early to pick up your tickets if you booked by telephone, as they may be sold to someone else at the last minute. If you are really keen and can't get hold of tickets, you can always turn up at the box office just before the performance in case there are unclaimed or returned tickets.

Listings Magazines

Paris has several good listings magazines. Among them are *Pariscope* and *L'Officiel des Spectacles*. They are published every Wednesday. *Le Figaro* has a good listings section on Wednesdays. *Télerama*, France's leading culture and listings weekly, has a Paris supplement called *Sortir*. For English listings, see the webzine *Paris Voice* at www.parisvoice.com.

Concert at Opéra National de Paris Garnier *(see p340)*

The Odéon Théâtre de l'Europe, a major theatre venue sometimes staging plays in English

Ticket Touts

If you must have a ticket to a sold-out performance, do as the French do: stand at the entrance with a sign that says *cherche une place (or deux,* etc). Many people have an extra ticket to sell. Often the people selling the extra tickets are doing so because a person in their party cannot come and they will simply sell the ticket on at face value. It is fine to buy these tickets, but do watch out for touts and be sure you don't buy a counterfeit or overpriced ticket.

Cut-Price Tickets

Half-price tickets to current plays are sold on the day of performance at **Kiosque Théâtre**. Credit cards are not accepted and a small commission is charged per ticket. There is a booth on the Place de la Madeleine *(see p218),* open 12.30–8pm, Tuesday–Saturday, 12.30–4pm Sunday, and on the Parvis de la Gare Montparnasse, which is open 12.30–8pm Tuesday–Saturday, 12.30–4pm Sunday. A third booth located on Place des Ternes is open 12.30–8pm Tuesday–Saturday, 12.30–4pm Sunday. The *kiosque* is a Parisian

institution and often has passes for the season's top shows.

Disabled Visitors' Facilities

Where facilities do exist, they are either very good or dreadful. Many venues have wheelchair space, but always phone in advance to make sure it's properly equipped. As far as public transport is concerned, the Metro, with its long stairways, is completely inaccessible to wheelchairs. Some bus lines are equipped with ramps to make them accessible to wheelchairs; check with the city's transport authority, the RATP, to find out which lines have facilities.

Pétanque players

The Grand Rex cinema *(see p346)*

DIRECTORY
Useful Addresses

FNAC
Forum des Halles, 1 Rue Pierre-Lescot 75001. **Map** 13 A2. **Tel** 0825 020 020.
26 Ave des Ternes 75017. **Map** 4 D3. **Tel** 0825 020 020.

G7 Taxis
Tel 36 07; 01 41 27 66 99 (in English).

Kiosque Theatre
Opposite 15 Pl de la Madeleine 75008.
W kiosquetheatre.com

Office du Tourisme
25 Rue des Pyramides 75001. **Map** 12 E1. **Tel** 08 9268 3000.
W parisinfo.com

Taxis Bleus
Tel 36 09 or 08 9170 1010.

Theatre

From the grandeur of the Comédie Française to slapstick farce and avant-garde drama, theatre is flourishing in Paris and the suburbs – the training ground for the best young actors and directors. The city also has a long tradition of playing host to visiting companies, and it attracts many foreign productions, often in the original languages.

There are theatres scattered throughout the city and the theatre season runs from September to July; national theatres close during August but many commercial ones stay open. For complete listings of what's on read *Pariscope* or *L'Officiel des Spectacles (see p332)*.

National Theatres

Founded in 1680 by royal decree, the **Comédie Française** *(see p130)*, with its strict conventions regarding the style of acting and interpretation, is the bastion of French theatre. Its aim is to keep classical drama in the public eye and also to perform works by the best modern playwrights.

The Comédie Française (inextricably linked in the national consciousness to Molière) is the oldest national theatre in the world and one of the few institutions of France's *ancien-régime* to have survived the Revolution. It settled into its present home after players occupied the Palais-Royal during the Revolution. The traditionally styled red velvet auditorium has a vast stage equipped with the latest technology.

The majority of the repertoire is classical, dominated by Corneille, Racine and Molière, followed by second strings Marivaux, Alfred de Musset and Victor Hugo. The company also performs modern plays by French and foreign playwrights.

The **Odéon Théâtre de l'Europe**, also known as the Théâtre National de l'Odéon *(see p142)*, was at one time the second theatre of the Comédie Française. It now has two sites and specializes in performing plays from other countries in their original languages.

Next door, the **Petit Odéon** is a studio space specializing in new plays.

The **Théâtre National de Chaillot** is a huge underground auditorium in the Art Deco Palais de Chaillot *(see p202)*. It stages experimental and contemporary theatre, lively dance productions and, occasionally, musical revues.

The **Théâtre National de la Colline** has two performance spaces and specializes in contemporary dramas.

Further Afield

A thriving multi-theatre complex in the Bois de Vincennes, the **Cartoucherie** houses five separate avant-garde theatres, including the internationally famous **Théâtre du Soleil**.

Independent Theatres

Among the most important of the serious independents are the **Comédie des Champs-Elysées**, the **Théâtre Hébertot** and the **Atelier**, which aims to be experimental. Other notable venues include the **Théâtre Marigny**, for excellent modern French drama, the **Théâtre Montparnasse** and the **Théâtre Antoine** which pioneered the use of realism on stage. The **Théâtre da la Madeleine** maintains consistently high standards and the **Théâtre de la Huchette** specializes in Ionesco plays. The British director Peter Brook has a loyal following at the **Théâtre des Bouffes du Nord**.

For over a hundred years, the **Théâtre du Palais-Royal** has been the temple of risqué farce. With fewer French Feydeau-style farce writers these days, translations of British and American sex comedies are filling the gap. Other notable venues include the **Bouffes Parisiens**, **La Bruyère**, the **Michel** and the **St-Georges**. The **Théâtre du Gymnase** presents popular one-man comedy shows.

Café-Theatres and Chansonniers

There is a long tradition of entertainment in cafés, but the café-theatres of today have nothing in common with the "café-concerts" of the late 19th century. These modern entertainments have originated because young actors and new playwrights could not find work, while drama students were unable to pay to hire established theatres. Don't be surprised if there is an element of audience participation, or alternatively, in small venues, if the actors can sometimes seem a little too close for comfort. This form of theatre is now so popular in Paris that one can often see posters advertising classes for café-theatre or notices inviting people to join small troupes. Café-theatres rose to prominence during the 1960s and 70s, when unknowns such as Coluche, Gérard Depardieu and Miou-Miou made their debut at the **Café de la Gare** before going on to success on the screen, so who knows who you might see at your local café.

Good venues for seeing new talent include the **Théâtre d'Edgar** and **Le Point Virgule**, while **Cabaret Michou** is an old-fashioned spot which is very popular and tends to specialize in broad caricature. Traditional *chansonniers* – cabarets where ballads, folk songs and humour abound – include **Au Lapin Agile** *(see p229)*, in the heart of Montmartre. Political satire is on offer at the **Caveau de la République** and the **Deux Anes**, also in Montmartre. Another form of café entertainment that often veers towards the theatrical is the *café-philosophique*. These are philosophical discussions or debates, held on topics such as justice, war and love, in which skilled orators take to the floor to declaim their positions. Audience participation is encouraged. Such events are held in many locations, including at **Les Editeurs**. Although debates take place in French, English language events also exist: play readings are a regular feature at the **Café de Flore**.

Children's Theatre

Some Paris theatres, such as the **Théâtre du Gymnase**, the **Théâtre de la Porte St-Martin** and the **Café d'Edgar**, have children's matinées on Wednesdays and weekends. In the city parks, there are several tiny puppet theatres (*marionnettes*), which are sure to delight children and adults alike. (*See* Independent Theatres *p336*.) The **Lido** also has an occasional children's season with shows at 2pm and 4pm (call for details).

Open-Air Theatre

During the summer, weather permitting, open-air perfor-mances of Shakespeare and classic French plays are held in the Shakespeare Garden in the Bois de Boulogne. There are also occasional performances in the Tuileries and in Montmartre as part of Paris's summer festival; check listings magazines for these events.

English-Language Theatre in Paris

The Improfessionals (improvo) and Mondays @ 7 are Paris-based companies who perform in English (details in listings magazines). There are also several English-language poetry societies which host poetry and play readings, the best is the Live Poets Society. **Kilometre Zero** is an interesting English-language arts collective that performs plays, publishes a magazine and hosts open-mike recital evenings. **La Java** puts on excellent stand-up comedy acts in English each month, courtesy of Anything Matters. Peter Brook occasionally puts on Shakespeare plays at the

Théâtre des Bouffes du Nord. A historic venue, it is much-loved by expatriates and plays host to some of the finest comic talent on the circuit at the moment.

Street Theatre

Street theatre thrives during the summer. Jugglers, mime artists, fire-eaters and musicians can be seen in tourist areas such as the Pompidou Centre (*see pp110–11*), St-Germain-des-Prés and Les Halles.

Cabaret

The music hall revue is the entertainment form most associated with late 19th-century Paris. It evokes images of Bohemian artists and absinthe-induced debauchery. Today, most of the women are likely to be non-French and the audience is made up mainly of foreign businessmen and tour groups.

When it comes to picking a cabaret, the rule of thumb is simple: the better-known places are the best. Lesser-known shows resemble nothing so much as Grade-B strip shows. All the cabarets listed here (*see p336*) guarantee topless women sporting outrageous feather and sequin-encrusted head-pieces, an assortment of vaudeville acts and, depending on your point of view, a specta-cularly entertaining evening or an exercise in high kitsch.

The **Lido** is the most Las Vegas-like of the cabarets and stars the legendary Bluebell Girls. The **Folies Bergère** is renowned for lively entertain-ment. It is the oldest music hall in Paris and probably the most famous in the world.

The **Crazy Horse** features some of the more risqué costumes and performances, and dancers with names such as Betty Buttocks, Fila Volcana and Nouka Bazooka. It has been transformed from its Wild West bar-room into a jewel-box theatre with a champagne bucket fastened to each seat. Here, the lowly striptease of burlesque shows has been refined into a vehicle for comedy

sketches and international beauties. **Paradis Latin** is the most "French" of all the city's cabaret shows. It has variety acts with remarkable special effects and scenery in a beautiful, old Left Bank theatre, partly designed by Gustave Eiffel.

The **Bobin'O** offers a commercial show that is inspired by all of Paris' cabarets. The **Moulin Rouge** (*see p230*), once the haunt of Toulouse-Lautrec, is the birthplace of the cancan. Today, the Moulin Rouge is less extravagant than the screen version portrayed in the famous film, but cabaret fans can still be certain of an evening of glamour, glitz and good times. Outrageously camp, transvestite parodies of these showgirl reviews can be seen at **Cabaret Michou**.

Booking Tickets

Tickets can be bought at the box office, by telephone or through theatre agencies. Box offices are open daily from about 11am–7pm; some accept credit card bookings by telephone or in person. Most tickets can also be bought online, via either theatre websites or Internet ticket agencies.

Ticket Prices

Ticket prices generally range from €7–€30 for the national theatres and €8–€38 for the inde-pendents. Reduced-price tickets and student standbys are available in some theatres 15 minutes before curtain-up. For cabaret, expect to pay from €23–€60; €68–€105 with dinner.

The **Kiosque Théâtre** offers half-price tickets on the day-of-performance; credit cards are not accepted and a small commission is charged for each ticket. There are booths in three locations (*see p333*).

Dress

These days, evening clothes are only worn to gala events at the Opéra National de Paris Garnier, the Comédie Française or the premiere of an up-market play.

DIRECTORY

National Theatres

Comédie Française
Salle Richelieu, 1 Pl
Colette 75001.
Map 12 E1.
Tel 08 25 10 16 80.
W comedie-francaise.fr

Odéon Théâtre
de l'Europe
Ateliers Berthier, 1 Rue
André Suares 75017.
Map 12 F5.
Tel 01 44 85 40 40.
Théâtre de l'Odéon, Pl de
l'Odéon 75006.
Map 12 F4.
W theatre-odeon.eu

Théâtre National
de Chaillot
1 Pl du Trocadéro 75016.
Map 9 C2.
Tel 01 53 65 30 00.
W theatre-chaillot.fr

Théâtre National de
la Colline
15 Rue Malte-Brun 75020.
Tel 01 44 62 52 52.
W colline.fr

Further Afield

Cartoucherie
Route du Champ-de-
Manoeuvre 75012.
Tel 01 43 74 87 63.
W cartoucherie.fr

Théâtre de
l'Aquarium
Tel 01 43 74 72 74.

Théâtre de l'Epée
de Bois
Tel 01 48 08 39 74.

Théâtre de la
Tempête
Tel 01 43 28 36 36.

Théâtre du Chaudron
Tel 01 43 28 97 04.

Théâtre du Soleil
Tel 01 43 74 24 08.

Independent
Theatres

Bobin'O
14–20 Rue de la Gaîté
75014.
Map 15 C2.
Tel 08 20 00 90 00
(tickets), 01 43 27 24 24
(general info).
W bobino.fr

Bouffes Parisiens
4 Rue Monsigny 75002.
Map 6 E5.
Tel 01 42 96 92 42.
W bouffesparisiens.com

Comédie des
Champs-Elysées
15 Ave Montaigne 75008.
Map 10 F1. **Tel** 01 53 23
99 19. W comediedes
champselysees.com

Théâtre Antoine
14 Blvd de Strasbourg
75010. **Map** 7 B5.
Tel 01 42 08 77 71.
W theatre-antoine.com

Théâtre de l'Atelier
1 Pl Charles Dullin 75018.
Map 6 F2.
Tel 01 46 06 49 24.
W theatre-atelier.com

Théâtre de la Gaîté
Montparnasse
26 Rue de la Gaîté 75014.
Map 15 C2.
Tel 01 43 20 60 56.

Théâtre de la
Huchette
23 Rue de la Huchette
75005. **Map** 13 A4.
Tel 01 43 26 38 99.
W theatre-
huchette.com

Théâtre de la
Madeleine
19 Rue de Surène 75008.
Map 5 C5.
Tel 01 42 65 07 09.
W theatre
madeleine.com

Théâtre de la Porte
St-Martin
18 Blvd St-Martin 75010.
Map 7 C5.
Tel 01 42 08 00 32.
W portestmartin.com

Théâtre des Bouffes
du Nord
37 bis Blvd de la Chapelle
75010. **Map** 7 C1.
Tel 01 46 07 34 50/ 01 46
07 33 00.
W bouffesdunord.
com/en

Théâtre du Gymnase
38 Blvd de Bonne-Nouvelle
75010. **Map** 7 A5.
Tel 01 42 46 79 79
W theatredu
gymnase.com

Théâtre du Palais-
Royal
38 Rue de Montpensier
75001. **Map** 12 E1.
Tel 01 42 97 59 76.

Théâtre Hébertot
78 bis Blvd des
Batignolles 75017.
Map 5 B2. **Tel** 01 43
87 23 23. W theatre
hebertot.com

Théâtre La Bruyère
5 Rue La Bruyère 75009.
Map 6 E3.
Tel 01 48 74 76 99.

Théâtre Marigny
Carré Marigny 75008.
Map 5 A5.
Tel 01 53 96 70 30.
W theatremarigny.fr

Théâtre Michel
38 Rue des Mathurins
75008. **Map** 5 C4.
Tel 01 42 65 35 02.
W theatre-michel.fr

Théâtre
Montparnasse
31 Rue de la Gaîté 75014.
Map 15 C2.
Tel 01 43 22 77 74.
W theatre
montparnasse.com

Théâtre St-Georges
51 Rue St-Georges 75009.
Map 6 E3.
Tel 01 48 78 63 47.
W theatre-saint-
georges.com

Théâtre Sudden
14 bis Rue Sainte-Isaure
75018. **Map** 2 F4.
Tel 01 42 62 35 00.

Café-Theatres
and Chansonniers

Au Lapin Agile
22 Rue des Saules 75018.
Map 2 F5.
Tel 01 46 06 85 87.
W au-lapin-agile.com

Café de la Gare
41 Rue du Temple
75004. **Map** 13 B2.
Tel 01 42 78 52 51.

Caveau de la
République
1 Blvd St-Martin 75003.
Map 8 D5.
Tel 01 42 78 44 45.

Deux Anes
100 Blvd de Clichy 75018.
Map 6 D1.
Tel 01 46 06 10 26.
W 2anes.com

La Java
105 Rue du Faubourg du
Temple 75010. **Map** 8 E5.
Tel 01 42 02 20 52.
W la-java.fr

Le Point Virgule
7 Rue St-Croix-de-la-
Bretonnerie 75004.
Map 13 C3.
Tel 01 42 78 67 03.
W lepointvirgule.com

Les Editeurs
4 Carrefour de l'Odéon
75006. **Map** 12 F4.
Tel 01 43 26 67 76.

Théâtre d'Edgar
58 Blvd Edgar-Quinet
75014. **Map** 16 D2.
Tel 01 43 22 11 02/ 01 42
79 97 97.

Cabaret

Cabaret Michou
80 Rue des Martyrs 75018.
Map 6 F3.
Tel 01 46 06 16 04.
W michou.com

Crazy Horse
12 Ave George V 75008.
Map 10 E1.
Tel 01 47 23 32 32.
W lecrazyhorse
paris.com

Folies Bergère
32 Rue Richer 75009.
Map 7 A4.
Tel 0892 681 650.
W foliesbergere.com

Lido
116 bis Ave des Champs-
Elysées 75008. **Map** 4 E4.
Tel 01 40 76 56 10
W lido.fr

Moulin Rouge
82 Blvd de Clichy 75018.
Map 6 E1.
Tel 01 53 09 82 82.
W moulinrouge.fr

Paradis Latin
28 Rue du Cardinal
Lemoine 75005. **Map** 13
B5. **Tel** 01 43 25 28 28.
W paradislatin.com

Classical Music

The music scene in Paris is busy and exciting, with many first-class venues offering an excellent range of opera, and classical and contemporary music productions. There are also numerous concerts in churches (some of which are free) and many music festivals, particularly during the summer months.

Information about what's on is listed in *Pariscope* and *L'Officiel des Spectacles*. A free monthly listing of musical events is given out at most concert halls. Also, try the Office du Tourisme in the Rue des Pyramides *(see pp332–3)* for details of many free and open-air classical music performances.

Opera

Opera lovers will find themselves well catered for, with many productions mounted at the Bastille and the beautifully renovated **Opéra National de Paris Garnier**. Opera is also an important part of the programming at the Théâtre du Châtelet, as well as being produced intermittently by a variety of small organizations, and there are occasional large-scale lavish productions at the **Palais Omnisports de Bercy** or POB *(see p351)*.

The Opéra de Paris's ultra-modern home is the **Opéra National de Paris Bastille** *(see p102)*, where performances make full use of the house's mind-boggling array of high-tech stage mechanisms. There are 2,700 seats, all with a good view of the stage, and the accoustics are excellent.

Productions feature classic and modern operas, and interpretations are often avant-garde: past examples include Philippe Mamoury's *K...*; Bob Wilson's production of *The Magic Flute*, done in the style of Japanese Noh; Messiaen's *St Francis of Assisi*, with video screens and neon added to bring the story up to date. On Thursday lunchtimes, they also offer free concerts, lectures and films as part of an occasional programme known as *Casse-Croûte à l'Opéra*.

There are also occasional dance performances, when the Bastille plays host to the ballet company from the Opéra National de Paris Garnier *(see p219)*. The house includes two smaller spaces, the **Auditorium** (500 seats) and the **Studio** (200 seats) for smaller-scale events connected to the current productions on the main stages here and at the Opéra Garnier.

The **Opéra Comique** (also known as the Salle Favart), directed by Jérôme Deschamps, no longer has opera, but stages a wide range of eccentric, light-weight productions, including some popular music-hall-style work and operetta.

North of the city centre, at St Denis, the **Stade de France** hosts occasional opera spectaculars. Past productions have included Verdi's *Aïda*, directed by Charles Roubaud, as well as Bizet's *Carmen* and *Nabucco* by Verdi.

Concerts

Paris is the home of three major symphony orchestras, and a good half-dozen other orchestras; it is also a major venue for touring European and American orchestras. Chamber music is also flourishing, either as part of the programming of the major venues, or in smaller halls and churches.

The **Salle Pleyel** is Paris's principal concert hall. After extensive renovation, it is now owned by the state-run Cité de la Musique and houses the Orchestre de Paris, directed by Christoph Eschenbach, as well as Radio France's Philharmonic Orchestra, led by Myung-Whun Chung. The Salle Pleyel has optimal acoustics for the classical and contemporary orchestra repertoire. In addition to running the Salle Pleyel, the Cité de la Musique also operates other venues at Parc de la Villette. These concert halls present a varied programme of music from all periods, genres and cultures.

The **Théâtre du Châtelet** has become one of the city's main venues for all kinds of concerts, opera and dance. The high-quality programme includes opera classics from Mozart's *Così fan tutte* to Verdi's *La Traviata*, and more modern works, such as Boessman's *Contes d'Hiver*, and occasional concerts by international opera stars. Great attention is also devoted to 20th-century music here, and throughout the season, there are lunchtime concerts and recitals in the foyer.

The beautiful Art Deco **Théâtre des Champs-Elysées** is a celebrated classical music venue which also produces some opera and dance. Radio-France is part-owner of the theatre, and its Orchestre National de France gives concerts here, as do many touring orchestras and soloists. The Orchestre des Champs-Elysées, directed by Philippe Herreweghe, is in residence here, and gives period-instrument performances.

Radio-France is the biggest single concert organizer in Paris, with a musical force that includes two major symphony orchestras: the Orchestre National de France and the Orchestre Philharmonique. Many of its concerts are given in Paris's other concert halls, but the **Maison de Radio-France** has a large hall and several smaller studios that are used for concerts and broadcasts open to the public *(see p204, Maison de Radio France)*.

The **Cité de la Musique** is a massive cultural centre devoted entirely to music – of all genres and from all eras. Classical music features heavily on its programme, with lots of chamber music and recitals, as well as more ambitious orchestral concerts.

The **Auditorium du Louvre** was built as part of the Grand Louvre project *(see pp122–9)* and it is used mostly for chamber, piano and vocal recitals. The Musée d'Orsay's *(see pp146–9)* **Auditorium du Musée d'Orsay** is a medium-sized auditorium, with an active concert programme. Concerts are usually held once or twice a week, and prices vary.

Other museums often hold concerts as part of an exhibition theme – such as troubadours at the Musée National du Moyen Age *(see pp154–7)* – so do check the listings magazines.

Musique à la Sorbonne is a concert series in the **Grand Amphithéâtre de la Sorbonne** and the **Amphithéâtre Richelieu de la Sorbonne**. Productions have included a Slavonic music festival, featuring the works of East European composers.

Occasionally concerts are given in the **Conservatoire d'Art Dramatique**, where Beethoven was introduced to Paris audiences in 1828 and where Hector Berlioz's major work, *La Symphonie Fantastique*, was first performed. Otherwise, it's not usually open to public.

Contemporary Music

Contemporary music in Paris has a high profile and is definitely alive and kicking. Although no longer at the head of any orchestra, Pierre Boulez is still a major figure in the capital's contemporary music scene. Jonathan Nott now directs the experimental Ensemble InterContemporain, which is lavishly supported by the French state in its home at the Cité de la Musique *(see pp238–9)*. **IRCAM** *(see p114)*, founded by Pierre Boulez, is a major centre for ground-breaking new musical forms. It organizes a programme of new music performances, talks and an annual festival in June.

Other bright stars among the many talented composers include Pascal Dusapin, Philippe Fénelon, George Benjamin and

Philippe Manoury, as well as Georges Aperghis, who specializes in musical theatre.

The fabulously designed **Cité de la Musique** complex at Parc de la Villette includes both a spectacularly domed *salle de concerts* surrounded by a glass-roofed arcade, and the **Conservatoire National de Musique** with its opera theatre and two small concert halls. The Chamber Orchestra of Europe plays regularly here. Both venues are used for regular performances, including jazz, ethnic and contemporary music, as well as *chanson* and Early Music.

For details, either phone the venue concerned or consult the listings magazines. For those interested in contemporary music, the quarterly magazine *Résonance* is published by IRCAM at the Pompidou Centre.

Festivals

Some of the most important music festivals are the result of the work of the **Festival d'Automne à Paris**, which acts as a behind-the-scenes stimulator, commissioning new works, subsidizing others and in general enlivening the Parisian musical, dance and theatrical scene from September to December.

The **Festival St-Denis** running throughout June and July holds concerts, with an emphasis on choral works. Most performances are given in the Basilique St-Denis.

Musique Baroque au Château de Versailles, from around the middle of March to the middle of June, is an offshoot of the Baroque Music Centre, founded in Versailles in 1988. Operas, concerts, recitals, chamber music, dance and theatre are on offer in the fabulous surroundings of Versailles *(see pp250–55)*.

Other interesting festivals include the Chopin festival, held in the Orangerie in the Bois de Boulogne from mid-June to mid-July, and the Quartier 25 d'Eté festival, which hosts a series of outdoor classical music

concerts. For tickets, it is usually necessary to go to the theatre box office or venue concerned, though some festivals may run an advance online or postal booking service.

Churches

Music is everywhere in Paris's churches, in the form of classical concerts, organ recitals or religious services. The most outstanding churches which hold regular concerts include **La Madeleine** *(see p218)*, **St- Germain-des-Prés** *(see p140)*, **St-Julien-le-Pauvre** *(see p158)* and **St-Roch** *(see p131)*. Music is also performed in the **Eglise des Billettes**, **St-Sulpice** *(see p174)*, **St-Gervais–St-Protais** *(see p103)*, **Notre-Dame** *(see pp82–5)*, **St-Louis-en-l'Ile** *(see p91)* and **Sainte-Chapelle** *(see pp88–9)*.

A great proportion, but not all, of these concerts are free. If you have any difficulty contacting the church in question, try the Office du Tourisme for information *(see pp332–3)*.

Early Music

A number of early-music ensembles have taken up residence in Paris. The Chapelle Royale gives a concert series at the **Théâtre des Champs-Elysées**, with programmes ranging from Renaissance vocal music to Mozart. Their enchanting sacred music concerts (look out for Bach cantatas) take place at **Notre-Dame-des-Blancs-Manteaux** *(see p104)*.

Baroque opera is more the domain of Les Arts Florissants, founded and directed by American-born William Christie, who perform French and Italian operas from Rossi to Rameau, and Les Musiciens du Louvre, directed by Marc Minkowski. Both companies perform regularly at the Théâtre du Châtelet and the Opera National Garnier. The **Théâtre de la Ville** is also an excellent venue in which to hear Baroque chamber music, as is the pretty **Eglise Saint-Germain l'Auxerrois**.

Booking Tickets

For tickets, it's always best to deal directly with the relevant box office. Booking tickets at the main venues is possible online or by post up to two months before the performance and by telephone two weeks to a month in advance. If you want a good seat, it's best to book in advance as tickets tend to sell quickly. Last-minute tickets may also be available at the box office, and certain venues, such as the Opéra National de Paris Bastille, keep some tickets

for the cheaper seats aside for the purpose. Ticket agents, notably in the **FNAC** stores (see p333), and a good hotel concierge can also help. These agencies accept credit card bookings – a useful service as not all venues are guaranteed to accept them.

Half-price tickets on the day of performance can be bought at one of three **Kiosque Théâtre** (see p333), located at Place de la Madeleine, the Parvis de la Gare Montparnasse and Place des Ternes. However, these agencies usually only deal for

performances taking place at private theatres.

Note, however, that many theatres and concert halls may be closed during the holiday season in August, so inquire first to avoid disappointment.

Ticket Prices

Ticket prices can range from €8–€85 for the Opéra de Paris Bastille and the principal classical music venues, and from €5–€25 for the smaller halls and concerts in churches around the city, such as Sainte-Chapelle.

DIRECTORY

Classical Music Venues

Amphithéâtre Richelieu de la Sorbonne
17 Rue de la Sorbonne 75005. **Map** 12 F5.
Tel 01 40 46 20 19.

Auditorium
See Opéra National de Paris Bastille.

Auditorium du Louvre
Musée du Louvre, Rue de Rivoli 75001. **Map** 12 E2.
Tel 01 40 20 55 00/55.

Auditorium du Musée d'Orsay
102 Rue de Lille 75007.
Map 12 D2.
Tel 01 53 63 04 63.

Centre de Musique Baroque de Versailles
22 Ave de Paris, Versailles.
Tel 01 39 20 78 10.

Cité de la Musique
Parc de La Villette, 221 Ave Jean-Jaurès 75019.
Tel 01 44 84 44 84.
W citedelamusique.fr

Conservatoire d'Art Dramatique
2 bis Rue du Conservatoire 75009.
Map 7 A4.
Tel 01 42 46 12 91.

Eglise des Billettes
24 Rue des Archives 75004. **Map** 13 C2.
Tel 01 42 72 38 79.

Eglise de la Madeleine
Pl de la Madeleine 75008.
Map 5 C5.
Tel 01 44 51 69 00 (church); 01 42 50 96 18 (concerts).

Eglise St-Germain l'Auxerrois
2 Place du Louvre 75001.
Map 12 F2.
Tel 01 42 60 13 96.

Festival d'Automne
156 Rue de Rivoli 75001.
Map 12 F2.
Tel 01 53 45 17 00.

Festival Chopin
Orangerie de Bagatelle Bois de Boulogne 75016.
Map 3 A4.
Tel 01 45 00 22 19.

Grand Amphithéâtre de la Sorbonne
45 Rue des Ecoles 75005.
Map 13 A5. **Tel** 01 42 62 71 71/ 01 40 46 33 72.

IRCAM
1 Pl Igor Stravinsky 75004.
Map 13 B2.
Tel 01 44 78 48 43.

Maison Radio-France
116 Ave du Président-Kennedy 75016.
Map 9 B4.
Tel 01 56 40 22 22.

Notre-Dame
Pl du Parvis-Notre-Dame 75004. **Map** 13 A4.
Tel 01 42 34 56 10.

Notre-Dame-des-Blancs-Manteaux
12 Rue des Blancs-Manteaux 75004.
Map 13 C3.
Tel 01 42 72 09 37.

Opéra Comique
5 Rue Favart 75002.
Map 6 F5.
Tel 08 25 01 01 23.

Opéra National de Paris Bastille
Pl de la Bastille 75012.
Map 14 E4.
Tel 08 92 89 90 90.
W operadeparis.fr

Opéra National de Paris Garnier
Pl de l'Opéra 75009. **Map** 6 E4.
Tel 08 92 89 90 90.
W operadeparis.fr

Pompidou Centre
Pl Georges Pompidou 75004. **Map** 13 B2.
Tel 01 44 78 12 33.

Quartier d'Eté Festival
Various venues.
Tel 01 44 94 98 00.

Sainte-Chapelle
48 Blvd du Palais. **Map** 13 A3. **Tel** 01 53 40 60 80.

St-Germain-des-Prés
3 Pl St-Germain-des-Prés 75006. **Map** 12 E4.
Tel 01 55 42 81 10.

St-Gervais–St-Protais
13 Rue des Barres 75004.
Map 13 B3.
Tel 01 48 87 32 02.

St-Julien-le-Pauvre
1 Rue St-Julien-le-Pauvre 75005. **Map** 13 A4.
Tel 01 43 54 52 16.

St-Louis-en-l'Ile
19 bis Rue St-Louis-en-l'Ile 75004. **Map** 13 C4.
Tel 01 46 34 11 60.

St-Roch
296 Rue St-Honoré 75001.
Map 12 D1.
Tel 01 42 44 13 20.

St-Sulpice
Pl St-Sulpice 75006.
Map 12 E4.
Tel 01 42 34 59 98.

Salle Pleyel
252 Rue du Faubourg St-Honoré 75008.
Map 4 E3. **Tel** 01 42 56 13 13. **W** sallepleyel.fr

Stade de France
Rue Henri Delaunay, La Plaine St-Denis 93210.
Tel 08 92 70 09 00.
W stadedefrance.com

Studio
See Opéra National de Paris Bastille.

Théâtre de la Ville
2 Pl du Châtelet 75004.
Map 13 A3.
Tel 01 42 74 22 77.

Théâtre des Champs-Élysées
15 Ave Montaigne 75008.
Map 10 F1.
Tel 01 49 52 50 50.

Théâtre du Châtelet
1 Pl du Châtelet 75001.
Map 13 A3.
Tel 01 40 28 28 40.

Dance

When it comes to dance, Paris is more a cultural crossroads than a cultural centre. Due to a deliberate government policy of decentralization, many of the top French dance companies are based in the provinces, although they frequently visit the capital. In addition, the greatest dance companies from all over the world perform here. Paris has a well-deserved reputation as a centre of excellence for modern and experimental dance, and has numerous workshops and places in which to learn its many forms.

Classical Ballet

The opulent **Opéra National de Paris Garnier** (see p219) is the home of the Ballet de l'Opéra de Paris which enjoys a reputation as one of the world's best classical dance companies.

Since the **Opéra National de Paris Bastille** opened in 1989, the Opéra National de Paris Garnier has been used almost exclusively for dance. Extensively restored both inside and out, it is one of the largest theatres in Europe, with performance space for 450 artists and a seating capacity of 2,200.

Modern dance companies such as the Martha Graham Company, Paul Taylor, Merce Cunningham, Alvin Ailey, Jerome Robbins and Roland Petit's Ballet de Marseille also regularly perform here. The Opéra National de Paris Garnier also shares operatic productions with the Opéra National de Paris Bastille.

Modern Dance

The **Théâtre de la Ville** (once run by Sarah Bernhardt) has become one of Paris's most important venues for modern dance. Through performances at the Théâtre de la Ville, modern choreographers such as Jean-Claude Gallotta, Regine Chopinot, Maguy Marin and Anne Teresa de Keersmaeker have gained international recognition. Here, you may also see troupes such as Pina Bausch's Wuppertal Dance Theatre, whose tormented, existential choreography may not be to everyone's taste, but is popular with Parisian audiences. Music performances also run throughout the season and

include chamber music, recitals, world music and jazz.

The **Maison des Arts et de la Culture de Créteil** presents some of the most interesting dance works in Paris. It is located in the modern, concrete, mid-20th-century Paris suburb of Créteil, south east of the city. Under artistic director Didier Fusillier, dance at MAC is part of an ambitious programme of avant-garde theatre, installations and performance as showcased at its annual festival EXIT, which is held in March. Acclaimed French choreographer Maguy Marin was MAC's resident dance guru for some years.

Set amid the opulent *couture* shops and embassies, the elegant Art Deco **Théâtre des Champs-Élysées** has 1,900 seats. It is frequented by an upmarket audience who watch major international companies perform here. It was here that Nijinsky first danced Stravinsky's iconoclastic *The Rite of Spring*, which led to rioting among the audience.

The theatre is more famous as a classical music venue, but visitors have included the Dance Theatre of Harlem and London's Royal Ballet, plus a strong Russian presence, notably the St Petersburg Ballet Theatre.

The lovely old **Théâtre du Châtelet** is a renowned opera and classical music venue, but it is also host to international contemporary dance companies such as the Tokyo Ballet and the Birmingham Royal Ballet.

Experimental dance companies perform in the **Théâtre de la Bastille**, where

innovative theatre is also staged. Many directors and companies start here, then go on to international fame.

The **Centre National de la Danse** in Pantin, a northeastern suburb of Paris, is France's national *conservatoire*. It hosts workshops, talks and performances, from classical ballet to experimental dance.

Events Listings

To find out what's on, read the inexpensive weekly entertainment guides *Pariscope* and *L'Officiel des Spectacles*. Posters advertising dance performances are widely displayed in the Metro and on the streets, especially on the green advertisement columns, the *colonnes Morris*.

Ticket Prices

Expect to pay €10–€195 for tickets to the ballet or opera at Opéra de Paris Garnier, €6–€75 for the Théâtre des Champs-Élysées, and anything from €9–€30 for other venues.

Rock, Jazz and World Music

Music lovers will find every imaginable form of music in Paris and its environs, from international pop stars in major venues to buskers of varying degrees of talent on the streets and in the Metro. There's a huge variety of styles on offer, with reggae, hip-hop, world music, blues, folk, rock and jazz – Paris is said to be second only to New York in the number of jazz clubs and jazz recordings made here, and there is always an excellent selection of bands and solo performers.

On the summer solstice (21 June) each year, the Fête de la Musique takes place. The whole city parties all night, with everything from huge outdoor stages and top bands to one-man buskers or accordionists playing traditional French songs invading Paris's streets, squares and cafés.

For complete listings of what's happening, buy *Pariscope* (published every Wednesday) at any kiosk. For jazz fans there's the monthly *Jazz* magazine for schedules and in-depth reviews.

Major Venues

The top international acts are often at the enormous arenas: **Palais Omnisports** at Bercy, **Stade de France** at St-Denis or the **Zénith**. Other venues such as the legendary *chanson* centre of the universe, the **Olympia**, or the **Grand Rex** (also a cinema), offer a more traditional concert-hall atmosphere. They host everyone from bewigged and cosmetically enhanced iconic first ladies of country to acid jazz stars. (*See* Directories *p342 and p351*).

Rock and Pop

Until recently, Paris's indigenous rock groups (Les Négresses Vertes, the hit fusion band of the nineties and noughties, are probably the best-known) drew foreign attention precisely because they were French.

For too long, Paris pop meant Johnny Hallyday and insipid covers of US and UK hits, or Serge Gainsbourg and his distinctive, decadent style. Paris rock traditionally (and deservedly) attracted either patronizing praise or outright mockery.

That is no longer the case. The international success of the groups Daft Punk and Air, and the contribution to the music scene of producer, songwriter and musician Bertrand Burgalat, led to a growth in confidence in the local music scene. The phrase "French Touch" often describes hip producers, writers or singers, now in demand all over the world. Banlieue- (suburb-) based rap, rai and reggae no longer sound like French versions of imported forms, instead they now have their own identity.

There is no shortage of gigs. The latest bands usually play at **Divan du Monde**, **Nouveau Casino** and **La Cigale** and its sister club, **La Boule Noire**. The **Bataclan** and the **Rex** club are the best places for R&B. The **Olympia** is the city's most famous rock venue, attracting top acts. Many nightclubs also double up as live music venues (*see pp343–5*).

Jazz

Paris is still jazz-crazy. Many American musicians have made the French capital their home because of its receptive atmosphere. All styles, from free-form to Dixieland and swing, and even hip-hop-jazz crossover, are on offer. Clubs range from quasi-concert halls to piano bars and pub-like venues. One of the most popular places, though not the most comfortable, is the **New Morning**. It's hot and the table service can be a little erratic, but all the great jazz musicians continue to perform here, as they have in the past. Arrive early to ensure a good seat. **Le Duc des Lombards** is a lively jazz club in Les Halles, which also features salsa.

Many jazz clubs are also cafés, bars or restaurants. The latter includes the intimate **Autour de Midi... et Minuit** in Montmartre, with its vaulted "cave". Dining might not be a requirement, but it's always wise to check first.

Other hotspots are **Le Petit Journal Montparnasse** for modern jazz, **Le Petit Journal St-Michel** for Dixieland. A trendy crowd is drawn to **La Bellevilloise's** Sunday jazz brunches in Ménilmontant. **Caveau de la Huchette** looks like the archetypal jazz joint, but today, it favours swing and big-band music, and is popular with students. The **Caveau des Oubliettes** has a growing reputation for cutting-edge jazz.

For a change, try the local talent at small, friendly bars such as the less expensive **Bistrot d'Eustache** and super cool **La Flèche d'Or**, set in an old railway station. The **Jazz Club Etoile** in the Méridien hotel is a well-respected venue which features Sunday jazz brunch. On the other side of town, the **La Trabendo** has an intriguing mix of up-and-comers and down-and-outers. Although the **Sunset-Sunside** is primarily known for jazz, it also includes blues nights on its programme.

Paris has two international jazz festivals in summer: the Paris Jazz Festival (*see p65*) and Jazz à la Villette in July. The Paris Jazz Festival is the mainstay of the summer calendar, and Jazz à la Villette offers films on jazz, debates and discussions and *boeufs* (jam sessions).

World Music

With its large populations from West Africa, the Maghreb, the Antilles and Latin America, Paris is a natural centre for world music. The **Chapelle des Lombards** has played host to top acts; it also has jazz, salsa and Brazilian music. **Aux Trois Mailletz** is a medieval cellar with everything from blues to tango and rock and roll covers, while **Kibélé** is a great place for North African sounds. Many jazz clubs intersperse their programmes with ethnic music. These include **New Morning**, which also has shows with South American artists, and **Baiser Salé**, for popular acts including Makossa, Kassav, Malavoi and Manu Dibango.

World music in a stunning setting can be found at the Institut du Monde Arabe, a wonderful architectural feat *(see p166)* which draws stars from the Arab music world to its concert hall.

Ticket Prices

Prices at jazz clubs can be steep, and there may be a cover charge of over €15 at the door, which usually includes the first drink. If there is no cover charge, the drinks will be expensive and at least one must be bought.

Tickets can be bought online on the FNAC website or from FNAC outlets *(see p333)*, or directly from venue box offices and at the door of the clubs themselves.

DIRECTORY

Major Venues

Grand Rex
1 Blvd Poissonnière 75002. **Map** 7 A5.
Tel 01 45 08 93 89.

Olympia
28 Blvd des Capucines 75009. **Map** 6 D5.
Tel 08 92 68 33 68.
W olympiahall.com

Palais Omnisports de Paris-Bercy
8 Blvd de Bercy 75012.
Map 18 F2.
W bercy.fr

Zénith
211 Ave de Jean-Jaurès 75019.
Tel 01 44 52 54 56.
W zenith-paris.com

Rock and Pop

Bataclan
50 Blvd Voltaire 75011.
Map 14 E1.
Tel 01 43 14 00 30.
W bataclan.fr

La Boule Noire
118 Blvd Rochechouart 75018. **Map** 6 F2.
Tel 01 49 25 81 75.
W laboule-noire.fr

La Cigale
120 Blvd Rochechouart 75018. **Map** 6 F2.
Tel 01 49 25 89 99.
W lacigale.fr

Divan du Monde
75 Rue des Martyrs 75018.
Map 6 F2.
Tel 01 40 05 06 99.
W divandumonde.com

Nouveau Casino
190 Rue Oberkampf 75011. **Map** 14 F1.
Tel 01 43 57 57 40.
W nouveaucasino.net

Rex Club
5 Blvd Poissonnière 75002. **Map** 7 A5.
Tel 01 42 36 10 96.
W rexclub.com

Jazz

Autour De Midi... et Minuit
11 Rue Lepic 75018.
Map 6 E1.
Tel 01 55 79 16 48.
W autourdemonde.fr

Baiser Salé
58 Rue des Lombards 75001.
Map 13 A2.
Tel 01 42 33 77 71.
W lebaisersale.com

Bellevilloise
19-21 Rue Boyer 75020.
Tel 01 46 36 07 07.
W labellevilloise.com

Bistrot d'Eustache
37 Rue Berger, Carré des Halles 75001.
Map 13 A2.
Tel 01 40 26 23 20.
W bistrotdeustache.fr

Caveau de la Huchette
5 Rue de la Huchette 75005. **Map** 13 A4.
Tel 01 43 26 65 05.
W caveaudela huchette.fr

Caveau des Oubliettes
52 Rue Galande 75005.
Map 13 A4.
Tel 01 46 34 23 09.
W caveaudes oubliettes.fr

Le Duc des Lombards
42 Rue des Lombards 75001. **Map** 13 A2.
Tel 01 42 33 22 88.
W ducdeslombards.com

La Flèche d'Or
102 bis Rue de Bagnolet 75020. **Tel** 01 44 64 01 02.
W flechedor.fr

La Grande Halle de la Villette
211 Ave Jean-Jaurès, Galerie de la Villette 75019.
Map 8 F1. **Tel** 01 40 03 75 75.
W villette.com

Jazz Club Etoile
Hôtel Méridien, 81 Blvd Gouvion-St-Cyr 75017.
Map 3 C3.
Tel 01 40 68 30 42.
W jazzclub-paris.com

New Morning
7–9 Rue des Petites-Écuries 75010. **Map** 7 B4.
Tel 01 45 23 51 41.
W newmorning.com

Paris Jazz Festival
Parc Floral Bois de Vincennes 75012.
W parisjazzfestival.fr

Le Petit Journal Montparnasse
13 Rue du Commandant-Mouchotte 75014.
Map 15 C2.
Tel 01 43 21 56 70.
W petitjournal montparnasse.com

Le Petit Journal St-Michel
71 Blvd St-Michel 75005.
Map 16 F1.
Tel 01 43 26 28 59.

Sunset-Sunside
60 Rue des Lombards 75001. **Map** 13 A2.
Tel 01 40 26 46 60.
W sunset-sunside.com

Le Trabendo
211 Ave Jean-Jaurès, Parc de la Villette 75019.
Map 8 F1.
Tel 01 42 06 05 52.
W letrabendo.net

World Music

Aux Trois Mailletz
56 Rue Galande 75005.
Map 13 A4.
Tel 01 43 25 96 86.
W lestroismailletz.fr

Baiser Salé
(see Jazz)

Chapelle des Lombards
19 Rue de Lappe 75011.
Map 14 F4.
Tel 01 43 57 24 24.
W la-chapelle-des-lombards.com

Institut du Monde Arabe
(see p166)

Kibélé
12 Rue de l'Echiquier 75010.
Map 7 B5.
Tel 01 48 24 57 74.
W kibele.fr

New Morning
(see Jazz)

Nightclubs

The club scene in Paris is now somewhat under siege as government legislation on noise levels hampers establishments' *modus operandi*. The city council is waging war on noise pollution and whilst this suits those with neighbours who possess large stereos, it's bad news for people who like to dance till dawn. They carry on regardless, albeit with fewer decibels, and you will still find every type of sound (and a great deal of creativity) on the club scene. There are clubs to suit every taste and it's worth noting that bouncers often treat foreign would-be entrants preferentially, so be sure to stand proud, ditch the attempts at French and speak English when you get near the door. The English website www.gogoparis.com reviews some of the capital's trendiest establishments. Alternatively, read the posters at the Bastille Metro station or listen to Radio NOVA 101.5 FM, which gives details of the night's best raves. Flyers advertising what's on at which clubs can be found on café, bar and shop counters. Popular nighttime options for the more mature set include social dancing and visits to suave piano bars. If you're wondering about what to wear, the smart side of the smart-casual approach is usually the safest bet. Attire for nightclubs varies; for upscale venues, be sure to put your designer-labelled best foot forward, whilst more relaxed ones will accept an urban look, but generally, tracksuits, jeans and trainers are definite no-nos.

Mainstream

A vast yet convivial venue, **Le Bataclan** is a showcase for current bands. After the show on Saturday nights, it becomes one of the best nightclubs in Paris, legendary for its varied mouth-watering choice of funk, soul and new jack swing.

Barrio Latino occupies three floors of a building designed by Gustav Eiffel. It combines Latin music with great cocktails and tapas served from trolleys by roaming staff. Dancers can perfect their moves at the Sunday salsa classes. The expensive **Le Baron** attracts a select crowd, and plays host to ultra-fashionable party producers. Linked to the **Alcazar**, which is a fashionable Terence Conran bar and restaurant very popular with a pre-club crowd, **Jane Club** just next door is a wonderful spot for some uninhibited dancing. It is unpretentious, although the door staff are discriminating, and the disco and soul played in the stone cellars make for a great night out. Five nights a week, Le

Paris Paris Club hosts music performances during the evening and then transforms into an all-night themed dance party after 11pm.

Le Cabaret Sauvage, a vast big-top circus-style venue in the Parc de la Villette, hosts club nights with famous DJs along with concerts and performances.

Located in the trendy South Pigalle area, **Le Bus Palladium** was founded in the 1960s for those looking for a place to dance. The club provided a bus that dropped party goers at certain points in the capital for just two francs. Today, there is a rock n' roll club on the ground floor. An American-themed restaurant on the first floor serves delicious dishes such as Argentinian beef or nachos throughout the night.

A mix of ages and trends frequent the **Rex Club**. Despite the essentially conservative nature of the clientele, the music on different nights ranges from glam rock and

house to "exotique" – funk, reggae and world music. The vast **La Machine** caters to mainstream tastes most nights, with rock, house, groove and dance music each occupying a different floor.

Exclusive

If you aren't rich, beautiful and at least super-hip (if not actually on the celebrity "A" list), gaining entry to Paris's more exclusive clubs will be difficult. If you are, be prepared for a degree of humiliation and snooty service all the same. **Castel's** is a strictly private club and the happy few who make it, dine in one of two restaurants before heading down to the dance floor.

Regine's is mostly full of besuited executives and wealthy foreigners who dine and dance to the easy-listening music. However, it is enjoying something of a renaissance, especially on ladies nights (Thursday), when a trained physiognomist picks out the best looking women for a girls-own session complete with a male strip show. Predictably, when the doors open to men later, it becomes one of Paris's top nightspots for seeing and being seen.

The wood-panelled, cosy **Ritz Club** in the legendary Ritz hotel is open only to members and hotel guests, though the chic and elegant are welcome. The ambience is upmarket and the music is easy listening. A younger, glamorous set have begun to make the Ritz Club their home, attracted, no doubt, by its old-fashioned star quality.

Located on Rue de Rivoli is the glamorous international club **Le VIP Room Theatre**, which also has branches in St Tropez, Cannes and Monaco. This club is one of the city's hippest venues and a great place for celebrity spotting. This club also hosts parties for big names from around the world.

Showcase is a hot venue on Paris's night-scene with over 3,000 sq metres (32,000 sq ft) of space below the Pont Alexandre III. It triples as a bar, nightclub and concert hall. Another extremely upscale spot is **L'Arc Paris** situated near the Arc de Triomphe. Be prepared to make the effort to look your best (and most-solvent) to get in here.

Trendy

Madam is known for its late-night sessions and beautiful, moneyed crowds. The music is very French, with lots of electro and disco, and the decor is sylish, with a members' club atmosphere. Located in "bobo" chic Montorgueil, the **Cafe Etienne Marcel** is one of the Costes brothers' most eclectic bars. Known for its original cocktails, 1970s decor and DJ-hosted weekends, it is a gathering place for young, cosmopolitan Parisians.

An ultra-hip young crowd come to enjoy cocktails and Asian fusion menu at the endur-ing **Buddha Bar** and restaurant near the Champs-Elysées.

Located in the northern part of the city, **Glazart** has regular hip-hop, drum and bass and electro nights. Club nights begin around midnight and continue until dawn. Live concerts usually take place from 7pm until midnight.

Paris's trendy clubs seem to have a longer shelf-life than those in some other cities and another hip venue that's still going strong is **Le Gibus**, which offers different dance styles throughout the week. Check the flyers to pick your own style of party. The **Batofar**, the scarlet lighthouse ship moored on the Seine in the 13th arrondissement, is a mainstay of the Paris club scene. The music here varies from underground techno to reggae depending on the night of the week, but the crowd are always friendly and relaxed. In the summer, try not to miss their wonderfully

chilled-out afternoon sessions on the quayside.

The **Nouveau Casino** behind the ever trendy Café Charbon (see p311) in Oberkampf pulls in an eclectic crowd for events varying from dub to air-guitar competitions. **Le Social Club** has made an impressive mark on the Paris club scene with both its mixed programming and excellent live music agenda.

Old-timer **La Flèche d'Or** also offers an eclectic array of concerts, DJ nights and concept evenings. Whilst if it's just a large dance floor that's needed, then **Mix Club** should suffice.

World Music

Le Cabaret Sauvage entertains a chic crowd under a big-top. Its eclectic programme includes jazz, African sounds and drum 'n' bass. **Le Casbah** is exclusive, jazzy and one of the best established venues on the Paris club scene. Its African-Middle Eastern decor has always been a magnet for models and trendies who, in between dances, do a little nocturnal shopping in the club's downstairs boutique. Le Casbah is at present deservedly enjoying something of a renaissance of its former "chicest of the chic" reputation.

If your nervous system responds favourably to the heaving rhythms and throbbing beat of authentic Latin music, you should head for **La Java**, which combines glorious sounds with the quaint appeal of a Belleville dance hall. **Barrio Latino** definitely is the place to go for salsa with soul. Spread out over four floors, it has a restaurant on the second floor, while the other three are given over to dancing. You can also take salsa lessons and then dance the night away at **La Pachanga**. **La Bellevilloise** often has eclectic world music (see p342). Other lively world music and rock nights are

held at **La Maroquinerie,** which attracts big stars and also houses a restaurant and literary café.

Gay and Lesbian

The gay scene in Paris is thriving. **Le Queen** boasts a great line-up of DJs. Monday is disco night, Friday and Saturday are garage and soul and the rest of the week is drum and bass and house. Some of the raunchier events are men-only. Girls should go with pretty boys. Some nights at **La Machine** draw in a gay crowd. **Le Champmeslé**, one of the most venerable fixtures of Paris's ever more upfront and confident lesbian scene, continues to evolve and attract a new clientele. **La Boite à Frissons – Le Tango** is a converted dance hall that features a wacky crowd, Madonna and accordion music.

One of the hippest and busiest lesbian pre-club events, **Le Troisième Lieu,** moves from venue to venue so has a big social media following. **Le So What** is a favourite haunt for cocktail lovers.

Le Club 18 is the oldest gay club in the city. A young and beautiful crowd come here for the fun music and very laid-back atmosphere. It's a small venue so it gets crowded at weekends, especially as the admission fee includes a drink. Entry is usually free on weeknights.

Admission Charges

Some clubs are strictly private, others have a more generous admission policy. Prices can range from €12 to €15 or €30, or more, and may be higher after midnight and on week-ends. But quite often, there are concessions for women.

In general, one drink (une consommation) tends to be included in the club's entry price; thereafter, it can become an extremely expensive evening.

DIRECTORY

Disco and Club Venues

Alcazar
62 Rue Mazarine 75006.
Map 12 F4.
Tel 01 53 10 19 99.
W alcazar.fr

L'Arc Paris
12 Rue de Presbourg
75016. **Map** 4 D4.
Tel 01 45 00 78 70.

Le Baron
6 Ave Marceau 75008.
Map 10 E1.
Tel 01 47 20 04 01.
W clublebaron.com

Barrio Latino
46-48 Rue du Faubourg
Saint Antoine
75012.
Map 14 F4.
Tel 01 55 78 84 75.
W barrio-latino.com

Le Bataclan
(see p342 – Rock and Pop)

Batofar
Moored opposite 11 Quai
Francois Mauriac 75013.
Tel 01 53 60 17 00.
W batofar.org

Buddha Bar
8/12 Rue Boissy d'Anglas
75008.
Map 4 E5.
Tel 01 53 05 90 00.
W buddhabar.com

Le Bus Palladium
6 Rue Pierre Fontaine
75009. **Map** 6 E2.
Tel 01 45 26 80 35.
W lebuspalladium.com

Cabaret Sauvage
211 Ave Jean Jaurès, Parc
de la Villette 75019.
Tel 01 42 09 03 09.
W cabaretsauvage.com

Cafe Etienne Marcel
34 Rue Etienne Marcel
75002. **Map** 12 E1.
Tel 01 45 08 01 03.

Castel
15 Rue Princesse 75006.
Map 12 E4.
Tel 01 40 51 52 80.

Chez Regine's
49–51 Rue Ponthieu
75008.
Map 5 A5.
Tel 01 43 59 21 13.

Le Duplex
2 bis Avenue Foch 75116.
Map 4 D4.
Tel 01 45 00 45 00.
W leduplex.com

La Flèche d'Or
(see p342 – Rock and Pop)

Glazart
7–15 Ave de la Porte de la
Villette 75019.
Tel 01 40 36 55 65.
W glazart.com

Le Gibus
18 Rue du Faubourg-du-
Temple 75011.
Map 8 E5.
Tel 01 47 00 78 88.
W gibus.fr

Hammam Club
94 Rue d'Amsterdam
75009.
Map 6 D2.
Tel 01 55 07 80 00.
W hammamclub.fr

Jane Club
62 Rue Mazarine 75006.
Map 12 F4.
Tel 01 55 42 22 01.

**La Machine du
Moulin Rouge**
90 Blvd de Clichy 75018.
Map 4 E4.
Tel 01 53 41 88 88.
W lamachinedu
moulinrouge.com

Madam
128 Rue de la Boétie
75008.
Tel 01 53 76 02 11.
Map 4 F5.
W lemadam.fr

Mix Club
24 Rue de l'Arrivée 75015.
Map 15 C1.
Tel 01 56 80 37 37.
W mixclub.fr

Nouveau Casino
(see p342 – Rock and Pop)

Le Paris Paris Club
5 Avenue de l'Opéra
75001.
Map 12 E1.
Tel 01 42 60 64 45.
W parisparisclub.com

Les Planches
40 Rue du Colisée 75008.
Map 5 A4.
Tel 01 42 25 11 68.

Red Light
34 Rue du Départ 75015.
Map 15 C2.
Tel 01 42 79 85 49.
W leredlight.com

Rex Club
(see p342 – Rock and Pop)

Ritz Club
Hôtel Ritz, 15 Pl Vendôme
75001.
Map 6 D5.
Tel 01 43 16 30 30.
W ritzparis.com

Showcase
Under Alexander III
Bridge, Port des Champs-
Elysées 75008.
Map 11 A1.
Tel 01 45 61 25 43.
W showcase.fr

Le Social Club
142 rue Montmartre
75002. **Map** 13 A1.
Tel 01 40 28 05 45.
W parissocialclub.com

Le VIP Room Theatre
188 bis Rue de Rivoli
75001.
Map 12 E1.
Tel 01 58 36 46 00.
W viproom.fr

World Music

Cabaret Sauvage
(see Disco and Club
venues)

Le Casbah
18-20 Rue de la Forge-
Royale 75011.
Tel 01 43 71 04 39.
W casbah.fr

La Java
(see p336 – Cafe-Theatres
and Chansonniers)

La Maroquinerie
23 Rue Boyer 75020.
Map 15 B4.
Tel 01 40 33 35 05.
W lamaroquinerie.fr

La Pachanga
8 Rue Vandamme 75014.
Map 15 C2.
Tel 01 56 80 11 40.

Gay and Lesbian Venues

**La Boite à Frissons –
Le Tango**
13 Rue au Maire 75003.
Map 13 C1.
Tel 01 42 72 17 78.
W boite-a-frisson.fr

La Champmeslé
4 Rue Chabanais 75002.
Map 12 E1.
Tel 01 42 96 85 20.
W lachampmesle.com

Le Club 18
18 Rue de Beaujolais
75001.
Map 12 F1.
Tel 01 42 97 52 13.
W club18.fr

Le Queen
102 Ave des Champs-
Elysées 75008.
Map 4 E4.
Tel 01 53 89 08 90.
W queen.fr

Le So What
30 Rue du Roi de Sicile
75008.
Map 13 C3.
Tel 01 42 71 24 59.

Le Troisième Lieu
Mobile disco.
W facebook.com/
letroisiemelieu

Cinema

Paris can justifiably claim to be one of the world's capitals of film appreciation. More than 370 screens within the city limits, distributed among over 100 cinemas and multiplexes, screen a fabulous cornucopia of films, both brand-new and classic. American movies share the limelight with home-grown dramas and comedies, and virtually every filmmaking industry in the world has found a niche in the city's art houses. Cinemas change their programmes on Wednesdays. The cheapest practical guides to what's on are *Pariscope* and *L'Officiel des Spectacles* (see p332) with complete cinema listings and timetables for some 300 films. Films shown in subtitled original language versions are coded "VO" *(version originale)*; dubbed films are coded "VF" *(version française)*. Paris's Film Festival is held for one week in late June/early July. The system is that you pay full price for one film, after which a special card gives access to unlimited films at just €3 a ticket, for the duration of the festival.

Movements in Cinema

Paris was the cradle of the cinematograph over 100 years ago, when Auguste and Louis Lumière invented the early film projector. Their screening of *L'Arrivée d'un Train en Gare de la Ciotat* (Arrival of a Train at la Ciotat Station) in Paris in 1895 is considered by many to mark the birth of the medium. The French reverence for film as a true art form is based on a theory of one of the world's first film critics, Ricciotto Canudo, an Italian intellectual living in France, who dubbed cine-matography "the Seventh Art" in 1922. The title holds true even today. The city was of course also the incubator of that very Parisian vanguard movement, the New Wave, when film directors such as Claude Chabrol, François Truffaut, Jean-Luc Godard and Eric Rohmer in the late 1950s and early 60s revolutionized the way films were made and perceived. The exploration of existential themes, the use of long tracking shots and the rejection of studios for outside locations are some of the characteristics of New Wave cinema. In 2001, the success of *Amélie Poulain* revitalized the Parisian filmmaking scene; many of its locations are easy to spot as you walk around town. The same is true of *The Da Vinci Code*, also featuring *Amélie* star Audrey Tautou.

Cinema Zones

Most Paris cinemas are concentrated in several cinema belts, which enjoy the added appeal of nearby restaurants and shops.

The Champs-Elysées remains the densest cinema strip in town, where you can see the latest Hollywood smash hit or French *auteur* triumph, as well as some classic reissues, in subtitled original language versions. Cinemas in the Grands Boulevards, in the vicinity of the Opéra de Paris Garnier, show films in both subtitled and dubbed versions. Boulevard de Clichy is home to two Pathé multiplexes with a total of 12 screens showing current dubbed, French and VO releases. A major hub of Right Bank cinema activity is in the Forum des Halles shopping mall.

The Left Bank, historically associated with the city's intel-lectual life, remains the centre of the art and repertory cinemas. Yet, it has equally as many of the latest blockbusters. Since the 1980s, many cinemas in the Latin Quarter have closed down and the main centre for Left Bank theatres is now the Odéon-St-Germain-des-Prés area. The Rue Champollion is an exception. It has enjoyed a revival as a mini-district for art and repertory films.

Further to the south, Mont-parnasse remains a lively district for new films in both dubbed and subtitled prints.

Big Screens and Picture Palaces

Among surviving landmark cinemas are two Grands Boulevards venues, the 2,800-seat **Le Grand Rex** with its Baroque decor, and the **Max Linder Panorama**, which was refurbished by a group of independent film buffs in the 1980s for both popular and art film programming.

The massive 14-screen **MK2 Bibliothèque** cinema (plus bar, shops and exhibition space), has opened up in the revitalised 13th arrondissement, and just across the river, the **Bercy Village** cinema complex is well worth a visit too.

In the Cité des Sciences et de l'Industrie at La Villette, scientific films are shown at **La Géode** (see p239). This has a hemispheric screen (once the world's largest) and an "omnimax" projector which uses 70-mm film shot horizontally to project an image which is nine times larger than the standard 35-mm print. Along the Canal St-Martin, **MK2**'s twin cinema complexes – **Quai de la Loire** and **Quai de la Seine** – are linked by a canal boat.

Revival and Repertory Houses

Each week, more than 150 titles representing the best of world cinema can be seen. For old Hollywood films, the independent **Grand Action** mini-chain can't be beaten. Other active and thoughtful repertory and reissue venues include the excellent **Reflets Médicis** screens in the Rue Champollion and the **Pagode**.

The latter is particularly striking; the Oriental pagoda was constructed in 1895. **Studio 28** in Montmartre is a lovely old movie house with lights in the theatre designed by Jean Cocteau and a charming garden bar full of fairy lights and kitsch cut-outs of old film stars. Opened in the 1920s, Studio 28 claims to be the first ever avant-garde cinema and once played host to film greats such as Luis Buñuel and Abel Gance. They screen everything from the latest releases through to Fellini festivals and documentary shows. There are at least ten films screened here each week, including art-house classics and pre-releases. The cinema also holds regular debates with well-known directors and actors. Another Parisian institution, **Studio Galande** has shown the *Rocky Horror Picture Show* to costumed movie-goers every Friday night for over 20 years.

Cinémathèque Française

The private "school" of the New Wave generation, this famous film archive and repertory cinema was created by Henri Langlois in 1936 *(see p348)*. It has lost its monopoly on classic film screenings, but it is still a must for cinephiles in search of that rare film no longer in theatrical circulation or, perhaps, recently restored or rescued. The association is now housed at 51 Rue de Bercy in a wonderfully futuristic-looking building designed by Frank Gehry. The sail-like façade has given the building its nickname: "dancer revealing her tutu". The film library has more than 18,000 digitalized movies, and there are enough exhibitions, projections, lectures and workshops to satisfy the appetite of any film enthusiast. For those interested in the building's architecture, there are tours on the first Sunday of each month.

Non-Theatrical Venues

In addition to the Cinémathèque Française, film programmes and festivals are integral parts of two highly popular Paris cultural institutions, the Musée d'Orsay *(see pp146–7)* and the Pompidou Centre *(see pp110–11)* with its two screening rooms. The Musée d'Orsay regularly schedules film programmes to complement current art exhibitions and is usually restricted to silent films. The Pompidou Centre organizes vast month-long retrospectives, devoted to national film industries and on occasion to some of the major companies.

Finally, the **Forum des Images** *(see p115)* in the heart of Les Halles is a hi-tech film and video library with a vast selection of films and documentaries featuring the city of Paris from the late 19th century to the present day. The archives here are amazing and include newsreels and advertisements featuring Paris alongside the feature films and documentaries. The Forum has three cinemas, all of which run daily screenings of feature films. One ticket allows the visitor access to both the video library and to the cinema screenings. The screenings are frequently grouped according to theme or director, making it possible to spend several hours enjoying a mini-retrospective. See website for details.

Ticket Prices

Expect to pay around €10–12 at first-run venues or even more for films of unusual length or special media attention. However, exhibitors practise a wide array of collective discount incentives, including cut-rate admissions for students, the unemployed, the elderly, old soldiers and large families. Wednesday is discount day for everybody at some cinemas – prices are slashed to as low as €4.

France's three exhibition giants, Gaumont, UGC and MK2, also sell special discount cards and accept credit card reservations for their flagship houses, while repertory houses issue "fidelity" cards.

Films Starring Paris

Historical Paris (studio-made)

An Italian Straw Hat
(René Clair, 1927)

Sous les toits de Paris
(René Clair, 1930)

Les Misérables
(Raymond Bernard, 1934)

Hôtel du Nord
(Marcel Carné, 1937)

Les Enfants du Paradis
(Marcel Carné, 1945)

Casque d'Or
(Jacques Becker, 1952)

La Traversée de Paris
(Claude Autant-Lara, 1956)

Playtime
(Jacques Tati, 1967)

New Wave Paris (location-made)

Breathless
(Jean-Luc Godard, 1959)

Les 400 coups
(François Truffaut, 1959)

Documentary Paris

Paris 1900
(Nicole Vedrès, 1948)

La Seine a rencontré Paris
(Joris Ivans, 1957)

Paris as seen by Hollywood

Seventh Heaven
(Frank Borzage, 1927)

Camille
(George Cukor, 1936)

An American in Paris
(Vincente Minnelli, 1951)

Gigi
(Vincente Minnelli, 1958)

Irma La Douce
(Billy Wilder, 1963)

Paris when it Sizzles
(Richard Quine, 1964)

Frantic *(Roman Polanski, 1988)*

French Kiss
(Lawrence Kasdan, 1995)

The Ninth Gate
(Roman Polanski, 1999)

Moulin Rouge
(Baz Luhrmann, 2001)

The Bourne Identity
(Doug Liman, 2002)

Before Sunset
(Richard Linklater, 2004)

The Da Vinci Code
(Ron Howard, 2006)

Midnight in Paris
(Woody Allen, 2011)

Film Festivals

Film festivals are a way of life for Parisian movie buffs. There are several major events each year and lots of small themed festivals happening at any given time around the city. The annual Paris Film Festival, held in late June/early July, may be dwarfed by its glitzier sister in Cannes, but the capital's version is a far friendlier event for the public to attend – and there are still more than enough opportunities to spot celebrities.

Open-Air Festivals

There are several outdoor cinema festivals throughout the summer, including the Festival Silhouette which shows short films in the lovely Buttes Chaumont (see p236), the Cinéma au Clair de Lune festival which has projections of films at Parisian sites which are relevant to the movie, and Le Cinéma en Plein Air which draws crowds to a lawn in La Villette (see pp238-9), where a giant inflatable screen shows old and contemporary classics. This is one of the summer's most popular events, so be sure to get there early and don't forget to take a hamper full of goodies to nibble on throughout the movie.

Indoor Festivals

During the annual Paris Film Festival, over 100 films are shown at the Gaumont Marignon on the Champs-Elysées. The city's gay and lesbian film festival at the Forum des Images usually takes place in November. Paris Tout Court is an impressive short film festival held at the Arlequin in St-Germain which also stages lectures and meetings with renowned directors and artists. Other film festivals include the L'Etrange festival, which shows weird and wonderful offbeat films from around the world to enthusiastic audiences.

DIRECTORY

Cinemas

Action Christine
4 Rue Christine 75006.
Map 12 F4.
Tel 01 43 25 85 78.

Arlequin
76 Rue de Rennes 75006.
Map 12 E4.
Tel 01 45 44 28 80.

Le Balzac
1 Rue Balzac 75008.
Map 4 E4.
Tel 01 45 61 10 60.

Centre Pompidou
19 Rue Beaubourg 75004.
Map 13 B2.
Tel 01 44 78 12 33.

Le Champo
51 Rue des Ecoles 75005.
Map 13 A5.
Tel 01 43 54 51 60.

Cinémathèque Française
51 Rue de Bercy 75013.
Tel 01 71 19 33 33.
ⓦ cinemateque.fr

Cinema Studio Galande
42 Rue Galande 75005.
Map 13 A4.
Tel 01 43 54 72 71.

Le Desperado
23 Rue des Ecoles 75005.
Map 13 A5.
Tel 01 43 25 72 07.

La Filmothèque du Quartier Latin
9 Rue Champollion 75005. **Map** 12 F5.
Tel 01 43 26 70 38.

Forum des Images
(see p115)

Gaumont Marignan
27 Ave Champs-Elysées 75008.
Map 5 A5.
Tel 08 92 69 66 96.

La Géode
26 Ave Corentin-Cariou 75019.
Tel 08 92 70 08 40.
ⓦ lageode.fr

Grand Action
5 Rue des Ecoles 75005.
Map 13 B5.
Tel 01 43 54 47 62.

Le Grand Rex
(see p342 – Major Venues)

Lucernaire
53 Rue Notre-Dame-des-Champs 75006.
Map 16 E2.
Tel 01 45 44 57 34.

Max Linder Panorama
24 Blvd Poissonnière 75009.
Map 7 A5.
Tel 01 48 00 90 24.

Majestic Bastille
2–4 Blvd Richard Lenoir 75011. **Map** 14 E4.
Tel 01 47 00 02 48.

MK2
Beaubourg: 50 Rue Rambuteau 75003.
Map 13 A2.
Tel 08 92 69 84 84.
Bibliothèque: 128-162 Ave de France 75013.
Map 18 F4.
Tel 08 92 69 84 84.
Quai de la Seine/Quai de la Loire: 7 Quai de la Seine; 14 Quai de la Loire 75019.
Map 8 F1.
Tel 08 92 69 84 84.
ⓦ mk2.com

Le Nouveau Latina
20 Rue du Temple 75004.
Map 13 A2.
Tel 01 42 78 47 86.

Le Nouvel Odeon
6 Rue de l'Ecole de Médecine
75006.
Map 12 F4.
Tel 01 46 33 43 71.

La Pagode
57 bis Rue de Babylone 75007.
Map 11 C4.
Tel 01 45 55 48 48.

Reflets Médicis
3 Rue Champollion 75005.
Map 12 F5.
Tel 01 43 54 42 54.

St-Andre des Arts
30 Rue St Andre des Arts (Salles 1&2) and 12 Rue Git-le-Coeur (Salle 3) 75006.
Map 12 F4.
Tel 01 43 26 48 18.

Studio 28
10 Rue Tholozé 75018.
Map 6 E1.
Tel 01 46 06 36 07.

UGC Ciné Cité Bercy
2 Cour St-Emilion 75012.
Tel 08 25 12 12 02.

UGC Ciné-Cité les Halles
7 Place de la Rotonde, Forum des Halles 75001.
Map 13 A2.
Tel 08 25 12 12 02.

Sport and Fitness

There is no end of sporting activities in Paris. Certain events such as the Roland Garros tennis tournament and the Tour de France bicycle race are national institutions. The only drawback is that many of the facilities are on the outskirts of the city.

For details regarding all sporting events in and around Paris, contact Paris's tourist office. The weekly entertainment guides *L'Officiel des Spectacles*, *Pariscope* and the Wednesday edition of *Le Figaro* also have good listings of the week's sporting events *(see p332)*. For in-depth sports coverage, there is the daily paper *L'Equipe*. See also *Children's Paris* on page 354.

Outdoor Sports

The annual Tour de France bicycle race finishes in July in Paris to a city-wide frenzy, when the French president awards the coveted *maillot jaune* (yellow jersey) to the winner. For over twenty years now the final stage of the tour has taken place over several laps of a circuit taking in the Louvre, the quais along the Seine and the Champs-Elysées. Finding a spot to watch can be extremely tough, it's best to hunt down your space several hours before the riders are expected.

For those brave enough to cycle through the city traffic, bikes may be hired throughout Paris, including at **Vélo Paris** in Montmartre or at around 1,500 locations across the city with the self-service **Vélib'** scheme. The first 30 minutes are free, after which there are additional charges: at a rate of €1 for the next 30 minutes, €2 for another 30 minutes and thereafter at €4 for every additional 30 minutes. Regular users can buy a one- or seven-day card.

The **Fédération Française de Cyclotourisme** in the Rue Louis Bertrand provides information on over 300 cycling clubs around Paris. Things are gradually improving for those who favour pedal power; the city council shuts down some of the quaysides on Sundays and national holidays to allow cyclists freewheeling next to the Seine and the Canal St-Martin. The city has also undertaken a programme of expansion for its cycle lanes *(pistes cyclables)*, and

Parisian drivers are becoming more respectful of cyclists as more people turn to travelling on two wheels. Those who can't wait for the quais along the Seine to be closed on Sundays should head over to the Bois de Vincennes or the Bois de Boulogne for a leisurely bike ride through the woods. The more ambitious can pick up a copy of the free *Paris à Vélo* map from a tourist office to find details of all the city's cycle lanes. If you'd prefer to take an organized cycle tour through the city, there are several organizations who run fun trips. **Fat Tire Bike Tours** in the Rue Edgar Faure are expensive but have daily trips in spring and summer in which knowledgeable guides shepherd cyclists around the streets whilst imparting interesting information on the city's landmarks. Their partner, **City Segway Tours**, offers guided tours on electric Segway scooters (over 12s only). **Paris à Vélo c'est Sympa!** runs multilingual tours to offbeat parts of the city.

Roller bladers can enjoy parades through the city on Friday nights. The police close off boulevards around the city allowing thousands of skate fans to join the trip every week. The parade usually starts at Place de la Bastille at 10pm, but you can join the route at any point if the whole circuit seems a little much. Contact www.pariroller.com for details of the route. Beginners can enjoy free tuition prior to the departure of the parade if they arrive at the

start point at 8pm. There are many good outlets in the city for rollerblade rental. The parade's website provides useful links to recommended outlets. As a safety precaution, the trip is cancelled if the weather is inclement and the roads are wet.

Parisians enjoy Sunday afternoon boating in the Bois de Vincennes *(see p237)*, the Bois de Boulogne *(see p256)* and the Parc des Buttes-Chaumont *(see p236)*. Just queue up to hire a boat.

All the golf courses are outside Paris. Many are private clubs, but some will admit non-members – for further information contact the **Fédération Française du Golf** in the Rue Anatole-France. Otherwise, try the **Golf de Chevry, Golf de Villeray, Golf de St-Quentin en Yvelines** or the **Golf de Villennes Sur Seine**. Expect to pay at least €25 each time you want to play.

You can go horse-riding in both the Bois de Boulogne and the Bois de Vincennes. For details, contact the **Comité Departemental d'Equitation de Paris** in the Rue Laugier.

Tennis can be played at municipal courts such as the **Tennis Luxembourg** in the Jardin du Luxembourg. Courts are available every day on a first-come first-served basis. **Tennis la Faluère** in the Bois de Vincennes has some of the better courts, but these must be booked at least 24 hours in advance.

Indoor Sports

There are plenty of gyms in Paris which you can use with a day pass. Expect to pay €20 or more, depending on the facilities.

Club Med Gym is a well-equipped, popular chain of gyms with more than twenty sites in Paris and the suburbs. Good choices include the branches in Rue de Berri and Rue de Rennes. **Club Jean de Beauvais** in the Rue Jean de Beauvais, is a state-of-the-art gym with personalized fitness programmes.

The **Ken Club** on Avenue President Kennedy is an upmarket gym complete with pool and sauna in the chic 16th arrondissement. Its proximity to France's public radio HQ means French media personalities are often to be found there working out on their lunch break. In theory, the **Ritz Gym**, which has the finest indoor swimming pool in Paris, is for guests or members only, but if the hotel is not too full, you can buy a day pass.

Skating is an inexpensive pastime and can be enjoyed year-round at the **Patinoire d'Asnières-sur-Seine** on Boulevard Pierre de Coubertin. Winter-only rinks include one at the Hôtel de Ville.

Squash can be played at **Squash Club Quartier Latin** in the Rue de Pontoise, where options also include billiards, gym and a sauna. Other good clubs include the **Squash Montmartre** and the **Jeu de Paume et de Squash**.

Spectator Sports

A day out at the races is a chance to see the rich in all their finery. The world-famous Prix de l'Arc de Triomphe is held at the **Hippodrome de Longchamp** in the Bois de Boulogne on the first Sunday in October. More flat racing takes place at the **Hippodrome de St-Cloud** and **Maisons-Laffitte**, which are a short drive west of Paris. For steeple-chasing, go to the **Hippodrome d'Auteuil** in the Bois de Boulogne. The **Hippodrome de Vincennes** on Route de la Ferne hosts the trotting races. For detailed information on all of these, consult **France Galop** by phone or check their website.

The 24-hour car race at Le Mans, 185 km (115 miles) southwest of Paris, is one of the best-known road races in the world. It takes place every year in mid-June. Contact the **Automobile Club de l'Ouest** for details. The **Palais Omnisports de Paris-Bercy** sports stadium in Boulevard Bercy is the venue for a vast range of events, including

the BNP Paribas Masters tennis tournament, cycle trials, showjumping, world-class martial arts demonstrations, tournaments in everything from figure skating to handball, and major rock concerts.

Parc des Princes can hold 50,000 people. It is home to the main Paris football team, Paris St-Germain.

The colossal **Stade de France** is a major venue for football, rugby and music concerts. Sports fans can go on a behind the scenes tour.

The **Stade Roland Garros** in Avenue Gordon-Bennett is famous for its international tennis tournament. From late May to mid-June, everyone lives and breathes tennis. Business meetings are transferred from the conference room to the stadium. Apply for tickets several months ahead. Don't miss a trip to the stadium's excellent museum of tennis featuring everything from prototype rackets to a Bjorn Bjorg headband. Also, be sure to book a table at one of the swanky restaurants here, which are transformed into a place to see and be seen during the tournament. Tennis fans should also be sure to catch the mens' masters series at the Palais Omnisports de Paris Bercy in November and the womens' Open Gaz de France tournament, which takes place at the **Stade Pierre de Coubertin** on Avenue Georges Lafont, in March.

Swimming

There is a massive aquatic fun park, known as **Aquaboulevard**, in south Paris (see p354). Besides an exotic artificial beach, swimming pools and water toboggans and rapids, there are tennis and squash courts, golf, bowling, table tennis, billiards, a gym, bars and shops.

Of the many municipal swimming pools, one of the best is the **Piscine Suzanne Berlioux** in Place de la Rotonde, with an Olympic-sized swimming pool in the underground shopping

complex. For a lovely 1930s mosaic decor with two levels of private changing cabins, a whirlpool, sauna and water jets, go to the **Piscine Pontoise-Quartier Latin**. This complex also has a small gym overlooking the pool, where fitness fans can pump a little iron before taking a dip. The **Piscine Henry de Montherlant** is part of a municipal sports complex that includes tennis courts and a gym. The beautiful Art Nouveau pool in the Butte aux Cailles (see pp274–5) is a treat for serious swimmers and sunbathers. A decent-sized indoor pool is perfect for laps whilst the two outdoor swimming areas are great for lounging. The villagey atmosphere of the surrounding area only serves to reinforce the feeling of relaxing on holiday miles away from the city. The **Piscine Josephine Baker** near the Bibliothèque F. Mitterand is a pleasing addition which floats on the Seine. In the summer, the rooftop terrace is a good spot for sunbathing.

Some of the smarter hotels and gyms also have their own pools. It is possible to buy a day pass to the chic **Club Med Gym** in the Rue Louis Armand and have access to their 15-metre pool. Similarly at the **Novotel Tour Eiffel**, non-guests are welcomed to their health club and pool which has a retractable roof for swimming under the sun in spring and summer. It is important to note that all municipal pools and some private ones insist that bathers wear swimming caps and that male swimmers wear swimming trunks rather than baggy shorts.

Miscellaneous

Baseball, fencing, jogging in the parks, volleyball, windsurfing at La Villette (see pp238–9) and bowling are just some of the other sporting activities that can be enjoyed during your stay.

Fishing on the Seine (with the appropriate permits) is fast becoming a popular pastime with Parisians. The Seine is home to a variety of freshwater fish.

DIRECTORY

Outdoor Sports

Comité Départemental d'Equitation de Paris
69 Rue Laugier 75017.
Tel 01 42 12 03 43.

Fat Tire Bike Tours & City Segway Tours
24 Rue Edgar Faure 75015. **Map** 10 D4.
Tel 01 56 58 10 54.
W paris.fattirebike tours.com
W citysegway tours. com

Fédération Française de Cyclotourisme
12 Rue Louis Bertrand 94207 Ivry-sur-Seine.
Tel 01 56 20 88 88.
W ffct.org

Fédération Française du Golf
68 Rue Anatole France, 92309 Levallois Perret.
Tel 01 41 49 77 00.
W ffgolf.org

France Galop
46 Place Abel Gance Boulogne 92100.
Tel 01 49 10 20 30.
W france-galop.com

Golf de Chevry
91190 Gif-sur-Yvette.
Tel 01 60 12 40 33.

Golf de St-Quentin en Yvelines
78190 Trappes.
Tel 01 30 50 86 40.

Golf de Villennes-sur-Seine
Route d'Orgeval Villennes-sur-Seine 78670.
Tel 01 39 08 18 18.

Golf de Villeray
91280 St-Pierre du Perray.
Tel 01 60 75 17 47.
W bluegreen.com

Paris à Vélo c'est Sympa!
22 Rue Alphonse Baudin 75011. **Map** 14 E2.
Tel 01 48 87 60 01.
W parisvelosympa.com

Paris Tourist Office
Tel 01 49 52 42 63.
(see p359).

Indoor Sports

Club Jean de Beauvais
5 Rue Jean de Beauvais 75005. **Map** 13 A5.
Tel 01 46 33 16 80.

Club Med Gym
26 Rue de Berri 75008.
Map 4 F4.
Tel 01 43 59 04 58.
149 Rue de Rennes 75006. **Map** 15 C1.
Tel 01 45 44 24 35.
W clubmedgym.com

Jeu de Paume et de Squash
74ter Rue Lauriston 75116. **Map** 4 D4.
Tel 01 47 27 46 86.
W jdpsquash.com

Ken Club
100 Ave President Kennedy 75016.
Tel 01 46 47 41 41.

Patinoire d'Asnières-sur-Seine
Blvd Pierre de Coubertin, Asnières 92600.
Tel 01 47 99 96 06.

Ritz Gym
Ritz Hotel, 15 Pl Vendôme 75001. **Map** 6 D5.
Tel 01 43 16 30 30.

Squash Club Quartier Latin
19 Rue de Pontoise 75005. **Map** 13 B5.
Tel 01 55 42 77 88.

Squash Montmartre
14 Rue Achille-Martinet 75018. **Map** 2 E4.
Tel 01 42 55 38 30.

Tennis la Faluère
113 Route de la Pyramide, Bois de Vincennes 75012.
Tel 01 43 74 40 93.

Tennis Luxembourg
Blvd St-Michel, Jardins du Luxembourg 75006.
Map 12 E5.
Tel 01 43 25 79 18.

Vélib'
Tel 01 30 79 74 30.
W velib.paris.fr

Vélo Paris
44 Rue d'Orsel 75018.
Map 6 F2.
Tel 01 42 64 97 39.
W veloparis.com

Spectator Sports

Automobile Club de l'Ouest
Tel 02 43 40 24 24.
W lemans.org

Hippodrome d'Auteuil
Route d'Auteuil aux Lac, Bois de Boulogne 75016.
Tel 01 40 71 47 47.

Hippodrome de Longchamp
Routes des Tribunes, Bois de Boulogne 75016.
Tel 01 44 30 75 00.

Hippodrome Maisons-Laffitte
1 Ave de la Pelouze, Maisons-Laffitte 78600.
Tel 01 39 12 81 70.

Hippodrome de St-Cloud
1 Rue de Camp Canadien, St-Cloud 92210.
Tel 01 47 71 69 26.

Hippodrome de Vincennes
2 Route de la Ferme, Vincennes 75012.
Tel 01 49 77 17 17.

Palais Omnisports de Paris-Bercy
8 Blvd Bercy 75012.
Map 18 F2.
Tel 01 40 02 60 60.

Parc des Princes
24 Rue du Commandant-Guilbaud 75016.
Tel 01 47 43 71 71.
W leparcdesprinces.fr

Stade de France
Rue Henri Delaunay, La Plaine St-Denis 93210.
Tel 08 92 70 09 00.
W stadedefrance.com

Stade Pierre de Coubertin
82 Ave Georges Lafont 75016.
Tel 01 45 27 79 12.

Stade Roland Garros
2 Ave Gordon-Bennett 75016.
Tel 01 47 43 48 00.
W rolandgarros.com

Swimming

Aquaboulevard
4 Rue Louis-Armand 75015.
Tel 01 40 60 10 00.

Club Med Gym
8 Rue Frémicourt 75015.
Tel 01 45 75 34 00.

Novotel Tour Eiffel
61 Quai de Grenelle 75015.
Map 9 B5.
Tel 01 40 58 20 00.

Piscine Butte-aux-Cailles
5 Pl Paul-Verlaine 75013.
Map 17 A5.
Tel 01 45 89 60 05.

Piscine des Amiraux
6 Rue Hermann-Lachapelle 75018.
Tel 01 46 06 46 47.

Piscine Henry de Montherlant
30 Blvd de Lannes 75016.
Tel 01 40 72 28 30.

Piscine Josephine Baker
Quai François Mauriac 75013.
Tel 01 56 61 96 50.

Piscine Pontoise-Quartier Latin
Rue de Pontoise 75005.
Map 13 B5.
Tel 01 55 42 77 88.

Piscine St Germain
12 Rue Lobineau 75006.
Map 12 E4.
Tel 01 56 81 25 40.

Piscine Saint-Merri
16 Rue de Renard 75004.
Map 13 B3.
Tel 01 42 72 83 67.

Piscine Suzanne Berlioux
10 Pl de la Rotonde, Niveau 3, Entrance Porte St Eustache, Les Halles 75001.
Map 13 A2.
Tel 01 42 36 98 44.

CHILDREN'S PARIS

It's never too early to instil a lifelong taste for this magical city in your children. Scaling the dizzy heights of the Eiffel Tower (see pp196–7), boating down the Seine (see pp74–5) or a visit to Notre-Dame (see pp82–5) are fun at any age, and with children in tow, you will see old haunts through new eyes. The historic parks are probably best appreciated by older children and adults, but everyone will love the technological wizardry of Disneyland® Paris (see pp244–7). During the summer, funfairs, circuses and all sorts of impromptu events are staged in gardens and parks, notably in the Bois de Boulogne (see pp256–7). Or, take children to an entertainment centre, museum, adventure playground, or zoo, or to a show at one of the café-theatres.

La Cité des Enfants at La Villette

Practical Advice

Paris welcomes young families in hotels (see p280) and most restaurants (see p291). Many sights and attractions offer child reductions, while infants under three or four enter free. Children under 18 are admitted free of charge to all state-run museums throughout the year. Ask at the Office du Tourisme (see p282) for full details of child reductions, or check in the weekly entertainment guides such as Pariscope, L'Officiel des Spectacles and Paris Mômes.

A lot of the children's activities are geared to end-of-school times, including Wednesday afternoons when French children have time off. For information on museum workshops, contact the museums individually.

Babychou and **Kidizen** are specialist babysitting organizations in the city. They also offer a wide range of other services, including hiring out cots, strollers and other equipment.

Museums

Top of the museum list for children is undoubtedly the **Cité des Sciences et de l'Industrie** (see pp238–9) at Parc de la Villette. Hands-on activities and frequently changing exhibitions illuminate many aspects of science and modern technology in this immense complex. There are sections for children called La Cité des Enfants and Techno Cité. In central Paris, the Palais de la Découverte, within the Grand Palais (see p210), is an old-fashioned but lively science museum where staff entertain the children by adopting the role of mad inventors.

The Louvre (see pp122–9) organizes thematic art trails around the museum for all ages, as well as special sessions designed to introduce children to various aspects of art. It is possible to download art trails from the website. The Musée D'Orsay (see pp146–7) has a variety of fun, interactive museum tours for children aged 5 to 12 to enjoy while The Galerie des Enfants at the Pompidou Centre (see pp110–13) also offers special sessions with a focus on modern art.

Other enjoyable museums for children include the Musée National de la Marine (see p203) and the Musée de la Poupée (see p116). The former covers the history of the French maritime tradition and includes scale models of some of France's finest battleships, dreadnoughts and submarines. The latter displays a collection of hand-made dolls dating from the mid-19th century, and also offers workshops for both adults and children.

Parks, Zoos and Adventure Playgrounds

The best children's park within Paris is the Jardin d'Acclimatation in the Bois de Boulogne (see pp256–7), with a children's theatre, a circus, a pony club, a mini railway and

The Café d'Edgar theatre

The Guignol marionnettes

boats, and the Musée en Herbe, a museum created especially for children offering entertaining educational activities. Out of town at Elancourt, **France Miniature** recreates France on a small scale, with fascinating mini monuments.

The Bois de Vincennes *(see p237)* has simple amusements for children in the inexpensive Parc Floral. It also has the largest funfair in France, open from Palm Sunday through to the end of May. Perhaps the most appealing zoo is the small

Ménagerie in the Jardin des Plantes *(see p166)*.

Entertainment Centres

There are many supervised children's activity centres in Paris. The Atelier des Enfants in the Pompidou Centre *(see pp110–11)* has a workshop on Wednesday and Saturday afternoons from 2.30 to 4pm. The medium of instruction is French but the circuses, mime-shows, marionnettes and craft or museum workshops focus on actions rather than words. Several café-theatres, including Café d'Edgar *(see p335)* and Abricadabra at the Antipode Barge on the Canal de L'Ourcq offer children's shows with mime, dance or music. The most spectacular cinematic experience is in La Géode at the Cité des Sciences et de l'Industrie *(see p239)*. The cinema **Le Saint Lambert** specializes in children's films and comic strips in French, though most films for children will not have English subtitles. Cinema tickets are cheaper on Wednesdays, with no child reductions at weekends.

Paris Miniature

Une Journée au Cirque offers children a day's entertainment when they can meet the animals, put on clown make-up or practise tightrope walking. Shows are in the afternoon, after lunch with the *artistes*.

The Guignol marionnette puppet shows are a summer tradition. Guignol himself is a far gentler character than the traditional English Mr Punch. Most of the main parks hold Guignol shows in summer on Wednesday afternoons and at weekends. Consult the entertainment guides such as *Pariscope*, *L'Officiel des Spectacles* and *Paris Mômes*.

DIRECTORY

Addresses

Babychou Services
Tel 01 43 13 33 23.
W babychou.com.

France Miniature
Blvd André Malraux,
Elancourt 78990.
Tel 01 30 16 16 30.
W franceminiature.com

Une Journée au Cirque
115 Blvd Charles de Gaulle,
Ville-neuve-la-Garenne 92390.
Tel 01 47 99 40 40.
W journeeaucirque.com.

Kidizen
Tel 06 38 10 97 42.
W kidizen.fr

Le Chaplin Saint Lambert
6 Rue Peclet 75015.
Tel 01 42 50 23 32.
W lescinemaschaplin.fr

The 'Le Dragon' ride in the Jardin d'Acclimation

Fireworks over Sleeping Beauty Castle, Disneyland® Paris

Theme Parks

The two parks of Disneyland® Paris (see pp244–7) are the biggest and most spectacular of the Paris theme parks. Seven hotels, each with a different, imaginative theme, and a campsite provide on-site accommodation. The complex also includes a golf course, shops and restaurants.

Parc Asterix is a French theme park centring around the legendary world of Asterix the Gaul. Here, six themed "worlds" feature gladiators, slave auctions and rides among the many attractions. The park is situated 38 km (24 miles) northeast of Paris. Take the RER line B to Charles de Gaulle Airport then the shuttle bus to Parc Asterix.

Sports and Recreation

The giant waterpark **Aquaboulevard** is one of the best places to take energetic youngsters. Also good is the indoor pool at **Forum des Halles**. The weekly entertainment guide *Pariscope* lists the swimming pools in and around Paris. Remember that it is compulsory to wear a swimming cap.

Accomplished rollerskaters and skateboarders practise outside the Palais de Chaillot (see p202). On Sundays, in summer, the roads along the Seine (between Chatelêt and Bercy) are closed to traffic; bikers and rollerbladers descend en masse. Disneyland® Paris (see pp244–7) has ice-skating rinks and a range of other sports facilities.

Donald Duck

Old-fashioned fairground carousels are situated near Sacré-Coeur (see pp226–7) and Forum des Halles (see p115). A great way of inspiring interest in the city's history, and great fun too, is a boat trip. Several companies compete (see pp74–5) from different departure points, and pass a host of waterfront sites including Notre-Dame, the Louvre and the Musée d'Orsay. Boats departing from La Villette travel along the Paris canal system. Radio-controlled model boats are popular on the ponds of the Jardin du Luxembourg (see p174). Or, take the family boating on the lakes of the Bois de Boulogne (see pp256–7) or the Bois de Vincennes (see p237). Riding is also popular in these parks (see p351 Directory).

Street Life and Markets

Outside the Pompidou Centre (see pp110–11), street entertainers draw the crowds on sunny afternoons. Musicians, conjurors, fire-eaters and artists of all kinds perform here. In Montmartre, there is a tradition of street-painting, predominantly in the Place du Tertre (see p228) where someone will always be willing to draw your child's portrait. It's also fun to take the funicular up the hill to Sacré-Coeur (see pp226–7), then walk down through the pretty streets.

Parisian markets are colourful and animated. Try taking children to the Marché aux

Children's Shops

There is no shortage of chic children's fashion in Paris. The Rue du Jour in Beaubourg and Les Halles has a number of boutiques for young fashionistas. The city has many appealing children's shops, such as the kid's concept store, Bonton (see p318), but, like the clothes shops, they can be prohibitively expensive.

Toy characters from *Tintin*, the popular comic book series

Skate-boarders near the Eiffel Tower

Fleurs et aux Oiseaux Cité on the Ile de la Cité *(see p87)* or to the food markets on the Rue Mouffetard, in the Jardin des Plantes Quarter *(see p168 and p331)*, or the Rue de Buci in St-Germain-des-Prés. The biggest flea market, Marché aux Puces de St-Ouen, is at weekends *(see p235 and p331)*.

Alternatively, take children to the quiet Ile de la Cité or Ile St-Louis on the Seine.

Viewpoints and Sightseeing

Top of the sightseeing list for children is a trip up the Eiffel Tower *(see pp196–7)*. On a clear day, spectacular views over Paris will enable you to point out a number of sights, and at night the city is magically lit up. Lifts run until 11pm and queues are much shorter in the evenings. If you are pushing a baby buggy, bear in mind that the ascent is in three stages, using two separate lifts.

Other interesting sights for children include Sacré-Coeur *(see pp226–7)* with its ovoid dome – the second highest point in Paris after the Eiffel Tower – and Notre-Dame cathedral *(see pp82–5)* on the Ile de la Cité. Children will enjoy feeding the pigeons in the cathedral square, visiting the gargoyles on the West Front and listening to you recount the story of the hunchback of Notre-Dame. There are incomparable views from the towers. Children and adults alike will appreciate the enchanting Sainte-Chapelle *(see pp88–9)*, also on the Ile de la Cité. Children under the age of 18 almost always go free.

Contrast ancient and modern Paris with a visit to the Pompidou Centre *(see pp110–13)* and enjoy a ride on the cater-pillar-like escalators outside, or go to the café on the roof terrace for the views. There is also the 56-storey Montparnasse Tower *(see p180)* with some spectacular telescopic views from the top terrace; and there is the huge arch at La Défense *(see p257)* which has lifts to exhibition

Carousel near Sacré-Coeur

platforms where visitors can overlook the whole complex.

Other Interests

Children are quick to see the funny side of unusual spectacles. Les Egouts, Paris's sewers, offer a short tour of the city's sewerage system *(see p192)*. Display boards in several languages explain the processes.

The Catacombs *(see p181)* are a long series of quarry tunnels built in Roman times, and lined with ancient skulls in the 18th century.

On the Ile de la Cité is the Conciergerie *(see p87)*, a turreted prison where many hapless aristocrats spent their final days. The Grévin waxworks are in Boulevard Montmartre *(see p220)*. The museum's Revolution rooms will especially appeal to older children, with gruesome scenes and grisly

Model boats for hire in the Jardin du Luxembourg

sound effects, demonstrating the reality of social upheaval.

Emergencies

Enfance et Partage is a free 24-hour child helpline (also for adults). One of Paris's largest children's hospitals is **Hôpital Necker**.

DIRECTORY

Useful Addresses

Aquaboulevard
4 Rue Louis Armand 75015.
Tel 01 40 60 10 00.
Open 9am–9pm Mon–Fri,
8am–9pm Sat, Sun & public hols.

Piscine Suzanne Berlioux
Forum des Halles, 10 Pl de la Rotonde, Les Halles 75001.
Map 12 F2. **Tel** 01 42 36 98 44.
Open 11.30am–10pm Mon,
Tue, Thu, Fri (to 11pm Mon);
7–8.15am, 10am–11pm Wed;
9am–7pm Sat & Sun (times vary during school hols). ⓦ **carilis.fr**

Parc Asterix
BP8 Plailly 60128. **Tel** 08 26 46 66 26. **Open** mid-Apr–Nov: 10am–6pm daily. ⓦ **parcasterix.fr**

Emergencies

Enfance et Partage
Tel 08 00 05 12 34.
ⓦ **enfance-et-partage.org**

Hôpital Necker
149 Rue de Sèvres 75015.
Map 15 B1. **Tel** 01 44 49 40 00.
ⓦ **aphp.fr**

SURVIVAL GUIDE

PRACTICAL INFORMATION

Paris offers a vast wealth of things to see and do. A little forward planning can save time and inconvenience. Make use of tourist offices and ring in advance to confirm a sight is open and is not closed for refurbishment or holidays. Guided tours are often the best way to see the essential sights while you get your bearings *(see p375)*. Buying a *Paris Pass* will give you unlimited access to the city's many attractions, and cuts down on time spent in

queues *(see p359)*. If you're on a tight budget, note that admission prices are sometimes lower at certain times of day, or on Sundays. Beware that some shops and museums are closed all day on Monday. Card-carrying students and senior travellers can obtain discounts on some tickets *(see p360)*. Purchase a *carnet* or travel pass to economize and simplify travel on the Metro and buses *(see p374 and pp376–9)*.

Visas and Passports

France is part of the Schengen common European border treaty, which means that travellers moving from one Schengen country to another are not subject to border controls. Schengen residents need only to show an identity card when entering France. Visitors from the UK, Ireland, the US, Canada, Australia and New Zealand need to show a full passport. Tourists from these countries may stay in France without a visa for 90 days within a continuous 180-day period. For more information and to check visa requirements, visitors should consult the website of their embassy in France.

Tax-free Goods and Customs Information

Visitors resident outside the EU can reclaim the sales tax (TVA, or VAT) they pay on French goods if they spend more than €175 in the same shop in one day and take the goods out of France *(see p312)*. Détaxe receipts can be issued on purchase to reclaim the tax paid (this is usually 12 per cent). The documents need to be endorsed at a détaxe office (located at airports) on exiting the EU within three months of purchase, then posted in the envelope provided. There are some goods on which a rebate cannot be claimed including food and drink, medicines, tobacco, cars and motorbikes. The **Centre des Renseignements des Douanes** provides full information about this.

In general, all personal goods, including cars and bicycles, may be imported to France if they are obviously for personal use and not for sale. There are no restrictions on the quantities of duty-paid and VAT-paid goods that can be taken from one EU country to another, as long as they are for personal use. Visitors under the age of 17 are not allowed to import duty-paid tobacco or alcohol into France. Duty-free purchases of liquids carried by travellers arriving in Paris from a non-EU country and connecting directly onto another flight will be confiscated at security check.

The maximum value of currency that can be brought into or taken out of France is €10,000. Sums in excess of this must be declared to the customs authority.

Tourist Information

The main tourist office in Paris, the **Office du Tourisme et des Congrès de Paris**, is near the Jardin des Tuileries *(see p132)*. It will have the latest maps, information and brochures, and can provide comprehensive information about events in the city.

There are other tourist offices at Place du Tertre, at the **Gare du Nord**, **Gare de l'Est** and **Gare de Lyon**, at **Anvers** Metro station and at the **Paris Expo** exhibition centre at Porte de Versailles during trade fairs. There are also summer-only kiosks at sights such as Notre-Dame and the Hôtel de Ville.

Admission Charges

An admission fee is usually charged, or a donation

Le Musée d'Orsay, where entry is free on the first Sunday of the month

◀ A busy platform next to the TGV Bullet train

expected, at museums. The entrance fee to some national and municipal museums is waived on the first Sunday of each month for their permanent collections. Some museums reduce their rates for an evening visit (for example, the entrance fee to the Louvre is reduced after 6pm on Wednesday and Friday, when the museum stays open until 10pm). Visitors under 18 years of age and European passport holders aged 18–26 years are usually admitted free to museums, and there are sometimes discounts for students and seniors who have ID showing their date of birth.

The *Paris Pass* gives the bearer unlimited access to over 60 of the city's attractions for 2, 4 or 6 days, without having to queue (temporary exhibitions are not included). It also offers unlimited travel on the Metro, buses and RER within central Paris, and a ticket for a hop-on hop-off bus tour. The pass must be bought in advance through the website (www.parispass. com) and is either posted (allow time for delivery) or can be collected in Paris (see website for details).

Opening Hours

Most of the city's museums and monuments open from 10am to 6pm. Municipal museums, such as those run by the city of Paris, are usually closed on Monday. The national museums are closed on Tuesday, except Versailles and the Musée d'Orsay, which are closed on Monday. Most ticket counters close 30–45 minutes before the official closing time. To avoid queues and packed museums, take advantage of the *nocturnes* (late-night opening) that many of the major museums offer or visit on weekday mornings.

Most Paris shops and businesses are open from 9am to 7pm. Some close for an hour or two from around 1pm. Smaller food shops tend to open earlier, around 7am, and take a longer midday break. Most businesses are closed on Sunday,

Kiosque Théâtre booking kiosk

but Sunday trading is allowed in tourist areas. Many shops close on Monday.

Listings and Tickets

The main listings magazines, available at all newsagents, are *Pariscope* and *L'Officiel des Spectacles (see p332)*. Each Wednesday, they publish full information on the week's theatre, cinema and exhibits, as well as on cabarets, dinner clubs and some restaurants. FNAC ticket agencies take bookings for all entertainment venues, including temporary museum shows. There are FNAC branches throughout Paris. For further details, call one of their branches *(see p333)*.

For booking the theatre only, the Kiosque Théâtre sells same-day tickets at 50 per cent discount. There are kiosks at Place de la Madeleine and the Parvis de la Gare Montparnasse *(see p333)*.

DIRECTORY

Customs Information

Centre des Renseignements des Douanes
Tel 08 11 20 44 44
Open 8.30am–6pm Mon–Fri. **W** douane.gouv.fr

Tourist Information

Office du Tourisme et des Congrès de Paris
25 Rue des Pyramides 75001. **Map** 12 E1.
Open 1 Nov–30 Apr: 10am–7pm daily (2 May–31 Oct: 9am daily).
W parisinfo.com

Anvers
72 Blvd Rochechouart 75018. **Map** 7 A2.
Open 10am–6pm daily

Gare de l'Est
Pl du 11 Novembre 1918, 75010. **Map** 18 F1.
Open 8am–7pm Mon–Sat.

Gare de Lyon
20 Blvd Diderot 75012.
Map 18 F1.
Open 8am–6pm Mon–Sat.

Gare du Nord
18 Rue de Dunkerque 75010. **Map** 7 B2.
Open 8am–6pm daily.

Paris Expo
1 Pl Porte de Versailles 75015. **Open** 11am–7pm during trade fairs.

Paris Rendez-Vous
29 Rue de Rivoli 75004.
Map 13 B3.
Open 10am–7pm Mon–Sat.

French Tourist Office Abroad

Australia
Level 13, 25 Bligh St, Sydney NSW 2000.
Tel 02 92 10 54 00.
W au.rendezvous enfrance.com

Canada
1800 Ave McGill College, Suite 1010, Montréal, Quebec H3A 3J6.
Tel 514 288 2026.
W ca.rendezvous enfrance.com

United Kingdom
Lincoln House, 300 High Holborn, London WC1V 7JH.
Tel 0207 061 66 00.
W uk.rendezvous enfrance.com

United States
825 Third Ave New York, NY 10022.
Tel 1 212 838 7800.
info.us@franceguide.com
W us.rendezvous enfrance.com

Embassies

Australia
4 Rue Jean Rey 75015.
Map 10 D3. **Tel** 01 40 59 33 00. **W** france. embassy.gov.au

Canada
35 Ave Montaigne 75008.
Map 10 F1. **Tel** 01 44 43 29 00. **W** canadainter-national. gc.ca/france

Great Britain
35 Rue du Faubourg St-Honoré 75008. **Map** 5 C5. **Tel** 01 44 51 31 00.
W gov.uk/government/ world/france.fr

Ireland (Eire)
12 Ave Foch 75016. **Map** 3 B4. **Tel** 01 44 17 67 00.
W embassyofireland.fr

New Zealand
7ter Rue Léonard de Vinci 75016. **Map** 3 C5.
Tel 01 45 01 43 43.
W nzembassy.com/ france

USA
2 Ave Gabriel 75008.
Map 5 B5. **Tel** 01 43 12 22 22. **W** france. usembassy.gov

Travellers with Special Needs

Services for people with special needs are improving in Paris. Most pavements are contoured to allow wheelchairs an easier passage, and restaurants, hotels and museums are adapting their facilities. There is, for example, wheelchair access to the first and second floor of the Eiffel Tower, at a reduced tariff, while the Louvre and Musée d'Orsay are free to disabled visitors and their escorts.

Increasingly, sights are sporting the *Tourisme & Handicap* label denoting that they are accessible to people with physical, mental, hearing and visual impediments. The Office du Tourisme et des Congrès *(see p359)* has a guide (*Les Sites Labellisés "Tourisme & Handicap" à Paris et en Ile-de-France*) listing these. The association **J'accede** has details (in French and English) of accessible museums, hotels, bars, restaurants and cinemas in Paris and other French cities.

Metro stations and bus routes accessible to travellers with limited mobility are marked with a wheelchair symbol on their maps. The RATP's **Infomobi** website details all their accessible public transport and stations. Paris's international train stations have lifts, ramps, courtesy wheelchairs, signs in Braille, and a magnetic loop at ticket counters for the hearing impaired. **Accès Plus** is a free service to greet and accompany disabled travellers on their journey. **Les Compagnons du Voyage** will provide an escort for persons with limited mobility on any form of public transport, for a fee.

Some Paris taxi companies (such as G7, *see p381*), have vehicles suited to travellers with limited mobility; taxis are bound by law to assist disabled travellers.

For further up-to-date information on public facilities for the disabled, contact the **GIHP**.

Tourisme & Handicap sign

Student Travellers

Students with valid ID cards benefit from discounts of 25–50 per cent at theatres, museums, cinemas and many public monuments. An ISIC card (International Student ID card) may be bought from the main travel agencies and the **CIDJ**. The **BVJ** has two reasonably priced hostels in Paris *(see p281)*.

Senior Travellers

Some museums and monuments, theatres and independent cinemas offer reductions for visitors aged over 60. Théâtre du Chatelet *(see p339)*, for example, offers discounted tickets 15 minutes before showtime to over-65s. Expect to be asked for ID, such as a passport, to prove your date of birth. Canal tour operators **Canauxrama and Paris Canal** offer reduced tariffs. Over-60s are eligible for a 25 per cent discount from state railway **SNCF** on off-peak travel. Check their website for details.

Etiquette and Smoking

Etiquette (*la politesse*) is everything to Parisians. On entering a shop or cafe, you're expected to say *"bonjour Madame"* or *"bonjour Monsieur"* to staff, and when leaving to say *"au revoir"*. Be sure to add *"s'il vous plaît"* (please) when ordering something, and *"pardon"* if you accidentally bump someone.

The French shake hands on meeting someone for the first time, and when greeting workmates or acquaintances. Friends and colleagues who know each other well usually greet each other with a kiss on each cheek. If you are unsure, wait to see if they proffer a hand or a cheek.

Smoking is prohibited in all public places, but is allowed on restaurant, café and pub terraces, as long as they are not enclosed.

Public Conveniences

Automated, self-cleaning toilets can be found across the city. They have been upgraded to be larger than previously, wheelchair-usable and free. Children under ten are not allowed into these toilets on their own because the automated cleaning function can be a danger to small children. There are also more than 30 free public toilet facilities in Paris; locations are listed on the **Mairie de Paris** website.

Paris Time

Paris is 1 hour ahead of Greenwich Mean Time (GMT) or British Summer Time (BST). New York is 6 hours behind Paris, Los Angeles is 9 hours behind and Auckland is 11 hours ahead. France observes Daylight Saving in summer; clocks are put forward by 1 hour on the last weekend in March and put back by 1 hour on the last weekend in October. The French use the 24-hour clock.

The Eiffel Tower, a wheelchair-accessible attraction

Electrical Adaptors

The voltage in France is 220 volts. Plugs have two small round pins; heavier-duty appliances have two large round pins. Better hotels offer built-in adaptors for shavers only or will lend you an adaptor. Adaptors can also be bought at department stores, such as BHV (see p313).

Conversion Chart

Imperial to Metric
1 inch = 2.54 centimetres
1 foot = 30 centimetres
1 mile = 1.6 kilometres
1 ounce = 28 grams
1 pound = 454 grams
1 pint = 0.6 litre
1 gallon = 4.6 litres

Metric to Imperial
1 millimetre = 0.04 inch
1 centimetre = 0.4 inch
1 metre = 3 feet 3 inches
1 kilometre = 0.6 mile
1 gram = 0.04 ounce
1 kilogram = 2.2 pounds
1 litre = 1.8 pints

Responsible Tourism

A great green wave has been quietly rolling over Paris. Compost boxes are appearing on tiny apartment balconies, organic markets are thriving, recycling bins are popping up in public transport stations, hotels use eco-friendly products and skincare devotees are scooping up chemical-free creams by the potful.

Paris has over 400 parks and gardens to help the city breathe, and sustainable development is a priority. "Eco-quartiers" are emerging, an example of which is the Rungis development in the 13th arrondissement, which has solar panels powering hot water and electricity and where 50 per cent of water on the roof is

Fresh produce at one of Paris's organic markets

collected for gardens, recycling is prevalent and priority is given to pedestrians, cyclists and public transport. Even the Eiffel Tower is eco-alert – its power is 100 per cent renewable. The addition of solar panels on some shop roofs in 2011 have further reduced energy consumption.

An increasing number of hotels, such as **Hotel Garvarni**, are sporting the European Ecolabel or the Clef Verte (Green Key), as a mark of their commitment to efficient energy and water consumption, waste separation and reduction in chemical use.

Organic, or "bio", cafés and restaurants are flourishing, including **Le Bio d'Adam et Eve**, a deli serving fresh meals and sandwiches for sit-down or takeout, and **Le So**, an organic gourmet restaurant with a tiny épicerie at the back. **Le Petit Bazar** also sells fair trade coffee and recycled toys.

There are weekly organic markets at Boulevard Raspail, Place Brancusi and Boulevard Batignolles. Organic super-markets, such as Naturalia and Biocoop, can be found across the city. **Canal Bio** is an independent store selling organic and fairtrade produce.

Personal Security and Health

Paris is as safe or as dangerous as you make it – common sense is usually sufficient to keep you out of trouble. If you fall sick during your visit, pharmacists are an excellent source of advice. In France, pharmacists can diagnose many health problems and suggest appropriate treatment. For more serious medical help, someone at the emergency numbers in the box below will be able to deal with most enquiries. There are many specialist services available, including a general advice line for English-speakers in crisis and a phoneline for psychiatric help.

French pharmacy sign

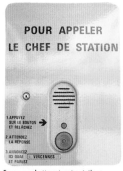

Emergency button at metro stations

DIRECTORY

Emergency Numbers

SAMU (ambulance)
Tel 15 or 112 (freecall)

Police
Tel 17 or 112 (freecall).

**Sapeurs-Pompiers
(fire department)**
Tel 18 or 112 (freecall).

SOS – all services
Tel 112 (freecall).

**SOS Médecins
(doctor, house calls)**
Tel 36 24.
🌐 sosmedecins-france.fr

SOS Dentaire (dentist)
Tel 01 43 37 51 00.

Burn Specialists
Hôpital Cochin 75014.
Tel 01 5841 4141.

**SOS Help (English-
language crisis line)**
Tel 01 46 21 46 46.

**SOS Psychiatrie (for
psychiatric help)**
Tel 01 47 07 24 24.
🌐 soshelpline.org

Sexual Disease Screening
Tel 01 40 78 26 00.

Police

As Paris is one of the most visited capitals in the world, the police are no strangers to dealing with tourists. If you need assistance, look for bilingual officers sporting a badge identifying the languages they speak. Thefts, assaults, loss of property and missing persons must be reported in person at the nearest police station; central police stations *(Commissariat de Police)* within the 20 arrondissements are open 24 hours a day, 7 days a week. Bilingual officers are usually available, but if not, there is a software programme called SAVE *(Système d'Accueil des Victimes Etrangères)* available in 20 languages, which allows tourists to record their complaint in their own language. For lost or stolen passports, call your embassy or consulate *(see p359)*.

What to be Aware of

Paris is, on the whole, a safe city. The centre, in particular, experiences little violent crime. Muggings and brawls do occur, but they are rare compared to many other world capitals. However, do try to avoid poorly lit or isolated places. Beware of pickpockets, especially on the Metro and on buses during the rush hour and in major tourist areas. Keep all valuables securely concealed and if you carry a handbag or case, never let it out of your sight. Take only as much cash as you think you will need and remember that most places accept credit cards. Travellers' cheques are a safe method of carrying large sums of money.

When travelling late at night, avoid long transfers in Metro stations, such as Châtelet-Les-Halles and Montparnasse. Generally, areas around RER

Parisian fireman

Policewoman

Policeman

Typical Paris police car

Paris fire engine

Paris ambulance

train stations tend to attract groups of youths from outlying areas who come to Paris for entertainment and may become unruly. The last RER trains to and from outlying areas should also be avoided.

Make sure you insure your possessions before arrival. On sightseeing or entertainment trips, do not carry valuables with you. You should never leave luggage unattended in Metro or train stations because it could cause a bomb scare.

In an Emergency

The telephone number for the police is 17 and for an ambulance it is 15. In the event of an emergency in the Metro, call the station agent by using the yellow telephone marked *Chef de Station* on all Metro and RER platforms, or go to the ticket booth at the entrance. Most Metro stations have emergency buttons and train carriages have alarm pulls.

The RAPT is continually upgrading security and has some 7,000 video cameras in stations and on trains, as well as 17,300 in the rail and bus network. Transport police patrol stations, and a small team of police officers survey the network electronically. Visitors

should be vigilant in heavy tourist areas for pickpockets and not let themselves be distracted. Caution should be exercised in the Les Halles area at night and at weekends.

In the case of a medical emergency, call **SAMU** (ambulance) or the **Sapeurs-Pompiers** (fire department). Fire department ambulances are often the quickest to arrive at an emergency. First-aid and emergency treatment is provided at all fire stations.

If you have been the victim of a physical assault, the police will ask that you undergo an examination at the medical-legal emergency unit near Notre-Dame.

Hospitals and Pharmacies

All EU nationals holding a European Health Insurance Card (EHIC) are entitled to use the French national health service. Patients must pay for all treatments and can then reclaim most of the cost from the health authorities. The process may be lengthy and travellers should therefore consider purchasing private travel insurance. Non-EU nationals must have full private medical insurance while in France and pay for services, claiming their costs back in full from their insurance company.

Hospitals with casualty departments are shown on the Street Finder maps *(see pp382–415)*. For English-language visitors, there are two private hospitals with bilingual staff and doctors: the **American Hospital of Paris** and the **Franco-Britannique Hospital**. The **Centre Médical Europe** is an inexpensive private clinic, which also has a dental practice.

There are many pharmacies throughout the city, and a short list is provided opposite. Pharmacies are indicated by a green cross on the shop front.

DIRECTORY

Medical Centres

American Hospital of Paris
63 Blvd Victor-Hugo 92200, Neuilly-sur-Seine.
Map 1 A3.
Tel 01 46 41 25 25.
Private hospital. Enquire about insurance and costs.
w american-hospital.org

Centre Médical Europe
44 Rue d'Amsterdam 75009.
Map 6 D3.
Tel 01 42 81 93 33.
Open 8am–8pm Mon–Sat.
Private clinic. Appointments, or walk-in.

Franco-Britannique Hospital
3 Rue Barbès 92300, Levallois-Perret.
Map 7 A1.
Tel 01 47 59 59 59.
Private hospital.
w ihfb.org

Pharmacies

British and American Pharmacy
1 Rue Auber 75009.
Map 6 D4.
Tel 01 42 65 88 29.
Open 9am–8pm Mon–Sat.

Pharmacie Anglo-Americaine
37 Ave Marceau 75016.
Map 10 E1.
Tel 01 47 20 57 37.
Open 8.30am–8.30pm Mon–Fri, 9am–8pm Sat.

Pharmacie Bader
10–12 Blvd St-Michel 75006.
Map 12 F5.
Tel 01 43 26 92 66.
Open 9am–9pm daily.

Pharmacie des Halles
10 Blvd Sebastopol 75004.
Map 13 A3.
Tel 01 42 72 03 23.
Open 9am–midnight Mon–Sat, 9am–10pm Sun.

Pharmacie Les Champs
84 Ave des Champs-Elysées 75008.
Map 4 F5.
Tel 01 45 62 02 41.
Open 24 hours daily.

Banking and Local Currency

Visitors to Paris will find that the banks usually offer them the best rates of exchange. Privately owned bureaux de change, on the other hand, have variable rates, and care should be taken to check small print details relating to commission and minimum charges before any transaction is completed.

Société Générale bank

Banks and Bureaux de Change

Most banks will exchange foreign currency and traveller's cheques. Make sure you have ID with you. The main French banks are BNP Paribas, Société Générale, Crédit Agricole and Crédit Mutuel (CIC). Banks generally offer the best exchange rates but the commission rates vary. Private bureaux de change offer poorer exchange rates than banks. Central Paris non-bank exchanges are usually open 9am–6pm Mon–Sat, and are found along the Champs-Elysées, around the Opéra and near some tourist attractions and monuments. They are also at all main railway stations, where they are generally open 8am–9pm daily. Airport exchange offices tend to open 7am–11pm daily. Private exchange offices can also be found in some hotels and shops.

Credit and Debit Cards

Major credit cards such as Visa and MasterCard, and debit cards such as Switch, Maestro and Cirrus, are widely accepted by most businesses. Most banks have ATMs (outside or in an indoor area) which accept these cards. This is the quickest and easiest way of obtaining money in local currency, although a small charge for this service will

be deducted from your account. Many French businesses do not accept American Express credit cards.

French credit and debit cards operate on a chip-and-PIN system, so you will need to know your PIN *(code personnel)* for making purchases in shops. If you have a card that does not use chip-and-PIN technology, you should ask that your card be swiped in the magnetic reader.

Be sure to notify your bank and credit card providers before you leave for France. Some banks forbid foreign transactions for security reasons unless they have been notified ahead of time.

Credit and debit card reader

Wiring Money

Money can be transferred via companies such as Western Union or MoneyGram, or bank to bank. **Banque Postale**, the post office bank, is an agent for Western Union. A transfer can be made online at Western Union or Banque Postale using a credit card, or by going to a main Banque Postale office. Depending on opening hours, the money can be picked up 10–15 minutes after it is wired. Make sure you have ID when you collect the funds and, if available, the transfer reference number. Charges are paid by the sender.

MoneyGram has its own offices in Paris. For a bank transfer, you

will need the French IBAN number, SWIFT/BIC code, bank name and address and name of the account holder. Often, the money is transferred to the main bank, then on to the relevant branch and can take 2–5 business days to arrive in the French account.

DIRECTORY

Foreign Banks

American Express
11 Rue Scribe 75009.
Map 6 D5.

Barclays
6 Rond-Point des Champs-Elysées 75008. **Map** 4 D4.

HSBC
103 Ave des Champs-Elysées 75008. **Map** 5 A5.

Bureaux de Change

Le Comptoir des Tuileries
53 Rue Vivienne 75002.
Map 12 F1. **Tel** 01 42 60 17 16.

Change Group
134 Blvd St-Germain 75006.
Map 12 F4. **Tel** 01 40 46 87 75.

49 Ave de l'Opéra 75002.
Map 6 E5. **Tel** 01 58 18 34 82.

Travelex
45 Ave de l'Opéra 75001.
Map 6 E5.

Gare du Nord (opposite Eurostar arrivals), 18 Rue de Dunkerque.
Map 7 B2.

Lost Cards and Traveller's Cheques

American Express
Tel 01 47 77 70 00 (cards).
Tel 08 00 83 28 20 (cheques).

MasterCard
Tel 08 92 70 57 05.

Visa
Tel 08 00 90 11 79 (cards).

Wiring Money

**Banque Postale
(Western Union)**
111 Rue des Sèvres 75006.
Map 15 B1.
🖥 labanquepostale.fr

MoneyGram
29 Bld de la Chapelle 75010.
Map 7 C1.
🖥 moneygram.com

The Euro

The euro (€) is the common currency of the European Union (EU). It went into general circulation on 1 January 2002, initially for 12 participating countries, including France. EU members using the euro as sole official currency are known as the eurozone. Several EU members have opted out of joining this common currency. Euro notes are identical throughout the eurozone countries, each one including designs of fictional architectural structures and monuments. The coins, however, have one side identical (the value side), and one side with an image unique to each country. Both notes and coins are exchangeable in all of the participating eurozone countries.

Bank Notes

Euro bank notes have seven denominations. The €5 note (grey in colour) is the smallest, followed by the €10 note, €20 note, €50 note, €100 note, €200 note and €500 note.

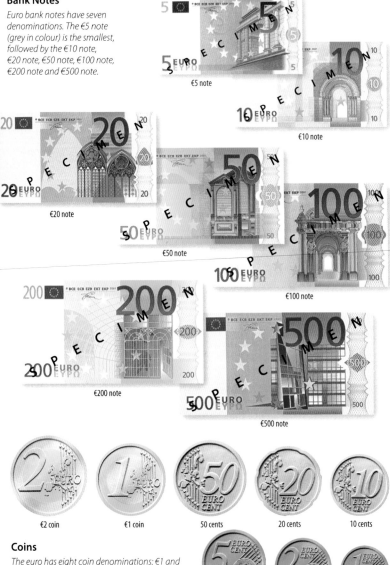

€5 note

€10 note

€20 note

€50 note

€100 note

€200 note

€500 note

Coins

The euro has eight coin denominations: €1 and €2; 50 cents, 20 cents, 10 cents, 5 cents, 2 cents and 1 cent. The €1 and €2 coins are both silver and gold in colour. The 50-, 20- and 10-cent coins are gold. The 5-, 2- and 1-cent coins are bronze.

€2 coin

€1 coin

50 cents

20 cents

10 cents

5 cents

2 cents

1 cent

Communications and Media

The main French telecommunications agency is France Télécom. The postal service is La Poste. Both work efficiently. Public telephones are located in most public places and usually require a phonecard (télécarte). Post offices have "hot stations" for customer information, and automatic vending machines for stamps and weighing packages. There are numerous post offices (bureaux de poste), identified by the blue-on-yellow La Poste sign, scattered around the city. Foreign-language newspapers can be bought at newsagents throughout Paris, and some TV channels and radio stations broadcast foreign-language programmes.

French Telephone Numbers

Telephone numbers in France have ten digits. The first two digits indicate the region: 01 and 09 are for Paris and the Ile de France; 02 for the northwest; 03 for the northeast; 04 for the southeast; 05 for the southwest. French mobile numbers begin with 06, 07 and 08 indicates a special rate number. Toll-free numbers (numéro vert) begin with 0800. For useful telephone numbers and codes, please see the box below.

Public Telephones

Paris has a large number of public telephones. To use one, you need a phonecard (télécarte), although some do accept credit cards. Sold in tabacs, post offices, France Télécom agencies and some newsagents, there are two kinds of télécartes – smart cards, available in 50 or 120 telephone units, which you simply insert in the phone, and code cards for which you tap in a code. For international calls, the International Telephone Card provides good value for money. If using a credit card, you will receive credit for calls up to €15. When the limit is reached, the call is cut off. Most telephone boxes can also receive calls – the box number is displayed above the phone unit.

Mobile Telephones

In order to use your mobile phone in France, it must be compatible with the European-standard dual-band GSM 900 or 1800 MHz frequencies. Contact your provider before leaving home to check your phone's compatibility.

Alert your network before travelling so that they can set your phone to allow "roaming". If you don't do this, your phone may not work. Always check roaming charges with your service provider before travelling, as making and receiving calls can be very expensive. Some companies offer "packages" for foreign calls which can work out better value for money.

If your phone is GSM and unlocked, you can insert a local SIM card into it, which can be obtained in Paris from one of the main local providers such as **Orange, Bouygues Télécom** or **SFR** and topped up as required. This way, you get a French phone number and pay normal, local mobile rates.

Internet Access

Internet access is widely available in Paris. There are a huge number of Internet cafés. Public libraries also provide Internet access. There are many free Wi-Fi spots around the city, including in parks, gardens and town halls. Thanks to the Pass Paris-Wi-Fi, a free wireless broad-band service set up by the Paris City Council (Mairie de Paris), you can connect instantly to the Internet by selecting the option "Paris wi-fi 2h" with your navigator. The Mairie de Paris has a list of 260 free Wi-Fi sites (Localisation des points Wi-Fi) on their website (www.paris.fr), while www.cafes-wifi.com lists cafés with Wi-Fi Internet access. Many hotels offer Wi-Fi connections, but these are rarely free.

Using the Internet in a library

Useful Telephone Numbers and Codes

- **To call the police**, dial 17; **for an ambulance**, 15.

- **Directory enquiries**, dial 118 712.

- **International directory enquiries**, for all countries, dial 118 700.

- **To make direct international calls**, dial 00 followed by the country code, area code (omit the initial 0) and the number.

- **To make a reverse charge call (PCV)**, dial 0800 99 00 followed by the country code.

- Country telephone codes: **Australia**: 61; **Canada** and **USA**: 1; **Eire**: 353; **New Zealand**: 64; **UK**: 44.

- **Low-rate period**: 7pm–8am Mon–Fri, all day Sun and public holidays.

- **To telephone France from your home country**, dial: from the UK 00 33; from the US 011 33; from Australia: 00 11 33. Omit the first 0 of the French area code.

There are pay-for-service Internet kiosks and Wi-Fi hotspots at Charles de Gaulle and Orly airports. Wi-Fi cards are available from bookstores in the terminals or you can purchase a session ahead of time on the Paris airports site (www.adp.fr).

Postal Services

The postal service in France is fast and usually reliable. Postage stamps (*timbres*) can be bought at post offices and are sold individually or in *carnets* of ten. They can be bought either at a post office counter or vending machine. Post offices also have self-service machines on which you can weigh letters and parcels, both domestic and international, which will then dispense the appropriate stamps. There are eight different price zones for international mail. Alternatively, you can buy stamps online and print them at home, or they can be bought at *tabacs*. Post offices also sell phonecards, and will cash or send inter-national money orders. They usually open 8am–7pm Mon–Fri and 9am–1pm Sat. Be prepared for long queues during peak times (early morning, lunch time and early evening).

For *poste restante* (mail holding), the sender should write the recipient's name in block letters, then "Poste Restante", followed by the address of the Paris-Louvre post office (*see Directory*).

Further information on all mail services is provided on the **La Poste** website.

Postcodes

The first three digits of Paris postcodes (750 or 751) indicate Paris; the last two numbers indicate the arrondissement (district) number. Paris's arrondis-sements are numbered from 1 to 20 (*see p382*). The postcode of the first arrondissement is 75001.

TV and Radio

The French TV channels are *TF1* and *France 2*, both with a lightweight mix; *France 3*, with documentaries, debate and classic films; *5e ("La Cinquième")* with discussion programmes; the Franco-German high-culture *ARTE*, specializing in arts, classical music and films; and *M6* airing mainly music, reality TV shows and commercial series. Cable and satellite channels include CNN, Sky, a variety of BBC channels and the English- and French-language news channel *France 24*. *BBC Radio 4* can be picked up during the day, while *BBC World Service* broadcasts at night. *Radio France International* (738 AM), along with live broadcasting in French and English, gives daily news in English on their website (www.rfi.fr).

Parisian letter box

Newspapers and Magazines

British and other European newspapers can be bought on the day of publication at newsagents (*maisons de la presse*) or newsstands (*kiosques*) throughout the city. These include European or international editions, such as *Financial Times Europe*, the *Guardian International*, *The Weekly Telegraph*, *USA Today*, *The Economist* and *The International Herald Tribune*.

The main French national dailies are – from right to left

A *kiosque* selling newspapers and magazines

on the political spectrum – *Le Figaro*, *Le Monde*, *Libération* and *L'Humanité*. The weeklies include the satirical *Le Canard Enchaîné*, news magazines *Le Nouvel Observateur*, *Marianne* and *L'Express*, as well as listings magazines (*see p359*).

(*see p382*)

DIRECTORY

Mobile Telephones

Bouygues Télécom
Tel 1034.
Ⓦ bouyguestelecom.fr

Orange
Tel 09 69 36 39 00 (English speaking).
Ⓦ orange.com

SFR
Tel 1026 (from a landline phone in France).
Ⓦ sfr.com

Internet Access

Cyber Cube
5 Rue Mignon, 75006.
Map 12 F4. **Tel** 01 82 09 04 46.
Ⓦ cybercube.fr

Luxembourg Micro
81 Blvd St Michel, 75005.
Map 16 F1. **Tel** 01 46 33 27 98.

Milk
5 Rue d'Odessa, 75005.
Map 15 C2. **Tel** 01 43 20 10 37.
Ⓦ milklub.com

Postal Services

La Poste
Ⓦ laposte.fr

Paris-Forum des Halles
1 Rue Pierre Lescot, Forum des Halles, 75001. **Map** 13 A2. **Tel** 3631.

Paris-Louvre
52 Rue de Louvre 75001.
Map 12 F1. **Tel** 3631.

Paris Saint-Lazare
7 Rue de la Pépinière 75008.
Map 5 C4. **Tel** 3631.

Couriers

Chronopost
Tel 08 25 80 18 01.
Ⓦ chronopost.fr

DHL
Tel 08 20 20 25 25,
Ⓦ dhl.fr

FedEx
Tel 08 20 12 38 00.

GETTING TO PARIS

Paris is a major hub of European air, road and rail travel. Direct flights from all over the world serve the French capital's two main international airports. Paris is also at the centre of France's vast internal rail network and of Europe's high-speed train network, with regular, fast Eurostar services under the Channel from London, Thalys from Brussels, Amsterdam and Cologne, and TGVs from Marseille and Geneva, as well as many other cities. Motorways (autoroutes) converge on Paris from all directions, including the UK via the Eurotunnel.

Arriving by Air

Paris is served by nearly all international airlines. It has two major airports, Charles de Gaulle (CDG) and Orly (ORY), and one secondary airport, Beauvais.

The main airlines with regular flights between the UK and Paris are **British Airways** and **Air France**, along with low-cost carriers **easyJet, Flybe** and **Jet2**. From the United States, there are regular flights direct to Paris, mainly on **American Airlines, United, Delta** and Air France. From Canada, **Air Canada** and Air France fly direct to Paris.

Qantas provides flights to Paris from Australia and New Zealand. **Air Austral** has flights from Australia via Réunion. **Emirates** and **Etihad Airways** fly from Australia via the Middle East, while **Cathay Pacific, Thai Airways** and **Singapore Air** fly from Asia.

Ryanair flies from Dublin, Shannon and Glasgow, and **Wizz Air** from parts of Eastern Europe to Beauvais airport.

For contact details of all these airlines, see page 369.

Tickets and Fares

The peak summer season in Paris is from July to September. Airline fares are at their highest at this time. Different airlines may have slightly varying high summer season periods. Generally, airlines offer their lowest fares to passengers booking on the Internet via their websites. It often pays to book far in advance. However, last-minute deals are sometimes available. Addresses of some discount agencies in Paris are listed on page 371. These agencies offer flights to Paris at competitive prices. Travel reservation Internet companies such as Expedia book airline tickets at discounted prices.

Charles de Gaulle (CDG) Airport

Paris's main airport, Charles de Gaulle (also known as Roissy), lies 30 km (19 miles) north of the city. It has two main terminals, CDG1 and CDG2, and a charter flight terminal, T3. A free CDGVAL shuttle train connects the three terminals.

Charles de Gaulle airport RER station

Buses, trains and taxis all run to central Paris from Charles de Gaulle airport. **Air France Buses** operates two bus services from both CDG1 and CDG2: one goes to Porte Maillot and Charles de Gaulle-Etoile (running about every 12 minutes, with a journey time of about 40 minutes); the other runs to the Gare de Lyon and Montparnasse TGV train station every 30 minutes, with a journey time of about 50 minutes.

The **RATP Roissybus** serves all three terminals, and departs every 20 minutes from 6am until 11pm for L'Opéra, taking about 50 minutes.

Airport Shuttle provides a door-to-door private transfer service in a minibus between Charles de Gaulle, Orly and Beauvais airports and individual hotels. It costs €40 per person, or €21–5 each for two or more people. Book at least 48 hours ahead, then call them after landing to confirm your journey. They also drop off at the Arc de Triomphe for €18 per person.

Disneyland® Paris runs the VEA shuttle bus service from 8.30am until 7.45pm daily (until 10pm Friday and 9.30pm Sunday) every 30–45 minutes from CDG1 and CDG2.

Access to central Paris by train is from **RER** stations (Line B) at CDG1 and CDG2. RER trains leave regularly every 5–15 minutes

Waiting area at Charles de Gaulle airport

and take 40 minutes to Gare du Nord and 45 minutes to Châtelet-Les-Halles, and then continue to several other major stations including Luxembourg, St-Michel and Port Royal.

Taxis take 25–45 minutes to the centre of Paris and cost €45–55. Queues for taxis can be long.

Orly Airport (ORY)

Paris's other main airport, Orly, is located 15 km (9 miles) south of the capital. It has two terminals, Orly Sud and Orly Ouest.

Travellers arriving at Orly can take a bus, train or taxi to central Paris. The buses are run by **Air France Buses** and **RATP Orlybus**. Air France buses take about 30 minutes to reach the city centre, stopping at Les Invalides and Gare de Montparnasse. The Orlybus runs every 12–20 minutes and takes about 25 minutes to reach the city centre at Denfert-Rochereau. The shuttle Jet Bus service takes

Orlyval train leaving Orly Airport

travellers from the airport to Villejuif-Louis Aragon Metro station every 15–20 minutes.

A shuttle bus service (VEA) links the airport with Disneyland® Paris. It runs every 45 minutes between 8.30am and 7.30pm.

Orlyrail bus service links the airport with **RER** Line C at Pont de Rungis. Trains leave from here every 15 minutes (every 30 minutes after 9pm), taking

25 minutes to reach the Gare d'Austerlitz. An automatic train, ORLYVAL, links the airport with RER Line B at Antony station, from where trains leave every 4–8 minutes for Châtelet-les-Halles.

Taxis to the city centre take about 25–45 minutes and cost €25–30.

Beauvais Airport

Beauvais airport serves mainly budget airlines. It is 70 km (44 miles) from Paris. A shuttle bus service operates between Beauvais and Porte-Maillot – buses leave 20 minutes after a flight has landed. Tickets are available in the arrivals lounge, or at the sales points outside. Trains run from Beauvais station to Gare du Nord, but the station is a 15-minute taxi-ride from the airport, and the train journey takes 75 minutes into Paris. Taxis take 1–1½ hours and cost about €100–130.

DIRECTORY

Main Airlines Serving Paris

Air Austral
Tel 0825 013 012 (France).
W **air-austral.com**

Air Canada
Tel 01 888 247 2262 (Canada),
0825 880 881 (France).
W **aircanada.ca**

Air France
Tel 36 54 (France).
W **airfrance.fr**

American Airlines
Tel 01 800 433 7300 (USA),
0821 980 999 (France).
W **aa.com**

British Airways
Tel 0844 493 0787 (UK),
0825 825 400 (France).
W **britishairways.com**

Cathay Pacific
W **cathaypacific.com**

Delta
Tel 0871 221 12 22 (UK),
08 92 70 26 09 (France).
W **delta.com**

easyJet
Tel 0330 365 5000 (UK),
0820 420 315 (France).
W **easyjet.com**

Emirates
Tel 01 57 32 49 99.
W **emirates.com**

Etihad Airways
Tel 01 57 32 43 43.
W **etihadairways.com**

Flybe
Tel 0371 700 2000 (UK),
+44 1392 683152 (outside UK) W **flybe.com**

Jet2
Tel 0333 300 0042 (UK),
0821 230 203 (France).
W **jet2.com**

Qantas
Tel 0845 7 747 767 (UK),
01 57 32 92 83 (France)
W **qantas.com**

Ryanair
Tel 0871 246 0000 (UK),
0892 562 150 (France).

Singapore Air
Tel 08 21 23 03 80.
W **singaporeair.com**

Thai Airways
Tel 01 800 426 5204 (USA),
01 55 68 80 00 (France).
W **thaiairways.fr**

United
Tel 01 800 864 8331 (USA), 01 71 23 03 35 (France).
W **united.com**

Wizz Air
Tel 08 99 19 00 37.
W **wizzair.com**

Airport Transfer Information

Air France Cars
W **cars-airfrance.com**

Airport Shuttle
Tel 01 82 28 38 70.
W **parishuttle.com**

RATP Roissybus/ Orlybus
Tel 3246 (information).
W **ratp.fr**

RER Trains
Tel 3246.

CDG Airport Hotels

Holiday Inn
Tel 01 30 18 22 00.
W **holidayinn.com**

Ibis
Tel 01 57 32 38 29.
W **ibishotel.com**

Novotel
Tel 01 49 19 27 27.
W **novotel.com**

Sheraton
Tel 01 49 19 70 70.
W **starwoodhotels.com**

Orly Airport Hotels

Hilton Hotel
Tel 01 45 12 45 12.
W **hilton.com**

Ibis
Tel 01 56 70 50 50.
W **ibishotel.com**

Mercure
Tel 08 25 80 69 69.
W **mercure.com**

Arriving by Rail

Eurostar trains travel directly from central London (St Pancras), Ashford and Ebbsfleet (both in Kent) to central Paris (Gare du Nord) in 2 hours and 15 minutes. There are up to 24 departures daily. Other high-speed services into Paris include Thalys trains from Brussels, Amsterdam and Cologne, and **TGVs** from throughout France. Pre-booking is essential. **Rail Europe** offers a comprehensive information and booking service for these and other trains throughout Europe.

As the railway hub of France and the Continent, Paris has six major international railway stations operated by the French state railways, known as **SNCF** (see p380). The Gare de Lyon (Map 18 F1) is the city's main station, serving the south of France, the Alps, Italy and Switzerland. The Gare de l'Est (Map 7 C3) serves eastern France, Austria, Switzerland and Germany. Trains from Britain, Holland, Belgium, Scandinavia and northeast France arrive at the Gare du Nord (Map 7 B3). Trains from some Channel ports and Normandy arrive at the Gare St-Lazare (Map 5 C3). The termini for trains from Spain, as well as from the Brittany ports, are the Gare Montparnasse (Map 15 C2) and Gare d'Austerlitz

Gare du Nord station concourse

(Map 18 D2). Trains from south-west France arrive at Gare d'Austerlitz. Other main stations are: Gare de Bercy; Massy-Palaiseau; Marne-la-Vallée for Disneyland® Paris; and Aéroport Charles-de-Gaulle.

There is a tourist office at the Gare de Lyon where accommodation can be booked (see p359). All the railway stations are served by city buses, the Metro and RER trains. Directional signs show where to make connections.

Eurotunnel

Travellers coming to Paris from Britain by road will need to cross the English Channel. The simplest and most popular way to do so is on the vehicle-carrying train shuttles which travel through the Channel Tunnel. Operated by **Eurotunnel**, these run

between the terminals at Folkestone and Calais.

Passengers are directed onto the trains and remain with their vehicle, though they may get out of their car and walk about inside the train during the journey.

The journey through the Tunnel takes about 30 minutes and is unaffected by sea conditions. Trains depart every 15–30 minutes, depending on demand. The Tunnel terminal has direct motorway access on both the English and the French side.

Arriving by Sea

Ship and catamaran car ferry companies operate across the Channel each day. On the short Dover–Calais route alone, there are up to 100 crossings per day, including those run by **Condor Ferries** and **P&O**, which offer fast frequent services taking 90 minutes to cross the Channel. **Transmanche Ferries**, part of Corsica Ferries, runs a route between Newhaven and Dieppe that takes nearly 4 hours. **DFDS Seaways/Norfolkline** operates a 2-hour crossing between Dover and Dunkerque.

Two companies ply the longer western routes across the Channel. **Brittany Ferries** crossings from Plymouth to Roscoff take up to 8 hours, and from Poole to Cherbourg they

Main entrance of the Gare du Nord, one of the busiest train stations in Europe

A high-speed TGV train

The TGV

Trains à Grande Vitesse, or TGV high-speed trains, travel at speeds up to 300 km/h (186mph). Paris is the nucleus for the TGV network and it is possible to connect from the Eurostar to other TGVs serving 150 destinations in France as well as Switzerland, Germany and Northern Europe. All of France's major cities can be reached by TGV and the number of stations is growing all the time, making this an ever-more convenient form of transport *(see pp372–3)*.

take 4¼ hours on a conventional ferry, or 3 hours on the *Condor Vitesse* (fast ferry). From Portsmouth, Brittany Ferries take 6 hours to travel to Caen, and 11 hours overnight to St-Malo. **LD Lines/DFDS Seaways** runs ferries from Portsmouth to Le Havre in 5½ hours. Driving to Paris from Cherbourg takes 4–5 hours; from Dieppe or Le Havre, about 2½–3 hours; and from Calais, 2 hours.

Arriving by Road

The main coach operator to Paris is **Eurolines**, based at the Gare Routière Internationale above the Galleini Metro station in eastern Paris. Its coaches travel from Belgium, Holland, Ireland, Germany, Scandinavia,

the UK, Italy and Portugal. The Eurolines terminus in London is the centrally located Victoria Coach Station, from where there are between three and five departures for Paris each day, depending on the season. The journey from London to Paris takes between 8 and 9 hours.

Paris is an oval-shaped city. It is surrounded by an outer ring road called the Boulevard Périphérique. All motorways leading to the capital link in to the Périphérique, which separates the city from the suburbs. Each former city gate, called a *porte*, now corresponds to an exit from (or entrance to) the Périphérique. Arriving motorists should take time to check their destination address and consult a map

of central Paris to find the closest corresponding *porte*. For example, a motorist who wants to get to the Arc de Triomphe should exit at Porte Maillot.

For the uninitiated, driving to the centre of Paris in heavy traffic and then parking can be a difficult experience *(see p381)*, which is why public transport is a more appealing option *(see pp374–80)*.

A long-haul international Eurolines coach

DIRECTORY

Arriving by Rail

Eurostar
Tel 03448 224 777 (UK).
W eurostar.com

Rail Europe
W raileurope.com

SNCF
Tel 3635. W sncf.com or voyages-sncf.com

TGV
W voyages-sncf.com

Arriving by Sea

Brittany Ferries
Tel 0871 244 0744 (UK).
W brittany-ferries.co.uk

Condor Ferries
Tel 0845 609 1024.
W condorferries.co.uk

DFDS Seaways/ Norfolkline
Tel 0871 574 7235 (UK).
W norfolkline.com

LD Lines/DFDS Seaways
Tel 0844 576 88 36 (UK).
W ldlines.com

P&O
Tel 0871 664 64 64 (UK).
W poferries.com

Transmanche Ferries
Tel 08 25 30 43 04. (France),

0800 917 1201 (UK).
W transmanche.ferries.com

Arriving by Road

Eurolines
Galieni Metro Station,
Ave de Général de Gaulle,
93541 Bagnolet. Tel 0892 899 091.

Victoria Coach Station,
London SW1. Tel 0870 5808 080. W eurolines.com

Eurotunnel
Tel 0871 781 8178 (UK),
0892 89 90 91 (France).
W eurotunnel.com

Traffic Reports around Paris
W sytadin.tm.fr

Discount Travel Agencies

Directours
Tel 01 45 62 62 62.
W directours.com

Havas Voyages
Tel 08 26 08 10 20.
W havas-voyages.fr

Jet Tours
Tel 08 20 83 08 80.
W jettours.com

Nouvelles Frontières
Tel 08 25 00 07 47.
W nouvelles-frontieres.fr

Arriving in Paris

This map depicts the bus and rail services between the two main airports and the city. It shows the ferry–rail links from the UK, the main railway links from other parts of France and Europe, and the long-haul coach services from other European countries. It also shows the main city railway and coach termini, the airport shuttle connections and the airport bus and rail stops. The frequency of services and journey times from the airport are provided, as are the approximate times of rail journeys from other cities. Metro and RER line connections to other parts of Paris are indicated at the termini and route stops.

🚢 **Calais**
Ferry and Eurotunnel links with Dover and Folkestone. Eurostar train London–Paris. *Gare du Nord* (2 hrs 15 mins) passes through here on the way to St Pancras and Ashford from Paris. *SNCF* train to *Gare du Nord* (1 hr 30 mins–3 hrs 30 mins).

🚢 **Le Havre**
Ferry links with Portsmouth. *SNCF* train to *Gare St-Lazare* (2 hrs 10 mins).

🚢 **Dieppe**
Ferry links with Newhaven (summer) *SNCF* train to *Gare St-Lazare* (2 hrs 20 mins).

🚢 **Caen**
Ferry links with Portsmouth. *SNCF* train to *Gare St-Lazare* (1 hr 50 mins).

🚢 **Cherbourg**
Ferry links with Portsmouth and Poole. *SNCF* train to *Gare St-Lazare* (3 hrs).

Gare St-Lazare
Rouen (1 hr 30 mins) .

Gare Montparnasse
Bordeaux (3 hrs 30 mins).
Brest (4 hrs 30 mins).
Lisbon (19 hrs 40 mins).
Madrid (12 hrs 25 mins).
Nantes (2 hrs 15 mins).
Rennes (2 hrs 15 mins).

Porte Maillot
M ①
RER Ⓐ Ⓒ

Charles de Gaulle-Etoile
M ①②⑥
RER Ⓐ

Gare St-Laza
M ③⑫⑬

Op.
Qu.

Champs-Elysées

Chaillot Quarter

Tuile
Quar

Invalides
M ⑧ ⑬
RER Ⓒ

Invalides and
Eiffel Tower
Quarter

Sei

St-Ger
des-

Luxembc
Quarte

Gare Montparnasse
④ ⑥ ⑫ ⑬ ⑭ M

Montparnas

Denfert-
Rochereau
RER M
Ⓑ ⑥ ④

Porte de Orléans
M ④

Key

— SNCF *see pp370–71*
— Coaches *see p371*
— Roissybus *see p368*
— Air France bus *see p368*
— RER *see p368*
— Orlyrail *see p369*
— Orlyval *see p369*
— Orlybus *see p369*
— Jet bus *see p369*

For additional map symbols *see back flap*

0 km   1
0 mile   1

Gare TGV de Massypalaiseau
Bordeaux (3 hrs 30 mins).
Lille (1 hr 50 mins).
London (4 hrs 15 mins).
Lyon (2 hrs 10 mins).
Nantes (2 hrs 30 mins).
Rennes (2 hrs 10 mins).

Antony
RER Ⓑ

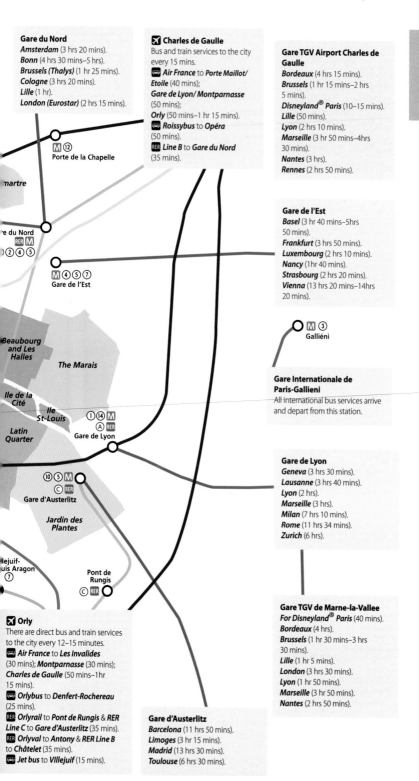

Gare du Nord
Amsterdam (3 hrs 20 mins).
Bonn (4 hrs 30 mins–5 hrs).
Brussels (Thalys) (1 hr 25 mins).
Cologne (3 hrs 20 mins).
Lille (1 hr).
London (Eurostar) (2 hrs 15 mins).

🛫 **Charles de Gaulle**
Bus and train services to the city
every 15 mins.
🚌 *Air France* to *Porte Maillot/
Etoile* (40 mins);
Gare de Lyon/ Montparnasse
(50 mins);
Orly (50 mins–1 hr 15 mins).
🚌 *Roissybus* to *Opéra*
(50 mins).
🚆 *Line B* to *Gare du Nord*
(35 mins).

Gare TGV Airport Charles de Gaulle
Bordeaux (4 hrs 15 mins).
Brussels (1 hr 15 mins–2 hrs
5 mins).
Disneyland® Paris (10–15 mins).
Lille (50 mins).
Lyon (2 hrs 10 mins).
Marseille (3 hr 50 mins–4hrs
30 mins).
Nantes (3 hrs).
Rennes (2 hrs 50 mins).

Ⓜ ⑫
Porte de la Chapelle

martre

re du Nord
🚇🅼
②④⑤

Ⓜ ④⑤⑦
Gare de l'Est

Gare de l'Est
Basel (3 hr 40 mins–5hrs
50 mins).
Frankfurt (3 hrs 50 mins).
Luxembourg (2 hrs 10 mins).
Nancy (1hr 40 mins).
Strasbourg (2 hrs 20 mins).
Vienna (13 hrs 20 mins–14hrs
20 mins).

Beaubourg
and Les
Halles

The Marais

Ⓜ ③
Galliéni

Ile de la
Cité

Ile
St-Louis

Latin
Quarter

①⑭ Ⓜ
Ⓐ 🚆
Gare de Lyon

Gare Internationale de Paris-Gallieni
All international bus services arrive
and depart from this station.

Gare de Lyon
Geneva (3 hrs 30 mins).
Lausanne (3 hrs 40 mins).
Lyon (2 hrs).
Marseille (3 hrs).
Milan (7 hrs 10 mins).
Rome (11 hrs 34 mins).
Zurich (6 hrs).

⑩⑤ Ⓜ
Ⓒ 🚆
Gare d'Austerlitz

Jardin des
Plantes

ejuif-
uis Aragon
⑦

Pont de
Rungis
Ⓒ 🚆

Gare TGV de Marne-la-Vallee
For Disneyland® Paris (40 mins).
Bordeaux (4 hrs).
Brussels (1 hr 30 mins–3 hrs
30 mins).
Lille (1 hr 5 mins).
London (3 hrs 30 mins).
Lyon (1 hr 50 mins).
Marseille (3 hrs 50 mins).
Nantes (2 hrs 50 mins).

🛫 **Orly**
There are direct bus and train services
to the city every 12–15 minutes.
🚌 *Air France* to *Les Invalides*
(30 mins); *Montparnasse* (30 mins);
Charles de Gaulle (50 mins–1hr
15 mins).
🚌 *Orlybus* to *Denfert-Rochereau*
(25 mins).
🚆 *Orlyrail* to *Pont de Rungis* & *RER
Line C* to *Gare d'Austerlitz* (35 mins).
🚆 *Orlyval* to *Antony* & *RER Line B*
to *Châtelet* (35 mins).
🚌 *Jet bus* to *Villejuif* (15 mins).

Gare d'Austerlitz
Barcelona (11 hrs 50 mins).
Limoges (3 hr 15 mins).
Madrid (13 hrs 30 mins).
Toulouse (6 hrs 30 mins).

GETTING AROUND PARIS

Central Paris is compact. The best way to get around is to walk. Cycling and rollerblading are also popular with Parisians and tourists alike. Public transport is very efficient. The Metro, RER train and bus system operated by the RATP makes getting around Paris cheap and easy, and the city authorities are working on green travel initiatives. The city is divided into six travel zones: zones 1 and 2 correspond to the centre and zones 3, 4, 5 and 6 to the suburbs and the airport. Some suburbs are served by a tramway. River boats make for a scenic mode of transport. By contrast driving a car in the city centre can be an unpleasant experience. Traffic is often heavy, there are many one-way streets and parking is notoriously difficult and expensive.

Green Travel

Paris has one of the world's most efficient and dependable public transport systems and city authorities are keen to make the capital more environmentally friendly. Residents and visitors alike are encouraged to swap cars for bicycles, and to strap on rollerblades or walking shoes as busy thoroughfares shut down to traffic at weekends as part of the *Paris-Respire* (Paris Breathes) initiative. The Mairie de Paris (Paris City Council) is enlarging footpaths, declaring more streets pedestrian-only, increasing bike lanes and planting trees in an effort to cut down on parking spaces and wean Parisians off cars. Around 55 per cent of city dwellers don't own a car.

In a bid to reduce carbon dioxide emissions by 22,000 tons a year and in order to improve traffic congestion, the Mairie is making 3,000 electric cars (Autolibs: www. autolib.eu) available for Parisians to pick up and drop off at rental stands throughout the city.

An eco-friendly Vélo taxi

The RATP is testing buses that run on second-generation bio-fuels and plans to gradually introduce vehicles equipped with hybrid electric-thermic engines in an effort to reduce fuel consumption along with noise and air pollution. The electric tramway is punctual, silent, and super green – for every three trees removed during its construction, four new ones were planted.

On the Paris Metro, the MF01 trains running on some lines have been designed to recover two-thirds of all energy lost during braking operations. In addition, a proportion of the water building up in the under-ground network is returned to nature instead of down city drains, and recycling bins have been placed in RER and a number of Metro stations.

Taxis G7 has introduced hybrid cars to their fleet and is putting drivers through eco-training courses while Taxis Bleus is promoting the use of biofuels, hybrid engines, particle filters and better driving techniques to reduce fuel consumption. Verture has a fleet composed entirely of hybrid vehicles, and offsets its carbon dioxide via an association that funds sustainable development *(see p381)*.

To estimate your carbon footprint, click onto the *ecocomparateur* on the SNCF website *(see p371)*. This helps you work out how much carbon dioxide your trip produces according to your transport method. Vélo taxis are electrically assisted tricycle rickshaws that are slower than traditional taxis, but are adept at zipping in and out of traffic.

The introduction of the Vélib' self-service bike hire system has spawned a new generation of street-savvy cyclists.

Tickets and Travel Passes

Tickets can be purchased at all main Metro and RER stations, at the airports and several tourist offices. Individual tickets are relatively cheap and you can buy a block of ten *(carnet)* for ease. The *Paris Visite* pass for one, two, three or five days includes discounted entry to some sights, but is comparatively expensive unless you intend to travel extensively.

To get a *Passe Navigo Découverte*, you do not need to be a resident of Paris but you will need a passport photo and to pay €5. A *Passe Navigo* requires a Paris address. It has replaced all travel cards. Visitors can also buy a one-day Mobilis card, valid for travel on most public transport.

Paris Visite pass

Mobilis card

Navigo travel card

Navigo Découverte pass

Walking In Paris

One of the best and easiest ways of getting around central Paris is to walk. Australian, British, Irish and New Zealand visitors need to remember that cars drive on the right-hand side of the road. There are many two-stage road crossings where pedestrians wait on an island in the centre of the road before proceeding. These are marked *piétons traversez en deux temps*.

Cycling in Paris

Paris is well equipped for cyclists. It's reasonably flat, manageably small, has many backstreets where car traffic is restricted as well as more than 370 km (230 miles) of cycle lanes *(pistes cyclables)*. Parisian motorists are increasingly respectful of cyclists as more and more of their fellow citizens turn to two wheels.

Vélib', a self-service bike scheme, offers both residents and visitors the cheapest way of getting around the city. Bike stands are located every 300 m (330 yds) and payment is by credit card at the access terminals, which operate in eight different languages. See page 357 for rates.

Bicycles (apart from Vélibs) may be taken on SNCF trains, and suburban stations also rent bicycles. There are bicycle shops throughout Paris, and many also organize guided tours by bike.

Bikes for hire by residents or tourists, at a Vélib' bike stand

Travelling by Boat

Paris's main river-boat shuttle service, the **Batobus**, runs every 15–30 minutes, with stops at eight of the city's most famous attractions – Eiffel Tower, Musée d'Orsay, St-Germain des Près, Louvre, Hôtel de Ville, Champs Elysées, Jardin des Plantes, and Notre Dame. Tickets can be bought at Batobus stops, RATP and tourist offices. The service shuts down annually from early January to early February *(see pp74–5)*.

Paris Vision tour bus

Guided Tours

Double-decker bus tours with commentaries in English, Italian, Japanese and German are organized by **France Tourisme** and Paris City Vision which runs **Cityrama** and **Paris Vision**. The tours begin from the city centre and take about 2 hours. They pass the main sights but do not stop at all of them. **Big Bus Paris** runs bus tours stopping at many of the sights in Paris. Each ticket is valid for 2 days and allows you to hop on or off at any of the stops.

Bike tours are run by a number of companies. **Paris Charms and Secrets** runs 4-hour tours in English on electric bikes departing from Place Vendôme. **Paris Bike Tour** departs from the Marais, **Paris à Velo C'est Sympa!** leaves from near the Bastille, while **Bike About Tours** starts from close to the Hôtel de Ville.

Paris Walks conducts daily tours in English, including a "Chocolate Walk" and a "Fashion Walk". The **Comité Départemental de la Randonée Pédestre de Paris** runs free thematic walks in French.

More information on guided tours is available at the Office du Tourisme *(see p359)*.

DIRECTORY

River Boats

Batobus
Port de la Bourdonnais 75007.
Map 10 D2. **Tel** 08 25 05 0101.
W batobus.com

Bus Tour Operators

Big Bus Paris
17 Quai de Grenelle 75015.
Map 9 C4. **Tel** 01 53 95 39 53.
W eng.bigbustours.com

Cityrama
2 Place des Pyramides 75001.
Map 12 E1. **Tel** 01 44 55 61 00.
W pariscityvision.com

France Tourisme
33 Quai des Grands Augustins
75006. **Map** 12 F4.
Tel 01 53 10 35 35.
W francetourisme.fr

Paris Vision
214 Rue de Rivoli 75001.
Map 12 D1. **Tel** 01 44 55 61 00.
W pariscityvision.com

Bicycle Hire & Tours

Bike About Tours
4 Rue de Lobau 75004.
Map 13 B3. **Tel** 06 18 80 84 92.
W bikeabouttours.com

Fat Tire Bike Tours
(see p351 - Outdoor Sports)

Paris à Vélo C'est Sympa!
22 Rue Alphonse Baudin 75011.
Map 14 E2. **Tel** 01 48 87 60 01.
W parisvelosympa.com

Paris Bike Tour
13 Rue Brantôme 75003.
Map 14 D2. **Tel** 01 42 74 22 14.
W parisbiketour.net

Paris Charms and Secrets
106 Rue Vielle du Temple, 75003.
Map 14 D2. **Tel** 01 40 29 00 00.
W parischarmssecrets.com

Vélib'
Tel 01 30 79 79 30.
W en.velib.paris.fr

Walking Tours

Comité Départemental de la Randonée Pédestre de Paris
6 Rue Paul Enfert 75013.
Tel 01 46 36 95 70.
W rando-paris.org

Paris Walks
12 Passage Meunier 93200 St Denis.
Map 17 B5. **Tel** 01 48 09 21 40.
W paris-walks.com

Travelling by Metro and RER

The RATP (Paris transport company) operates 14 main metro lines, referred to by their number and terminus names, which criss-cross Paris and its suburbs. There are also two minor lines – 3b (Gambetta–Porte de Lilas) and 7b (Louis Blanc–Pré St Gervais). The metro is often the fastest and cheapest way to get across the capital, as there are hundreds of stations *(see map on inside back cover)*. Metro stations are easily identified by their logo, a large circled "M", and some by their Art Nouveau entrances. The metro and RER (Paris rail network) systems operate in much the same way. The trains run from 4.45am to between 12.40am and 1.30am (1 hour later on weekends).

Art Nouveau metro sign

Modern metro sign

Reading the Metro Map

Metro and RER lines are shown in various colours on the metro map. Metro lines are identified by a number, which is located on the map at either end of a line. Some metro stations serve only one line, others serve more than one. There are stations sharing both metro and RER lines and some are linked to one another by inter-connecting passages.

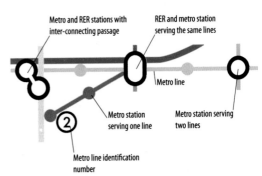

Metro and RER stations with inter-connecting passage

RER and metro station serving the same lines

Metro line

Metro station serving one line

Metro station serving two lines

Metro line identification number

Using the RER

The RER is a system of commuter trains which travel underground in central Paris and above ground in outlying areas. Metro tickets and passes are valid on it. There are five lines, known by their letters: A, B, C, D and E. Each line forks. For example, Line C has six forks, labelled C1, C2 etc. All RER trains bear names (for example, ALEX or VERA) to make it easier to read RER timetables in the station halls and on platforms. Digital panels on all RER platforms indicate train name, direction of travel (terminus) and upcoming stations. RER stations are identified by a large circled logo. The main city stations are: Charles de Gaulle-Etoile, Châtelet-Les-Halles, Gare de Lyon, Nation, St-Michel-Notre-Dame, Auber-Haussmann St-Lazare and the Gare du Nord-Magenta.

The RER and metro systems overlap in central Paris. It is

often quicker to take an RER train to a station served by both, as in the case of La Défense and Nation. However, getting into the RER stations, which are often linked to the metro by a maze of corridors, can be very time-consuming.

The RER is particularly useful for getting to Paris airports and to many of the outlying towns and tourist attractions. Line B serves Charles de Gaulle airport and Orly airport; Line A goes to Disneyland Resort Paris; and Line C runs to Versailles and Orly airport.

RER logo

Buying a Ticket

Ordinary metro and RER tickets can be bought either singly or as a *carnet* of ten, from ticket booths or ticket machines in the booking halls (carry some €1 and €2 coins). The useful Paris Visite bus, metro and RER pass *(see p374)* is widely available, and you can also buy it in advance at certain travel agencies and rail ticket agents abroad (e.g. Rail Europe in London). There is also the Passe Navigo Découverte *(see p374)* which requires a passport photo. One metro ticket entitles you to travel anywhere on the metro, and on RER trains in central Paris. RER trips outside the centre (such as to airports) require special tickets. Fares to suburbs and nearby towns vary. Consult the fare charts posted in RER stations. You must retain your ticket during the trip, as regular inspections are made and you can be fined for not having a ticket.

Making a Journey by Metro

1 To determine which metro line to take, travellers should first find their destination on a metro map. (Maps can be found inside stations and also on the inside back cover of this book.) Trace the metro line by following the colour coding and the number of the line. At the end of the line you will see the number of the terminus – remember this, as it will help you to find the correct train.

2 Metro tickets are sold at all stations. These are equipped with coin-operated automatic machines. One metro ticket allows the bearer travel for one journey, including any transfers on the metro system, and on RER trains in central Paris.

Insert the train ticket in the first slot.

Remove the ticket from the second slot.

3 To enter the platform area, insert the metro ticket, with the magnetic strip facing down, into the first barrier slot. Remove the ticket from the second slot, then walk through. Alternatively, swipe your *Passe Navigo Découverte* over the reader in the barrier.

4 At the entrance to each station platform, and in the station corridors, there are lists of upcoming stations corresponding to a given terminus. Terminus names are also indicated on the platform and should be checked before boarding the train.

5 To change lines, get off at the appropriate transfer station and follow the *correspondance* (connections) signs on the platform indicating the appropriate direction.

DIRECTION

(M) (1)

CHÂTEAU DE VINCENNES

6 There is a release button which you press to open the metro doors. Before the doors open and close, a single tone will sound.

7 Inside the trains are charts of the line being served by the train. The station stops are plotted on the chart, so travellers can track their journeys.

8 The "Sortie" sign indicates the way out. At all metro exits there are neighbourhood maps.

← SORTIE

Travelling by Bus

The bus is an excellent way to see the great sights of Paris. The bus system is run by the RATP, which also runs the metro, so you can use the same tickets for both. There are more than 350 bus lines in greater Paris and over 4,300 buses in daily circulation at rush hour. Buses can be the fastest way to travel short distances, especially now that there are more bus-only lanes. However, during peak hours buses may get caught in heavy traffic and are often crowded. Visitors should check the times for the first and last buses as they vary widely, depending on the line. Night buses run throughout the night.

Ticket-cancelling machine

Bus Stop Signs

Signs at bus stops display route numbers. A white background indicates a service every day all year; a black one means no service on Sundays or public holidays.

Bus stop sign

Night bus sign

Bus stop

Tickets and Passes

A single bus ticket entitles the bearer to a single journey on a single line. If you want to make a change, you'll need another ticket. (Exceptions to this rule are the buses Balabus, Noctambus, Orlybus and Roissybus, and lines 221, 297, 299, 350 and 351.) Children under four travel for free, and those aged between four and ten may travel at half price.

Bus-only tickets are purchased from the bus driver and must be cancelled to be valid. To do this, insert the ticket into the cancelling machine inside the bus. Hold on to your ticket until the end of the journey; inspectors do make random checks and are empowered to levy on-the-spot fines if you cannot produce a valid cancelled ticket for your journey.

You can also purchase a *carnet* of ten tickets, each of

Cancelling a Bus Ticket

Insert the ticket into the machine in the direction of the arrow, then withdraw it.

them valid for a single bus, metro or RER journey. However, a carnet cannot be purchased on buses, and can only be bought at metro stations.

Travel passes are a good idea if you are planning a number of journeys during your stay. For a set fee, you can enjoy unlimited travel on Paris buses with a *Paris Visite* pass *(see p374).* Never cancel these as it will render them invalid. They should be shown to the bus driver whenever you board a bus, and to a ticket inspector on request. If you have a *Passe Navigo Découverte (see p374),* swipe it across the card-reading machine as you board the bus.

Paris's Buses

Passengers can identify the route and destination of a bus from the information on the panels at the front. It's possible to enter some buses from the middle door; there's a button on the exterior of the bus.

Bus route number

Bus destination

Gare du Nord

Passengers enter the bus at the front door

Bus front displaying information

Using the Buses

Bus stops and shelters are identified by the number shields of the buses that stop at them, and by the distinctive RATP logo. Route maps at bus stops indicate transfers and nearby metro and RER stops. Bus stops also display timetables, and show first and last buses. Neighbourhood maps are also displayed at most bus shelters.

Most buses must be flagged down. Some models have multiple doors which must be opened by pressing a red button inside the bus to exit, or outside the bus to enter. All buses have buttons and bells to signal for a stop. Some buses do not go all the way to their terminus, in which case there will be a slash through the name of the destination on the front panel.

All of central Paris's 60 bus routes are equipped to allow wheelchair access; this means that at least 70 per cent of stops on the route are accessible; suitable stops are designated by a wheelchair symbol on the bus route sign. All buses have some seats reserved for disabled and elderly persons. These seats are identified by a sign and must be given up on request.

Night and Summer Buses

There are 31 night bus lines, called Noctilien, serving Paris and its suburbs (from 12:30am– 5:30am Monday to Thursday and 1am–5.30am Friday and Saturday). The network is laid out around the five major transfer stations of Gare de Lyon, Gare de l'Est, St Lazare, Montparnasse and Châtelet. The terminus for most lines is Châtelet, at Avenue Victoria or Rue St-Martin. Noctilien stops are identified by a letter "N" set

in a white circle on a blue background. Noctilien buses must be flagged down. Travel passes are valid, as are normal metro tickets, which must be cancelled on board. Travellers may buy tickets on board the bus. See www.noctilien.fr for more details.

In summer, the RATP also operates buses in the Bois de Vincennes and Bois de Boulogne, and the Balabus which stops at major tourist sites. **RATP Information** has useful details about these and the best ways to get around.

RATP Information
54 Quai de la Rapée 75012.
Tel 32 46. W **ratp.fr**

Tramway

There are three RATP tramways operating in Paris –T1 (Gare de St Denis–Noisy le Sec), T2 (La Défense–Porte de Versailles) and T3 (Pont du Garigliano– Porte d'Ivry), and the network is expected to grow. T3, dubbed the *Tramway des Maréchaux* as it follows the wide boulevards named after military marshals, is handy for exploring the outer reaches of the 13th, 14th and 15th arrondissements.

The T4 (Aulnay-sous-Bois– Bondy) is run by SNCF and is a tram-train line.

RATP metro and public bus tickets are valid for use on tramways.

Passengers embarking at an RATP tram stop

Useful Bus Routes

Here is a selection of some of the most useful bus routes around the centre of Paris, taking in some of the great sights of the city. The routes show the major bus stops, and locations of some of the notable sights.

Key

- ▦ Major sight
- ▬ Bus route
- ○ Bus stop *(selected stops only)*
- Balabus Balabus (Apr–Sep)

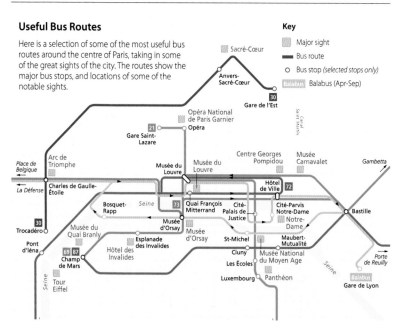

Using SNCF Trains

The French state railway, Société Nationale des Chemins de Fer (SNCF), has two services in Paris: the *Banlieue* suburban service and the *Grandes Lignes*, or long-distance service. The suburban services all operate within the five-zone network *(see p374)*. The long-distance services operate throughout France. These services allow visitors to travel to parts of France close to Paris in a day round trip. The TGV high-speed service is particularly useful for such journeys, as it is capable of travelling about twice as fast as standard trains *(see pp370–71)*.

Gare de l'Est railway station in 1920

Railway Stations

France has always been known for the punctuality of its trains, and has maintained a high level of investment in the state-owned rail system, SNCF.

As the railway hub of France, Paris boasts six major international railway stations operated by the SNCF: the Gare du Nord, Gare de l'Est, Gare de Lyon, Gare d'Austerlitz, Gare St-Lazare and Gare Montparnasse *(see p370)*.

All the main train stations have long-distance and suburban destinations. Some of the main suburban locations, such as Versailles and Chantilly, are served by both long-distance and suburban trains.

Stations have departures and arrivals boards showing the train number, departure and arrival times, delay, platform number, place of departure and main stops en route. For those with heavy luggage, there are trolleys, requiring a €1 coin (refunded when the trolley is returned). See the SNCF website for further information *(see p371)*.

Tickets

Tickets to suburban destinations can be purchased at automatic machines located inside station halls (the machines give change; most also take credit cards). You can also buy tickets at the ticket counters. These are marked with panels indicating the kind of tickets *(billets)* sold: *Banlieue* for suburban tickets, *Grandes Lignes* for mainline tickets and *Internationale* for international tickets. Fare rates vary according to the type of train.

For all trains that can be booked online through the SNCF or Rail Europe websites, there are two or three basic fare rates for each class. The cheapest tickets are called *PREMs*, which are advance-purchase fares that cannot be altered after payment; weekend and last-minute specials are also offered as *PREMs*. On some trains, fares are cheaper at off-peak times *(périodes bleues)*. Peak times *(périodes blanches)* are from 5am until 10am on Monday and from 3pm until 8pm on Friday and Sunday.

Composteur Machine

The composteur *machines are located in station halls and at the head of each platform. Tickets and reservations must be inserted face up.*

A time-punched ticket

SNCF sells several travel cards that give fare reductions of around 50 per cent, including the *Carte 12–25* for young people, *Carte Senior* for people over 60 years of age, *Carte Escapades* for frequent travellers and *Carte Enfant +* for parents with small children. Further details of fares are available on the SNCF website *(see p371)*.

Before boarding a train, travellers must remember to time-punch *(composter)* their tickets and reservations in a *composteur* machine. Beware that inspectors do check travellers' tickets and anyone who fails to time-punch their ticket can be fined.

A double-decker Banlieue train

Suburban Trains

Suburban lines are found at all main Paris train stations and are clearly marked *Banlieue*. Tickets for city transport cannot be used on *Banlieue* trains, with the exception of some RER tickets to stations with both SNCF and RER lines. Several tourist destinations are served by *Banlieue* trains, including Chantilly, Chartres, Giverny and Versailles *(see pp250–55)*. For further destinations, look at the SNCF website *(see p371)*.

Travelling by Car

Although driving and parking can be difficult in central Paris, a hire car might be useful for visiting outlying areas. Taxis are a more expensive way of getting around than trains or buses, but can be an advantage late at night when the Metro has stopped running. There are about 800 taxi ranks *(station de taxis)* throughout Paris.

Driving

To hire a car, a valid driving licence, passport and proof of insurance are required (most firms also require one major credit card). International driving licences are not needed for short-term visitors (up to 90 days) from the EU, North America, Australia and New Zealand.

Cars drive on the right-hand side and must yield to traffic merging from the right, even on thoroughfares, unless marked by a *priorité* sign, which indicates right of way. Cars on a roundabout usually have right of way, though the Arc de Triomphe is a hair-raising exception as cars give way to traffic on the right.

Parking

Parking in Paris is difficult and expensive. Never park where there are *Parking (Stationnement) Interdit* signs or yellow painted lines on the road or curb. Park only in areas with a large "P" or a *Payant* sign on the pavement or road, and pay at the *horodateur* (parking meter). Buy a *carte de stationnement* or "*Paris Carte*" (€15 or €40 from a *tabac*) to use in the meter, and place the parking ticket so that it is clearly visible through the windscreen. Parking meters *(horodateurs)* operate from 9am until 7pm Monday to Friday. Unless otherwise indicated, parking is free on Saturday, Sunday and public holidays.

Illuminated sign on a taxi

Taxis

There are over 15,000 taxis operating in central Paris, yet there never seem to be enough to meet demand, particularly during rush hours and on Friday and Saturday nights. The city is now thought to have more than 19,000 taxis.

Taxis can be hailed in the street, but not within 50 m (55 yards) of a taxi rank. Since ranks always take priority over street stops, the easiest way to get a cab is to find a rank and join the queue. Ranks are located at many busy crossroads, at main Metro and RER stations, hospitals, train stations and airports. An illuminated white light on the taxi roof shows that it is available. A small light lit below means that the taxi is occupied. If the white light is covered the taxi is off duty. Taxis on their last run can refuse to take passengers.

The meter should have a specified initial amount showing at the rank, or when it is hailed. If you order a taxi, the metre will show the charge from where the driver started his journey to collect you. Initial charges for radio taxis vary widely, depending on the distance the taxi covers to arrive at the pick-up point. Payment by cheque is not accepted but many vehicles take credit cards.

Rates vary according to the city area and the time of day. Rate A, in the city centre, is charged per kilometre. The higher rate B applies in the city centre on Sundays, holidays and at night (7pm–7am), or daytime in the suburbs or airports. The highest rate, C, applies to the suburbs and airports at night. Taxis charge for each piece of luggage, and for a fourth passenger. Drivers expect fares to be "rounded up".

DIRECTORY

Car Hire Agencies

Car hire agencies abound in Paris. Here is a list of major firms with agencies at Charles de Gaulle and Orly airports, main railway stations and city-centre locations. Call for information and reservations.

Avis
Tel 0821 230 760.

Budget
Tel 0825 003 564.

Citer
Tel 01 49 75 36 38 (Orly);
01 48 62 64 84 (CDG).

Europcar
Tel 0825 358 358.

Hertz
Tel 08 25 88 92 65 (Orly), 08 25 88 97 55 (CDG).

Sixt
Tel 0820 007 498.

Taxis and Car Services

Citybird
Tel 0826 100 100. Motorbike taxis and chauffeur driven cars-.
W city-bird.com (Bookings can be made online).

Les Taxis Bleus
Tel 3609. W taxis-bleus.com (Bookings can be made online).

Taxis G7
Tel 01 41 27 66 99, 01 47 39 00 91 (special needs). W taxisg7.com (Bookings can be made online).

Urban Driver
Tel 0825 625 100. Motorcycle taxi service. W urban-driver.com (Bookings can be made online).

No entry sign

INTERDIT
SUR TOUTE LA LONGUEUR DE LA VOIE
Parking Interdit (no parking)

AXE ROUGE
ARRÊT GÊNANT
Tow-away zone

30
Speed limit sign in km

STREET FINDER

The map references given with all sights, hotels, restaurants, shops and entertainment venues described in this book refer to the maps in this section (see How the Map References Work *opposite*). A complete index of street names and all the places of interest marked on the maps can be found on the following pages. The key map shows the area of Paris covered by the *Street Finder*, with the arrondissement numbers for each district. The maps include not only the sightseeing areas (which are colour-coded), but the whole of central Paris with all the districts important for hotels, restaurants, shopping and entertainment venues. The symbols used to represent sights and features on the *Street Finder* maps are listed opposite.

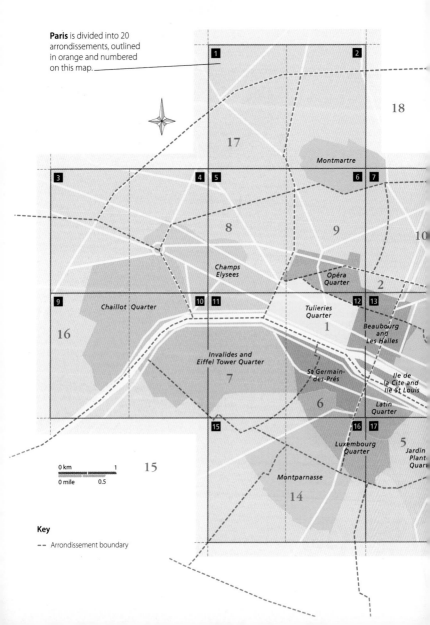

Paris is divided into 20 arrondissements, outlined in orange and numbered on this map.

Key

-- Arrondissement boundary

How the Map References Work

The first figure tells you which *Street Finder* map to turn to.

⓳ Hotel de Ville

4 Pl de l'Hôtel-de-Ville 75004.
Map 13 B3. **Tel** 01 42 76 50 49.
Ⓜ Hotel de Ville. **Open** groups: by arrangement. **Closed** public hols, official functions &

The letter and number give the grid reference. Letters go across the map's top and bottom; figures on its sides.

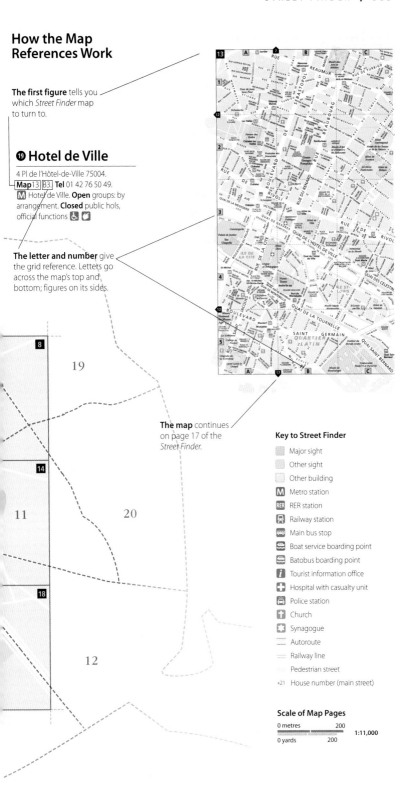

The map continues on page 17 of the *Street Finder*.

Key to Street Finder

- Major sight
- Other sight
- Other building
- Ⓜ Metro station
- RER RER station
- Railway station
- Main bus stop
- Boat service boarding point
- Batobus boarding point
- *i* Tourist information office
- Hospital with casualty unit
- Police station
- Church
- Synagogue
- Autoroute
- Railway line
- Pedestrian street
- «21 House number (main street)

Scale of Map Pages

0 metres	200
0 yards	200

1:11,000

Street Finder Index

Each place name is followed by its arrondissement number and then by its Street Finder reference

Each place name is followed by its arrondissement number and then by its Street Finder reference

Each place name is followed by its arrondissement number and then by its Street Finder reference

Each place name is followed by its arrondissement number and then by its Street Finder reference

R

Each place name is followed by its arrondissement number and then by its Street Finder reference

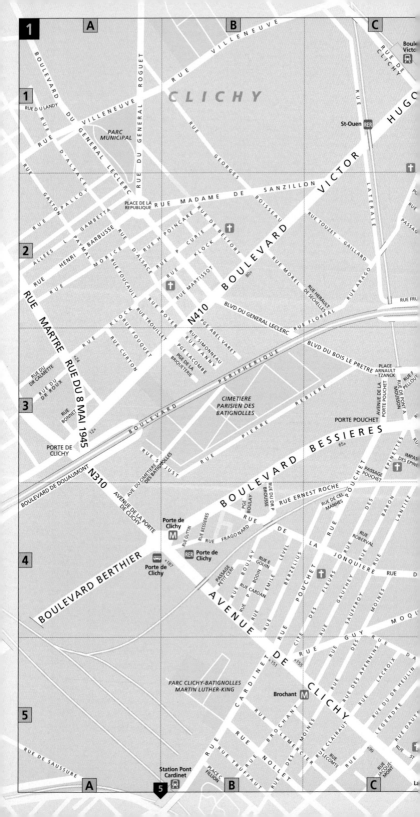

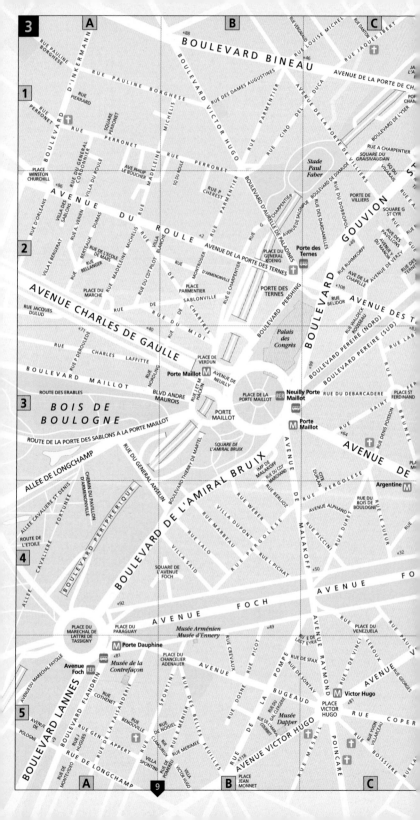

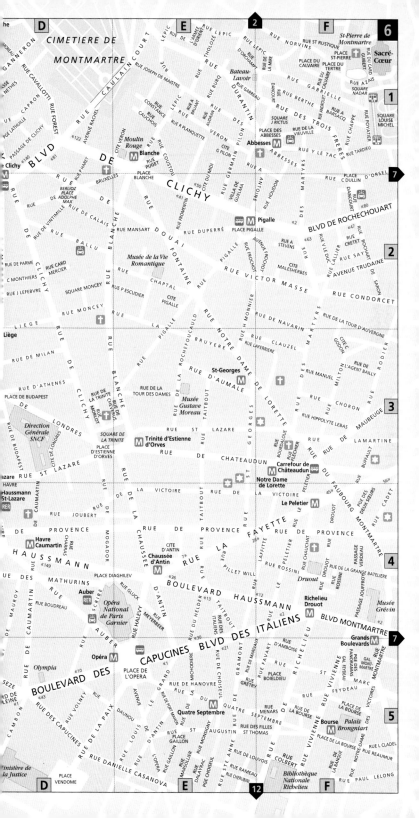

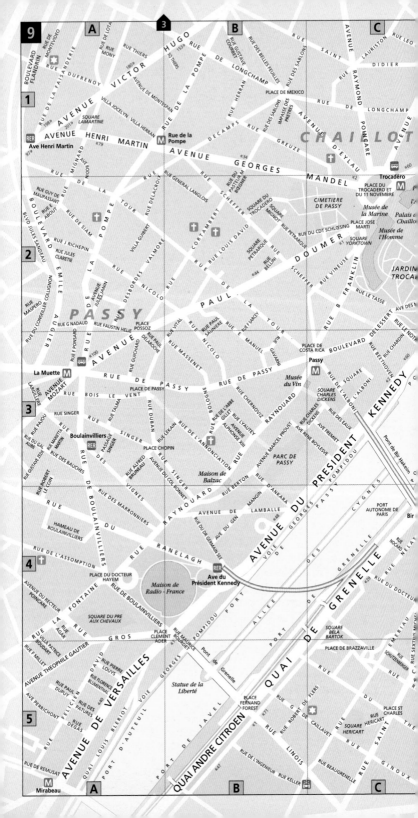

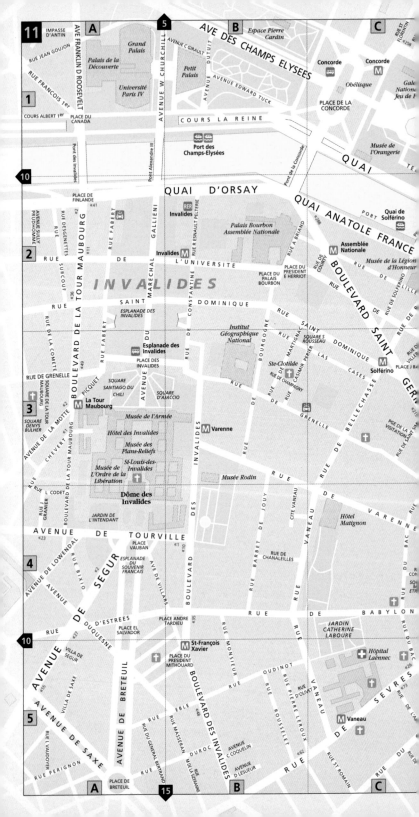

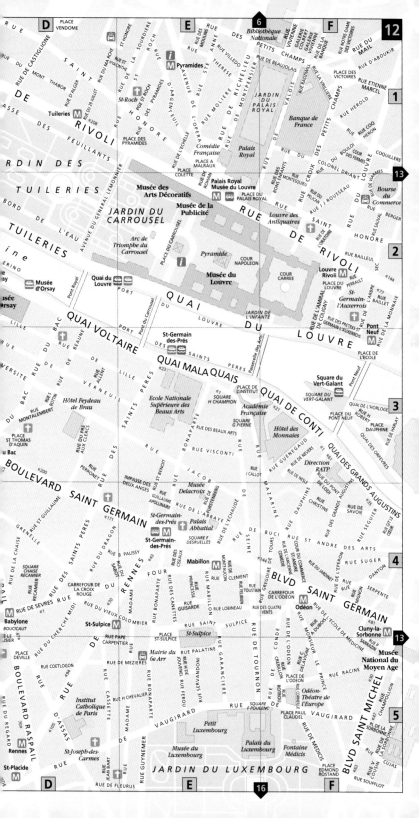

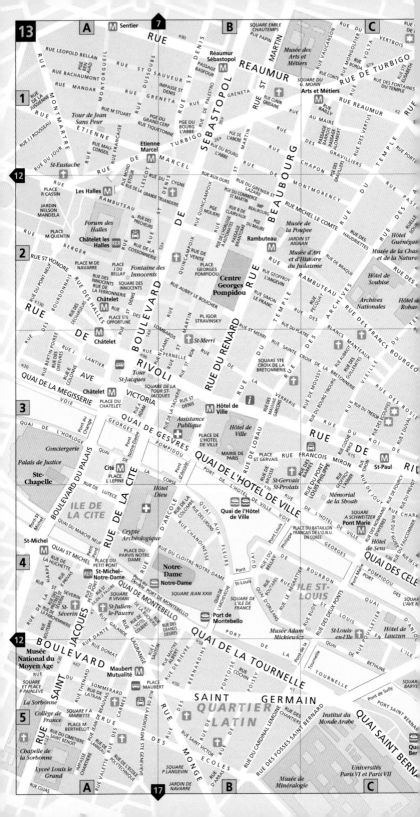

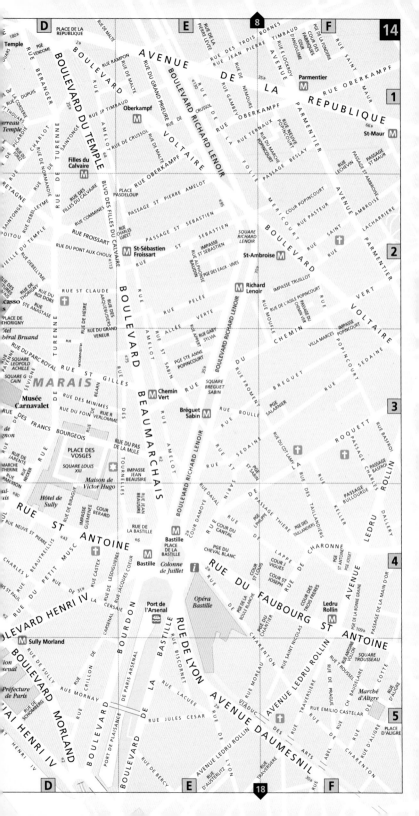

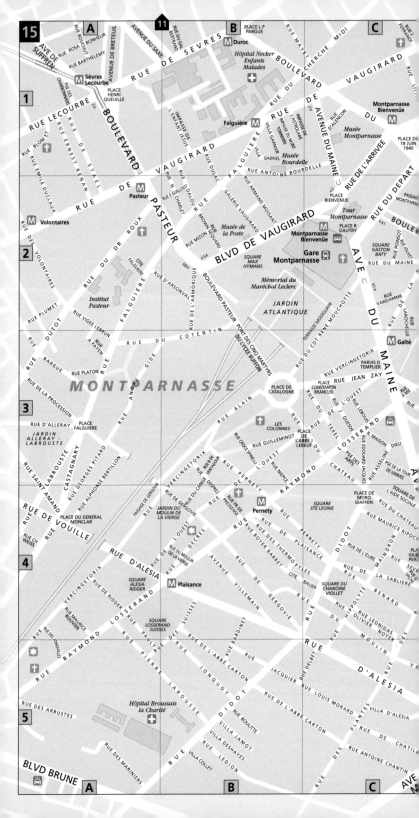

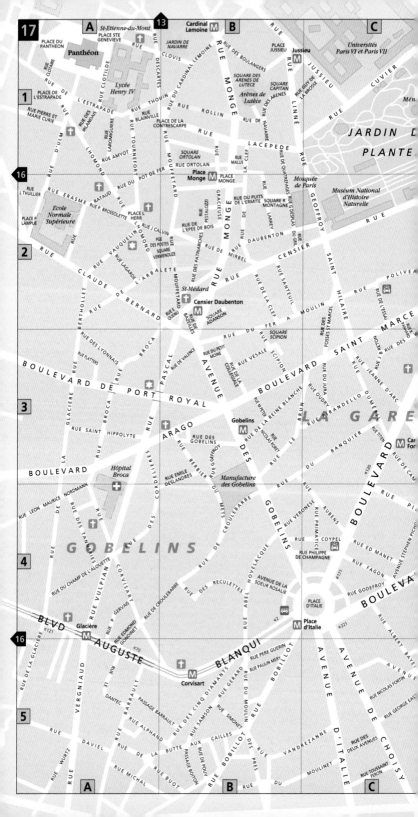

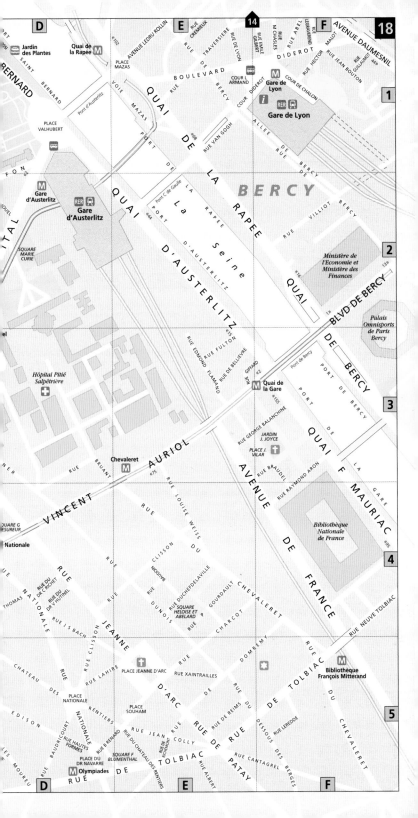

General Index

Acknowledgments

Dorling Kindersley would like to thank the many people whose help and assistance contributed to the preparation of this book.

Main Contributor
Alan Tillier has lived in all the main areas of Paris for 25 years, during which time he has been Paris correspondent for several journals including *Newsweek*, *The Times* and the *International Herald Tribune*. He is the author of several *Herald Tribune* guides for business travellers to Europe.

Contributors
Lenny Borger, Karen Burshtein, Thomas Quinn Curtiss, David Downie, Fiona Dunlop, Heidi Ellison, Leonie Glass, Alexandre Lazareff, Robert Noah, Nick Rider, Andrew Sanger, Martha Rose Shulman, David Stevens, Ian Williams, Jude Welton.

Dorling Kindersley wishes to thank the following editors and researchers at Websters International Publishers: Sandy Carr, Siobhan Bremner, Valeria Fabbri, Gemma Hancock, Sara Harper, Annie Hubert, Celia Woolfrey.

Additional Photography
Marta Bescos, Anna Brooke, Andy Crawford, Michael Crockett, Lucy Davies, Mike Dunning, Philip Gatward, Steve Gorton, Alison Harris, Andrew Holligan, Chas Howson, Britta Jaschinski, Dave King, Ranald MacKechnie, Oliver Knight, Michael Lin, Eric Meacher, Neil Mersh, Ian O'Leary, Stephen Oliver, Poppy, Susannah Price, Tim Ridley, Rough Guides/Lydia Evans, Rough Guides/James McConnachie, Philippe Sebert, Jules Selmes, Sheillee Shah, Steve Shott, Valerio Vincenzo, Peter Wilson, Steven Wooster.

Additional Illustrations
John Fox, Nick Gibbard, David Harris, Kevin Jones Associates, John Woodcock.

Cartography
Jasneet Arora, Mohammad Hassan, Andrew Heritage, James Mills-Hicks, Suresh Kumar, Alok Pathak, John Plumer, Chez Picthall (DK Cartography). Advanced Illustration (Cheshire), Contour Publishing (Derby), Euromap Limited (Berkshire). Street Finder maps: ERA-Maptec Ltd (Dublin) adapted with permission from original survey and mapping by Shobunsha (Japan).

Cartographic Research
Roger Bullen, Tony Chambers, Paul Dempsey, Ruth Duxbury, Ailsa Heritage, Margeret Hynes, Jayne Parsons, Donna Rispoli, Andrew Thompson.

Design and Editorial
Managing Editor Douglas Amrine
Managing Art Editor Geoff Manders
Senior Editor Georgina Matthews
Series Design Consultant Peter Luff
Editorial Director David Lamb
Art Director Anne-Marie Bulat
Production Controller Hilary Stephens

Picture Research Naomi Peck
Production Controller Hilary Stephens
Proofreader Stewart Wild
DTP Designer Andy Wilkinson

Revisions Team
Janet Abbott, Emma Ainsworth, Shruti Bahl, Claire Baranowski, Vandana Bhagra, Sonal Bhatt, Hilary Bird, Anna Brooke, Vanessa Courtier, Maggie Crowley, Lisa Davidson, Simon Davis, Guy Dimond, Neha Dinghra, Nicola Erdpresser, Elizabeth Eyre, Simon Farbrother, Fay Franklin, Michelle Arness Frederic, Anna Freiberger, Rhiannon Furber, Eric Gibory, Lydia Halliday, Amy Harrison, Kaberi Hazarika, Lilly Heise, Paul Hines, Fiona Holman, Gail Jones, Laura Jones, Nancy Jones, Bharti Karakoti, Sumita Khatwani, Stephen Knowlden, Rahul Kumar, Kim Laidlaw Adrey, Maite Lantaron, Chris Lascelles, Delphine Lawrance, Jude Ledger, Darren Longley, Carly Madden, Hayley Maher, Nicola Malone, Alison McGill, Sam Merrell, Rebecca Milner, Fiona Morgan, Rakesh Kurma Pal, Lyn Parry, Shirin Patel, Susie Peachey, Khushboo Priya, Pure Content, Rada Radojicic, Pamposh Raina, Lucy Richards, Philippa Richmond, Louise Rogers, Ellen Root, Philippe Rouin, Shreya Sarkar, Azeem Siddiqui, Sands Publishing Solutions, Beverly Smart, Meredith Smith, Andrew Szudek, Alka Thakur, Roseen Teare, Ajay Verma, Nikhil Verma, Dora Whitaker.

Special Assistance
Miranda Dewer at Bridgeman Art Library, Editions Gallimard, Lindsay Hunt, Emma Hutton at Cooling Brown, Janet Todd at DACS.

Photographic Reference
Musée Carnavalet, Thomas d'Hoste.

Photography Permissions
Dorling Kindersley would like to thank the following for their kind permission to photograph at their establishments: Aéroports de Paris, Basilique du Sacré-Coeur de Montmartre, Beauvilliers, Benoit, Bibliothèque Historique de la Ville de Paris, Bibliothèque Polonaise, Bofinger, Brasserie Lipp, Café de Flore, Caisse Nationale des Monuments Historiques et des Sites, Les Catacombes, Centre National d'Art et de Culture Georges Pompidou, Chartier, Chiberta, La Cité des Sciences et de l'Industrie and L'EPPV, La Coupole, Les Deux Magots, Fondation Cousteau, Le Grand Colbert, Hôtel Atala, Hôtel Liberal Bruand, Hôtel Meurice, Hôtel Relais Christine, Kenzo, Lucas-Carton, La Madeleine, Mariage Frères, Memorial de la Shoah, Thierry Mugler, Musée Armenien de France, Musée de l'Art Juif, Musée Bourdelle, Musée du Cabinet des Medailles, Musée Carnavalet, Musée Cernuschi: Ville de Paris, Musée du Cinema Henri Langlois, Musée Cognacq-Jay, Musée de Cristal de Baccarat, Musée d'Ennery, Musée Grévin, Musée Jacquemart-André, Musée de la Musique Méchanique, Musée National des Châteaux de Malmaison et Bois-Préau, Collections du Musée National de la Légion d'Honneur, Musée de Notre-Dame de Paris, Musée de l'Opéra, Musée de l'Ordre de la Libération, Musée d'Orsay, Musée de la Préfecture de la Police

Musée de Radio France, Musée Ro-din, Musée des Transports Urbains, Musée Zadkine, Notre-Dame du Travail, A l'Olivier, Palais de la Découverte, Palais de Luxembourg, Pharamond, Pied de Cochon, Lionel Poilanê, St Germain-des-Prés, St Louis en l'Ile, St Médard, St Merry, St Paul–St-Louis, St-Roch, St-Sulpice, La Société Nouvelle d'Exploitation de La Tour Eiffel, La Tour Montparnasse, Unesco, and all the other museums, churches, hotels, restaurants, shops, galleries and sights too numerous to thank individually.

Picture Credits

a-above; b-below/bottom; c-centre; f-far; l-left; r-right; t-top. Works of art have been reproduced with the permission of the following copyright holders:

© ADAGP/SPADEM, Paris and DACS, London 2011: 46cla; © ADAGP, Paris and DACS, London 2011: 63tr, 63br, 109br, 111tc, 111crb, 112bl, 112cla, 112br, 113bl, 113br, 115br, 182br, 183crb; © DACS 2011: 47cr, 52br, 57cr, 59tl, 100t, 100br, 100clb, 100cl, 100cra, 101t, 101crb, 101bl, 109t, 113c, 139tl, 224bc.

Christo–The Pont Neuf wrapped, Paris, 1975-85: 42cl; © Christo 1985, by kind permission of the artist. Photos achieved with the assistance of the Courtesy of the l'Etablissement Public du Musee et du Domaine National de Versailles 250–255; EPPV and the CSI pp 238-241; Courtesy of Erben Otto Dix: 110bl; Fondation Le Corbusier: 61t, 256bl; Courtesy of The Estate of Joan Mitchell: 113t; © Henry Moore Foundation 1993: 193br. Reproduced by kind permission of the Henry Moore Foundation; Courtesy of the Maison Victor Hugo, Ville de Paris: 99cl; Musée Carnavalet: 216br; Musée de L'Orangerie: 133tr; Musée du Louvre: 125br, 128c; Courtesy of Musée de la Poste 181tl; Musée de La Poupée 116tl; Musée National des Châteaux de Malmaison et Bois-Préau: 256cr; Musée Marmottan: 60c, 60cb, 61c; Musée de la Mode et du Costume Palais Galliera: 59br; Musée de Montmartre: 225t; Musée des Monuments Français: 201tc, 202cr; Musée National de la Légion d'Honneur: 34bc, 145bl; Courtesy of Musée National du Moyen-Age Thermes de Cluny 154 -7; Musée de la Ville de Paris: Musée du Petit Palais: 56cl, 209crb; Courtesy of the Musée du Vin, Paris 203bc; © Sundancer: 354bl.

The Publishers are grateful to the following individuals, companies and picture libraries for permission to reproduce their photographs:

Les Abeilles: 274br; **Académie de la Grande Chaumiére**: 179tc; **Aeroports De Paris**: 369tc; **Agapé Substance/Maryse Masse Communications**: Thai Toutain 305tl; **Agence Républic**: 374bc, 374br; **Alain Ducasse Entreprise**: 297tl, Matt Aletti 303tl, C. Sarramon 290cra; **Alamy**: Martin Bache 214; Tibor Bognar 117tr; Christel Broque 203cra; Bertrand Collet 271cl; Directphoto.org 299tl, 364tl; Franck Guizou/hemis.fr 103br; Glenn Harper 216tr; hemis.fr / Bertrand Rieger 307br; hemis.fr / Jean-Claude Amiel 288bl, 302bc; hemis.fr / René Mattes 92; imageimage 180cl; Image State 272br; John Kellerman 136; Lautaro 83cr; Paris Cafe 306br; A la Poste 367c; GA Rousseau 221br; Sylvain Sonnet/hemis.fr 105cr; Jack Sullivan 363cla; Travel Pictures 222; Justin Kase Zfivez 363tl; worldimages 300tl; **Allsport UK**: Sean Botterill 43bl; **The Ancient Art and Architecture Collection**: 24clb. **Banque de France**: 135t; **Bateaux Parisiens**: 74crb; **Brasserie**

Bofinger: 290tl; **Gérard Boullay**: 84tr, 84bl, 84br, 85 all; **Bridgeman Art Library, London**: 23br, 24cr, 25cl, 32cr–33cl, (detail) 37br; British Library, London (detail) 20br, (detail) 25bl, B N, Paris 21bl, (detail) 25tr, (detail) 25cr; Château de Versailles, France 21ftr, 21bc, (detail) 21br, (detail) 32br, (detail) 155b; Christie's, London (detail) 26cb, 36cla, 46cla; Delomosne, London 34clb; Giraudon 18, 27cra, (detail) 28bl, (detail) 28clb, (detail) 29br, (detail) 32bl, (detail) 32cla, (detail) 33bl, 35cb, 60br, (detail) 62bl, 62cra, 62cb; Lauros– Giraudon 25tc; Louvre, Paris 27cb, 58b, 62br, 63clb, 63tl; Roy Miles Gallery 29tr; Musée de L'Armée, Paris (detail) 83bc; Musée Condé, Chantilly (detail) 4tr, 20bl, 21tc, (detail) 21tr, (detail) 21cb, (detail) 28bc; Musée Crozatier, Le Puy en Velay, France (detail) 27bl; Musée Gustave Moreau, Paris 58tr, 235c; Musee National d'Art Moderne, Centre Pompidou, Paris 111ca; National Gallery (detail) 31tl; (detail) 46bl, Musée de la Ville de Paris, Musée Carnavalet (detail) 33br, (detail) 33tr, 33crb, 97cb. CineAqua: 202bl. Collection Painton Cowen 42cl; Palais du Tokyo, Paris 61b; Temples Newsham House, Leeds 27cr; Uffizi Gallery, Florence (detail) 26br; © British Museum: 32ca.

Camping International Maisons Laffitte: 282br; **Cité de la Musique**: Eric Mahondieu 239br; **Cité des Sciences et de l'Industrie**: EPPDCSI P. Sorin - A.Robin 241crb; Sophie Chivet 241bc; NASA/ESA 240bc; Sylvain Sonnet 240ca; **Cliché Photothèque des Musées de la Ville de Paris – © DACS 2011**: 23ca, 23crb, 30cr–31cb, 97tl; **Collections du Mobilier National-Cliché du Mobilier National**: 169br; **Corbis**: The Art Archive/Alfredo Dagli Ort 8–9; Bettmann 243tl; Jose Fuste Raga 368bl; Hemis/René Mattes 298bl; Hemis / Sylvain Sonnet 150, 304br; JAI/David Bank 291bl; Jasper Juinen 65cra; Ray Juno 10cla; Richard List 11cl; Robert Harding World Imagery/Richard Nebesky 198; Ocean 12tl, Christine Osborne 12cr; Bertrand Rieger 94cal; Sylvain Saustier 270b; **Tom Craig**: 273tr, 275tl, 275br.

Les Degrés de Notre-Dame: 278cr; **Disneyland ® Paris**: 244tr, 245bl, 245cr, 318t, 354tl, 354c. The characters, architectural works and trademarks are the property of The Walt Disney Company. All rights reserved; **Dreamstime.com**: Aoo3771 98b; Michal Bednarek 72tc; Dan Breckwoldt 45cr; Dennis Dolkens 106; Roberto Giovannini 206; Rostislav Glinsky 74cla; Jianqing Gu 45clb; K0tk0t9 236br; Kemaltaner 219tc; Ladiras81 90t; Laraslk 76-7; James Mackenzie 118; Maisicon 132bl; 00000000Nightman1965 276-7; Photogolfer 217tl; Tatiana Savvateeva 73bl; Sborisov 68; Jozef Sedmak 44; Nigel Spiers 230tl; Tupungato 162; Lestoquoy Véronique 232; Vvoevale 94clb; Roman Zaremba 184; Adrian Zenz 87br.

Espace Montmartre: 224cb; **Eurolines**: 371cr; **Mary Evans Picture Library**: 40bl, 89tl, 143cl, 192cr, 197crb, 213b, 227tl, 249br, 253t, 254bl, 380tr. **Four Seasons Hotel George V**: 279bl; **France Miniature**: Stefan Meyer 353tr.

Getty Images: AFP/Pierre Verdy 108clb; Fred Dufour 194clb; Boris Horvat 180; Miguel Medina 294tr; Craig Pershouse 156tl; FilmMagic/Marc Piasecki 301bc, 307tl; Gamma-Rapho/ Maurice ROUGEMONT 300tr, 305br; Yvan Travert 83tl; **Giraudon**: (detail) 24bl, (detail) 25crb; Lauros–Giraudon (detail) 35bl; Sami Sarkis 13br; **Le Grand Véfour**: 289tr, 299br. **Roland Halbe**: 194tr; La Halle Saint Pierre 229bc; **Robert**

Harding Picture Library: 24br, 31ca, 31br, 38cla, 43tl, 47cr, 67br, 243br, 373cr; B M 29cra; B N 193tr, 212bc; Biblioteco Reale, Turin 127t; Bulloz 212cb; P Craven 372b; Stuart Dee 170; Directphoto 356-7; Neil Emmerson 78; R Francis 82br; H Josse 212br; Musée National des Châteaux de Malmaison et Bois-Préau 35tc; Musée de Versailles 28cl; P Tetrel 253crb; Explorer 14bl; F. Chazot 333b; Girard 67cr; P Gleizes 64bl; J Moatti 340bl, 332c, 332bl; Roy Rainford 2-3; Walter Rawlings 45bc; A Wolf 123br, 123tl; Alison Harris: Le Village Royale 134tl; Hôtel d'Aubusson: 278bl; Hotel Le Bristol/Oetker Collection: Eric Deniset 285tr; Hôtel Duc de Saint Simon: 286tl; Hotel Caron De Beaumarchais: 284bc; Hôtel du Jeu de Paume: 281br; Hotel Lancaster/PRCo France: 279tr; Hotels Paris Rive Gauche/Hôtel des Grands Hommes: 280br; Hulton Getty: 47cl, 101cl, 183tc, ; Charles Hewitt 42clb; Lancaster 183tc.

© IGN Paris 1990 Authorisation N° 90–2067: 15b; Institut du Monde Arabe: Georges Fessey 167tl. The Kobal Collection: 46t, 142b; Columbia Pictures 183br; Société Générale de Films 40ca; Kong: Patricia Bailer 10br. Leonardo Media Ltd.: 281tl.

Magnum: Bruno Barbey 66b; Philippe Halsmann 47b; Le Meurice: Peter Hebeisen 280tl; Ministère de L'Economie et des Finances: 365c; Ministère de l'Intérieur SGAP de Paris: 362b; © photo Musée de L'Armée, Paris: 189cr; Musée des Arts Décoratifs, Paris: L Sully Jaulmes 56t, Cabinet (1922-1923) Jacques-Emile Ruhlmann 59tr; Musée Cantonal des Beaux-Arts, Lausanne: 117br; Musée Carnavalet: Dac Karin Mau-cotel 96tr; Musée D'Orsay: Jim Purcell 147crb; Musée National de L'Histoire Naturelle: D Serrette 169cla; © Musée de L'Homme, Paris: D Ponsard 203c; © Photo Musée de la Marine, Paris: 34bl, 200cl; Musée National d'Art Moderne – Centre Georges Pompidou, Paris: 63tr, 110br, 110bl, 111t, 111crb, 112cla, 112bl, 112br, 113t, 113c, 113bl, 113br; Musée des Plans-Reliefs, Paris: 190cra; Musée du Quai Branly: 194cla, 195cb, 195br; Patrick Gries/Bruno Descoings 56cb, 194br.

The Odéon-Théâtre de L'Europe: 333t.

Paris Convention & Visitors Bureau: Marc Bertrand 224br, 375bl; Fabian Charaffi 367bc; Amélie Dupont 57tr,164cl, 315bl, 374ca; David Lefranc 358br, 360bl; Alain Potigon 361c, 366crb; © Paris Tourist Office: Catherine Balet 272cla; David Lefranc 270c, 271t, 271br, 272tr, 273cr, 274cl, 274cb; Paris Vision & Cityrama: 375ca; Le Petit Moulin/MangoPR: 287br; Photolibrary: F1 Online/Widmann Widmann 364c; Photononstop/Jean-Marc Romain 363cl; Philippe Perdereau: 135b; courtesy of Poilâne: 313bl; Le Pre Verre: 288cr;

PunchStock: Thinkstock/Ron Chapple 82cla. Qui Plume La Lune/PimliCom: 290bc, 296bl.

Paul Raferty: 248bl; Rapho: R Doisneau: 145tl.RATP: 374crb, 377ca, 377cb, 379cr; Redferns: W Gottlieb 40cb; © Photo Réunion des Musées Nationaux: Grand Trianon 28crb; Musée Guimet 204cr; Musée du Louvre 29cb, (detail) 34cr–35cl, 57tl, 124t, 124bl, 125t, 125c, 126cl, 126bl, 126br, 127b, 128tr, 128br, 129tr, 129cl; Musée Picasso 57cr, 100t, 100cra, 100cl, 100clb, 100br, 101bl, 101crb, 101t; Roger-Viollet: (detail) 26clb, (detail) 41bl, (detail) 196c, (detail) 213tl; Philippe Ruault: Fondation Cartier 31bc; Photo Scala, Florence: Musée du Quai Branly/Patrick Gries/Valérie Torre 195tl, 195cr; Sipapress: 228c; SNCF – Service Presse Voyages France Europe: 5tl, 380bl; CAV/Christophe Recoura 370b; CAV/Jean-Marc Fabbro 370tc; /French railways 368crca; Frank Spooner Pictures: F Reglain 66cra; P Renault 66cr; SuperStock: Hemis.fr 13ca, 115t; Nordic Photos 258, Photononstop 176; Sygma: 37cb, 242c; Keystone 42br, 243cra; Keler 43crb; J Van Hasselt 43tr; P. Habans 64cra; P Vauthey 67bl; Y Forestier 188tr; Sunset Blvd 243bc.

Tallandier: 27bc, 27tl, 30cl, 30clb, 30bl, 31bl, 33cr, 33tl, 34cb, 34br, 40cla, 41ca, 41br, 42cb, 54cla; B N 30br, 34crb, 40bc; Brigaud 41crb; Brimeur 36bl; Charmet 38clb; Dubout 19b, 26ca, 28br, 32cb, 35crb, 35tr, 36br, 37bl, 38cb, 38bl, 38br, 39bl, 39br, 39cb, 39tl, 40br; Josse 22 all, 23tl, 38bc; Joubert 40clb; Tildier 39ca; Vigne 36clb; Tourisme & Handicaps: 360tr; Le Train Bleu: 291t.

Vedettes de Paris: 74clb; Agence Vu: Didier Lefèvre 332cr.

Front Endpaper
Alamy Images: BonkersAboutTravel Rbr, hemis.fr/René Mattes Rcrb, John Kellerman Lbc, Iain Masterton Rcra, Travel Pictures Rtr; Corbis: Hemis/Sylvain Sonnet Rbc, Robert Harding World Imagery/Richard Nebesky Lfclb, Sygma/Bernard Annebicque Rfbr, Sygma/Nathalie Darbellay Rtc; Dreamstime.com: James Mackenzie Lclb, Tomas Marek Ltr, Roman Zaremba Lbl; SuperStock: Hemis.fr Rbl, Photononstop Lbr; Back endpaper: RATP CML Agence Cartographique.

Map Cover
Superstock: age fotostock.

Jacket
Front, Main and Spine t – Illuminated Eiffel Tower © Gavin Hellier/Robert Harding.

Special Editions of DK Travel Guides

DK Travel Guides can be purchased in bulk quantities at discounted prices for use in promotions or as premiums. We are also able to offer special editions and personalized jackets, corporate imprints, and excerpts from all of our books, tailored specifically to meet your own needs.

To find out more, please contact:
in the United States SpecialSales@dk.com
in the UK travelspecialsales@uk.dk.com
in Canada DK Special Sales at general@tourmaline.ca
in Australia business.development@pearson.com.au

Phrase Book

In Emergency

Help!	**Au secours!**	*oh sekoor*
Stop!	**Arrêtez!**	*aret-ay*
Call a doctor!	**Appelez un médecin!**	*apuh-lay uñ medsañ*
Call an ambulance!	**Appelez une ambulance!**	*apuh-lay oon oñboo-loñs*
Call the police!	**Appelez la police!**	*apuh-lay lah poh-lees*
Call the fire brigade!	**Appelez les pompiers!**	*apuh-lay leh poñ-peeyay*
Where is the nearest telephone?	**Où est le téléphone le plus proche?**	*oo ay luh tehlehfon luh ploo prosh*
Where is the nearest hospital?	**Où est l'hôpital le plus proche?**	*oo ay l'opeetal luh ploo prosh*

Communication Essentials

Yes	**Oui**	*wee*
No	**Non**	*noñ*
Please	**S'il vous plaît**	*seel voo play*
Thank you	**Merci**	*mer-see*
Excuse me	**Excusez-moi**	*exkoo-zay mwah*
Hello	**Bonjour**	*boñzhoor*
Goodbye	**Au revoir**	*oh ruh-vwar*
Good night	**Bonsoir**	*boñ-swar*
Morning	**Le matin**	*matañ*
Afternoon	**L'après-midi**	*l'apreh-meedee*
Evening	**Le soir**	*swar*
Yesterday	**Hier**	*eeyehr*
Today	**Aujourd'hui**	*oh-zhoor-dwee*
Tomorrow	**Demain**	*duhmañ*
Here	**Ici**	*ee-see*
There	**Là**	*lah*
What?	**Quoi, quel, quelle?**	*kwah, kel, kel*
When?	**Quand?**	*koñ*
Why?	**Pourquoi?**	*poor-kwah*
Where?	**Où?**	*oo*

Useful Phrases

How are you?	**Comment allez-vous?**	*kom-moñ talay voo*
Very well, thank you.	**Très bien, merci.**	*treh byañ, mer-see*
Pleased to meet you.	**Enchanté de faire votre connaissance.**	*oñshoñ-tay duh fehr votr kon-ay-sans*
See you soon.	**A bientôt.**	*byañ-toh*
That's fine	**C'est bon**	*say bon*
Where is/are...?	**Où est/sont...?**	*ooay/soñ*
How far is it to...?	**Combien de kilomètres d'ici à...?**	*kom-byañ duh keelo-metr d'ee-see ah*
Which way to...?	**Quelle est la direction pour...?**	*kel ay lah deer-ek-syoñ poor*
Do you speak English?	**Parlez-vous anglais?**	*par-lay voo oñg-lay*
I don't understand.	**Je ne comprends pas.**	*zhuh nuh kom-proñ pah*
Could you speak slowly please?	**Pouvez-vous parler moins vite s'il vous plaît?**	*poo-vay voo par-lay mwañ veet seel voo play*
I'm sorry.	**Excusez-moi.**	*exkoo-zay mwah*

Useful Words

big	**grand**	*groñ*
small	**petit**	*puh-tee*
hot	**chaud**	*show*
cold	**froid**	*frwah*
good	**bon/bien**	*boñ/byañ*
bad	**mauvais**	*moh-veh*
enough	**assez**	*assay*
well	**bien**	*byañ*
open	**ouvert**	*oo-ver*
closed	**fermé**	*fer-meh*
left	**gauche**	*gohsh*
right	**droite**	*drwaht*
straight on	**tout droite**	*too drwaht*
near	**près**	*preh*
far	**loin**	*lwañ*
up	**en haut**	*oñ oh*
down	**en bas**	*oñ bah*
early	**de bonne heure**	*duh bon urr*
late	**en retard**	*oñ ruh-tar*
entrance	**l'entrée**	*l'on-tray*
exit	**la sortie**	*sor-tee*
toilet	**les toilettes, le WC**	*twah-let, vay-see*
free, unoccupied	**libre**	*leebr*
free, no charge	**gratuit**	*grah-twee*

Making a Telephone Call

I'd like to place a long-distance call.	**Je voudrais faire un appel á l'étranger.**	*zhuh voo-dreh fehr uñ apel a laytroñ-zhay*
I'd like to make a reverse charge call.	**Je voudrais faire une communication en PCV.**	*zhuh voo-dreh fehr oon komoonikah-syoñ oñ peh-seh-veh*
I'll try again later.	**Je rappelerai plus tard.**	*zhuh rapel-eray ploo tar*
Can I leave a message?	**Est-ce que je peux laisser un message?**	*es-keh zhuh puh leh-say uñ mehsazh*
Hold on.	**Ne quittez pas, s'il vous plaît.**	*nuh kee-tay pah seel voo play*
Could you speak up a little please?	**Pouvez-vous parler un peu plus fort?**	*poo-vay voo par-lay uñ puh ploo for*
local call	**la communication locale**	*komoonikah-syoñ low-kal*

Shopping

How much does this cost?	**C'est combien s'il vous plaît?**	*say kom-byañ seel voo play*
I would like ...	**je voudrais...**	*zhuh voo-dray*
Do you have?	**Est-ce que vous avez**	*es-kuh voo zavay*
I'm just looking.	**Je regarde seulement.**	*zhuh ruhgar suhlmoñ*
Do you take credit cards?	**Est-ce que vous acceptez les cartes de crédit?**	*es-kuh voo zaksept-ay leh kart duh kreh-dee*
Do you take travellers' cheques?	**Est-ce que vous acceptez les cheques de voyages?**	*es-kuh voo zaksept-ay leh shek duh vwayazh*
What time do you open?	**A quelle heure vous êtes ouvert?**	*ah kel urr voo zet oo-ver*
What time do you close?	**A quelle heure vous êtes fermé?**	*ah kel urr voo zet fer-may*
This one.	**Celui-ci.**	*suhl-wee-see*
That one.	**Celui-là.**	*suhl-wee-lah*
expensive	**cher**	*shehr*
cheap	**pas cher, bon marché**	*pah shehr, boñ mar-shay*
size, clothes	**la taille**	*tye*
size, shoes	**la pointure**	*pwañ-tur*
white	**blanc**	*bloñ*
black	**noir**	*nwahr*
red	**rouge**	*roozh*
yellow	**jaune**	*zhohwn*
green	**vert**	*vehr*
blue	**bleu**	*bluh*

Types of Shop

antique shop	**le magasin d'antiquités**	*maga-zañ d'oñteekee-tay*
bakery	**la boulangerie**	*booloñ-zhuree*
bank	**la banque**	*boñk*
book shop	**la librairie**	*lee-brehree*
butcher	**la boucherie**	*boo-shehree*
cake shop	**la pâtisserie**	*patee-sree*
cheese shop	**la fromagerie**	*fromazh-ree*
chemist	**la pharmacie**	*farmah-see*
dairy	**la crémerie**	*krem-ree*
department store	**le grand magasin**	*groñ maga-zañ*
delicatessen	**la charcuterie**	*sharkoot-ree*
fishmonger	**la poissonnerie**	*pwasson-ree*
gift shop	**le magasin de cadeaux**	*maga-zañ duh kadoh*
greengrocer	**le marchand de légumes**	*mar-shoñ duh lay-goom*
grocery	**l'alimentation**	*alee-moñta-syoñ*
hairdresser	**le coiffeur**	*kwafuhr*
market	**le marché**	*marsh-ay*
newsagent	**le magasin de journaux**	*maga-zañ duh zhoor-no*
post office	**la poste, le bureau de poste, le PTT**	*pohst, booroh duh pohst, peh-teh-teh*
shoe shop	**le magasin de chaussures**	*maga-zañ duh show-soor*
supermarket	**le supermarché**	*soo pehr-marshay*
tobacconist	**le tabac**	*tabah*
travel agent	**l'agence de voyages**	*l'azhoñs duh vwayazh*

Sightseeing

abbey	**l'abbaye**	*l'abay-ee*
art gallery	**la galerie d'art**	*galer-ree dart*
bus station	**la gare routière**	*gahr roo-tee-yehr*

cathedral	**la cathédrale**	*katay-dral*
church	**l'église**	*l'aygleez*
garden	**le jardin**	*zhar-dañ*
library	**la bibliothèque**	*beebleeo-tek*
museum	**le musée**	*moo-zay*
railway station	**la gare (SNCF)**	*gahr (es-en-say-ef)*
tourist information office	**les renseignements touristiques, le syndicat d'initiative**	*roñsayn-moñ toorees-teek, sandee-ka d'eenee-syateev*
town hall	**l'hôtel de ville**	*l'ohtel duh veel*
closed for public holiday	**fermeture jour férié**	*fehrmeh-tur zhoor fehree-ay*

Staying in a Hotel

Do you have a vacant room?	**Est-ce que vous avez une chambre?**	*es-kuh voo-zavay oon shambr*
double room, with double bed	**la chambre à deux personnes, avec un grand lit**	*shambr ah duh pehr-son avek un groññ lee*
twin room	**la chambre à deux lits**	*shambr ah duh lee*
single room	**la chambre à une personne**	*shambr ah oon pehr-son*
room with a bath, shower	**la chambre avec salle de bains, une douche**	*shambr avek sal duh bañ, oon doosh*
porter	**le garçon**	*gar-soñ*
key	**la clef**	*klay*
I have a reservation.	**J'ai fait une réservation.**	*zhay fay oon rayzehrva-syoñ*

Eating Out

Have you got a table?	**Avez-vous une table de libre?**	*avay-voo oon tahbl duh leebr*
I want to reserve a table.	**Je voudrais réserver une table.**	*zhuh voo-dray rayzehr-vay oon tahbl*
The bill please.	**L'addition s'il vous plaît.**	*l'adee-syoñ seel voo play*
I am a vegetarian.	**Je suis végétarien.**	*zhuh swee vezhay-tehryañ*
Waitress/ waiter	**Madame, Mademoiselle/ Monsieur**	*mah-dam, mah-demwahzel/ muh-syuh*
menu	**le menu, la carte**	*men-oo, kart*
fixed-price menu	**le menu à prix fixe**	*men-oo ah pree feeks*
cover charge	**le couvert**	*koo-vehr*
wine list	**la carte des vins**	*kart-deh vañ*
glass	**le verre**	*vehr*
bottle	**la bouteille**	*boo-tay*
knife	**le couteau**	*koo-toh*
fork	**la fourchette**	*for-shet*
spoon	**la cuillère**	*kwee-yehr*
breakfast	**le petit déjeuner**	*puh-tee deh-zhuh-nay*
lunch	**le déjeuner**	*deh-zhuh-nay*
dinner	**le dîner**	*dee-nay*
main course	**le plat principal**	*plah prañsee-pal*
starter, first course	**l'entrée, le hors d'oeuvre**	*l'oñ-tray, or-duhvr*
dish of the day	**le plat du jour**	*plah doo zhoor*
wine bar	**le bar à vin**	*bar ah vañ*
café	**le café**	*ka-fay*
rare	**saignant**	*say-noñ*
medium	**à point**	*ah pwañ*
well done	**bien cuit**	*byañ kwee*

Menu Decoder

apple	**la pomme**	*pom*
baked	**cuit au four**	*kweet oh foor*
banana	**la banane**	*banan*
beef	**le boeuf**	*buhf*
beer, draught	**la bière, bière**	*bee-yehr, bee-yehr*
beer	**à la pression**	*ah lah pres-syoñ*
boiled	**bouilli**	*boo-yee*
bread	**le pain**	*pan*
butter	**le beurre**	*burr*
cake	**le gâteau**	*gah-toh*
cheese	**le fromage**	*from-azh*
chicken	**le poulet**	*poo-lay*
chips	**les frites**	*freet*
chocolate	**le chocolat**	*shoko-lah*
cocktail	**le cocktail**	*cocktail*
coffee	**le café**	*kah-fay*
dessert	**le dessert**	*deh-ser*
dry	**sec**	*sek*
duck	**le canard**	*kanar*
egg	**l'oeuf**	*l'uf*

fish	**le poisson**	*pwah-ssoñ*
fresh fruit	**le fruit frais**	*frwee freh*
garlic	**l'ail**	*l'eye*
grilled	**grillé**	*gree-yay*
ham	**le jambon**	*zhoñ-boñ*
ice, ice cream	**la glace**	*glas*
lamb	**l'agneau**	*l'anyoh*
lemon	**le citron**	*see-troñ*
lobster	**le homard**	*omahr*
meat	**la viande**	*vee-yand*
milk	**le lait**	*leh*
mineral water	**l'eau minérale**	*l'oh meeney-ral*
mustard	**la moutarde**	*moo-tard*
oil	**l'huile**	*l'weel*
olives	**les olives**	*leh zoleev*
onions	**les oignons**	*leh zonyoñ*
orange	**l'orange**	*l'oroñzh*
fresh orange juice	**l'orange pressée**	*l'oroñzh press-eh*
fresh lemon juice	**le citron pressé**	*see-troñ press-eh*
pepper	**le poivre**	*pwavr*
poached	**poché**	*posh-ay*
pork	**le porc**	*por*
potatoes	**les pommes de terre**	*pom-duh tehr*
prawns	**les crevettes**	*kruh-vet*
rice	**le riz**	*ree*
roast	**rôti**	*row-tee*
roll	**le petit pain**	*puh-tee pañ*
salt	**le sel**	*sel*
sauce	**la sauce**	*sohs*
sausage, fresh	**la saucisse**	*sohsees*
seafood	**les fruits de mer**	*frwee duh mer*
shellfish	**les crustaces**	*kroos-tas*
snails	**les escargots**	*leh zes-kar-goh*
soup	**la soupe, le potage**	*soop, poh-tazh*
steak	**le bifteck, le steack**	*beef-tek, stek*
sugar	**le sucre**	*sookr*
tea	**le thé**	*tay*
toast	**pain grillé**	*pan greeyay*
vegetables	**les légumes**	*lay-goom*
vinegar	**le vinaigre**	*veenaygr*
water	**l'eau**	*l'oh*
red wine	**le vin rouge**	*vañ roozh*
white wine	**le vin blanc**	*vañ bloñ*

Numbers

0	**zéro**	*zeh-roh*
1	**un, une**	*uñ, oon*
2	**deux**	*duh*
3	**trois**	*trwah*
4	**quatre**	*katr*
5	**cinq**	*sañk*
6	**six**	*sees*
7	**sept**	*set*
8	**huit**	*weet*
9	**neuf**	*nerf*
10	**dix**	*dees*
11	**onze**	*oñz*
12	**douze**	*dooz*
13	**treize**	*trehz*
14	**quatorze**	*katorz*
15	**quinze**	*kañz*
16	**seize**	*sehz*
17	**dix-sept**	*dees-set*
18	**dix-huit**	*dees-weet*
19	**dix-neuf**	*dees-nerf*
20	**vingt**	*vañ*
30	**trente**	*tront*
40	**quarante**	*karoñt*
50	**cinquante**	*sañkoñt*
60	**soixante**	*swasoñt*
70	**soixante-dix**	*swasoñt-dees*
80	**quatre-vingts**	*katr-vañ*
90	**quatre-vingt-dix**	*katr-vañ-dees*
100	**cent**	*soñ*
1,000	**mille**	*meel*

Time

one minute	**une minute**	*oon mee-noot*
one hour	**une heure**	*oon urr*
half an hour	**une demi-heure**	*oon duh-mee urr*
Monday	**lundi**	*luñ-dee*
Tuesday	**mardi**	*mar-dee*
Wednesday	**mercredi**	*mehrkruh-dee*
Thursday	**jeudi**	*zhuh-dee*
Friday	**vendredi**	*voñdruh-dee*
Saturday	**samedi**	*sam-dee*
Sunday	**dimanche**	*dee-moñsh*

Paris Metro and Regional Express Railway (RER)

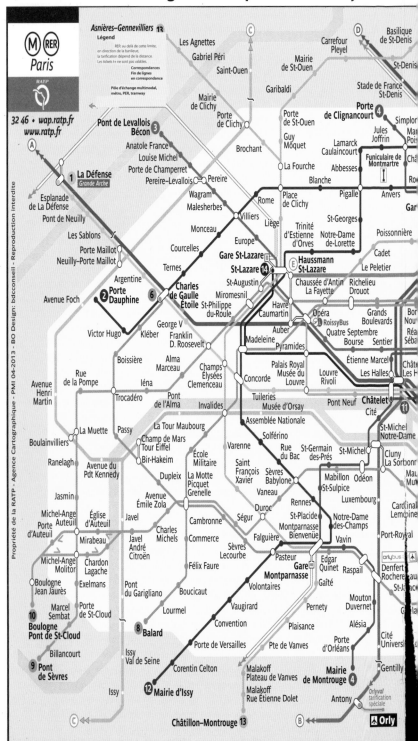